Accounting
An Introduction
Parts I and II

ccounting

An Introduction

Parts I and II

Nanci Lee
American River College

Jane Kelley
Dallas County Community College District

THE DRYDEN PRESS
Chicago   New York   San Francisco
Philadelphia   Montreal   Toronto
London   Sydney   Tokyo

Acquisitions Editor: Mike Reynolds
Developmental Editor: Penny Gaffney
Project Editor: Paula Dempsey
Design Director: Alan Wendt
Production Manager: Barb Bahnsen
Permissions Editor: Doris Milligan
Director of Editing, Design, and Production: Jane Perkins

Text and Cover Designer: Jeanne Wolfgeher
Copy Editor: Kathy Pruno
Indexer: Lois Oster
Compositor: The Clarinda Company
Text Type: 11 point ITC Cheltenham Book

Library of Congress Cataloging-in-Publication Data
Lee, Nanci.
   Accounting, an introduction. Parts I and II.

   Pt. I also issued separately.
   Includes index.
   1. Accounting.   I. Kelley, Jane.   II. Title.
HF5635.L3876   1989   657'.042   88-25621
ISBN 0-03-013072-7

Printed in the United States of America
890-039-987654321
Copyright © 1989 by The Dryden Press, a division of Holt,
Rinehart and Winston, Inc.

Address orders:
The Dryden Press
Orlando, FL 32887

Address editorial correspondence:
The Dryden Press
908 N. Elm Street
Hinsdale, IL 60521

The Dryden Press
Holt, Rinehart and Winston
Saunders College Publishing

Cover Photo by Michael Regnier

To our accounting students, whose enthusiastic assistance in all phases of development has been invaluable, and especially to Brenda Myers and Karen Rogers.

The Dryden Press Series in Accounting

Bierman and Swieringa
Financial Accounting: An Introduction

Clowes
EDP Auditing

Davidson, Maher, Stickney, and Weil
**Managerial Accounting: An Introduction
to Concepts, Methods, and Uses**
Third Edition

Davidson, Stickney, and Weil
**Financial Accounting: An Introduction to
Concepts, Methods, and Uses**
Fifth Edition

Hillman, Kochanek, and Reynolds
Principles of Accounting
Fifth Edition

Hoskin and Hughes
Financial Accounting Cases

Huefner and Largay
Advanced Financial Accounting
Second Edition

Lee
Accounting: An Introduction, Part I
Revised Edition

Lee and Kelley
**Accounting: An Introduction, Parts I
and II**

Reynolds, Sanders, and Hillman
Financial Accounting
Second Edition

Titard
Managerial Accounting
Second Edition

Preface

Accounting: An Introduction, Parts I and II, is designed to make learning as easy as possible. The new material presented in each chapter is kept to a minimum so that readers can absorb the content thoroughly before continuing. Difficult concepts are broken down into small segments where feasible so that readers can master the concepts a little at a time.

CHAPTER ORGANIZATION

Each chapter contains the following features.

"Learning Objectives" are listed at the beginning of each chapter. They clearly delineate for the reader and instructor what skills and concepts are to be gained from the chapter.

Marginal definitions are provided whenever a new accounting word or term is mentioned. The word is boldfaced in the text and defined in the margin next to its application. This enhances the readers' comprehension of the material and reduces the number of questions about content.

Discussion material is followed by illustrations. T-accounts, ledgers, journal entries, financial statements, and worksheets are used throughout the text to aid the reader in visually comprehending the written material, and color is used to highlight illustrations and forms.

Chapter summaries contain a concise review of the material presented in the chapter.

A "Review of Accounting Terminology" follows each chapter. Two exercises are designed specifically to help the reader learn the definitions of the accounting and accounting-related words and terms.

"Exercises" and "Problems" follow each chapter. There are approximately ten exercises for each chapter, and each is designed to review one specific point covered in the chapter.

The problems are more comprehensive than the exercises and progress from easy to more difficult. The exercises and problems cover all the major points discussed in the chapter.

TO THE STUDENT

From the beginning, *Accounting: An Introduction* was written in close cooperation with the students using the book. It has been thoroughly class tested, refined, and class tested again over several semesters. Literally every suggestion for improvement made by a student was taken into consideration as instructions to problems were changed, paragraphs were rewritten, exercises were added or deleted, and so on. The first thought in writing the material was to be completely clear to facilitate your learning.

Where students were weak in understanding, more exercise or problem material was added, the emphasis was slightly altered, or the discussion material was revised.

To help you comprehend the material, marginal definitions have been included that define new accounting words or terms as they are used. These allow you to comprehend what is being read without breaking your train of thought to leaf through the chapters looking for a glossary. The marginal definitions also provide an excellent way to review and thus enhance your business vocabulary.

LEARNING AIDS

Study Guides

The *Study Guides* to accompany *Accounting: An Introduction* thoroughly review each chapter. They contain a summary of chapter highlights, a review of accounting terminology, exercises that stress each of the new points covered in the chapter, and reviews of mathematical calculations where they are used in the text. *Study Guide I* covers Chapters 1–14. *Study Guide II* covers Chapters 15–28.

Working Papers

The *Working Papers* provide answer spaces and appropriate forms for all the exercises, problems, and comprehensive problems in the text. *Working Papers I* should be used with Chapters 1–14. *Working Papers II* should be used with Chapters 15–28.

Practice Sets

Three new practice sets have been prepared by Donald R. Davis to accompany *Accounting: An Introduction. Consulting Unlimited* (Practice Set One) covers the accounting cycle for a service business. *Software Mart* (Practice Set Two) covers the accounting cycle for a retail business and contains appropriate business documents. *Sandy Night, Inc.* (Practice Set Three) covers the corporate form of ownership. Software for completing all the practice sets on IBM and Apple microcomputers is available.

ACKNOWLEDGMENTS

This book could not have been written without the help of hundreds of students who were more than willing to be a part of the development of the book; who were willing to tolerate the inconvenience of an unfinished book, working papers, and solutions; and who were extremely helpful with their suggestions and criticisms. They have made the text what it is.

The reviewers, too, gave many valuable suggestions for improving the text. We are indebted to the following:

Diane B. Birch
Becker Community College

Donna Bleck
Middlesex Community College

Anthony Cilano
Erie Community College

Marlin Gerber
Kalamazoo Valley Community College

Helen M. Gerrard
Miami University

Marie Gressel
Santa Barbara City College

Robert S. Johnson
Jefferson College

Philippe Joyal
Massachusetts Bay Community College

Frances Kubicek
Kalamazoo Valley Community College

Sharon Niblock
Spokane Community College

Billy S. Sexton
York Technical College

Leslie Thysell
John Taylor Community College

Donald Whisler
Spokane Falls Community College

We would also like to thank the staff of The Dryden Press—Mike Reynolds, Penny Gaffney, Alan Wendt, Marj Hughes, and Paula Dempsey—and the copy editor, Kathy Pruno.

Nanci Lee
American River College

Jane Kelley
Dallas County Community College District

Brief Contents

Contents

8 | The Purchases Journal and the Accounts Payable Subsidiary Ledger 266

9 | The Cash Receipts, Cash Payments, and Combined Cash Journals 304

10 The Checking Account and Cash Funds 356

11 Worksheets, Financial Statements, and Closing Entries for a Merchandising Business 394

16 Accounts Receivable Valuation 580

17 Notes Receivable and Notes Payable 606

18 Valuation of Plant and Equipment 640

19　Disposition of Plant and Equipment, Natural Resources, and Intangible Assets　676

20　Partnership Accounting　708

21　Corporations: Characteristics and Formation　752

CHAPTER 1

Starting a Business and the Balance Sheet

LEARNING OBJECTIVES

When you have completed this chapter, you should

1. have an increased understanding of accounting terminology, particularly as it relates to the balance sheet.

2. know how management and accountants work together to make business decisions.

3. have a basic knowledge of the fundamental accounting equation.

4. be able to prepare a balance sheet.

Many people have dreamed of opening their own business—maybe a restaurant, a riding school, an auto repair shop, or a consulting firm. While starting a business is relatively easy, keeping the business alive and healthy is much more difficult.

The accountant and the accounting records play an important role in the life of any business. Accounting provides financial information about an economic entity (a business enterprise, a church, a club, a government organization, and so on). The daily **transactions,** such as buying or selling goods and services, making a payment on a loan, or borrowing money—in short, anything that can be measured objectively in **monetary** terms—are recorded and classified. To make the information more usable, it is summarized in accounting reports, which are the basic tools for financial decision making.

Accounting is called the "language of business" because owners, managers, investors, creditors, bankers, and so on, communicate with each other by using terms such as *cost of goods sold, book value, net profit, operating expenses, return on net assets,* and *inventory turnover.* They read financial statements and make business decisions based on the information contained in them. Management needs financial statements and other detailed accounting data to make intelligent decisions, such as: What price shall be charged? Shall we expand our hours? Hire new people? Take on new products? Offer new services? Borrow money? Cut back? Open another store? Take on a partner? Get out of the business altogether?

Without good records, a business would have difficulty remaining **solvent.** Many new businesses close their doors in failure before the first year has passed, and poor management is frequently cited as the reason. Management must work hand in hand with accountants in analyzing the records to make the daily decisions that keep a business successful. In addition, many persons outside the business are interested in the accounting records.

The various taxing agencies may want to see a firm's books regularly to audit, for example, payroll tax and sales tax records, or the **Internal Revenue Service (IRS)** may want to verify claims for expenses and revenue. Good records can help keep a business out of trouble with various government agencies.

Accountants and bookkeepers provide a valuable service for both businesses and individuals. Accountants are often hired to set up an accounting system for businesses; they are called on to audit

---

transaction
any business occurrence that can be measured in dollars and cents and that must be recorded in the accounting records

monetary
pertaining to money

solvent
able to pay bills when they become due

Internal Revenue Service (IRS)
the federal agency responsible for, among other things, the collecting of personal and business income taxes

the records of companies to determine whether their figures are arrived at fairly; they are called on at the beginning of every year to calculate the income taxes for millions of Americans; and they are hired regularly to prepare payroll and sales tax returns for businesses. Accountants may work for the Internal Revenue Service, where their work might include (among other things) auditing income tax returns for businesses and individuals. Accountants may be hired to tell an individual how to best invest money, how to pay the least amount of income taxes, or how to plan for retirement. Accountants are an important segment of our society, and their services are constantly sought after.

The job of the accountant is normally to interpret the data in the accounting records, perhaps to help management make decisions, to project future business trends, or to suggest several plans of action designed to give the best tax options. The job of a bookkeeper, on the other hand, is one of record keeping. Record keeping entails regularly recording all the transactions of a business, classifying that information, and summarizing the data for presentation to the accountant, who will interpret the results.

STARTING A BUSINESS

service business
a business that sells a service rather than a product; examples include doctors, counselors, beauticians, accountants

After attending school and working for a few years to save enough money, Ms. Florence Hansen decides to start her own business. She plans to purchase a word processor, hire an assistant, and then provide secretarial services to other businesses. She will call her business The Instant Secretary. The business will not be selling a product as such (other than the talents and skills of Ms. Hansen and her employee), and thus the business is a **service business.** Because Florence (or, simply, Flo) has studied accounting and knows she must keep track of all business transactions carefully, she is ahead of many people who start a new business.

fundamental accounting equation
Assets = Liabilities + Owner's Equity

The **fundamental accounting equation** governs how transactions are recorded. The equation is:

$$Assets = Liabilities + Owner's\ Equity.$$

assets
the economic resources owned by a business

tangible
capable of being touched

liabilities
debts

owner's equity
the owner's claim on the assets of the business; Assets − Liabilities = Owner's Equity

creditor
a person or business to whom a debt is owed

Assets are the economic resources owned by a business (whether or not they are fully paid for). They may be **tangible,** that is, have a definite physical form, such as office equipment, buildings, land, furniture, or cash, or they may be an investment, a copyright or patent, or amounts due from customers. Assets are expected to benefit future operations.

Liabilities are debts owed by the business.

Owner's equity is the difference between the assets and the liabilities. Therefore, the fundamental accounting equation may also be stated as:

$$\text{Assets} - \text{Liabilities} = \text{Owner's Equity.}$$

The assets of a business are owned either by the owner or by some other person or company. That portion of the assets to which the owner has a claim is called the *owner's equity.* That portion to which creditors have a claim is called *liabilities.* If, for example, a business owner purchased new equipment costing $10,000 by making a $6,000 down payment and agreeing to pay the other $4,000 over a year's time, the owner's equity in that asset at the time of purchase is $6,000; the rest is a liability. Thus, the equipment is owned by both the owner of the business and by a **creditor.** Each has an equity in the equipment until it is fully paid for.

Development of Accounting Standards

Financial Accounting Standards Board (FASB)
a seven-member board influential in improving accounting practices

Persons involved in accounting education and professional accountancy are continually conducting research so that accounting principles and practices may be developed or updated. This research results in the development of generally accepted accounting principles (GAAP), which are the concepts and standards used when financial statements are prepared. The American Accounting Association, the Securities and Exchange Commission, the American Institute of Certified Public Accountants, and the **Financial Accounting Standards Board (FASB)** have all been influential in improving accounting practices and in developing standards.

The FASB consists of seven full-time members who represent education, industry, and public accounting. These members conduct extensive research on matters of importance to accountants and issue Statements of Financial Accounting Standards, which form

business entity concept
an accounting principle that states that a firm's assets and liabilities be kept separate from those of the owner(s)

the basis for generally accepted accounting principles, which in turn govern in part how certain matters are handled.

One GAAP that will affect Flo right away is the **business entity concept.** This principle states that a business is an entity separate from its owner and that it is an economic unit that may enter into transactions that must be recorded, summarized, and reported.

Transactions of a New Business

Now let's trace the transactions for The Instant Secretary to see how Flo went about getting ready to begin this business venture. We will see how every transaction affects the fundamental accounting equation. Because of the business entity concept, Flo has kept all of her personal records separate from her business records. She owns her own home, a car, furniture, appliances, cameras, and so on, but these personal items do not reflect on the accounting records of The Instant Secretary.

account
a separate record that is kept for each asset, liability, and the owner's equity

A separate record called an **account** is kept for each business asset and liability and for the owner's equity. All increases and decreases are recorded in these individual accounts.

Transaction 1: Owner Establishes a Business Bank Account   Flo withdrew $10,000 from her personal savings account, deposited the money in a business account, and ordered personalized checks for The Instant Secretary. The fundamental accounting equation looks like this after the deposit.

	Assets	**=**	**Liabilities + Owner's Equity**
	Cash	**=**	**Hansen, Capital**
(1)	$10,000	=	$10,000

The original investment, additional investments at a later date, withdrawals by the owner, and all profits and losses of the business are recorded in a separate account called Capital. After this initial deposit, Assets = Owner's Equity, because at this point there are no debts.

Transaction 2: Owner Purchases Office Equipment on Account
Flo purchased a word processor and printer from Business Equipment Company (BECO) at a total cost of $9,500. Flo does not pay

for the equipment now, but agrees to pay the full amount within 12 months. Amounts owed to creditors are recorded in the liability account titled Accounts Payable. After this transaction, the equation looks like this.

	Assets			=	**Liabilities + Owner's Equity**		
	Cash	+	**Equipment**	=	**Accounts Payable**	+	**Hansen, Capital**
Previous Balance	$10,000			=			$10,000
(2)			+9,500	=	+9,500		
New Balance	$10,000	+	$9,500	=	$9,500	+	$10,000

The liabilities are now $9,500. This means that of the total assets of $19,500 ($10,000 + $9,500), the owner's share is $10,000.

Transaction 3: Owner Purchases Office Furniture Making a Cash Down Payment Flo bought $4,500 worth of furniture from Andrews Office Furniture Company. She paid $2,500 down and agreed to pay the balance in six months' time. The equation now looks like this.

	Assets					=	**Liabilities + Owner's Equity**		
	Cash	+	**Equipment**	+	**Furniture**	=	**Accounts Payable**	+	**Hansen, Capital**
Previous Balance	$10,000		$9,500				$ 9,500		$10,000
(3)	−2,500				+4,500	=	+ 2,000		
New Balance	$ 7,500	+	$9,500	+	$4,500	=	$11,500	+	$10,000

Any time a transaction has been recorded, total assets will equal total liabilities and owner's equity. The accuracy of recording a transaction may be checked by simply adding.

Assets		**Liabilities and Owner's Equity**	
Cash	$ 7,500	Accounts Payable	$11,500
Equipment	9,500	Hansen, Capital	10,000
Furniture	4,500		
Total	$21,500	Total	$21,500

Transaction 4: Owner Purchases Office Supplies Using Cash

Flo purchased $800 worth of office supplies and wrote a check for the total. The equation after that transaction is as follows.

	Assets				=	Liabilities + Owner's Equity		
	Cash	+ Equipment	+ Furniture	+ Supplies	=	Accounts Payable	+	Hansen, Capital
Previous								
Balance	$7,500 +	$9,500	+ $4,500		=	$11,500	+	$10,000
(4)	− 800			+800				
New								
Balance	$6,700 +	$9,500	+ $4,500	+ $800	=	$11,500	+	$10,000

Transaction 5: Owner Contributes Personal Assets to the Business

Flo has several up-to-date dictionaries, office procedures manuals, and word division guides that she contributes to the business. Since these books come from her personal library to the business, their value increases the owner's capital account. The estimated value of the books is $200.

	Assets					=	Liabilities +	Owner's Equity
							Accounts	Hansen,
	Cash	+ Equipment	+ Furniture	+ Supplies	+ Library	=	Payable +	Capital
Previous								
Balance	$6,700 +	$9,500	+ $4,500	+ $800		=	$11,500 +	$10,000
(5)					+200			+ 200
New								
Balance	$6,700 +	$9,500	+ $4,500	+ $800	+ $200	=	$11,500 +	$10,200

Do the total assets equal the total of the liabilities and owner's equity? This question should be asked after every transaction.

Transaction 6: Owner Pays Money to a Creditor

Flo pays $500 to BECO as a partial payment of the $9,500 owed for the purchase of office equipment (see Transaction 2). Now the equation appears as follows.

		Assets				= Liabilities	+ Owner's Equity
Cash	+ Equipment	+ Furniture	+ Supplies	+ Library =	Accounts Payable +	Hansen, Capital
Previous Balance	$6,700 +	$9,500	+ $4,500	+ $800	+ $200 =	$11,500 +	$10,200
(6)	− 500					− 500	
New Balance	$6,200 +	$9,500	+ $4,500	+ $800	+ $200 =	$11,000 +	$10,200

Manipulating the Fundamental Accounting Equation   The transaction shows that total assets equal $21,200, total liabilities equal $11,000, and owner's equity equals $10,200. The equation looks like this.

Assets	=	Liabilities	+	Owner's Equity
$21,200	=	$11,000	+	$10,200

If any two parts of the equation are known, the missing part can easily be found.

Illustration 1: Assets − Liabilities = Owner's Equity (A − L = OE)
Assets are $21,200 and liabilities are $11,000. What is the amount of the owner's equity?

Assets	−	Liabilities	=	Owner's Equity
$21,200	−	$11,000	=	$10,200

Illustration 2: Assets − Owner's Equity = Liabilities (A − OE = L)
Assets are $21,200 and owner's equity is $10,200. What is the amount of the liabilities?

Assets	−	Owner's Equity	=	Liabilities
$21,200	−	$10,200	=	$11,000

discrepancy
disagreement, as be-
tween facts and
claims

Total assets should always equal total liabilities plus owner's equity. If for some reason there is a **discrepancy,** a mistake in
recording has occurred, and the error must be located before continuing.

Where total assets increase, total liabilities and owner's equity
must also increase by the same amount (see Transactions 1, 2, 3,
and 5). If total assets decrease, total liabilities and owner's equity
must decrease by the same amount (see Transaction 6). However,
one asset may increase and another may decrease by the same
amount, thus causing no change in the totals of the fundamental
accounting equation (see Transaction 4).

THE BALANCE SHEET

Flo has now purchased most of what she needs to begin her business and is ready to prepare her first financial statement, the balance sheet. The balance sheet contains a complete listing of all asset, liability, and owner's equity accounts and is called balance
sheet because it proves that total assets equal total liabilities and
owner's equity or that the fundamental accounting equation is in
balance. The balance sheet for The Instant Secretary on January 31
follows.

THE INSTANT SECRETARY BALANCE SHEET JANUARY 31, 19XX		
Assets		
Cash	$6 2 0 0 —	
Supplies	8 0 0 —	
Equipment	9 5 0 0 —	
Furniture	4 5 0 0 —	
Library	2 0 0 —	
Total Assets		$2 1 2 0 0 —
Liabilities		
Accounts Payable		$1 1 0 0 0 —
Owner's Equity		
Florence Hansen, Capital, January 31, 19XX		1 0 2 0 0 —
Total Liabilities and Owner's Equity		$2 1 2 0 0 —

Assets are recorded on the balance sheet at their original, or historic, cost. This is significant because many assets are worth an amount that is different from the one reflected on the balance sheet; such assets as land and buildings often **appreciate** in value over the years. The **cost principle** of accounting, however, requires that assets be recorded at the amount originally paid for them. Thus, the balance sheet does not necessarily reflect what the business is actually worth.

appreciate
to increase in value

cost principle
assets must be recorded at their historical cost

Because assets are economic resources that are expected to benefit future operations, such assets as land, buildings, and equipment are for use and are not for sale. Most assets could not be sold without disrupting normal business activity. The business is considered to be ongoing, so the market values of assets are not of immediate significance. This concept is the **going concern assumption.**

going concern assumption
a business will be ongoing for an indefinite period of time and therefore the current market value of assets is not of immediate concern

The cost principle illustrates how important it is for accountants to be objective in their valuation of assets; they must have factual information that can be verified by interested persons outside the business. If business owners were to change land or building values on the balance sheet every year as market prices fluctuate, it would be very confusing for the readers of the financial statements. Appraisals of value are constantly changing as market conditions change. For these reasons, accountants use the **objectivity principle,** which states that asset values must be determined by factual evidence, and they must be verifiable by independent experts.

objectivity principle
factual evidence that is verifiable by independent experts must be used in determining the value of assets

Guidelines for Preparing the Balance Sheet

The Heading   The balance sheet has a three-part heading, which is centered and always includes, in this order, (1) the name of the business, (2) the name of the financial statement, and (3) the day for which the statement is prepared.

Assets   This form of the balance sheet is called the *report form.* The word *Assets* is centered on the top line, and **current assets** begins the listing of accounts; these are cash or assets that will be used up or converted into cash within a year's time. (Supplies is an example of an asset that will be used up.) The first asset listed is Cash, and it is followed by Notes Receivable and then Accounts Receivable. Receivables represent amounts owed to the business. The other current assets are listed following the receivables, in no particular order.

current assets
an asset that is cash or that will be converted into cash or used up within a year's time

The plant and equipment titles are listed after the current assets. If there is a Land account, it is shown last, following the other plant and equipment titles (Furniture, Fixtures, Equipment, Buildings, etc.), which are listed in no particular order. Account titles are written next to the double vertical line, amounts to be added are entered in the left-hand column, and totals are entered in the right-hand column. A single line is drawn all the way across the column (from double vertical lines to double vertical lines) to indicate addition, then the total dollar amounts are entered, and *Total Assets* is written opposite that figure.

Liabilities   One blank line should be left before centering the word *Liabilities* over the listing of account titles. Other account titles might include Payroll Taxes Payable, Notes Payable, or Mortgage Payable. Debts that are due within a year are listed first and are called **current liabilities.** In this category, Notes Payable is usually listed first and is followed by Accounts Payable. Notes Payable represents debt evidenced by the signing of a formal document in which the borrower promises to pay back a certain amount of money by a certain time and usually with interest. Other current liabilities are listed in any order after Notes Payable.

current liabilities
debts due within a year

Amounts to be added are written in the left-hand column, and column totals are entered in the right-hand column. In cases where there is only one account, the amount may be entered directly into the right-hand column as it is not necessary to find a column total.

Owner's Equity   Another blank line should be left before centering the words *Owner's Equity* over the last section. The Capital account is listed beneath the heading. A single line is drawn beneath the amount for the Capital account and the figures are added. *Total Liabilities and Owner's Equity* is then written opposite the sum obtained.

When a total for the assets and a total for liabilities and owner's equity is determined, and the amounts are equal, a double horizontal line is drawn across the columns to indicate that the work is in balance and complete.

Dollar Signs and Rulings   A dollar sign appears at the beginning of each column and at totals or subtotals. A ruling must extend all the way across a column. A single ruling indicates addition or subtraction, and a double ruling indicates that work is completed and in balance. Always use a ruler for drawing lines. Neatness is very important in accounting.

Cents Column   When money amounts are in even dollars, two ze-
roes should be written in the cents column. *XX's should not be
used.* However, a straight line may be used to indicate even money
amounts. For example, seven hundred forty-eight dollars may be
written as $748.00 or $748.—.

SUMMARY

Accounting is the language of business and as such is used by
owners, managers, investors, bankers—in short, nearly everyone
concerned with business—to communicate vital information to
one another. Daily transactions of economic units must be recorded, classified, and summarized into useful reports for management to make intelligent business decisions. Good accounting
records help enable an organization to be profitable and remain
solvent.

Accounting practices and procedures must be standard and updated for records to be intelligently read and compared. Several
organizations in the United States are influential in improving and
standardizing accounting practices. Some of these are the American Accounting Association, the Securities and Exchange Commission, the American Institute of Certified Public Accountants, and
the Financial Accounting Standards Board.

The fundamental accounting equation states that assets equal liabilities plus owner's equity. Assets are the economic resources
owned by a business and include such tangible items as land,
buildings, furniture, equipment, and cash, and such intangible
items as patents or copyrights. Liabilities are the debts incurred by
the business. Owner's equity is the owner's share in the assets, or
that portion of the total asset value to which the owner has a direct claim. The business entity concept requires that a business
owner keep his or her personal assets, liabilities, and owner's equity records separate from those of the business.

The relationship of assets, liabilities, and owner's equity is
shown on the balance sheet, where a listing of these accounts and
their dollar amounts is prepared to show the financial position of a
firm on a particular date. Current assets are listed first, followed by
land and items of plant and equipment. In the liabilities section,
current liabilities are listed first, followed by those due after a
year's time.

Assets are listed on the balance sheet at their historic cost. The objectivity principle states that asset values must be determined by factual evidence and must be verifiable by independent, outside experts. Because the business is a going concern, asset values are not changed according to fluctuations in market value.

Review of Accounting Terminology

Following is a list of the accounting terminology for this chapter.

account	going concern assumption
appreciate	IRS
assets	liabilities
business entity concept	monetary
cost principle	objectivity principle
creditor	owner's equity
current assets	service business
current liabilities	solvent
discrepancy	tangible
Financial Accounting Standards Board	transaction
fundamental accounting equation	

Fill in the blank with the correct word or term from the list.

1. The word _____ means pertaining to money.
2. _____ are economic resources owned by a business.
3. Debts owed by a business are called _____.
4. A business that is able to pay its bills when they become due is said to be _____.
5. A purchase or sale, receipt or payment of cash, or any business occurrence that can be measured in dollars and cents and that must be recorded on the books is called a/an _____.
6. A/an _____ exists when facts are not in agreement.
7. _____ are assets that are cash or will be converted into cash or used up within a year's time.
8. A person or business to whom money is owed is called a/an _____.

9. The organization that develops Statements of Financial Accounting Standards is the _____.

10. A = L + OE is the _____.

11. The federal agency responsible for collecting income taxes is the _____.

12. An accounting firm is an example of a/an _____.

13. The owner's claim on the assets of the business is called _____.

14. The separate record for each asset and liability and the owner's equity is called a/an _____.

15. An accounting principle that states that a business is an entity separate from its owners is called the _____.

16. Debts due within a year's time are _____.

17. _____ means capable of being touched.

18. An accounting principle that requires factual evidence and not a current market appraisal to be used in determining the value of assets is referred to as the _____.

19. The _____ states that the market values of assets are not particularly significant because the business is a continuing enterprise.

20. An accounting principle that states that assets must be recorded at the amount actually paid for them is referred to as the _____.

21. To rise in value is to _____.

Match the following words and terms with the definitions at the top of page 17.

22. solvent	33. current asset
23. monetary	34. business entity concept
24. discrepancy	35. service business
25. transaction	36. owner's equity
26. creditor	37. fundamental accounting equation
27. assets	
28. FASB	38. objectivity principle
29. liabilities	39. tangible
30. IRS	40. appreciate
31. account	41. going concern assumption
32. current liabilities	42. cost principle

a. things owned
b. to rise in value
c. one to whom money is owed
d. Internal Revenue Service
e. the owner's share of the assets
f. disagreement between facts
g. capable of being touched
h. able to pay bills when they become due
i. debts
j. an individual record for assets, liabilities, and the owner's capital account
k. an accounting principle that states that assets must be recorded at their historic cost
l. an asset that is either cash or will be converted to cash within a year's time
m. a business occurrence that can be measured in monetary terms

n. a principle that states that assets need not be recorded at their current market value because the business is ongoing, and thus that value is not particularly significant
o. pertaining to money
p. a business that provides a service
q. A = L + OE
r. debts due in a year's time
s. Financial Accounting Standards Board
t. an accounting principle that states that asset values must be verifiable by factual evidence
u. an accounting principle that states that a business's accounting records must be kept separate from the records of the owner

Exercises

Exercise 1.1
using the fundamental accounting equation

Complete the following equations.

a. Assets = Liabilities + _____
b. Liabilities + Owner's Equity = _____
c. A − L = _____
d. A − OE = _____
e. OE + L = _____
f. A − _____ = OE
g. A − _____ = L
h. A = L + _____
i. _____ − L = OE
j. _____ − OE = L

Exercise 1.2
using the fundamental accounting equation

Use the fundamental accounting equation to find the missing element in each of the following.

a. A = _____
     L = \$4,200
     OE = \$7,100

b. A = \$18,000
     L = \$6,800
     OE = _____

c. A = \$21,000
     L = \$8,000
     OE = _____

d. A = \$7,500
     L = _____
     OE = \$4,000

e. A = _____
     L = \$5,800
     OE = \$9,470

f. A = \$17,600
     L = _____
     OE = \$12,000

Exercise 1.3
identifying accounts

Identify the following as an asset (A), a liability (L), or an owner's equity (OE) account.

_____ a. Cash
_____ b. Accounts Payable
_____ c. Juan Martinez, Capital
_____ d. Supplies
_____ e. Furniture
_____ f. Building
_____ g. Equipment
_____ h. Wages Payable
_____ i. Library
_____ j. Payroll Taxes Payable

Exercise 1.4
manipulating the fundamental accounting equation

Find answers for the following.

a. The assets of the Dallas Riding School were \$510,000, and the owner's equity was \$275,000. What was the total amount of the liabilities?

b. The liabilities of the Peoria Parochial School were \$35,000. This amounted to one-fourth of the total assets. What was the amount of the owner's equity?

c. On December 31 of Year 1, the assets of the Oxford Counseling Center were \$180,000. At the end of Year 2, they had increased by \$32,000. The owner's equity at the end of Year 1 was one-third the value of the assets. The liabilities increased by \$15,000 from Year 1 to Year 2. What is the value of the owner's equity at the end of Year 2?

Exercise 1.5
analyzing transactions in equation form

Study the individual transactions in the equation and describe briefly what has occurred in each. Then determine the dollar value of the total assets and the dollar value of the total liabilities and owner's equity.

	Assets				=	Liabilities	+	Owner's Equity
	Cash	+	Equipment	+	Furniture =	Accounts Payable	+	Capital
a.	$15,000				=			$15,000
b.	− 4,000		+ 4,000					
	$11,000	+	$ 4,000			=		$15,000
c.					+500 =	+ 500		
	$11,000	+	$ 4,000	+	$500 =	$ 500	+	$15,000
d.	− 2,000		+ 6,000		=	+4,000		
	$ 9,000	+	$10,000	+	$500 =	$4,500	+	$15,000
e.	− 1,000				=	−1,000		
	$ 8,000	+	$10,000	+	$500 =	$3,500	+	$15,000

Exercise 1.6
analyzing transactions in terms of increases and decreases in the accounts

Determine what kind of a business transaction might occur to cause the following.

a. increase one asset and decrease another asset by the same amount
b. increase an asset and a liability by the same amount
c. increase an asset and increase owner's equity by the same amount
d. decrease an asset and decrease a liability by the same amount
e. increase one asset, decrease another asset, and increase a liability

Exercise 1.7
analyzing effects of transactions on total assets

Indicate whether the following transactions will cause total assets to increase (+), decrease (−), or not change (NC).

_____ a. purchased office equipment for cash
_____ b. purchased office equipment on account
_____ c. invested cash in the business
_____ d. purchased supplies for cash
_____ e. purchased furniture on account
_____ f. purchased a typewriter; made a cash down payment and agreed to pay the balance in six months
_____ g. paid money on account
_____ h. donated personal assets to the business

Exercise 1.8

analyzing effects of transactions on total assets, liabilities, and owner's equity

Determine the effect of each transaction on the total assets, total liabilities, and owner's equity. Indicate an increase by (+), a decrease by (−), and no change by (NC). The first transaction has been completed for you.

	Transaction	Total Assets	Total Liabilities	Owner's Equity
a.	owner invested money from personal funds into the business	+	NC	+
b.	purchased office equipment for cash			
c.	purchased equipment on account			
d.	paid money on account			
e.	owner donated personal library to the business			
f.	purchased equipment; made a cash down payment and agreed to pay the balance in three months			

Problems

Problem 1.1

recording transactions in equation form

Harvey Yee began a landscaping business on March 1, 19XX. The first transactions of the business were completed by Harvey as follows.

a. withdrew $5,000 from his personal savings account and deposited it in a business bank account

b. purchased two power mowers for cash at a total cost of $1,200

c. bought a power edger from Steinman's Hardware, paying no money down but agreeing to pay the $250 cost within 60 days

d. purchased supplies for cash at a cost of $375

e. acquired additional equipment at a total cost of $900, paying $600 down and agreeing to pay the balance within 90 days

f. purchased lawn tools for cash, $800

g. purchased a trailer costing $3,000 in which to transport equipment, tools, and supplies; paid $1,000 cash down and agreed to pay the balance within one year

h. donated to the business lawn equipment owned personally by him and valued at $2,000

Instructions   1. *Record the transactions in equation form showing the increases, decreases, and balance for each account after each transaction.*

2. *Prove the accuracy of your work by showing that total assets is equal to total liabilities and owner's equity.*

Problem 1.2
preparing a balance sheet

The following is a list of the accounts for Sharon Christensen, public accountant.

Cash	$ 8,000
Supplies	500
Office Furniture	3,500
Office Machines	4,700
Accounts Payable	4,500
Sharon Christensen, Capital	12,200

Instructions   1. *Prepare a balance sheet as of February 28, 19XX. Before you begin, review the form on page 11 and the rules for preparing the balance sheet.*

2. *After completing the balance sheet, check the following.*
    a. *Is the heading centered and does it contain three lines?*
    b. *Is the word* Assets *centered over the asset accounts?*
    c. *Does a dollar sign appear at the beginning of each column and at totals?*
    d. *Did you leave one blank space before you centered the headings* Liabilities *and* Owner's Equity?
    e. *Are the account titles for assets, liabilities, and owner's equity listed close to the double vertical lines?*
    f. *Is there a single ruling that extends all the way across the column beneath the last asset listed and beneath the Capital account amount?*
    g. *Is there a double ruling beneath the total assets figure and beneath the total liabilities and owner's equity figure?*

Problem 1.3
recording transactions and preparing a balance sheet

Paul Schmidt, an attorney, opened a business on October 1, 19XX. Paul completed the following transactions in October.

a. deposited $15,000 into a business bank account

b. paid $5,000 cash for books for the law library

c. bought office furniture costing $4,500; paid $2,000 cash down and agreed to pay the balance in six months

d. donated his personal law library worth $3,000 to the business

e. wrote a check for $500 in partial payment of the debt acquired in Transaction c

f. purchased office equipment costing $2,800; paid $1,600 cash down and agreed to pay the balance within one year

Instructions *1. Record the transactions in equation form showing the increases, decreases, and balances after each transaction. The equation should contain the following account titles.*

Cash + Library + Furniture + Equipment = Accounts Payable + Schmidt, Capital

2. Prove the accuracy of your work by showing that total assets equal total liabilities and owner's equity.

3. Prepare a balance sheet for Paul Schmidt, Attorney, as of October 31, 19XX.

Problem 1.4

determining amount of capital and preparing a balance sheet

Nancy Samuels just opened an exercise salon called No Weighting. The cost of her exercise equipment was $9,500; the exercise mats cost $2,200; the stereo system cost $3,500; furniture cost $1,800; and special lighting fixtures cost $875. Nancy owes $5,000 on the exercise equipment and $2,000 on the stereo, and both of these amounts are due within one year. She has $2,700 cash in the bank.

Instructions *1. Calculate the amount of Nancy's Capital account, following this procedure:*

    a. List the asset accounts (six in all) and their balances, and then determine the dollar value of the total assets.

    b. Determine the total amount of accounts payable.

    c. Subtract the total liabilities from the total assets.

2. Prepare a balance sheet for No Weighting as of March 31, 19XX.

Problem 1.5

analyzing effects of transactions on the balance sheet

Following is a partially completed balance sheet for S. P. Brocke Accountancy Company on January 31, 19XX.

S.P. BROCKE ACCOUNTANCY COMPANY
BALANCE SHEET
JANUARY 31, 19XX

Assets		
Cash	$ 8 1 4 0 —	
Office Supplies	4 2 5 —	
Furniture	6 9 5 0 —	
Lighting Fixtures	8 5 0 —	
Computers	1 7 6 0 0 —	
Library	8 2 0 0 —	
Office Equipment	3 6 4 0 —	
Total Assets		
Liabilities		
Accounts Payable	$ 1 4 9 7 0 —	
Payroll Taxes Payable	9 0 0 —	
Total Liabilities		
Owner's Equity		
Susan P. Brocke, Capital, January 31, 19XX		

Susan completed the following transactions on February 1.

a.   paid $500 cash for office supplies

b.   wrote checks to various creditors totaling $1,500

c.   purchased a new computer for $3,000; paid $700 cash down and agreed to pay the balance in 12 months' time

Instructions

1.   *Determine the amount of the owner's capital on January 31.*

2.   *Determine the effect of each transaction on the accounts.*

3.   *Prepare a balance sheet on February 1 that shows the results of the February 1 transactions.*

CHAPTER 2

Profitability and the Income Statement

LEARNING OBJECTIVES

When you have completed this chapter, you should

1. have a better understanding of accounting terminology, particularly as it relates to the income statement.

2. understand how owner's equity is increased or decreased.

3. understand how revenue and expenses affect owner's equity.

4. be able to prepare an income statement.

5. be able to prepare a statement of owner's equity detailing the changes that have occurred.

In Chapter 1 we learned that Ms. Florence Hansen was willing to invest $10,000 of her own money into a business venture called The Instant Secretary. Ms. Hansen, and many others like her, are willing to take such financial risks for many reasons; the most likely reason, though, is that Flo thinks The Instant Secretary will earn a healthy **profit.** Other reasons might be that she likes the idea of setting her own work hours or she has decided that if she must work hard, she wants the benefits to **accrue** to herself. She believes that her idea is a good one and that people will pay for the service she intends to provide.

profit
the return received on a business undertaking after costs have been met

accrue
to be gained or attained

proprietor
an owner

incur
to become subject to

For a business to be profitable, the revenue must be greater than the expenses. When this is the case, the **proprietor** benefits by the gain. However, if expenses become too large compared with revenue, and if the cash on hand is reduced to a small amount, the business may not remain solvent. In this case, the proprietor **incurs** the loss.

REVENUE

revenue
the inflow of cash and receivables for services performed

Flo begins her business with just herself and one other employee. She plans to prepare letters, memos, and reports for individuals and businesses and has advertised in the local newspapers. She receives many inquiries and orders for work right away. **Revenue** for The Instant Secretary results when services are performed and cash is received for those services, or when services are performed and an account receivable results. Revenue increases owner's equity, but it is recorded in a separate revenue account.

An account receivable is a promise by a customer to pay at some future date. The company selling the service stipulates when the account receivable must be paid; Flo requires that all accounts receivable be paid within 30 days.

Cash must not be confused with revenue; not all cash coming into a business is revenue. Revenue results for Flo's business only when services are sold, but *cash* may come into the business from many other sources. Assume, for example, that in February The Instant Secretary performs services for the Legal Services Company in the amount of $800. The Legal Services Company does not pay for the work in February, but the $800 is nevertheless recorded as revenue in the month in which it is earned. When in March the Legal Services Company pays the $800 owed to The Instant Secretary, it is logically *not* counted as revenue again. In March the transaction simply increases one asset, Cash, while decreasing another, Accounts Receivable. Other examples of cash coming into the business that is not revenue include the owner withdrawing cash from a personal savings account and depositing that money into the business account or the business borrowing from a bank.

EXPENSES

expenses
the necessary costs incurred in obtaining revenue

Expenses are the necessary costs that relate to earning revenue. Examples are salaries for employees, payroll taxes, utilities, phone bills, advertising costs, delivery charges, and so on. Expenses may be paid in cash as they are incurred, or the business may promise to pay at a later date. This results in an Account Payable.

Not all payments of cash are considered to be expenses. Paying back a loan, for example, is not an expense; rather, it is a reduction in an asset and a liability. Money paid for purchasing equipment is not an expense, but causes an increase in one asset and a decrease in another. Expenses decrease owner's equity and are recorded in separate accounts.

NET INCOME

When a business is making money, it is said to be operating profitably, and earning a profit is probably the most important motive urging people to open their own businesses. The accounting term used to describe profits is **net income,** the excess of revenue over expenses.

net income
the excess of revenue over expenses

Net income must be measured for a specific period of time (say, one month or one year) for it to be meaningful. For example, the statement "Our company earned $5,000" would not be particularly significant without knowing whether it took one year, one month, or one week to earn the $5,000.

accounting period
the time span covered by the income statement

All businesses prepare financial statements yearly and many prepare them monthly or quarterly. An **accounting period** refers to the span of time covered by an income statement. The period of time covered by the financial statements must be the same, so that management can make comparisons of revenue and expenses from year to year or from one month of the current year to the corresponding month of the previous year. Such comparisons might be: Is revenue this December greater than that of last December? Have expenses increased this year? How does our net income compare with that of similar businesses?

MATCHING REVENUE AND EXPENSES

matching principle
expenses incurred during an accounting period must be deducted from the revenue for that same time period to determine the net income or loss

When preparing an income statement, the accountant must take into consideration the **matching principle,** which recognizes that during a particular time period, expenses are incurred to produce revenue. Those expenses must be deducted from the revenue for that accounting period so that the measurement of net income for that period is valid. To compare this year's revenue with last year's expenses would not be an accurate measurement of what the business has done in either year.

Assume that The Instant Secretary sells $75,000 in services the first year. If Flo did not deduct the year's advertising, salaries, utilities, and other expenses related to earning the $75,000, she would not have an accurate picture of The Instant Secretary's earning power.

OWNER'S WITHDRAWALS

single proprietorship
a business owned by an individual

With a **single proprietorship,** the owner is *not* considered to be a regular employee of the business. The salaries of employees are business expenses, and income taxes and payroll taxes are deducted from their paychecks. A proprietor of a small business, on the other hand, pays personal income taxes based on the net income for the year; that net income is considered to be the owner's salary for income tax purposes.

When the owner decides to withdraw cash from the business for personal use, the withdrawal is *not* considered to be an expense. Rather, it is a reduction in the owner's equity and is recorded in a separate account called Drawing. The drawing account is used to record

1. all cash taken from the business by the owner for personal use.

2. any payments of personal bills by the owner with the business checkbook.

3. removal by the owner of business assets for personal use (for example, taking a computer from the business for home use).

OWNER'S EQUITY

The owner's equity account increases when the owner invests cash from personal savings into the business or when she or he donates personal assets to the business. When the business becomes profitable, the owner may choose to withdraw cash from the business for personal use or may remove equipment, supplies, furniture, or other business assets for personal use. All withdrawals of assets by the owner are recorded in the drawing account and reduce the owner's equity. The owner's equity may be affected only by the following:

Increases in Owner's Equity

1. The owner invests cash or other assets in the business.

2. The business earns a net income.

Decreases in Owner's Equity

1. The owner withdraws cash or other assets from the business.

2. The business incurs a net loss.

THE FUNDAMENTAL ACCOUNTING EQUATION WITH REVENUE, EXPENSES, AND WITHDRAWALS

Revenue increases owner's equity; expenses and withdrawals decrease owner's equity; and revenue, expenses, and withdrawals are each recorded in separate accounts. Because revenue, expenses, and drawing directly affect owner's equity, the fundamental accounting equation now looks like this:

Assets = Liabilities + Owner's Equity + Revenue − Expenses − Withdrawals.

Transactions for Revenue, Expenses, and Drawing

Now let's look at some typical transactions for The Instant Secretary.

Transaction 1: Sale of Services for Cash　Flo agreed to do some work for another local business. The work was completed in three days, and the charge for the service was $150. The customer paid cash. The fundamental accounting equation is shown with the previous balances from Chapter 1. This particular transaction increases cash and increases revenue and affects the equation as follows.

					Assets		=		Liabilities + Owner's Equity				
			Accts.					Accts.					
	Cash +	Rec. +	Equip. +	Furn. +	Sup. +	Lib. =	Pay.	+ Capital +	Rev.	− Exp.	− Draw.		
Previous													
Balance	$6,200 +	0	+ $9,500 +	$4,500 +	$800 +	$200 =	$11,000 +	$10,200					
(1)	+ 150								+150				
New													
Balance	$6,350 +	0	+ $9,500 +	$4,500 +	$800 +	$200 =	$11,000 +	$10,200 +	$150				

Transaction 2: Sale of Services on Account　The Instant Secretary agreed to do some work for Allen's Engineering Company over a two-week period. The total cost of The Instant Secretary's services for this job was $750. Allen's paid no money when the work was delivered but agreed to pay within 30 days, thus creating an Account Receivable for The Instant Secretary. The equation looks like this after Revenue and the asset Accounts Receivable have both been increased.

					Assets		=		Liabilities + Owner's Equity				
			Accts.					Accts.					
	Cash +	Rec. +	Equip. +	Furn. +	Sup. +	Lib. =	Pay.	+ Capital +	Rev.	− Exp.	− Draw.		
Previous													
Balance	$6,350 +	0	+ $9,500 +	$4,500 +	$800 +	$200 =	$11,000 +	$10,200 +	$150				
(2)		+750							+750				
New													
Balance	$6,350 +	$750	+ $9,500 +	$4,500 +	$800 +	$200 =	$11,000 +	$10,200 +	$900				

The work performed was recognized as revenue at the time the work was done even though the money had not yet been collected for the service.

Transaction 3: Cash Payment for an Expense   Flo pays a $60 phone bill for The Instant Secretary. The equation looks like this after the transaction.

		Assets				=	Liabilities + Owner's Equity				
	Accts.						Accts.				
Cash +	Rec. +	Equip. +	Furn. +	Sup. +	Lib. =		Pay. +	Capital +	Rev. –	Exp. –	Draw.
Previous											
Balance $6,350 +	$750 +	$9,500 +	$4,500 +	$800 +	$200 =		$11,000 +	$10,200 +	$900		
(3) – 60										–60	
New											
Balance $6,290 +	$750 +	$9,500 +	$4,500 +	$800 +	$200 =		$11,000 +	$10,200 +	$900 –	$60	

A careful look at the equation shows that expenses are subtracted from revenue to keep the equation in balance. Total assets are equal to total liabilities plus owner's equity plus revenue minus expenses.

$$\text{Assets} = \text{Liabilities} + \text{Capital} + \text{Revenue} - \text{Expenses}$$
$$\$22{,}040 = \$11{,}000 + \$10{,}200 + \$900 \qquad \$60$$

$$\$22{,}040$$

Transaction 4: Owner Withdraws Cash for Personal Use   Flo withdrew $250 cash for her personal use. Owner's withdrawals are not considered to be an expense of the business and are recorded in a separate account called Drawing or Owner's Withdrawals.

		Assets				=	Liabilities + Owner's Equity				
	Accts.						Accts.				
Cash +	Rec. +	Equip. +	Furn. +	Sup. +	Lib. =		Pay. +	Capital +	Rev. –	Exp. –	Draw.
Previous											
Balance $6,290 +	$750 +	$9,500 +	$4,500 +	$800 +	$200 =		$11,000 +	$10,200 +	$900 –	$60	
(4) – 250											–250
New											
Balance $6,040 +	$750 +	$9,500 +	$4,500 +	$800 +	$200 =		$11,000 +	$10,200 +	$900 –	$60 –	$250

Transaction 5: An Expense Is Incurred but Payment Is Delayed
Flo has some radio advertising done for The Instant Secretary for $375 and agrees to pay the bill within 60 days. This transaction

does not affect assets at all. On the liabilities and owner's equity side of the equation, the $375 is added as a liability and will be subtracted as an expense, thus causing no change in the right side of the equation.

			Assets				=		Liabilities + Owner's Equity			
		Accts.							Accts.			
Cash	+ Rec.	+ Equip.	+ Furn.	+ Sup.	+ Lib.	=		Pay.	+ Capital	+ Rev.	− Exp.	− Draw.
Previous												
Balance $6,040	+ $750	+ $9,500	+ $4,500	+ $800	+ $200	=		$11,000	+ $10,200	+ $900	− $ 60	− $250
(5)								+ 375			−375	
New												
Balance $6,040	+ $750	+ $9,500	+ $4,500	+ $800	+ $200	=		$11,375	+ $10,200	+ $900	− $435	− $250

As required by the matching principle, expenses are recognized when incurred, *not* when they are paid.

Transaction 6: Money Is Received on Account   Allen's Engineering Service (see Transaction 2) paid $500 to The Instant Secretary as a partial settlement of its account.

			Assets				=		Liabilities + Owner's Equity			
		Accts.							Accts.			
Cash	+ Rec.	+ Equip.	+ Furn.	+ Sup.	+ Lib.	=		Pay.	+ Capital	+ Rev.	− Exp.	− Draw.
Previous												
Balance $6,040	+ $750	+ $9,500	+ $4,500	+ $800	+ $200	=		$11,375	+ $10,200	+ $900	− $435	− $250
(6)	+ 500	−500										
New												
Balance $6,540	+ $250	+ $9,500	+ $4,500	+ $800	+ $200	=		$11,375	+ $10,200	+ $900	− $435	− $250

One asset, Cash, has increased by $500 while another asset, Accounts Receivable, has decreased by $500, thus keeping the total assets the same. Money received on account is *not* revenue, but a reduction in the asset Accounts Receivable. In this particular case, Transaction 2 recorded the $750 as revenue, and it would not be appropriate to recognize it as revenue again at this point.

Transaction 7: Owner Makes an Additional Cash Investment
Flo decided to take an additional $1,000 from her personal savings account and deposit it in the business account.

	Assets					=	Liabilities + Owner's Equity				
Cash +	Accts. Rec. +	Equip. +	Furn. +	Sup. +	Lib. =		Accts. Pay. +	Capital +	Rev. −	Exp. −	Draw.
Previous											
Balance $6,540 +	$250 +	$9,500 +	$4,500 +	$800 +	$200 =		$11,375 +	$10,200 +	$900 −	$435 −	$250
(7) +1,000								+ 1,000			
New											
Balance $7,540 +	$250 +	$9,500 +	$4,500 +	$800 +	$200 =		$11,375 +	$11,200 +	$900 −	$435 −	$250

This additional investment of $1,000 increases the capital account but does not affect revenue.

THE INCOME STATEMENT

The preceding seven transactions are typical of those that occurred during the entire month for The Instant Secretary. In addition to the revenue shown in the equation, The Instant Secretary performed additional services for cash in the amount of $2,400, thus bringing the Cash balance from $7,540 to $9,940 and increasing the revenue earned from $900 to $3,300. Flo also paid cash for the following expenses, which are not shown in the equation.

Equipment Rental	$ 100
Wages	800
Utilities	90
Newspaper Advertising	72
Delivery	18
Total Other Expenses	$1,080

Payment for these additional expenses brings the amount of cash on hand to $8,860.

Balance after Transaction 7	$7,540
Additional Services Performed for Cash	+2,400
Subtotal	$9,940
Additional Expenses Paid with Cash	−1,080
Cash Balance	$8,860

The owner's withdrawal (Transaction 4) is *not* an expense; it will appear on the balance sheet as a deduction from capital.

The income statement is the financial statement that shows total revenue, total expenses, and net income (or net loss) for an accounting period. The income statement for The Instant Secretary, showing in detail all the revenue and expenses for the month of February, follows.

THE INSTANT SECRETARY INCOME STATEMENT FOR MONTH ENDED FEBRUARY 28, 19XX		
Revenue		
Revenue from Services		$ 3300 —
Expenses		
Telephone Expense	$ 60 —	
Equipment Rental Expense	100 —	
*Advertising Expense**	447 —	
Wages Expense	800 —	
Utilities Expense	90 —	
Delivery Expense	18 —	
Total Expenses		1515 —
Net Income		$ 1785 —

*Note that newspaper and radio advertising expense are combined for the income statement under one account titled Advertising Expense.

Guidelines for Preparing the Income Statement

The Heading   The income statement has a three-part heading, which is centered and always includes, in this order, (1) the name of the business, (2) the name of the financial statement, and (3) the time period or the length of time for which the net income is measured.

Revenue   The word *Revenue* is written at the left next to the double vertical lines, and the name of the revenue account is indented about one-half inch. If there is more than one revenue account, list the amounts in the left-hand column. *Total Revenue* is written immediately below the last revenue account listed, and the total amount is written in the right-hand column as illustrated.

Revenue							
Revenue from Consulting			$1 4 5 0 —				
Revenue from Teaching			2 7 0 0 —				
Total Revenue					$4 1 5 0 —		

Expenses   One blank line should be left before writing the word *Expenses* at the left. Again, indent about one-half inch and list the expense accounts. There is no particular order for listing expenses. The amounts are entered in the left-hand column, and the total of the expenses is written in the right-hand column beneath the total revenue figure.

Net Income   The total of expenses is subtracted from the total revenue to obtain net income. If total expenses are larger than total revenue, then a **net loss** has been incurred. Another blank line should be left before writing *Net Income* or *Net Loss.*

net loss
the excess of
expenses over
revenue

Dollar Signs and Rulings   A dollar sign appears at the beginning of each column and next to the net income figure. A single ruling appears under the amount for the last expense listed to indicate addition, and a single ruling appears beneath the figure for total expenses to indicate subtraction. A double ruling appears beneath net income to show that work is completed. Remember, all rulings are drawn with a ruler and extend all the way across the column.

STATEMENT OF OWNER'S EQUITY

Because revenue and expense accounts affect owner's equity, the income statement must be prepared *before* the balance sheet so that results of operations (net income or net loss) can be included in the owner's equity section of the balance sheet. Some people prefer, however, to prepare a statement of owner's equity separate from the balance sheet. This is the procedure that Flo chooses, and following is the statement of owner's equity for The Instant Secretary detailing the changes in owner's equity for February.

THE INSTANT SECRETARY STATEMENT OF OWNER'S EQUITY FOR MONTH ENDED FEBRUARY 28, 19XX		
Florence Hansen, Capital, February 1, 19XX	$10200—	
Add: Net Income for February	1785—	
Additional Investment	1000—	
Subtotal	12985—	
Deduct: Florence Hansen, Drawing	250—	
Florence Hansen, Capital, February 28, 19XX		$12735—

Net income and Flo's additional investment have increased owner's equity, and the withdrawals have caused a decrease. A net loss would also cause a decrease in owner's equity.

The following statement of owner's equity shows how a loss is handled for the A & M Consulting Service.

A & M CONSULTING SERVICE STATEMENT OF OWNER'S EQUITY FOR MONTH ENDED JULY 31, 19XX			
T. A. Adams, Capital, July 1, 19XX		$42000—	
Add: Additional Investment		3600—	
Subtotal		45600—	
Deduct: Net Loss for July	$4,280—		
T. A. Adams, Drawing	2,700—		
Total Deductions		6980—	
T. A. Adams, Capital, July 31, 19XX			$38620—

Guidelines for Preparing the Statement of Owner's Equity

The statement of owner's equity has a three-part heading similar to the heading on the balance sheet. It contains (1) the name of the company, (2) the name of the statement, and (3) the time period during which the changes have occurred.

Calculations are completed in the left-hand column, and the total capital is entered directly into the right-hand column. Often a third column is required for calculating, as is the case when the net loss must be added to the withdrawals.

THE BALANCE SHEET—NOT DETAILING CHANGES IN OWNER'S EQUITY

The balance sheet for The Instant Secretary looks as it did before, except that when a separate statement of owner's equity is prepared, those changes are not reflected again on the balance sheet; only the ending capital figure appears in the owner's equity section.

THE INSTANT SECRETARY
BALANCE SHEET
FEBRUARY 28, 19XX

Assets		
Cash	$8860 —	
Accounts Receivable	250 —	
Supplies	800 —	
Equipment	9500 —	
Furniture	4500 —	
Library	200 —	
Total Assets		$24110 —
Liabilities		
Accounts Payable		$11375 —
Owner's Equity		
Florence Hansen, Capital, February 28, 19XX		12735 —
Total Liabilities and Owner's Equity		$24110 —

THE BALANCE SHEET—DETAILING CHANGES IN OWNER'S EQUITY

If Flo were to choose not to prepare a separate statement of owner's equity, the balance sheet would reflect all the changes in the owner's capital account. The balance sheet for The Instant Secretary showing the changes in owner's equity for February follows.

THE INSTANT SECRETARY BALANCE SHEET FEBRUARY 28, 19XX		
Assets		
Cash	$8 8 6 0 —	
Accounts Receivable	2 5 0 —	
Supplies	8 0 0 —	
Equipment	9 5 0 0 —	
Furniture	4 5 0 0 —	
Library	2 0 0 —	
Total Assets		$2 4 1 1 0 —
Liabilities		
Accounts Payable		$1 1 3 7 5 —
Owner's Equity		
Florence Hansen, Capital, February 1, 19XX	$1 0 2 0 0 —	
Add: Net Income for February	1 7 8 5 —	
Additional Investment	1 0 0 0 —	
Subtotal	1 2 9 8 5 —	
Deduct: Florence Hansen, Drawing	2 5 0 —	
Florence Hansen, Capital, February 28, 19XX		1 2 7 3 5 —
Total Liabilities and Owner's Equity		$2 4 1 1 0 —

THE ACCRUAL METHOD AND THE CASH METHOD OF MEASURING NET INCOME

accrual method
revenue is recognized in the period in which it is earned, and expenses are recognized in the period in which they are incurred

The **accrual method** of accounting is a method whereby all revenue is recognized in the period in which the services are performed (or in the period in which the revenue is earned), whether or not cash is received right away. Likewise, expenses are recognized as expenses in the period in which they are incurred, whether or not cash payment for them is made in the same accounting period. Revenue may be included in accounts receivable and expenses may show up in accounts payable. For example, a landscape contractor agreed to do some work for a client and send the bill for the services after all the work was completed. The job was started on November 1 and completed on February 28 of the following year. The contractor would recognize a portion of the total revenue as being earned during each of the four months and would simply record an account receivable for amounts to be received after completion of the entire job. By the same token, the contractor would record *all* expenses related to this job when they are incurred, even if creditors agree to accept payment at a later date.

The cash basis of accounting, on the other hand, recognizes revenue when cash is actually received and recognizes expenses when cash is paid out. In the preceding example of the landscape contractor, revenue for that particular job would not be recognized until March, when the cash was received, and expenses would be recognized when paid, not when they were incurred. This would distort the firm's financial position, because the contractor was actually performing landscape services from November through February, yet all the revenue for this job by this method would be recognized in March, making that month's income as greatly overstated as the four preceding months' income was understated. An obvious advantage to the cash basis of accounting is its simplicity, and its use is widespread among professionals. Because accounting by the cash basis does, however, have a tendency to distort income earned and expenses incurred for a particular time period, the accrual method of accounting will be used exclusively in this text.

SUMMARY

Revenue is the inflow of cash and other assets into the business for services performed; expenses are the necessary costs related to earning revenue. The fundamental accounting equation is now expanded to include revenue and expenses and the owner's withdrawals.

Assets = Liabilities + Owner's Equity + Revenue − Expenses − Drawing.

To earn a profit, revenue must be greater than related expenses. The matching principle requires that all expenses for an accounting period be deducted from the revenue earned for that same accounting period to determine the net income.

The proprietor of a business gains all the profits but must also sustain all the losses. He or she may be required to invest additional sums of money from time to time and may withdraw cash or other assets as needed. A transaction that involves the owner removing cash or other assets from the business will be recorded in the owner's drawing account.

The income statement is the financial statement that shows whether the business is operating profitably. It lists the revenue accounts and total revenue, the expense accounts and total expenses, and the net income or net loss for the period. The span of time covered by the income statement is referred to as an *accounting period.* Accounting periods are of equal length so that comparisons may be made from period to period.

The balance sheet reflects a firm's position on a certain date and may detail the changes in owner's equity, or a separate statement of owner's equity may be prepared. The owner's equity account may be increased by a net income or an additional investment by the owner, and it may be decreased by a net loss or by the owner's withdrawals.

Review of Accounting Terminology

Following is a list of the accounting terminology for this chapter.

accounting period	net income
accrual method	net loss
accrue	profit
expenses	proprietor
incur	revenue
matching principle	single proprietorship

Fill in the blank with the correct word or term from the list.

1. The word that means to increase or accumulate is
    _____.

2. An owner of a business is referred to as a/an _____.

3. To _____ means to become subject to.

4. The amount by which expenses are greater than revenue is referred to as _____.

5. _____ is defined as the inflow of cash and receivables for services performed.

6. The costs incurred in obtaining revenue are called
    _____.

7. A business owned by an individual is referred to as a/an
    _____.

8. Revenue minus expenses equals _____.

9. The return received by a business after costs have been met is called _____.

10. A designated time period for which a company's net income or net loss is calculated is called a/an _____.

11. An accounting principle that states that revenue must be matched with related expenses incurred during an accounting period is referred to as the _____.

12. A method of accounting whereby revenue is recognized in the period earned and expenses are recognized when incurred is called the _____ of accounting.

Match the following words and terms on the left with the definitions on the right.

13. accrue
14. profit
15. proprietor
16. net income
17. matching principle
18. expenses
19. net loss
20. incur
21. accrual method
22. single proprietorship
23. revenue
24. accounting period

a. to increase or accumulate
b. the excess of expenses over revenue
c. the return received on a business undertaking after costs have been met
d. inflow of cash and receivables for services performed
e. costs incurred in obtaining revenue
f. to become subject to
g. the excess of revenue over expenses
h. a time period of a month, quarter, year, and so on, for which a company's net income or loss is determined
i. an owner
j. a business owned by one person
k. when expenses for a particular time period are deducted from the revenue earned for that time period to determine net income
l. an accounting method that recognizes revenue in the period earned and expenses in the period incurred

Exercises

Exercise 2.1
identifying accounts

Identify the following as asset (A), liability (L), owner's equity (OE), revenue (R), or expense (E) accounts.

_____ a.	Accounts Receivable	_____ h.	Utilities Expense
_____ b.	Furniture	_____ i.	Taxes Payable
_____ c.	Don Jones, Capital	_____ j.	Rent Expense
_____ d.	Accounts Payable	_____ k.	Don Jones, Drawing
_____ e.	Equipment	_____ l.	Salaries Expense
_____ f.	Cash	_____ m.	Office Machines
_____ g.	Revenue from Services	_____ n.	Consulting Revenue

Exercise 2.2
*analyzing transactions
in equation form*

Study the following carefully, then answer the questions that relate to Transactions a through i.

	Cash	+	Accts. Rec.	+	Equip.	=	Accts. Pay.	+	Capital	+	Rev.	−	Exp.	−	Draw.
a.	+10,000								+10,000						
b.	− 2,000				+2,000										
	8,000	+			2,000	=			10,000						
c.	+ 500										+500				
	8,500			+	2,000	=			10,000	+	500				
d.			+800								+800				
	8,500	+	800	+	2,000	=			10,000	+	1,300				
e.	− 400												−400		
	8,100	+	800	+	2,000	=			10,000	+	1,300	−	400		
f.	− 800														−800
	7,300	+	800	+	2,000	=			10,000	+	1,300	−	400	−	800
g.					+ 900	=	+900								
	7,300	+	800	+	2,900	=	900	+	10,000	+	1,300	−	400	−	800
h.							+300						−300		
	7,300	+	800	+	2,900	=	1,200	+	10,000	+	1,300	−	700	−	800
i.	+ 100		−100												
	7,400	+	700	+	2,900	=	1,200	+	10,000	+	1,300	−	700	−	800

1. Is the equation in balance, i.e., do total assets equal liabilities plus capital plus revenue minus expenses minus drawing?
2. Tell what has occurred for each transaction.
3. What is the amount of net income?
4. What is the amount of ending capital?

Exercise 2.3
analyzing transactions in terms of increases and decreases in accounts

Describe a transaction that could cause the following to occur.

a. increase one asset and decrease another asset by the same amount

b. increase an asset and increase revenue by the same amount

c. increase an asset and increase owner's equity by the same amount

d. decrease an asset and increase the drawing account by the same amount

e. decrease an asset and increase an expense by the same amount

f. decrease an asset and decrease a liability by the same amount

g. increase a liability and increase an expense

Exercise 2.4
describing transactions that cause increases and decreases in the accounts

Describe a situation that may have caused the following for Leslie Andrews, veterinarian.

a. Cash is increased by $800 and Revenue is increased by $800

b. Accounts Receivable is increased by $600 and Revenue is increased by $600

c. Equipment is increased by $750 and Accounts Payable is increased by $750

d. Cash is increased by $225 and Accounts Receivable is decreased by $225

e. Cash is decreased by $600 and Drawing is increased by $600

f. Equipment is increased by $2,500, Cash is decreased by $1,000, and Accounts Payable is increased by $1,500

g. Accounts Payable is decreased by $500 and Cash is decreased by $500

h. Utilities Expense is increased by $175 and Cash is decreased by $175

i.   Cash is decreased by $1,000 and Office Equipment is increased by $1,000

j.   Advertising Expense is increased by $220 and Accounts Payable is increased by $220

Exercise 2.5
determining whether a transaction represents revenue

During May, Harry Brown, proprietor of Poodle Pruners, carried out the transactions listed below. In each case, determine whether the transaction represents revenue for the month of May.

a.   obtained a $5,000 business loan for the purchase of equipment and furniture

b.   trimmed the fur of 14 poodles on May 10 and received $280 cash for the service

c.   invested an additional $2,500 into the business

d.   received $750 cash on account from customers whose dogs he had trimmed in April

e.   trimmed and bathed eight poodles on May 31 at a total cost to customers of $450; five customers paid cash for the service amounting to $150, and the others agreed to pay within 30 days

Exercise 2.6
determining whether a transaction represents expense

During July, Harry Brown, proprietor of Poodle Pruners, carried out the following transactions. Determine which of the following represent expenses for July.

a.   on July 1, wrote a check for $1,500 in payment of the rent for July

b.   on July 3, wrote a $500 check to himself to be deposited in his personal checking account

c.   on July 10, wrote a check for $725 in payment of an account payable resulting from radio advertising done in June

d.   on July 15, wrote a check for $450 in payment for a desk for the computer and printer

e.   on July 20, wrote a check for $1,000 to repay a non-interest-bearing loan obtained in February

f.   on July 31, wrote a check for $120 for gasoline purchases for the business van for July

Exercise 2.7
preparing statement of owner's equity

Heather Bullock is a certified public account (CPA). Heather's Capital account on May 1 had a balance of $7,800. During May, Heather invested an additional $2,000 into the business from her personal savings. Revenue for the month was $10,740, and expenses were $8,340. The balance in the drawing account on May 31 was $800. Prepare a statement of owner's equity for Heather Bullock, CPA, on May 31, 19XX.

Exercise 2.8
preparing statement of owner's equity

Roger Barnes has a small business called Horse Hair Care. Roger grooms horses before their shows and gives advice about the proper care of horses. His Capital account on November 1 showed a balance of $2,800. Revenue for November was $4,325, and expenses were $4,885. Roger's drawing account showed a balance on November 30 of $480. Prepare a statement of owner's equity for the month ended November 30, 19XX, for Horse Hair Care.

Exercise 2.9
manipulating the fundamental accounting equation

Following are several possibilities for the statement of owner's equity. Determine in each case the dollar value of the missing figure.

a.	Capital, February 1	$8,000
	Net Loss for the Month	1,500
	Owner's Withdrawals	800
	Capital, February 28	5700
b.	Capital, May 1	$6,100
	Net Income for the Month	1,800
	Capital, May 31	7,000
	Owner's Withdrawals	900
c.	Capital, October 31	$8,700
	Net Income for the Month	1,650
	Owner's Withdrawals	1,000
	Capital, October 1	8050
d.	Capital, March 1	$10,600
	Owner's Withdrawals	2,300
	Net Income for the Month	1,700
	Additional Investment	1,000
	Capital, March 31	11000
e.	Capital, September 1	$4,900
	Owner's Withdrawals	900
	Capital, September 30	3,200
	Net Loss for the Month	800

Problems

Problem 2.1
recording transactions in equation form, preparing statement of owner's equity

Albert Mar, a decorator, began his own business on September 1, and he performed the following transactions in the first month.

a. deposited $5,500 in a bank account for Mar's Home Decorating

b. bought furniture for the office at a total cost of $3,500; made a $1,000 cash down payment and agreed to pay the rest within six months

c. purchased office equipment for $650 cash

d. paid rent, $450

e. received $800 cash for services rendered

f. paid cash for supplies for the office, $280

g. paid salary of part-time employee, $250

h. received a bill for advertising, $380, and decided to pay it later (remember, expenses are recorded when incurred, not necessarily when paid)

i. bought a typewriter, $1,000, and paid no money down; full amount is due in 90 days

j. performed services for a customer and sent a bill for $1,250; the customer agrees to pay within 30 days

k. paid $100 on account (see Transaction h)

l. withdrew $500 from the business for his personal use

m. received check for $475 from a customer in partial settlement of the account

Instructions

1. Using the following headings, record each transaction and the new balances after each.

Cash + Accts. Rec. + Sup. + Furn. + Equip. = Accts. Pay. + Capital + Rev. − Exp. − Draw.

2. After recording all the transactions, check to make sure that the equation is in balance.

3. Determine the amount of the net income or net loss for the month.

4. Prepare a statement of owner's equity for the month ended September 30, 19XX.

Problem 2.2

preparing financial statements from account balances

Following is a list of the accounts and their balances on June 30 for Toni Sanchez, Child Psychologist.

Cash	$3,000	Counseling Revenue	$3,200
Accounts Receivable	1,500	Advertising Expense	500
Furniture	4,500	Wages Expense	1,560
Equipment	1,940	Utilities Expense	85
Accounts Payable	2,800	Telephone Expense	140
Sanchez, Drawing	1,000	Rent Expense	875
Sanchez, Capital, June 1	7,205	Equipment Rental Expense	260
Consulting Revenue	2,200	Miscellaneous Expense	45

Instructions

1. *Prepare an income statement for Toni Sanchez, Child Psychologist, for the month ended June 30, 19XX.*

2. *Prepare a statement of owner's equity for the month ended June 30, 19XX.*

3. *Prepare a balance sheet as of June 30, 19XX. Include only the ending capital figure in the Owner's Equity section.*

Problem 2.3

recording transactions in equation form, preparing balance sheet

Paul Padilla established his own business, Paul's Parking. Transactions for September are as follows:

a. deposited $6,000 into the business account

b. purchased office equipment from J. R.'s Office Supply Company for $1,800; paid $800 cash down and agreed to pay the balance within 90 days

c. paid rent, $1,000

d. paid $240 cash for supplies

e. paid wages, $300

f. received parking lot revenue, $2,000 cash

g. purchased office furniture from J. R.'s Office Supply Company for $2,000; paid $1,000 cash down and agreed to pay the balance within 60 days

h. paid $350 for advertising

i. Paul wrote a business check in payment of his personal phone bill, $126

j. paid utilities bill, $60

k. paid phone bill, $85

l. received $500 in cash revenue

m. sent bills totaling $650 to regular customers who have been using the parking lot but have not yet paid

n. paid wages, $300

o. wrote a check for $200 in partial settlement of the account owed to J. R.'s Office Supply Company (see Transactions b and g)

p. received a bill for advertising, $35; recorded it now to be paid later

q. Paul withdrew $400 for his personal use

Instructions 1. *Using the following headings, record each transaction and the new balance after each.*

Cash + Accts. Rec. + Sup. + Equip. + Furn. = Accts. Pay. + Capital + Rev. − Exp. − Draw.

2. *After recording all the transactions, check to see if the equation is in balance.*

3. *Determine the amount of net income or net loss for the month.*

4. *Prepare a balance sheet as of September 30 that shows the changes that have occurred in owner's equity. Do not prepare a separate statement of owner's equity.*

Problem 2.4
*identifying accounts
and preparing
financial statements*

The accounts and their balances for Jesse Brown, accountant, follow.

Jesse Brown, Drawing	$ 800
Revenue from Services	2,000
Cash	1,850
Accounts Payable	5,400
Supplies	520
Rent Expense	475
Wages Expense	800
Office Furniture	3,800
Office Equipment	4,700
Advertising Expense	160
Utilities Expense	295
Insurance Expense	80
Accounts Receivable	700
Jesse Brown, Capital, December 1, 19XX	5,580
Revenue from Consulting	1,200

Instructions 1. *Identify each of the accounts as either asset (A), liability (L), owner's equity (OE), revenue (R), or expense (E).*

2. *Prepare an income statement for the month ended December 31, 19XX.*

3. *Prepare a statement of owner's equity for the month ended December 31, 19XX.*

4. *Prepare a balance sheet as of December 31, 19XX. Include only the ending capital figure in the owner's equity section.*

Problem 2.5
analyzing the effects of errors on net income

Rita Roth owns the Roth Real Estate Company. The income statement for the month of November shows a net income of $1,762. When the transactions were recorded for the month, however, several errors were made.

a. Rita withdrew $1,200 during the month for personal use. The $1,200 was recorded as a deduction from cash and as an expense.

b. The Roth Real Estate Company performed services amounting to $2,400 for Andy Blake during November, but since he would not be paying for the service until December, the bookkeeper decided to wait until then to record the transaction.

c. A check for $700 in payment of an account payable to a local radio station for advertising done in October was recorded as an expense and as a deduction from cash.

d. Rita performed services for E. Z. Agnos Company in November in the amount of $3,700. Agnos paid $2,000 cash and agreed to pay the balance in 60 days. The bookkeeper recorded the transaction by increasing cash by $2,000, increasing accounts payable by $1,700, and by increasing revenue by $3,700.

e. Rita made a $250 payment on a non-interest-bearing loan obtained in February. The bookkeeper recorded the payment as an expense and as a deduction from cash.

f. A $375 bill was received for delivery services for the month of November. The bookkeeper decided to put off paying the debt until December, and thus did not record the liability.

g. Rita donated office equipment valued at $5,000 to the Roth Real Estate Company. The transaction was recorded as an increase to assets and as an increase to revenue.

Instructions

1. *Analyze each incorrect transaction and determine whether the error would cause net income to be overstated (O), understated (U), or not affected (NA).*

CHAPTER 3

Recording Changes in Financial Position

LEARNING OBJECTIVES

When you have completed this chapter, you should

1. have a better understanding of accounting terminology.

2. have an understanding of debits and credits in the accounts.

3. be able to record transactions in T-accounts.

4. be able to prepare a trial balance from the T-accounts.

In a large business, hundreds or even thousands of transactions may occur daily. So that information about each account is readily available, a separate record is kept for every balance sheet and income statement account. A quick look at the Cash account, for example, would reveal how much cash was on hand at the beginning of the accounting period, all increases and decreases during the period, and the current balance.

THE T-ACCOUNT

debit
an entry on the left-hand side of an account

credit
an entry on the right-hand side of an account

The simplest form of an account is the T-account and is called such because it is drawn to look like a T. A T-account has three basic parts: (1) the title, (2) a left-hand side, and (3) a right-hand side. The left-hand side of an account is called the **debit** side, and the right-hand side is called the **credit** side.

Account Title

Left-hand side Debit side	Right-hand side Credit side

Guidelines for Debits and Credits in Asset, Liability, and Owner's Equity Accounts

The debit and credit sides are used to record increases and decreases in the accounts. An entry on the left-hand side is a debit to the account; an entry on the right-hand side of an account is a credit. A debit entry may cause an increase in the account or it may cause a decrease; the same is true for a credit entry. An easy way to remember the rules for debits and credits is to keep the fundamental accounting equation in mind:

$$\text{Assets} = \text{Liabilities} + \text{Owner's Equity.}$$

Assets appear on the left-hand side of the equation; assets increase by a left-hand, or debit, entry.

Asset Accounts

Debit side For recording **increases**	**Credit** side For recording decreases

When a debit entry causes an increase to an account, a credit entry must cause a decrease to the same account.

Again, let's look at the fundamental accounting equation:

Assets = Liabilities + Owner's Equity.

Liabilities and owner's equity appear on the right-hand side of the equation; increases in liability and the owner's equity account are recorded on the right-hand, or credit, side.

Asset Accounts		=	Liability Accounts		+	Owner's Equity Account	
Debit side for recording increases	**Credit** side		**Debit** side	**Credit** side for recording increases		**Debit** side	**Credit** side for recording increases

Again, when a credit records an increase in an account, a debit will record a decrease.

Assets		=	Liabilities		+	Owner's Equity	
Debit +	Credit −		Debit −	Credit +		Debit −	Credit +

account balance the figure obtained when the total of the smaller side of an account is subtracted from the total of the larger side

The **account balance** is determined by subtracting the total of the smaller side from the total of the larger side. If the debit side is larger, the account has a debit balance; if the credit side is larger, the account has a credit balance.

Let's look in detail at the asset account Cash. All the left-hand or debit entries in the account represent increases, or in this case, deposits of cash into the bank. All the right-hand or credit entries represent checks written or cash withdrawn. A quick glance at the Cash account shows how much cash is on hand or the balance of the account.

The Cash account looks like this at the end of October:

Cash

10/1	Balance 25,000	10/5	4,000
10/7	3,000	10/10	2,200
10/14	3,500	10/14	500
10/21	2,800	10/19	1,000
10/28	3,900	10/26	1,400
	28,800	38,200	10/31	300
			9,400

Debit entries { ... } Credit entries

Debit balance → 28,800

Pencil footings → 38,200 ... 9,400

The account balance is determined as follows:

1. Total the debit entries.
2. Total the credit entries.
3. Subtract the smaller total from the larger.
4. Enter the balance on the side of the account with the larger total.

The balance should be written in pencil and circled so that it will not be confused with a transaction entry. The small pencil-written totals beneath the debit and credit columns are called *pencil footings* and are entered in small figures to avoid confusing them with transactions; they may be easily erased if a mistake is made. The actual transactions are entered in ink and should never be erased.

normal balance
the debit or credit balance that an account is expected to have

The debit balance of $28,800 in the Cash account represents cash in the bank. Asset accounts have a **normal balance** that is a debit. A credit balance in the Cash account would indicate that more cash had been spent than deposited, a situation that could not continue for long. All asset accounts have normal debit balances, and liabilities and the owner's capital account have normal credit balances.

The following T-accounts review the relationship between the fundamental accounting equation and the rules for debit and credit in the accounts. Assets appear on the left-hand side of the equation and increase on the left-hand or debit side of the account. Liabilities and owner's equity appear on the right-hand side of the equation and increase on the right-hand side or credit side of the account.

Assets	=	Liabilities	+	Owner's Equity

Cash		Notes Payable		Owner's Capital
Debit +	*Credit* −	*Debit* −	*Credit* +	*Debit* −	*Credit* +

Accounts Receivable		Accounts Payable
Debit +	*Credit* −	*Debit* −	*Credit* +

	Assets	=	Liabilities	+	Owner's Equity

Office Supplies

Debit	Credit
+	−

Taxes Payable

Debit	Credit
−	+

Equipment

Debit	Credit
+	−

Mortgage Payable

Debit	Credit
−	+

Land

Debit	Credit
+	−

RECORDING TRANSACTIONS IN THE ACCOUNTS

Before entering the debit and credit amounts, the following questions must be answered:

double-entry system of bookkeeping
a system where an equal and corresponding credit entry is required for every debit entry

1. Which accounts are affected?
2. Will the accounts increase or decrease?
3. Which accounts will be debited and which will be credited?
4. Do the debit entries equal the credit entries?

corresponding
to be similar; to be in agreement

The **double-entry system of bookkeeping** requires that every debit entry must have a **corresponding** credit entry or entries that will be equal. Debits always equal credits (unless a mistake has been made).

Transactions Affecting the Balance Sheet

Transaction 1 On November 1, 19XX, Eppie Kondos opened a janitorial service called Scrub-a-Dub-Dub by depositing $15,000 into the business account.

Analysis. The entry increases Cash and increases Owner's Capital. An increase to Cash requires a debit to the account and an increase to Owner's Capital requires a credit.

Cash	110				Eppie Kondos, Capital	310
+		−		−		+
11/1 15,000						11/1 15,000
(Debit						*(Credit*
increase)						*increase)*

Transaction 2   On November 2, Eppie purchased cleaning equipment for $5,000 cash.

Analysis.   This entry must increase the asset Equipment; therefore, a debit to that account is required. To decrease the asset Cash, that account must be credited.

Equipment	150		Cash			110
+		−		+		−
11/2 5,000			11/1 15,000		11/2 5,000	
(Debit					*(Credit*	
increase)					*decrease)*	

Double-entry bookkeeping requires that every debit entry must have a corresponding and equal credit entry.

Transaction 3   On November 5, Eppie purchased $1,200 worth of cleaning supplies on account and agreed to pay within 60 days.

Analysis.   This entry will increase the asset account Supplies by a debit and will increase the liability Accounts Payable by a credit.

Supplies	130				Accounts Payable	220
+		−		−		+
11/5 1,200						11/5 1,200
(Debit						*(Credit*
increase)						*increase)*

Transaction 4   On November 6, Eppie agreed to sell an unneeded vacuum cleaner to a friend for $650, its original cost. The friend agreed to sign a non-interest-bearing note stipulating that the $650 would be paid in full in six months.

Analysis. The Equipment account must be decreased, or credited, for $650. Notes Receivable must be increased, or debited, for $650.

Notes Receivable	120	Equipment	150
+	–	+	–
11/6 650		11/2 5,000	11/6 650
(Debits increase assets)			*(Credits decrease assets)*

Transaction 5 On November 6, Eppie purchased a pickup truck costing $15,000 to haul the equipment for Scrub-a-Dub-Dub. He paid $5,000 down and signed an interest-bearing note payable for the remainder.

Analysis. This entry increases the asset account Truck, decreases the asset account Cash, and increases the liability account Notes Payable. *Total* assets will increase by $10,000 and *total* liabilities will increase by $10,000, thus ensuring that the debits equal the credits.

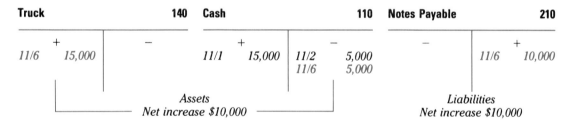

On any individual entry, there may be more than one debit or credit entry, but the *total debits* must equal the *total credits.*

Notes Payable and Notes Receivable are similar to Accounts Payable and Accounts Receivable, except that notes are formal, legal instruments signed by their makers (borrowers). Notes may state an amount of interest that must be paid back along with the amount borrowed.

Transaction 6 On November 9, Eppie made a $300 payment on the cleaning supplies purchased in Transaction 3.

Analysis. The Cash account must be decreased (requiring a credit entry) and Accounts Payable must be decreased (requiring a debit entry).

Accounts Payable		220	Cash		110
−	+		+	−	
11/9 300	11/5 1,200		11/1 15,000	11/2 5,000	
				11/6 5,000	
				11/9 300	
(Debit decrease)			(Credit decrease)		

Transaction 7   On November 10, Eppie withdrew $800 from the business for his personal use.

Analysis.   Remember that in the fundamental accounting equation, drawing is subtracted from the liabilities and owner's equity side. Also, in the statement of owner's equity, drawing is subtracted from the balance in the capital account. Since credit entries increase the capital account and debit entries decrease the capital account, entries to the drawing account are debits.

Eppie Kondos, Drawing		320	Cash		110
+	−		+	−	
11/10 800			11/1 15,000	11/2 5,000	
				11/6 5,000	
				11/9 300	
				11/10 800	
(Debit increases Drawing)			(Credit decreases Cash)		

Transaction 8   On November 10, Eppie received a check for $65 in partial payment of the note receivable that resulted from selling the vacuum cleaner (see Transaction 4).

Analysis.   The asset Cash must be increased by recording a debit entry, and the asset Notes Receivable must be decreased by recording a credit.

Cash		110	Notes Receivable		120
+	−		+	−	
11/1 15,000	11/2 5,000		11/6 650	11/10 65	
11/10 65	11/6 5,000				
	11/9 300				
	11/10 800				
(Debit increases cash)			(Credit decreases notes receivable)		

Rules for Debit and Credit in Revenue and Expense Accounts

A quick look at the Cash account for Scrub-a-Dub-Dub reveals that the only debits are the $15,000 original investment that Eppie made and the $65 received from the sale of an extra vacuum cleaner. Once the business has been established and the necessary equipment and supplies have been purchased, the source for additional cash will be selling the service or product. Let's briefly review the fundamental accounting equation to see how revenue and expense are handled.

Assets = Liabilities + Owner's Equity + Revenue − Expenses − Drawing.

Revenue is added in the equation because it causes an increase in the owner's capital account, and expenses are subtracted because they cause a decrease. The rules for debiting and crediting these accounts are directly related to how they affect owner's capital.

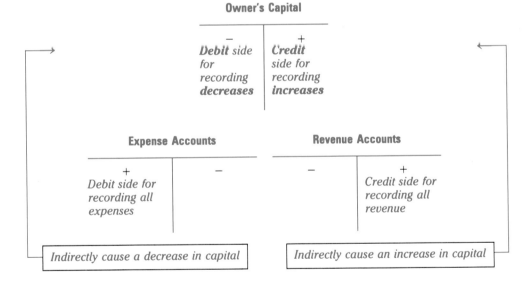

Transactions Affecting the Income Statement

Transaction 9   On November 12, Eppie advertised the services of Scrub-a-Dub-Dub in the local newspaper and paid $95 cash for those services.

   Analysis.   Expenses are recorded as debit entries, because they indirectly cause a decrease in owner's capital. Cash is decreased by a credit entry.

Advertising Expense		610	Cash			110
+		−	+		−	
11/12	95		11/1	15,000	11/2	5,000
			11/10	65	11/6	5,000
					11/9	300
					11/10	800
					11/12	95
(Expenses are recorded as debits)			(Credits decrease cash)			

Transaction 10 On November 14, Eppie received a call from a local business and agreed to shampoo its carpets for $350 cash.

Analysis. An increase of $350 must be recorded in the asset account Cash; therefore, Cash must be debited. An increase in Revenue is recorded by a credit.

Cash				110	Cleaning Revenue		410
+		−			−	+	
11/1	15,000	11/2	5,000			11/14	350
11/12	65	11/6	5,000				
11/14	350	11/9	300				
		11/10	800				
		11/12	95				
(Cash is increased by debits)					(Revenue is recorded as a credit)		

Transaction 11 On November 15, Eppie agreed to clean the floors for a local clinic for $150. The clinic will pay on the 15th of the following month.

Analysis. The accrual method of accounting recognizes revenue when earned (when the services are performed), even though the cash may be forthcoming later. This entry debits Accounts Receivable to record the increase in the asset and credits Revenue to recognize services performed.

Accounts Receivable		125	Cleaning Revenue		410
+		−	−	+	
11/15	150			11/14	350
				11/15	150
(Debits increase assets)			(Credits increase revenue)		

Transaction 12   On November 18, Eppie decided to advertise the services of Scrub-a-Dub-Dub on a local radio station for $425. Eppie agreed to pay in 30 days.

 Analysis.   Expenses have again increased, as have Accounts Payable. Increases in Expenses are recorded as debits, and increases in Accounts Payable are recorded as credits.

Advertising Expense		**610**	**Accounts Payable**			**220**
+		−		−	+	
11/12	95		11/9	300	11/5	1,200
11/18	425				11/18	425
(Expenses					(Liabilities	
increase by					increase by	
debits)					credits)	

Transaction 13   On November 20, Eppie made a $492 payment on the note payable for the truck (see Transaction 5). Of the total payment, $295 applies toward reduction of the amount borrowed and the rest, $197, is payment for interest. Interest is the charge to the borrower for the use of money. It will be discussed in more detail later.

 Analysis.   This transaction represents a compound entry because more than two accounts are involved. The increase in Interest Expense will be recorded as a debit; the reduction of the liability Notes Payable will be recorded as a debit; and the reduction in the asset Cash will be recorded as a credit.

Interest Expense		**650**	**Notes Payable**			**210**	**Cash**				**110**
+		−	−		+		+		−		
11/20	197		11/20	295	11/6	10,000	11/1	15,000	11/2	5,000	
							11/12	65	11/6	5,000	
							11/14	350	11/9	300	
									11/10	800	
									11/12	95	
									11/20	492	
(Expenses			(Liabilities				(Assets				
increase by			decrease by				decrease by				
debits)			debits)				credits)				

In this compound entry, as in all compound entries, the total debits ($197 + $295) equal the total credits ($492).

Summary of the Rules for Debit and Credit

Accountants do not customarily refer to accounts as either increasing or decreasing. They automatically know that a debit to Cash is an increase, a credit to Accounts Payable is an increase, and so on. This information is second nature to them.

The following chart summarizes the debit and credit rules.

Accounts That Increase by Debits		Accounts That Increase by Credits	
Assets		**Liabilities**	
Debit side +	Credit side −	Debit side −	Credit side +
Owner's Withdrawals		**Owner's Capital**	
Debit side +	Credit side −	Debit side −	Credit side +
Expense Accounts		**Revenue**	
Debit side +	Credit side −	Debit side −	Credit side +

THE CHART OF ACCOUNTS

chart of accounts
a list of all the general ledger accounts in financial statement order

Each business has its own **chart of accounts.** Each one is assigned an identification number and a specific name that is used when transactions are recorded. The accounts are arranged in financial statement order with the balance sheet accounts listed first, followed by the income statement accounts. Numbers are assigned to the accounts in family groups with, for example, all the assets numbered in the 100s, all the liabilities in the 200s, the owner's equity accounts in the 300s, revenue in the 400s, and expenses in the 600s. Account numbers in the 500s will be assigned to a category of accounts titled *Cost of Goods Sold,* to be discussed in a later chapter. Some numbers in each family group are left unassigned to allow for adding new accounts. Following is the chart of accounts for Scrub-a-Dub-Dub. (Some accounts have been added to the ones mentioned earlier.)

Scrub-a-Dub-Dub
Chart of Accounts

Account Title	Account Number
Cash	110
Notes Receivable	120
Accounts Receivable	125
Supplies	130
Truck	140
Equipment	150
Notes Payable	210
Accounts Payable	220
Eppie Kondos, Capital	310
Eppie Kondos, Drawing	320
Cleaning Revenue	410
Advertising Expense	610
Gas and Oil Expense	620
Wages Expense	630
Utilities Expense	640
Interest Expense	650

THE TRIAL BALANCE

For every transaction recorded in the T-accounts, total debits equal total credits. At the end of the accounting period, the total of all the debit entries will equal the total of all the credit entries. If they do not, a mistake has been made.

trial balance
a list of accounts and their balances, in financial statement order, used to prove the equality of debits and credits in the ledger

The **trial balance** is the device used by accountants to **verify** that total debits are equal to total credits. The trial balance is prepared directly from the T-accounts on a two-column form. The steps in preparing the trial balance are:

1. The balance of each T-account is determined.

verify
test the accuracy of

2. On the two-column schedule the three-part heading is centered. It consists of the company name on the first line, the name *Trial Balance* on the second line, and the day for which the trial balance is being prepared on the third line.

3. The account titles and their balances are listed in chart of accounts order. Debit balances are entered in the first column, and credit balances are entered in the second column.

4. Both columns are totaled and the totals are compared to determine whether they are equal.

5. If the debit column equals the credit column, a double-ruled line is drawn across both columns to indicate that they are in balance.

The ledger accounts for Scrub-a-Dub-Dub follow. Some transactions have been added to the original ones so that the entire month's transactions can be shown.

Cash   **110**

11/1	15,000	11/2	5,000
11/12	65	11/6	5,000
11/14	350	11/9	300
11/20	5,000	11/10	800
11/21	680	11/12	95
11/30	545	11/20	492
	21,640	11/21	38
(9,079)		11/22	250
		11/23	46
		11/24	40
		11/28	315
		11/29	140
		11/30	45
			12,561

Notes Receivable   **120**

11/6	650	11/10	65
(585)			

Accounts Receivable   **125**

11/15	150		
11/27	570		
	720		

Supplies   **130**

11/5	1,200		

Truck   **140**

11/6	15,000		

Equipment   **150**

11/2	5,000	11/6	650
(4,350)			

Notes Payable   **210**

11/20	295	11/6	10,000
		(9,705)	

Accounts Payable   **220**

11/9	300	11/5	1,200
		11/18	425
			1,625
		(1,325)	

Eppie Kondos, Capital			310
	11/1	15,000	
	11/20	5,000	
		20,000	

Eppie Kondos, Drawing		320
11/10	800	

Cleaning Revenue			410
	11/14	350	
	11/15	150	
	11/21	680	
	11/27	570	
	11/30	545	
		2,295	

Advertising Expense		610
11/12	95	
11/18	425	
	520	

Gas and Oil Expense		620
11/14	38	
11/21	46	
11/24	40	
11/30	45	
	169	

Wages Expense		630
11/20	250	
11/28	315	
	565	

Utilities Expense		640
11/29	140	

Interest Expense		650
11/20	197	

The trial balance for Scrub-a-Dub-Dub, taken directly from the T-accounts, follows.

SCRUB-A-DUB-DUB TRIAL BALANCE NOVEMBER 30, 19XX		
Cash	$ 9 0 7 9 —	
Notes Receivable	5 8 5 —	
Accounts Receivable	7 2 0 —	
Supplies	1 2 0 0 —	
Truck	1 5 0 0 0 —	
Equipment	4 3 5 0 —	
Notes Payable		$ 9 7 0 5 —
Accounts Payable		1 3 2 5 —
Eppie Kondos, Capital		2 0 0 0 0 —
Eppie Kondos, Drawing	8 0 0 —	
Cleaning Revenue		2 2 9 5 —
Advertising Expense	5 2 0 —	
Gas and Oil Expense	1 6 9 —	
Wages Expense	5 6 5 —	
Utilities Expense	1 4 0 —	
Interest Expense	1 9 7 —	
Totals	$ 3 3 3 2 5 —	$ 3 3 3 2 5 —

Trial Balance Limitations

The trial balance shows whether debit entries equal credit entries, but does not necessarily prove that no errors have been made. For example, if an entire entry is omitted from the ledger, the trial balance will not reveal that. If the bookkeeper debits Office Equipment rather than the Office Furniture account, the trial balance will still show that total debits equal total credits, even though there are errors in both accounts. Also, the same wrong figure may be entered both as a debit and a credit in the ledger. In short, the trial balance is useful only for proving that debits equal credits in the ledger.

Trial Balance Errors

If the debits and credits are not equal when the trial balance is complete, the following procedure is used for locating any errors.

1. Check to make sure that accounts with debit balances are correctly entered in the debit column of the trial balance and that

accounts with credit balances are correctly entered in the credit column.

2. Re-add the debit and credit columns.

3. Check to make sure that the balance of each account has been transferred correctly from the T-account to the trial balance.

4. Recalculate the balances in the T-accounts.

5. Check to make sure the correct debits and credits are entered in the T-accounts for each transaction.

SUMMARY

A separate record is kept for each asset, liability, owner's equity, revenue, and expense account. The T-account is the simplest form of an account; it has a title, a left (debit) side, and a right (credit) side. Debits and credits are used for recording increases and decreases in the accounts.

Double-entry bookkeeping requires that every debit entry must have an equal and corresponding credit entry. The fundamental accounting equation may be used to help remember the rules for recording increases and decreases in the accounts.

Assets that appear on the left-hand side of the equation increase on the left, or debit, side of the account. Liabilities and owner's capital, which appear on the right-hand side of the equation, increase on the right, or credit, side of the account.

Revenue, which indirectly increases capital, increases on the same side as the capital account, the credit side; expenses and owner's withdrawals, which indirectly decrease the owner's capital account, are recorded as debits.

The balance of an account may be determined by subtracting the total of the smaller side from the total of the larger side. Assets, owner's drawing, and expense accounts have normal debit balances; liabilities, owner's capital, and revenue have normal credit balances.

The chart of accounts lists all the accounts used by a particular business in financial statement order and assigns a number to each.

The trial balance is prepared by listing all the accounts and their balances in appropriate debit or credit columns. It will show whether total debits equal total credits, but it does not reveal many other types of errors.

Review of Accounting Terminology

Following is a list of the accounting terminology for this chapter.

account balance   double-entry bookkeeping
chart of accounts   normal balance
corresponding   trial balance
credit   verify
debit

Fill in the blank with the correct word or term from the list.

1. An entry on the right-hand side of an account is called a/an

   _____.

2. The formal list of a company's accounts and their numbers is called a/an _____.

3. A system of bookkeeping that requires a corresponding and equal credit entry for every debit entry is called _____.

4. An entry on the left-hand side of an account is called a/an

   _____.

5. The debit or credit balance that an account is usually expected to have is referred to as its _____.

6. The figure that is obtained when the smaller side of an account is subtracted from the larger side is called the

   _____.

7. A schedule that lists all the accounts in financial statement order and their balances and that proves the equality of debits and credits is called a/an _____.

8. To determine or test the truth of, by comparison or investigation, is to _____.

9. A word that means similar or equivalent is _____.

Match the following words and terms on the left with the definitions on the right.

10. debit
11. credit
12. double-entry bookkeeping
13. trial balance
14. account balance
15. normal balance

a. a corresponding and equal credit entry is required for every debit entry
b. the formal list of a company's accounts and account numbers

16. chart of accounts
17. corresponding
18. verify

c. an entry on the right-hand side of an account
d. a list of all the accounts in financial statement order, their balances, and the total of the debit and credit entries
e. an entry on the left-hand side of an account
f. the figure that is obtained when the smaller side of an account is subtracted from the larger side
g. the debit or credit balance that an account normally has
h. similar or equivalent
i. to test the accuracy of

Exercises

Exercise 3.1
determining how debits and credits affect accounts

The debit and credit sides of the following T-accounts are identified. Indicate the correct side for recording increases (+) and the correct side for recording decreases (−) for each T-account. The solution to the first one is given as an example.

Example

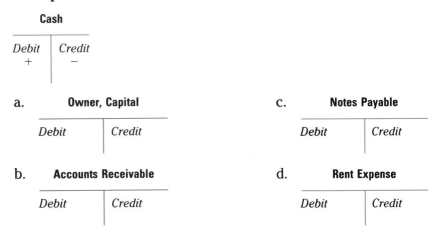

Cash

Debit	Credit
+	−

a. Owner, Capital

Debit	Credit

b. Accounts Receivable

Debit	Credit

c. Notes Payable

Debit	Credit

d. Rent Expense

Debit	Credit

e.   **Commission Revenue**

Debit	Credit

h.   **Accounts Payable**

Debit	Credit

f.   **Owner, Drawing**

Debit	Credit

i.   **Rental Revenue**

Debit	Credit

g.   **Supplies**

Debit	Credit

j.   **Utilities Expense**

Debit	Credit

Exercise 3.2

analyzing debits and credits to the accounts

a. Tell whether the following would cause an increase (+) or a decrease (−) to the account mentioned.

- __+__ 1. a debit to Cash
- __+__ 2. a debit to Drawing
- __+__ 3. a debit to Salary Expense
- __−__ 4. a credit to Accounts Receivable
- __−__ 5. a credit to Capital
- __−__ 6. a credit to Land
- __+__ 7. a debit to Accounts Payable
- __−__ 8. a credit to Cash
- __−__ 9. a credit to Commissions Revenue
- __+__ 10. a debit to Rent Expense
- ____ 11. a credit to Accounts Payable
- ____ 12. a credit to Rental Revenue
- __+__ 13. a debit to Mortgage Payable
- __+__ 14. a debit to Accounts Receivable
- __+__ 15. a debit to Capital

b. For each account listed, indicate whether the account has a normal debit balance or a normal credit balance.

- __+__ 1. Accounts Payable
- __+__ 2. Capital
- __−__ 3. Furniture
- __+__ 4. Drawing
- __+__ 5. Wages Expense
- __−__ 6. Cash
- __+__ 7. Revenue from Sales
- __+__ 8. Taxes Payable
- __−__ 9. Supplies
- ____ 10. Equipment
- __+__ 11. Gas and Oil Expense
- __+__ 12. Commissions Revenue
- __−__ 13. Accounts Receivable
- __−__ 14. Automobile
- __+__ 15. Advertising Expense

Exercise 3.3
determining account
balances and
preparing trial balance

Determine the balance for each account listed, and then prepare a trial balance for Gretchen Klint, accountant, as of November 30, 19XX.

Cash			101
a.	25,000	b.	5,000
e.	900	c.	850
m.	650	d.	2,000
o.	400	f.	750
		g.	290
		i.	500
		j.	1,200
		k.	95
		l.	200
		n.	620

Accounts Receivable			110
h.	800	o.	400

Supplies		120
c.	850	

Equipment		140
b.	5,000	
d.	8,000	

Accounts Payable			210
i.	500	d.	6,000

Grotohon Klint, Capital		310
	a.	25,000

Gretchen Klint, Drawing		320
n.	620	

Sales Revenue		410
	e.	900
	h.	800
	m.	650

Rent Expense		620
f.	750	

Salary Expense		630
j.	1,200	
l.	200	

Utilities Expense		640
k.	95	

Advertising Expense		650
g.	290	

Exercise 3.4
describing what has occurred in T-accounts

Using the T-accounts in Exercise 3.3, briefly describe what has happened for each lettered transaction. The first one has been completed as an example.

Example Transaction a. The owner invested $25,000 cash into the business.

Exercise 3.5
recording transactions in T-accounts

Following are the chart of accounts and T-accounts for Jack Feder, consultant. Analyze each transaction separately, decide which accounts must be debited and credited, title the T-accounts, and enter the correct amounts. In each case, enter the account(s) to be debited first. The first transaction has been completed.

Jack Feder, Consultant
Chart of Accounts

Assets		**Revenue**	
100	Cash	410	Consulting Revenue
105	Accounts Receivable		
109	Supplies		
120	Office Equipment		
150	Land		

Liabilities		**Expenses**	
205	Notes Payable	606	Wages Expense
210	Accounts Payable	610	Insurance Expense
215	Payroll Taxes Payable	620	Utilities Expense
		625	Advertising Expense
		630	Automobile Expense
Owner's Equity		635	Rent Expense
		645	Interest Expense
301	Jack Feder, Capital		
310	Jack Feder, Drawing		

Transactions

	Cash	Land	Jack Feder, Capital
Example Owner invested $10,000 in cash and donated a parcel of property worth $75,000 to establish consulting business	10,000	75,000	85,000

a. purchased $20,000 in office equipment; paid $5,000 cash down and signed a three-year interest-bearing note for $15,000

Office Equip		cash		note Payable	
20000			5000		15000

b. paid $200 cash for an ad in a local magazine

cash		Advertizing	
	200	200	

c. bought $1,200 in supplies; paid $400 down and agreed to pay the balance in 30 days

Supplies		cash		Acct Payable	
1200			400		800

d. paid $800 for the first month's rent

cash		rent expense	
	800	800	

e. borrowed $10,000 from the bank; signed a two-year interest-bearing note

cash		note payable	
10000			10000

f. performed consulting services and received $1,400 cash

cash		consulting Revenue	
1400			1400

g. paid the insurance premium for one month, $105

cash		Insurance Expense	
	105	105	

h. performed $800 in consulting services for a customer who agreed to pay within 30 days

Acct Receivable		consulting Revenue	
800			800

i. paid $500 on the supplies purchased in Transaction c

cash		Account Payable	
	500	500	

j. paid the bill for electricity, $175

cash		Utilities	
	175	175	

k. paid $625 on the note in Transaction e; $415 is for repayment of the principal, and the rest is for payment of interest

cash		Note Payable		Interest Expense	
	625	415		210	

Continued.

l. performed $1,500 in consulting services for a customer who paid $900 in cash and agreed to pay the rest in 60 days

Cash	Consulting Rev.	Acct. Rec.
900	1500	600

m. received $400 on account from a customer (see Transaction h)

Cash	Acct Receivable
400	400

n. paid for gasoline and oil for the car for the month, $250

Cash	Gas & Oil expense
250	250

o. withdrew $1,000 for personal use

Cash	Drawing
1000	1000

p. made a $730 monthly payment on the note for the office equipment (see Transaction a); $417 is for repayment of the principal, and the rest is for payment of interest

Cash	Note Payable	Interest
730	417	313

Exercise 3.6
finding errors in a trial balance

Following is the trial balance for Joe Sanchez, designer, on May 31, 19XX. Joe has a new bookkeeper who is not entirely familiar with the process for preparing a trial balance. Find the errors and prepare a corrected trial balance for May 31, 19XX.

Trial Balance

		Debit	Credit
120	Accounts Receivable	$ 2,500	
210	Accounts Payable		$ 5,000
110	Cash	8,000	
130	Equipment	12,000	
320	Joe Sanchez, Drawing	600	600
310	Joe Sanchez, Capital		27,000
610	Rent Expense	600	
630	Wages Expense	400	
410	Designing Revenue		2,670
640	Advertising Expense	350	
620	Gas and Oil Expense	220	
140	Truck		10,000

Exercise 3.7

analyzing effects of errors on trial balance totals

Assume that a trial balance has been prepared and that the debit column does not equal the credit column. Considering each of the following errors separately, indicate whether the error would cause the trial balance totals to be unequal; and if so, which side, debit or credit, would be larger because of the error; and by how much? The first item has been completed as an example.

Error	Will trial balance totals be unequal?	If so, which column will be larger?	How much larger will it be?
Example A $50 debit to Cash was not recorded.	yes	credit	$50
a. A $25 debit to Accounts Receivable was recorded as a $25 debit to Cash.	yes	debit	25
b. A $150 debit to Drawing was not recorded.	yes	credit	150
c. A $75 credit to Accounts Payable was recorded twice.	yes	credit	75
d. A $1,000 credit to Capital was recorded as a $100 credit to Capital.	yes	debit	900
e. A $70 debit to Cash was recorded as a $700 debit to Cash.	yes	debit	630
f. A $60 credit to Taxes Payable was not recorded.	yes	debit	60
g. A $600 debit to Equipment was recorded as a $600 credit.	yes	credit	1200
h. A $90 credit to Notes Payable was recorded as a $90 debit.	yes	debit	90
i. A $200 debit to Accounts Receivable was recorded as a $200 credit.	yes	credit	200
j. A $10 debit to Accounts Payable was recorded as a $10 credit.	yes	credit	10

Exercise 3.8

determining which transactions represent revenue and which represent expense for the period

Determine for Lester Douglas, a lawyer, which of the following actions represent revenue, expenses, or neither for the month of July 19XX.

_____ a.   received $500 in the mail from a client whose will he prepared in February

_____ b.   invested an additional $3,000 into his law practice

_____ c.   made a $450 payment on a note; $200 applies to reduction of the principal and $250 is interest for July

_____ d.   bought a new couch for the office, $970 cash

_____ e.   advised a client in July, received $200 cash

_____ f.   withdrew $2,200 for personal use in July

_____ g.   paid wages for July, $2,000

_____ h.   donated a law library worth $3,500 to the business

_____ i.   paid $300 for advertising done in May

_____ j.   performed legal services for a client during the last two weeks in July and sent the client a bill for $600

Exercise 3.9

determining effect of errors on revenue and expense

The following transactions were recorded in error for the Black Canyon Tour Guide Company in April. Determine how each affects revenue and expense. For each, indicate whether revenue and expense will be overstated (O), understated (U), or not affected (NA) because of the error.

	Revenue	Expense
a. On April 5, the owner performed services on account amounting to $630. The bookkeeper debited Cash and credited Revenue.	_____	_____
b. The owner purchased office supplies on account for $320. The bookkeeper debited Office Supplies and credited Accounts Payable for $230.	_____	_____
c. The owner wrote a check for $196 for the April phone bill. The bookkeeper debited Rent Expense and credited Cash.	_____	_____

Continued.

	Revenue	Expense
d. On April 30, a bill was received for electricity for the month of April. The bookkeeper did not pay it or record it.	_____	_____
e. The owner invested $6,000 additional cash into the business. The bookkeeper debited Cash and credited Revenue.	_____	_____

Problems

Problem 3.1

analyzing transactions in T-accounts; preparing trial balance

The T-accounts and the transactions for November 19XX for the Tree Doctors follow.

Cash				110	Accounts Receivable				120
a.	10,000	b.	6,000		p.	600	t.	250	
f.	800	c.	2,000		s.	400			
j.	5,000	e.	600						
k.	1,200	g.	400						
s.	300	h.	150		**Supplies**				**130**
t.	250	i.	900						
		l.	250		d.	1,000			
		m.	140						
		n.	200						
		o.	900		**Equipment**				**140**
		q.	300						
		r.	500		c.	5,000			
		u.	175						
		v.	200						

Truck			150	Notes Payable				210
b.	12,000			o.	500	b.	6,000	
						c.	3,000	

Accounts Payable				220	Jack Pine, Capital				310
q.	300	d.	1,000				a.	10,000	
v.	200						j.	5,000	

Continued.

Jack Pine, Drawing	320	Revenue from Services 410
i.	900	f.	800
r.	500	k.	1,200
		p.	600
		s.	700

Truck Repairs Expense 610	Rent Expense	620
l.	250	e.	600

Utilities Expense	630	Advertising Expense	640
m.	140	g.	400
		n.	200

Interest Expense	650	Gas and Oil Expense	660
o.	400	h.	150
		u.	175

Instructions

1. *Analyze each transaction and write a brief description telling what has occurred.*

2. *Determine the balance for each account.*

3. *Prepare a trial balance for the month ended November 30, 19XX.*

Problem 3.2

recording transactions in T-accounts; preparing trial balance

The chart of accounts and the transactions for the month of January 19XX for Shawn O'Brien follow.

Chart of Accounts

100	Cash	310	Shawn O'Brien, Capital
110	Accounts Receivable	320	Shawn O'Brien, Drawing
120	Medical Supplies	410	Revenue
130	Office Supplies	610	Rent Expense
140	Equipment	620	Salary Expense
210	Notes Payable	630	Utilities Expense
220	Accounts Payable	650	Insurance Expense

Transactions

a. wrote a personal check for $18,000 and deposited it in a business account titled Shawn O'Brien, M.D.
b. purchased medical supplies, $5,000 cash
c. purchased office supplies costing $400 and agreed to pay for them within 30 days
d. purchased office equipment costing $19,000; paid $3,000 cash down and signed a three-year, non-interest-bearing note for the rest
e. received cash revenue for the first week, $1,200
f. paid rent, $1,500
g. paid insurance premium, $800
h. paid office salaries, $375
i. made a $200 payment on office supplies purchased in Transaction c
j. performed $2,000 in medical services for the week; $1,100 was received in cash and the rest is due in 30 days
k. bought examining room equipment costing $22,000; paid $5,000 cash down and signed a two-year, non-interest-bearing note for the rest
l. received $450 on account from charge customers
m. performed $2,400 in medical services; received $1,700 in cash and the rest is due in 30 days
n. bought office supplies, $620, on account
o. paid electricity bill, $210
p. paid office salaries, $375
q. received $500 from charge customers
r. paid $1,063 on the equipment purchased in Transaction k
s. paid $780 on the equipment purchased in Transaction d
t. performed $3,000 in medical services; received $1,700 cash and the rest is due in 30 days
u. received $470 from charge customers
v. Shawn withdrew $1,500 for personal use

Instructions

1. *Record a plus (+) or a minus (−) on the debit and credit side of each T-account to indicate where the increases and decreases will be recorded.*

2. *Record the transactions in the T-accounts, identifying each by letter.*

3. *Determine the balance for each account.*

4. *Prepare a trial balance as of January 31, 19XX.*

Problem 3.3

*recording transactions
in T-accounts;
preparing trial balance*

David Custer owns David's Delivery, which has been in operation for nine months. The chart of accounts, account balances, and transactions for the month of October 19XX follow.

Chart of Accounts

101	Cash	$ 8,500	
105	Accounts Receivable	4,100	
110	Office Supplies	870	
120	Delivery Van	25,000	
130	Delivery Equipment	9,500	
140	Office Equipment	12,000	
205	Notes Payable		$35,000
210	Accounts Payable		6,000
300	David Custer, Capital		18,970
310	David Custer, Drawing		
400	Delivery Revenue		
601	Rent Expense		
610	Advertising Expense		
614	Insurance Expense		
620	Repairs Expense		
630	Gas and Oil Expense		
640	Utilities Expense		

Transactions

a. paid $650 for rent

b. paid $800 to creditors to reduce Accounts Payable

c. received checks in the mail totaling $700 from charge customers

d. paid $46 to fill the van with gas and add oil

e. performed delivery services and received $460 in cash

f. performed delivery services in the amount of $1,500 for which customers will pay within 30 days

g. David withdrew $1,000 cash for personal use

h. paid $400 for insurance premium

i. paid $270 for repairs to delivery van

j. performed $800 in delivery services; received cash

k. bought a computer for the office; paid $1,800 cash down and signed a note for $4,000

l. paid $85 for a newspaper ad

m. performed $600 in delivery services; customers will pay within 30 days

n. received checks in the mail totaling $500 from charge customers

o. paid $180 for a tune-up for the van

p. paid $1,100 to reduce Notes Payable

q. paid $930 for radio advertising
r. performed $780 in delivery services; received cash
s. David withdrew $600 for personal use
t. paid $210 for the electricity bill for the office
u. received a $285 bill for gasoline for the delivery van for October (record the bill now to be paid later)
v. paid $165 for the phone bill
w. bought office supplies costing $250; will pay in 30 days
x. performed $380 in delivery services; payment to be received in 30 days

Instructions

1. *Record a plus (+) or a minus (−) on the debit and credit side of each T-account to indicate where the increases and decreases will be recorded.*

2. *Enter the balance from the chart of accounts into the T-accounts.*

3. *Record the transactions in the T-accounts, identifying each by letter.*

4. *Determine the new balance of each account.*

5. *Prepare a trial balance as of October 31, 19XX*

Problem 3.4

recording transactions in T-accounts; preparing trial balance and financial statements

Frances Schultz operates a dog-grooming business called Pet's Pride. The chart of accounts, account balances, and transactions for September 19XX for Pet's Pride follow.

Chart of Accounts

100	Cash	$ 2,000	
105	Accounts Receivable	1,800	
110	Grooming Supplies	800	
115	Grooming Equipment	5,700	
120	Office Furniture	4,900	
125	Van	18,000	
201	Notes Payable		$12,000
210	Accounts Payable		3,200
305	Frances Schultz, Capital		18,000
310	Frances Schultz, Drawing		
401	Grooming Revenue		
605	Rent Expense		
610	Utilities Expense		
612	Insurance Expense		
615	Advertising Expense		
620	Repairs Expense		
625	Gas and Oil Expense		
630	Interest Expense		

Transactions

a. borrowed $5,000 from a local bank; signed a note agreeing to repay the money within 24 months

b. paid $550 rent

c. received $200 cash from customers for services performed

d. bought a new couch for the waiting room; paid $400 cash down and signed a 12-month, non-interest-bearing note for $600 for the rest

e. wrote a check for $800 to reduce amount owed on account to creditors

f. performed grooming services totaling $350; received $120 in cash, the rest is due in 30 days

g. paid $95 for electricity for the office

h. bought gasoline for the van, $36

i. received a bill for $480 for radio advertising for September (record it now to be paid later)

j. paid monthly insurance premium of $90

k. performed grooming services totaling $275; received $175 in cash, the rest is due in 30 days

l. received $400 in the mail from charge customers

m. Frances wrote a check for $500 for personal use

n. paid $40 for a newspaper ad

o. paid $300 for repairs to equipment

p. performed grooming services and received $110 in cash

q. made a loan payment of $800; $450 is interest, the rest applies to reduce the balance in Notes Payable

r. Frances withdrew $600 for personal use

s. paid $120 for phone bill

t. performed grooming services totaling $530; received $300 in cash, the rest is due in 30 days

u. wrote a check for $700 to reduce amount owed on account to creditors

v. paid $200 for a tune-up for the van

w. received checks in the mail totaling $470 from charge customers

x. Frances withdrew $300 for personal use

Instructions

1. *Enter the beginning balances in the T-accounts.*

2. *Record September's transactions in the T-accounts.*

3. *Determine the balance of each account.*

4. *Prepare a trial balance as of September 30, 19XX.*

5. *Prepare an income statement for the month ended September 30, 19XX.*

6. *Prepare a statement of owner's equity for the month ended September 30, 19XX.*

7. *Prepare a balance sheet as of September 30, 19XX. Include only the ending capital figure in the owner's equity section.*

Problem 3.5
analyzing errors in trial balance and preparing corrected one

The T-accounts and trial balance for Maria's Appliance Repair follow. The trial balance, however, indicates that one or more mistakes have been made.

Cash		110			Accounts Receivable		120
a.	25,000	b.	4,000		j.	520	q.	520
i.	450	d.	5,000		p.	750	
m.	1,050	e.	3,200				
q.	520	f.	800				
v.	1,500	g.	1,200		**Supplies**		130
		k.	150				
		l.	370		c.	4,500	
		o.	2,500		e.	3,200	
		r.	1,000				
		s.	290				
		t.	370		**Equipment**		140
		u.	900				
					b.	10,000	
					d.	8,000	

Notes Payable		210			Accounts Payable		220
r.	1,000	b.	6,000		o.	2,500	c.	4,500
		d.	3,000		s.	290	h.	600
							n.	290

Maria Acevedo, Capital		310			Maria Acevedo, Drawing		320
		a.	25,000		u.	900	

Continued.

Repair Revenue		410
	i.	450
	j.	2 520
	m.	1,050
	p.	750
	v.	1,500
		4270

Rent Expense		610
f.	800	

Utilities Expense		620
k.	150	

Salary Expense		630
l.	370	
t.	370	
	740	

Repair Parts Expense		640
n.	290	

Advertising Expense		650
g.	1,200	
h.	600	
	1800	

Maria's Appliance Repair
Trial Balance
November 30, 19XX

	Debit	Credit
Cash	$ 8,470	
Accounts Receivable	850	
Supplies	7,700	
Equipment	18000	$18,000
Notes Payable		8,000
Accounts Payable		2,600
Maria Acevedo, Capital		25,000
Maria Acevedo, Drawing	900	900
Repair Revenue		4,720
Rent Expense	800	
Utilities Expense	150	
Salary Expense	640	
Repair Parts Expense	290	
Advertising Expense	1,800	
Totals	$56,700	$59,220

Instructions   1. *Locate the errors in the trial balance using the following procedure:*

   a. *Re-add the debit and credit columns of the trial balance.*

   b. *If the trial balance does not balance at this point, check to make sure that the balance of each account has been properly transferred to the trial balance and that the balance is entered in the correct debit or credit column.*

   c. *If the trial balance does not balance at this point, recalculate the balances in the individual accounts.*

   d. *If the trial balance still does not balance, check the individual entries to make sure there is a corresponding and equal credit entry for each debit entry.*

2. *Prepare a corrected trial balance.*

Problem 3.6
analyzing effects of errors on revenue and expense

An income statement showing a net income of $7,200 was prepared for Seymour Enterprises for the month of April 19XX. When the bookkeeper was recording the transactions, however, some errors were made. The errors are as follows.

a. The owner, Carl Seymour, withdrew $1,000 for his personal use, but the $1,000 was debited to Wages Expense and credited to Cash.

b. Customers sent checks totaling $2,500 to apply on their accounts from previous months. The bookkeeper debited Cash for $2,500 and credited Revenue for $2,500.

c. Carl wrote a $300 check to pay for utilities for April. The bookkeeper debited Advertising Expense for $300 and credited Cash for $300.

d. Carl wrote a check for $900 to a creditor to reduce the amount owed for supplies purchased in February. The bookkeeper debited Supplies for $900 and credited Cash for $900.

e. Carl performed services on account in April totaling $3,000. The bookkeeper recorded this transaction by debiting Cash for $3,000 and crediting Accounts Payable for $3,000.

f. A $900 bill for repairs to equipment was paid and recorded as a debit to Repairs Expense for $90 and a credit to Cash for $90.

g. A check for $75 was received from a customer who was paying on account. The bookkeeper debited Accounts Receivable for $75 and credited Cash for $75.

h. Carl donated his personal computer and printer valued at $3,500 to the business. The bookkeeper recorded this transaction by debiting Equipment for $3,500 and crediting Revenue for $3,500.

Instructions *Considering each situation separately, analyze the incorrect entry to determine whether the errors (1) will cause expenses to be overstated, understated, or not affected or (2) will cause revenue to be overstated, understated, or not affected. If expenses or revenue are affected, determine by how much each is overstated or understated. Your answers should be recorded with the following headings. The first one has been completed as an example.*

Error	Will expenses be overstated? By how much?	Will expenses be understated? By how much?	Will revenue be overstated? By how much?	Will revenue be understated? By how much?
a.	Yes, by $1,000			

CHAPTER 4

The General Journal and the General Ledger

When you have completed this chapter, you should

1. have a better understanding of accounting and accounting-related terminology.

2. be able to analyze and record transactions in a general journal.

3. be able to post general journal entries to the general ledger.

4. be able to prepare a trial balance directly from the general ledger and make an organized search for errors if the columns do not balance.

journal
a book in which transactions are first recorded

general journal
a journal that is used to record many different types of transactions

In Chapter 3 transactions were recorded directly in T-accounts, and a trial balance was prepared from the balances calculated at the end of the period. Except for illustrating, however, transactions are not recorded directly into the accounts, but are first recorded in a **journal.** The **general journal** is used to record all different types of transactions, and there are many kinds of journals. The journal is called the *book of original entry* because transactions are first recorded there.

JOURNALIZING

chronologically
in date order

journalizing
recording entries into a journal

Transactions are recorded **chronologically** in the general journal. The process itself is called **journalizing.** To illustrate, the first transaction of Eppie Kondos of Scrub-a-Dub-Dub will be used, in which Eppie deposits $15,000 into the business account. This requires a debit to Cash and a credit to Capital of $15,000 and looks as follows.

GENERAL JOURNAL														Page *1*
Date			Description		Post. Ref.		Debit				Credit			
19XX *Nov.*	*1*	*Cash*					*1*	*5*	*0*	*0*	*0* —			
			Eppie Kondos, Capital									*1*	*5*	*0*	*0*	*0* —
			To Record Original Investment												

Guidelines for General Journal Entries

1. The year is written at the top of the date column in small figures.

2. The month and day on which the transaction occurs follows. The name of the month may be abbreviated and is written once at the top of the page. Transactions are recorded chronologically.

3. The debit entry (or entries) is always entered first and appears at the extreme left side of the description column. The

account title is written exactly as it appears in the chart of accounts.

4. The dollar amount of the debit entry is entered in the debit column.

5. The credit entry (or entries) follows the debit entry on the next line. In the description column, the titles of the accounts to be credited are indented about one-half inch. Again, the account titles are written exactly as they appear in the chart of accounts.

6. The dollar amount of the credit entry is entered in the credit column.

7. A brief explanation of the transaction is written beneath the credit entry, and should not be indented.

8. For ease of reading, one blank line in the journal should be left between entries.

9. Dollar signs are not used in the general journal.

compound journal entry
a journal entry with more than one debit and/or credit

10. An entry with more than one debit and/or credit is called a **compound journal entry.** The debits are entered first (in no particular order) and appear at the extreme left-hand side of the description column. The credits follow on the lines below the debits (again in no particular order) and are all indented one-half inch.

posting reference
a cross-reference notation entered into the journal and the ledger after posting has been completed

11. The **posting reference** column (Post. Ref., which is blank in this entry) is used to record the account number only after the dollar amount is transferred to the corresponding account in the ledger.

The following are the general journal entries for November 1 through 6 for Scrub-a-Dub-Dub.

		GENERAL JOURNAL			Page*1*
Date		**Description**	Post. Ref.	**Debit**	**Credit**
19XX Nov.	1	Cash		15000 —	
		Eppie Kondos, Capital			15000 —
		To Record Original Investment			
	2	Equipment		5000 —	
		Cash			5000 —
		Purchased Cleaning Equipment			
	5	Supplies		1200 —	
		Accounts Payable			1200 —
		Purchased Supplies; Due in 60 Days			
	6	Notes Receivable		650 —	
		Equipment			650 —
		Sold Equipment; Customer Signed 6-Month Non-Interest-Bearing Note			
	6	Truck		15000 —	
		Cash			5000 —
		Notes Payable			10000 —
		Bought Truck; Signed 2-Year Non-Interest-Bearing Note			

THE RUNNING BALANCE FORM OF ACCOUNT

T-accounts are used by bookkeepers because they are basic and easy to use. Formally, however, in manual accounting systems, an account with special rulings replaces the T-account in the ledger. The Cash account that follows illustrates the running balance form of ledger account. Debit amounts are entered in the debit column, credit amounts in the credit column, and a balance is calculated after each entry.

CASH   Acct. No. *110*

Date		Explanation	PR	Debit	Credit	Balance
19XX Nov.	1		GJ1	15000 —		15000 —
	2		GJ1		5000 —	10000 —
	6		GJ1		5000 —	5000 —
	9		GJ1		300 —	4700 —
	10		GJ1		800 —	3900 —
	10		GJ1		95 —	3805 —
	10		GJ1	65 —		3870 —
	14		GJ2		38 —	3832 —
	14		GJ2	350 —		4182 —
	20		GJ2		250 —	3932 —

POSTING

accumulates
gathers; collects

general ledger
a ledger that contains
a separate record for
each asset, liability,
owner's equity,
revenue, and expense
account

posting
transferring
information from the
journal to the ledger

The ledger is a book with a separate page for each account title that appears in the chart of accounts. While the journal **accumulates** all the information about a particular transaction in one place, the ledger contains all the information about a particular account in one place. For example, all the increases and decreases to cash are shown in the Cash account in the **general ledger,** which contains a separate page for every asset, liability, owner's equity, revenue, and expense account.

The process of transferring the information about transactions from the journal to the ledger is called **posting.**

The first transaction for Scrub-a-Dub-Dub is repeated now; the general journal entry is followed by the ledger accounts that are affected.

GENERAL JOURNAL					Page *1*
Date	Description	Post. Ref.	Debit		Credit
19XX Nov. 1	Cash	110	1 5 0 0 0 —		
	Eppie Kondos, Capital	310			1 5 0 0 0 —
	To Record Original Investment				

CASH   Acct. No. *110*

Date	Explanation	PR	Debit	Credit	Balance
19XX Nov. 1		GJ1	1 5 0 0 0 —		1 5 0 0 0 —

EPPIE KONDOS, CAPITAL   Acct. No. *310*

Date	Explanation	PR	Debit	Credit	Balance
19XX Nov. 1		GJ1		1 5 0 0 0 —	1 5 0 0 0 —

Guidelines for Posting

1. In the appropriate ledger account, the year is entered in small figures at the top of the date column. The month and day are entered as they appear in the journal; the month may be abbreviated.

2. The dollar amount from the debit column of the journal is entered in the debit column of the ledger account. Dollar signs are not used in the ledger.

3. The balance of the account is calculated and entered in the balance column. The balance may be a debit or a credit, and it is necessary to recall which accounts have normal debit balances and which have normal credit balances.

4. In the posting reference column (PR) of the ledger account, the initials GJ (general journal) are entered along with the journal page number from which the transaction was taken.

5. *After posting has been completed,* the account number is entered in the posting reference column of the journal.

6. Steps 1 through 5 are repeated until each account is posted.

7. Extra care when posting may save time later, as errors may be avoided.

GENERAL LEDGER AFTER POSTING HAS BEEN COMPLETED

Following is the general ledger for Scrub-a-Dub-Dub showing all the transactions for November.

CASH   Acct. No. *110*

Date		Explanation	PR	Debit	Credit	Balance
Nov.	*1*		GJ1	15000 —		15000 —
	2		GJ1		5000 —	10000 —
	6		GJ1		5000 —	5000 —
	9		GJ1		300 —	4700 —
	10		GJ1		800 —	3900 —
	12		GJ1	65 —		3965 —
	12		GJ1		95 —	3870 —
	14		GJ2	350 —		4220 —
	20		GJ2	5000 —		9220 —
	20		GJ2		492 —	8728 —
	21		GJ2	680 —		9408 —
	21		GJ2		38 —	9370 —
	22		GJ2		250 —	9120 —
	23		GJ2		46 —	9074 —
	24		GJ3		40 —	9034 —
	28		GJ3		315 —	8719 —
	29		GJ3		140 —	8579 —
	30		GJ3	545 —		9124 —
	30		GJ3		45 —	9079 —

NOTES RECEIVABLE   Acct. No. *120*

Date	Explanation	PR	Debit	Credit	Balance
19XX Nov. 6		GJ1	650 —		650 —
10		GJ1		65 —	585 —

ACCOUNTS RECEIVABLE   Acct. No. *125*

Date	Explanation	PR	Debit	Credit	Balance
19XX Nov. 15		GJ2	150 —		150 —
27		GJ3	570 —		720 —

SUPPLIES   Acct. No. *130*

Date	Explanation	PR	Debit	Credit	Balance
19XX Nov. 5		GJ1	1200 —		1200 —

TRUCK   Acct. No. *140*

Date	Explanation	PR	Debit	Credit	Balance
19XX Nov. 6		GJ1	15000 —		15000 —

EQUIPMENT   Acct. No. *150*

Date	Explanation	PR	Debit	Credit	Balance
19XX Nov. 2		GJ1	5000 —		5000 —
6		GJ1		650 —	4350 —

NOTES PAYABLE   Acct. No. *210*

Date	Explanation	PR	Debit	Credit	Balance
19XX Nov. 6		GJ1		10000 —	10000 —
20		GJ3	295 —		9705 —

ACCOUNTS PAYABLE   Acct. No. *220*

Date		Explanation	PR	Debit	Credit	Balance
19XX Nov.	5		GJ1		1200 —	1200 —
	9		GJ1	300 —		900 —
	18		GJ2		425 —	1325 —

EPPIE KONDOS, CAPITAL   Acct. No. *310*

Date		Explanation	PR	Debit	Credit	Balance
19XX Nov.	1		GJ1		15000 —	15000 —
	20		GJ3		5000 —	20000 —

EPPIE KONDOS, DRAWING   Acct. No. *320*

Date		Explanation	PR	Debit	Credit	Balance
19XX Nov.	10		GJ1	800 —		800 —

CLEANING REVENUE   Acct. No. *410*

Date		Explanation	PR	Debit	Credit	Balance
19XX Nov.	14		GJ1		350 —	350 —
	15		GJ2		150 —	500 —
	21		GJ2		680 —	1180 —
	27		GJ3		570 —	1750 —
	30		GJ3		545 —	2295 —

ADVERTISING EXPENSE   Acct. No. *610*

Date		Explanation	PR	Debit	Credit	Balance
19XX Nov.	12		GJ1	95 —		95 —
	18		GJ2	425 —		520 —

GAS AND OIL EXPENSE   Acct. No. *620*

Date		Explanation	PR	Debit	Credit	Balance
Nov.	*14*		*GJ1*	3 8 —		3 8 —
	21		*GJ2*	4 6 —		8 4 —
	24		*GJ3*	4 0 —		1 2 4 —
	30		*GJ3*	4 5 —		1 6 9 —

WAGES EXPENSE   Acct. No. *630*

Date		Explanation	PR	Debit	Credit	Balance
Nov.	*20*		*GJ2*	2 5 0 —		2 5 0 —
	28		*GJ3*	3 1 5 —		5 6 5 —

UTILITIES EXPENSE   Acct. No. *640*

Date		Explanation	PR	Debit	Credit	Balance
Nov.	*29*		*GJ3*	1 4 0 —		1 4 0 —

INTEREST EXPENSE   Acct. No. *650*

Date		Explanation	PR	Debit	Credit	Balance
Nov.	*20*		*GJ2*	1 9 7 —		1 9 7 —

THE TRIAL BALANCE

Once the journalizing and posting have been completed, the accountant is ready to prepare a trial balance to verify that debit entries equal credit entries. The dollar amounts appearing on the trial balance are taken directly from the ledger.

SCRUB-A-DUB-DUB TRIAL BALANCE NOVEMBER 30, 19XX		
Cash	$ 9079 —	
Notes Receivable	585 —	
Accounts Receivable	720 —	
Supplies	1200 —	
Truck	15000 —	
Equipment	4350 —	
Notes Payable		$ 9705 —
Accounts Payable		1325 —
Eppie Kondos, Capital		20000 —
Eppie Kondos, Drawing	800 —	
Cleaning Revenue		2295 —
Advertising Expense	520 —	
Gas and Oil Expense	169 —	
Wages Expense	565 —	
Utilities Expense	140 —	
Interest Expense	197 —	
Totals	$33325 —	$33325 —

If the columns of the trial balance do not equal each other, the smaller side can be subtracted from the larger side to determine the difference. If, for example, the debit side totals $8,275 and the credit side totals $8,250, the difference is $25. The bookkeeper can then look for a $25 figure in the journal to see if one-half of the entry was posted to the ledger. He or she could also look for a $12.50 amount (one-half the amount of the difference); such a discrepancy could occur by posting $12.50 as a credit to Accounts Receivable when a $12.50 debit should have been recorded.

TRANSPOSITIONS AND SLIDES

transposition
when the order of digits is reversed as they are copied

A **transposition** occurs when the order of digits is reversed when copying. For example, 357 is recorded as 375. When a transposition occurs, the difference between the number as it should be and the transposed number will always be evenly divisible by 9. The difference, for example, between 375 and 357 is 18, and the number 18 is evenly divisible by 9. Another example is 1,192 copied as 1,912. The difference between the two (1,912 − 1,192) is 720, which is evenly divisible by 9 (720 ÷ 9 = 80).

Transpositions

Number as It Should Be	Number Transposed	Difference	Divide Difference by 9
357	537	537 − 357 = 180	180 ÷ 9 = 20
978	789	978 − 789 = 189	189 ÷ 9 = 21
1,042	1,024	1,042 − 1,024 = 18	18 ÷ 9 = 2
14	41	41 − 14 = 27	27 ÷ 9 = 3

Note: Always subtract the smaller number from the larger to avoid negative numbers.

slide
when the position of the decimal point is moved as the number is copied

A **slide** occurs when the decimal point is accidentally moved when copying from one place to another. For example, the number 754.15 is copied as 7,541.50 or as 75.415. As with a transposition, the difference between the number as it should be and the number as it is recorded will be evenly divisible by 9. Subtract 754.15 from 7,541.50 and the difference is 6,787.35, which is evenly divisible by 9 (6,787.35 ÷ 9 = 754.15).

An easy way to tell whether a number is evenly divisible by 9 is to simply add the digits of the number. For example, to determine if the number 6,787.35 is evenly divisible by 9, add the digits: 6 + 7 + 8 + 7 + 3 + 5 = 36. The number 36 is evenly divisible by 9; so is the number 6,787.35.

Slides

Number as It Should Be	Number as It Is Recorded	Difference	Divide Difference by 9
7.85	78.5	78.5 − 7.85 = 70.65	70.65 ÷ 9 = 7.85
204	2.04	204 − 2.04 = 201.96	201.96 ÷ 9 = 22.44
60,469	604.69	60,469 − 604.69 = 59,864.31	59,864.31 ÷ 9 = 6,651.59
10,250	1,025	10,250 − 1,025 = 9,225	9,225 ÷ 9 = 1,025

Note: Always subtract the smaller number from the larger to avoid negative numbers.

This information may be helpful when the totals for the trial balance columns are not the same. Assume, for example, that the debit total is $10,072 and that the credit total is $10,108. The difference between those two numbers ($10,108 − $10,072), $36, is evenly divisible by 9. The reason for the trial balance columns not being equal in this case may be a transposed number or a slide.

SUMMARY

The journal is called the book of original entry because transactions are first recorded there. To record a transaction in the journal is called journalizing, and the first step requires the accountant to enter the year at the top of the date column followed by the month and day on which the transaction occurred. The account titles to be debited are always entered first and are written at the extreme left side of the description column. The accounts to be credited are entered on the lines immediately below the debit entry and are indented one-half inch. A short explanation follows on the line below the credit entry; it is not indented. A blank line is left between journal entries.

Posting is the second step in the accounting cycle and is the process of transferring the dates and amounts from the journal to the specific accounts in the ledger. After the amounts have been posted, the journal page number is written in the posting reference column of the ledger account and the ledger account number is entered in the posting reference column of the journal. No posting reference notations should be made until posting is complete.

Preparing a trial balance is the third step in the accounting cycle. It is prepared to prove the equality of debits and credits in the ledger and involves listing the account titles and their balances in the appropriate debit or credit column and totaling the columns. If the trial balance columns are not equal, the bookkeeper should calculate the difference between the columns and look for that figure in the journal. A figure one-half the amount of the difference may indicate that a debit amount was posted as a credit or a credit amount as a debit. If the trial balance totals are not equal and the difference between them is evenly divisible by 9, the error may be a transposition or a slide.

Review of Accounting Terminology

Following is a list of the accounting terminology for this chapter.

accumulates	journalizing
chronologically	posting
compound journal entry	posting reference
general journal	slide
general ledger	transposition
journal	

Fill in the blank with the correct word or term from the list.

1. A cross-reference from the journal to the ledger and vice versa is referred to as a/an _____.

2. A book of original entry is called a/an _____.

3. Another word for gathers or piles up is _____.

4. A word that means arranged in date order is _____.

5. A/an _____ contains a separate record for each asset, liability, owner's equity, revenue, and expense account.

6. The process of transferring information from the journal to the ledger is called _____.

7. When the position of the decimal point is changed as the number is written down, a/an _____ has occurred.

8. The number 652 copied as 625 is an example of a/an

_____.

9. A journal entry with more than one debit and/or credit entry is referred to as a/an _____.

10. A journal that is used to record many different types of transactions is a/an _____.

11. The process of recording entries into the journal is called

_____.

Match the following words and terms on the left with the definitions on the right.

12. accumulates
13. chronologically
14. compound journal entry
15. general journal
16. general ledger
17. journal
18. journalizing
19. posting
20. posting reference

a. when the position of the decimal point is changed as the number is written down
b. in date order
c. a book of original entry
d. gathers
e. when the order of numbers is changed as they are written down

21. slide
22. transposition

f. the process of transferring information from the journal to the ledger
g. the process of recording transactions into a journal
h. a journal used to record many different kinds of transactions
i. a journal entry with more than one debit and/or credit
j. a ledger with separate accounts for asset, liability, owner's equity, revenue, and expense accounts
k. a cross-reference between the journal and the ledger

Exercises

Exercise 4.1
transferring T-account information to three-column balance ledger accounts

Following are the T-accounts representing the ledger for The Tree Pruners. Transfer chronologically the transactions entered in the T-accounts into three-column balance ledger accounts in the following manner.

a. Write the account title and number at the top of the individual accounts.
b. Write the current year in small figures at the top of the date column.
c. Enter the month and day in the date column.
d. Write the amount in the appropriate debit or credit column.
e. Calculate the account balance after each entry.
f. Prepare a trial balance for The Tree Pruners on December 31, 19XX.

Cash						101
12/1	GJ1	10,000	12/2	GJ1	5,000	
12/10	GJ2	800	12/3	GJ1	1,000	
12/26	GJ4	700	12/12	GJ2	1,500	
12/27	GJ4	500	12/18	GJ3	85	
			12/20	GJ3	250	
			12/28	GJ4	420	
			12/30	GJ5	1,000	

Accounts Receivable					110
12/5	GJ1	500	12/27	GJ4	500
12/10	GJ2	300			
12/26	GJ4	900			

Supplies			120
12/3	GJ1	3,000	

Equipment			130
12/2	GJ1	5,000	

Accounts Payable					210
12/30	GJ5	1,000	12/3	GJ1	2,000

Yale Goldstein, Capital					310
			12/1	GJ1	10,000

Yale Goldstein, Drawing			320
12/12	GJ2	1,500	

Revenue					405
			12/5	GJ1	500
			12/10	GJ2	1,100
			12/26	GJ4	1,600

Insurance Expense			610
12/28	GJ4	420	

Utilities Expense			620
12/18	GJ3	85	

Advertising Expense			630
12/20	GJ3	250	

Exercise 4.2
posting

Post the following general journal entries into three-column balance ledger accounts, calculating a new balance after each posting. Then enter the journal page number into the posting reference column of the ledger account. The account titles and numbers are: Cash, 101; Accounts Receivable, 110; Supplies 120; Equipment, 130; Accounts Payable, 210; Pat O'Henry, Capital, 310; Pat O'Henry, Drawing, 320; Revenue from Services, 410; and Utilities Expense, 610.

GENERAL JOURNAL						Page 28
Date		Description	Post. Ref.	Debit	Credit	
19XX Nov.	1	Cash		8000 —		
		Pat O'Henry, Capital			8000 —	
		To Record Original Investment				
	3	Equipment		3000 —		
		Cash			1000 —	
		Accounts Payable			2000 —	
		Purchased Equipment: Balance Due in 90 Days				
	5	Supplies		400 —		
		Accounts Payable			400 —	
		Purchased Supplies on Account				
	9	Cash		270 —		
		Revenue from Services			270	
		Performed Services for Cash				
	10	Pat O'Henry, Drawing		650 —		
		Cash			650 —	
		To Record Owner's Withdrawal				
	12	Accounts Receivable		400 —		
		Cash		250 —		
		Revenue from Services			650 —	
		Performed Services for Cash and on Account				
	14	Utilities Expense		90 —		
		Cash			90 —	
		Paid Bill for Electricity				
	18	Accounts Payable		400 —		
		Cash			400 —	
		Paid Money to Creditor				
	20	Cash		100 —		
		Accounts Receivable			100 —	
		Received Money on Account				

Exercise 4.3

Determining balance of general ledger accounts and preparing a trial balance

Determine the balance for each of the following accounts for Buck Jensen, trail guide. Then prepare a trial balance as of June 30, 19XX. (A check mark in the posting reference column of the ledger account indicates that the figure in that column has not been posted from a journal, but is a balance from the previous month.)

CASH   Acct. No. *101*

Date		Explanation	PR	Debit	Credit	Balance
19XX May	31	Balance	✔			2 0 0 0 —
June	1		GJ20	5 0 —		
	7		GJ20	3 7 5 —		
	8		GJ20		1 3 0 —	
	10		GJ20		4 0 0 —	
	14		GJ20	4 0 0 —		
	15		GJ21		5 0 0 —	
	15		GJ21		3 0 0 —	
	16		GJ21		1 4 0 —	
	18		GJ21		4 0 0 —	
	25		GJ22		3 0 0 —	
	28		GJ22	5 2 0 —		
	29		GJ22		8 5 —	
	30		GJ22	1 0 0 —		

ACCOUNTS RECEIVABLE   Acct. No. *105*

Date		Explanation	PR	Debit	Credit	Balance
19XX May	31	Balance	✔			5 0 0 —
June	1		GJ20		5 0 —	
	21		GJ21	2 5 0 —		
	30		GJ22		1 0 0 —	

SUPPLIES   Acct. No. *108*

Date		Explanation	PR	Debit	Credit	Balance
19XX May	31	Balance	✔			4 0 0 —
June	8		GJ20	1 3 0 —		

EQUIPMENT

Acct. No. 110

Date		Explanation	PR	Debit	Credit	Balance
19XX May	31	Balance	✔			5000 —

ACCOUNTS PAYABLE

Acct. No. 205

Date		Explanation	PR	Debit	Credit	Balance
19XX May	31	Balance	✔			2000 —
June	10		GJ20	400 —		
	18		GJ21	400 —		

BUCK JENSEN, CAPITAL

Acct. No. 310

Date		Explanation	PR	Debit	Credit	Balance
19XX May	31	Balance	✔			5900 —

BUCK JENSEN, DRAWING

Acct. No. 320

Date		Explanation	PR	Debit	Credit	Balance
19XX June	15		GJ21	500 —		
	25		GJ22	300 —		

GUIDE REVENUE

Acct. No. 401

Date		Explanation	PR	Debit	Credit	Balance
19XX June	7		GJ20		375 —	
	14		GJ20		400 —	
	21		GJ21		250 —	
	28		GJ21		520 —	

STABLE EXPENSE   Acct. No. *610*

Date	Explanation	PR	Debit	Credit	Balance
19XX *June* 16		GJ21	1 4 0 —		
29		GJ22	8 5 —		

RENT EXPENSE   Acct. No. *620*

Date	Explanation	PR	Debit	Credit	Balance
19XX *June* 15		GJ21	3 0 0 —		

Exercise 4.4
journalizing

The chart of accounts for Sylvia Song, photographer, follows. Journalize the transactions for the month of April 19XX. Begin numbering with journal page 18.

Chart of Accounts

101	Cash
105	Accounts Receivable
110	Supplies
120	Photographic Equipment
215	Notes Payable
220	Accounts Payable
305	Sylvia Song, Capital
310	Sylvia Song, Drawing
410	Photographic Revenue
620	Rent Expense
625	Utilities Expense
630	Insurance Expense
640	Advertising Expense

Transactions

April 1 photographed a wedding; $500 fee to be received within 10 days

April 2 paid $650 rent

April 3 received $420 from charge customers

April 4   took senior portraits; received $200 in cash, $300 is due within 30 days

April 5   made a loan payment of $150; the note is non-interest-bearing

April 8   paid $80 to reduce Accounts Payable

April 9   Sylvia withdrew $700 for personal use

April 10   paid a monthly insurance premium of $95

April 12   portrait revenue for the week is $1,200; $500 received in cash, the rest is due within 30 days

April 14   paid telephone bill, $120

April 18   paid for advertising in high-school newspaper, $50

April 20   bought a new lens for $825; paid $200 cash down and agreed to pay the balance within 60 days

April 25   portrait revenue is $1,450; $800 received in cash, the rest is due in 30 days

April 26   received $500 from charge customers

April 28   paid bill for electricity, $75

April 29   paid cash for photographic supplies, $250

April 30   Sylvia withdrew $500 for personal use

Exercise 4.5
posting

Following are the general journal entries for July 1, 19XX, and a partial general ledger for The House Painter, a business owned by Roy Magneson. Post the journal entries to the general ledger. As you post, enter the account number in the posting reference column of the general journal and enter GJ19 in the posting reference column of the ledger. Calculate a new balance in the ledger after each posting.

Account Number	Account Title	Debit Balance	Credit Balance
101	Cash	$ 4,780	
110	Accounts Receivable	2,785	
150	Office Equipment	10,800	
220	Accounts Payable		$1,760
310	Roy Magneson, Capital		6,740
410	Revenue from Painting		0

GENERAL JOURNAL				Page 19	
Date	Description	Post. Ref.	Debit	Credit	
19XX *July* 2	**Cash**		795 —		
	Revenue from Painting			795 —	
	To Record Painting Revenue				
2	**Cash**		420 —		
	Accounts Receivable			420 —	
	To Record Cash Received on Account				
2	**Accounts Payable**		315 —		
	Cash			315 —	
	To Record Cash Paid on Account				
2	**Office Equipment**		7420 —		
	Cash			2000 —	
	Accounts Payable			5420 —	
	Purchased Office Equipment; Balance				
	Due in Six Months				
2	**Cash**		5000 —		
	Roy Magneson, Capital			5000 —	
	To Record Additional Investment				

CASH   Acct. No. 101

Date	Explanation	PR	Debit	Credit	Balance
19XX *July* 1	**Balance**	✔			4780 —

ACCOUNTS RECEIVABLE   Acct. No. 110

Date	Explanation	PR	Debit	Credit	Balance
19XX *July* 1	**Balance**	✔			2785 —

OFFICE EQUIPMENT   Acct. No. **150**

Date		Explanation	PR	Debit	Credit	Balance
July^{19XX}	1	*Balance*	✔			10800 —

ACCOUNTS PAYABLE   Acct. No. **220**

Date		Explanation	PR	Debit	Credit	Balance
July^{19XX}	1	*Balance*	✔			1760 —

ROY MAGNESON, CAPITAL   Acct. No. **310**

Date		Explanation	PR	Debit	Credit	Balance
July^{19XX}	1	*Balance*	✔			6740 —

REVENUE FROM PAINTING   Acct. No. **410**

Date		Explanation	PR	Debit	Credit	Balance

Exercise 4.6
*determining whether a
number is evenly
divisible by 9*

Tell whether the following numbers are evenly divisible by 9 using
the following procedure.

a. Find the sum of the digits of each number and write the sum in
    the space provided.
b. Determine whether the sum of the digits is evenly divisible by
    9. If it is, the number itself is evenly divisible by 9.

Number	Sum of the Digits	Is the Number Evenly Divisible by 9?
Example 64.783	28	no
1. 306.42	_____	_____
2. 7,234.12	_____	_____
3. 46,728	_____	_____

Continued.

Number	Sum of the Digits	Is the Number Evenly Divisible by 9?
4. 416,732.85	_____	_____
5. 8,334.00	_____	_____
6. 3,939.93	_____	_____
7. 423	_____	_____
8. 5,721	_____	_____
9. 46,901.30	_____	_____
10. 74,615.91	_____	_____

Exercise 4.7
analyzing transposition and slide errors

For each of the following, find the difference between the number as it should be recorded and the number as it is actually recorded. Then divide the difference by 9 to prove that transposition or slide errors are evenly divisible by 9. The first one has been completed as an example.

Number as It Should Be Recorded	Number as It Is Recorded	Difference	Divide Difference by 9
Example 873	837	36	36 ÷ 9 = 4
1. 749	794	_____	_____
2. 105.20	1,052.00	_____	_____
3. 37,654	37,645	_____	_____
4. 10.97	1.097	_____	_____
5. 52	25	_____	_____
6. 1.28	2.18	_____	_____
7. 204	2,040	_____	_____
8. 7.39	7.93	_____	_____
9. 40,639	46,039	_____	_____
10. 10,828	10,288	_____	_____

Exercise 4.8
determining how errors affect trial balance totals

The following transactions were journalized correctly, but errors were made when posting. For each, tell whether the errors would cause the trial balance totals to be unequal, and if so, by how much the columns will differ. Also indicate which column of the trial balance, debit or credit, will be larger.

	Will trial balance totals be unequal?	If so, by how much?	Which column will be larger?
a. A journal entry debiting Cash and crediting Accounts Receivable for $670 was posted as a debit to Cash of $760 and a credit to Accounts Receivable of $760.	———	———	———
b. A journal entry debiting Cash and crediting Revenue for $200 was posted as a debit to Cash for $200 and a credit to Revenue for $2,000.	———	———	———
c. A journal entry debiting Rent Expense and crediting Cash for $1,600 was posted as a debit to Advertising Expense for $1,600 and a credit to Cash for $1,600.	———	———	———
d. A journal entry debiting Accounts Payable and crediting Cash for $350 was posted as a debit to Accounts Payable of $350 and a credit to Cash of $530.	———	———	———
e. A journal entry debiting Accounts Receivable and crediting Revenue for $340 was posted as a debit to Accounts Receivable of $430 and a credit to Revenue of $430.	———	———	———
f. A journal entry debiting Drawing and crediting Cash for $600 was posted as a debit to Drawing of $600 and as a debit to Cash for $600.	———	———	———
g. A journal entry debiting Equipment and crediting Accounts Payable for $2,400 was posted as a debit to Equipment of $2,400 and as a credit to Accounts Payable of $3,400.	———	———	———
h. A journal entry debiting Cash and crediting Furniture for $460 was posted as a debit to Cash of $640 and a credit to Furniture of $460.	———	———	———

Exercise 4.9

determining how errors affect revenue, expenses, and net income

The following transactions were journalized and posted in error. Considering each separately, determine whether the error will cause total revenue, total expenses, and net income to be overstated (O), understated (U), or not affected (NA). (If revenue is overstated, then net income will also be overstated; likewise, if revenue is understated, net income will be understated. If expenses are overstated, net income will be understated; and if expenses are understated, net income will be overstated.) The first one has been completed as an example.

	Total Revenue	Total Expenses	Total Net Income
Example The owner withdrew $750 for personal use. The bookkeeper debited Wages Expense and credited Cash for $750.	NA	O	U
a. The owner invested an additional $5,000 in the business. The bookkeeper debited Cash and credited Revenue for $5,000.	——	——	——
b. A check for $950 was written in payment of rent. The bookkeeper debited Repairs Expense and credited Cash for $950.	——	——	——
c. A check for $375 was written in payment of an account. The bookkeeper debited Insurance Expense and credited Cash for $375.	——	——	——
d. $620 was received from charge customers. The bookkeeper debited Accounts Receivable and credited Revenue for $620.	——	——	——
e. $840 in services were performed on account. The bookkeeper debited Accounts Receivable and credited Capital for $840.	——	——	——
f. A check was written for $775 in payment of the rent. The bookkeeper debited Building and credited Cash for $775.	——	——	——
g. Salaries amounting to $415 were paid with cash. The bookkeeper debited Drawing and credited Cash for $415.	——	——	——
h. A check was written for $62 in payment of the current month's phone bill. The bookkeeper debited Utilities Expense and credited Cash for $42.	——	——	——

Problems

Problem 4.1
journalizing, posting, and preparing trial balance

The chart of accounts and the transactions for June 19XX for Dizzy's Flying School follow.

Chart of Accounts

101	Cash
105	Accounts Receivable
110	Supplies
115	Equipment
120	Airplane
220	Notes Payable
230	Accounts Payable
301	Dizzy Dawson, Capital
310	Dizzy Dawson, Drawing
401	Flying Revenue
615	Insurance Expense
630	Fuel Expense
640	Rent Expense
650	Interest Expense

Transactions

June 1 deposited $150,000 cash into the business account

June 2 purchased an airplane for instruction purposes; paid $75,000 cash down and signed a five-year, 12 percent note for $200,000 for the balance

June 3 bought office supplies on account for $350

June 4 bought fuel costing $3,870; agreed to pay within 30 days

June 6 bought office equipment on account for $5,000; paid $2,500 cash down and agreed to pay the balance in 30 days

June 9 paid office rent, $1,750

June 10 paid monthly insurance premium, $900

June 12 Dizzy withdrew $3,500 for personal use

June 15 Flying Revenue for the first half of the month is $7,000; $4,300 is received in cash, the rest is due within 30 days

June 17 paid $850 due on Accounts Payable

June 19 received a $265 bill for fuel (record it now to be paid later)

June 20 received $1,800 from charge customers

June 29 paid $6,170 on the note for the amount due on the airplane; of that amount, $2,834 is for payment of interest

June 30 flying revenue for the second half of the month is $4,700; $3,500 is received in cash, the rest is due within 30 days

1. *Journalize the transactions in a general journal beginning with page number 28.*

2. *Post to the general ledger.*

3. *Prepare a trial balance as of June 30, 19XX.*

Problem 4.2
journalizing, posting, and preparing trial balance

The chart of accounts and the account balances as of August 1, 19XX, for Kwik Kleaners follows.

Chart of Accounts

101	Cash	$ 6,500	
110	Accounts Receivable	2,100	
114	Cleaning Supplies	1,950	
115	Cleaning Equipment	95,000	
120	Office Equipment	8,000	
210	Notes Payable		$50,000
220	Accounts Payable		4,500
310	Nathaniel Emerson, Capital		59,050
320	Nathaniel Emerson, Drawing		
410	Cleaning Revenue		
601	Rent Expense		
605	Insurance Expense		
610	Advertising Expense		
620	Salary Expense		
630	Utilities Expense		
635	Interest Expense		

Transactions

August 1   paid rent for August, $1,500

August 1   bought a new typewriter for the office; paid $500 cash down and agreed to pay the balance of $700 within 60 days

August 4   placed an ad in the newspaper costing $100 (record it now to be paid within 30 days)

August 8   paid $125 for August insurance premium

August 10   bought $400 in cleaning supplies; will pay within 30 days

August 15   paid semimonthly salaries, $1,080

August 15   cleaning revenue for the first two weeks is $3,300; $1,600 is received in cash

August 17   received $2,225 from charge customers

August 18   paid $700 of the amount owed on the typewriter purchased on August 1

August 22   paid $1,000 to reduce the amount owed on a note; $425 of the amount is for interest expense

August 25   paid the telephone bill, $305

August 28   cleaning revenue for the second two weeks is $3,800; $2,300 is received in cash

August 29   paid bill for electricity, $120

August 31   paid semimonthly salaries, $1,090

August 31   Nathaniel withdrew $1,800 for personal use

Instructions

1. *Enter the balances from the chart of accounts into the ledger. Write "Balance" in the account description column and place a check mark (√) in the posting reference column of each account for which a balance is entered.*

2. *Journalize the August transactions in the general journal beginning with page number 39.*

3. *Post the transactions.*

4. *Prepare a trial balance as of August 31, 19XX.*

Problem 4.3
analyzing and correcting journal entries; posting and preparing trial balance

The bookkeeper for David's Dance Studio was new and made several errors when journalizing the transactions for the first month of business. The entries have not been posted. The chart of accounts and the general journal for the month of December follow.

Chart of Accounts

110	Cash
120	Accounts Receivable
130	Supplies
140	Equipment
150	Furniture
210	Notes Payable
220	Accounts Payable
310	David Starsky, Capital
320	David Starsky, Drawing
410	Dance Revenue
610	Utilities Expense
620	Wages Expense
630	Advertising Expense

General Journal for Problem 4.3

		GENERAL JOURNAL				Page *1*	
Date		Description	Post. Ref.	Debit		Credit	
19XX *Dec.*	*1*	Cash		12000 —			
		David Starsky, Capital				12000 —	
		To Record Owner's Investment					
	2	Equipment		4000 —			
		Cash				1000 —	
		Accounts Receivable				3000 —	
		Bought Equipment: Paid $1,000 Down; Balance					
		Due in 90 Days					
	4	Furniture		2000 —			
		Notes Payable				2000 —	
		Bought Furniture: Signed a 6-Month, 12% Note					
		for $2,000					
	5	Cash		500 —			
		Supplies				500 —	
		Paid Cash for Supplies					
	6	Cash		400 —			
		Dance Revenue				400 —	
		To Record Week's Revenue: $400 Received in					
		Cash; $300 Balance Due within 30 Days					
	9	Utilities Expense		105 —			
		Cash				105 —	
		Paid Bill for Electricity					
	10	Cash		370 —			
		David Starsky, Drawing				370 —	
		To Record Owner's Withdrawal					
	12	Utilities Expense		75 —			
		Accounts Payable				75 —	
		Received Phone Bill (Record Now to Be Paid					
		Later)					
	15	Wages Expense		1200 —			
		Cash				1200 —	
		To Record Wages of $800 and Owner's					
		Withdrawal of $400					

General Journal for Problem 4.3 *(continued)*

		GENERAL JOURNAL			Page 2
Date		**Description**	**Post. Ref.**	**Debit**	**Credit**
19XX *Dec.*	*18*	*Utilities Expense*		*75 —*	
		Cash			*75 —*
		To Record Payment of Phone Bill Received and			
		Recorded on December 12			
	20	*Cash*		*300 —*	
		David Starsky, Capital			*300 —*
		To Record Cash Received from Charge Customers			
	23	*Advertising Expense*		*175 —*	
		Accounts Receivable			*175 —*
		To Record Bill Received for Newspaper Ad in			
		December			
	24	*Equipment*		*1000 —*	
		David Starsky, Capital			*1000 —*
		Owner Donated a Typewriter to the Business			
	26	*Wages Expense*		*700 —*	
		Cash			*700 —*
		To Record Payment of Wages			
	28	*Cash*		*500 —*	
		Accounts Payable		*600 —*	
		Dance Revenue			*1100 —*
		To Record Revenue of $1,100: $500 Received in			
		Cash			
	30	*Accounts Receivable*		*500 —*	
		Cash			*500 —*
		To Record Payment Made on Equipment			
		Purchased on December 2			

Instructions

1. *Look over each journal entry carefully, including the description. If the entry is not correct, draw a line with a ruler through either the account title or the amount (or both) and enter the correct title or amount above the incorrect one.*

2. *When the incorrect entries have been corrected, post all the transactions to the general ledger.*

3. *Prepare a trial balance as of December 31, 19XX.*

4. *Determine the amount of the net income or net loss for December. Do not prepare a formal income statement.*

Problem 4.4
calculating ledger account balances; preparing trial balance, income statement, and balance sheet

Following is the ledger for Rainbow Painting, owned by Elvin Smythe, showing the transactions for the month of November 19XX.

CASH   Acct. No. *110*

Date		Explanation	PR	Debit	Credit	Balance
19XX Nov.	1	*Balance*	✔			6 2 9 0 —
	2		GJ14	5 5 0 —		
	5		GJ14		1 0 0 0 —	
	7		GJ14		2 0 0 0 —	
	7		GJ14	2 0 0 0 —		
	9		GJ14		4 0 0 —	
	11		GJ14		7 7 5 —	
	12		GJ14		1 9 0 —	
	14		GJ14	2 6 0 —		
	15		GJ15		1 5 0 0 —	
	15		GJ15	1 6 9 0 —		
	17		GJ15		2 1 0 —	
	19		GJ15		5 2 0 —	
	21		GJ16		2 7 5 —	
	21		GJ16	2 2 8 0 —		
	23		GJ16	4 7 5 —		
	24		GJ16		1 0 0 0 —	
	26		GJ17		3 7 5 —	
	27		GJ17		8 2 0 —	
	28		GJ17	1 3 0 —		
	30		GJ17		1 5 0 0 —	
	30		GJ17		1 0 0 0 —	
	30		GJ17	2 4 9 0 —		
	30		GJ17	1 1 5 0 —		

ACCOUNTS RECEIVABLE   Acct. No. **120**

Date		Explanation	PR	Debit	Credit	Balance
19XX Nov.	1	Balance	✔			4240 —
	2		GJ14		550 —	
	7		GJ14	1740 —		
	15		GJ15	500 —		
	21		GJ16	760 —		
	23		GJ16		475 —	
	30		GJ17	2200 —		
	30		GJ17		1150 —	

SUPPLIES   Acct. No. **130**

Date		Explanation	PR	Debit	Credit	Balance
19XX Nov.	1	Balance	✔			3730 —
	3		GJ14	200 —		

EQUIPMENT   Acct. No. **150**

Date		Explanation	PR	Debit	Credit	Balance
19XX Nov.	1	Balance	✔			29700 —

FURNITURE   Acct. No. **160**

Date		Explanation	PR	Debit	Credit	Balance
19XX Nov.	1	Balance	✔			9600 —
	21		GJ15	820 —		

NOTES PAYABLE   Acct. No. **210**

Date		Explanation	PR	Debit	Credit	Balance
19XX Nov.	1	Balance	✔			11400 —
	5		GJ14	1000 —		

ACCOUNTS PAYABLE   Acct. No. *220*

Date		Explanation	PR	Debit	Credit	Balance
*Nov.*¹⁹ˣˣ	1	Balance	✔			2 1 5 0 —
	3		GJ14		2 0 0 —	
	9		GJ14	4 0 0 —		
	21		GJ15		8 2 0 —	
	26		GJ17	3 7 5 —		

ELVIN SMYTHE, CAPITAL   Acct. No. *310*

Date		Explanation	PR	Debit	Credit	Balance
*Nov.*¹⁹ˣˣ	1	Balance	✔			4 0 0 1 0 —

ELVIN SMYTHE, DRAWING   Acct. No. *320*

Date		Explanation	PR	Debit	Credit	Balance
*Nov.*¹⁹ˣˣ	23		GJ16	1 0 0 0 —		
	30		GJ17	1 0 0 0 —		

REVENUE FROM PAINTING   Acct. No. *410*

Date		Explanation	PR	Debit	Credit	Balance
*Nov.*¹⁹ˣˣ	7		GJ14		3 7 4 0 —	
	15		GJ15		2 1 9 0 —	
	21		GJ16		3 0 4 0 —	
	30		GJ17		4 6 9 0 —	

REVENUE FROM INSTRUCTION   Acct. No. *420*

Date		Explanation	PR	Debit	Credit	Balance
*Nov.*¹⁹ˣˣ	14		GJ14		2 6 0 —	
	28		GJ17		1 3 0 —	

UTILITIES EXPENSE

Acct. No. **610**

Date		Explanation	PR	Debit	Credit	Balance
19XX Nov.	12		GJ14	1 9 0 —		
	17		GJ15	2 1 0 —		

ADVERTISING EXPENSE

Acct. No. **620**

Date		Explanation	PR	Debit	Credit	Balance
19XX Nov.	19		GJ15	5 2 0 —		

WAGES EXPENSE

Acct. No. **630**

Date		Explanation	PR	Debit	Credit	Balance
19XX Nov.	15		GJ15	1 5 0 0 —		
	30		GJ17	1 5 0 0 —		

RENT EXPENSE

Acct. No. **640**

Date		Explanation	PR	Debit	Credit	Balance
19XX Nov.	7		GJ14	2 0 0 0 —		

REPAIRS EXPENSE

Acct. No. **650**

Date		Explanation	PR	Debit	Credit	Balance
19XX Nov.	11		GJ14	7 7 5 —		
	27		GJ17	8 2 0 —		

INSURANCE EXPENSE

Acct. No. **660**

Date		Explanation	PR	Debit	Credit	Balance
19XX Nov.	21		GJ16	2 7 5 —		

Instructions

1. *Calculate the balance for each account.*
2. *Prepare a trial balance for Rainbow Painting as of November 30, 19XX.*
3. *Prepare an income statement for the month ended November 30, 19XX.*
4. *Prepare a balance sheet as of November 30. Include a complete statement of owner's equity on it.*

Problem 4.5
analyzing how errors affect net income.

An income statement prepared for the Bowmer Company for the month of February 19XX showed a net income of $2,100. The following errors were made by the bookkeeper in journalizing and posting the transactions for the month.

a. A $700 withdrawal of cash by Barbara Bowmer was recorded by debiting Salary Expense for $700 and crediting Cash for $700.
b. A bill was received for February advertising for $500, but it was not paid or recorded on the books.
c. $950 was received from clients who received services in January. It was recorded as a debit to Cash of $950 and a credit to Revenue of $950.
d. $1,200 in rent was paid; it was recorded as a debit to Rent Expense of $120 and a credit to Cash of $120.
e. $1,500 in cash was received for services performed in February; it was recorded as a debit to Cash of $1,500 and a credit to Capital of $1,500.
f. Services performed on account amounting to $1,100 was recorded as an $1,100 debit to Revenue and an $1,100 credit to Accounts Receivable.

Instructions

Considering each situation separately, analyze the incorrect entry to determine whether the error(s) will cause revenue or expenses to be overstated or understated. If revenue or expenses are affected by the error, determine by how much each is overstated or understated. The first one has been completed as an example. Answers should be recorded with the following headings.

Error	Will revenue be overstated? By how much?	Will revenue be understated? By how much?	Will expenses be overstated? By how much?	Will expenses be understated? By how much?
a.	_____	_____	yes, $700	_____

CHAPTER 5

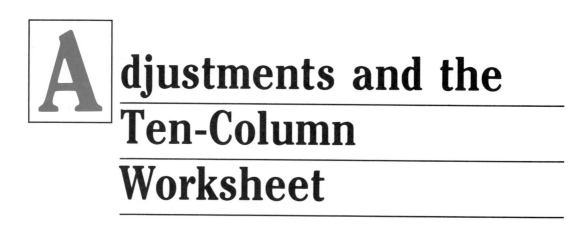

Adjustments and the Ten-Column Worksheet

accounting cycle
the step-by-step procedure that begins with a transaction and ends with the closing of the books

The **accounting cycle** is a series of steps that are repeated for every accounting period. The accounting cycle begins when the first transaction occurs and ends when the bookkeeper closes the books for the period; the cycle is repeated for each accounting period.

The first steps in the accounting cycle are journalizing, posting, and preparing a trial balance. In this chapter, the trial balance will be placed directly onto a **worksheet,** which is a ten-column form used by the bookkeeper to organize the data necessary for preparing the adjusting and closing entries and the financial statements. After the trial balance has been completed and is in balance, the next steps in the accounting cycle are calculating adjustments and completing a worksheet.

worksheet
a ten-column form on which the trial balance is entered, adjustments are prepared, and the necessary information for preparing the income statement and balance sheet is accumulated

An accounting period, which is the time span covered by the income statement, determines when (for example, a month, a quarter, a year) financial statements are prepared. Accounting periods must be equal in length, so that comparisons can be made from one period to another. The measurement of net income should be as precise as possible, and the matching principle requires that all expenses incurred during an accounting period be subtracted from the revenue earned for that same period. Past or future revenue or expenses must not be recorded on current financial statements.

To help ensure accuracy in reporting net income, certain adjustments to the accounts are made before the financial statements are prepared. These adjusting entries are recorded first on the worksheet, next in the general journal, and finally are posted to the general ledger.

PREPAID EXPENSES

Businesses often make expenditures that will benefit more than one accounting period. For example, when supplies are purchased, they are expected to last for several accounting periods; insurance policies are frequently purchased for one-, two-, or three-year periods; and rent is often prepaid for several months. Such expenditures in advance are called **prepaid expenses** and are debited to an asset account at the time of payment; at the end of the accounting period, a portion of the cost will be recognized as expense for the current period. The *unused* portion will remain on the books as an asset, but will eventually be converted to expense.

prepaid expenses
expenses paid in advance and recorded initially as assets

ADJUSTING ENTRIES

adjusting entry
an entry made at the end of the accounting period for which no transaction occurs and which brings certain accounts up to date

Up until now, when a transaction has been recorded, something has happened to prompt a journal entry. For example, a customer makes a payment on account, services are sold for cash, the owner withdraws money, the rent is paid. With an **adjusting entry,** however, nothing external happens. Adjusting entries are made simply to bring certain accounts up to date or to make certain accounts accurately reflect their value. For example, the Office Supplies account is debited whenever supplies are purchased, but *no credit to the account is made when supplies are used up* until an adjusting entry is recorded. At the time a one-, two-, or three-year insurance policy is purchased, the total cost is debited to an asset account called Prepaid Insurance, but *no credits are recorded* to the account until an adjusting entry is made. Adjustments to the accounts are made at the end of the accounting period, which may be one month, three months, a year, or some other time.

Adjustment for Supplies Used

Assume that on January 1, the Supplies account for Mary Tyus, M.D., had a balance of $255. Assume also that two purchases of supplies were made in January: one on January 14 for $60 and one on January 26 for $35. The general journal entries to record the purchases of supplies are as follows.

GENERAL JOURNAL					Page 5
Date	Description	Post. Ref.	Debit		Credit
Jan. 14	**Supplies**		6 0 —		
	Cash				6 0 —
	To Record Purchase of Supplies				
26	**Supplies**		3 5 —		
	Cash				3 5 —
	To Record Purchase of Supplies				

At the end of January, the Supplies account looks like this.

Supplies   **130**

1/1	Balance	255
1/14	GJ5	60
1/26	GJ8	35
		350

On January 31, a physical count of the supplies on hand showed their dollar balance to be $260, yet it appears from the account that $350 worth of supplies is on hand; this is not the case, because some of the supplies have been used. To reflect the accurate value ($260) of the account on January 31, an adjusting entry is made transferring the used-up portion to Supplies Used, an expense account. The entry is as follows.

	GENERAL JOURNAL			Page *14*
Date	**Description**	**Post. Ref.**	**Debit**	**Credit**
	Adjusting Entries			
19XX *Jan.* **31**	**Supplies Used**		90 —	
	Supplies			90 —
	To Record Supplies Used for the Month			

The $90 figure used in the adjusting entry was determined by subtracting the ending value of supplies from the balance in the account ($350 − $260 = $90). The Supplies account should reflect the value of the ending inventory after the adjusting entry has been journalized and posted.

Supplies   **130**

1/1	Balance	255	1/31	GJ14	Adjusting	90
1/14	GJ5	60				
1/26	GJ8	35				
	260	350				

Supplies Used   **605**

1/31	GJ14	Adjusting	90

The Supplies account is an asset and will appear on the balance sheet; Supplies Used is an expense and will appear on the income statement. Every adjusting entry will involve both a balance sheet account and an income statement account.

Adjustment for Prepaid Insurance

Assume that on January 2, 19XX, Mary Tyus, M.D., purchased a 12-month fire insurance policy for $360. The entry in the general journal is as follows.

	GENERAL JOURNAL			Page *1*
Date	**Description**	**Post. Ref.**	**Debit**	**Credit**
Jan. 2	*Prepaid Insurance*		3 6 0 —	
	Cash			3 6 0 —
	To Record Purchase of 12-Month Fire Insurance			
	Policy			

The Prepaid Insurance account is an asset and will appear on the balance sheet. Insurance expense should not be debited at the time the policy is purchased, because the expense should logically be spread out over the 12-month period for which the policy is in force.

At the end of the month (or the accounting period), the adjusting entry for insurance is calculated as follows:

$$\$360 \div 12 \text{ Months} = \$30 \text{ Cost per Month.}$$

The general journal entry to transfer a portion of the asset Prepaid Insurance to Insurance Expense is as follows.

GENERAL JOURNAL				Page *14*
Date	Description	Post. Ref.	Debit	Credit
19XX	*Adjusting Entries*			
Jan. *31*	*Insurance Expense*		3 0 —	
	Prepaid Insurance			3 0 —
	To Record Insurance Expense for Month			

After the entry has been posted, the T-accounts look like this.

Prepaid Insurance   **120**

1/2 GJ1	360	1/31 GJ14 Adjusting 30
⟨330⟩		

Insurance Expense   **660**

1/31 GJ14 Adjusting 30	

Twelve $30 credits will be journalized and posted, one each month, until the entire $360 has been transferred to Insurance Expense.

Adjustment for Depreciation

The balance sheet is divided into two main categories of assets called *current assets* and *plant and equipment.* Plant and equipment items include assets such as buildings, furniture, office or store equipment, autos, and trucks. Plant and equipment assets are used in the production of other assets (for example, cash or accounts receivable) and are generally not for sale.

When an asset is purchased for use in the business, an asset account is debited. By recording **depreciation,** the cost of these assets is converted to expense over time. Assume, for example, that Mary Tyus purchases office equipment costing $10,600 on January 2. It is expected to have a **useful life** of four years and then have a

depreciation
the transferring of the cost of an asset to expense over the asset's useful life

useful life
the number of years over which an asset is depreciated

salvage value
the estimated worth of an asset at the end of its useful life

acquisition
the act of acquiring possession

salvage value of $1,000. In the general journal, the entry to record the **acquisition** of the asset is as follows.

GENERAL JOURNAL				Page *1*
Date	Description	Post. Ref.	Debit	Credit
19XX *Jan.* *2*	*Office Equipment*		*10600 —*	
	Cash			*3000 —*
	Notes Payable			*7600 —*
	To Record Purchase of Office Equipment;			
	Signed a 12-Month, 10% Note			

Accountants may use several methods to determine how much depreciation expense may be recognized for an accounting period. The straight-line depreciation method recognizes the same amount of expense each accounting period. The bookkeeper must know three things to calculate the straight-line depreciation expense: (1) the cost of the asset, (2) the useful life of the asset, and (3) the estimated salvage value. Depreciation is calculated as follows.

1. Subtract the salvage value from the cost to determine the depreciable amount:

$$\$10,600 - \$1,000 = \$9,600$$

2. Divide the depreciable amount by the number of years in the useful life to determine the annual depreciation:

$$\$9,600 \div 4 = \$2,400$$

3. Divide yearly depreciation by 12 (if necessary) to determine monthly depreciation:

$$\$2,400 \div 12 = \$200$$

The adjusting entry to record the depreciation is as follows.

GENERAL JOURNAL				Page *14*
Date	Description	Post. Ref.	Debit	Credit
19XX	*Adjusting Entries*			
Jan. 31	*Depreciation Expense*		2 0 0 —	
	Accumulated Depreciation: Office Equipment			2 0 0 —
	To Record Depreciation on Office Equipment			

contra asset
an account with a credit balance that subtracts from its related asset account balance on the balance sheet

When depreciation is recorded, credits are not entered directly into the asset account because accounts for depreciable assets show the historical cost. Depreciation amounts are recorded in an account called Accumulated Depreciation; it is a **contra asset** because it subtracts from its related asset on the balance sheet.

After the adjusting entry for depreciation has been posted, the T-accounts look like this.

Office Equipment				150
1/2	*GJ1*	*10,600*		

Accumulated Depreciation: Office Equipment				150A
		1/31 *Adjusting*	*GJ14*	*200*

Depreciation Expense				670
1/31 *Adjusting*	*GJ14*	*200*		

The Accumulated Depreciation account accumulates the depreciation for its related asset. The Office Equipment account and the contra asset account, Accumulated Depreciation, look like this six months after the purchase of the equipment.

Office Equipment 150

1/2	GJ1	10,600	

Accumulated Depreciation: Office Equipment 150A

1/31	Adjusting	GJ14	200
2/28	Adjusting	GJ18	200
3/31	Adjusting	GJ22	200
4/30	Adjusting	GJ27	200
5/31	Adjusting	GJ32	200
6/30	Adjusting	GJ37	200

book value
the cost of an asset minus its accumulated depreciation

The cost of an asset minus its accumulated depreciation is called the **book value.** The balance sheet will show cost, accumulated depreciation, and book value for every depreciable asset. A portion of the balance sheet on June 30 for the preceding purchase and six months' depreciation would appear as follows.

MARY TYUS, M.D.
BALANCE SHEET
JUNE 30, 19XX

Assets			
Cash		$ 8 1 0 0 —	

Office Equipment	$10,600 —		
Less Accumulated Depreciation: Office Equipment	1,200 —	9 4 0 0 —	

Adjustment for Wages Payable

Assume that Mary Tyus incurs $150 in wages every day, Monday through Friday, and that paydays fall on Friday of each week. The end of the accounting period, however, falls on Tuesday, which is January 31, the end of the month. For January expenses to be properly recorded, two days of wages expense (Monday and Tuesday, January 30 and 31) must be recorded for January.

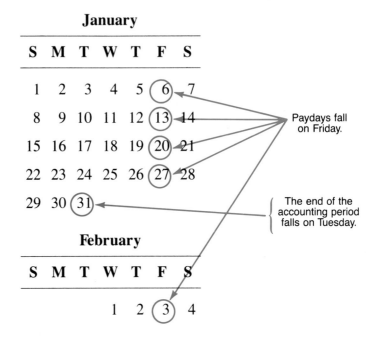

The adjusting entry to record this is as follows.

GENERAL JOURNAL				Page *14*
Date	Description	Post. Ref.	Debit	Credit
19XX	*Adjusting Entries*			
Jan. *31*	*Wages Expense*		*3 0 0 —*	
	Wages Payable			*3 0 0 —*
	To Record Wages Expense for January 30			
	and 31			

Wages Payable is credited because the wages will not actually be paid until Friday, thus creating a short-term liability. After the adjusting entry is posted, the T-accounts look like this.

Wages Expense   **640**

1/6		GJ2	750
1/13		GJ5	750
1/20		GJ7	750
1/27		GJ9	750
1/31	Adjusting	GJ14	300

Wages Payable   **230**

1/31	Adjusting	GJ14	300

On Friday, when the wages are actually paid, the balance from the Wages Payable account must be removed and three days' wages expense must be recognized for February. The entry to record payment of the wages is as follows.

	GENERAL JOURNAL				Page *15*
Date	**Description**	**Post. Ref.**	**Debit**		**Credit**
Feb. *3*	*Wages Expense*		4 5 0 —		
	Wages Payable		3 0 0 —		
	Cash				7 5 0 —
	To Record Payment of Wages for Period				
	January 30–February 3				

After posting the entry for payment of the wages, the T-accounts for Wages Payable and Wages Expense look like this.

Wages Payable   **230**

2/3		GJ15	300	1/31	Adjusting	GJ14	300

Wages Expense   **640**

1/6		GJ2	750
1/13		GJ5	750
1/20		GJ7	750
1/27		GJ9	750
1/31	Adjusting	GJ14	300
2/3		GJ15	450

The Wages Expense account now accurately reflects $450 for the first week in February, and $300 of that week's total wages of $750 has been allocated to January.

Adjustment for Unearned Revenue

Often, a business receives money in advance for services it plans to deliver later. For example, magazine subscriptions are paid in advance, theaters sell season tickets, and dormitories collect room and board at the beginning of the quarter or semester. Cash received in advance of performing the services should not be recognized as revenue.

Assume that Mary Tyus received $1,000 from Jorge Sanders on January 3 for consulting services that she will perform in the future. The entry to record the $1,000 received is as follows.

		GENERAL JOURNAL			Page 2
Date		Description	Post. Ref.	Debit	Credit
19XX Jan. 3		Cash		1000 —	
		Unearned Consulting Revenue			1000 —
		Cash Received for Services to Be Performed			
		in the Future			

The Unearned Revenue account is a liability, because Mary owes the services to the customer and the $1,000 will not be recognized as revenue until the services are performed.

Assume that by the end of January, Mary performs $600 of consulting services for Jorge Sanders. Through an adjusting entry, the $600 will be transferred from an Unearned Revenue account to Earned Revenue.

GENERAL JOURNAL				Page **14**
Date	Description	Post. Ref.	Debit	Credit
19XX	*Adjusting Entries*			
Jan. *31*	*Unearned Consulting Revenue*		*6 0 0 —*	
	Consulting Revenue			*6 0 0 —*
	To Transfer $600 into Consulting Revenue			

After the adjusting entry has been posted, the T-accounts appear as follows.

Unearned Consulting Revenue   **220**

1/31 Adjusting GJ14 600	*1/3* *GJ2 1,000*
	400

Consulting Revenue   **405**

	1/15 GJ11 900
	1/31 Adjusting GJ14 600

The balance in the Unearned Consulting Revenue account on January 31 is $400. When Mary performs the remainder of the consulting services, that balance, too, will be transferred to Consulting Revenue.

Adjustment for the Accrual of Revenue

In the previous example, Mary Tyus was paid for consulting before the services were performed. A more common occurrence would be where Mary had performed services but had not yet received payment at the end of the accounting period in which the financial statements were prepared. Assume that in January, Mary had performed medical services for a customer amounting to $2,000. At the end of the month, a bill was sent to the customer and the following adjusting entry to recognize the revenue earned was prepared.

		GENERAL JOURNAL			Page *14*
Date		Description	Post. Ref.	Debit	Credit
19XX					

Jan.	31	Accounts Receivable		2000 —	
		Medical Revenue			2000 —
		To Record Services Performed and Bills			
		Sent to Customers			

The T-accounts look as follows after the adjusting entry has been prepared.

Accounts Receivable   **110**

1/1	Balance		400
1/15		GJ7	700
1/31	Adjusting	GJ14	2,000

Medical Revenue   **401**

	1/8		GJ5	2,700
	1/15		GJ6	3,100
	1/22		GJ8	3,300
	1/29		GJ10	2,500
	1/31	Adjusting	GJ14	2,000

DEFERRALS

Deferrals fall into two main categories called *deferred expenses* and *deferred revenue.* Deferred expenses are originally recorded as assets, but are converted to expense over an appropriate time, as when rent paid in advance and recorded in the Prepaid Rent account is transferred to the Rent Expense account through an adjusting entry. The recording of the rent expense is deferred, or postponed, until some future accounting period. Adjustments for prepaid advertising, supplies used, and depreciation fall into the deferred expense category.

Deferred revenue indicates that cash has been received for services that have not yet been performed. At the time the cash is received, an Unearned Revenue account is credited, creating a short-term liability. When the services are performed, the appropriate amount will be transferred from Unearned Revenue to Earned Revenue through an adjusting entry.

Adjusting entries for deferrals will record either an expense or revenue; failure to record a deferral will understate expenses or revenue, thus making the net income figure incorrect.

ACCRUALS

Whereas the information for recording deferrals is contained in the accounting records, the information for recording accruals is not. An accrual will record an asset that exists at the end of the accounting period but does not yet show on the accounting records, or it will record a liability that exists but does not reflect on the books. The adjusting entry debiting Accounts Receivable and crediting Medical Revenue is an example of the first type; until the adjusting entry is made, both Accounts Receivable and Medical Revenue are understated. The adjusting entry to record Wages Expense and Wages Payable records an expense and a liability that were not previously on the books. To omit this adjustment would cause an understatement of expenses and liabilities.

EFFECTS OF THE FAILURE TO RECORD ADJUSTING ENTRIES

Every adjusting entry involves both an income statement account and a balance sheet account. Failure to record an adjustment causes an overstatement or understatement of either expenses or revenue and an overstatement or understatement of net income.

For example, failure to record an adjustment for an expense (such as the entry that debits Insurance Expense and credits Prepaid Insurance) would cause an understatement of expenses and a resulting overstatement of net income, while failure to record an adjustment for accrued revenue (such as the entry debiting Accounts Receivable and crediting Revenue) would cause an understatement of revenue and an understatement of net income.

Any time there is a failure to record an adjustment, net income will be affected. Owner's equity will also be affected, because net income is added to the Owner's Capital account at the end of the accounting period. If net income is overstated, owner's capital will also be overstated; and if net income is understated, owner's capital will be understated.

Other accounts, too, will be affected. For example, the failure to record the adjustment for supplies used (a debit to Supplies Used and a credit to Supplies) would cause an overstatement of total assets, an understatement of total expenses, and an overstatement of net income.

THE TEN-COLUMN WORKSHEET

The worksheet is a ten-column form on which the trial balance, the adjustments, an adjusted trial balance, the income statement, and the balance sheet are first prepared. It is prepared in pencil because it is not a formal statement; rather, it is the bookkeeper's tool and proves that the general ledger is in balance, and it accumulates the information for the adjustments and for the income statement and balance sheet *before* the adjustments are journalized and the formal statements are prepared in ink.

Trial Balance Columns of the Worksheet

The ten-column worksheet that follows is for Mary Tyus, M.D. The first two columns of the worksheet are for preparing the trial balance. The figures are taken directly from the ledger after all the posting for the period has been completed. The trial balance must be complete and in balance before continuing on to the adjustments columns of the worksheet. A single line to indicate addition is drawn across the debit and credit columns beneath the last item listed, and a double line extends across the debit and credit columns beneath the trial balance totals.

	MARY TYUS, M.D. WORKSHEET FOR MONTH ENDING JANUARY 31, 19XX				
Acct. No.	Account Titles	Trial Balance			
		Debit		Credit	
101	Cash	12500 —			
105	Notes Receivable	4700 —			
110	Accounts Receivable	1100 —			
120	Prepaid Insurance	360 —			
130	Supplies	350 —			
150	Office Equipment	10600 —			
150A	Accumulated Depreciation: OE				
201	Notes Payable			7600 —	
210	Accounts Payable			2950 —	
215	Payroll Taxes Payable			210 —	
220	Unearned Consulting Revenue			1000 —	
301	Mary Tyus, Capital			21692 —	
310	Mary Tyus, Drawing	4800 —			
401	Medical Revenue			11600 —	
405	Consulting Revenue			900 —	
601	Rent Expense	3900 —			
610	Interest Expense	76 —			
615	Utilities Expense	1420 —			
620	Repairs Expense	2416 —			
630	Uniforms Expense	500 —			
640	Wages Expense	3000 —			
650	Payroll Tax Expense	230 —			
	Totals	45952 —		45952 —	

Adjustments Columns of the Worksheet

Once the trial balance is complete and in balance, the data for the adjustments are entered directly in the adjustments columns opposite their account titles. If the account title does not appear on the original trial balance, it may be added at the bottom of the worksheet.

The letter *a* is written next to the debit and credit amounts for the first adjustment, the letter *b* beside the next adjustment, and so on. The letters identify the adjustments and make them easier to journalize after the worksheet is complete.

The adjustment data for Mary Tyus, M.D., is as follows.

a. The Supplies Used account is debited and Supplies is credited for $90 to recognize supplies used in January.

b. The Insurance Expense account is debited and Prepaid Insurance is credited for $30 to recognize insurance expense for January.

c. Depreciation Expense is debited and Accumulated Depreciation is credited for $200 to record depreciation expense for January.

d. Wages Expense is debited and Wages Payable is credited for $300 to record accrued wages expense.

e. The liability account Unearned Consulting Revenue is debited and Consulting Revenue is credited for $600 to recognize that portion of the consulting revenue that has been earned in January.

f. Accounts Receivable has been debited and Medical Revenue has been credited for $2,000 to recognize services performed but for which payment has not been received.

The worksheet on page 145 shows the trial balance and the adjustments columns.

Adjusted Trial Balance Columns of the Worksheet

The figures in the adjusted trial balance columns, not the ones on the original trial balance, are the ones that will be used by the accountant for preparing the financial statements. The correct procedure for completing the adjusted trial balance is to start with the first account, Cash, and if there is no adjustment, simply extend the balance to its correct debit or credit column of the adjusted trial balance. All accounts without adjustments are treated in the same fashion.

Accounts with adjustments are handled in one of four ways.

1. If the original account has a debit balance and the adjustment is also a debit, add the amounts together and extend the total to the adjusted trial balance as a debit. The adjustment to the Accounts Receivable account (f) is an example.

2. If the original account has a credit balance and the adjustment is also a credit, add the figures and extend the total to the adjusted trial balance as a credit. The adjustment to Medical Revenue (f) is an example.

3. If the account on the original trial balance has a debit balance and the adjustment is a credit, subtract and enter the new but

MARY TYUS, M.D.
WORKSHEET
FOR MONTH ENDED JANUARY 31, 19XX

Acct. No.	Account Titles	Trial Balance Debit	Trial Balance Credit	Adjustments Debit	Adjustments Credit
101	Cash	12500 —			
105	Notes Receivable	4700 —			
110	Accounts Receivable	1100 —		f. 2000 —	
120	Prepaid Insurance	360 —			b. 30 —
130	Supplies	350 —			a. 90 —
150	Office Equipment	10600 —			
150A	Accumulated Depr.: OE				c. 200 —
201	Notes Payable		7600 —		
210	Accounts Payable		2950 —		
215	Payroll Taxes Payable		210 —		
220	Unearned Consulting Rev.		1000 —	e. 600 —	
301	Mary Tyus, Capital		21692 —		
310	Mary Tyus, Drawing	4800 —			
401	Medical Revenue		11600 —		f. 2000 —
405	Consulting Revenue		900 —		e. 600 —
601	Rent Expense	3900 —			
610	Interest Expense	76 —			
615	Utilities Expense	1420 —			
620	Repairs Expense	2416 —			
630	Uniforms Expense	500 —			
640	Wages Expense	3000 —		d. 300 —	
650	Payroll Tax Expense	230 —			
	Totals	45952 —	45952 —		
605	Supplies Used			a. 90 —	
660	Insurance Expense			b. 30 —	
670	Depreciation Expense			c. 200 —	
230	Wages Payable				d. 300 —
				3220 —	3220 —

smaller debit balance onto the adjusted trial balance. The adjustment to Supplies (a) is an example.

4. If the account on the original trial balance has a credit balance and the adjustment is a debit, subtract and extend the smaller balance to the credit side of the adjusted trial balance. The adjustment to Unearned Consulting Revenue (e) is an example.

The adjusted trial balance appears in the following worksheet.

MARY TYUS, M.D.
WORKSHEET
FOR MONTH ENDED JANUARY 31, 19XX

Acct. No.	Account Titles	Trial Balance Debit	Trial Balance Credit
101	Cash	12500 —	
105	Notes Receivable	4700 —	
110	Accounts Receivable	1100 —	
120	Prepaid Insurance	360 —	
130	Supplies	350 —	
150	Office Equipment	10600 —	
150A	Accumulated Depreciation: OE		
201	Notes Payable		7600 —
210	Accounts Payable		2950 —
215	Payroll Taxes Payable		210 —
220	Unearned Consulting Revenue		1000 —
301	Mary Tyus, Capital		21692 —
310	Mary Tyus, Drawing	4800 —	
401	Medical Revenue		11600 —
405	Consulting Revenue		900 —
601	Rent Expense	3900 —	
610	Interest Expense	76 —	
615	Utilities Expense	1420 —	
620	Repairs Expense	2416 —	
630	Uniforms Expense	500 —	
640	Wages Expense	3000 —	
650	Payroll Tax Expense	230 —	
	Totals	45952 —	45952 —
605	Supplies Used		
660	Insurance Expense		
670	Depreciation Expense		
230	Wages Payable		

Adjustments				Adjusted Trial Balance			
Debit		Credit		Debit		Credit	
				12500 —			
				4700 —			
f.	2000 —			3100 —			
		b.	30 —	330 —			
		a.	90 —	260 —			
				10600 —			
		c.	200 —			200 —	
						7600 —	
						2950 —	
						210 —	
e.	600 —					400 —	
						21692 —	
				4800 —			
		f.	2000 —			13600 —	
		e.	600 —			1500 —	
				3900 —			
				76 —			
				1420 —			
				2416 —			
				500 —			
d.	300 —			3300 —			
				230 —			
a.	90 —			90 —			
b.	30 —			30 —			
c.	200 —			200 —			
		d.	300 —			300 —	
	3220 —		3220 —	48452 —		48452 —	

Income Statement and Balance Sheet Columns of the Worksheet

Once the adjusted trial balance is complete and in balance, each figure is extended to the columns for either the balance sheet or the income statement. The procedure for extending the figures is as follows.

1. Starting at the top with Cash, extend the figures to their correct debit or credit column of the balance sheet. Repeat this procedure for each asset, liability, and owner's equity account that appears on the adjusted trial balance.

2. Beginning with the first revenue account, extend that balance into the credit column of the income statement, and extend all expense account balances into the debit column of the income statement.

3. Do not omit any of the accounts with adjustments that appear at the bottom of the original trial balance. Some are income statement accounts and others are balance sheet accounts. Supplies Used, Insurance Expense, and Depreciation Expense are all extended to the debit column of the income statement, while Wages Payable is a liability and must be extended to the credit column of the balance sheet.

4. Total the four columns of the income statement and the balance sheet and enter totals on the worksheet beneath a single ruled line.

Carefully study the worksheet as it appears after all figures have been extended from the adjusted trial balance columns to the balance sheet and income statement columns.

MARY TYUS, M.D.
WORKSHEET
FOR MONTH ENDED JANUARY 31, 19XX

Acct. No.	Account Titles	Trial Balance Debit	Trial Balance Credit	Adjustments Debit	Adjustments Credit
101	Cash	12500 —			
105	Notes Receivable	4700 —			
110	Accounts Receivable	1100 —		f. 2000 —	
120	Prepaid Insurance	360 —			b. 30 —
130	Supplies	350 —			a. 90 —
150	Office Equipment	10600 —			
150A	Accumulated Depr.: OE				c. 200 —
201	Notes Payable		7600 —		
210	Accounts Payable		2950 —		
215	Payroll Taxes Payable		210 —		
220	Unearned Consulting Rev.		1000 —	e. 600 —	
301	Mary Tyus, Capital		21692 —		
310	Mary Tyus, Drawing	4800 —			
401	Medical Revenue		11600 —		f. 2000 —
405	Consulting Revenue		900 —		e. 600 —
601	Rent Expense	3900 —			
610	Interest Expense	76 —			
615	Utilities Expense	1420 —			
620	Repairs Expense	2416 —			
630	Uniforms Expense	500 —			
640	Wages Expense	3000 —		d. 300 —	
650	Payroll Tax Expense	230 —			
	Totals	45952 —	45952 —		
605	Supplies Used			a. 90 —	
660	Insurance Expense			b. 30 —	
670	Depreciation Expense			c. 200 —	
230	Wages Payable				d. 300 —
				3220 —	3220 —

Adjusted Trial Balance		Income Statement		Balance Sheet	
Debit	Credit	Debit	Credit	Debit	Credit
12500 —				12500 —	
4700 —				4700 —	
3100 —				3100 —	
330 —				330 —	
260 —				260 —	
10600 —				10600 —	
	200 —				200 —
	7600 —				7600 —
	2950 —				2950 —
	210 —				210 —
	400 —				400 —
	21692 —				21692 —
4800 —				4800 —	
	13600 —		13600 —		
	1500 —		1500 —		
3900 —		3900 —			
76 —		76 —			
1420 —		1420 —			
2416 —		2416 —			
500 —		500 —			
3300 —		3300 —			
230 —		230 —			
90 —		90 —			
30 —		30 —			
200 —		200 —			
	300 —				300 —
48452 —	48452 —	12162 —	15100 —	36290 —	33352 —

Net Income on the Worksheet

The next steps will verify the accuracy of the bookkeeper's work and will complete the worksheet.

5. Determine the difference between the income statement debit and credit columns. If the credit total (revenue) is larger than the debit total (expenses), then a net income has been earned. Enter the net income figure beneath the total on the debit side of the income statement and write the words *Net Income* in the Account Titles column of the worksheet on the same line.

6. Next enter the net income figure obtained in Step 5 beneath the credit column total on the balance sheet. This is required because the net income is added to the Owner's Capital account (which has a credit balance) in the owner's equity section of the balance sheet.

7. Draw a single ruling beneath the four columns of the income statement and the balance sheet beneath the net income figure.

8. Total the balance sheet columns. At this point, they must equal each other. If they do not, a mistake has been made and the bookkeeper must find it before continuing.

9. Total the income statement columns and draw a double ruling across the income statement and balance sheet columns.

The debit column equals the credit column on the income statement, and the debit column equals the credit column on the balance sheet, but *the columns of the income statement do not equal the columns of the balance sheet.*

MARY TYUS, M.D.
WORKSHEET
FOR MONTH ENDED JANUARY 31, 19XX

Acct. No.	Account Titles	Trial Balance Debit	Trial Balance Credit	Adjustments Debit	Adjustments Credit
101	Cash	12500 —			
105	Notes Receivable	4700 —			
110	Accounts Receivable	1100 —		f. 2000 —	
120	Prepaid Insurance	360 —			b. 30 —
130	Supplies	350 —			a. 90 —
150	Office Equipment	10600 —			
150A	Accumulated Depr.: OE				c. 200 —
201	Notes Payable		7600 —		
210	Accounts Payable		2950 —		
215	Payroll Taxes Payable		210 —		
220	Unearned Consulting Rev.		1000 —	e. 600 —	
301	Mary Tyus, Capital		21692 —		
310	Mary Tyus, Drawing	4800 —			
401	Medical Revenue		11600 —		f. 2000 —
405	Consulting Revenue		900 —		e. 600 —
601	Rent Expense	3900 —			
610	Interest Expense	76 —			
615	Utilities Expense	1420 —			
620	Repairs Expense	2416 —			
630	Uniforms Expense	500 —			
640	Wages Expense	3000 —		d. 300 —	
650	Payroll Tax Expense	230 —			
	Totals	45952 —	45952 —		
605	Supplies Used			a. 90 —	
660	Insurance Expense			b. 30 —	
670	Depreciation Expense			c. 200 —	
230	Wages Payable				d. 300 —
				3220 —	3220 —
	Net Income				

Adjusted Trial Balance		Income Statement		Balance Sheet	
Debit	Credit	Debit	Credit	Debit	Credit
12500 —				12500 —	
4700 —				4700 —	
3100 —				3100 —	
330 —				330 —	
260 —				260 —	
10600 —				10600 —	
	200 —				200 —
	7600 —				7600 —
	2950 —				2950 —
	210 —				210 —
	400 —				400 —
	21692 —				21692 —
4800 —				4800 —	
	13600 —		13600 —		
	1500 —		1500 —		
3900 —		3900 —			
76 —		76 —			
1420 —		1420 —			
2416 —		2416 —			
500 —		500 —			
3300 —		3300 —			
230 —		230 —			
90 —		90 —			
30 —		30 —			
200 —		200 —			
	300 —				300 —
48452 —	48452 —	12162 —	15100 —	36290 —	33352 —
		2938 —			2938 —
		15100 —	15100 —	36290 —	36290 —

A NET LOSS ON THE WORKSHEET

A net *income* figure is added to the credit column of the balance sheet because net income is added to capital when preparing the statement of owner's equity (credits increase the Capital account). If, however, after totaling the income statement columns of the worksheet, the debit column (expenses) is larger than the credit

PAUL'S PRESCHOOL
WORKSHEET
FOR MONTH ENDED MARCH 31, 19XX

Acct. No.	Account Titles	Adjusted Trial Balance Debit	Credit
110	Cash	6720—	
115	Notes Receivable	905—	
120	Accounts Receivable	1200—	
130	Prepaid Insurance	600—	
140	Supplies	400—	
145	Playground Equipment	16190—	
145A	Accumulated Depreciation: PE		900—
200	Notes Payable		9600—
201	Accounts Payable		860—
210	Unearned Revenue		2500—
220	Wages Payable		220—
301	Paul Pinchen, Capital		14334—
310	Paul Pinchen, Drawing	1560—	
410	Revenue		2780—
601	Advertising Expense	105—	
610	Rent Expense	800—	
615	Utilities Expense	150—	
620	Repairs Expense	235—	
630	Depreciation Expense	300—	
640	Wages Expense	1700—	
660	Payroll Tax Expense	102—	
670	Interest Expense	127—	
680	Supplies Used	60—	
690	Insurance Expense	40—	
	Totals	31194—	31194—
	Net Loss		

column (revenue), then a net loss has occurred; the amount of the net loss is entered beneath the debit column total on the balance sheet to complete the worksheet. A net loss will be subtracted from the Owner's Capital account when the statement of owner's equity is prepared. Study the partial worksheet for Paul's Preschool for March 19XX.

	Income Statement		Balance Sheet	
	Debit	Credit	Debit	Credit
			6720 —	
			905 —	
			1200 —	
			600 —	
			100	
			16190 —	
				900 —
				9600 —
				860 —
				2500 —
				220 —
				14334 —
			1560 —	
		2780 —		
	105 —			
	800 —			
	150 —			
	235 —			
	300 —			
	1700 —			
	102 —			
	127 —			
	60 —			
	40 —			
	3619 —	2780 —	27575 —	28414 —
		839 —	839 —	
	3619 —	3619 —	28414 —	28414 —

FINDING ERRORS IN THE INCOME STATEMENT AND BALANCE SHEET COLUMNS

Totaling the columns of the income statement and determining the net income or net loss will not show whether an error has been made. Only after totaling the balance sheet columns and adding the net income or loss to the appropriate column will a mistake become apparent. If, for example, the credit column of the balance sheet does not equal the debit column after adding the net income to the credit column of the balance sheet, then a mistake has been made. The error probably is *not* on the adjusted trial balance, because it was in balance before any figures were extended to the balance sheet and income statement. (The trial balance, and thus the adjusted trial balance, does not reveal all errors, however. It only proves the equality of debits and credits.) The following procedure can be used to locate errors on the worksheet.

1. Quickly look at each account on the adjusted trial balance to make sure that each has been extended to the right financial statement column and in the right debit or credit column. For example, the balance of the Drawing account may have been extended to the credit column of the balance sheet rather than to the debit column.

2. Check also to make sure that the amounts as extended are correct. A number can easily be transposed or a decimal point misplaced when numbers are transferred from one column to another.

3. Check the accounts at the bottom of the original trial balance to make sure their balances have been extended to the correct income statement or balance sheet column.

4. Re-add the income statement columns.

5. Recalculate the net income or net loss figure.

6. Re-add the balance sheet columns.

7. Make sure that a net income figure appears in the credit column of the balance sheet and that a net loss figure appears in the debit column.

8. Finally, re-add the net income or loss figure to its correct balance sheet column total.

JOURNALIZING THE ADJUSTING ENTRIES

Once the worksheet is complete, the bookkeeper must journalize and post the adjusting entries; the adjustments will not appear in the accounts until these steps have been completed. The worksheet is used simply to accumulate the information needed to journalize the adjusting entries and to prepare the financial statements.

To begin, center the words *Adjusting Entries* in the description column of the general journal. To journalize the adjustments, refer to the adjustments columns of the worksheet and, starting with the first adjustment (a), copy the debit account title and amount and the credit account title and amount into the general journal. After entering a concise explanation, continue with adjustments b, c, and so on. The general journal entries for the adjustments of Mary Tyus, M.D., are illustrated here. The general ledger after posting the adjustments appears in the next chapter.

GENERAL JOURNAL				Page *14*	
Date	Description	Post. Ref.	Debit	Credit	
19XX	*Adjusting Entries*				
Jan. 31	Supplies Used		90 —		
	Supplies			90 —	
	To Record Supplies Used for the Month				
31	Insurance Expense		30 —		
	Prepaid Insurance			30 —	
	To Record Insurance Expense for the Month				
31	Depreciation Expense		200 —		
	Accumulated Depreciation: Office Equipment			200 —	
	To Record Depreciation on Office Equipment				
31	Wages Expense		300 —		
	Wages Payable			300 —	
	To Record Wages Expense for January 30 and 31				
31	Unearned Consulting Revenue		600 —		
	Consulting Revenue			600 —	
	To Transfer $600 into Consulting Revenue				
31	Accounts Receivable		2000 —		
	Medical Revenue			2000 —	
	To Record Services Performed and Bill Sent to Customer				

SUMMARY

The accounting cycle is a series of steps that are completed each accounting period. The steps covered so far include journalizing, posting, preparing the worksheet with adjustments, preparing the financial statements, and journalizing and posting the adjustments.

The worksheet is the ten-column form used by accountants to accumulate data for the adjusting entries and the financial statements. Adjustments fall into two main categories called *deferrals* and *accruals*.

Deferrals occur when certain expenses or revenue are deferred, or postponed, until some future accounting period. The following are examples of deferrals.

1. When supplies are purchased, the amount is debited to the asset account Supplies. As supplies are used up, however, no credit entries are made to the account to indicate this. An adjusting entry is required to record the supplies expense; it is recorded as a debit to the expense account Supplies Used and a credit to the asset account Supplies.

2. When an insurance policy is purchased, the amount is debited to the asset account Prepaid Insurance. A portion of the cost of the policy is transferred to expense at the end of each accounting period by an adjustment that debits Insurance Expense and credits Prepaid Insurance.

3. When an asset such as equipment, furniture, buildings, automobiles, or trucks is purchased, its historical cost is recorded in the asset account. At the end of each accounting period, a portion of the cost of each depreciable asset is transferred to expense by a debit to Depreciation Expense and a credit to the contra-asset account Accumulated Depreciation. Accumulated Depreciation subtracts from the balance of its related asset account on the balance sheet; the balance sheet shows the cost of each asset, its accumulated depreciation, and the difference between the two, the book value.

4. When a customer pays in advance for services, the recognition of the revenue must be deferred until the services are actually performed. To achieve this, the original entry debits Cash and credits a liability account (the *services* are owed to the customer) called Unearned Revenue. When the services are actually performed, the cash value of the work done is removed from the Unearned Revenue account by a debit and is entered into an Earned Revenue account by a credit.

Adjusting entries for accruals result in recording an asset or a liability that has accrued over the accounting period but does not show on the books. The following are examples of accruals.

1. At the end of the accounting period, services performed for which no payment has been received must be recorded. This is accomplished by an adjusting entry that debits the asset Accounts Receivable and credits Revenue.

2. Any liabilities that have accrued during the period but do not show on the books must be recorded as adjustments. The entry to record accrued wages is typical; Wages Expense is debited and Wages Payable is credited.

The adjusting entries are first entered in the adjustments columns of the worksheet. The amounts are combined with the figures on the original trial balance to produce an adjusted trial balance from which the figures used to prepare the income statement and balance sheet are obtained.

Review of Accounting Terminology

Following is a list of the accounting terminology for this chapter.

accounting cycle   depreciation
acquisition   prepaid expenses
adjusting entry   salvage value
book value   useful life
contra asset   worksheet

Fill in the blank with the correct word or term from the list.

1. The number of years over which an asset is depreciated is the asset's _____.

2. An account that subtracts from its related asset account on the balance sheet is a/an _____.

3. A/an _____ is the act of acquiring possession.

4. The cost of an asset minus its accumulated depreciation is the asset's _____.

5. The periodic transferring of plant and equipment asset cost to expense is called _____.

6. The step-by-step procedure that begins with recording transactions and is repeated for each accounting period is the _____.

7. The ten-column form used to organize the data necessary for journalizing the adjustments and preparing the financial statements is the _____.

8. An accrual or deferral recorded at the end of the accounting period to bring the ledger up to date is a/an _____.

9. Expense items that are paid for prior to their use are called _____.

10. The expected worth of an asset at the end of its useful life is its _____.

Match the following words and terms on the left with the definitions on the right.

11. accounting cycle	a. the act of acquiring
12. acquisition	b. the number of years over which an asset is depreciated
13. adjusting entry	
14. contra asset	c. an account that subtracts from its related asset on the balance sheet
15. book value	
16. depreciation	d. the accounting procedure that is repeated for each accounting period
17. prepaid expenses	
18. salvage value	e. the form on which the data for adjustments and the financial statements are first accumulated
19. useful life	
20. worksheet	f. the transferring of plant and equipment cost to expense
	g. the value of an asset at the end of its useful life
	h. a journal entry made at the end of the accounting period to record accruals and deferrals and for which no transaction occurs
	i. the cost minus the accumulated depreciation of an asset
	j. expense items that are paid for before they are incurred

Exercises

Exercise 5.1
journalizing adjustment for Insurance Expense

On January 2, Phil's Automotive Engineering Company purchased a 12-month insurance policy for $540 cash.

a. Prepare the general journal entry required on January 2 to record the purchase of the policy.

b. Prepare the adjusting entry required on January 31 to record January's insurance expense.

Exercise 5.2
journalizing adjustment for Wages Expense

Every Friday, Acme Personnel pays its employees weekly salaries amounting to $25,000 ($5,000 per day, Monday through Friday).

a. Prepare the necessary entry on Wednesday, September 30, to record the wages expense for the last three days of September.
b. Prepare the general journal entry required on Friday, October 2, to record payment of the week's wages.

Exercise 5.3
journalizing adjustment for Unearned Revenue

On July 1, Andy's Delivery Service received a check for $1,500 from Pete's Laundry for delivery services to be performed in July, August, and September.

a. Record the journal entry required on July 1 to record the liability for the services and the receipt of the cash.
b. Prepare the required adjusting entry on July 31, assuming that Andy performs $400 of delivery services for Pete in July.

Exercise 5.4
journalizing adjustment for Supplies Used

The balance in the Supplies account for The Queen's Limos on September 1 was $235. Purchases of supplies for cash were recorded on September 5 for $110 and on September 19 for $185. The supplies inventory on September 30 as determined by a physical count was $215.

a. Prepare the two journal entries to record purchasing supplies on September 5 and 19.
b. Prepare the adjusting entry required on September 30 to record the supplies used during September.

Exercise 5.5
journalizing adjustment for Depreciation

Sandra Smythe, public accountant, purchased a computer costing $12,000 for her office on January 3. It has a useful life of four years and no salvage value. Sandra paid $5,000 cash down for the computer and signed a 24-month, non-interest-bearing note for the remainder.

a. Prepare the general journal entry necessary to record the acquisition of the asset.
b. Prepare the adjusting entry on January 31 to record the depreciation on the computer.
c. Assuming that Sandra's accounting period is one year instead of one month, prepare the adjusting entry required on December 31 to record the depreciation.

Exercise 5.6
journalizing adjustment for Revenue Earned

Mac's Repair Service performed $2,500 in services for T. A. Luong during the month of December for which no cash was received. On December 31, Mac sent a bill to Luong for $2,500 for the services performed; the bill stipulated that payment should be made within 30 days. Prepare the adjusting entry necessary on December 31 to record earning the revenue.

Exercise 5.7
calculating net income or loss and ruling worksheet

Following is a portion of a worksheet for Ron Lee, Educational Consultant, on August 31, 19XX. The worksheet has been completed except for calculating the net income or net loss for the month and the final ruling.

a. Calculate the net income or net loss, label it in the account titles column, and enter the amount in the appropriate income statement and balance sheet columns.
b. Total and rule the worksheet.

Exercise 5.8
calculating net income or loss and ruling worksheet

Following is a portion of a worksheet for Juanita Barbosa, Accountant, on November 30, 19XX. The worksheet has been completed except for calculating the net income or net loss for the month and the final ruling.

a. Calculate the net income or net loss, label it in the account titles column, and enter the amount in the appropriate income statement and balance sheet columns.
b. Total and rule the worksheet.

Worksheet for Exercise 5.7

RON LEE, EDUCATIONAL CONSULTANT
WORKSHEET
FOR MONTH ENDED AUGUST 31, 19XX

Acct. No.	Account Titles	Adjusted Trial Balance Debit	Adjusted Trial Balance Credit
101	Cash	1980 —	
110	Notes Receivable	500 —	
120	Accounts Receivable	970 —	
640	Wages Expense	1110 —	
650	Supplies Used	70 —	
660	Insurance Expense	40 —	
670	Advertising Expense	150 —	
	Totals	24620 —	24620 —

Worksheet for Exercise 5.8

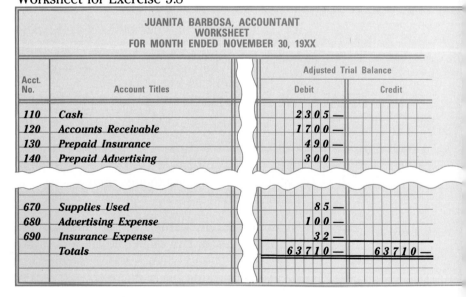

JUANITA BARBOSA, ACCOUNTANT
WORKSHEET
FOR MONTH ENDED NOVEMBER 30, 19XX

Acct. No.	Account Titles	Adjusted Trial Balance Debit	Adjusted Trial Balance Credit
110	Cash	2305 —	
120	Accounts Receivable	1700 —	
130	Prepaid Insurance	490 —	
140	Prepaid Advertising	300 —	
670	Supplies Used	85 —	
680	Advertising Expense	100 —	
690	Insurance Expense	32 —	
	Totals	63710 —	63710 —

| Income Statement | | Balance Sheet | |
Debit	Credit	Debit	Credit
		1980 —	
		500 —	
		970 —	
1110 —			
70 —			
40 —			
150 —			
4205 —	7811 —	39050 —	35444 —

| Income Statement | | Balance Sheet | |
Debit	Credit	Debit	Credit
		2305 —	
		1700 —	
		490 —	
		300 —	
85 —			
100 —			
32 —			
3810 —	3160 —	58640 —	59290 —

Exercise 5.9
identifying accounts

Identify the following accounts as asset (A), contra asset (CA), liability (L), owner's equity (OE), revenue (R), or expense (E). Indicate whether the account has a normal debit or credit balance, and tell on which financial statement, the balance sheet (BS) or income statement (IS), each account will appear.

	Account Classification	Normal Debit or Credit Balance	Which Financial Statement?
Example Accounts Receivable	A	debit	BS
a. Notes Payable			
b. Rent Expense			
c. Revenue from Consulting			
d. Office Equipment			
e. Supplies			
f. Supplies Used			
g. Accumulated Depreciation			
h. Prepaid Advertising			
i. Owner's Drawing			
j. Delivery Revenue			
k. Unearned Delivery Revenue			
l. Prepaid Rent			
m. Automobile			
n. Wages Payable			
o. Unearned Consulting Revenue			

Exercise 5.10
completing worksheet after adjustments are calculated

Following are the trial balance and adjustments columns of the worksheet for George Atkinson, consultant, for the month of September, 19XX. Recopy the information onto a ten-column worksheet and complete it.

Worksheet for Exercise 5.10

GEORGE ATKINSON, CONSULTANT
WORKSHEET
FOR MONTH ENDED SEPTEMBER 30, 19XX

Acct. No.	Account Titles	Trial Balance Debit	Trial Balance Credit	Adjustments Debit	Adjustments Credit
101	Cash	12000 —			
105	Notes Receivable	14000 —			
110	Accounts Receivable	8500 —		e. 1250 —	
115	Office Supplies	1500 —			a. 400 —
120	Prepaid Insurance	1290 —			b. 100 —
128	Office Equipment	22000 —			
128A	Accumulated Depr.: OE		5520 —		d. 460 —
201	Notes Payable		9800 —		
205	Accounts Payable		1750 —		
206	Payroll Taxes Payable		520 —		
210	Unearned Consulting Rev.		1500 —	f. 900 —	
301	George Atkinson, Capital		42260 —		
310	George Atkinson, Drawing	5000 —			
401	Revenue from Teaching		8500 —		e. 1250 —
405	Revenue from Consulting		1500 —		f. 900 —
601	Rent Expense	2200 —			
603	Utilities Expense	470 —			
620	Advertising Expense	500 —			
630	Wages Expense	3800 —		c. 350 —	
640	Interest Expense	90 —			
	Totals	71350 —	71350 —		
650	Office Supplies Used			a. 400 —	
615	Insurance Expense			b. 100 —	
220	Wages Payable				c. 350 —
660	Depreciation Expense			d. 460 —	
				3460 —	3460 —

Exercise 5.11

analyzing effect on revenue, expense, and net income when adjusting entries are not recorded

Following are several circumstances where the accountant failed to record adjusting entries. For each tell whether the failure to record the adjustment would cause an overstatement of expenses and by how much; an understatement of expenses and by how much; an overstatement of revenue and by how much; an understatement of revenue and by how much; an overstatement of net income and by how much; or an understatement of net income and by how much. The first one has been completed as an example.

	Overstatement of Expenses	Understatement of Expenses	Overstatement of Revenue	Understatement of Revenue	Overstatement of Net Income	Understatement of Net Income
Example Accountant did not record adjusting entry for depreciation of $1,000.		$1,000			$1,000	
a. Accountant did not record supplies used for the period for $500.						
b. Accountant transferred $1,000 from Prepaid Advertising to Advertising Expense when the amount transferred should have been $100.						
c. Accountant did not record accrued wages of $700.						
d. Accountant did not record revenue performed for which cash had not yet been received, but for which bills had been sent for $5,000.						
e. Accountant did not record depreciation of $850 on the equipment.						
f. Accountant did not transfer $150 from Prepaid Insurance to Insurance Expense.						
g. Accountant debited Accounts Receivable and credited Revenue for $650 at the end of the month when a check for $650 was received from a customer who was paying on account.						

Problems ══

Problem 5.1

completing worksheet after adjustments are calculated and journalizing adjusting entries

Following on page 172 are the trial balance and adjustments columns of the worksheet prepared on May 31, 19XX, for the Linowitz Trucking Company, owned by Paula Linowitz. The accounting period covers one month.

Instructions

1. *Copy the trial balance and adjustments columns onto a ten-column worksheet.*

2. *Extend the figures to the adjusted trial balance and add the debit and credit columns. If they are equal, place the correct totals on the worksheet and rule the adjusted trial balance. In adjustments e, the three amounts for Accumulated Depreciation are combined into one amount for Depreciation Expense. The two credits to Trucking Revenue (g and h) are written on one line in the adjustments credit column. When extending, add both credit amounts to Trucking Revenue.*

3. *Starting with Cash, extend the asset, liability, and owner's equity account balances to the balance sheet columns of the worksheet.*

4. *Starting with Trucking Revenue, extend the revenue and expense account balances to the income statement columns of the worksheet.*

5. *Total the income statement columns of the worksheet, determine the net income, and total the balance sheet columns.*

6. *Enter the net income beneath the debit column total of the income statement and beneath the credit column total of the balance sheet. Add the column totals to the net income. The balance sheet debit and credit totals should be the same, as should the income statement debit and credit totals. If they are not, look for the error.*

7. *When the worksheet is complete and in balance, draw the correct rulings across the income statement and balance sheet columns.*

8. *Journalize the adjusting entries on page 30 in the general journal.*

Worksheet for Problem 5.1

Acct. No.	Account Titles	Trial Balance Debit	Trial Balance Credit	Adjustments Debit	Adjustments Credit
	LINOWITZ TRUCKING COMPANY **WORKSHEET** **FOR MONTH ENDED MAY 31, 19XX**				
110	Cash	28000 —			
115	Notes Receivable	7600 —			
120	Accounts Receivable	4320 —		g. 4900 —	
125	Office Supplies	1490 —			a. 560 —
130	Trucking Supplies	7130 —			b. 1840 —
140	Prepaid Insurance	4700 —			c. 300 —
150	Prepaid Advertising	6900 —			d. 2300 —
160	Equipment	142000 —			
160A	Accumulated Depr.: Equip.		37760 —		e. 2360 —
170	Trucks	732000 —			
170A	Accumulated Depr.: Trucks		195200 —		e. 12200 —
180	Office Furniture	3970 —			
180A	Accumulated Depr.: OF		1120 —		e. 70 —
200	Notes Payable		416500 —		
210	Accounts Payable		6900 —		
220	Payroll Taxes Payable		800 —		
230	Unearned Revenue		4250 —	h. 2000 —	
300	Paula Linowitz, Capital		264101 —		
310	Paula Linowitz, Drawing	3250 —			
400	Trucking Revenue		37650 —		g. 4900 — h. 2000 —
610	Interest Expense	6247 —			
620	Rent Expense	1800 —			
630	Repairs Expense	2404 —			
640	Gas and Oil Expense	3170 —			
650	Utilities Expense	1200 —			
660	Wages Expense	8100 —		f. 950 —	
	Totals	964281 —	964281 —		
605	Office Supplies Used			a. 560 —	
615	Trucking Supplies Used			b. 1840 —	
625	Insurance Expense			c. 300 —	
635	Advertising Expense			d. 2300 —	
645	Depreciation Expense			e. 14630 —	
240	Wages Payable				f. 950 —
				27480 —	27480 —

Problem 5.2
*preparing worksheet
and journalizing
adjusting entries*

Following is the trial balance for Carol's Exercise Clinic on June 30, 19XX. The business is owned by Carol Goren, and the accounting period covers one month.

CAROL'S EXERCISE CLINIC
TRIAL BALANCE
JUNE 30, 19XX

Acct. No.	Account Titles	Debit	Credit
101	Cash	$ 4,250	
105	Notes Receivable	1,690	
110	Accounts Receivable	1,535	
120	Supplies	615	
130	Prepaid Insurance	500	
140	Van	23,600	
140A	Accumulated Depreciation: Van		$10,200
150	Equipment	48,000	
150A	Accumulated Depreciation: Equipment		2,000
201	Notes Payable		10,000
205	Accounts Payable		400
210	Unearned Revenue		1,000
220	Mortgage Payable		43,000
305	Carol Goren, Capital		14,590
310	Carol Goren, Drawing	2,600	
401	Revenue from Teaching		750
410	Revenue from Exercise Clinic		6,200
602	Utilities Expense	195	
604	Advertising Expense	250	
610	Interest Expense	760	
620	Wages Expense	2,800	
630	Payroll Tax Expense	170	
635	Gas and Oil Expense	130	
650	Repairs Expense	225	
660	Insurance Expense	820	
	Totals	$88,140	$88,140

Instructions

1. *Copy the trial balance onto a ten-column worksheet.*

2. *Calculate the adjustments from the following data and enter them in the adjustments columns of the worksheet. Label the adjustments a, b, c, and so on. Additional account titles and numbers that will be required in this problem are: Supplies Used, 670; Depreciation Expense, 685; and Wages Payable, 230.*

a. The beginning inventory of supplies was $475. A purchase
    of supplies was made on June 21 for $140, and the ending
    inventory of supplies was $270.

b. The insurance policy was purchased on April 1 of this year
    for $600. It prepaid the insurance for one year.

c. The van was purchased on January 2 of last year. It has a
    useful life of five years and a salvage value of $2,000. The
    equipment was purchased on February 5 of this year. It is
    expected to last eight years and will have no salvage
    value.

d. June 30 falls on a Thursday. Wages of $100 a day are paid
    on each Friday. Record the wages expense for Monday
    through Thursday, June 27 through 30.

e. On June 1, Carol received a check for $1,000 from a local
    exercise firm to give ten aerobics lessons to its new instruc-
    tors. Carol taught five of the lessons in June.

f. On June 30, services had been performed in the clinic total-
    ing $1,200 for which no payment had been received.

3. Complete the worksheet.

4. Journalize the adjusting entries on page 42 of the general jour-
    nal.

Problem 5.3

*preparing worksheet
and statement of
owner's equity and
journalizing adjusting
entries*

Following is the trial balance for Dancing Dynamics on March 31,
19XX. The business is owned by Jon Phillips, and the accounting
period covers three months.

DANCING DYNAMICS
TRIAL BALANCE
MARCH 31, 19XX

Acct. No.	Account Titles	Debit	Credit
101	Cash	$ 1,950	
105	Accounts Receivable	2,700	
110	Supplies	560	
115	Prepaid Insurance	400	
120	Office Equipment	11,500	
120A	Accumulated Depreciation: Office Equip.		
145	Van	18,000	
145A	Accumulated Depreciation: Van		
201	Notes Payable		$15,500
210	Accounts Payable		3,520

Continued.

Acct. No.	Account Titles	Debit	Credit
215	Payroll Taxes Payable		145
220	Interest Payable		335
230	Unearned Lecturing Revenue		1,500
301	Jon Phillips, Capital		16,370
310	Jon Phillips, Drawing	4,000	
401	Revenue from Dancing		10,520
410	Revenue from Lecturing		840
601	Rent Expense	2,400	
610	Utilities Expense	600	
615	Advertising Expense	450	
620	Repairs Expense	420	
630	Gas and Oil Expense	550	
640	Interest Expense	1,000	
650	Wages Expense	4,200	
	Totals	$48,730	$48,730

Instructions

1. Copy the trial balance onto a ten-column worksheet.

2. Calculate the adjustments for a three-month period from the following data and enter them onto the adjustments columns of the worksheet. Label the adjustments a, b, c, and so on. Additional account titles and numbers required in this problem are: Supplies Used, 660; Insurance Expense, 670; Depreciation Expense, 680; and Wages Payable, 240.

    a. The beginning inventory of supplies on January 1 was $400. One purchase of supplies was made on February 27 for $160. The ending inventory of supplies on March 31, determined by a physical count, was $355.

    b. The insurance policy was purchased on January 2 of this year. Its cost was $400, and it prepaid the insurance for six months.

    c. Wages for Dancing Dynamics are $85 a day and are paid every Friday. March 31 falls on a Tuesday.

    d. The office equipment was purchased on January 2 of this year. It has an expected useful life of four years and a salvage value of $1,500. The van was purchased on January 4 of this year and has an expected useful life of four years and a salvage value of $2,000.

    e. Maybelle Johnson paid Jon $1,500 for five lectures he would be delivering during February, March, and April. Jon has delivered three of the lectures by the end of March.

f. *On March 31, $2,100 in dancing revenue services have been performed for which no cash has been received and no bills have been sent.*

3. *Complete the worksheet.*

4. *Prepare a statement of owner's equity for the three-month period January 1 through March 31.*

5. *Journalize the adjusting entries on general journal page 66.*

Problem 5.4

preparing worksheet and statement of owner's equity and journalizing adjusting entries

The trial balance columns of the worksheet for Marie's Bookkeeping Service for the third quarter of 19XX follow.

MARIE'S BOOKKEEPING SERVICE
TRIAL BALANCE
SEPTEMBER 30, 19XX

Acct. No.	Account Titles	Debit	Credit
101	Cash	$ 4,120	
110	Accounts Receivable	1,780	
115	Office Supplies	920	
120	Prepaid Insurance	300	
125	Prepaid Advertising	600	
130	Office Equipment	18,050	
130A	Accumulated Depreciation: Office Equip.		$ 3,000
150	Automobile	14,800	
150A	Accumulated Depreciation: Auto.		4,500
201	Notes Payable		12,000
210	Accounts Payable		1,100
215	Payroll Taxes Payable		144
230	Unearned Consulting Revenue		900
301	Marie Himler, Capital		15,066
310	Marie Himler, Drawing	3,600	
401	Revenue from Bookkeeping		8,950
410	Revenue from Consulting		4,750
601	Rent Expense	1,800	
610	Repairs Expense	475	
620	Utilities Expense	450	
630	Advertising Expense	600	
640	Insurance Expense	305	
650	Gas and Oil Expense	210	
660	Wages Expense	2,400	
	Totals	$50,410	$50,410

Instructions   1. *Copy the trial balance onto a ten-column worksheet.*

2. *Record the adjustments from the following data. Label the adjustments a, b, c, and so on. The accounting period covers three months. Additional account titles and numbers required in the problem are: Supplies Used, 670; Depreciation Expense, 680; and Wages Payable, 250.*

   a. *The inventory of office supplies on September 30 is $520.*

   b. *The advertising was prepaid on July 1 for a six-month period. (Remember that the adjustment period is three months.)*

   c. *The $300 figure in Prepaid Insurance represents a six-month policy purchased on July 1.*

   d. *The auto was purchased on January 1 of the previous year. It has a useful life of four years and a salvage value of $2,800. The office equipment was purchased on July 1 of the previous year. It has a useful life of five years and a salvage value of $3,050.*

   e. *$700 of the unearned consulting revenue has been earned this period.*

   f. *Bookkeeping services for $2,200 have been performed but no cash has been received and no bills have been sent to customers.*

   g. *Wages totaling $75 per day are paid every Friday. September 30 falls on a Thursday.*

3. *Complete the worksheet for the three-month period.*

4. *Prepare a statement of owner's equity for the third quarter.*

5. *Journalize the adjusting entries on general journal page 39.*

Problem 5.5
locating errors on worksheet

Following is the worksheet for Lori's Landscape Service for the month of April, 19XX. The trial balance and adjustments columns are without error, but the bookkeeper made several mistakes when extending the figures to the adjusted trial balance. The bookkeeper did not total the adjusted trial balance, but continued on, again making errors when extending figures to the income statement and balance sheet columns. As a result, when the net income was added to the credit column of the balance sheet, it did not balance.

Worksheet for Problem 5.5

LORI'S LANDSCAPE SERVICE
WORKSHEET
FOR MONTH ENDED APRIL 30, 19XX

Acct. No.	Account Titles	Trial Balance Debit	Trial Balance Credit	Adjustments Debit		Adjustments Credit	
101	Cash	3050 —					
105	Accounts Receivable	1605 —		g.	500 —		
115	Office Supplies	495 —				b.	205 —
120	Garden Supplies	1840 —				a.	720 —
130	Prepaid Insurance	900 —				c.	100 —
140	Prepaid Advertising	800 —				d.	200 —
150	Office Equipment	8500 —					
150A	Accumulated Depr.: OE		2300 —			e.	150 —
160	Garden Equipment	10000 —					
160A	Accumulated Depr.: GE		4900 —			e.	230 —
170	Truck	25500 —					
170A	Accumulated Depr.: Truck		10600 —			e.	400 —
201	Notes Payable		15200 —				
210	Accounts Payable		1400 —				
215	Payroll Taxes Payable		160 —				
220	Unearned Landscape Rev.		1000 —	h.	600 —		
301	Lori Salzman, Capital		17970 —				
310	Lori Salzman, Drawing	2000 —					
401	Landscape Revenue		4750 —			g. / h.	500 — / 600 —
601	Truck Expense	760 —					
610	Repairs Expense	290 —					
620	Rent Expense	550 —					
630	Wages Expense	1600 —		f.	340 —		
640	Utilities Expense	390 —					
	Totals	58280 —	58280 —				
650	Garden Supplies Used			a.	720 —		
660	Office Supplies Used			b.	205 —		
670	Insurance Expense			c.	100 —		
680	Advertising Expense			d.	200 —		
690	Depreciation Expense			e.	780 —		
230	Wages Payable			f.			340 —
					3445 —		3445 —

	Adjusted Trial Balance		Income Statement		Balance Sheet	
	Debit	Credit	Debit	Credit	Debit	Credit
	3050 —				3050 —	
	1105 —				1105 —	
	290 —				290 —	
	1130 —				1310 —	
	800 —				800 —	
	1000 —				1000 —	
	8500 —				8500 —	
		2450 —				2450 —
	10000 —				10000 —	
		5220 —				5220 —
	25500 —				25500 —	
		1100 —				1100 —
		15200 —				15200 —
		1400 —				1400 —
		160 —				160 —
		1600 —				1000 —
		19790 —				19970 —
	2000 —					
		4750 —		4750 —		
	670 —		670 —			
	290 —		290 —			
	550 —		550 —			
	1600 —		1600 —			
	390 —		390 —			
	720 —		720 —			
	250 —		250 —			
	100 —		100 —			
	200 —		200 —			
	780 —		870 —			
		340 —	340 —			

1. *Look over the worksheet carefully. Check to make sure that the adjusted trial balance is correct. Look for transpositions as well as miscalculations and omissions. Write in all your corrections.*

2. *Re-add the adjusted trial balance. Do not continue until it is in balance.*

3. *Check extensions to the balance sheet and income statement columns. Carry forward all corrections made on the adjusted trial balance and check for other errors in these columns.*

4. *Re-add the balance sheet and income statement columns, write in correct figures, and rule the worksheet.*

Problem 5.6

analyzing effect of adjusting entries on net income and revising net income figure

Before preparing adjusting entries, Jon Smythe, Flight Trainer, calculated his net income for November to be $5,700. His accountant, however, calculated the following necessary adjustments to the accounts.

a. depreciation on the airplane, $3,500
b. services performed for which payment had not been received and for which no bills had yet been sent, $1,400
c. accrued wages expense, $425
d. supplies used in November, $190
e. insurance expense, $1,500
f. $500 of the balance of $1,300 in unearned revenue had been earned in November

1. *Consider the effect each adjusting entry will have on net income. Determine whether the adjustment will cause net income to be reduced (and by how much) or whether the adjustment will cause net income to increase (and by how much). The first transaction has been recorded as an example.*

Adjustment	Reduces Net Income by This Amount	Increases Net Income by This Amount
a	$3,500	

2. *Considering the effect the adjusting entries will have, determine the correct amount of net income or loss for the month.*

CHAPTER 6

Correcting and Closing Entries

LEARNING OBJECTIVES

When you have completed this chapter, you should

1. have a better understanding of accounting terminology.

2. be able to analyze an incorrect journal entry and determine how to correct it.

3. be able to journalize and post the closing entries.

4. be able to prepare financial statements directly from the worksheet.

5. be able to prepare a post-closing trial balance.

counteract
to reverse the effects
of a previous act

closing entries
journal entries that,
when posted, bring
the account balances
of revenue and ex-
pense accounts and
the drawing account
to zero and update
the Capital account

If an error is made when journalizing and that incorrect journal entry is posted, the bookkeeper must prepare a new journal entry
that will **counteract** the effects of the first entry. Once the correcting entry is posted, the general ledger will be correct.

The last chapter showed how bookkeepers have developed the
worksheet to help them sort out and organize the information required for the adjusting entries and financial statements. The worksheet is also used to help in one of the last steps in the accounting
cycle—journalizing the closing entries. The **closing entries** bring
all revenue and expense account balances and the owner's drawing account balance to zero and update the Capital account.

CORRECTING ENTRIES

When an error is made in a journal entry and it is discovered before it is posted, it may be corrected by drawing a line through the
incorrect account title(s) and amount(s) and writing the correct
title(s) and amount(s) in small letters and figures immediately
above the incorrect entry. It is not acceptable in actual practice to
erase in the journal or ledger.

		GENERAL JOURNAL			Page *25*
Date		Description	Post. Ref.	Debit	Credit
19XX Jan. 11		Cash		1 6 0 —	
		Receivable Accounts ~~Payable~~			1 6 0 —
		Received Cash on Account			

Often, however, the error is not discovered right away and the
incorrect amounts are posted. When this happens, the easiest way
to correct the entry is to make a new entry that will counteract the
effects of the first entry. For example, assume that on January 4 a
firm pays $250 cash for office supplies. The bookkeeper debits
Medical Supplies and credits Cash for $250. The entry is posted to
the ledger. Before the accounting cycle has been completed, the
wrong entry is discovered and corrected by debiting Office Supplies and crediting Medical Supplies for $250 in the general journal.

Once this entry has been posted, the general ledger will be correct. The entry looks like this.

GENERAL JOURNAL				Page 26	
Date	Description	Post. Ref.	Debit	Credit	
19XX	*Correcting Entry*				
Jan. 28	*Office Supplies*		2 5 0 —		
	Medical Supplies			2 5 0 —	
	To Correct Entry of January 4				

Debiting Office Supplies for $250 puts the correct amount in that account for the first time, and crediting Medical Supplies for $250 removes the incorrect amount from that account. Another example might be when a customer sends in a check for $500 on February 10 to apply on his or her account, and the bookkeeper debits Accounts Receivable and credits Cash for $500 and posts the figures. This error, when discovered on February 28, will be corrected in the following manner.

GENERAL JOURNAL				Page 34	
Date	Description	Post. Ref.	Debit	Credit	
19XX	*Correcting Entry*				
Feb. 28	*Cash*		1 0 0 0 —		
	Accounts Receivable			1 0 0 0 —	
	To Correct Entry of February 10				

By debiting Cash for $1,000, the effects of the incorrect entry will have been counteracted: a $500 debit is required to reverse the effects of the incorrect $500 credit to Cash and another $500 debit is required for the correct entry. The same logic holds true for the error in Accounts Receivable.

Incorrect amounts, as well as incorrect account titles, may be recorded in error. For example, on March 3, $1,100 is spent on a

erroneous
wrong or inaccurate

new typewriter for the office. The bookkeeper **erroneously** records a debit to Office Equipment of $1,000 and a credit to Cash of $1,000 and posts the incorrect amounts. When the error is discovered at the end of the month, it will be handled this way.

GENERAL JOURNAL				Page *43*
Date	Description	Post. Ref.	Debit	Credit
19XX	*Correcting Entry*			
Mar. *31*	*Office Equipment*		*1 0 0* —	
	Cash			*1 0 0* —
	To Correct Entry of March 3			

Correcting entries may occur at any time, and they vary a great deal. Both what was done and what should have been done must be considered before journalizing. Each incorrect entry must be carefully analyzed to determine its effects on the accounts involved; using T-accounts may be helpful in the analysis. In each case, the words *Correcting Entry* must be centered in the description column of the general journal before making the actual entry.

CLOSING ENTRIES

Closing an account means bringing it to a zero balance, and the journal entries that accomplish this are called closing entries. All the revenue and expense accounts are closed and the net income or net loss is transferred to the owner's capital account by closing entries; for this reason, revenue and expense accounts are called temporary proprietorship accounts or **nominal accounts.**

nominal accounts
the income statement accounts

By bringing the revenue and expense account balances to zero at the end of each accounting period, a new net income or loss figure can more easily be calculated for the next accounting period. The revenue and expense figures of one accounting period should not be running into those of the next.

Closing entries also update the Capital account by crediting it for the amount of the net income and debiting it for the amount of the drawing. This procedure is repeated in the statement of owner's equity. If the accounting period shows a net loss, the Owner's Capital account will be debited for that amount in the closing process.

The illustrations in this chapter show the closing process at month's end, but many businesses close their books quarterly or at the end of the **fiscal year.** A fiscal year is any 12-month period chosen by a business owner during which the yearly net income or loss is determined and federal and state income taxes are calculated. A **calendar year** is the period beginning January 1 and ending December 31. A fiscal year and a calendar year may be the same.

fiscal year
a 12-month period used for determining net income or loss by a business

calendar year
January 1 through December 31

The closing process involves recording the entries in the general journal and posting them to the general ledger. The four closing entries (1) close all revenue accounts; (2) close all expense accounts; (3) transfer the net income or net loss to the owner's capital account; and (4) transfer the balance of the drawing account to the owner's capital account.

THE INCOME SUMMARY ACCOUNT

The Income Summary account is a special account used only in the closing process. Though it is given an account number in the owner's equity category, this account does not appear on the trial balance or on the balance sheet. It is both opened and closed in the closing process and is not used again until the end of the next accounting period.

THE WORKSHEET AND THE CLOSING PROCESS

Because the worksheet accumulates all the revenue and expense accounts and the net income in one place, it may be used when journalizing the closing entries. The bookkeeper uses the debit and credit columns of the income statement to determine the account titles and amounts to be used in the closing process. As the closing entries are journalized, check marks ($\sqrt{}$) are placed by the amounts in the debit or credit columns. A check mark by each amount in the income statement columns of the worksheet ensures that no accounts have been omitted in the closing process.

Closing the Revenue Accounts

The bookkeeper will close all revenue accounts in the first closing entry. Because revenue accounts have credit balances, debits are required for closing them. The corresponding credit will be to the Income Summary account. Consult the income statement columns

MARY TYUS, M.D.
WORKSHEET
FOR MONTH ENDING JANUARY 31, 19XX

Acct. No.	Account Titles	Adjusted Trial Balance Debit	Adjusted Trial Balance Credit	Income Statement Debit	Income Statement Credit
101	Cash	12500 —			
105	Notes Receivable	4700 —			
110	Accounts Receivable	3100 —			
120	Prepaid Insurance	330 —			
130	Supplies	260 —			
150	Office Equipment	10600 —			
150A	Accumulated Depreciation: OE		200 —		
201	Notes Payable		7600 —		
210	Accounts Payable		2950 —		
215	Payroll Taxes Payable		210 —		
220	Unearned Consulting Revenue		400 —		
301	Mary Tyus, Capital		21692 —		
310	Mary Tyus, Drawing	4800 —			
401	Medical Revenue		13600 —		13600 —
405	Consulting Revenue		1500 —		1500 —
601	Rent Expense	3900 —		3900 —	
610	Interest Expense	76 —		76 —	
615	Utilities Expense	1420 —		1420 —	
620	Repairs Expense	2416 —		2416 —	
630	Uniforms Expense	500 —		500 —	
640	Wages Expense	3300 —		3300 —	
650	Payroll Tax Expense	230 —		230 —	
	Totals				
605	Supplies Used	90 —		90 —	
660	Insurance Expense	30 —		30 —	
670	Depreciation Expense	200 —		200 —	
230	Wages Payable		300 —		
		48452 —	48452 —	12162 —	15100 —
	Net Income			2938 —	
				15100 —	15100 —

of the worksheet to determine the number of revenue accounts, their account titles, and their balances. A portion of the worksheet and the required entry to close the revenue accounts for Mary Tyus, M.D., appear on page 188.

	GENERAL JOURNAL				Page 15
Date	Description	Post. Ref.	Debit		Credit
19XX	**Closing Entries**				
Jan. 31	**Medical Revenue**		13600 —		
	Consulting Revenue		1500 —		
	Income Summary				15100 —
	To Close Revenue Accounts				

As the first closing entry is journalized, check marks (√) are placed by the revenue amounts on the worksheet to indicate that those accounts have been closed. The following T-accounts for Medical Revenue, Consulting Revenue, and Income Summary look like this after the first closing entry is posted.

Medical Revenue   401

1/31	Closing	13,600	1/31	Balance	11,600
			1/31	Adjusting	2,000

Income Summary   315

		1/31	Closing	15,100

Consulting Revenue   405

1/31	Closing	1,500	1/31	Balance	900
			1/31	Adjusting	600

Total revenue on credit side of Income Summary

The debit and credit sides of the revenue accounts are now equal, and the accounts have a zero balance. The Income Summary account contains on its credit side a total of all the revenue for the period.

Closing the Expense Accounts

The account titles and amounts necessary for preparing the second closing entry may be taken directly from the income statement debit column of the worksheet. The journal entry to close the expense accounts is as follows.

Date	Description	Post. Ref.	Debit	Credit
	GENERAL JOURNAL Page **15**			
19XX	*Closing Entries*			
Jan. *31*	*Income Summary*		12162 —	
	Rent Expense			3900 —
	Interest Expense			76 —
	Utilities Expense			1420 —
	Repairs Expense			2416 —
	Uniforms Expense			500 —
	Wages Expense			3300 —
	Payroll Tax Expense			230 —
	Supplies Used			90 —
	Insurance Expense			30 —
	Depreciation Expense			200 —
	To Close Expense Accounts			

The adjusted trial balance and the income statement columns of the worksheet for Mary Tyus, M.D., follow. Look at it carefully; pay special attention to the check marks that have been entered on the worksheet opposite the revenue and expense amounts. The T-accounts also follow to show how they appear after the closing entries have been posted.

MARY TYUS, M.D.
WORKSHEET
FOR MONTH ENDING JANUARY 31, 19XX

Acct. No.	Account Titles	Adjusted Trial Balance Debit	Adjusted Trial Balance Credit	Income Statement Debit	Income Statement Credit
101	Cash	12500 —			
105	Notes Receivable	4700 —			
110	Accounts Receivable	3100 —			
120	Prepaid Insurance	330 —			
130	Supplies	260 —			
150	Office Equipment	10600 —			
150A	Accumulated				
	Depreciation: OE		200 —		
201	Notes Payable		7600 —		
210	Accounts Payable		2950 —		
215	Payroll Taxes Payable		210 —		
220	Unearned Consulting				
	Revenue		400 —		
301	Mary Tyus, Capital		21692 —		
310	Mary Tyus, Drawing	4800 —			
401	Medical Revenue		13600 —		13600 ✓
405	Consulting Revenue		1500 —		1500 ✓
601	Rent Expense	3900 —		3900 ✓	
610	Interest Expense	76 —		76 ✓	
615	Utilities Expense	1420 —		1420 ✓	
620	Repairs Expense	2416 —		2416 ✓	
630	Uniforms Expense	500 —		500 ✓	
640	Wages Expense	3300 —		3300 ✓	
650	Payroll Tax Expense	230 —		230 ✓	
	Totals				
605	Supplies Used	90 —		90 ✓	
660	Insurance Expense	30 —		30 ✓	
670	Depreciation Expense	200 —		200 ✓	
230	Wages Payable		300 —		
		48452 —	48452 —	12162 —	15100 —
	Net Income			2938 —	
				15100 —	15100 —

Income Summary 315

1/31 Closing	12,162	1/31 Closing	15,100
Total expenses on debit side		*Total revenue on credit side*	

Rent Expense 601

1/31 Balance	3,900	1/31 Closing	3,900

Wages Expense 640

1/31 Balance	3,000	1/31 Closing	3,300
1/31 Adjusting	300		

Interest Expense 610

1/31 Balance	76	1/31 Closing	76

Payroll Tax Expense 650

1/31 Balance	230	1/31 Closing	230

Utilities Expense 615

1/31 Balance	1,420	1/31 Closing	1,420

Supplies Used 605

1/31 Adjusting	90	1/31 Closing	90

Repairs Expense 620

1/31 Balance	2,416	1/31 Closing	2,416

Insurance Expense 660

1/31 Adjusting	30	1/31 Closing	30

Uniforms Expense 630

1/31 Balance	500	1/31 Closing	500

Depreciation Expense 670

1/31 Adjusting	200	1/31 Closing	200

After the second closing entry has been posted, the Income Summary account has a debit balance of $2,938, the net income for the period. The balance is logical, because the total revenue appears on the credit side of the Income Summary account and total expenses appear on the debit side. After the first two closing entries have been posted, the balance in the Income Summary account will always represent the net income or net loss for the period.

Transferring the Net Income (or Loss) to Owner's Capital

The third closing entry transfers the net income or net loss to the owner's capital account. A net income must be added to capital, which requires a credit to the Capital account; a net loss, on the other hand, requires a debit to capital to reduce the Capital account by the amount of the loss. This third closing entry begins the process of updating the Capital account in the general ledger by adding to it the net income or subtracting from it the net loss.

The actual dollar amount of the net income or loss is obtained from the income statement columns of the worksheet, where it is first calculated. The third closing entry transferring the net income to capital for Mary Tyus, M.D., follows.

GENERAL JOURNAL					Page 15
Date	Description	Post. Ref.	Debit		Credit
19XX	**Closing Entries**				
Jan. 31	*Income Summary*		2938 —		
	Mary Tyus, Capital				2938 —
	To Transfer Net Income to Capital				

After this third closing entry has been posted, the Income Summary account is closed and the Capital account is increased by the amount of the net income for the period, $2,938.

Income Summary   315

	1/31	Closing	12,162	1/31 Closing	15,100
	1/31	Closing	2,938		
All expenses					
and net income			15,100	15,100	All revenue

Mary Tyus, Capital   301

1/1	Balance	21,692	
1/31	Closing	2,938	(Net income)

Transferring Drawing to Capital

The owner's drawing account is the only balance sheet account that is closed. Drawing is subtracted from capital in the statement of owner's equity and in the ledger as one of the steps to determine the ending capital figure. The last closing entry closes drawing and transfers its balance to the Capital account.

GENERAL JOURNAL					Page 15
Date	Description	Post. Ref.	Debit		Credit
19XX	**Closing Entries**				
Jan. 31	**Mary Tyus, Capital**		4 8 0 0 —		
	Mary Tyus, Drawing				4 8 0 0 —
	To Transfer Balance of Drawing to Capital				

A check mark by the $4,800 Drawing account figure on the worksheet completes the journalizing of the closing entries. The Drawing account and Capital account look like this after the entry has been posted.

Mary Tyus, Drawing   **310**

1/31	Balance	4,800	1/31	Closing	4,800

Mary Tyus, Capital   **301**

(Drawing subtracted)	1/31	Closing	4,800	1/1	Balance	21,692	
				1/31	Closing	2,938	(Net income
					⟨19,830⟩		added)

The ending balance of the Capital account is $19,830. The financial statements may be prepared at any time after the worksheet has been completed. They will be accurate and up to date if their source of information is the worksheet, even though the adjusting and closing entries have not yet been journalized and posted. Following are the income statement, statement of owner's equity, and balance sheet for Mary Tyus, M.D. Each has been prepared from information presented in the income statement and balance sheet columns of the worksheet in Chapter 5.

MARY TYUS, M.D.
INCOME STATEMENT
FOR MONTH ENDED JANUARY 31, 19XX

Revenue		
Medical Revenue	$13 600 —	
Consulting Revenue	1 500 —	
Total Revenue		$15 100 —
Expenses		
Rent Expense	$ 3 900 —	
Interest Expense	76 —	
Utilities Expense	1 420 —	
Repairs Expense	2 416 —	
Uniforms Expense	500 —	
Wages Expense	3 300 —	
Payroll Tax Expense	230 —	
Supplies Used	90 —	
Insurance Expense	30 —	
Depreciation Expense	200 —	
Total Expenses		12 162 —
Net Income		$ 2 938 —

MARY TYUS, M.D.
STATEMENT OF OWNER'S EQUITY
FOR MONTH ENDED JANUARY 31, 19XX

Mary Tyus, Capital, January 1, 19XX	$21 692 —	
Add: Net Income for January	2 938 —	
Subtotal	24 630 —	
Deduct: Mary Tyus, Drawing	4 800 —	
Mary Tyus, Capital, January 31, 19XX		$19 830 —

MARY TYUS, M.D. BALANCE SHEET JANUARY 31, 19XX																			
Assets																			
Cash					$	1	2	5	0	0	—								
Notes Receivable							4	7	0	0	—								
Accounts Receivable							3	1	0	0	—								
Prepaid Insurance								3	3	0	—								
Supplies								2	6	0	—								
Office Equipment	$10,600.—																		
Less: Accumulated Depreciation	200.—					1	0	4	0	0	—								
Total Assets												$	3	1	2	9	0	—	
Liabilities																			
Notes Payable					$		7	6	0	0	—								
Accounts Payable							2	9	5	0	—								
Payroll Taxes Payable								2	1	0	—								
Unearned Consulting Revenue								4	0	0	—								
Wages Payable								3	0	0	—								
Total Liabilities												$	1	1	4	6	0	—	
Owner's Equity																			
Mary Tyus, Capital, January 31, 19XX													1	9	8	3	0	—	
Total Liabilities and Owner's Equity												$	3	1	2	9	0	—	

THE JOURNAL AND LEDGER ILLUSTRATED

The closing entries are recorded in the general journal immediately following the adjusting entries. Adjusting entries are always posted before closing entries. Either the word *Adjusting* or *Closing* is entered in the explanation column of the ledger account. The closing entries and the general ledger accounts for Mary Tyus, M.D., follow. Those accounts that have not been affected by the adjusting or closing entries are shown with only their January 31 balances.

GENERAL JOURNAL				Page *14*

Date		Description	Post. Ref.	Debit	Credit
19XX		***Adjusting Entries***			
Jan.	*31*	**Supplies Used**	*605*	90 —	
		Supplies	*130*		90 —
		To Record Supplies Used for Month			

Date		Description	Post. Ref.	Debit	Credit
		Closing Entries			
	31	**Medical Revenue**	*401*	13600 —	
		Consulting Revenue	*405*	1500 —	
		Income Summary	*315*		15100 —
		To Close Revenue Accounts			
	31	**Income Summary**	*315*	12162 —	
		Rent Expense	*601*		3900 —
		Interest Expense	*610*		76 —
		Utilities Expense	*615*		1420 —
		Repairs Expense	*620*		2416 —
		Uniforms Expense	*630*		500 —
		Wages Expense	*040*		3300 —
		Payroll Tax Expense	*650*		230 —
		Supplies Used	*605*		90 —
		Insurance Expense	*660*		30 —
		Depreciation Expense	*670*		200 —
		To Close Expense Accounts			
	31	**Income Summary**	*315*	2938 —	
		Mary Tyus, Capital	*301*		2938 —
		To Transfer Net Income to Capital			
	31	**Mary Tyus, Capital**	*301*	4800 —	
		Mary Tyus, Drawing	*310*		4800 —
		To Transfer Balance of Drawing to Capital			

CASH   Acct. No. *101*

Date		Explanation	PR	Debit	Credit	Balance
19XX						
Jan.	*31*	**Balance**	✔			12500 —

NOTES RECEIVABLE   Acct. No. *105*

Date		Explanation	PR	Debit	Credit	Balance
Jan.^{19XX}	31	Balance	✔			4 7 0 0 —

ACCOUNTS RECEIVABLE   Acct. No. *110*

Date		Explanation	PR	Debit	Credit	Balance
Jan.^{19XX}	31	Balance	✔			1 1 0 0 —
	31	Adjusting	GJ14	2 0 0 0 —		3 1 0 0 —

PREPAID INSURANCE   Acct. No. *120*

Date		Explanation	PR	Debit	Credit	Balance
Jan.^{19XX}	2		GJ5	3 6 0 —		3 6 0 —
	31	Adjusting	GJ14		3 0 —	3 3 0 —

SUPPLIES   Acct. No. *130*

Date		Explanation	PR	Debit	Credit	Balance
Jan.^{19XX}	1	Balance	✔	2 5 5 —		2 5 5 —
	14		GJ5	6 0 —		3 1 5 —
	26		GJ8	3 5 —		3 5 0 —
	31	Adjusting	GJ14		9 0 —	2 6 0 —

OFFICE EQUIPMENT   Acct. No. *150*

Date		Explanation	PR	Debit	Credit	Balance
Jan.^{19XX}	2		GJ5	1 0 6 0 0 —		1 0 6 0 0 —

ACCUMULATED DEPRECIATION: OFFICE EQUIPMENT   Acct. No. **150A**

Date		Explanation	PR	Debit	Credit	Balance
Jan.^19XX	31	Adjusting	GJ14		200 —	200 —

NOTES PAYABLE   Acct. No. **201**

Date		Explanation	PR	Debit	Credit	Balance
Jan.^19XX	31	Balance	✔			7600 —

ACCOUNTS PAYABLE   Acct. No. **210**

Date		Explanation	PR	Debit	Credit	Balance
Jan.^19XX	31	Balance	✔			2950 —

PAYROLL TAXES PAYABLE   Acct. No. **215**

Date		Explanation	PR	Debit	Credit	Balance
Jan.^19XX	31	Balance	✔			210 —

UNEARNED CONSULTING REVENUE   Acct. No. **220**

Date		Explanation	PR	Debit	Credit	Balance
Jan.^19XX	3		GJ5		1000 —	1000 —
	31	Adjusting	GJ14	600 —		400 —

WAGES PAYABLE   Acct. No. **230**

Date		Explanation	PR	Debit	Credit	Balance
Jan.^19XX	31	Adjusting	GJ14		300 —	300 —

MARY TYUS, CAPITAL   Acct. No. *301*

Date		Explanation	PR	Debit	Credit	Balance
Jan. ^{19XX}	*31*	Balance	✔			21692 —
	31	Closing	GJ15		2938 —	24630 —
	31	Closing	GJ15	4800 —		19830 —

MARY TYUS, DRAWING   Acct. No. *310*

Date		Explanation	PR	Debit	Credit	Balance
Jan. ^{19XX}	*31*	Balance	✔			4800 —
	31	Closing	GJ15		4800 —	0

INCOME SUMMARY   Acct. No. *315*

Date		Explanation	PR	Debit	Credit	Balance
Jan. ^{19XX}	*31*	Closing	GJ15		15100 —	15100 —
	31	Closing	GJ15	12162 —		2938 —
	31	Closing	GJ15	2938 —		0

MEDICAL REVENUE   Acct. No. *401*

Date		Explanation	PR	Debit	Credit	Balance
Jan. ^{19XX}	*31*	Balance	✔			11600 —
	31	Adjusting	GJ14		2000 —	13600 —
	31	Closing	GJ15	13600 —		0

CONSULTING REVENUE   Acct. No. *405*

Date		Explanation	PR	Debit	Credit	Balance
Jan. ^{19XX}	*31*	Balance	✔			900 —
	31	Adjusting	GJ14		600 —	1500 —
	31	Closing	GJ15	1500 —		0

RENT EXPENSE Acct. No. *601*

Date		Explanation	PR	Debit	Credit	Balance
Jan.^{19XX}	*31*	*Balance*	✔			3 9 0 0 —
	31	*Closing*	*GJ15*		3 9 0 0 —	0

SUPPLIES USED Acct. No. *605*

Date		Explanation	PR	Debit	Credit	Balance
Jan.^{19XX}	*31*	*Adjusting*	*GJ14*	9 0 —		9 0 —
	31	*Closing*	*GJ15*		9 0 —	0

INTEREST EXPENSE Acct. No. *610*

Date		Explanation	PR	Debit	Credit	Balance
Jan.^{19XX}	*31*	*Balance*	✔			7 6 —
	31	*Closing*	*GJ15*		7 6 —	0

UTILITIES EXPENSE Acct. No. *615*

Date		Explanation	PR	Debit	Credit	Balance
Jan.^{19XX}	*31*	*Balance*	✔			1 4 2 0 —
	31	*Closing*	*GJ15*		1 4 2 0 —	0

REPAIRS EXPENSE Acct. No. *620*

Date		Explanation	PR	Debit	Credit	Balance
Jan.^{19XX}	*31*	*Balance*	✔			2 4 1 6 —
	31	*Closing*	*GJ15*		2 4 1 6 —	0

UNIFORMS EXPENSE Acct. No. *630*

Date		Explanation	PR	Debit	Credit	Balance
¹⁹ˣˣ Jan.	31	Balance	✔			500 —
	31	Closing	GJ15		500 —	0

WAGES EXPENSE Acct. No. *640*

Date		Explanation	PR	Debit	Credit	Balance
¹⁹ˣˣ Jan.	6		GJ2	750 —		750 —
	13		GJ6	750 —		1500 —
	20		GJ9	750 —		2250 —
	27		GJ12	750 —		3000 —
	31	Adjusting	GJ14	300 —		3300 —
	31	Closing	GJ15		3300 —	0

PAYROLL TAX EXPENSE Acct. No. *650*

Date		Explanation	PR	Debit	Credit	Balance
¹⁹ˣˣ Jan.	31	Balance	✔			230 —
	31	Closing	GJ15		230 —	0

INSURANCE EXPENSE Acct. No. *660*

Date		Explanation	PR	Debit	Credit	Balance
¹⁹ˣˣ Jan.	31	Adjusting	GJ14	30 —		30 —
	31	Closing	GJ15		30 —	0

DEPRECIATION EXPENSE Acct. No. *670*

Date		Explanation	PR	Debit	Credit	Balance
¹⁹ˣˣ Jan.	31	Adjusting	GJ14	200 —		200 —
		Closing	GJ15		200 —	0

THE POST-CLOSING TRIAL BALANCE

post-closing
after closing

real accounts
assets, liabilities, and
the owner's capital
account

Once the closing entries have been posted, the remaining step in the accounting cycle is preparing the **post-closing** trial balance. The accounts that appear on the post-closing trial balance are the **real accounts** and include assets, liabilities, and the owner's capital account. The post-closing trial balance is prepared as a last check to ensure that after the adjusting and closing entries have been posted, the ledger is in balance. The post-closing trial balance for Mary Tyus, M.D., follows.

MARY TYUS, M.D. POST-CLOSING TRIAL BALANCE JANUARY 31, 19XX		
Cash	$ 12500 —	
Notes Receivable	4700 —	
Accounts Receivable	3100 —	
Prepaid Insurance	330 —	
Supplies	260 —	
Office Equipment	10600 —	
Accumulated Depreciation: Office Equipment		$ 200 —
Notes Payable		7600 —
Accounts Payable		2950 —
Payroll Taxes Payable		210 —
Unearned Consulting Revenue		400 —
Wages Payable		300 —
Mary Tyus, Capital		19830 —
Totals	$ 31490 —	$ 31490 —

STEPS IN THE ACCOUNTING CYCLE

The accounting cycle begins with a transaction and the journalizing of it and ends with the closing of the books and the post-closing trial balance. The steps in the accounting cycle are:

1. Journalize the transactions.
2. Post the transactions.
3. Prepare a worksheet.
   a. Prepare a trial balance.
   b. Prepare the adjustments.

  c. Prepare an adjusted trial balance.

  d. Complete the worksheet by extending figures first to the balance sheet and then to the income statement columns.

4. Prepare the financial statements.

5. Journalize the adjusting entries.

6. Post the adjusting entries.

7. Journalize the closing entries.

8. Post the closing entries.

9. Prepare the post-closing trial balance.

SUMMARY

If a general journal entry has not been posted, any errors that have been made when journalizing may be corrected simply by drawing a line through the incorrect account title(s) and/or amount(s) and entering the correct title(s) and/or amount(s) above. If the journal entry has been posted, however, a new entry must be made that will counteract the effects of the first entry. When the error is discovered, the bookkeeper simply centers the words *Correcting Entry* in the description column of the journal and journalizes the entry required to correct the one in error.

The closing entries are journalized following the adjusting entries. All the nominal accounts, or the temporary proprietorship accounts, are brought to a zero balance during the closing process, and the owner's capital account is updated. Temporary proprietorship accounts include drawing, revenue, and expense accounts. The closing process takes place at the end of the accounting period, which may be at the end of a month, a quarter, or a fiscal year. The four closing entries (1) close all revenue accounts, (2) close all expense accounts, (3) transfer net income or loss to capital, and (4) transfer the balance of drawing to capital.

The Income Summary account is used only in the closing process. All the revenue, expenses, and net income or loss are transferred to it during closing. The Income Summary account opens and closes when the first three closing entries have been journalized and posted.

The information for the closing entries is available in the income statement and balance sheet columns of the worksheet. Check marks should be placed next to all of the amounts in the income statement columns as they are journalized and next to the drawing account balance as it is closed.

Only the real accounts (assets, liabilities, and owner's capital) remain open after the closing entries have been posted. A post-closing trial balance verifies that they are in balance before the next accounting cycle is begun.

Review of Accounting Terminology

Following is a list of the accounting terminology for this chapter.

calendar year	fiscal year
closing entries	nominal accounts
counteract	post-closing
erroneous	real accounts

Fill in the blank with the correct word or term from the list.

1. All the revenue and expense accounts are referred to as
   _____.

2. Journal entries that bring account balances to zero are called
   _____.

3. All the asset and liability accounts and the owner's capital account are called _____.

4. "After closing" means _____.

5. To perform an act that will reverse the effects of a previous act is to _____.

6. January 1 through December 31 is a/an _____.

7. Something that is wrong or inaccurate is _____.

8. Any 12-month period chosen by a business owner for determining net income is a/an _____.

Match the following words and terms on the left with the definitions on the right (lists are continued on the following page).

9. closing entries	a. asset, liability, and the owner's capital account
10. counteract	
11. erroneous	b. to reverse the effects of a previous act
12. post-closing	

13. nominal accounts
14. real accounts
15. fiscal year
16. calendar year

c. revenue and expense accounts
d. wrong or inaccurate
e. January 1 through December 31
f. after closing
g. journal entries that bring revenue and expense account balances to zero and update the Capital account
h. April 1 through March 31

Exercises

Exercise 6.1
journalizing correcting entries

Ly Vo owns The Reading School. Following are examples of transactions that have been erroneously journalized and posted by the bookkeeper. Prepare the correcting entry for each. Write the letter of each entry in the date column on page 6 of the general journal. You may omit explanations.

a. Ly Vo wrote a check for $220 for office supplies. The bookkeeper debits Office Supplies for $200 and credits Cash for $200.

b. A check for $89 is received from a customer of The Reading School who is paying on account. The bookkeeper debits Cash for $89 and credits Accounts Payable for $89.

c. A check for $440 is received from a customer of The Reading School who is paying on account. The bookkeeper debits Accounts Payable for $440 and credits Cash for $440.

d. Ly Vo wrote a check for $50 to pay an outstanding account. The bookkeeper debits Accounts Receivable for $50 and credits Cash for $50.

e. Ly Vo wrote a check for $250 for office furniture. The bookkeeper debits Office Equipment for $250 and credits Accounts Payable for $250.

Exercise 6.2
posting closing entries

Following are the closing entries on July 31, 19XX, for Reliable Answering Service. Post them to accounts with the following titles and account balances.

301	Daniel Black, Capital	$8,750
310	Daniel Black, Drawing	2,400
315	Income Summary	0
401	Revenue	4,000
601	Utilities Expense	190
605	Rent Expense	575
610	Wages Expense	900
615	Advertising Expense	250
620	Payroll Tax Expense	55
630	Supplies Used	70
640	Depreciation Expense	50

GENERAL JOURNAL				Page 24
Date	Description	Post. Ref.	Debit	Credit
19XX	**Closing Entries**			
July 31	Revenue		4000 —	
	Income Summary			4000 —
	To Close Revenue Account			
31	Income Summary		2090 —	
	Utilities Expense			190 —
	Rent Expense			575 —
	Wages Expense			900 —
	Advertising Expense			250 —
	Payroll Tax Expense			55 —
	Supplies Used			70 —
	Depreciation Expense			50 —
	To Close Expense Accounts			
31	Income Summary		1910 —	
	Daniel Black, Capital			1910 —
	To Transfer Net Income To Capital			
31	Daniel Black, Capital		2400 —	
	Daniel Black, Drawing			2400 —
	To Transfer Balance of Drawing to Capital			

Exercise 6.3
journalizing and posting closing entries

Following are the balances of the T-accounts for Wayne's Wind-surfers on June 30, 19XX. Journalize the closing entries on page 14. The four entries will (1) close all revenue accounts, (2) close all expense accounts, (3) transfer the profit or loss to the capital account, and (4) transfer the balance of drawing to the capital account. Post the entries to the T-accounts and determine the amount of the ending capital balance.

Wayne Werner, Capital	301
	6/1 Balance 5,250

Revenue	401
	6/30 Balance 2,100

Wayne Werner, Drawing	310
6/30 Balance 1,000	

Rent Expense	601
6/30 Balance 400	

Income Summary	315

Insurance Expense	605
6/30 Balance 75	

Advertising Expense	610
6/30 Balance 250	

Repairs Expense	615
6/30 Balance 320	

Depreciation Expense	650
6/30 Balance 450	

Supplies Used	660
6/30 Balance 30	

Exercise 6.4
determining how transactions affect net income

Tell whether each of the following will cause an increase (+), cause a decrease (−), or have no effect (NE) on net income for March. Assume that adjusting and closing entries are prepared monthly.

_____ a.   withdrawals in March by the owner for personal use
_____ b.   a purchase of equipment for cash on March 31
_____ c.   a bill for electricity for March is received and recorded but not paid
_____ d.   an additional investment by the owner on March 9
_____ e.   cash paid on an account payable on March 29
_____ f.   an adjusting entry to record wages payable
_____ g.   an adjusting entry on March 31 to record depreciation on the automobile
_____ h.   a receipt of $3,000 cash on March 1 from a customer who is paying in advance for services to be performed in April, May, and June
_____ i.   a $10,000 business loan is obtained on March 13
_____ j.   an adjusting entry to record $500 of services performed for which no cash has been received

Exercise 6.5
classifying accounts

For the following accounts indicate on which financial statement each will appear (income statement or balance sheet) and whether the account has a normal debit or credit balance. The first one has been completed as an example.

	Which Financial Statement?	Normal Debit or Credit Balance?
Example Capital	balance sheet	credit
a. Equipment		
b. Wages Payable		
c. Supplies Used		
d. Accumulated Depreciation		
e. Unearned Consulting Revenue		
f. Prepaid Advertising		
g. Wages Expense		
h. Supplies		
i. Revenue from Services		
j. Advertising Expense		
k. Prepaid Insurance		
l. Depreciation Expense		
m. Unearned Medical Revenue		
n. Insurance Expense		
o. Consulting Revenue		

Exercise 6.6
journalizing closing entries

Following are selected ledger accounts for the Tri-More Company on January 31, 19XX. All of the revenue and expense accounts are listed. Journalize the four required closing entries on journal page 27.

230	Unearned Consulting Revenue	$1,000
601	Rent Expense	900
201	Accounts Payable	2,740
310	Sandra Nielsen, Drawing	2,770
401	Revenue	3,055
301	Sandra Nielsen, Capital, January 1, 19XX	6,120
605	Insurance Expense	275
170A	Accumulated Depreciation: Office Equipment	1,000
610	Advertising Expense	350
615	Wages Expense	1,890
620	Payroll Tax Expense	114
315	Income Summary	0
640	Depreciation Expense	200
160	Supplies	190
660	Supplies Used	75

Exercise 6.7
preparing statement of owner's equity

Using the information in Exercise 6.6, prepare a statement of owner's equity on January 31, 19XX, for the Tri-More Company.

Exercise 6.8
analyzing Income Summary account

Following is the Income Summary account for Kay Song, Consultant, on April 30, 19XX, after the first two closing entries have been posted.

Income Summary   **315**

4/30 Closing 15,820	4/30 Closing 12,485

a. What is the balance of the account before the third closing entry is posted to it?

b. Is the account balance a debit or a credit?

c. After the first two entries have been posted to the Income Summary account, does a debit balance represent a net income or a net loss for the period?

d. After the first two closing entries have been posted, does the credit side of the Income Summary account represent total revenue or total expenses for the period?

e. Will the third closing entry, which transfers net loss to capital, be recorded as a debit or as a credit to Capital? To Income Summary?

f. If there is a net income for the period, will the amount of the net income be recorded as a debit or as a credit to Capital? To Income Summary?

Exercise 6.9
analyzing errors in closing entries

Following are the closing entries for Gregory Bronski, Counselor, on May 31, 19XX. The entries have not been posted. Assuming that the first two entries are correct, determine what is wrong, if anything, with the last two. If you find one or both of them to be incorrect, draw a line through the account title and/or amount and enter the correct account title and/or amount directly above the line. The balance of the Capital account on May 1 was $6,240, and the balance of Drawing on May 31 was $1,800.

GENERAL JOURNAL					Page 4
Date	Description	Post. Ref.	Debit	Credit	
19XX	**Closing Entries**				
May 31	Revenue from Counseling		1916 —		
	Income Summary			1916 —	
	To Close Revenue Account				
31	Income Summary		2334 —		
	Rent Expense			890 —	
	Utilities Expense			225 —	
	Wages Expense			800 —	
	Payroll Tax Expense			79 —	
	Supplies Used			45 —	
	Insurance Expense			75 —	
	Depreciation Expense			220 —	
	To Close Expense Accounts				
31	Income Summary		318 —		
	Gregory Bronski, Capital			318 —	
	To Transfer Net Income to Capital				
31	Gregory Bronski, Drawing		1800 —		
	Gregory Bronski, Capital			1800 —	
	To Transfer Balance of Drawing to Capital				

Exercise 6.10

determining how errors affect net income

Following are several examples of incorrect journal entries that have already been posted to the ledger. Tell whether the incorrect entry will affect net income for the month. If so, determine whether it will be overstated (O) or understated (U) and determine by how much the net income will be overstated or understated.

	Will error affect net income?	If so, will it be overstated or understated?	By how much?
a. Services were performed for $500 cash; recorded by a $500 debit to Accounts Receivable and a $500 credit to Revenue.	_____	_____	_____
b. $100 was received from a customer who was paying on account; recorded by a $110 debit to Cash and a $110 credit to Accounts Receivable.	_____	_____	_____
c. Owner's withdrawal of $900 was recorded as a $900 debit to Salary Expense and a $900 credit to Cash.	_____	_____	_____
d. A check was written for $175 for payment on account; recorded as a $175 debit to Utilities Expense and a $175 credit to Cash.	_____	_____	_____
e. $800 in services were performed on account; recorded as an $800 debit to Accounts Receivable and an $800 credit to Owner's Capital.	_____	_____	_____
f. $1,200 in services were performed on account; recorded as a $1,200 debit to Cash and a $1,200 credit to Revenue.	_____	_____	_____
g. A $168 telephone bill was paid and recorded as a $186 debit to Utilities Expense and a $186 credit to Cash.	_____	_____	_____
h. The owner invested an additional $1,000 in the business. It was recorded as a $1,000 debit to Cash and a $1,000 credit to Revenue.	_____	_____	_____
i. A $250 cash payment was made for equipment repairs. It was recorded as a $250 debit to Equipment and a $250 credit to Cash.	_____	_____	_____
j. A $190 payment was made for gas and oil for a delivery van. Utilities Expense was debited for $190 and Cash was credited for $190.	_____	_____	_____

Problems

Problem 6.1
journalizing correcting entries

Following are several examples of journalizing errors that have been posted.

a. A firm writes a check for $550 for shop supplies. The book-keeper records a debit of $550 to Office Supplies and a credit of $550 to Cash.

b. A firm writes a check for $550 for shop supplies. The book-keeper records a debit of $505 to Shop Supplies and a credit of $505 to Cash.

c. A firm writes a check for $550 for shop supplies. The book-keeper records a debit of $650 to Shop Supplies and a credit of $650 to Cash.

d. A check for $420 is received from a customer paying on account. The bookkeeper records a debit to Cash of $402 and a credit to Accounts Receivable for $402.

e. A check for $420 is received from a customer paying on account. The bookkeeper records a debit to Accounts Receivable for $420 and a credit to Cash for $420.

f   A check for $420 is received from a customer paying on account. The bookkeeper records a debit to Accounts Receivable for $410 and a credit to Cash for $410.

g. A firm writes a check for $840 to pay an outstanding debt. The bookkeeper records a debit to Accounts Payable for $860 and a credit to Cash for $860.

h. A firm writes a check for $840 to pay an outstanding debt. The bookkeeper records a debit to Cash of $840 and a credit to Accounts Payable of $840.

i. A firm writes a check for $840 to pay an outstanding debt. The bookkeeper records a debit to Accounts Receivable of $840 and a credit to Cash for $840.

j. A firm writes a check for $840 to pay an outstanding debt. The bookkeeper records a debit to Accounts Receivable of $480 and a credit to Cash for $480.

Instructions   *Prepare correcting entries in the general journal on page 49. Explanations may be omitted. Enter the letter of the transaction in the date column of the journal.*

Problem 6.2
journalizing and posting closing entries and preparing post-closing trial balance

The trial balance and income statement columns of the worksheet for Dandee Delivery Service for the month of September 19XX follow.

Dandee Delivery Service
Worksheet (Partial)
For Month Ended September 30, 19XX

Acct. No.	Account Titles	Adjusted Trial Balance Debit	Adjusted Trial Balance Credit	Income Statement Debit	Income Statement Credit
101	Cash	4,020			
105	Accounts Receivable	850			
110	Supplies	490			
115	Prepaid Insurance	300			
120	Equipment	3,465			
120A	Accumulated Depreciation: Equipment		1,590		
130	Truck	18,500			
130A	Accumulated Depreciation: Truck		8,200		
201	Notes Payable		10,550		
210	Accounts Payable		300		
220	Unearned Delivery Revenue		800		
301	Dee Snyder, Capital		7,870		
310	Dee Snyder, Drawing	3,200			
401	Revenue from Delivery		4,720		4,720
601	Truck Expense	310		310	
610	Rent Expense	950		950	
615	Utilities Expense	255		255	
630	Advertising Expense	580		580	
640	Interest Expense	260		260	
650	Insurance Expense	100		100	
660	Supplies Used	75		75	
670	Depreciation Expense	675		675	
	Totals	34,030	34,030	3,205	4,720
	Net Income			1,515	
				4,720	4,720

Instructions

1. *Prepare the four closing entries required on September 30, 19XX, on journal page 39. The account number for Income Summary is 315.*

2. *Post the entries to the general ledger.*

3. *Prepare a post-closing trial balance.*

Problem 6.3
journalizing closing entries and preparing financial statements

The income statement and balance sheet columns of the worksheet for Softee Diaper Service for the year ended December 31, 19XX, follow.

Softee Diaper Service
Worksheet (Partial)
For Year Ended December 31, 19XX

Acct. No.	Account Titles	Income Statement Debit	Income Statement Credit	Balance Sheet Debit	Balance Sheet Credit
101	Cash			7,064	
110	Notes Receivable			3,002	
115	Accounts Receivable			1,500	
120	Supplies			775	
125	Prepaid Insurance			400	
135	Prepaid Advertising			1,550	
136	Equipment			24,000	
136A	Accumulated Depreciation: Equipment				4,500
140	Furniture			4,540	
140A	Accumulated Depreciation: Furniture				1,600
150	Truck			22,000	
150A	Accumulated Depreciation: Truck				7,000
201	Notes Payable				30,000
210	Accounts Payable				1,765
220	Unearned Consulting Revenue				3,500
301	Alex Agnos, Capital				37,041
310	Alex Agnos, Drawing			12,000	
401	Revenue from Services		42,625		
601	Delivery Expense	5,100			
605	Repairs Expense	6,204			
610	Rent Expense	12,000			
615	Interest Expense	6,396			
620	Advertising Expense	1,000			
630	Utilities Expense	2,400			
640	Insurance Expense	100			
650	Wages Expense	15,000			
660	Payroll Tax Expense	900			
670	Supplies Used	600			
680	Depreciation Expense	1,500			
		51,200	42,625	76,831	85,406
	Net Loss		8,575	8,575	
		51,200	51,200	85,406	85,406

Instructions   1. *Journalize the four closing entries required on December 31, 19XX. The account number for Income Summary is 315.*

2. *Prepare a statement of owner's equity for the year ended December 31, 19XX.*

3. *Prepare a balance sheet as of December 31, 19XX.*

4. *Prepare an income statement for the year ended December 31, 19XX.*

Problem 6.4

journalizing and posting adjusting and closing entries and preparing financial statements and post-closing trial balance

Following on pages 218–219 is the worksheet for Robert's Hair Styling for the month of December 19XX.

Worksheet for Problem 6.4

ROBERT'S HAIR STYLING
WORKSHEET
FOR MONTH ENDED DECEMBER 31, 19XX

Acct. No.	Account Titles	Trial Balance Debit	Credit	Adjustments Debit	Credit
101	Cash	6400—			
110	Accounts Receivable	1250—		f. 300—	
120	Beauty Supplies	2800—			a. 1290—
125	Office Supplies	980—			b. 430—
130	Prepaid Insurance	1440—			c. 240—
135	Hair Styling Equipment	18000—			
135A	Accumulated Depr.: HSE		5500—		e. 250—
140	Office Equipment	10500—			
140A	Accumulated Depr.: OE		1837—		e. 167—
150	Furniture	6200—			
150A	Accumulated Depr.: Furn.		1100—		e. 100—
160	Automobile	18200—			
160A	Accumulated Depr.: Auto.		3663—		e. 333—
205	Notes Payable		15600—		
220	Accounts Payable		2940—		
230	Unearned Hair Styling Rev.		500—	g. 200—	
301	Robert Goodwin, Capital		36526—		
310	Robert Goodwin, Drawing	2500—			
401	Hair Styling Revenue		6150—		f. 300— / g. 200—
601	Rent Expense	1800—			
610	Advertising Expense	500—			
620	Utilities Expense	470—			
630	Repairs Expense	220—			
640	Interest Expense	156—			
650	Wages Expense	2200—		d. 330—	
655	Payroll Tax Expense	200—			
	Totals	73816—	73816—		
615	Beauty Supplies Used			a. 1290—	
625	Office Supplies Used			b. 430—	
635	Insurance Expense			c. 240—	
240	Wages Payable				d. 330—
670	Depreciation Expense			e. 850—	
				3640—	3640—
	Net Loss				

| Adjusted Trial Balance | | Income Statement | | Balance Sheet | |
Debit	Credit	Debit	Credit	Debit	Credit
6400 —				6400 —	
1550 —				1550 —	
1510 —				1510 —	
550 —				550 —	
1200 —				1200 —	
18000 —				18000 —	
	5750 —				5750 —
10500 —				10500 —	
	2004 —				2004 —
6200 —				6200 —	
	1200 —				1200 —
18200 —				18200 —	
	3996 —				3996 —
	15600 —				15600 —
	2940 —				2940 —
	300 —				300 —
	36526 —				36526 —
2500 —				2500 —	
	6650 —		6650 —		
1800 —		1800 —			
500 —		500 —			
470 —		470 —			
220 —		220 —			
156 —		156 —			
2530 —		2530 —			
200 —		200 —			
1290 —		1290 —			
430 —		430 —			
240 —		240 —			
	330 —				330 —
850 —		850 —			
75296 —	75296 —	8686 —	6650 —	66610 —	68646 —
			2036 —	2036 —	
		8686 —	8686 —	68646 —	68646 —

Instructions

1. *Journalize and post the adjusting entries. Write* Adjusting *in the explanation column of each ledger account as you post. Use general journal page 27.*

2. *Journalize and post the closing entries. Write* Closing *in the explanation column of each ledger account as you post. Continue on general journal page 27. The account number for Income Summary is 315.*

3. *Prepare an income statement for the month of December 19XX.*

4. *Prepare a balance sheet as of December 31. Include the statement of owner's equity on the balance sheet.*

5. *Prepare a post-closing trial balance.*

Problem 6.5

preparing worksheet and journalizing and posting adjusting and closing entries

Following is the trial balance for Uncle Ray's Party Service for the third quarter of 19XX.

Uncle Ray's Party Service
Trial Balance
For Quarter Ended September 30, 19XX

Acct. No.	Account Titles	Debit	Credit
101	Cash	$ 5,214	
110	Accounts Receivable	279	
115	Party Supplies	895	
116	Prepaid Insurance	300	
120	Party Equipment	6,500	
120A	Accumulated Depreciation: Party Equipment		$ 750
130	Van	18,000	
130A	Accumulated Depreciation: Van		1,250
201	Notes Payable		11,404
205	Accounts Payable		756
210	Unearned Party Revenue		600
301	Ray Whittier, Capital		19,714
310	Ray Whittier, Drawing	4,500	
401	Revenue from Party Services		8,742
601	Salary Expense	2,046	
610	Repairs Expense	750	
620	Rent Expense	1,500	
630	Payroll Tax Expense	125	
640	Utilities Expense	507	
670	Advertising Expense	600	
685	Wages Expense	2,000	
	Totals	$43,216	$43,216

Instructions

1. *Copy the trial balance onto the trial balance columns of a ten-column worksheet.*

2. *Record the adjustments from the following data for the three-month period ending September 30, 19XX. Account numbers you will need to complete this problem include: Party Supplies Used, 680; Insurance Expense, 690; Depreciation Expense, 675; Wages Payable, 220; and Income Summary, 320.*

   a. *The inventory of party supplies on September 30 is $585.*

   b. *The insurance policy was purchased on July 1 for $300 for a 12-month period.*

   c. *The party equipment was purchased on January 2 of this year. It has a useful life of four years and a salvage value of $500. The van was purchased on April 1 of this year. It has a useful life of three years and a salvage value of $3,000.*

   d. *One-half of the balance in the Unearned Party Revenue account has been earned this quarter.*

   e. *September 30 falls on a Wednesday. Record three days' wages expense at $100 a day for September 28 through 30.*

   f. *Ray performed services amounting to $900 for which no cash has been received or bills sent.*

3. *Complete the worksheet.*

4. *Journalize the adjusting entries. Assign page number 84 to the journal.*

5. *Journalize the closing entries. Continue on page 84.*

Comprehensive Problem 1

for Review of Chapters 1

through 6

Following are the chart of accounts and account balances on October 1, Year 3, for the Ozark Reporter, a newspaper. Also following are the transactions for the month of October, Year 3.

Chart of Accounts

110	Cash	$ 17,540.63	
120	Accounts Receivable	12,409.15	
130	Supplies	1,962.00	
135	Prepaid Insurance	600.00	
140	Equipment	75,000.00	
140A	Accumulated Depreciation: Equipment		$ 19,800.00
150	Delivery Van	21,640.00	
150A	Accumulated Depreciation: Del. Van		10,800.00
160	Furniture	4,300.00	
160A	Accumulated Depreciation: Furniture		2,145.00
170	Building	195,000.00	
170A	Accumulated Depreciation: Building		24,750.00
180	Land	36,000.00	
210	Notes Payable		31,490.60
220	Accounts Payable		4,203.32
225	Unearned Consulting Revenue		
230	Mortgage Payable: Building		122,400.00
240	Wages Payable		
310	Emerson Browne, Capital		148,862.86

Continued.

320	Emerson Browne, Drawing
330	Income Summary
410	Revenue from Subscriptions
420	Consulting Revenue
610	Utilities Expense
620	Wages Expense
630	Advertising Expense
640	Gasoline and Oil Expense
650	Building Repairs Expense
655	Van Repairs Expense
660	Interest Expense
670	Supplies Used
680	Insurance Expense
690	Depreciation Expense

Transactions

Oct. 1   wrote check #2169 for $2,400 for the personal use of Emerson Browne

Oct. 2   received $1,000 in cash from the Missouri Center for Learning for ten hours of consulting services to be provided by Emerson Browne in the future (credit to Unearned Consulting Revenue)

Oct. 3   wrote check #2170 for $375.62 for payment of telephone bill

Oct. 5   wrote check #2171 for $147.70 for payment for gasoline for the van

Oct. 6   bought $420 in supplies; agreed to pay within 30 days

Oct. 7   wrote check #2172 for $570.61 to pay bill for electricity

Oct. 7   recorded $5,200 in subscription revenue for the week; $4,010 was received in cash and the rest is due within 30 days

Oct. 9   wrote check #2173 for $1,760.50 in payment of monthly mortgage on building; $1,240.10 is for payment of interest, and the rest applies toward reduction of the principal (the amount borrowed)

Oct. 10   wrote check #2174 for $1,460.82 for repairs to the building

Oct. 12   received checks totaling $2,060.49 from charge customers

Oct. 13   purchased office supplies costing $1,540.22; wrote check #2175 for $850.22 as a cash down payment and agreed to pay the balance in 60 days

Oct. 14   wrote check #2176 for $2,100 for personal use of Emerson Browne

Oct. 14   wrote check #2177 for $3,410.77 to pay wages from October 1 through 14

Oct. 15   recorded $6,100 in subscription revenue for the week; $4,650.25 was received in cash, and the rest is due within 30 days

Oct. 16   wrote check #2178 for $217.40 to pay for repairs to the van

Oct. 17   wrote check #2179 for $168.40 for gasoline and oil for the van

Oct. 19   received checks from charge customers totaling $1,971.14

Oct. 20   wrote check #2180 for $2,462.90 to pay for television advertising

Oct. 21   recorded $4,742.80 in subscription revenue for the week; $3,960.20 was received in cash, and the rest is due within 30 days

Oct. 23   received a bill for radio advertising for $950 (record it now to be paid within 30 days)

Oct. 24   wrote check #2181 for $1,500 for personal use of Emerson Browne

Oct. 25   wrote check #2182 for $542.68 for building repairs

Oct. 26   wrote check #2183 for $650 to reduce the amount owed on account

Oct. 28   recorded $5,001 in subscription revenue for the week; $4,019.50 was received in cash, and the rest is due within 30 days

Oct. 28   wrote check #2184 for $3,410.77 to pay wages from October 15 through 28

Oct. 29   wrote check #2185 for $822.86 for payment on note; $640.32 is payment for interest, and the rest applies to reduction of the principal

Oct. 30   wrote check #2186 for $260.14 for gasoline and oil for the van

Oct. 31   wrote check #2187 for $420 to reduce the amount owed to creditors

Instructions

1. Enter the account names, numbers, and balances into the general ledger.

2. Record October's transactions in a general journal. Begin numbering with page 20.

3. Post the transactions to the general ledger.

4. Prepare a trial balance on the first two columns of a ten-column worksheet.

5. Prepare the adjustments from the following data.
   a. The inventory of supplies on October 31, determined by a physical count, is $1,140.75.
   b. The $600 figure in the Prepaid Insurance account on October 1 represents the remaining balance of a 12-month in-

surance policy purchased on April 1 of this year for
$1,200.

c. The equipment was purchased in January of Year 1. It has
a useful life of ten years and a salvage value of $3,000.

d. The delivery van was purchased in July of Year 1. It has a
useful life of four years and a salvage value of $2,440.

e. The furniture was purchased in January of Year 1. It has a
useful life of five years and a salvage value of $400.

f. The building was purchased in January of Year 1. It has a
useful life of 20 years and a salvage value of $15,000.

g. Three hours of consulting (at $100 per hour) were per-
formed by Emerson Browne during October for the Mis-
souri Center for Learning. (Refer to October 2 transaction.)

h. October 31 falls on a Monday. Record one day's wages
expense at $341.07.

i. Unrecorded Subscription Revenue during October (for
which customers have not paid) is $2,017.15.

6. Complete the worksheet.

7. Prepare an income statement for the month of October 19XX.

8. Prepare a statement of owner's equity for the month of October 19XX.

9. Prepare a balance sheet as of October 31, 19XX. Include only
the ending capital figure in the owner's equity section.

10. Journalize the adjusting entries in the general journal. Continue in the same journal. Center the words Adjusting Entries
in the description column of the journal before recording the
entries.

11. Post the adjusting entries to the general ledger.

12. Journalize the closing entries in the general journal. Continue
in the same journal as before. Center the words Closing Entries in the description column of the journal before recording
the entries.

13. Post the closing entries to the general ledger.

14. Prepare a post-closing trial balance.

CHAPTER 7

The Sales Journal and the Accounts Receivable Subsidiary Ledger

LEARNING OBJECTIVES

When you have completed this chapter, you should

1. have a better understanding of accounting terminology.

2. have an increased understanding of merchandising businesses.

3. be able to record entries directly into the special sales journal and perform summary posting.

4. be able to post to the accounts receivable subsidiary ledger and prepare a schedule of accounts receivable.

5. be able to calculate and account for sales tax.

6. be able to account for sales returns and allowances and sales discounts.

So far, our discussion has centered on service businesses. From now on, however, our focus will be on merchandising businesses and the special kinds of accounting procedures required by such businesses.

merchandising business
a business that buys and sells a product

merchant
a person who operates a business

merchandise
goods that may be bought or sold

While a service business sells the services of its owner and/or employees, a **merchandising business** sells a product, sometimes along with a service. The product usually has to be bought by the **merchant** before it can be resold; therefore, when determining a price, the merchant must consider the related selling expenses, the cost price of the **merchandise** to be sold, and the amount of profit desired. In this and the chapters to come, new accounts relating to merchandising businesses will be introduced, as well as two new ledgers.

SPECIAL JOURNALS

In addition to the general journal, many firms use special journals because of the time saved by the bookkeeper when journalizing and posting. Another advantage to using more than one journal is that more than one person may record journal entries at the same time. There are four special journals; their names, functions, and posting reference notations follow.

Journal	Function	Posting Reference
Sales Journal	Used to record all sales of merchandise on account	S
Purchases Journal	Used to record all credit purchases of merchandise for resale	P
Cash Receipts Journal	Used to record all incoming cash	CR
Cash Payments Journal	Used to record all checks written	CP

The special journals may be designed to fit the needs of the individual business. While each one may be different, the principles for recording and posting remain the same.

THE SALES ACCOUNT

When merchandise is sold, the amount is credited to a revenue account called Sales. It is handled in the same way as Revenue from Consulting, Medical Revenue, or any of the other revenue accounts used to record services performed. The Sales account appears as the first item on the income statement under the Revenue from Sales heading. Assume that merchandise is sold on November 28 for $500 cash. The T-accounts would look like this after the sale is posted.

Cash	105	Sales	400
11/28 500			11/28 500

THE SALES INVOICE

retail
the sale of goods in small quantities to the consumer

wholesale
the sale of goods in large quantities to the retailer

markup
the amount added to the cost price to determine the selling price

Frank Phelps owns a **retail** sporting goods store called Sports Haven. He purchases tennis rackets, racquetball shoes, running shorts, exercise bikes, and so on, from **a wholesale** dealer. He then calculates how much he needs to add to the cost price of each item purchased to determine the selling price. Frank must consider three things when determining the **markup:** (1) the cost of the merchandise, (2) the related expenses that will be incurred in selling the item, and (3) the average amount of net income desired on merchandise sold.

In general journal form, a sale on account to P. R. Collins would look like this.

GENERAL JOURNAL					Page *13*
Date	Description	Post. Ref.	Debit	Credit	
19XX June 1	Accounts Receivable/P. R. Collins		1 2 5 —		
	Sales			1 2 5 —	
	Invoice 507				

Frank does not, however, use a general journal for recording sales, because for each entry:

1. the words *accounts receivable* (or *cash*) and *sales* must be written into the journal.
2. two amounts must be posted to the general ledger.

Both of these tasks take up valuable time for the bookkeeper. Much of this time is saved, however, by using a special sales journal.

Entries in the sales journal may be made directly from sales invoices. The invoice shows the quantity of the item sold, a brief description of the item, the unit price, and the total price. The customer's name appears on the invoice and, for credit sales, the customer's address. Sales invoices are **consecutively** prenumbered and multiple copies are prepared; one copy goes to the accounting department so that the sale may be recorded. A sample invoice for Sports Haven follows.

consecutively
in uninterrupted order

SPORTS HAVEN   No. 507

740 Main Street
Des Moines, Iowa 50265
(515) 555-0773

Invoice
Terms: *net 30*
Date: *6/1/xx*

Sold to: *P.R. Collins*
176 Oak Avenue
Des Moines, IA 50265

Quantity	Description	Unit Price	Total Price
2	Running Shorts	5.00	10.00
1	Running Shoes	45.00	45.00
1	Tennis Racket	70.00	70.00
			125.00

THE SINGLE-COLUMN SALES JOURNAL

A sales journal is used only for recording sales of merchandise on account. Therefore, every entry in the sales journal is a debit to Accounts Receivable and a credit to Sales. The bookkeeper does not need to record a separate debit to Accounts Receivable and credit to Sales each time a credit sale is made. Carefully study the single-column sales journal for the month of June 19XX for Sports Haven.

		SALES JOURNAL				Page **6**
Date	Sales Invoice Number	Customer's Name	Terms	Post. Ref.		Amount
19XX *June* 1	507	P. R. Collins	*Net 30*			1 2 5 —
3	508	A. O. Brickner	*Net 30*			2 7 5 —
7	509	Z. A. Mysine	*Net 30*			4 5 —
10	510	B. L. Laws	*Net 30*			7 6 —
13	511	J. R. Custer	*Net 30*			1 9 5 —
16	512	A. O. Brickner	*Net 30*			1 0 9 —
20	513	C. L. Lindsay	*Net 30*			1 7 —
25	514	J. R. Custer	*Net 30*			4 7 5 —
30	515	W. W. Ho	*Net 30*			2 6 6 —
		Total				1 5 8 3 —

For the sale to P. R. Collins on June 1, the bookkeeper wrote in the sales journal the date of the invoice, the invoice number, the terms of the sale, and the amount. The term *net 30* indicates that no discount will be granted for prompt payment and that the invoice amount is due within 30 days of the invoice date.

At the end of the month, the sales journal is totaled. Special care must be taken when totaling a single-column journal, because there is no self-check as there is with both a debit and a credit column. Adding the column twice is usually sufficient to ensure that the total is correct. A double rule is then placed across all columns of the sales journal except the customer's name column.

THE ACCOUNTS RECEIVABLE SUBSIDIARY LEDGER

The Accounts Receivable account in the general ledger shows the total owed by all customers; it does *not* show the amounts owed by individuals. These amounts could be kept in the general ledger, and it might then read: Accounts Receivable—Adams; Accounts Receivable—Brown; Accounts Receivable—Coulson, and so on.

control account
the Accounts Receivable (or Accounts Payable) account in the general ledger whose balance must equal the total of the individual balances in the accounts receivable subsidiary ledger

subsidiary
secondary in importance

This would be unwieldy, and the trial balance might have hundreds or thousands of account titles. This would make the trial balance nearly impossible to prepare and read, and the chances for making errors would be much greater. Therefore, accountants keep the Accounts Receivable account in the general ledger simple by showing only the totals owed by charge customers. It is called a **control account** because its balance provides a check; the total of all the *individual* customer's balances must equal the balance in the Accounts Receivable control account in the general ledger.

Accounts for individual customers are kept alphabetically in a separate ledger called the accounts receivable subsidiary ledger. It is called a **subsidiary** ledger because it is under the control of the Accounts Receivable account in the general ledger. A separate page is assigned to each customer, and all sales made to the customer and payments received or items returned are recorded in his or her account in this ledger. When the bookkeeper needs to know how much a particular customer owes (for example, at billing time), he or she can refer to that customer's account in the accounts receivable subsidiary ledger.

The accounts receivable subsidiary ledger is not meant to replace the general ledger; it is designed to give specific information that the general ledger does not give. Study the following account for Tyler Petrie, which appears in the accounts receivable subsidiary ledger of Action Clothes.

TYLER PETRIE

Date		Explanation	PR	Debit	Credit	Balance
19XX Oct.	1		S10	500 —		500 —
	9		S10	750 —		1250 —
	10		GJ40		100 —	1150 —
	19		S10	800 —		1950 —
	20		GJ41		375 —	1575 —

POSTING THE SINGLE-COLUMN SALES JOURNAL

Each time a transaction is recorded in the sales journal, it is a debit to Accounts Receivable and a credit to Sales. The debit amount must be posted to the accounts receivable subsidiary ledger immediately, but postings to the general ledger are made at the end of the accounting period when the sales journal is totaled and ruled.

Immediately after a transaction is journalized the customer's name must be found in the accounts receivable subsidiary ledger, the debit amount posted to his or her account, and a new balance calculated. The posting reference S and the journal page number are entered in the ledger account, and a check mark ($\sqrt{}$) is placed in the posting reference column of the sales journal to indicate that the amount has been posted. This procedure is repeated for each transaction.

summary posting
posting journal totals rather than the individual amounts in the columns

At the end of the accounting period, the *total* of the sales journal must be posted to the general ledger accounts for Accounts Receivable and Sales. When journal totals are posted, rather than individual amounts, it is referred to as **summary posting.**

After the debit amount is posted to Accounts Receivable, the notation S and the journal page number are entered in the posting reference column of the Accounts Receivable account. The account number for Accounts Receivable is then entered in the posting reference column of the sales journal. The procedure is repeated when posting the credit amount to the Sales account.

Again, posting to the accounts receivable subsidiary ledger from the sales journal is done *immediately* after the transaction is journalized, while the totals of the sales journal are posted at the end of the accounting period as a debit to Accounts Receivable and as a credit to Sales in the general ledger.

Postings to the accounts receivable subsidiary ledger come primarily from the sales journal, where the charge sales are recorded; from the cash receipts journal, where customers' payments on account are recorded; and from the general journal, where customer returns are recorded. The sales journal, the general ledger accounts affected, and the accounts receivable subsidiary ledger (arranged in alphabetical order) for Sports Haven follow.

SALES JOURNAL

Date		Sales Invoice Number	Customer's Name	Terms	Post. Ref.	Amount
19XX *June*	1	507	P. R. Collins	Net 30	✓	125 —
	3	508	A. O. Brickner	Net 30	✓	275 —
	7	509	Z. A. Mysine	Net 30	✓	45 —
	10	510	B. L. Laws	Net 30	✓	76 —
	13	511	J. R. Custer	Net 30	✓	195 —
	16	512	A. O. Brickner	Net 30	✓	109 —
	20	513	C. L. Lindsay	Net 30	✓	17 —
	25	514	J. R. Custer	Net 30	✓	475 —
	30	515	W. W. Ho	Net 30	✓	266 —
			Total		110/401	1583 —

General Ledger

Accounts Receivable   110

6/30   S6   1,583

Sales   401

6/30   S6   1,583

Accounts Receivable Subsidiary Ledger

A. O. Brickner

6/3   S6   275
6/16   S6   109

P. R. Collins

6/1   S6   125

J. R. Custer

6/13   S6   195
6/25   S6   475

W. W. Ho

6/30   S6   266

B. L. Laws

6/10   S6   76

C. L. Lindsay

6/20   S6   17

Z. A. Mysine

6/7   S6   45

THE SCHEDULE OF ACCOUNTS RECEIVABLE

At the end of the accounting period, a schedule of accounts receivable is prepared directly from the accounts receivable subsidiary ledger. Each customer and the balance owed is listed on the schedule. The total owed by customers as shown on the schedule of accounts receivable must equal the balance in the Accounts Receivable control account in the general ledger. If the totals do not agree, then a mistake has been made.

The accounts receivable subsidiary ledger, the schedule of accounts receivable, and the Accounts Receivable control account from the general ledger follow. The accounts show only debit entries, even though normally they would also have credit entries. Payments on account and returns are omitted here for simplicity.

ACCOUNTS RECEIVABLE SUBSIDIARY LEDGER

A. O. BRICKNER

Date	Explanation	PR	Debit	Credit	Balance
19XX June 9		S0	2 7 5 —		2 7 5 —
16		S6	1 0 9 —		3 8 4 —

P. R. COLLINS

Date	Explanation	PR	Debit	Credit	Balance
19XX June 1		S6	1 2 5 —		1 2 5 —

J. R. CUSTER

Date	Explanation	PR	Debit	Credit	Balance
19XX June 13		S6	1 9 5 —		1 9 5 —
25		S6	4 7 5 —		6 7 0 —

W. W. HO

Date	Explanation	PR	Debit	Credit	Balance
June 30		S6	266 —		266 —

June 30 (19XX)

B. L. LAWS

Date	Explanation	PR	Debit	Credit	Balance
June 10		S6	76 —		76 —

June 10 (19XX)

C. L. LINDSAY

Date	Explanation	PR	Debit	Credit	Balance
June 20		S6	17 —		17 —

June 20 (19XX)

Z. A. MYSINE

Date	Explanation	PR	Debit	Credit	Balance
June 7		S6	45 —		45 —

June 7 (19XX)

SPORTS HAVEN
SCHEDULE OF ACCOUNTS RECEIVABLE
JUNE 30,19XX

A. O. Brickner	$384 —	
P. R. Collins	125 —	
J. R. Custer	670 —	
W. W. Ho	266 —	
B. L. Laws	76 —	
C. L. Lindsay	17 —	
Z. A. Mysine	45 —	
Total		$1583 —

GENERAL LEDGER

ACCOUNTS RECEIVABLE   Acct. No. *110*

Date	Explanation	PR	Debit	Credit	Balance
19XX *June* *30*		*S6*	*1 5 8 3* —		*1 5 8 3* —

SALES TAX PAYABLE

Many retail merchants are required by law to collect sales taxes from their customers; this tax is then remitted to the various taxing agencies by the merchant. Wholesalers are not usually required to collect sales tax when they sell to retailers, because the end-user, the final customer, usually pays it. The requirements for sales tax collection vary from state to state and sometimes from city to city within the states. Regardless of varying exemptions and amounts, the accounting principles remain the same.

Assume that in a certain area, sales taxes are 5 percent and that on July 9, a retailer makes a $240 taxable sale on account to Spencer Chatterly. To calculate the tax

1. change 5 percent to its decimal equivalent by moving the decimal point two places to the left: 5% = 0.5. = .05

2. multiply $240 by the decimal equivalent for 5 percent: $240 × .05 = $12

The customer will be charged for the amount of the sale ($240) and the amount of the tax ($12). The journal entry for this sale would require a debit to Accounts Receivable for the amount of the sale plus the tax, a credit to Sales for the amount of the merchandise sold, and a credit to Sales Tax Payable for the amount of the tax. The Accounts Receivable account is always debited for both the amount of the sale and the amount of the tax, because the customer pays the tax.

Amount Credited to Sales	$240
Amount Credited to Sales Tax Payable	12
Amount Debited to Accounts Receivable	$252

The sales tax collected from the customer is recorded in an account called Sales Tax Payable. It is a current liability and will reflect on the balance sheet with the other liabilities. The sales tax collected by the business is not a business expense, because it is the customer who pays it; the business owner merely collects the tax and sends it to the proper taxing agency. The entry to pay the sales tax to the taxing authority is recorded as a debit to Sales Tax Payable and as a credit to Cash.

THE MULTI-COLUMN SALES JOURNAL

If sales tax is collected regularly, then the sales journal should be designed with a special column for it. Such a journal might look like this.

		SALES JOURNAL					Page 43
Date	Sales Invoice Number	Customer's Name	Terms	Post. Ref.	Accounts Receivable Debit	Sales Tax Payable Credit	Sales Credit
19XX Oct. 1	7643	P. R. Jones	Net 30		4 1 6 —	1 6 —	4 0 0 —
4	7644	C. Y. Little	Net 30		1 5 6 —	6 —	1 5 0 —
9	7645	J. L. King	Net 30		7 8 0 —	3 0 —	7 5 0 —
15	7646	J. M. Alvarez	Net 30		6 2 4 —	2 4 —	6 0 0 —
		Totals			1 9 7 6 —	7 6 —	1 9 0 0 —

crossfooting
proving the equality of debit and credit columns in a journal before posting

After the multi-column sales journal is totaled, the bookkeeper must prove that the debit column is equal to the total of the two credit columns. This process is called **crossfooting.** The bookkeeper enters in small, pencil figures the column totals and then proves that total debits equal total credits before continuing.

Sales Credit Column Total	$1,900
Sales Tax Payable Credit Column Total	76
Accounts Receivable Debit Column Total	$1,976

Since the total of the two credit columns equals the total of the debit column, crossfooting is complete and the journal totals may be posted.

POSTING THE MULTI-COLUMN SALES JOURNAL

As with the single-column sales journal, the debit postings to the accounts receivable subsidiary ledger must be done immediately after journalizing to keep the accounts up to date. After posting to the subsidiary ledger, a check mark ($\checkmark$) is placed in the posting reference column of the sales journal.

Summary posting is performed at the end of the month, after crossfooting has been completed and the journal has been ruled. The total of the accounts receivable column is posted as a debit to the Accounts Receivable account in the general ledger, and the notation S and the journal page number are entered in the ledger account. The account number for Accounts Receivable is entered in parentheses beneath the double-ruled line under the column total. This procedure is repeated for the credit column totals. The multi-column sales journal looks like this after posting is complete.

SALES JOURNAL										**Page 43**
Date	Sales Invoice Number	Customer's Name	Terms	Post. Ref.	Accounts Receivable Debit			Sales Tax Payable Credit		Sales Credit
19XX Oct. 1	7643	P. R. Jones	Net 30	✔	4 1 6 —			1 6 —		4 0 0 —
4	7644	C. Y. Little	Net 30	✔	1 5 6 —			6 —		1 5 0 —
9	7645	J. L. King	Net 30	✔	7 8 0 —			3 0 —		7 5 0 —
15	7646	J. M. Alvarez	Net 30	✔	6 2 4 —			2 4 —		6 0 0 —
		Totals			1 9 7 6 —			7 6 —		1 9 0 0 —
					(1 1 0)			(2 2 5)		(4 0 1)

SALES RETURNS AND ALLOWANCES

credit memorandum
a document issued by the seller indicating that the buyer's Accounts Receivable is being reduced

The Sales Returns and Allowances account is used to record a return of merchandise by the customer or an allowance granted by the seller because of inferior, defective, or damaged merchandise. When such returns or allowances occur, a **credit memorandum** is given to the customer. It is called credit memorandum because it indicates that the customer's account receivable will be credited. The credit memorandum is prepared with multiple copies with one copy going to the accounting department. Although sales returns and allowances could be debited directly to the Sales account, it is not desirable because owners and managers need to keep a record of the number of returns, by whom, and of which merchandise. Too many returns may indicate customer dissatisfaction with the merchandise and may require obtaining a new supplier.

A sales return reverses the effects on the books of the original sale. Therefore, the Sales Returns and Allowances account has a debit balance; ultimately it is subtracted from sales on the income statement. For this reason, the Sales Returns and Allowances account is called a **contra**-revenue account. It is included in the revenue category on the chart of accounts.

contra
opposing

Assume that on October 3, 19XX, Schwartz Company purchased four tennis rackets on account from Sports Haven for $110 each. The transaction was recorded in Sports Haven's sales journal. On October 10, 19XX, Schwartz Company returned one of the rackets because the strings were faulty. When sales returns relate to credit sales, they are recorded in the general journal. The entry to record the return on Sports Haven's books follows.

Date		Description	Post. Ref.	Debit	Credit
19XX *Oct.*	*10*	*Sales Returns and Allowances*		*1 1 0 —*	
		Accounts Receivable—Schwartz Co.			*1 1 0 —*
		To Record Return of Faulty Tennis Racket			

GENERAL JOURNAL — Page **47**

If a customer returns merchandise on which he or she paid sales tax, credit must be given to the customer for the merchandise returned and for any sales tax charged. For example, assume that on October 4, 19XX, Sports Haven sold two warm-up suits on account to Arlene Davidson for $70 each, plus 4 percent sales tax. The entry in the sales journal looks as follows.

							SALES JOURNAL											Page **22**	
Date	Sales Invoice Number	Customer's Name	Terms	Post. Ref.	Accounts Receivable Debit				Sales Tax Payable Credit			Sales Credit			
19XX Oct. 4	*6143*	*A. Davidson*	*Net 30*				*1 4 5 60*				*5 60*				*1 4 0 —*	

Assume that on October 6, Arlene returned one of the warm-up suits for credit. The entry to record the return is as follows.

				GENERAL JOURNAL					Page **47**	
Date		Description		Post. Ref.	Debit			Credit		
19XX Oct. 6		*Sales Returns and Allowances*			*7 0 —*					
		Sales Tax Payable			*2 80*					
		Accounts Receivable—Arlene Davidson						*7 2 80*		
		To Record Return of Merchandise								

Sales Returns and Allowances is debited for the amount of the original selling price of the returned item, and Sales Tax Payable is debited for the amount of the tax relating to the returned item. The Sales Tax Payable account must be reduced, because if the merchandise is returned, a sale has been reversed and no sales tax is required.

POSTING TO ACCOUNTS RECEIVABLE FROM THE GENERAL JOURNAL

When any general journal entry is made that involves accounts receivable, the amount must be posted immediately to both the control account in the general ledger and the customer's account in the accounts receivable subsidiary ledger. When posting, the debits to Sales Returns and Allowances and Sales Tax Payable will be posted to the general ledger in the usual manner. The credit to Accounts Receivable, however, must be posted twice: once to the Accounts Receivable account in the general ledger and once to the customer's account in the accounts receivable subsidiary ledger. After the amount is posted as a credit to the Accounts Receivable control account in the general ledger, the account number is placed in the posting reference column of the general journal, followed by a diagonal line 110/ . After the amount is posted as a credit to the customer's account in the accounts receivable subsidiary ledger, a check mark is placed in the posting reference column of the general journal following the diagonal line 110/✓ . The two notations indicate that the amount has correctly been posted twice, once to the general ledger and once to the accounts receivable subsidiary ledger. The proper posting reference notations must be made in the accounts, too.

Following are the entries in the general journal and the ledger accounts to record the return of merchandise by Arlene Davidson. Study these accounts carefully and pay special attention to the posting reference notations.

GENERAL JOURNAL					Page 47
Date	Description	Post. Ref.	Debit	Credit	
19XX Oct. 6	Sales Returns and Allowances	420	70 —		
	Sales Tax Payable	250	2 80		
	Accounts Receivable—Arlene Davidson	110/✓		72 80	
	To Record Return of Merchandise				

ACCOUNTS RECEIVABLE SUBSIDIARY LEDGER

ARLENE DAVIDSON

Date	Explanation	PR	Debit	Credit	Balance
19XX Oct. 4		S22	145 60		145 60
6		GJ47		72 80	72 80

GENERAL LEDGER (PARTIAL)

ACCOUNTS RECEIVABLE   Acct. No. *110*

Date	Explanation	PR	Debit	Credit	Balance
19XX Oct. 1	**Balance**	✔			5 2 0 0 —
6		GJ47		7 2 80	5 1 2 7 20

SALES TAX PAYABLE   Acct. No. *250*

Date	Explanation	PR	Debit	Credit	Balance
19XX Oct. 1	**Balance**	✔			7 4 0 50
6		GJ14	2 80		7 3 7 70

SALES RETURNS AND ALLOWANCES   Acct. No. *420*

Date	Explanation	PR	Debit	Credit	Balance
19XX Oct. 6		GJ47	7 0 —		7 0 —

The original sale to Arlene Davidson is not recorded in the Accounts Receivable account in the general ledger, because only the *total* of the accounts receivable column in the sales journal will be posted to the control account.

SALES DISCOUNTS

When a credit sale is made and no discount for paying early is offered, the terms may be expressed on the invoice as *net 30,* which means that the full amount of the invoice is due within 30 days. Often, however, the seller will grant discount terms to credit buyers. The terms will indicate that a certain percent of the purchase price will be deducted if the buyer pays the invoice within a certain time. Such terms might read: 2/10, n/30 (read as *two-ten, net-thirty*), which means that a 2 percent discount will be allowed if paid within 10 days of the invoice date. If the invoice is not paid within 10 days, then the total invoice price must be paid within 30 days of the invoice date.

When the sale is made, the seller does not know whether the buyer will take advantage of credit terms. Therefore, sales are recorded in the sales journal at their full invoice price. It is only when the customer pays that it becomes evident whether a discount has been earned. If the discount has been taken, it is recorded in a special account called Sales Discounts, which has a debit balance and subtracts from sales on the income statement. Sales Discounts is a contra-revenue account and is assigned a number in the revenue category on the chart of accounts.

Assume that on October 3 a credit sale is made by A-1 Plumbing Supplies to Joe's Hardware in the amount of $5,000. Terms are 1/10, n/30 (a 1 percent discount is allowed if the invoice is paid within 10 days, or the net amount is due within 30 days). The entry was recorded on page 30 of the sales journal as illustrated.

			SALES JOURNAL			Page 30
Date	Sales Invoice Number		Customer's Name	Terms	Post. Ref.	Amount
_19XX_ Oct. 3	1046		_Joe's Hardware_	_1/10, n/30_	✔	5000 —

Joe's Hardware has 10 days from the day of the invoice to pay and receive the 1 percent discount; it has until October 13 (3 + 10). (When calculating a due date, do not count the first day.) Assume that on October 13, a check is received by A-1 Plumbing Supplies from Joe's Hardware. The check is for the amount of the sale on October 3 minus the 1 percent discount. To calculate the discount

1. change 1 percent to its decimal equivalent (1% = 0 1. = .01) by moving the decimal point two places to the left:
2. multiply the invoice amount by the decimal equivalent for 1 percent: $5,000 × .01 = $50

The entry in the general journal is as follows.

GENERAL JOURNAL				Page **20**
Date	Description	Post. Ref.	Debit	Credit
19XX Oct. 13	Cash	101	4950 —	
	Sales Discount	430	50 —	
	Accounts Receivable—Joe's Hardware	110/✔		5000 —
	To Record Payment of Invoice 1046, Less 1%			
	Discount			

Accounts Receivable is credited for the full amount of the sale, $5,000, even though the customer remitted only $4,950. If this were not done, the Accounts Receivable account would show a $50 balance still owing, even though the customer had paid in full by taking advantage of the sales discount. The T-accounts after posting has been completed look like this.

General Ledger

Cash   **101**

| 10/1 | Balance | 16,450 | |
| 10/13 | GJ20 | 4,950 | |

Accounts Receivable   **110**

| 10/1 | Balance | 12,900 | 10/13 | GJ20 | 5,000 |

Sales   **401**

| | | | 10/3 | S30 | 5,000 |

Sales Discount   **430**

| 10/13 | GJ20 | 50 | |

Accounts Receivable Subsidiary Ledger

Joe's Hardware

| 10/3 | S30 | 5,000 | 10/13 | GJ20 | 5,000 |

SALES RETURNS AND ALLOWANCES AND SALES DISCOUNTS ON THE INCOME STATEMENT

Both Sales Discounts and Sales Returns and Allowances are contra-revenue accounts and subtract from sales on the income statement. A portion of the income statement for A-1 Plumbing Supplies follows.

A-1 PLUMBING SUPPLIES PARTIAL INCOME STATEMENT FOR MONTH ENDED OCTOBER 31, 19XX			
Revenue			
Sales		$1 2 5 7 0 —	
Less: Sales Returns and Allowances	$75.00		
Sales Discounts	60.00	1 3 5 —	
Net Sales			$1 2 4 3 5 —

Net sales represents gross sales minus all returns, allowances, and discounts.

SUMMARY

A merchandising business sells a product and perhaps a service, too. A retailing business sells small quantities to the final consumer, while a wholesaling business sells in large quantities to the retailers. Once the merchandise is purchased, the merchant must determine the selling price by establishing the markup necessary to cover the cost of the merchandise, the related selling expenses, and the net income the merchant wants to receive.

Sales of merchandise are recorded in a revenue account called Sales. All sales of merchandise on account are recorded in a special sales journal; every entry in the sales journal is a debit to Accounts Receivable and a credit to Sales. At the end of the accounting period, summary posting of the sales journal is performed. Its total is posted as a debit to Accounts Receivable and as a credit to Sales in the general ledger.

The accounts receivable subsidiary ledger records all transactions to individual customers. As a transaction is entered in the sales journal, it is immediately posted as a debit to the customer's account in the accounts receivable subsidiary ledger. At the end of the accounting period, the customers' names and the account balances are listed on a schedule of accounts receivable. The total of all the individual customers' account balances must be the same as the balance in the Accounts Receivable control account in the general ledger. The schedule of accounts receivable is prepared as a self-check.

When a merchant is required to collect sales tax, the sales journal will have several columns to record this special type of transaction. The columns include one for Accounts Receivable (debit), one for Sales (credit), and one for Sales Tax Payable (credit). Each transaction entered in a multi-column sales journal is a debit to Accounts Receivable and must be posted to the accounts receivable subsidiary ledger immediately. At the end of the accounting period, the columns are totaled and crossfooting is performed before the column totals are posted to the general ledger. Sales tax is recorded as a credit to the account Sales Tax Payable. It is a current liability and reflects on the balance sheet.

When a customer returns merchandise, the amount of the return is debited to Sales Returns and Allowances. This account is classified as a contra-revenue account and subtracts from Sales on the income statement. If sales tax is involved in the original sale, then the sales tax must also be returned to the customer.

Often, sellers offer credit terms to encourage buyers to pay early. For example, if the terms are 2/10, n/30, the buyer will be granted a 2 percent discount if he or she pays within 10 days; otherwise, the net amount of the invoice is due within 30 days of the invoice date. If the invoice is paid within the discount period, the discount is deducted by the buyer from the total amount owed. The discount is recorded in an account called Sales Discounts. Sales Discounts is a contra-revenue account and subtracts from sales on the income statement.

For every entry to Accounts Receivable, two postings must be made: one to the general ledger Accounts Receivable control account, and one to the customer's account in the accounts receivable subsidiary ledger. If the entry involving Accounts Receivable is recorded in the general journal, the account number of the Accounts Receivable account is placed in the posting reference column followed by a diagonal line $\boxed{110/}$. When the amount is recorded in the accounts receivable subsidiary ledger, a check mark is placed next to the diagonal line to indicate that posting is complete $\boxed{110/\checkmark}$.

Review of Accounting Terminology

Following is a list of the accounting terminology for this chapter.

consecutively   merchandising business
contra   merchant
control account   retail
credit memorandum   subsidiary
crossfooting   summary posting
markup   wholesale
merchandise

Fill in the blank with the correct word or term from the list.

1. The word _____ means opposing.

2. The sale of goods in small quantities directly to the consumer is referred to as _____ sales.

3. One who operates a store is called a _____.

4. When the seller needs to inform the buyer that his or her Accounts Receivable account is being reduced, the seller will issue a _____.

5. When journal totals are posted rather than individual amounts within the columns, it is called _____.

6. Goods sold in a retail store are called _____.

7. The sale of goods in large quantities to retailers rather than to the final consumer is called _____ sales.

8. The _____ is the amount added to the cost price to determine the selling price.

9. Because the total of the customers' accounts in the accounts receivable subsidiary ledger must equal the balance in the Accounts Receivable account in the general ledger, the Accounts Receivable account is called a/an _____.

10. A/an _____ is a business that sells a product.

11. Proving the equality of the debit and credit column totals of a journal is called _____.

12. Invoices that are numbered in uninterrupted order are said to be _____ numbered.

13. The word _____ means subordinate to or of secondary importance.

Match the following words and terms on the left with the definitions on the right.

14. consecutively	a. one who operates a retail store
15. contra	b. a form issued by the seller indicating that the buyer's Accounts Receivable account is being reduced
16. control account	
17. credit memorandum	
18. crossfooting	
19. markup	c. opposing
20. merchandise	d. in uninterrupted order
21. merchandising business	e. the sale of goods in small quantities to the consumer
22. merchant	f. proving the equality of debit and credit journal column totals
23. retail	
24. subsidiary	
25. summary posting	g. the business that sells in large quantities to retailers
26. wholesale	h. of secondary importance
	i. a business that sells a product
	j. the Accounts Receivable account in the general ledger
	k. the amount added to the cost price to establish selling price
	l. when journal totals are posted
	m. goods for sale

Exercises

Exercise 7.1
finding due dates and the amounts of discounts

In each case, determine the amount of the sales discount and the last day on which the discount may be taken. The months of the year and the number of days in each is included for your reference.

Month	Number of Days	Month	Number of Days
January	31	July	31
February*	28	August	31
March	31	September	30
April	30	October	31
May	31	November	30
June	30	December	31

*February has 29 days in leap years. An easy way to tell whether any particular year is a leap year is to determine if the year is evenly divisible by 4. For example, 1996 is a leap year because 1996 ÷ 4 = 499.

	Invoice Amount	Invoice Date	Terms	Amount of Discount	Last Day to Pay and Receive Discount
a.	$ 1,200	January 26	1/15, n/60	_____	_____
b.	3,780	March 22	2/10, n/30	_____	_____
c.	10,460	June 20	2/15, n/30	_____	_____
d.	475	July 29	1/10, n/60	_____	_____
e.	520	August 30	2/15, n/60	_____	_____
f.	1,650	September 30	2/10, n/30	_____	_____
g.	5,720	November 16	1/15, n/60	_____	_____
h.	15,240	October 19	2/15, n/60	_____	_____

Exercise 7.2

posting the sales journal

Following is the sales journal for The Book Worm for the month of May 19XX. It has been totaled and ruled, but not posted.

a. Post each transaction to the customer's account in the accounts receivable subsidiary ledger and place a check mark in the posting reference column of the journal as you post. Place the posting reference notation S17 in the subsidiary ledger as you post.

b. Post the total of the sales journal to the general ledger as a debit to Accounts Receivable (Account No. 110) and a credit to Sales (Account No. 410). Enter the account numbers in the posting reference column of the sales journal after posting has been completed and enter the posting reference S17 in the general ledger accounts.

SALES JOURNAL						Page *17*
Date	Sales Invoice Number	Customer's Name	Terms	Post. Ref.	Amount	
19XX *May* 1	*1743*	*Luan Ying*	*2/10, n/30*		1400 —	
5	*1744*	*William Reimer*	*2/10, n/30*		1760 —	
7	*1745*	*Katherine Olds*	*2/10, n/30*		2745 —	
15	*1746*	*Marilyn Andrews*	*2/10, n/30*		590 —	
21	*1747*	*Luan Ying*	*2/10, n/30*		3120 —	
29	*1748*	*Katherine Olds*	*2/10, n/30*		1230 —	
31	*1749*	*William Reimer*	*2/10, n/30*		2630 —	
		Total			13475 —	

Exercise 7.3

posting to the general ledger and the accounts receivable ledger from the general journal

On the following page are two general journal entries recording customers' returns of merchandise. Account titles used and balances are as follows.

Account Title—General Ledger	Debit Balance	Credit Balance
115 Accounts Receivable	$2,740.00	
250 Sales Tax Payable		$745.00
430 Sales Returns and Allowances	394.00	

Accounts Receivable Subsidiary Ledger

J. Jackson	$ 540.00
N. Petrovich	284.08

a. Post to the accounts receivable subsidiary ledger for customers Jackson and Petrovich. Place a check mark in the posting reference column of the general journal behind a diagonal line as you post ☐ . Enter GJ49 as the posting reference in the subsidiary ledger.

b. Post to the Accounts Receivable account in the general ledger and enter the account number before the diagonal line as you post ☐ . Enter GJ49 in the general ledger accounts as the posting reference.

c. Post to Sales Returns and Allowances and Sales Tax Payable in the general ledger. Enter the account numbers in the posting reference column of the general journal and enter GJ49 in the posting reference column of the ledger.

GENERAL JOURNAL					Page 49
Date	Description	Post. Ref.	Debit	Credit	
1988 *July* 7	*Sales Returns and Allowances*	430	1 2 0 —		
	Sales Tax Payable	250	7 20		
	Accounts Receivable/J. Jackson	115 ✓		1 2 7 20	
	To Record Return of Item 42-016-D				
9	*Sales Returns and Allowances*	430	2 6 8 —		
	Sales Tax Payable	250	1 6 08		
	Accounts Receivable/N. Petrovich	115 ✓		2 8 4 08	
	To Record Return of Item 46-019-A				

Exercise 7.4
describing what has occurred in T-accounts

Following are T-accounts for Pop's Candy Store with a series of transactions related to the sale on account to one customer. The posting reference CR indicates that a payment on account has been received by Pop's and has been recorded in the cash receipts journal. Briefly describe what has occurred on June 3, June 6, and June 13.

Cash   101

6/13 CR9 106	

Accounts Receivable   110

6/3 S6 159	6/6 GJ8 53
	6/13 CR9 106

Sales Tax Payable   220

6/6 GJ8 3	6/3 S6 9

Sales   **401**

| | 6/3 | S6 | 150 |

Sales Returns and Allowances   405

| 6/6 | GJ8 | 50 | |

Exercise 7.5
*analyzing entries
relating to sales and
sales returns and
allowances*

Following is the sales journal for Clay Pots for November 19XX and the general journal entries relating to Sales Returns and Allowances.

			SALES JOURNAL				Page **14**
Date	Sales Invoice Number		Customer's Name	Terms	Post. Ref.		Amount
19XX Nov.	1	1762	Barbara Boone	2/10, n/30	✔		1 4 0 —
	3	1763	Buster Jayne	2/10, n/30	✔		7 5 —
	8	1764	Jana Trickle	2/10, n/30	✔		8 0 —
	10	1765	Barbara Boone	2/10, n/30	✔		1 8 5 —
	15	1766	Bud Marengo	2/10, n/30	✔		5 0 —
	18	1767	John Stamas	2/10, n/30	✔		2 7 5 —
	25	1768	Jana Trickle	2/10, n/30	✔		9 4 —
	30	1769	Barbara Boone	2/10, n/30	✔		4 2 0 —
			Total				1 3 1 9 —

		GENERAL JOURNAL				Page **9**
Date		Description	Post. Ref.	Debit		Credit
19XX Nov.	5	Sales Returns and Allowances	405	4 0 —		
		Accounts Receivable—Barbara Boone	110/✔			4 0 —
		To Record Return of Merchandise				
	10	Sales Returns and Allowances	405	3 0 —		
		Accounts Receivable—Jana Trickle	110/✔			3 0 —
		To Record Return of Merchandise				

a. Where will the total of the sales journal be posted?
b. Including both the sales and general journals, how many separate postings must be made to the accounts receivable subsidiary ledger? To the Accounts Receivable control account in the general ledger?
c. If Barbara Boone sends a check to Clay Pots on November 11 to cover her total purchases up until that date, how much should she remit?
d. If Jana Trickle sends a check to Clay Pots on November 23, how much should she remit?
e. What is the last day on which Bud Marengo may pay and still receive the discount? How much will be due on that date?
f. What is the last day on which Barbara Boone may pay and still receive the discount for her November 30 purchase? How much will be due on that date?

Exercise 7.6
calculating net sales

Pete Agnos owns a retail men's clothing store called Man's Choice. Pete's total sales for October 19XX were $28,700. Sales returns and allowances were 1 percent of gross sales and sales discounts were 2 percent of the credit sales, which were $12,700. Prepare the revenue section of the income statement for Man's Choice for the month of October 19XX.

Exercise 7.7
preparing schedule of accounts receivable

Following is the accounts receivable subsidiary ledger for Marie's Auto Parts. Calculate the balance after each transaction and prepare a schedule of accounts receivable on March 31, 19XX. The balance in the Accounts Receivable control account on March 31 is $1,480. CR in the posting reference column indicates that a payment on account has been recorded in the cash receipts journal.

ACCOUNTS RECEIVABLE SUBSIDIARY LEDGER

BUG REPAIR SHOP

Date	Explanation	PR	Debit	Credit	Balance
19XX *Mar.* 1		S3	8 7 0 —		
11		CR4		4 0 0 —	
15		S4	5 5 0 —		
19		GJ5		1 5 0 —	

FOREIGN AUTO REPAIR

Date	Explanation	PR	Debit	Credit	Balance
19XX Mar. 12		S4	6 5 —		
14		S4	1 7 0 —		
15		GJ5		4 0 —	

JOANNA GRIMM

Date	Explanation	PR	Debit	Credit	Balance
19XX Mar. 15		S4	3 7 5 —		
25		CR4		3 7 5 —	
28		S4	4 2 5 —		
31		GJ6		1 2 5 —	

KURT ZANDER

Date	Explanation	PR	Debit	Credit	Balance
19XX Mar. 20		S4	2 0 6 —		
24		S4	1 1 5 —		
25		S4	6 5 —		
26		GJ6		6 5 —	
30		CR4		2 0 6 —	

Exercise 7.8

journalizing and posting sales with sales tax, return, and subsequent payment

Claudia Shayne owns a retail shop called Pick-A-Wick; she sells unusual candles. Sales tax is 5 percent. Record the following sales on account in the sales journal (page 12) and the returns and payments received in the general journal (page 24). Credit terms are n/30. After journalizing, total, crossfoot, and rule the sales journal. Use check marks and account numbers to show how the sales journal and general journal would appear if they had been posted. Use the following account titles and numbers: Cash, 101; Accounts Receivable, 110; Sales Tax Payable, 210; Sales, 405; and Sales Returns and Allowances, 410.

Dec. 5   sold ten candles to Roger Merino on account; $215 plus 5 percent sales tax; invoice 16432

Dec. 6   issued credit memorandum 203 to Roger Merino, who returned two candles priced at $15 each plus sales tax

Dec. 7   sold five candles to Henry Winklebean on account; $96 plus sales tax; invoice 16433

Dec. 10   sold four candles to Patsy Browne on account; $65 plus sales tax; invoice 16434

Dec. 26   received payment in full from Roger Merino for the balance owed on invoice 16432 less the December 6 return

Exercise 7.9
journalizing and posting sale, return, and payment within the discount period

Lee Kawasaki owns a wholesale waterbed store. He sells to retailers and offers credit terms of 2/10, n/30. No sales tax is collected. Record the following sale in the sales journal (page 16) and record the return and the receipt of payment in the general journal (page 55). Use check marks and account numbers to show how the entries would look if posting were done. It is not necessary to total the sales journal. Use the following account titles and numbers: Cash, 101; Accounts Receivable, 110; Sales, 401; Sales Returns and Allowances, 405; and Sales Discount, 410.

Apr. 2   sold $4,000 worth of merchandise on account to Waterbeds Galore; terms 2/10, n/30; invoice 2111-40

Apr. 4   issued credit memorandum 40-32 for $75 to Waterbeds Galore because three frames from the April 2 purchase were damaged in shipment

Apr. 12   received a check from Waterbeds Galore for the total amount owed minus the April 4 return and the discount

Problems

Problem 7.1
posting from the sales journal and the general journal

Following are the sales journal and the general journal for the month of January for Photo Supplies.

Sales Journal for Problem 7.1

		SALES JOURNAL			Page 10	
Date	Sales Invoice Number	Customer's Name	Terms	Post. Ref.	Amount	
19XX Jan. 2	3650	Pete Jones	2/10, n/30		2500	—
5	3651	Wanda Lander	2/10, n/30		1200	—
9	3652	Hans Zander	2/10, n/30		3960	—
22	3653	Pete Jones	2/10, n/30		1675	—
23	3654	Bill Greene	2/10, n/30		500	—
28	3655	Nancy Christensen	2/10, n/30		4720	—
31	3656	Wanda Lander	2/10, n/30		740	—

General Journal for Problem 7.1

		GENERAL JOURNAL			Page 31	
Date		Description	Post. Ref.	Debit	Credit	
19XX Jan. 3		Sales Returns and Allowances		400 —		
		Accounts Receivable—Jones			400	—
		Credit Memo; Invoice 3650				
	11	Cash		2058 —		
		Sales Discounts		42 —		
		Accounts Receivable—Jones			2100	—
		Payment in Full; Invoice 3650				
	11	Sales Returns and Allowances		720 —		
		Accounts Receivable—Zander			720	—
		Credit Memo; Invoice 3652				
	15	Cash		1176 —		
		Sales Discounts		24 —		
		Accounts Receivable—Lander			1200	—
		Payment in Full; Invoice 3651				
	30	Cash		1500 —		
		Accounts Receivable—Andrews			1500	—
		Partial Payment; Invoice 3615				

Instructions

1. *Enter the following accounts and balances in the general ledger.*

101	Cash	$7,640
110	Accounts Receivable	6,800
400	Sales	0
410	Sales Returns and Allowances	0
415	Sales Discounts	0

2. *Enter the following names and account balances in the accounts receivable subsidiary ledger.*

William Andrews	$2,750
Nancy Christensen	0
Bill Greene	0
Pete Jones	0
Wanda Lander	0
Katherine Munro	1,975
Allen Potsdorf	1,075
Hans Zander	1,000

3. *Post to the accounts receivable subsidiary ledger from the sales journal and from the general journal chronologically. Place a check mark in the posting reference column of the sales journal as you post, and place S10 in the subsidiary ledger accounts. In the general journal, place a diagonal line followed by a check mark as you post and place GJ31 in the subsidiary ledger accounts.*

4. *Post to the general ledger from the general journal chronologically. Enter the account numbers in the general journal as you post and enter GJ31 in the ledger accounts.*

5. *Total and rule the sales journal.*

6. *Post the total of the sales journal as a debit to Accounts Receivable and a credit to Sales in the general ledger. Enter the account numbers in the posting reference column of the journal and enter S10 in the ledger accounts.*

7. *Prepare a schedule of accounts receivable and compare its total with the balance in the Accounts Receivable control account.*

Problem 7.2

journalizing and posting sales and returns

Roxanne Simas owns a feed store called R & S Feed and Supplies. Roxanne sells to ranchers and is not required to collect sales tax. Following are the transactions relating to credit sales for March 19XX.

Mar. 1 sold alfalfa to Bar-D Ranch; $800; invoice 1660

Mar. 3 sold grain to Sleepy River Ranch; $180; invoice 1661

Mar. 5 sold supplies to Oak Hill Ranch; $570; invoice 1662

Mar. 7 sold supplies to Sleepy River Ranch; $270; invoice 1663

Mar. 8 issued credit memorandum 420-D to Oak Hill Ranch for supplies returned; $150

Mar. 11 sold supplies to Bar-D Ranch; $950; invoice 1664

Mar. 15 issued credit memorandum 421-D to Bar-D Ranch for supplies returned; $200

Mar. 20 sold hay to Angus Acres; $1,500; invoice 1665

Mar. 24 sold salt blocks to Sleepy River Ranch; $120; invoice 1666.

Mar. 25 issued credit memorandum 422-D to Sleepy River Ranch for merchandise returned; $60

Mar. 29 sold grain to Angus Acres; $550; invoice 1667

Instructions

1. *Enter the following account titles, numbers, and March balances into the general ledger and the accounts receivable subsidiary ledger.*

	General Ledger		Accounts Receivable Subsidiary Ledger	
110	Accounts Receivable	$1,005	Angus Acres	$250
400	Sales	0	Bar-D Ranch	175
410	Sales Returns and Allowances	0	Oak Hill Ranch	460
			Sleepy River Ranch	120

2. *Use page 3 for the sales journal and page 7 for the general journal.*

3. *Assuming that the terms of sales are net 30, record sales on account in the sales journal and record sales returns and allowances in the general journal.*

4. *Post to the accounts receivable subsidiary ledger immediately after each transaction. Enter S3 or GJ7 in the posting reference column of the subsidiary ledger accounts and place a check mark in the posting reference column of the sales journal or the general journal after posting.*

5. *Post to the general ledger from the general journal immediately after journalizing. Enter the account numbers in the posting reference column of the journal and enter GJ7 in the ledger accounts.*

6. *After carefully checking the addition, total and rule the sales journal.*

7. *Post the total of the sales journal as a debit to Accounts Receivable and a credit to Sales in the general ledger. Enter the account numbers in the posting reference column of the journal and enter S3 in the ledger accounts.*

8. *Prepare a schedule of accounts receivable as of March 31 and compare its total with the balance in the Accounts Receivable control account.*

Problem 7.3

journalizing and posting sales with sales tax, returns, and payments on account

The transactions relating to credit sales for August 19XX for Wanda's Beauty Supplies follow. Wanda is a retailer who sells directly to consumers and is required to collect 4 percent sales tax on all sales.

Aug. 1   sold supplies to Andy Johnson; $50 plus 4 percent sales tax; invoice 4302 $52

Aug. 4   sold supplies to Georgia Keene; $125 plus 4 percent sales tax; invoice 4303   130

Aug. 6   sold supplies to Byron Metzinger; $75 plus 4 percent sales tax; invoice 4304   78

Aug. 8   issued credit memorandum 16032-A to Georgia Keene for supplies returned; $30 plus 4 percent sales tax   31.2

Aug. 10   sold supplies to Andy Johnson; $30 plus 4 percent sales tax; invoice 4305   31.20

Aug. 14   sold supplies to Joe Nagasaki; $220 plus 4 percent sales tax; invoice 4306   228.80

Aug. 18   issued credit memorandum 16033-A to Byron Metzinger for damaged merchandise; $10 plus 4 percent sales tax   10.40

Aug. 22   sold supplies to Andy Johnson; $40 plus 4 percent sales tax; invoice 4307   41.60

Aug. 24   issued credit memorandum 16034-A to Joe Nagasaki; $20 plus 4 percent sales tax

Aug. 26   sold supplies to Byron Metzinger; $75 plus 4 percent sales tax; invoice 4308

Aug. 29   sold supplies to Georgia Keene; $165 plus 4 percent sales tax; invoice 4309

Aug. 30   issued credit memorandum 16035-A to Georgia Keene for merchandise returned; $50 plus 4 percent sales tax

Instructions   *1. Enter the following account titles, numbers, and August 1 balances into the general ledger and the accounts receivable subsidiary ledger.*

	General Ledger		Accounts Receivable Subsidiary Ledger	
110	Accounts Receivable	$500	Andy Johnson	$125
210	Sales Tax Payable	120	Georgia Keene	80
410	Sales	0	Byron Metzinger	240
420	Sales Returns and Allowances	0	Joe Nagasaki	55

2. Use page 8 for the sales journal and page 14 for the general journal.

3. Assuming that terms of sale are net 30, record sales plus 4 percent sales tax in the multi-column sales journal and record sales returns in the general journal.

4. Post to the accounts receivable ledger immediately after each transaction. Enter S8 or GJ14 in the posting reference column of the subsidiary ledger accounts and place a check mark in the posting reference column of the sales journal or the general journal after posting.

5. Post to the general ledger from the general journal immediately after journalizing. Enter the account numbers in the posting reference column of the journal and enter GJ14 in the ledger accounts.

6. Total, crossfoot, and rule the sales journal.

7. Post the totals of the sales journal. Enter the account numbers in parentheses beneath the column totals and enter S8 in the posting reference column of the ledger accounts.

8. Prepare a schedule of accounts receivable as of August 31 and compare its total with the balance in the Accounts Receivable control account.

Problem 7.4
journalizing and posting sales with credit terms, returns, and payments on account

Wiley Manual owns a wholesale furniture warehouse called Wooden Legs. No sales tax is charged his customers. The following transactions relating to credit sales took place during the month of May 19XX. Be sure to read through all the instructions before beginning the problem.

May 1   sold merchandise on account to Mack's Bar Stools; $3,000; terms 2/10, n/30; invoice 2000

May 4   sold merchandise on account to Kitchen Korner; $4,500; terms 2/10, n/30; invoice 2001

May 6   issued credit memorandum 14-280 to grant a $200 allowance to Mack's Bar Stools on the May 1 purchase because of damage to several stools

May 10 received a check from Mack's Bar Stools for the balance owed on May 1 purchase less the return on May 6

May 15 sold merchandise on account to House of Maple; $970; terms 2/10, n/30; invoice 2002

May 16 received a check from Kitchen Korner for the balance owed on its May 4 purchase

May 19 sold merchandise on account to Mack's Bar Stools; $1,500; terms 2/10, n/30; invoice 2003

May 22 issued credit memorandum 14-281 to House of Maple; it returned $200 of its May 15 purchase

May 24 sold merchandise on account to Chairs, Inc.; $1,050; terms 2/10, n/30; invoice 2004

May 25 received a check from House of Maple for payment of the balance owed on May 15 invoice less the return on May 22

May 27 sold merchandise on account to Chairs, Inc.; $500; terms 2/10, n/30; invoice 2005

May 30 sold merchandise on account to House of Maple; $700; terms 2/10, n/30; invoice 2006

Instructions   *1. Enter the following account titles and balances into the general ledger and the accounts receivable subsidiary ledger.*

	General Ledger		**Accounts Receivable Subsidiary Ledger**	
101	Cash	$4,620	Chairs, Inc.	$1,760
110	Accounts Receivable	9,170	Discount Furniture	2,650
401	Sales	0	House of Maple	2,170
406	Sales Discounts	0	Kitchen Korner	1,890
411	Sales Returns and Allowances	0	Leather Products	700
			Mack's Bar Stools	0

2. *Use page 5 for the sales journal and page 11 for the general journal.*

3. *Record sales on account in the sales journal and record sales returns and allowances, receipts of cash, and sales discounts in the general journal. (Later, you will record all incoming cash in the cash receipts journal.)*

4. *Post to the accounts receivable subsidiary ledger immediately after each transaction. Enter S5 or GJ11 in the posting reference column of the subsidiary ledger accounts and place a check mark in the posting reference column of the sales journal or the general journal after posting.*

5. *Post to the general ledger from the general journal immediately after journalizing. Enter the account numbers in the posting reference column of the journal and enter GJ14 in the ledger accounts.*

6. *Total, crossfoot, and rule the sales journal.*

7. *Post the totals of the sales journal. Enter the account numbers in parentheses beneath the column totals and enter S5 or GJ11 in the posting reference column of the ledger accounts.*

8. *Prepare a schedule of accounts receivable as of May 31 and compare its total with the balance in the Accounts Receivable control account.*

Problem 7.5
journalizing and posting sales with credit terms, returns, and payment on account

Following are the transactions for Super Shirts, a wholesale shirt and sweater store, relating to credit sales for the month of November 19XX. No sales tax is collected by Super Shirts. Credit terms for all customers are 3/10, n/30.

Nov. 1   sold merchandise to College Town; $1,250; invoice 3301
Nov. 3   sold merchandise to Shirt Shack; $1,560; invoice 3302

Nov. 5   sold merchandise to Sweaters Exclusively; $1,650; invoice 3303

Nov. 9   issued credit memorandum 4062-A to Shirt Shack for damaged merchandise; $230

Nov. 10   received a check from College Town for payment of its November 1 invoice

Nov. 13   received a check from Shirt Shack in payment of its November 3 invoice less the November 9 return

Nov. 14   received a check from Sweaters Exclusively in full payment of the balance owed on November 1

Nov. 15   sold merchandise to Roy's Apparel; $950; invoice 3304

Nov. 18   sold merchandise to College Town; $805; invoice 3305

Nov. 20   sold merchandise to Sweaters Exclusively; $450; invoice 3306

Nov. 22   received a check from Sweaters Exclusively in payment of its November 5 invoice

Nov. 24   issued credit memorandum 4063-A to Roy's Apparel for merchandise returned; $200

Nov. 25   received a check from Roy's Apparel in payment of its November 15 invoice less the return of November 24

Nov. 27   issued credit memorandum 4064-A to Sweaters Exclusively for damaged merchandise; $50

Nov. 29   sold merchandise to Shirt Shack; $740; invoice 3307

Nov. 30   received a check from Sweaters Exclusively in payment of its November 20 invoice less the return of November 27

Instructions   *1. Enter the following account titles and balances into the general ledger and the accounts receivable subsidiary ledger.*

	General Ledger		**Accounts Receivable Subsidiary Ledger**	
101	Cash	$3,740	College Town	0
110	Accounts Receivable	8,150	John's Jeans	$ 870
401	Sales	0	Roy's Apparel	1,950
405	Sales Discounts	0	Shirt Shack	1,760
410	Sales Returns and Allowances	0	Sweaters Exclusively	720
			Woolen Wear	2,850

2. Use page 11 for the sales journal and page 26 for the general journal.

3. Record sales on account in the sales journal and record sales returns and allowances in the general journal. Record receipt of cash and sales discounts in the general journal. (Later, you will record all incoming cash in the cash receipts journal.)

4. Post to the accounts receivable subsidiary ledger immediately after each transaction.

5. Post to the general ledger from the general journal immediately after journalizing.

6. After carefully checking the addition, total and rule the sales journal.

7. Post the total of the sales journal.

8. Prepare a schedule of accounts receivable.

CHAPTER 8

The Purchases Journal and the Accounts Payable Subsidiary Ledger

LEARNING OBJECTIVES

When you have completed this chapter, you should

1. have a better understanding of accounting terminology.

2. be able to record entries directly into the purchases journal and perform summary posting.

3. be able to post to the accounts payable subsidiary ledger and prepare a schedule of accounts payable.

4. be able to account for freight charges.

5. be able to account for purchases returns and allowances.

6. be able to calculate and account for purchases discounts.

7. be able to calculate trade discounts.

8. recognize several different forms of credit terms.

A business that sells a product must first buy the merchandise and determine the markup before offering it for sale. While the preceding chapter dealt with the sales of merchandise, this chapter will deal with the purchasing of merchandise for resale and the special accounting procedures involved with purchases.

PURCHASES AND THE PURCHASE INVOICE

In a small firm, a purchase order may be made directly and simply. Often, the sales representative will obtain an order from the owner or manager when he or she makes a sales call. A purchase order may also be placed by phone. When the merchandise is delivered, the buyer should check the goods received against the seller's invoice.

purchase requisition
a form made out by a department requesting the purchasing department to prepare a formal purchase order

Large firms use a more formal approach to purchasing. A **purchase requisition** is prepared with multiple copies; one of the copies is sent to the purchasing department, and one is kept by the department issuing the request. No accounting entry is made at this time. When the proper authority in the purchasing department approves the requisition, a formal **purchase order** is prepared. Purchase orders are numbered consecutively and are carefully accounted for. Multiple copies are usually prepared: one copy is retained by the purchasing department, one copy goes to the supplier, one copy goes to the department that originated the order, and one copy goes to the receiving clerk. When the merchandise is received, the receiving clerk will check the actual sales invoice from the vendor against the purchase order to make sure everything ordered was actually delivered and to verify that the terms on the sales invoice are the same as those originally agreed on. Copies of purchase orders should be sent to the accounting department, too, so that invoice calculations may be verified and prices may be checked against the sales invoice.

purchase order
a form prepared by the purchasing department that gives written authorization to buy merchandise

purchase invoice
the invoice that is received when ordered goods are shipped to the buyer; from the seller's viewpoint, it is a sales invoice and is prepared by the seller

When the sales invoice arrives, either with the merchandise ordered or before it, a copy of the invoice is sent to the accounting department to be recorded. From the point of view of the buyer, the sales invoice received from the vendor is a **purchase invoice.** At this point the accountant will record the purchase of merchandise. Following is the purchase invoice that arrived with the shipment when Frank Phelps ordered skis and bindings from Cold Weather Sports, Inc.

Cold Weather Sports, Inc.			Invoice No. 5307
1421 First Avenue Boston, MA 02109 (617) 555-1300	Invoice Date	Order No.	Order Date
	June 4	*608*	*June 1*

Terms	FOB	Shipped via:	Shipped from:
2/15, n/30	*Destination*	*Spartan Delivery*	*Boston*

Sold to:	Ship to:
Sports Haven 740 Main Street Des Moines, IA 50265	*Same*

Quantity Shipped	Description	Unit Price	Extension
6	*Tuf-Lite, 170 mm, Skis, # S46130*	*85.00*	*510.00*
10	*Tuf-Lite, 190 mm, Skis, # S46132*	*85.00*	*850.00*
8	*Ski-Rite, 150 mm, Skis, # Q04329*	*50.00*	*400.00*
20	*Eazy-On Bindings, # J46523*	*40.00*	*800.00*
			2,560.00

When this shipment arrives from Cold Weather Sports, Inc., the person receiving the goods should check to make sure that everything that appears on the invoice is included with the shipment. The receiving clerk will be asked to sign the invoice indicating that the goods are in satisfactory condition and that they are all there. If a careful check is not made at this point, it may be discovered too late that a portion of the shipment is missing or that some items have been damaged **in transit.**

in transit
in the process of being moved from one place to another

THE PURCHASES ACCOUNT

All merchandise that is purchased for resale is debited to an account called Purchases; it is assigned a number in a new category, Cost of Goods Sold. Cost of Goods Sold accounts are used on the income statement for calculating the actual cost of the merchandise that is sold. Cost of goods sold will be discussed in detail in a later chapter.

Assume that Sports Haven recorded the credit purchase of ski equipment from Cold Weather Sports, Inc. The T-accounts would look like this after posting.

Purchases	511	Accounts Payable	215
6/8 P6 2,560			6/8 P6 2,560

The Purchases account is debited only for the purchase of merchandise for resale. When merchandise is purchased that is *not* for resale, it is debited to its appropriate asset account. For example, assume that Frank purchased a small computer on account for use by his bookkeeper. The entry would be a debit to Office Equipment and a credit to Accounts Payable and would be recorded in the general journal.

MERCHANDISE INVENTORY

The Purchases account is debited for all merchandise purchased for resale, but it is not credited when merchandise is sold. Therefore, at the end of the accounting period, the balance in the Purchases account represents all the merchandise purchased for resale during the period. The actual value of merchandise on hand is determined at the end of the accounting period by estimating or by physically counting it.

periodic inventory
the counting and pricing of merchandise on hand at regular intervals

A **periodic inventory** is when the value of the merchandise on hand is determined by an actual count at regular intervals. There are two steps involved when counting the merchandise on hand: (1) the quantity of merchandise on hand must be determined and (2) the cost of each item must be multiplied by the quantity on hand. The first step is called taking the inventory, and the second step is called pricing the inventory. Electronic cash registers used in many stores keep track of merchandise sold and prepare inventory reports. However, even with the use of computers, a physical count of the merchandise on hand must be made periodically; the cash registers do not record theft or damaged merchandise.

Once the value of the merchandise on hand is determined, it is entered directly onto the worksheet. From there, it is transferred during the closing process to an account called Merchandise Inventory. No transactions are recorded in the Merchandise Inventory account except those that record the value of the ending inventory and remove the value of the beginning inventory each accounting period. Specific instructions for doing this will be given in a later chapter. Merchandise Inventory is a current asset and appears on the balance sheet.

THE PURCHASES JOURNAL

Sports Haven uses special journals to record sales, purchases, cash receipts, and cash payments. All credit purchases of merchandise for resale are recorded in the purchases journal. Each entry in the purchases journal is a debit to Purchases and a credit to Accounts Payable, but as with the sales journal, the words *Purchases* and *Accounts Payable* do not have to be written each time. Only the date, the supplier's name, the invoice number and date, the terms, and the amount need to be entered. This saves a great deal of time in both journalizing and posting. Following is the purchases journal for Sports Haven for the month of June 19XX.

PURCHASES JOURNAL						Page **6**
Date	Supplier's Name	Invoice Number	Invoice Date	Terms	Post. Ref.	Amount
19XX June 8	Cold Weather Sports, Inc.	5307	June 4	2/10, n/30		2 5 6 0 —
10	Running World	1042	June 8	1/10, n/30		5 7 4 —
12	Racquet Warehouse	879	June 10	1/10, n/60		7 4 0 —
16	Running World	1078	June 14	1/10, n/30		7 6 0 —
20	Sports Supplies	7061	June 19	n/EOM		1 4 0 9 —
25	Cold Weather Sports, Inc.	5390	June 21	2/10, n/30		9 6 2 —
30	Running World	1091	June 28	1/10, n/30		4 1 6 —
	Total					7 4 2 1 —

Because a single-column journal has no self-check, the column should be added at least twice. When the total is determined, a single line is placed across the amount column beneath the last figure in that column, the column is totaled, and a double rule is drawn beneath the total across all columns of the journal except the supplier's name column.

THE ACCOUNTS PAYABLE SUBSIDIARY LEDGER

The Accounts Payable account in the general ledger shows the total owed to all creditors, while the accounts payable subsidiary ledger shows the amounts owed to individuals. Accounts for individual creditors are kept alphabetically, and all charge purchases, purchases returns and allowances, and payments made to creditors appear in the accounts payable subsidiary ledger. The Accounts Payable account in the general ledger is, like Accounts Receivable, a control account, because its balance represents the *total* amount owed to all creditors, and the total of the individual creditors' balances must equal the balance in the control account.

The accounts payable subsidiary ledger is a supplement to the general ledger; it provides specific information that the general ledger does not have. Study the following account for Runners' Warehouse in the accounts payable subsidiary ledger of Sports Supply House.

RUNNER'S WAREHOUSE

Date		Explanation	PR	Debit	Credit	Balance
19XX Aug.	1		P9		500 —	500 —
	2		GJ20	100 —		400 —
	10		CP14	400 —		0 —
	24		P9		1000 —	1000 —

The three ledgers that will be used from now on are:

1. The general ledger, which contains separate records for all assets, liabilities, owner's equity, revenue, cost of goods sold, and expense accounts.

2. The accounts receivable subsidiary ledger, which contains individual accounts for all charge customers, showing all credit sales made to them, their sales returns and allowances, and all payments received.

3. The accounts payable subsidiary ledger, which contains individual accounts for all creditors, showing all credit purchases, purchases returns and allowances, and all payments made. The accounts receivable and accounts payable subsidiary ledgers are frequently referred to as simply the accounts receivable ledger and the accounts payable ledger.

POSTING THE SINGLE-COLUMN PURCHASES JOURNAL

Each time a transaction is recorded in the purchases journal, it is a debit to Purchases and a credit to Accounts Payable. Immediately after each journal entry, the credit amount must be posted to the accounts payable subsidiary ledger. Simply locate the creditor's name in the subsidiary ledger, post the amount as a credit to the account, calculate the new account balance, enter the posting reference P and the page number in the ledger, and place a check mark in the posting reference column of the purchases journal. This procedure must be repeated for every transaction entered in the purchases journal.

At the end of the accounting period, summary posting is performed as the total of the purchases journal is posted to the general ledger as a debit to Purchases and a credit to Accounts Payable. Enter P and the journal page number in the general ledger accounts and enter the account numbers for Purchases and Accounts Payable in the posting reference column of the purchases journal.

Postings to the accounts payable subsidiary ledger come primarily from the purchases journal, where the purchase is recorded; from the general journal, where returns are recorded; and from the cash payments journal, where payments on account are recorded. The purchases journal, the general ledger accounts affected, and the accounts payable subsidiary ledger (arranged in alphabetical order) for Sports Haven follow.

PURCHASES JOURNAL						Page 6
Date	Supplier's Name	Invoice Number	Invoice Date	Terms	Post. Ref.	Amount
June 8	Cold Weather Sports, Inc.	5307	June 4	2/10, n/30	✔	2 5 6 0 —
10	Running World	1042	June 8	1/10, n/30	✔	5 7 4 —
12	Racquet Warehouse	879	June 10	1/10, n/60	✔	7 4 0 —
16	Running World	1078	June 14	1/10, n/30	✔	7 6 0 —
20	Sports Supplies	7061	June 19	n/EOM	✔	1 4 0 9 —
25	Cold Weather Sports, Inc.	5390	June 21	2/10, n/30	✔	9 6 2 —
30	Running World	1091	June 28	1/10, n/30	✔	4 1 6 —
	Total				511/205	7 4 2 1 —

General Ledger

Accounts Payable   205

		6/30	P6	7,421

Purchases   511

6/30	P6	7,421		

Accounts Payable Ledger

Cold Weather Sports, Inc.

		6/8	P6	2,560
		6/25	P6	962

Racquet Warehouse

		6/12	P6	740

Running World

		6/10	P6	574
		6/16	P6	760
		6/30	P6	416

Sports Supplies

		6/20	P6	1,409

THE SCHEDULE OF ACCOUNTS PAYABLE

A schedule of accounts payable is prepared at the end of the accounting period listing alphabetically each creditor and the amount owed. When the total of the schedule of accounts payable is compared with the balance in the Accounts Payable control account, the two figures must be the same; if they are not, the bookkeeper must search for the error.

The accounts payable ledger, the schedule of accounts payable, and the Accounts Payable control account for Sports Haven follow. The accounts show only credit entries, even though normally they would have debit entries, too. Payments on account and returns are omitted here for simplicity.

ACCOUNTS PAYABLE LEDGER

COLD WEATHER SPORTS, INC.

Date	Explanation	PR	Debit	Credit	Balance
19XX June 8		P6		2 5 6 0 —	2 5 6 0 —
25		P6		9 6 2 —	3 5 2 2 —

RACQUET WAREHOUSE

Date	Explanation	PR	Debit	Credit	Balance
19XX June 12		P6		7 4 0 —	7 4 0 —

RUNNING WORLD

Date	Explanation	PR	Debit	Credit	Balance
19XX June 10		P6		5 7 4 —	5 7 4 —
16		P6		7 6 0 —	1 3 3 4 —
30		P6		4 1 6 —	1 7 5 0 —

SPORTS SUPPLIES

Date	Explanation	PR	Debit	Credit	Balance
_19XX_ June 20		P6		1 4 0 9 —	1 4 0 9 —

SPORTS HAVEN **SCHEDULE OF ACCOUNTS PAYABLE** **JUNE 30, 19XX**			
Cold Weather Sports, Inc.		$ 3 5 2 2 —	
Racquet Warehouse		7 4 0 —	
Running World		1 7 5 0 —	
Sports Supplies		1 4 0 9 —	
Total			$ 7 4 2 1 —

GENERAL LEDGER

ACCOUNTS PAYABLE   Acct. No. **205**

Date	Explanation	PR	Debit	Credit	Balance
_19XX_ June 30		P6		7 4 2 1 —	7 4 2 1 —

THE FREIGHT IN ACCOUNT

Often, freight charges are incurred when merchandise is purchased. Such charges are considered to be an added cost of the merchandise purchased, because the buyer usually pays the freight charges, either directly or indirectly through higher prices for the merchandise purchased. For this reason, an account called Freight In is debited for freight costs. Although the cost of freight could be debited directly to the Purchases account, most businesses prefer to keep freight costs separate. Knowing exactly how much is spent for various methods of transporting goods is essential to management in controlling costs. Decisions have to be made concerning which type of transportation to use, such as air, truck, or rail. Keeping careful accounting records of freight costs provides invaluable information necessary for making those decisions.

The T-accounts reflecting Sports Haven's transportation charge on the shipment of skis and bindings from Boston are as follows.

Freight In	411	Cash	110
6/8 CP10 175			6/8 CP10 175

The Freight In account is a cost of goods sold account, and its balance will be added to the balance of Purchases on the income statement as follows.

Purchases	$7,421
Freight In	+ 175
Delivered Cost of Purchases	$7,596

FOB SHIPPING POINT AND FOB DESTINATION

FOB shipping point
free on board to the shipping point; the seller will pay for the cost of loading the goods at the shipping point, where title of the goods passes to the buyer; buyer will pay freight charges

FOB destination
free on board to the destination; the seller will pay the freight charges to the destination of the goods, where title then passes to the buyer

Before goods are shipped, an agreement must be made between buyer and seller as to which party will pay the freight charges. The seller's invoice will stipulate either *FOB shipping point* or *FOB destination*. **FOB shipping point** means free on board to the shipping point, or that the seller will pay to have the goods loaded at the point of shipment, but will not pay the transportation costs from the shipping point to the destination. Title to the goods passes to the buyer at the shipping point, and the buyer will pay the freight charges on arrival of the merchandise. **FOB destination** means free on board to the destination agreed on, and the seller will pay the freight charges. Title to the goods passes to the buyer when the goods arrive.

DEBIT AND CREDIT MEMORANDA

When damaged or unsatisfactory merchandise is returned, or when the buyer is given an allowance for such, the buyer will issue a

**debit
memorandum**
a document issued by
the buyer indicating
that the buyer's Ac-
counts Payable ac-
count is being
reduced because of a
return of merchandise
or an allowance

debit memorandum to the seller indicating that the buyer's Accounts Payable account has been debited or reduced. When the bookkeeper receives the debit memorandum, she or he records it by crediting an account called Purchases Returns and Allowances and debiting Accounts Payable. This same transaction on the books of the seller would be recorded as a debit to Sales Returns and Allowances and as a credit to Accounts Receivable. If the seller (instead of the buyer) had issued the memo, it would have been called a credit memorandum, because on the books of the seller, a credit to Accounts Receivable is being recorded.

PURCHASES RETURNS AND ALLOWANCES

Although simply crediting the Purchases account for returns and allowances is possible, keeping a separate record of them is good accounting practice. Management can use this information to make decisions about which merchandise to buy in the future or which vendor to contact for a particular product. An excessive number of returns of any one product or to any one vendor may indicate that the purchasing policy needs to be revised.

Assume that on June 9, Frank Phelps, owner of Sports Haven, contacted the manager of Cold Weather Sports in Boston by telephone to tell him that the Eazy-On Bindings sent were factory damaged and had to be adjusted before they could be used. The manager of Cold Weather Sports suggested that if Frank would keep the bindings and make the necessary adjustments, he would give Sports Haven a $10 allowance on each binding ordered. Frank agreed, and a $200 debit memorandum was issued by Sports Haven on June 9. The general journal entry for Sports Haven's recording of the allowance follows.

GENERAL JOURNAL				Page **6**	
Date	Description	Post. Ref.	Debit	Credit	
19XX *June* **9**	*Accounts Payable—Cold Weather Sports, Inc.*	205/✓	2 0 0 —		
	Purchases Returns and Allowances	512		2 0 0 —	
	To Record Debit Memorandum, Invoice 5307				

The debit to Accounts Payable must be posted to both the general ledger and Cold Weather Sports' account in the accounts payable subsidiary ledger.

The Purchases Returns and Allowances account appears in the cost of goods sold category on the chart of accounts along with purchases. Purchases Returns and Allowances is a contra-purchases account, because its balance subtracts from the balance of purchases on the income statement.

PURCHASES DISCOUNTS

The buyer is often granted a discount if the invoice is paid within a certain number of days. The terms indicated on invoice 5307 from Cold Weather Sports, Inc., are 2/15, n/30. If Sports Haven pays within 15 days of the invoice date, a 2 percent discount may be deducted from the total invoice price. Remember that Sports Haven received a $200 allowance for damaged merchandise on invoice 5307. The procedure for calculating the amount due if paid within the discount period is as follows.

1. Calculate the last day for payment within the discount period. Terms are 2/15, n/30 and the invoice date is June 4.

June 4	
+15	(2/15, n/30)
June 19	(last day for payment within discount period)

2. Calculate the balance owed on the invoice.

June 8 (original purchase)	$2,560.00
June 9 (purchase allowance)	− 200.00
June 19 (balance owed)	$2,360.00

3. Calculate the cash discount.
   a. Change 2 percent to its decimal equivalent by moving the decimal point two places to the left:

$$2\% = 0\,2. = .02$$

   b. Multiply .02 times the balance of the invoice:

$$.02 \times \$2,360.00 = \$47.20$$

4. Calculate the amount owed by subtracting the amount of the discount from the balance owed:

$$\$2,360.00 - \$47.20 = \$2,312.80$$

The invoice must be paid by June 19 to receive the 2 percent discount. On or before that date, a check for $2,312.80 may be remitted to Cold Weather Sports, Inc. The discount is recorded as a credit to an account called Purchases Discounts. It is shown in the cost of goods sold category on the chart of accounts. Purchases Discounts is a contra-purchases account and will subtract from the balance of purchases on the income statement. The general journal entry on Sports Haven's books to record the payment of Cold Weather Sports' invoice 5307 is as follows:

GENERAL JOURNAL					Page **6**
Date	Description	Post. Ref.		Debit	Credit
19XX June 19	*Accounts Payable—Cold Weather Sports, Inc.*	205/✓		2 3 6 0 —	
	Cash	*101*			2 3 1 2 80
	Purchases Discounts	*513*			4 7 20
	To Record Payment in Full of Invoice 5307				

Accounts Payable has been debited for $2,360.00, the balance owed on the invoice, even though only $2,312.80 was actually paid. This is necessary so that Sports Haven's account in the subsidiary ledger will show a zero balance. Sports Haven has saved $47.20 by taking advantage of the discount and does not owe any more on this particular invoice.

The following T-accounts outline Sports Haven's original purchase from Cold Weather Sports, the purchase allowance, and the payment of the invoice within the discount period. The entries are outlined as follows:

a. a debit to Purchases and a credit to Accounts Payable to record the original purchase

b. a debit to Accounts Payable and a credit to Purchases Returns and Allowances to record the $200 debit memorandum from Cold Weather Sports

c. a debit to Accounts Payable and credits to Purchases Discounts and Cash to record payment of the invoice within the discount period

General Ledger							Accounts Payable Ledger						

Cash   101

6/1	Balance	10,000	6/19	GJ6	2,312.80	(c)

Cold Weather Sports, Inc.

(b)	6/9	GJ6	200	6/8	P6	2,560	(a)
(c)	6/19	GJ6	2,360				

Accounts Payable   205

(b)	6/9	GJ6	200	6/8	P6	2,560	(a)
(c)	6/19	GJ6	2,360				

Purchases   511

(a)	6/8	P6	2,560

Purchases Returns and Allowances   512

	6/9	GJ6	200 (b)

Purchases Discount   513

	6/19	GJ6	47.20 (c)

Purchases Discounts and Purchases Returns and Allowances are subtracted from Purchases on the income statement, because a return or an allowance is like a purchase not made, and the purchases discount reduces the cost of the merchandise. The portion of the income statement that shows Purchases and its related accounts follows.

PARTIAL INCOME STATEMENT			
Revenue			
Cost of Goods Sold			
Purchases		$4 5 0 0 0 —$	
Add: Freight In		$1 2 0 0 —$	
Delivered Cost of Purchases		$4 6 2 0 0 —$	
Less: Purchases Returns and			
Allowances	$2,700—$		
Purchases Discounts	$900—$	$3 6 0 0 —$	
Net Purchases			$4 2 6 0 0 —$

TRADE DISCOUNTS

list price
the price listed in the seller's catalog

trade discount
a discount given to the buyer by the seller at the time of purchase

Most sellers print catalogs from which buyers may choose their merchandise. The catalogs list the seller's prices, and the catalog price is called the **list price.** Sellers may grant a discount at the time of the sale to the buyer, and if so, that discount is called a **trade discount.** By changing the trade discount offered, the seller may easily change the price charged. Changing the discount offered is easier and more economical for the seller than changing the entire catalog. Also, different trade discounts may be offered to different customers, thus allowing the seller to charge a lower price, for example, to a volume buyer.

Trade discounts are not recorded on the books of the seller or the buyer. Only the actual price charged for the merchandise is recorded. However, the bookkeeper must be able to calculate trade discounts so that invoices may be checked for accuracy.

Assume that on June 21, a sales representative from Running World calls on Frank Phelps of Sports Haven. Frank orders 30 pairs of running shoes with a list price of $25 per pair minus a 10 percent trade discount. The total price paid for the shoes is calculated as follows.

1. Calculate total list price.

$$30 \text{ pairs} \times \$25 = \$750$$

2. Calculate trade discount.
   a. Move decimal point two places to the left in 10 percent:

$$10\% = 1\ 0. = .10$$

   b. Multiply list price times trade discount:

$$\$750 \times .10 = \$75$$

3. Calculate net price of invoice by subtracting the trade discount from the list price:

$$\$750 - \$75 = \$675$$

net price
the list price minus the discount

The **net price** of the invoice is $675. On the books of Sports Haven, the entry will be recorded as a debit to Purchases and a credit to Accounts Payable for $675. On the books of Running World, the entry will be recorded as a debit to Accounts Receivable and a credit to Sales of $675. Remember, the trade discount is not recorded on the books of the buyer or the seller.

TRADE DISCOUNTS AND CREDIT TERMS ON THE SAME INVOICE

Frequently, a trade discount will be offered to the buyer along with credit terms to encourage early payment of the invoice. For example, assume that on July 11 Sports Haven purchased merchandise from Racquet Warehouse with a list price of $1,500 minus a trade discount of 5 percent. In addition, credit terms of 2/10, n/30 were offered. The net price for the purchase is

1. $\$1,500 \times .05 = \$75$
2. $\$1,500 - \$75 = \$1,425$

The entry will be recorded in the purchases journal as follows.

	PURCHASES JOURNAL						Page **7**
Date	Supplier's Name	Invoice Number	Invoice Date	Terms	Post. Ref.	Amount	
19XX *July* **11**	*Racquet Warehouse*	**956**	*July 11*	*2/10, n/30*		1 4 2 5 —	

The last day for payment of the invoice within the discount period is July 21 (July 11 + 10 days). The discount is 2 percent of $1,425 or $28.50. The entry in the general journal to record the payment of the invoice is as follows.

Date	Description	Post. Ref.	Debit	Credit
	GENERAL JOURNAL			**Page 8**
19XX *July* 21	*Accounts Payable—Racquet Warehouse*		1425 —	
	Cash			1396 50
	Purchases Discounts			28 50
	To Record Payment of Invoice 956			

The trade discount was not recorded on the books. Rather, it was calculated and subtracted from the list price ($1,500 − $75 = $1,425). The purchases discount was calculated on the actual purchase price of $1,425.

CREDIT TERMS

Many different credit terms are offered to buyers. Some of the more common ones are listed here.

Terms	
2/10, n/30	A 2 percent discount is offered if the invoice is paid within 10 days of the invoice date; otherwise, the full amount of the invoice is due within 30 days of the invoice date.
2/10, EOM	A 2 percent discount is allowed if the invoice is paid within 10 days after the end of the current month; otherwise, the full amount is due at the end of the month following the date of the invoice.
n/10, EOM	No discount is allowed; the net amount is due within 10 days after the end of the current month.
30 days	No discount is allowed; the net amount is due within 30 days after the date of the invoice.
COD	Cash on delivery or collect on delivery; the amount of the invoice must be paid at the time the goods are delivered.

SUMMARY

In many large firms, the purchasing process requires that a purchase requisition be filled out by the department making the request, followed by a purchase order filled out by the purchasing department. The accounting entry is recorded when the seller sends the goods ordered along with the sales invoice (which is a purchase invoice to the buyer).

All merchandise bought for resale is debited to an account called Purchases. Purchases belongs to a new category of accounts called cost of goods sold. It has a debit balance and appears on the income statement.

A special journal, the purchases journal, is used to record all credit purchases of merchandise for resale. Summary posting is used in the purchases journal: the total is posted as a debit to Purchases and a credit to Accounts Payable. In addition, each entry in the purchases journal is posted as a credit to the individual creditor's accounts in the accounts payable subsidiary ledger. At the end of the accounting period, a schedule of accounts payable is prepared and the total is compared with the balance of the Accounts Payable account in the general ledger. The figures must be the same or an error has been made.

Freight charges are considered to be part of the cost of the merchandise purchased and are debited to an account called Freight In. The balance of the Freight In account is added to the balance of the Purchases Account on the Income Statement to arrive at a figure called delivered cost of purchases. On the seller's invoice, either the terms *FOB shipping point* or *FOB destination* are indicated. FOB shipping point means free on board to the point of shipment, and the buyer will reimburse the carrier; FOB destination means free on board to the destination, and the seller will pay the carrier.

When merchandise that has been purchased has to be returned or when it is damaged, the buyer issues a debit memorandum to the seller indicating that the buyer's Accounts Payable account is being reduced by a debit. When the seller receives the debit memorandum, the Accounts Receivable account on the seller's books must be reduced by the same amount. The return of merchandise is recorded on the buyer's books as a credit to Purchases Returns and Allowances and as a debit to Accounts Payable (or Cash); the same return on the seller's books is recorded as a debit to Sales

Returns and Allowances and a credit to Accounts Receivable (or Cash).

If a trade discount is granted to the buyer, the buyer subtracts the amount of the trade discount from the list price of the merchandise and records only the actual purchase price. Trade discounts are not recorded on the books of the buyer or the seller.

Credit terms may be offered on the same invoice by the seller to encourage prompt payment. If the buyer pays within the discount period, the amount of the discount is credited to an account called Purchases Discounts. Purchases Discounts and Purchases Returns and Allowances subtract from Purchases on the income statement. Both accounts are contra-purchases accounts and appear in the cost of goods sold section of the income statement.

Review of Accounting Terminology

Following is a list of the accounting terminology for this chapter.

debit memorandum
FOB destination
FOB shipping point
in transit
list price
net price

periodic inventory
purchase invoice
purchase order
purchase requisition
trade discount

Fill in the blank with the correct word or term from the list.

1. In the process of being moved from one place to another is called _____.

2. The invoice that is received by the buyer when goods ordered have been shipped is called a _____.

3. The process of physically counting merchandise on hand at regular intervals is called a/an _____.

4. The form a purchasing department prepares to order merchandise is a/an _____.

5. A form made out by a department requesting the purchasing department to order merchandise is a/an _____.

6. A discount granted to the buyer at the time of purchase is a/an _____.

7. The price of merchandise that is shown in the seller's catalog is the _____.

8. The catalog price minus the trade discount is the

   _____.

9. When the seller pays the freight charges all the way to the buyer's destination, the freight terms are _____.

10. When the seller pays only for loading the merchandise at the point of shipment, the freight terms are _____.

11. A document issued by the buyer to the seller indicating that the buyer's Accounts Payable account is being reduced is a

   _____.

Match the following words and terms on the left with the definitions on the right.

12. debit memorandum
13. FOB destination
14. FOB shipping point
15. in transit
16. list price
17. net price
18. periodic inventory
19. purchase invoice
20. purchase order
21. purchase requisition
22. trade discount

a. freight charges paid by seller to buyer's destination

b. the invoice that is received with the ordered merchandise

c. a request to the purchasing department that merchandise be ordered

d. catalog price minus trade discount

e. in the process of being moved

f. a formal order of merchandise made by the purchasing department

g. the catalog price

h. cost of loading merchandise at the point of shipment is paid by seller; buyer pays to destination

i. a document indicating that the buyer's Accounts Payable account is being reduced

j. a discount granted to the buyer at the time of purchase

k. a counting of merchandise on hand at regular intervals

Exercises

Exercise 8.1

determining due dates and discounts

In each case, determine the last day on which the invoice may be paid to receive the discount, the last day on which the invoice may be paid after the discount has passed, and the amount of the discount. For a list of the months and the number of days in each, refer to Chapter 7, Exercise 7.1, page 250.

	Invoice Amount	Invoice Date	Terms	Last Day for Discount	Last Day for Payment after Discount	Amount of Discount
a.	$1,000	January 18	1/15, n/60	2/2	3/19	$10
b.	4,750	February 20	2/10, EOM	3/10	3/31	95
c.	500	April 25	2/10, n/30	5/5	5/25	10
d.	8,040	June 27	1/15, n/30	7/12	7/27	80.40
e.	3,000	July 29	60 days	—	9/27	0
f.	5,500	September 11	2/10, n/60	9/21	11/10	110
g.	7,420	November 21	1/15, n/60	12/6	1/20	74.20
h.	9,000	December 14	1/10, EOM	1/10	1/31	90

Exercise 8.2

journalizing purchase of merchandise, return, and subsequent payment of the invoice

Charlene Woodbridge owns a sandwich shop called No Baloney. Record the following purchase in the purchases journal (page 4) and the subsequent return and payment in the general journal (page 8). Account titles required are: Cash, Accounts Payable, Purchases, Purchases Returns and Allowances, and Purchases Discounts.

Apr. 10   No Baloney purchased 40 pounds of prime rib for $160 from Restaurant Supplies, Inc.; terms, 2/10, EOM; invoice 9041.

Apr. 11   Charlene called the manager of Restaurant Supplies, Inc., to complain about the quality of the prime rib delivered on April 10. She suggested that Restaurant Supplies, Inc., grant No Baloney a 20 percent allowance. They agreed, and No Baloney issued a debit memorandum for $32 to Restaurant Supplies, Inc.

Apr. 30   Charlene issued a check to Restaurant Supplies, Inc., to pay the balance owed on the April 10 purchase.

Exercise 8.3

journalizing sale of merchandise, return, and subsequent receipt of payment for the invoice

In Exercise 8.2, you recorded three transactions for No Baloney relating to a purchase, a return, and a payment. Now record the same transactions for Restaurant Supplies, Inc., as they relate to the same sale (invoice 6092), return, and receipt of payment on April 10, 11, and 30. Record the sale in the sales journal (page 10) and the return and subsequent payment in the general journal (page 17). Account titles required are: Cash, Accounts Receivable, Sales, Sales Returns and Allowances, and Sales Discounts.

Exercise 8.4

journalizing credit purchase, return of merchandise, and subsequent payment of invoice within discount period

Record the following purchase in a purchases journal (page 5) and the payments of cash and returns in the general journal (page 9) for Charlene Woodbridge, owner of the No Baloney sandwich shop. Account titles required are: Cash, Accounts Payable, Purchases, Freight In, Purchases Returns and Allowances, and Purchases Discounts. Round discount amounts to the nearest penny.

May 1 Purchased 100 pounds of whole-wheat flour and 50 pounds of cake flour on invoice 9089 from Nature's Products, an out-of-town vendor. The list price for the whole-wheat flour was $50, and the list price for the cake flour was $26. Nature's Products allowed a 10 percent trade discount. Credit terms were 2/15, n/30.

May 1 Charlene wrote a check to United Delivery Service for $10 for delivering the goods ordered from Nature's Products.

May 2 No Baloney issued a $50 debit memorandum to Nature's Products because of returned merchandise.

May 16 Charlene sent a check to Nature's Products for the amount owed on the May 1 purchase.

Exercise 8.5

journalizing credit sale, return of merchandise, and subsequent receipt of payment within discount period

In Exercise 8.4, you recorded four transactions for No Baloney relating to a purchase, payment for freight, return, and payment for the purchase. Now record the same transaction for Nature's Products as they relate to the sale (invoice 6032), the return, and the receipt of payment. Record the sale in the sales journal (page 20) and the return and payment in the general journal (page 42). Account titles required are: Cash, Accounts Receivable, Sales, Sales Returns and Allowances, and Sales Discounts.

Exercise 8.6

posting from the purchases journal and the general journal

Following are the purchases journal for Plant City for the month of September 19XX and the general journal entries relating to purchases returns and allowances.

				PURCHASES JOURNAL				Page 9
Date		Supplier's Name	Invoice Number	Invoice Date	Terms	Post. Ref.		Amount
19XX *Sept.*	*1*	*Planters Unlimited*	*9721*	*Sept.* *1*	*1/10, n/30*			*2 7 0 —*
	6	*Green Growers*	*10649*	*Sept.* *6*	*1/15, n/60*			*5 0 0 —*
	16	*Plant Food, Inc.*	*4298*	*Sept. 16*	*1/10, EOM*			*1 9 0 —*
	21	*Planters Unlimited*	*9846*	*Sept. 20*	*1/10, n/30*			*9 4 0 —*
	26	*ABC Nursery*	*17408*	*Sept. 26*	*1/10, EOM*			*1 6 2 0 —*
	30	*Green Growers*	*10841*	*Sept. 29*	*1/15, n/60*			*6 5 0 —*
		Total						*4 1 7 0 —*

			GENERAL JOURNAL				Page 14
Date		Description	Post. Ref.		Debit		Credit
19XX *Sept.*	*2*	*Accounts Payable—Planters Unlimited*			*1 0 0 —*		
		Purchases Returns and Allowances					*1 0 0 —*
		To Record Debit Memo 604–C; Invoice 9721					
	27	*Accounts Payable—ABC Nursery*			*2 0 0 —*		
		Purchases Returns and Allowances					*2 0 0 —*
		To Record Debit Memo 605–C; Invoice 17408					

Post from the purchases journal and the general journal following these directions.

a. Post to the accounts payable subsidiary ledger chronologically from the purchases journal and from the general journal. Place a check mark in the posting reference column of the journal as you post and place either P9 or GJ14 in the ledger accounts. Account names and balances are as follows.

ABC Nursery	$500
Green Growers	750
Plant Food, Inc.	0
Planters Unlimited	0

b. Post to the general ledger from the general journal. Enter GJ14 in the ledger accounts and enter the account numbers in the posting reference column of the general journal.

c. Post the total of the purchases journal as a debit to Purchases and a credit to Accounts Payable in the general ledger. Enter P9 in the ledger accounts and the account numbers (separated by a diagonal line) in the purchases journal. Account titles and balances required are as follows.

220	Accounts Payable	$1,250
501	Purchases	0
515	Purchases Returns and Allowances	0

Exercise 8.7
analyzing purchases journal and general journal entries

Answer the following questions about the journals in Exercise 8.6.

a. Where will the total of the purchases journal be posted?

b. Including both the purchases journal and the general journal, how many separate postings must be made to the accounts payable subsidiary ledger? To the Accounts Payable control account in the general ledger?

c. How much money must be sent on September 11 to Planters Unlimited in full payment of invoice 9721?

d. What is the last day for payment within the discount period on the September 16 purchase from Plant Food, Inc., invoice 4298? What amount must be remitted to Plant Food, Inc., on that date?

e. Assuming that Plant City takes advantage of each purchases discount offered, how much will actually be paid for the September charge purchases?

Exercise 8.8
calculating net purchases

In July 19XX Fashion Jewelry recorded a total of $14,500 in the purchases journal. Purchases returns and allowances for the same period were $275, purchases discounts were $260, and freight charges were $570. Calculate the amount of net purchases.

Exercise 8.9
preparing a schedule of accounts payable

Following is the accounts payable subsidiary ledger for Kid's Klothes. Calculate the balance after each transaction and prepare a schedule of accounts payable on August 31, 19XX. CP in the posting reference column indicates a payment on account recorded in the cash payments journal. The balance in the Accounts Payable control account on August 31, 19XX, is $3,195.

ACCOUNTS PAYABLE SUBSIDIARY LEDGER

ALL WEATHER COATS

Date		Explanation	PR	Debit	Credit	Balance
19XX Aug.	1		P8		500 —	
	3		GJ10	150 —		
	5		P8		700 —	
	11		CP14	350 —		

CANVAS CLOTHES

Date		Explanation	PR	Debit	Credit	Balance
19XX Aug.	4		P8		250 —	
	9		P8		460 —	
	10		GJ10	100 —		
	14		P8		150 —	
	20		P8		300 —	

KIDDIE KORNER

Date		Explanation	PR	Debit	Credit	Balance
19XX Aug.	7		P8		260 —	
	9		P8		410 —	
	10		P8		520 —	
	17		CP14	260 —		

LITTLE MEN

Date		Explanation	PR	Debit	Credit	Balance
19XX Aug.	15		P8		305 —	
	16		GJ10	305 —		
	17		P8		420 —	
	27		CP14	420 —		
	31		P8		505 —	

Exercise 8.10
classifying accounts

Give the account classification for each of the following accounts. Classifications are asset, contra asset, liability, owner's equity, revenue, contra revenue, cost of goods sold, contra purchases, and expense. Also indicate whether the account has a normal debit or credit balance and on which financial statement, income statement or balance sheet, it appears. The first one has been completed as an example.

Account Title	Classification	Normal Debit or Credit Balance?	Which Financial Statement?
Example			
Accumulated Depreciation	contra asset	credit	balance sheet
a. Mortgage Payable			
b. Sales			
c. Unearned Revenue			
d. Supplies Used			
e. Purchases Discounts			
f. Equipment			
g. Freight In			
h. Depreciation Expense			
i. Purchases Returns and Allowances			
j. Prepaid Advertising			
k. Sales Discounts			
l. Supplies			
m. Merchandise Inventory			
n. Accounts Receivable			
o. Wages Payable			
p. Purchases			
q. Sales Returns and Allowances			
r. Drawing			
s. Prepaid Insurance			
t. Accounts Payable			

Problems

Problem 8.1
journalizing purchases in purchases journal and returns in general journal; posting

Carol Ruckle owns a small jewelry store called Rings 'n Things. Following are the transactions relating to credit purchases for the month of May 19XX.

May 1 purchased 14K gold chains from M & M Jewelry on invoice 17-420 dated May 1; list price was $3,000 minus a 5 percent trade discount

May 3   purchased 18K gold rings from Ring Warehouse on invoice 48260 dated May 2; list price was $2,500 minus a trade discount of 10 percent.

May 4   issued a $300 debit memorandum 620-A to Ring Warehouse relating to the May 3 purchase

May 9   purchased pendants from Gold Products Company on invoice 12411 dated May 7; list price was $1,100 minus a trade discount of 5 percent

May 18 purchased earrings from Silver Supplies on invoice 9072-8 dated May 16; list price was $450; no trade discount was granted

May 20 issued a $50 debit memorandum 621-A to Silver Supplies relating to May 18 purchase

May 26 purchased rings and bracelets from Silver Supplies on invoice 9159-A dated May 25; list price was $570; no trade discount was granted

May 28 purchased ankle bracelets from Rich's Supplies on invoice 1049 dated May 27; list price was $400 minus a 10 percent trade discount

Instructions   1.   *Enter the following account titles, numbers, and May 1 balances in the general ledger and the accounts payable subsidiary ledger.*

General Ledger		Accounts Payable Ledger	
101 Cash	$8,700	Gold Products Company	0
210 Accounts Payable	7,600	M & M Jewelry	$2,000
511 Purchases	0	Rich's Supplies	4,500
515 Purchases Returns and		Ring Warehouse	0
Allowances	0	Silver Supplies	1,100

2.   *Use page 5 for the purchases journal and page 21 for the general journal.*

3.   *Assuming that purchase terms are net 30, record purchases on account in the purchases journal and purchases returns and allowances in the general journal.*

4.   *Post to the accounts payable ledger immediately after each transaction is journalized. Use P5 or GJ21 in the posting refer-*

ence column of the subsidiary ledger accounts and place a check mark in the posting reference column of the purchases journal or the general journal after posting.

5. Post to the general ledger from the general journal immediately after journalizing. Enter the account numbers in the posting reference column of the journal and enter GJ21 in the ledger accounts.

6. Post the total of the purchases journal as a debit to Purchases and a credit to Accounts Payable in the general ledger. Use P5 for the posting reference in the ledger accounts and enter the account numbers in the posting reference column of the purchases journal.

7. Prepare a schedule of accounts payable and compare the total with the balance in the Accounts Payable control account on May 31.

Problem 8.2
journalizing purchases with credit terms in purchases journal and returns and payments in general journal; posting

Curt Cristofferson owns a western clothing store called Curt's Country Clothes. Following are the transactions relating to credit purchases for the month of February 19XX.

Feb. 1   purchased jeans from Cowhand Supplies on invoice 7612 dated February 1; list price was $500; terms were 2/10, n/30

Feb. 4   purchased leather vests from Leather Products on invoice 1039 dated February 3; list price was $1,200; terms were 1/15, n/30

Feb. 8   issued debit memorandum 16-123 to Leather Products for $300 relating to its invoice 1039

Feb. 9   purchased shirts from Cowhand Supplies on invoice 7690 dated February 7; list price was $490; terms were 2/10, n/30

Feb. 11   wrote a check to Cowhand Supplies in full payment of February 1 invoice 7612

Feb. 12   purchased coats from Double R Supplies on invoice 6401 dated February 12; list price was $2,500; terms were 2/10, EOM

Feb. 13   issued debit memorandum 16-124 to Double R Supplies for $150 relating to its invoice 6401 dated February 12

Feb. 14   wrote a check to Leather Products in full payment of the February 3 invoice 1039 minus the February 8 return

Feb. 24   wrote a check to Cowhand Supplies in full payment of invoice 7690 dated February 7

Feb. 26 purchased boots from Ringo Western Wear on invoice 5622 dated February 25; list price was $1,000; terms were 1/15, n/60

Feb. 28 wrote a check to Double R Supplies in full payment of February 12 invoice 6401 minus the February 13 return

Instructions 1. *Enter the following account titles, numbers, and February 1 balances in the general ledger and the accounts payable subsidiary ledger.*

	General Ledger		Accounts Payable Ledger	
101	Cash	$7,230	Cowhand Supplies	$3,000
211	Accounts Payable	6,430	Double R Supplies	2,000
511	Purchases	0	Leather Products	1,430
515	Purchases Returns and Allowances	0	Ringo Western Wear	0
520	Purchases Discounts	0		

2. *Use page 2 for the purchases journal and page 5 for the general journal.*

3. *Record purchases on account in the purchases journal, purchases returns and allowances in the general journal, and cash payments (including purchases discounts) in the general journal. (Later, you will record all payments of cash in the cash payments journal.)*

4. *Post to the accounts payable ledger immediately after each transaction is journalized. Use P2 or GJ5 in the posting reference column of the subsidiary ledger accounts and place a check mark in the posting reference column of the purchases journal or the general journal after posting.*

5. *Post to the general ledger from the general journal immediately after journalizing. Enter the account numbers in the posting reference column of the journal and enter GJ5 in the ledger accounts.*

6. *After carefully checking the addition, total and rule the purchases journal.*

7. *Post the total of the purchases journal as a debit to Purchases and a credit to Accounts Payable in the general ledger. Use P2 for the posting reference in the ledger accounts and enter the account numbers in the posting reference column of the purchases journal.*

8. *Prepare a schedule of accounts payable and compare the total with the balance in the Accounts Payable control account on February 28.*

Problem 8.3
journalizing purchases with trade discounts and credit terms in purchases journal and returns and payments in general journal; posting

Following are the transactions relating to credit purchases for Household Supplies for the month of January 19XX.

Jan. 2 purchased merchandise from A-1 Products on invoice 76403 dated January 2; list price was $5,000 minus a 10 percent trade discount; terms were 1/15, n/30

Jan. 2 wrote a check to Intra-State Delivery Company for $75 relating to A-1 Products' purchase invoice 76403 dated January 2

Jan. 3 purchased merchandise from Zumwalt's on invoice 1240 dated January 3; list price was $4,000; no trade discount was allowed; terms were 2/10, n/30

Jan. 4 issued debit memorandum 643-B for $500 to Zumwalt's relating to its January 3 invoice 1240; merchandise was damaged

Jan. 8 purchased merchandise from Best Products on invoice 6243 dated January 8; list price was $3,500 less trade discount of 10 percent; terms were 2/10, EOM

Jan. 12 wrote a check to Zumwalt's in full payment of its January 3 invoice 1240 less the January 4 return

Jan. 15 purchased merchandise from The White House on invoice 1649 dated January 15; list price was $8,000 less a 5 percent trade discount; terms were 1/10, EOM

Jan. 17 wrote a check to A-1 Products in full payment of its January 2 invoice 76403

Jan. 18 purchased merchandise from The White House on invoice 1701 dated January 18; list price was $2,600 less a 5 percent trade discount; terms were 1/10, EOM

Jan. 19 issued debit memorandum 644-B for $400 to The White House relating to its January 18 invoice 1701

Jan. 22 purchased merchandise from Zumwalt's on invoice 1322 dated January 22; list price was $3,700; no trade discount was allowed; terms were 2/10, n/30

Jan. 24 purchased merchandise from Bargain Basement on invoice 16404 dated January 24; list price was $1,500 less a trade discount of 5 percent; terms were n/30

Jan. 28 purchased merchandise from A-1 Products on invoice 77106 dated January 28; list price was $4,700 minus a 10 percent trade discount; terms were 1/15, n/30

Jan. 28 wrote a check to Intra-State Delivery Company for $75 relating to A-1 Products' January 28 purchase invoice 77106

Instructions　　1.　*Enter the following account titles, numbers, and January 1 balances in the general ledger and the accounts payable subsidiary ledger.*

General Ledger		Accounts Payable Ledger	
101　Cash	$16,100	A-1 Products	$3,000
211　Accounts Payable	8,900	Bargain Basement	2,500
501　Purchases	0	Best Products	0
505　Freight In	0	The White House	2,000
510　Purchases Returns and Allowances	0	Zumwalt's	1,400
520　Purchases Discounts	0		

2.　*Use page 31 for the purchases journal and page 49 for the general journal.*

3.　*Record purchases on account in the purchases journal, purchases returns and allowances in the general journal, and cash payments in the general journal. Remember, trade discounts are not recorded on the books of the buyer or the seller.*

4.　*Post to the accounts payable ledger immediately after each transaction is journalized. Use P31 or GJ49 in the posting reference column of the subsidiary ledger accounts and place a check mark in the posting reference column of the purchases journal or the general journal after posting.*

5.　*Post to the general ledger from the general journal immediately after journalizing. Enter the account numbers in the posting reference column of the journal and enter GJ49 in the ledger accounts.*

6.　*After carefully checking the addition, total and rule the purchases journal.*

7.　*Post the total of the purchases journal as a debit to Purchases and a credit to Accounts Payable in the general ledger. Use P31 for the posting reference in the ledger accounts and enter the account numbers in the posting reference column of the purchases journal.*

8.　*Prepare a schedule of accounts payable and compare the total with the balance in the Accounts Payable control account on January 31.*

Problem 8.4

journalizing purchases in purchases journal, sales with sales tax in sales journal, and debit and credit memoranda and payments made and received in general journal; posting

Following are the transactions relating to credit sales and credit purchases for Ray's Sewing Center for the month of October 19XX.

Oct. 1   purchased merchandise from Kathy's Sewright Machines on invoice 60213 dated October 1; list price was $5,720; terms were n/30

Oct. 1   wrote a $70 check to Speedee Delivery Company for delivering the purchase from Kathy's Sewright Machines

Oct. 5   sold merchandise to B. L. Botham; invoice 8037; list price was $60 plus 6 percent sales tax; terms were n/30

Oct. 9   purchased merchandise from G & B Fabrics on invoice 9160 dated October 9; list price was $4,200; terms were n/30

Oct. 10   issued debit memorandum 581 for $1,000 to G & B Fabrics relating to invoice 9160; merchandise was returned

Oct. 14   wrote a check to Kathy's Sewright Machines in full payment of its October 1 invoice 60213.

Oct. 17   sold merchandise to The Sewing Corner; invoice 8038; list price was $980 plus 6 percent sales tax; terms were n/30

Oct. 19   issued credit memorandum 603 for $318 to The Sewing Corner relating to invoice 8038 dated October 17; $300 of the amount relates to the list price of the merchandise and $18 relates to the sales tax

Oct. 22   received a check from B. L. Botham in full payment of invoice 8037 dated October 5

Oct. 25   wrote a check to G & B Fabrics in full payment of invoice 9160 dated October 9 less the return on October 10

Oct. 27   sold merchandise to The Sewing Corner; invoice 8039; list price was $850 plus 6 percent sales tax; terms were n/30

Oct. 28   received a check from The Sewing Corner in full payment of invoice 8038 dated October 17 less the return on October 19

Oct. 29   purchased merchandise from Kwik-Sew on invoice 1641 dated October 29; list price was $880; terms were n/30

Oct. 29   wrote a check for $50 to Fast Freight for delivering the purchase from Kwik-Sew on October 29

Oct. 30   issued debit memorandum 582 for $106 to Kwik-Sew relating to invoice 1641 dated October 29

Oct. 31   received a check from The Sewing Corner in full payment of invoice 8039 dated October 27

Oct. 31   wrote a check to Kwik-Sew in full payment of invoice 1641 dated October 29 less the return on October 30

Instructions   1. *Listed below is a partial chart of accounts for Ray's Sewing Center.*

101	Cash
110	Accounts Receivable
210	Accounts Payable
220	Sales Tax Payable
405	Sales
410	Sales Returns and Allowances
505	Purchases
515	Freight In
520	Purchases Returns and Allowances

2. *Enter the following names into the accounts receivable and accounts payable subsidiary ledgers.*

Accounts Receivable Ledger	Accounts Payable Ledger
B. L. Botham	G & B Fabrics
The Sewing Corner	Kathy's Sewright Machines
	Kwik-Sew

3. *Record all sales on account in a sales journal (page 18). Record all purchases on account in a purchases journal (page 10). Record all other transactions in a general journal; begin numbering with page 28.*

4. *Post to the accounts receivable and accounts payable subsidiary ledgers immediately after any transaction involving Accounts Receivable or Accounts Payable. Enter S18, P10, or GJ28 in the subsidiary ledger accounts and place a check mark in the journal after posting has been completed.*

5. *Total, crossfoot, and rule the sales journal.*

6. *Total and rule the purchases journal.*

Problem 8.5
journalizing in purchases, sales, and general journals; posting to subsidiary and general ledgers

Following are the transactions relating to credit sales and credit purchases for Wing's Mercantile for the month of June 19XX. On all credit sales, Wing's grants charge customers credit terms of 2/10, n/30. Wing's is not required to collect sales tax.

June 1   purchased merchandise from Wilson Supplies on invoice 1643 dated June 1; list price was $500; terms were n/30

June 2   sold merchandise to A. G. Rogers; invoice 7029; list price was $120; terms were 2/10, n/30

June 3   issued debit memorandum 603 to Wilson Supplies for $25 relating to June 1 purchase

June 5   sold merchandise on account to B. B. Ulrich; invoice 7030; list price was $250; terms were 2/10, n/30

June 6   issued credit memorandum 804 to B. B. Ulrich for $50 relating to June 5 sale

June 8   purchased merchandise from Moreno's Appliances on invoice 32961 dated June 8; list price was $3,000 less a 5 percent trade discount; terms were n/30

June 8   wrote a check to Van's Delivery for $100 relating to the June 8 purchase from Moreno's Appliances

June 10   purchased merchandise from Van Riper Wholesale House on invoice 20396 dated June 10; list price was $1,650; terms were n/30

June 12   received a check from A. G. Rogers in full payment of the June 2 invoice 7029

June 14   sold merchandise on account to P. S. Tolstoy; invoice 7031; list price was $370; terms were 2/10, n/30

June 15   received a check from B. B. Ulrich in full payment of June 5 invoice 7030 minus the return on June 6

June 18   purchased merchandise from Wilson Supplies on invoice 1699 dated June 18; list price was $800; terms were n/30

June 20   issued debit memorandum 604 to Wilson Supplies for $100 relating to June 18 purchase

June 23   sold merchandise to A. G. Rogers; invoice 7032; list price was $325; terms were 2/10, n/30

June 24   wrote a check to Moreno's Appliances in full payment of June 8 purchase; invoice 32961

June 27   purchased merchandise from Moreno's Appliances on invoice 32998 dated June 27; list price was $1,800 less a 5 percent trade discount; terms were n/30

June 27   wrote a check to Van's Delivery for $75 relating to June 27 purchase from Moreno's Appliances

June 29   received a check from P. S. Tolstoy in full payment of June 14 invoice 7031

June 30   paid amount owed to Wilson Supplies for purchases on June 1 invoice 1643 and June 18 invoice 1699 minus the returns on June 3 and June 20

Instructions   1.   *Enter the following account titles and balances into the general ledger accounts for Wing's Mercantile. This is a partial list of accounts.*

101	Cash	$9,530
110	Accounts Receivable	2,955
210	Accounts Payable	4,215
405	Sales	0
410	Sales Discounts	0
415	Sales Returns and Allowances	0
545	Purchases	0
550	Freight In	0
560	Purchases Returns and Allowances	0

2.   *Enter the following names and account balances into the accounts receivable and accounts payable subsidiary ledgers.*

Accounts Receivable Ledger		Accounts Payable Ledger	
P. O. Dermott	$840	Hal's Electrics	$190
A. G. Rogers	0	Moreno's Appliances	450
B. A. Smoley	175	Nguyen Home Store	3,000
P. S. Tolstoy	490	Van Riper Wholesale House	200
B. B. Ulrich	0	Wilson Supplies	0
B. R. Ziolkowsky	1,450	Zanders Warehouse	375

3.   *Record sales on account in the sales journal (page 32). Record purchases on account in the purchases journal (page 19). Record sales returns and allowances, sales discounts, purchases returns and allowances, and cash transactions in the general journal; begin numbering with page 68.*

4.   *Post to the accounts receivable or the accounts payable subsidiary ledgers immediately after each transaction involving Accounts Receivable or Accounts Payable. Place a check mark in the posting reference column of the journal and enter S32, P19, or GJ68 in the subsidiary ledger accounts.*

5.   *Post to the general ledger from the general journal immediately after each transaction. Enter the account number in the posting reference column of the general journal and enter GJ68 in the general ledger accounts.*

6. *Total, rule, and post the sales journal.*

7. *Total, rule, and post the purchases journal.*

8. *Prepare schedules of accounts receivable and accounts payable and compare the totals with the balances in the control accounts in the general ledger.*

CHAPTER 9

The Cash Receipts, Cash Payments, and Combined Cash Journals

LEARNING OBJECTIVES

When you have completed this chapter, you should

1. have a better understanding of accounting terminology.

2. have a basic understanding of internal control.

3. have a basic understanding of cash management.

4. be able to account for credit card sales.

5. be able to record entries directly into the cash receipts, cash payments, and combined cash journals.

6. be able to post from the cash receipts, cash payments, and combined cash journals directly into the general ledger and subsidiary ledgers.

7. be able to calculate and account for interest received and interest paid.

The purchases and sales journals and the cash receipts and cash payments journals are designed to meet the needs of the particular company using them and save the bookkeeper a great deal of time in the journalizing and posting processes. In Chapters 7 and 8, we learned how Frank Phelps, owner of Sports Haven, handled sales and purchases, returns and allowances, sales tax, freight charges, and discounts. In this chapter, we will see how receipts and payments of cash are handled and how special precautions are taken to safeguard against the theft of cash.

INTERNAL CONTROL

Many management decisions are based in part on data obtained from the accounting records. For this reason, accounting information must be accurate. A strong system of internal control will help ensure that this is the case. Internal control refers to the steps taken by a company to: (1) protect its resources from theft, waste, and inefficiency; (2) ensure that accounting data is accurate; and (3) evaluate employees and departments to determine the level of their performance and whether they are complying with company policy. One important principle of internal control is that, whenever possible, no one employee should be responsible for handling all phases of a transaction from beginning to end. This is especially true with cash transactions, since cash is particularly susceptible to theft.

CASH MANAGEMENT

fraud
a dishonest act in which someone is cheated

Proper management of cash will minimize losses from theft or **fraud** and provide for the accurate accounting of cash. It will ensure that enough cash is on hand for the business to remain solvent and will allow a reserve for emergencies. Proper cash management will also provide for any extra cash to be invested.

For strong internal control of cash, the following guidelines should be observed.

1. Cash receipts should be deposited daily.
2. Cash payments should be made by check (not from the cash

register or cash on hand unless a petty cash fund has been established).

3. The functions of receiving cash, making cash payments, and accounting for cash should be kept separate.

4. One employee should be designated to verify the amount of every cash payment and to determine whether the payment is **valid;** another employee should be designated to write the checks. The same person should not be designated to verify the validity and amount of an **expenditure** *and* to write the checks.

5. Routines for handling cash should be established and carefully followed.

valid
sufficiently supported by facts; legally sound

expenditure
an amount spent

justify
to show or prove to be just, right, or fair

The reasons for these procedures are fairly obvious. When cash is deposited daily, it is not lying around as a temptation. Payments should not be made directly from the cash register, because it may be difficult or too time consuming to verify amounts and to **justify** payment; thus, unwarranted cash payments may be made. If more than one person is involved in receiving money at the cash register, the chance of error is greater and the chance of finding the person responsible for the error less likely. The functions of receiving cash should be kept separate from the paying of and the accounting for cash to help prevent employee theft. Such theft is made much more difficult when two or more persons have to be involved. When a specific routine has been established for handling cash, management can more easily check to see that the procedures are being followed.

Cash received is primarily from two sources: (1) cash sales and (2) money received on account. Cash sales are normally recorded on a cash register and should be plainly visible to the customer. If the employee fraudulently records an amount different from that charged the customer, management hopes that the customer will complain and thus provide an outside check on the employees.

Prenumbered sales tickets also help to strengthen internal control. One copy of the sales ticket is given to the customer and one copy is retained at the cash register. All tickets must be accounted for at the end of the day. The total of all the tickets must equal the total cash received that day, as verified by the manager or some employee other than the one who received the cash.

CASH SHORT AND OVER

Some small errors may be expected in handling cash. However, large cash discrepancies, errors made consistently by one employee, or errors that cannot be explained call for immediate attention by management. Assume that the total amount from the prenumbered sales tickets shows that cash sales on January 11 are $1,240. However, the actual cash in the cash register is only $1,230. (Perhaps the cashier accidentally gave a customer an extra $10 in change.) The general journal entry to record the day's cash sales would be as follows.

GENERAL JOURNAL				Page 1
Date	Description	Post. Ref.	Debit	Credit
19XX Jan. 11	Cash		1230 —	
	Cash Short and Over		10 —	
	Sales			1240 —
	To Record Cash Sales			

However, if the total of the sales ticket showed sales on January 11 to be $1,240, but the actual cash on hand proved to be $1,250, the general journal entry would appear as follows.

GENERAL JOURNAL				Page 1
Date	Description	Post. Ref.	Debit	Credit
19XX Jan. 11	Cash		1250 —	
	Cash Short and Over			10 —
	Sales			1240 —
	To Record Cash Sales			

The Cash Short and Over account is debited when cash is short and credited when cash is over. If the Cash Short and Over account has a credit balance at the end of the accounting period, it is shown on the income statement in a special category called Other Income; it follows the net income from operations section. If Cash Short and Over has a debit balance, it will appear in the category called Other Expense.

CREDIT CARD SALES

Credit cards such as MasterCard, Visa, and Diners Club are quite common. After credit approval, the customer is issued the card, which may then be used for purchases in many stores. When making a purchase, the customer signs a credit card draft. The customer then owes the money to the company issuing the credit card, *not* to the store making the sale. The credit card company will **reimburse** the store owner.

reimburse
to repay

The advantages to the merchant of offering credit card sales are many.

1. Cash from credit sales is received more quickly.
2. Costly credit checks are not required, because the customer owes money to the credit card company, not to the store making the sale.
3. No uncollectible accounts expense is incurred with credit card sales.

Bank credit card drafts (such as MasterCard or Visa) may be deposited directly into the merchant's bank account, similar to a deposit of a customer's check. At the end of the month, the fee for using the credit card company services is deducted directly from the merchant's checking account. This fee is debited to an account called Credit Card Discount Expense, which shows on the income statement along with the other expenses.

Nonbank credit card drafts (such as American Express or Diners Club) cannot be directly deposited into the merchant's checking account. The merchant must remit the credit card drafts to the issuing company, which will then send a check to the merchant for the amount of the drafts minus a fee.

Assume that Audrey Billings purchases merchandise on March 1 from Sports Haven totaling $300; she presents an Ultra Charge card for payment. The entry is a debit to Accounts Receivable and a credit to Sales and is recorded in the sales journal.

SALES JOURNAL						Page *18*
Date	Sales Invoice Number	Customer's Name	Terms	Post. Ref.		Amount
19XX **Mar.** 1	9612	*Ultra Charge*				3 0 0 —

Assume further that Sports Haven has nonbank credit card drafts of $1,000 at the end of the first week in March. These drafts are sent to the Ultra Charge Company, which deducts a 4 percent fee and sends a check for the difference to Sports Haven. The general journal entry to record the receipt of the check by Sports Haven would be as follows.

GENERAL JOURNAL					Page *17*
Date	Description	Post. Ref.	Debit		Credit
19XX **Mar.** 10	*Cash*		9 6 0 —		
	Credit Card Discount Expense		4 0 —		
	Accounts Receivable—Ultra Charge				1 0 0 0 —
	To Record Receipt of Cash for Ultra Charge				
	Sales, March 1–7, Less 4% Discount				

THE CASH RECEIPTS JOURNAL

The cash receipts journal is, like the other special journals, designed to meet the needs of the particular company using it. All cash received by the company is entered in the cash receipts journal, and every entry in it will be a debit to Cash. Thus, the first column (or the last, as the accountant prefers) will be a cash debit column. If the merchant allows nonbank credit card sales, a special debit column for credit card discount expense may be included. A special debit column may also be included to record sales discounts as customers take advantage of credit terms by paying their invoices early. Credit columns may include accounts receivable, sales, and sales tax payable. Other columns may be added if the need arises.

To determine which special columns to use in the cash receipts journal, the accountant must analyze the kinds of transactions that normally occur. For many businesses, the most common examples will be cash received from sales and cash received from customers who are paying on account. Less-frequent transactions might include a cash investment by the owner, a cash sale of assets, or a receipt of money on an outstanding note. When these transactions are recorded in the general journal, each must be recorded and posted separately—time-consuming chores. The following shows how these transactions, and some others as well, would appear in a multi-column cash receipts journal.

Date	Account Titles	Post. Ref.	Sundry Accounts Credit	Accounts Receivable Credit	Sales Credit	Sales Tax Payable Credit	Credit Card Discount Debit	Cash Debit
		CASH RECEIPTS JOURNAL						Page *1*
Jan. 4	Cash Sales				2 0 0 —	1 0 —		2 1 0 —
5	Jo Scott			5 0 —				5 0 —
6	B. J. King, Cap.		3 0 0 0 —					3 0 0 0 —
9	Office Equipment		5 0 0 —					5 0 0 —
11	Notes Receivable		7 5 0 —					7 5 0 —
15	Fast Charge			1 0 0 0 —			4 0 —	9 6 0 —
17	Cash Sales				5 5 0 —	2 7 50		5 7 7 50
19	Pat Kinghorn			8 0 —				8 0 —
21	Cash Sales				1 0 0 —	5 —		1 0 5 —
24	Phil Valentino			7 5 —				7 5 —
27	Cash Sales				4 0 —	2 —		4 2 —
30	Cash Sales				9 0 —	4 50		9 4 50
31	Fast Charge			2 0 0 0 —			8 0 —	1 9 2 0 —

Analysis of Individual Transactions

Jan. 4 This transaction is to record cash sales plus 5 percent sales tax and requires a debit to Cash and credits to Sales and Sales Tax Payable. Since there are special columns for each of these accounts, only the words *cash sales* and the amounts need to be entered. Similar transactions appear on January 17, 21, 27, and 30.

Jan. 5 A $50 check was received from Jo Scott to apply on her outstanding account. The $50 is entered in the accounts receivable credit column and the cash debit column. Her name is included in the account titles column so that the $50 may be posted to the accounts receivable subsidiary ledger. The January 19 and 24 transactions are similar.

sundry
miscellaneous

Jan. 6   B. J. King invested an additional $3,000 cash into the business. This entry requires a debit to Cash and a credit to Capital. Because there is no special column for the Capital account, the amount is entered in the **sundry** credit column and in the cash debit column. For all entries in the sundry column, the account title must be written in the account titles column, so that the amount can be posted to the correct general ledger account.

Jan. 9   Surplus office equipment was sold at cost. This requires a debit to Cash and a credit to Office Equipment. Again, because there is no special column for office equipment, the amount is entered in the sundry credit column and in the cash debit column. The account title, Office Equipment, must be written in the account titles column, so that the amount can be posted to the correct general ledger account.

Jan. 11 $750 was received on a non-interest-bearing note. The entry requires a debit to Cash and a credit to Notes Receivable. The amount is entered in the sundry credit and the cash debit columns and Notes Receivable is written in the account titles column, so that the amount can be posted to the general ledger.

Jan. 15   Fast Charge sent a check to cover the credit card charges minus a 4 percent fee for the first half of the month. The entry requires a debit to Cash, a debit to Credit Card Discount Expense, and a credit to Accounts Receivable. The amount of the fee, $40, is entered in the credit card discount debit column; the total cash received, $960, is entered in the cash debit column; and the amount of the total, $1,000, is entered in the accounts receivable credit column. The name, Fast Charge, is entered in the account titles column, so that the amount may be posted to the accounts receivable ledger. There is a similar entry on January 31.

Crossfooting the Cash Receipts Journal

Before performing the required summary posting, the bookkeeper must make sure that the totals of the debit columns are equal to the totals of the credit columns of the journal. Crossfooting will ensure that the journal is in balance. After adding each journal column, two columns should be listed on a sheet of paper: one for debit column totals and one for credit column totals. If the total of the journal's debit columns is equal to the total of its credit columns, the journal is ready to be ruled and posted. The cash receipts journal is reproduced here to illustrate crossfooting.

CASH RECEIPTS JOURNAL								Page *1*
Date	Account Titles	Post. Ref.	Sundry Accounts Credit	Accounts Receivable Credit	Sales Credit	Sales Tax Payable Credit	Credit Card Discount Debit	Cash Debit
19XX Jan. 4	Cash Sales				200 —	10 —		210 —
5	Jo Scott			50 —				50 —
6	B. J. King, Cap.		3000 —					3000 —
9	Office Equipment		500 —					500 —
11	Notes Receivable		750 —					750 —
15	Fast Charge			1000 —			40 —	960 —
17	Cash Sales				550 —	27 50		577 50
19	Pat Kinghorn			80 —				80 —
21	Cash Sales				100 —	5 —		105 —
24	Phil Valentino			75 —				75 —
27	Cash Sales				40 —	2 —		42 —
30	Cash Sales				90 —	4 50		94 50
31	Fast Charge			2000 —			80 —	1920 —
	Totals		4250 —	3205 —	980 —	49 —	120 —	8364 —

Column	Debit Total	Credit Total
Sundry		$4,250
Accounts Receivable		3,205
Sales		980
Sales Tax Payable		49
Credit Card Discount	$ 120	
Cash	8,364	
	$8,484	$8,484

Ruling and Posting the Cash Receipts Journal

When crossfooting has been completed, a single line is drawn that extends across all account columns beneath the last entry. Beneath the totals, a double line is drawn across all columns except the account titles column.

Three steps are involved in posting the cash receipts journal.

1. For every amount entered in the accounts receivable credit column, a posting to the accounts receivable ledger must be made immediately. A check mark is placed in the posting reference column of the journal after each posting is complete, and CR and the page number are entered in the ledger.

2. Daily postings must be made to the general ledger for the amounts that appear in the sundry column. The account numbers are entered in the posting reference column of the journal after each amount is posted, and CR and the page number are entered in the posting reference column of the general ledger accounts. An X is placed beneath the sundry column total at the end of the period to indicate that the column total is not posted.

3. At the end of the accounting period, summary posting is performed. All column totals (except the sundry column) are posted to the general ledger. As each amount is posted, the account number in parentheses is entered beneath the double-ruled line, and CR and the page number are entered in the posting reference column of the general ledger accounts.

The completed journal, the T-accounts for the general ledger, and T-accounts for the accounts receivable ledger are reproduced here with rulings and cross-reference notations indicated.

			CASH RECEIPTS JOURNAL						Page *1*
Date	Account Titles	Post. Ref.	Sundry Accounts Credit	Accounts Receivable Credit	Sales Credit	Sales Tax Payable Credit	Credit Card Discount Debit	Cash Debit	
19XX Jan. 4	Cash Sales				200 —	10 —		210 —	
5	Jo Scott	✔		50 —				50 —	
6	B. J. King, Cap.	310	3000 —					3000 —	
9	Office Equipment	130	500 —					500 —	
11	Notes Receivable	120	750 —					750 —	
15	Fast Charge	✔		1000 —			40 —	960 —	
17	Cash Sales				550 —	27 50		577 50	
19	Pat Kinghorn	✔		80 —				80 —	
21	Cash Sales				100 —	5 —		105 —	
24	Phil Valentino	✔		75 —				75 —	
27	Cash Sales				40 —	2 —		42 —	
30	Cash Sales				90 —	4 50		94 50	
31	Fast Charge	✔		2000 —			80 —	1920 —	
	Totals		4250 —	3205 —	980 —	49 —	120 —	8364 —	
			(X)	(110)	(401)	(215)	(630)	(101)	

Partial General Ledger　　　　　　**Partial Accounts Receivable Ledger**

Cash　　　　　　　　　　　　　　**101**　　　　　　　**Fast Charge**

1/1	Balance	4,500			1/1	Balance 3,000	1/15 CR1	1,000
1/31	CR1	8,364					1/31 CR1	2,000

Accounts Receivable　　　　　　**110**　　　　　　　**Pat Kinghorn**

1/1	Balance	6,000	1/31	CR1	3,205	1/1 Balance 300	1/19 CR1	80

Notes Receivable　　　　　　　　**120**　　　　　　　**Jo Scott**

1/1	Balance	2,000	1/11	CR1	750	1/1 Balance 120	1/5 CR1	50

Partial General Ledger		**Partial Accounts Receivable Ledger**	

Office Equipment   130

| 1/1 | Balance | 5,000 | 1/9 | CR1 | 500 |

Phil Valentino

| 1/1 | Balance | 75 | 1/24 | CR1 | 75 |

Sales Tax Payable   215

| | | 1/1 | Balance | 30 |
| | | 1/31 | CR1 | 49 |

B. J. King, Capital   310

| | | 1/1 | Balance | 6,000 |
| | | 1/6 | CR1 | 3,000 |

Sales   401

| | | 1/31 | CR1 | 980 |

Credit Card Discount Expense   630

| 1/31 | CR1 | 120 | | |

Recording Sales Discounts in the Cash Receipts Journal

If it is company policy to allow credit terms, then the cash receipts journal should be designed with a special debit column for sales discounts. Assume that on January 10, a sale of $500 is made to Joseph Lee and that credit terms are 2/10, n/30. On January 19, when Joseph Lee sends a check in full payment of the purchase, Cash is debited for $490, Sales Discounts is debited for $10, and Accounts Receivable is credited for $500. The transaction as entered in the cash receipts journal looks like this.

	CASH RECEIPTS JOURNAL						Page *11*
Date	Account Titles	Post. Ref.	Sundry Accounts Credit	Accounts Receivable Credit	Sales Credit	Sales Discount Debit	Cash Debit
19XX							
Jan. 19	**Joseph Lee**			5 0 0 —		1 0 —	4 9 0 —

THE CASH PAYMENTS JOURNAL

Good internal control of cash requires bills to be paid by check, and the cash payments journal is the special journal in which all checks written are recorded. It may be designed to meet the particular needs of any company; special columns may be added to the journal for those transactions that occur frequently.

In a typical business, cash must be spent in a large number of places, but incoming cash comes from only a few sources. For example, typical transactions where cash is paid out might include payments on account, payment for rent, wages, utilities, advertising, delivery, phone, and so on; while sources of money coming into a business are often limited primarily to cash sales or money received on account.

If a general journal is used to record cash transactions, rather than a cash payments journal, many postings to the Cash account are required each period as well as numerous postings to other general ledger accounts. Using the cash payments journal saves a great deal of time in both journalizing and posting. Following is a cash payments journal with some typical entries. The check number is included with every transaction; strong internal control requires that every check be accounted for. Even when a check is voided, it is recorded in the cash payments journal so that missing numbers can be noticed at a glance.

CASH PAYMENTS JOURNAL								**Page 7**
Date	Check No.	Account Titles	Post. Ref.	Sundry Accounts Debit	Accounts Payable Debit	Purchases Debit	Purchases Discount Credit	Cash Credit
July 1	1071	Rent Expense		750 —				750 —
2	1072	Purchases				800 —		800 —
5	1073	Roberta Smith, Drawing		500 —				500 —
7	1074	Payroll Taxes Payable		180 —				180 —
8	1075	Telephone Expense		140 —				140 —
11	1076	Unity Products			1200 —		24 —	1176 —
15	1077	Delivery Expense		30 —				30 —
18	1078	Joy Moroni Company			1000 —		10 —	990 —
20	1079	Roberta Smith, Drawing		500 —				500 —
24	1080	Freight In		75 —				75 —
27	1081	Purchases				1400 —		1400 —
31	1082	Unity Products			1600 —		32 —	1568 —
31	1083	Void						

Analysis of Individual Transactions

July 1 A check is written to pay the rent. This entry requires a debit to Rent Expense and a credit to Cash of $750. Since there is no special column for rent expense, the debit amount is entered in the sundry column; the credit amount is entered in the cash column. The account title is written in the account titles column, so that the amount for rent expense may be individually posted. Similar entries appear on July 5, 7, 8, 15, 20, and 24.

July 2 A check is written for a cash purchase of merchandise for resale. The entry requires a debit to Purchases and a credit to Cash. Since there are special columns for both, the amount, $800, is simply written in the special columns and *purchases* is written in the account titles column. A similar entry appears on July 27.

July 11 A check is written in payment of an outstanding account minus the purchases discount. The entry requires a debit to Accounts Payable of $1,200 and credits to Purchases Discounts of $24 and Cash of $1,176. There are special columns for each of these accounts, thus the amounts are simply entered in the columns. The name of the creditor, Unity Products, is written in the account titles column. Similar entries appear on July 18 and 31.

Totaling, Crossfooting, and Ruling the Cash Payments Journal

Once all the entries for the period have been completed, each column is totaled and crossfooting is performed. Once the equality of debits and credits has been proved, a single ruling is placed across all the amount columns and a double ruling is placed across all columns except the account titles column.

Posting the Cash Payments Journal

Following is the procedure used when posting the cash payments journal.

1. All debits to Accounts Payable must be posted immediately to the accounts payable ledger. A check mark is placed in the posting reference column of the journal to indicate that posting to the accounts payable ledger has taken place and CP and the page number are entered in the posting reference column of the ledger.

2. Each entry that is recorded in the sundry column as a debit is posted immediately to the appropriate general ledger account. The ledger account number is written in the posting reference column of the journal and CP and the page number are written in the posting reference column of the general ledger accounts.

3. The totals of the special columns are posted to the general ledger. The account number in parentheses is placed beneath the column total after posting has taken place and CP and the page number are written in the posting reference column of the general ledger account. An X must be placed in parentheses beneath the sundry column total to indicate that amounts in that column are posted individually.

The completed cash payments journal follows on page 322; pay special attention to the posting reference notations. T-accounts for the general ledger and the accounts payable ledger are also shown, on pages 322–323.

					CASH PAYMENTS JOURNAL				Page 7
Date	Check No.	Account Titles	Post. Ref.	Sundry Accounts Debit	Accounts Payable Debit	Purchases Debit	Purchases Discount Credit	Cash Credit
July 1	1071	Rent Expense	610	750 —				750 —
2	1072	Purchases				800 —		800 —
5	1073	Roberta Smith, Drawing	310	500 —				500 —
7	1074	Payroll Taxes Payable	210	180 —				180 —
8	1075	Telephone Expense	615	140 —				140 —
11	1076	Unity Products	✔		1200 —		24 —	1176 —
15	1077	Delivery Expense	630	30 —				30 —
18	1078	Joy Moroni Company	✔		1000 —		10 —	990 —
20	1079	Roberta Smith, Drawing	310	500 —				500 —
24	1080	Freight In	510	75 —				75 —
27	1081	Purchases				1400 —		1400 —
31	1082	Unity Products	✔		1600 —		32 —	1568 —
31	1083	Void						
				2175 —	3800 —	2200 —	66 —	8109 —
				(X)	(201)	(501)	(511)	(101)

Partial General Ledger

Cash   101

7/1	Balance	12,500	7/31	CP7	8,109

Roberta Smith, Drawing   310

7/5	CP7	500		
7/20	CP7	500		

Accounts Payable   201

7/31	CP7	3,800	7/1	Balance	8,500

Purchases   501

7/31	CP7	2,200		

Payroll Taxes Payable   210

7/7	CP7	180	7/1	Balance	180

Freight In   510

7/24	CP7	75		

Partial General Ledger (*continued*)					**Partial Accounts Payable Ledger**				

Purchases Discounts   **511**   **Joy Moroni Company**

			7/31	CP7	66	7/18	CP7	1,000	7/1	Balance	1,000

Rent Expense   **610**   **Unity Products**

7/1	CP7	750				7/11	CP7	1,200	7/1	Balance	2,800
						7/31	CP7	1,600			

Telephone Expense   **615**

7/8	CP7	140

Delivery Expense   **630**

7/15	CP7	30

THE COMBINED CASH JOURNAL

The combined cash journal uses features of the special journals and the general journal in a single record. It is often used by professional and service business owners when there are too many transactions to make using the general journal feasible, yet not enough transactions to make it worthwhile to use all the special journals.

All transactions may be recorded in the combined cash journal. Special columns are included as needed by the individual company for which the journal is designed. Typically, the combined cash journal includes debit and credit columns for Cash; debit and credit columns for Accounts Receivable and Accounts Payable; a column for Sales; and debit and credit sundry columns.

Study the combined cash journal for C. R. Riley, educational consultant, for the month of April 19XX.

			Cash				Accounts Receivable		
Date	Check No.	Description	Debit	Credit	✓		Debit	Credit	

COMBINED CASH JOURNAL

Date	Check No.	Description	Cash Debit	Cash Credit	✓	Acct Rec Debit	Acct Rec Credit
19XX Apr. 1	110	Paid Rent		800 —			
4	111	Owner Drawing		500 —			
6	112	Paid Telephone Bill		90 —			
7		Services Performed	2650 —				
7	113	Wages Paid		315 —			
9	114	Furniture Warehouse		250 —			
12		Office Supplies, Inc.					
14		Nancy Black	610 —		✓		610 —
14		Services/Pete Stone	2000 —		✓	1200 —	
14	115	Wages Paid		315 —			
17	116	Made Payment on Note					
		Plus Interest		275 —			
19		John Petersen	320 —		✓		320 —
21		Services Performed	1800 —				
21	117	Office Supplies, Inc.		440 —			
21	118	Wages Paid		315 —			
24	119	Purchased Supplies		60 —			
26	120	The Computer Store		100 —			
27		Wayne Rogers	300 —		✓		300 —
28	121	Wages Paid		315 —			
28		Services/Sue Paine	2900 —		✓	560 —	
29	122	Paid for Cleaning		50 —			
30		Received Partial					
		Payment on Note	1250 —				
			11830 —	3825 —		1760 —	1230 —
			(101)	(101)		(110)	(110)

Following is an explanation of some of the major types of entries included in the combined cash journal.

Expenses

During the month, C. R. Riley paid the following expenses: rent, April 1; telephone bill, April 6; wages, April 7, 14, 21, and 28; and cleaning, April 29. Each entry requires a debit to an expense account and a credit to Cash. Since there is a special debit column for wages expense, the amount may be entered in that column and in the cash credit column when wages are paid. A simple description of the transaction may be entered in the description column

Page **4**

✓	Accounts Payable		Wages Exp.	Prof. Fees	Sundry Accounts			
	Debit	Credit	Debit	Credit	Account Titles	PR	Debit	Credit
					Rent Expense	610	800 —	
					C. R. Riley, Drawing	320	500 —	
					Utilities Expense	630	90 —	
				2650 —				
			315 —					
✓	250 —							
✓		75 —			Supplies	140	75 —	
				3200 —				
			315 —					
					Notes Payable	205	250 —	
					Interest Expense	660	25 —	
				1800 —				
✓	440 —							
			315 —					
					Supplies	140	60 —	
✓	100 —							
			315 —					
				3460 —				
					Cleaning Expense	670	50 —	
					Notes Receivable	105		1250 —
	790 —	75 —	1260 —	11110 —			1850 —	1250 —
	(210)	(210)	(640)	(410)			(X)	(X)

of the journal. The other debits to expense accounts are entered in the sundry debit column along with the account title, and the credit amounts are entered in the cash credit column. Again, a short description of the transaction may be entered in the description column of the journal.

Services Performed

C. R. Riley recorded services performed for cash on April 7 and 21. Each entry requires a debit to Cash and a credit to Professional Fees. Since there are special columns for both of these account titles, the dollar amounts are entered in the correct columns and a brief description is written in the description column. On April 14 and 28, C. R. Riley performed services again; however, on these dates, part of the money was received in cash and the rest was on account. Debits to Cash and Accounts Receivable are required, along with the credit to Professional Fees. Again, there are special columns for each account title; the customer's name is entered in the description column, so that posting to Accounts Receivable ledger may take place.

Transactions Involving Accounts Payable

Payments made on account occurred on April 9, 21, and 26. In each case, the debit amount is entered in the accounts payable debit column and the credit amount in the cash credit column. The creditor's name is written in the description column, so that posting to the accounts payable ledger may take place.

On April 12, supplies were purchased on account. The $75 debit is entered in the sundry debit column along with the account title of Supplies. The credit amount is entered in the accounts payable credit column and the name of the creditor, Office Supplies, Inc., is written in the description column.

Transactions Involving Accounts Receivable

On April 14, 19, and 27, C. R. Riley received cash from customers paying on account. Each entry requires a debit to Cash and a credit to Accounts Receivable. The debit and credit amounts may be entered directly into the special columns, and the customer's name must be entered in the description column, so that posting to the accounts receivable ledger may take place. As has already been mentioned, on April 14 and 28 debits to Accounts Receivable are recorded when C. R. Riley performed services for customers and agreed to accept payment at a later date.

Payment Made on a Note

On April 17, C. R. Riley wrote a check for $275 in partial payment of a note and interest. The debit amounts to Notes Payable and Interest Expense are entered in the sundry debit column, along with the account titles; the corresponding credit is entered in the cash credit column. It is acceptable to use more than one line if necessary for any combined cash journal entry.

Crossfooting, Ruling, and Posting the Combined Cash Journal

Following is the proof of crossfooting for the combined cash journal.

Column	Debit Column Totals	Credit Column Totals
Cash	$11,830	$ 3,825
Accounts Receivable	1,760	1,230
Accounts Payable	790	75
Wages Expense	1,260	
Professional Fees		11,110
Sundry	1,850	1,250
Totals	$17,490	$17,490

Once crossfooting is complete, a single ruling is placed beneath all amount columns and a double ruling is placed beneath all columns except the description column and the account titles column preceding the sundry debit and credit columns.

Posting to the accounts receivable and accounts payable ledgers is done immediately after each transaction is journalized. A check mark is placed in the journal after posting to the subsidiary ledger, and J and the page number are placed in the posting reference column of the subsidiary ledger account. In a similar fashion, posting is performed immediately for all amounts entered in the sundry columns, and the account number is entered in the special posting reference column of the journal after posting has been completed. J and the page number is entered in the posting reference column of the general ledger accounts, and an X is placed beneath the sundry column totals to indicate that items have been posted individually.

Summary posting is performed at the end of the month; account numbers are placed in parentheses beneath the individual column totals, and J and the page number are entered in the posting reference column of the general ledger accounts.

RECORDING INTEREST PAID

negotiable
capable of being legally transferred from one person to another

collateral
property that is acceptable as security for a loan

repossess
to take back possession of

foreclose
to deprive the borrower of the right to retain ownership of the property when the borrower is behind in payments

interest
the charge made for a loan, usually expressed as a percent of the amount borrowed

promissory note
a legal document signed by the borrower (the maker) that specifies the amount borrowed, the interest rate, the time, and the due date of the loan

maker
the person who borrows money and who signs a promissory note

principal
the amount of money borrowed

payee
the person who lends the money; the person to whom payments of principal and interest will be made

Major purchases of equipment, inventory, vehicles, or other assets are often paid for partially through the issuance of a note. A note is a **negotiable** instrument; that is, it can be bought and sold. Usually, when a note is issued by the seller, the item sold is held as **collateral** for the note; in other words, title does not fully pass to the buyer until the note is paid in full. The seller normally retains the option to **repossess** the merchandise sold (or to **foreclose** on property) if the terms of the note are not met.

Assume, for example, that Valley Restaurant Supply sold booths and tables to Tony's Pizza on July 1, 19XX, at a total cost of $24,000. Tony paid $14,000 cash as a down payment and signed an **interest**-bearing note for the other $10,000; the interest rate agreed on was 10 percent per year. Tony agreed to pay the full amount of the note and the interest at the end of one year's time. Tony signed the following **promissory note.**

$ 10,000.00	Taos, New Mexico	July 1, 19XX
One year	after date	I promise to pay
to the order of	Valley Restaurant Supply	
	00	
	Ten thousand and 100 — — — — — — —	dollars
at	Bank of New Mexico	
Value received with interest at	10%	
No. 502 Due July 1, 19XX		Tony Agostini
	Tony's Pizza	

Tony Agostini is the borrower, or the **maker,** of the note; he signs the note and is required to pay back the **principal** plus the interest. Valley Restaurant Supply is referred to as the **payee** of the note and is the firm to which payment will be made. A purchase such as Tony's, with a cash down payment and the signing of a note, could be recorded in the general journal as follows.

		GENERAL JOURNAL			Page 18	
Date		Description	Post. Ref.	Debit	Credit	
July 1	1	Furniture		24000 —		
		Cash			14000 —	
		Notes Payable			10000 —	
		To Record Purchase of Booths and Tables from				
		Valley Restaurant Supply; Signed a 1-year,				
		10% Note				

19XX

Because all payments of cash should be recorded in the cash payments journal, the entry would best be recorded as follows.

				Sundry Accounts Debit	Accounts Payable Debit	Purchases Debit	Purchases Discount Credit	Cash Credit
Date	Check No.	Account Titles	Post. Ref.					
July 1	1768	Furniture		24000 —				14000 —
		Notes Payable		(10000 —)				

CASH PAYMENTS JOURNAL — Page 7

19XX

The debit to Furniture for $24,000 is entered as usual in the sundry column, and the $14,000 credit to Cash is entered in the cash credit column. Since there is no special credit column for Notes Payable or a sundry credit column, the $10,000 credit to Notes Payable is entered in brackets in the sundry debit column. The brackets indicate that the $10,000 is to be posted with a balance opposite the one indicated in the column head, or in this case, that the $10,000 is a *credit* rather than a *debit*.

At the end of the year, when Tony pays the $10,000 plus interest to Valley Restaurant Supply, the entry will be recorded in the cash payments journal. The ordinary simple interest on the note is calculated as follows.

Interest Formula

$$\text{Interest} = \text{Principal} \times \text{Rate} \times \text{Time}$$
$$I = P \times R \times T,$$
$$\text{where principal} = \text{amount borrowed}$$
$$\text{rate} = \text{interest rate}$$
$$\text{time} = \text{length of time for which money is kept}$$

Interest Calculation

1. Change interest rate into a decimal by moving the decimal point two places to the left:

$$10\% = \underset{\smile}{10.} = .10$$

2. Multiply:

$$I = P \times R \times T$$
$$I = \$10,000 \times .10 \times 1 \text{ (1 year)}^*$$
$$I = \$1,000$$

The cash payments journal entry to record the payment of the note plus the interest would look like this.

					Sundry Accounts Debit	Accounts Payable Debit	Purchases Debit	Purchases Discount Credit	Cash Credit
Date	Check No.	Account Titles	Post. Ref.						
July	1	*2691*	*Notes Payable*		10 0 0 0 —				11 0 0 0 —
			Interest Expense		1 0 0 0 —				

CASH PAYMENTS JOURNAL — Page *19*

Two or more lines may be used when recording an entry in the cash payments journal. Interest Expense is treated like any other expense account, except that it is shown at the bottom of the income statement in a category called Other Expenses. ("Other" refers to expenses not normally classified as regular operating expenses.)

---

*Note that 10 percent means 10 hundredths and may be expressed in decimal form as .10 or in fraction form as 10/100.

RECORDING INTEREST RECEIVED

The transaction between Tony Agostini and Valley Restaurant Supply may be used to illustrate the receipt of interest as well as the payment of interest. The following shows how the transaction would be handled on the books of Valley Restaurant Supply. The original sale of the booths and tables to Tony Agostini could be recorded in the general journal as follows.

		GENERAL JOURNAL			Page 9
Date		Description	Post. Ref.	Debit	Credit
19XX July	1	Notes Receivable		10000 —	
		Cash		14000 —	
		Sales			24000 —
		To Record Sale of Booths and Tables to Tony's			
		Pizza; Issued a 1-year, 10% Note			

However, the transaction should be recorded in a cash receipts journal.

		CASH RECEIPTS JOURNAL						Page 7
Date		Account Titles	Post. Ref.	Sundry Accounts Credit	Accounts Receivable Credit	Sales Credit	Sales Discount Debit	Cash Debit
19XX July	1	Notes Receivable		(10000 —)		24000 —		14000 —

Since there is no sundry debit column in the cash receipts journal, the $10,000 debit to Notes Receivable is entered in brackets in the sundry credit column to indicate that the amount is to be posted as a debit. When, one year later, Valley Restaurant Supply receives the check from Tony's Pizza, it will be recorded in the cash receipts journal as follows.

CASH RECEIPTS JOURNAL								Page 7
Date	Account Titles	Post. Ref.	Sundry Accounts Credit	Accounts Receivable Credit	Sales Credit	Sales Discount Debit	Cash Debit
July 19XX 1	*Notes Receivable*		10 0 0 0 —				11 0 0 0 —
	Interest Income		1 0 0 0 —				

Again, two or more lines may be used for the entry. Interest Income is a miscellaneous income item and is shown at the bottom of the income statement under Other Income.

OTHER EXPENSES AND OTHER INCOME ON THE INCOME STATEMENT

The net income with which you are already familiar refers to income from operations and is that regular income that results from the company selling its product or service. The net operating income figure is compared and analyzed from period to period, and net income must be compared from the same source. Therefore, income items that are irregular are listed at the bottom of the income statement as an addition after net income from operations has been calculated. Other income might result from interest being received, a credit balance in the Cash Short and Over account, rent income (resulting when the business rents out an unused portion of the premises), or a gain incurred on the sale or disposition of an asset.

Other expense items are those expenses not normally incurred in regular operations and may include interest expense or a debit balance in the Cash Short and Over account. A portion of an income statement, with sections for other income and other expense, is shown here.

Toy Warehouse
Income Statement
For Month Ended July 31, 19XX

Revenue			
Sales		$75,000	
Less: Sales Returns and Allowances	$4,000		
Sales Discounts	1,300	5,300	
Net Sales			$69,700

Net Income from Operations		$ 7,000
Other Income		
Interest Income	$ 800	
Miscellaneous Income	200	
Total Other Income	1,000	
Other Expenses		
Interest Expense	350	650
Net Income		$ 7,650

MISCELLANEOUS ORDINARY INTEREST CALCULATIONS

When money is borrowed for a period of time other than one year, the time portion of the interest formula will not be 1 (for one year). If, for example, money is borrowed for two years, the ordinary simple interest will be twice as much as if borrowed for one year.

Example $10,000 is borrowed at 9 percent for 2 years.

$$\text{Formula: } I = P \times R \times T$$
$$I = \$10,000 \times 9\% \times 2$$
$$I = \$10,000 \times .09 \times 2$$
$$I = \$1,800$$

If money is borrowed for half a year, the ordinary simple interest will be one-half of what it would be for a whole year. When the time is expressed in months, a fraction is used in the formula to express it. The numerator is the number of months for which the money is borrowed and the denominator is 12 (for one year).

Example $10,000 is borrowed at 8 percent for 6 months.

Formula: I = P × R × T

$$I = \$10{,}000 \times 8\% \times \frac{6}{12}$$

$$I = \frac{\overset{100}{\cancel{10{,}000}}}{1} \times \frac{\overset{4}{\cancel{8}}}{\underset{1}{\cancel{100}}} \times \frac{\overset{1}{\cancel{6}}}{\underset{\underset{1}{2}}{\cancel{12}}}$$

$$I = \$400$$

or, on a calculator,

$$I = P \times R \times T$$

$$I = \$10{,}000 \times .08 \times .5 \ (.5 \text{ is one-half or } \frac{6}{12} \text{ of a year})$$

$$I = \$400$$

When money is borrowed for a specific number of days, a fraction is also used in the formula to express the time. The numerator will be the number of days for which the money is borrowed and the denominator will be 360. (When calculating ordinary simple interest, a year is considered to have 360 days.)

Example $10,000 is borrowed at 6 percent for 60 days.

Formula: I = P × R × T

$$I = \frac{\overset{100}{\cancel{10{,}000}}}{1} \times \frac{\overset{1}{\cancel{6}}}{\underset{1}{\cancel{100}}} \times \frac{\overset{1}{\cancel{60}}}{\underset{\underset{1}{6}}{\cancel{360}}}$$

$$I = \$100$$

or, on a calculator,

$$I = \frac{10{,}000 \times .06}{6} \ (60 \text{ days is } \frac{1}{6} \text{ of a year; multiply } 10{,}000$$
$$\text{by .06 and divide the result by 6)}$$

SUMMARY

A strong system of internal control will help a business protect its resources from theft, waste, and inefficiency; ensure that accounting data is accurate; and evaluate employees and departments to determine their level of performance. Proper cash management provides for the accurate accounting of cash and minimizes losses from theft and fraud. It requires that cash receipts be deposited daily; that cash payments be made by check and only by an authorized individual; that no one person be responsible for receiving cash *and* making cash payments; that one person be designated to verify the amounts of cash payments and another to actually write the checks; and that someone be designated to enforce the cash handling procedures.

Cash registers should be in the plain view of the customer as a double check against fraudulent amounts being recorded. Prenumbered sales tickets should be used, and any missing sales tickets are a red flag to management that something is amiss.

At the end of an employee's shift, the sales tickets should be totaled and compared with the cash register tape total and the amount in the cash drawer. If more money is in the drawer than the total indicated by the tape and the sales tickets, then there is an overage and the amount is credited to an account called Cash Short and Over. If less money is in the cash register drawer than indicated by the tape and the sales tickets, then there is a shortage and the amount is debited to Cash Short and Over. At the end of the accounting period, the Cash Short and Over account may have either a debit or a credit balance. If it has a credit balance, it is listed on the income statement in a special category called other income, which follows net income from operations; if it has a debit balance, it is listed in a special category called other expenses, which follows other income.

Stores that allow the use of credit cards by customers may avoid costly credit checks and subsequent uncollectible accounts expense. The issuing company for the credit cards will charge the merchant a fee for the use of the credit card services; this fee is debited by the merchant to an account called Credit Card Discount Expense.

All cash received is recorded in the cash receipts journal, and all checks written are recorded in the cash payments journal. Every entry in the cash receipts journal is a debit to Cash, and every entry in the cash payments journal is a credit to Cash. Special columns are included in the journals as required. Immediate postings are required to the accounts receivable and accounts payable subsidiary ledgers, and daily postings are required from the sundry columns of both the cash receipts and cash payments journals. At the end of the accounting period, the journals are crossfooted and ruled before summary posting is performed.

The combined cash journal is used primarily by professionals who have too many transactions to conveniently use the general journal and too few to make use of the special journals feasible. The process for journalizing and posting from the combined cash journal is the same as for the cash receipts and cash payments journals.

Sometimes merchandise or services are sold by accepting a promissory note for a portion or all that is owed. The maker of the note normally agrees to pay back the principal and interest within a certain time. The formula for calculating interest is: Interest = Principal × Rate × Time (I = P × R × T). Interest rates are normally expressed in terms of a year. Interest paid is recorded in the cash payments journal, and interest received is recorded in the cash receipts journal.

Review of Accounting Terminology

Following is a list of the accounting terminology for this chapter.

collateral	payee
expenditure	principal
foreclose	promissory note
fraud	reimburse
interest	repossess
justify	sundry
maker	valid
negotiable	

Fill in the blank with the correct word or term from the list.

1. A legal document that shows the amount borrowed, the interest rate, and the due date of the money borrowed and that is signed by the maker is called a _____.

2. A person who borrows money and who signs a note is called the _____ of the note.
3. The lender is called the _____ of the note.
4. The amount of money borrowed is called the _____.
5. An amount spent is a/an _____.
6. Security that is given for a loan is called _____.
7. A dishonest act in which someone is cheated is called _____.
8. To show or prove that something is right is to _____.
9. To take back possession of is to _____.
10. Another word for miscellaneous is _____.
11. When a borrower is behind in payments, the lender may choose to _____ on the property, thus depriving the borrower of ownership rights.
12. A charge made for the use of money is called _____.
13. A document that may be transferred from one party to another is said to be _____.
14. To repay is to _____.
15. Having facts to support something makes it _____.

Match the following words and terms on the left with the definitions on the right (lists continue on the following page).

16. valid
17. sundry
18. repossess
19. reimburse
20. promissory note
21. principal
22. payee
23. negotiable
24. maker
25. justify
26. interest
27. fraud
28. foreclose

a. to take back possession of
b. the lender
c. a dishonest act to deceive someone
d. the amount borrowed
e. miscellaneous
f. to repay
g. transferable from one person or party to another
h. the borrower
i. an expense or amount spent
j. security for a loan
k. an amount charged for borrowing money

30. collateral

l. legally sound because of facts or evidence

m. a legal document indicating an amount of money borrowed, the interest rate, and the time; it is signed by the maker

n. to prove to be right or fair

o. to deprive a borrower of her or his ownership rights

Exercises

Exercise 9.1
posting the cash receipts journal

Following is a cash receipts journal with all the entries recorded for the month of August 19XX. A partial chart of accounts and account balances also follow.

				CASH RECEIPTS JOURNAL					Page 8
Date	Account Titles	Post. Ref.	Sundry Accounts Credit	Accounts Receivable Credit	Sales Credit	Sales Discount Debit	Cash Debit
19XX Aug. 1	A. A. Zorba			100 —			100 —
8	P. R. Swan			200 —		4 —	196 —
10	Office Furniture		1200 —				1200 —
15	A. A. Zorba			400 —			400 —
18	Cash Sales				650 —		650 —
24	Notes Receivable		5000 —				5000 —
27	Cash Sales				200 —		200 —
30	S. T. Tarnower, Capital		1500 —				1500 —
31	P. R. Swan			80 —		1 60	78 40

Partial General Ledger		**Balance**	**Partial Accounts Receivable Ledger**	**Balance**
101	Cash	$8,750	P. R. Swan	$600
105	Notes Receivable	5,000	A. A. Zorba	500
110	Accounts Receivable	1,400		
120	Office Furniture	3,200		
301	S. T. Tarnower, Capital	9,640		
401	Sales			
410	Sales Discounts			

Total each column and crossfoot the journal to prove the equality of the debit and credit columns. Rule the journal and post following these instructions.

a. Post all amounts in the accounts receivable credit column to the accounts receivable subsidiary ledger. Place a check mark in the journal after posting and enter CR8 in the subsidiary ledger accounts.

b. Post all amounts in the sundry credit column to the general ledger. Place the account numbers after posting in the posting reference column of the journal and enter CR8 in the posting reference column of the ledger accounts.

c. Perform the required summary posting. Place the account numbers in parentheses beneath the double ruling and place CR8 in the posting reference column of the general ledger accounts.

Exercise 9.2
posting the cash payments journal

Following is a cash payments journal with all the entries recorded for the month of March 19XX. Also following is a partial chart of accounts and account balances along with subsidiary ledger names and balances.

		CASH PAYMENTS JOURNAL						Page 3
Date	Check No.	Account Titles	Post. Ref.	Sundry Accounts Debit	Accounts Payable Debit	Purchases Debit	Purchases Discount Credit	Cash Credit
19XX *Mar.* 1	7012	*Freight In*		35 —				35 —
4	7013	*Lorraine Stewart,* *Drawing*		750 —				750 —
8	7014	*Smith Sisters, Inc.*			600 —		12 —	588 —
12	7015	*Hinsdale Products Co.*			1500 —		15 —	1485 —
17	7016	*Utilities Expense*		175 —				175 —
20	7017	*Purchases*				496 —		496 —
21	7018	*Void*						
21	7019	*Payroll Taxes Payable*		220 —				220 —
25	7020	*Purchases*				320 —		320 —
29	7021	*Smith Sisters, Inc.*			900 —		18 —	882 —

Partial General Ledger	Balance	Partial Accounts Payable Ledger	Balance
101 Cash	$7,221	Hinsdale Products Co.	$1,500
215 Accounts Payable	4,204	Smith Sisters, Inc.	1,500
225 Payroll Taxes Payable	220		
310 Lorraine Stewart, Drawing			
501 Purchases			
520 Purchases Discounts			
530 Freight In			
615 Utilities Expense			

Total each column and crossfoot the journal to prove the equality of the debit and credit columns. Rule the journal and post following these instructions.

a. Post all amounts in the accounts payable debit column to the accounts payable subsidiary ledger. Place a check mark in the journal after posting and enter CP3 in the subsidiary ledger accounts.

b. Post all amounts in the sundry debit column to the general ledger. Place the account numbers after posting in the posting reference column of the journal and enter CP3 in the posting reference column of the ledger accounts.

c. Perform the required summary posting. Place the account numbers in parentheses beneath the double ruling and place CP3 in the posting reference column of the general ledger accounts.

Exercise 9.3
journalizing and posting charge card sales and subsequent payment

Record the following cash sales and cash receipts for the month of October in a cash receipts journal (page 18) and the sales on account in the sales journal (page 25). Post immediately all transactions involving Accounts Receivable to the accounts receivable subsidiary ledger. You do not need to post to the general ledger. Account titles required are Cash, Accounts Receivable, Sales Tax Payable, Sales, and Credit Card Discount Expense.

Oct. 1   sold merchandise for cash to Rick Trevino; $90 plus $3.60 sales tax; invoice 143–L

Oct. 4   sold merchandise to Sandra Butler; $120 plus $4.80 sales tax; invoice 172–L; Sandra paid for the merchandise with her Ultra Charge card

Oct. 8   sold merchandise for cash to Andrew Bigg; $340 plus $13.60 sales tax; invoice 144–L

Oct. 10   sold merchandise on account to Tay Luong; $520 plus $20.80 sales tax; invoice 176–L; Tay paid for the merchandise with his Ultra Charge card

Oct. 15   received $573 from the Ultra Charge Company; this represents charge tickets totaling $600 minus a 4.5 percent fee

Exercise 9.4
journalizing cash sales with shortages and overages

a. Record the following cash sales in the cash receipts journal (page 10) for Geri's Jeans for the first week in March.

b. Determine whether the Cash Short and Over account has a debit or credit balance and the amount of the balance.

Date	Sales	Actual Cash on Hand	Cash Short Or (Over)
March 1	$2,754	$2,774	($20)
March 2	2,329	2,334	($5)
March 3	1,645	1,635	$10
March 4	1,520	1,519	$1
March 5	2,116	2,166	($50)
March 6	2,904	2,886	$18
March 7	1,592	1,590	$2

Exercise 9.5

calculating ordinary simple interest

Calculate the ordinary simple interest for the following. Round your answers to the nearest penny if necessary.

Interest	=	Principal	×	Rate	×	Time
1. _____	=	$ 5,000	×	10%	×	1 year
2. _____	=	3,000	×	7	×	3 years
3. _____	=	8,500	×	5	×	6 months
4. _____	=	12,000	×	11	×	3 months
5. _____	=	1,000	×	12	×	60 days
6. _____	=	2,400	×	8	×	30 days
7. _____	=	10,000	×	9	×	1 month
8. _____	=	25,000	×	13	×	5 years
9. _____	=	50,000	×	9	×	15 years
10. _____	=	14,000	×	7	×	6 months

Exercise 9.6

determining appropriate debits and credits for notes receivable and notes payable transactions

Indicate for the following transactions which accounts should be debited and credited and for how much. Also indicate into which journal (cash receipts, cash payments, or general journal) each transaction should be recorded. Account titles required are Cash, Notes Receivable, Notes Payable, Sales, Interest Income, and Interest Expense. Use the following headings for your answers.

Transaction Date	Account(s) Debited	Debit Amount	Account(s) Credited	Credit Amount	Journal

Feb. 1   borrowed $5,000 from Providence City Bank; signed a 6 month, 10 percent note

Mar. 3   sold $7,000 in merchandise to Boat House; accepted a 3 month, 9 percent note in payment

June 3   received a check from Boat House in full payment of the March 3 note plus the interest

Aug. 1   wrote a check to Providence City Bank in full payment of the February 1 note plus the 10 percent interest for 6 months

Exercise 9.7

totaling, crossfooting, ruling, and posting a combined cash journal

Following is a combined cash journal with the May transactions recorded in it. Total each column and crossfoot and rule the journal. Then post following these instructions.

a. Post all amounts in the accounts receivable and accounts payable columns to the appropriate subsidiary ledger account. Place a check mark in the column provided in the journal and place J6 in the subsidiary ledger accounts. A partial list of the names and balances in the subsidiary ledgers follows.

Partial Accounts Receivable Ledger	Balance	Partial Accounts Payable Ledger	Balance
Sandra Buchanan	0	Bud's Repairs	$500
Wilma Groggins	0	Office Furniture, Inc.	0
Patrick Nolen	$400	Supply Warehouse	0
Bill Price	100		

b. Post all amounts entered in the sundry debit and credit columns to the appropriate general ledger accounts. Enter the account number in the posting reference column of the journal and J6 in the general ledger accounts. A partial list of the general ledger accounts and balances follows.

Partial General Ledger		Balance
100	Cash	$6,428
110	Notes Receivable	3,250
120	Accounts Receivable	800
130	Supplies	290
140	Office Furniture	3,575
210	Accounts Payable	1,722
410	Professional Fees	
420	Interest Income	
610	Utilities Expense	
620	Rent Expense	
630	Wages Expense	

c. Perform the required summary posting and enter the general ledger account numbers in parentheses beneath the double-ruled line. Enter J6 in the posting reference column of the ledger accounts.

Journal for Exercise 9.7

			COMBINED CASH JOURNAL								
				Cash					Accounts Receivable		
Date	Check No.	Description		Debit		Credit	✓		Debit		Credit
19XX May 1	110	Paid phone bill				120 —					
1	111	Paid Rent				1000 —					
4	112	Bud's Repairs				500 —					
7		Performed Services		1300 —							
11		Bill Price		100 —							100 —
14		Performed Services		2100 —							
16		Supply Warehouse									
18	113	Paid Part-time Wages				90 —					
21		Wilma Groggins							1000 —		
23		Office Furniture, Inc.									
25		Purchased Supplies				200 —					
26		Supply Warehouse				100 —					
28		Patrick Nolen		50 —							50 —
29		Sandra Buchanan							500 —		
30	114	Paid Wages				120 —					
31		Wilma Groggins		300 —							300 —
31		Received Partial		650 —							
		Payment on Note		650 —							

Accounts Payable		Wages Exp.	Prof. Fees	Sundry Accounts			
Debit	Credit	Debit	Credit	Account Titles	PR	Debit	Credit
				Utilities Expense		120 —	
				Rent Expense		1000 —	
500 —			1300 —				
			2100 —				
	450 —			Supplies		450 —	
		90 —					
			1000 —				
	2500 —			Office Furniture		2500 —	
100 —				Supplies		200 —	
			500 —				
		120 —					
				Notes Receivable			600 —
				Interest Income			50 —

Exercise 9.8
determining which journal to use

After looking over the following transactions, determine into which journal each should be recorded. Identify the journals by their posting reference notations: sales journal, S; purchases journal, P; cash receipts journal, CR; cash payments journal, CP; and general journal, GJ.

Type of Transaction	Which Journal?
1. paid monthly telephone bill	_____
2. purchased merchandise for resale on account	_____
3. received cash from a customer who is paying on account	_____
4. purchased furniture on account	_____
5. sold merchandise on account	_____
6. withdrew cash for personal use	_____
7. made payment to a creditor	_____
8. sold extra item of office equipment; will receive payment within 90 days	_____
9. invested additional cash into the business	_____
10. made adjusting entries	_____
11. purchased office equipment for cash	_____
12. borrowed money from a bank	_____
13. issued credit memorandum to a customer to whom merchandise was originally sold on account	_____
14. made payment on a loan, plus interest	_____
15. purchased merchandise for resale for cash	_____
16. made cash sales plus 6 percent sales tax	_____
17. received payment less a 2 percent discount from a customer to whom merchandise was sold earlier	_____
18. invested personal property into the business	_____
19. recorded closing entries	_____
20. issued a debit memorandum to creditor from whom merchandise was purchased on account	_____

Problems

Problem 9.1
journalizing in cash receipts journal and posting

Suzie Niessen owns a retail gift shop. Suzie makes sales for cash, sales on account, and credit card sales through the Horizon Credit Card Company. A 5 percent sales tax is collected on all sales. Following are a partial chart of accounts, a partial list of the customers in the accounts receivable subsidiary ledger, and the transactions relating to cash received for the month of October 19XX.

Partial General Ledger		Balance	Partial Accounts Receivable Ledger	Balance
101	Cash	$ 4,621.90	Barbara Goode	$ 52.50
110	Notes Receivable	1,000.00	Ron King	189.00
120	Accounts Receivable	5,021.90	Horizon Credit Card Company	4,000.00
130	Office Equipment	10,420.00		
220	Sales Tax Payable	65.20		
301	Suzie Niessen, Capital	9,604.00		
401	Sales			
410	Interest Income			
610	Credit Card Discount Expense			

Transactions

Oct. 1   sold merchandise for cash; $175 plus 5 percent sales tax

Oct. 4   received a check for $189 from Ron King to apply on his account

Oct. 8   received a check from Horizon Credit Card Company for $1,432.50 for payment on account for credit card sales of $1,500 less a 4.5 percent discount

Oct. 12   cold merchandise for cash; $290 plus 5 percent sales tax

Oct. 15   invested an additional $6,000 into the business

Oct. 17   sold an extra item of office equipment to Al Torino for $5,500 cash, original cost of the equipment

Oct. 20   received a check for $52.50 from Barbara Goode to apply on her account

Oct. 24   received a check from Horizon Credit Card Company for $2,387.50 for credit card sales of $2,500 less a 4.5 percent discount

Oct. 27   sold merchandise for cash; $700 plus 5 percent sales tax

Oct. 31   received a check from Andrew Pate for $1,200 for full payment plus interest of his $1,000 outstanding note of a year ago

Instructions

1. Transfer the account balances to the general ledger and the subsidiary ledger accounts.

2. Journalize the transactions in a cash receipts journal. Use page 10.

3. Post immediately to the accounts receivable subsidiary ledger for all transactions involving accounts receivable. Enter a check mark in the posting reference column of the journal and enter CR10 in the subsidiary ledger accounts.

4. *Post immediately to the general ledger for all amounts entered in the sundry credit column. Place the account number in the posting reference column of the journal and enter CR10 in the general ledger accounts.*

5. *Total, crossfoot, and rule the journal.*

6. *Perform the required summary posting. Enter the account numbers in parentheses beneath the double ruling and enter CR10 in the posting reference column of the general ledger accounts.*

Problem 9.2
journalizing in cash payments journal and posting

Wayne Werner owns a retail store called Artists' Supply Shop. Wayne takes advantage of all purchases discounts offered. Following are a partial chart of accounts and account balances, a partial list of the creditors in the accounts payable subsidiary ledger, and the transactions relating to cash payments for the month of April 19XX.

Partial General Ledger		Balance	Partial Accounts Payable Ledger	Balance
101	Cash	$10,614	Art Corner	$2,100
220	Notes Payable	500	Sandberg's Paints	3,000
230	Accounts Payable	7,200		
240	Payroll Taxes Payable	175		
320	Wayne Werner, Drawing			
501	Purchases			
510	Purchases Discount			
520	Freight In			
605	Rent Expense			
610	Utilities Expense			
630	Interest Expense			

Transactions

Apr. 1 wrote check 5203 for $650 for April rent

Apr. 3 wrote check 5204 for $125 to Kwik Delivery when it delivered an out-of-town purchase

Apr. 6 withdrew $500 for personal use; check 5205

Apr. 8 paid payroll taxes due, $175; check 5206

Apr. 11 wrote check 5207 for $1,764 to Sandberg's Paints in payment of its invoice 1643-2 for $1,800 less a 2 percent discount

Apr. 13 wrote check 5208 for $2,460 for cash purchases of frames, mats, and paint brushes for resale

Apr. 15   wrote check 5209 for electricity bill; $140

Apr. 19   wrote check 5210 for $1,188 to Art Corner in payment of its invoice 469-20 for $1,200 less a 1 percent discount

Apr. 22   wrote check 5211 for $92 in payment of telephone bill

Apr. 25   wrote check 5212 for $510 in full payment of a $500 note plus interest

Apr. 28   withdrew $500 for personal use; check 5213

Apr. 30   wrote check 5214 for $490 to Sandberg's Paints in payment of its invoice 1740-2 for $500 less a 2 percent discount

Apr. 30   wrote check 5215 for $642 for purchase of art supplies for re-sale

Instructions

1. *Enter the account balances into the general ledger and the subsidiary ledger accounts*

2. *Journalize the transactions in a cash payments journal. Use page 4.*

3. *Post immediately to the accounts payable subsidiary ledger for all transactions involving accounts payable. Enter a check mark in the posting reference column of the journal and enter CP4 in the subsidiary ledger accounts.*

4. *Post immediately to the general ledger for all amounts entered in the sundry debit column. Place the account number in the posting reference column of the journal and enter CP4 in the general ledger accounts.*

5. *Total, crossfoot, and rule the journal.*

6. *Perform the required summary posting. Enter the account numbers in parentheses beneath the double ruling and enter CP4 in the posting reference column of the general ledger accounts.*

Problem 9.3

journalizing in cash receipts and cash payments journals and posting

Grace O'Brien owns a retail store called The Book Depot. Grace sells merchandise for cash and on account and also accepts credit card sales through the Wonder Charge Company. Grace takes advantage of all purchases discounts by paying within the discount period. A 6 percent sales tax is charged for each sale. Following are the cash transactions for December and a partial chart of accounts with balances for selected accounts as of December 1. Partial schedules of accounts receivable and accounts payable as of December 1 are also shown.

Partial Chart of Accounts

101	Cash	$3,800
110	Notes Receivable	400
120	Accounts Receivable	5,000
201	Notes Payable	2,500
210	Accounts Payable	3,000
220	Sales Tax Payable	600
301	Grace O'Brien, Capital	7,500
310	Grace O'Brien, Drawing	
401	Sales	
410	Interest Income	
501	Purchases	
510	Purchases Discounts	
601	Credit Card Discount Expense	
620	Utilities Expense	
630	Rent Expense	
640	Interest Expense	

Partial Schedule of Accounts Receivable		Partial Schedule of Accounts Payable	
Ellen Brown	$ 150	Book Wholesalers	$750
Kenneth Kong	180	Paperbacks, Inc.	900
Wonder Charge Company	3,300		

Transactions

Dec. 1 sold merchandise for cash; $320 plus 6 percent sales tax

Dec. 2 wrote check 9013 for December rent; $1,500

Dec. 5 received a $70 check from Ellen Brown to apply on her account

Dec. 6 wrote check 9014 to Book Wholesalers for $735 in full payment of its invoice 1620-A for $750 less a 2 percent discount

Dec. 9 received a check from Wonder Charge Company for $1,056 for credit card sales of $1,100 minus a 4 percent discount

Dec. 10 wrote check 9015 to pay sales tax from previous period; $600

Dec. 11 wrote check 9016 for $82 in payment of telephone bill

Dec. 12 invested an additional $4,500 into business

Dec. 15 sold merchandise for cash; $570 plus 6 percent sales tax

Dec. 16 withdrew $800 for personal use; check 9017

Dec. 17 wrote check 9018 to Paperbacks, Inc., for $891 for payment in full of its invoice 16204 for $900 less a 1 percent discount

Dec. 17   wrote check 9019 for $650 for purchase of books for resale

Dec. 18   received a $50 check from Kenneth Kong to apply on his account

Dec. 24   received a check from Thomas Payne for $440 for full payment of his outstanding note of $400 plus interest

Dec. 26   wrote check 9020 in payment of electric bill; $230

Dec. 26   wrote check 9021 for $520 for purchase of books for resale

Dec. 28   sold merchandise for cash; $900 plus 6 percent sales tax

Dec. 29   wrote check 9022 for $2,750 to Eastern Savings Company in full payment of outstanding note of $2,500 plus interest

Dec. 30   received a check from Ellen Brown for $80 to apply on her account

Dec. 31   received a check from Wonder Charge Company for $2,112 for credit card sales of $2,200 less a 4 percent discount

Instructions

1. *Transfer the account balances to the general ledger accounts and the subsidiary ledger accounts.*

2. *Journalize December's transactions into a cash receipts journal, page 16, and a cash payments journal, page 20.*

3. *As an entry is journalized to accounts receivable or accounts payable, post immediately to the appropriate account in either the accounts receivable or the accounts payable ledger.*

4. *Post immediately to the general ledger for all transactions entered in a sundry column.*

5. *When journalizing is complete, total, crossfoot, and rule the journals.*

6. *Perform the required summary posting from the cash receipts journal and the cash payments journal.*

Problem 9.4
journalizing in all five journals, totaling, crossfooting, and ruling

Willie Davis owns a retail store called Family Cycles. He sells bicycles and parts, both for cash and on account. Willie uses a cash receipts journal, a cash payments journal, sales and purchases journals, and a general journal. Willie is required to collect a 5 percent sales tax on all sales; terms of credit sales are net 30. Following are the partial chart of accounts and the transactions for Family Cycles for the month of May 19XX.

Partial Chart of Accounts

101 Cash
110 Accounts Receivable
130 Office Equipment
210 Accounts Payable
220 Sales Tax Payable
301 Willie Davis, Capital
310 Willie Davis, Drawing
401 Sales
410 Sales Returns and Allowances
501 Purchases
510 Purchases Returns and Allowances
601 Rent Expense
620 Utilities Expense

Transactions

May	1	purchased unassembled bicycles from Bike World on account; $1,750; invoice 72403 dated May 1; terms net 30.
May	2	wrote check 4039 for $800 for the May rent
May	3	sold a bicycle to Hortense Wiggins on account; $250 plus 5 percent sales tax; invoice 2031-14.
May	4	wrote check 4040 for $180 for utilities
May	5	received a $400 check from Bob Dole in partial payment of his account
May	10	purchased bicycle parts on account from The Cyclery; $800; invoice 6043-A dated May 10; terms net 30
May	11	sold a bicycle to Doc Smoley for $275 cash plus 5 percent sales tax; invoice 2031-15
May	12	withdrew $600 for personal use; check 4041
May	15	sold bicycle parts on account to Wayne Dyke; $50 plus 5 percent sales tax; invoice 2031-16
May	16	wrote check 4042 to Bike World in full payment of May 1 purchase; invoice 72403
May	18	sold five bicycles to Riders Anonymous for $1,250 cash plus 5 percent sales tax; invoice 2031-17
May	19	purchased bicycle parts on account from Cycle World; $570; invoice 42137 dated May 19; terms net 30
May	20	issued debit memorandum 231-B for $60 to Cycle World relating to its invoice 42137 of May 19; returned some parts to Cycle World
May	21	wrote check 4043 to The Cyclery in full payment of May 10 purchase, invoice 6043-A
May	21	wrote check 4044 for $922 for purchase of bicycle parts for resale

May 23   sold three bicycles to Rose Santiago on account; $950 plus 5 percent sales tax; invoice 2031-18

May 24   received a $100 check from Hortense Wiggins to apply on her account

May 25   wrote check 4045 for $800 for the purchase of bicycles for re-sale

May 26   purchased a small computer on account for office use from Computer World; $4,000; invoice 9034-21 dated May 26; terms net 30

May 27   wrote check 4046 for $90 in payment of phone bill

May 28   sold bicycle parts on account to Joe Yamaha; $160 plus 5 percent sales tax; invoice 2031-19

May 29   issued credit memorandum 603-C for $10 plus 5 percent sales tax to Joe Yamaha relating to May 28 invoice 2031-19; he returned a portion of the parts he had purchased

May 31   purchased bicycle parts on account from Bikes 'N Cycles; $350; invoice 30116 dated May 31; terms net 30

Instructions

1. *Journalize cash receipts in the cash receipts journal, page 5; cash payments in the cash payments journal, page 6; purchases of merchandise on account in the purchases journal, page 7; sales of merchandise on account in the sales journal, page 8; and miscellaneous entries in the general journal, page 15.*

2. *Total, crossfoot (where required), and rule each journal.*

3. *Indicate, by using check marks and account numbers, how the journals would look if posting were complete.*

Problem 9.5
journalizing in combined cash journal and posting

Lon Symond is a dentist and uses a combined cash journal for recording all transactions. Following are the partial chart of general ledger accounts, partial schedules of accounts receivable and payable, and transactions for the month of August 19XX.

Partial General Ledger		Balance	Partial General Ledger	
101	Cash	$7,325	320	Lon Symond, Drawing
110	Notes Receivable	1,500	410	Professional Fees
115	Accounts Receivable	1,042	420	Interest Income
120	Supplies	90	610	Rent Expense
125	Office Furniture	4,320	620	Utilities Expense
210	Notes Payable	2,000	630	Wages Expense
220	Accounts Payable	164	640	Interest Expense

Partial Schedule of Accounts Receivable	Balance	Partial Schedule of Accounts Payable	Balance
Sarah Blue	$500	Furniture Barn	0
Edna Farber	0	Professional Suppliers	0
John Hopper	0		
Bob Taylor	0		

Transactions

Aug. 1   wrote check 604 for $1,200 in payment of August rent

Aug. 3   received $70 from Sarah Blue in partial payment of her account

Aug. 5   bought office supplies on account from Professional Suppliers; $150

Aug. 7   sold services for cash; $2,720

Aug. 9   wrote check 605 in payment of telephone bill; $195

Aug. 12   wrote check 606 for personal use; $635

Aug. 13   bought new desk on account for the office from Furniture Barn; $320

Aug. 14   sold services for cash; $1,625; and on account to John Hopper; $960

Aug. 15   wrote check 607 for $816 for wages

Aug. 17   wrote check 608 for $2,040; $2,000 is for repayment of an outstanding note and $40 represents interest expense

Aug. 18   wrote check 609 to buy office supplies; $89

Aug. 19   received $300 on account from John Hopper

Aug. 21   performed services for cash; $875; and on account to Edna Farber; $730

Aug. 23   received $510 from a client in partial payment of a note; $500 applies to the principal and $10 represents interest income

Aug. 25   wrote check 610 for $100 in partial payment of the amount owed to Furniture Barn

Aug. 28   wrote check 611 for $816 for wages

Aug. 29   performed services for cash; $520; and on account to Bob Taylor; $810

Aug. 31   received $200 on account from Edna Farber

Instructions

1. *Enter the account titles and balances in the general ledger and enter the customer's names and balances in the accounts receivable ledger and the creditors' names in the accounts payable ledger.*

2. *Journalize all transactions in the combined cash journal, page 8.*

3. *Post immediately to the appropriate subsidiary ledger for all amounts entered in the accounts receivable or accounts payable columns. Place a check mark in the column provided in the journal and enter J8 in the subsidiary ledger accounts.*

4. *Post immediately to the appropriate general ledger account for all amounts entered in the sundry debit or credit column. Place the account number in the posting reference column of the journal and enter J8 in the general ledger accounts.*

5. *Total, crossfoot, and rule the journal.*

6. *Perform the required summary posting. Place the account numbers in parentheses beneath the double ruling and enter J8 in the general ledger accounts.*

CHAPTER 10

The Checking Account and Cash Funds

LEARNING OBJECTIVES

When you have completed this chapter, you should

1. have a better understanding of accounting terminology.

2. have a basic understanding of checking accounts.

3. be able to reconcile a bank statement.

4. be able to prepare the journal entries to bring the books up to date after bank statement reconciliation is complete.

5. be able to prepare the journal entries to establish and replenish a petty cash fund.

6. be able to prepare the journal entries to establish a change fund.

Most businesses pay their bills by check. The check and its accompanying stub provide information for the accountant. Entries are made in the cash payments journal from the check stubs, and the stubs are used when reconciling the bank statement. Paying bills by serially numbered checks provides an important element of internal control over cash; only certain persons should be authorized to write the checks, and the checks that are written are either returned to the business or kept on microfilm at the bank. If the checks are microfilmed, they are listed by number, amount, and date on the bank statement. The bookkeeper can then see if any checks are missing and if the information recorded on the check stub agrees with the information on the check itself.

OPENING A CHECKING ACCOUNT

Before a checking account may be opened, personal information (social security number, name, address, and so on) must be provided to the bank. A signature card is filled out and signed by each person who is authorized to write checks on the account. If there is any doubt about the validity of a signature on an incoming check, the bank employee will use the signature card to verify that the signature on the check is an authorized one.

serial
numbers arranged in a series

Checks are numbered **serially** and are provided by the bank with the depositor's name, address, and phone number printed on each. The numbered checks allow the business owner to easily discover any missing checks and thus help maintain internal control over cash. In addition to the serial numbers at the top of each check, each depositor is assigned an account number, which is printed on the check in magnetic ink so that checks may be processed by computer.

MAKING DEPOSITS

Cash should be deposited daily. Printed forms provided by the bank contain spaces to list currency, coins, and checks. Study the following deposit slip prepared by Robert's Pastries.

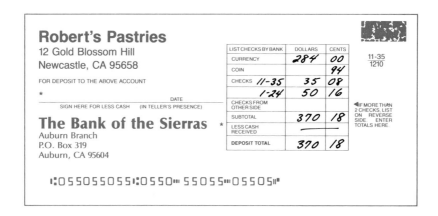

Checks are listed separately on the deposit slip and are identified by their American Banking Association (ABA) number, which appears on the upper-right portion of the check. The ABA number identifies the city or state in which the bank is located, the specific bank, and the Federal Reserve District, and it provides a routing number for the Federal Reserve's use.

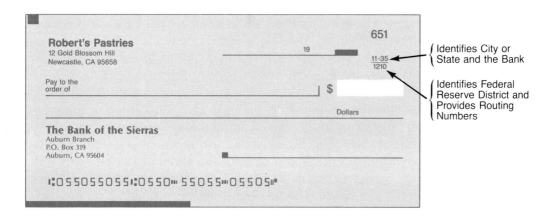

The depositor's account number is printed at the bottom of the deposit slip in magnetic ink that can be read by computers. The numbers are called MICR numbers (magnetic ink character recognition) and are also printed at the bottom of the depositor's checks.

If the depositor goes to the bank to make a deposit, he or she will receive a duplicate deposit slip or the teller will enter the amount of the deposit and the date in the depositor's checkbook, along with his or her initials. Deposits of checks may be made by mail, but with mail deposits there is always the possibility of the deposit being lost or stolen. Deposits may also be dropped into the night depository provided by the bank. In either case, the bank will mail a deposit receipt to the depositor.

automated
when electronic devices are used to control a machine

Automated teller machines (ATMs) are becoming increasingly common. ATMs are often conveniently located outside the bank or in its lobby, or at airports, college campuses, and shopping centers. To use the ATMs, the depositor must sign an agreement with the financial institution for ATM services. The institution will then issue a card to the depositor, along with a secret code number that must be used for every ATM transaction. ATMs are available 24 hours a day every day of the year, which makes it convenient to make deposits (or withdrawals) after normal banking hours and on weekends. While ATMs may be used by individuals, banks make them available only on a limited basis to businesses.

WRITING THE CHECK

Before a check is written, the accompanying check stub should be carefully filled in. The check stub should show the date the check was written, to whom, for what amount, and for what reason. In addition, it should show the balance in the cash account before and after the check is written. The check stubs are used as the source documents for entries in the cash payments journal, to verify the cash balance, and to reconcile the bank statement.

Care should be taken when writing the check. The date is entered first on the line provided, the name of the payee is entered next, and the dollar amount of the check in figures and then in words is entered. The amount in figures should be entered so that there is no space between the dollar sign that is printed on the check and the first digit of the amount. This prevents altering the check. In the same vein, the amount written in words should be entered at the extreme left end of the line provided so that no additional words may be added. After entering the amount for the cents (no/100, 12/100, and so on), a line should be drawn to the end of the line provided.

drawer
the person who signs the check

Last, the check is signed by the **drawer,** the person who will be paying the funds. (Organizations designate certain individuals to

drawee
the bank in which checking account funds are kept

write and sign checks for the company.) The bank in which the funds are deposited and out of which they will be paid is referred to as the **drawee.**

No. **652**	$ **547.00**	

Date: **March 1** 19 **XX**
To: **49'er Restaurant Supply**
For: **Equipment**

Balance Brought Forward $**2,330.80**
Amount Deposited **475.80**
TOTAL $**2,806.60**
Amount This Check **547.00**

Balance Brought Forward $**2,259.60**

Robert's Pastries
12 Gold Blossom Hill
Newcastle, CA 95658

March 1 19 **XX**   651   11-35 / 1210

Pay to the order of **49'er Restaurant Supply** $ **547.00**

Five Hundred Forty-seven **NO**/100 ————— Dollars

The Bank of the Sierras
Auburn Branch
P.O. Box 319
Auburn, CA 95604

Robert Cummings

⑆055055055⑆0550⑃ 55055⑃05505⑄

ENDORSEMENTS

endorsement
the signature of the payee of a check written on its back

blank endorsement
an endorsement that contains only a signature

full endorsement
an endorsement that names a new payee

restrictive endorsement
an endorsement that prohibits further circulation of the check

To be deposited, each check must have an **endorsement.** This is the process by which the payee of the check transfers ownership; by endorsing a check, the payee gives legal right to the bank to collect from the drawer of the check. There are several types of endorsements. The payee may sign just her or his name on the back of the check; this is referred to as a **blank endorsement.** A blank endorsement should not be used unless the payee is ready to cash or deposit the check, because once a blank endorsement appears on a check, anyone who possesses it may cash it. It is better to use a **full endorsement** which names a new payee. After a full endorsement, only the person or firm named in the endorsement may cash or deposit the check. A **restrictive endorsement** is the most appropriate for business use; it limits the further use of the check to a specific purpose. For example, a restrictive endorsement may specifically state "For Deposit Only." Most firms have rubber stamps made for their restrictive endorsements. Look carefully at the examples of each type of endorsement.

Blank Endorsement	Full Endorsement	Restrictive Endorsement
Robert Cummings	Pay to the Order of The Bank of the Sierras Robert's Pastries 08787-05514	Pay to the Order of The Bank of the Sierras For Deposit Only Robert's Pastries 08787-05514

ELECTRONIC FUNDS TRANSFERS

Rapidly expanding technology in the banking industry includes the development and widespread use of electronic funds transfers (EFT). Examples of EFTs include the routine transactions at an automated teller machine and paying for goods or services with a bank card. EFT services allow transactions to and from an account to be made electronically, rather than using paper checks or deposit slips. Individuals may instruct employers to deposit their paychecks automatically, sign an agreement with their insurance company to transfer funds from their checking account each month for the premium, or direct the bank to electronically transfer funds from checking to savings each month. All of these electronic funds transfers make banking quicker and more convenient, but each transaction must be taken into consideration when reconciling the bank statement each month.

STOP PAYMENT ORDERS

Once a check has been written and presented to someone as payment, it is the depositor's order to the bank to make payment. If the depositor changes his or her mind, a stop payment order may be issued that instructs the bank not to make the payment. The bank will charge the depositor a fee for the stop payment order, and it is most effective if issued soon after the check is written. The bank cannot stop payment if the check has already been paid.

THE BANK STATEMENT

Once a month the bank sends a statement to the depositor showing all the transactions that occurred in that account. Each check presented to the bank for payment and each deposit made is listed; and each miscellaneous transaction is shown (sometimes with a code letter, sometimes with a prepared list). Miscellaneous transactions are referred to as debits or credits to the account. Debit entries are deductions from the account (such as checks), and credit entries are additions to the account (such as deposits). On the accounting records of the bank, each depositor's account is handled like an account payable.

BANK STATEMENT RECONCILIATION

When the bank statement is received, it will show the cash balance (according to the bank) at the beginning and at the end of the period. In most cases, the ending cash balance will not agree with the depositor's checkbook balance. There are many causes for this difference, and the depositor must prepare a bank statement **reconciliation** to bring the bank statement balance and the checkbook balance into agreement. Once reconciliation is complete, the depositor knows the correct cash balance. If reconciliation is completed at the end of the month, the cash balance determined by reconciliation will appear on the balance sheet.

reconciliation
the act of bringing into agreement

Some causes for the discrepancy between the ending bank balance and the checkbook balance follow.

outstanding checks
checks that have not been presented to the bank for payment

1. **Outstanding checks:** those that have not yet been presented to the bank for payment. They must be subtracted from the bank statement balance when reconciling.

deposits in transit
deposits that do not appear on the bank statement

2. **Deposits in transit:** those that have been made but do not appear on the bank statement. All such deposits must be added to the bank balance when reconciling.

3. **Service charges:** made by the bank for handling the account. The service charge is usually based on the amount of the average daily balance in the account and the number of transactions that occur each month. A service charge will show on the bank statement as a debit entry (reducing the depositor's balance) and must be subtracted from the balance in the checkbook when reconciling.

4. **Special collections:** made by the bank for the depositor. They appear on the bank statement as miscellaneous credits (increasing the depositor's balance). For example, a depositor may designate the bank as payee on an outstanding note receivable. When the note becomes due, the maker will pay the face amount of the note plus the interest to the lender's bank, who will in turn deposit the money into the lender's account. Special collections will be added to the checkbook balance when reconciling.

5. **Miscellaneous charges:** made by the bank and appear on the bank statement as miscellaneous debits (reducing the depositor's balance). Such miscellaneous charges might include a safe deposit box rental fee, check printing charge, or stop payment order fee. In addition to bank charges, the depositor might authorize another firm to deduct money from the account on a regular basis. Such deductions might be for a loan payment, an insurance premium, or a savings account and will appear on the bank statement as debits or deductions from the depositor's balance. Miscellaneous charges subtracted from the checkbook balance when reconciling.

6. **Errors:** may be made either by the bank or the depositor and will cause a discrepancy when reconciling. When a bank error is discovered, the depositor should notify the bank right away. Errors on the depositor's books should be corrected when reconciling.

Steps in Preparing a Bank Statement Reconciliation

canceled checks
checks that have
been paid by the bank

Before reconciliation can take place, the depositor needs the bank statement, the **canceled checks,** and the check stubs. A canceled check is one that has been paid by the bank and is then in some way, with perforations or other distinctive markings, marked Paid. (If the canceled checks are not returned by the bank, they will all be listed on the bank statement by check number, date, and amount.) Most banks provide a reconciliation form on the back of the statement. Basically, the depositor must do the following.

1. Check to make sure that all deposits recorded in the check stubs are entered on the bank statement. Those deposits that do not appear on the bank statement are called deposits in

transit and are added to the bank balance. A deposit may appear on the bank statement but not in the check stubs, indicating that the depositor forgot to record the deposit when it was made. If this is the case, the depositor must add the deposit to the check stubs when reconciling.

2. Place all the canceled checks in numerical order. Compare the amounts on the checks with the amounts written in the check stubs to make sure they are the same.

3. Check the miscellaneous debits and credits (subtractions and additions) on the bank statement. The debit entries will be subtracted from the checkbook balance, and the credit entries will be added to the checkbook balance when reconciling (if this has not been done already).

Illustration of a Bank Statement Reconciliation

The bank statement for Robert's Pastries showed a balance on March 31 of $5,575.39. The checkbook balance on this date was $5,957.88. Robert took the following steps to reconcile the bank statement.

1. He compared the deposits in the checkbook with those on the bank statement. There was one deposit in transit on March 31 for $371.50.

2. He put the canceled checks in numerical order and compared the amounts on the checks with the amounts entered in the check stubs. Robert noticed that check 1872 written for $60 in payment of the electricity bill was recorded in the check stubs and in the journal for $90.

3. He compared the canceled checks with the check stubs and found there were five outstanding checks:

   1885 $ 20.00
   1888 $ 32.14
   1893 $150.16
   1894 $ 10.00
   1896 $ 48.50

4. Robert noted the following debit entries listed on the bank statement.
   a. March 10—a withdrawal of $160 (made by Robert for personal use) at the Bank of the Sierras' automated teller.

b. March 12—a life insurance check for $137.79 cleared the bank. This is an automatic check that comes directly from the insurance company; it is a policy on the manager's life. Robert made the agreement and signed the necessary papers some time ago.

c. Bank service charge—$4.

None of these debit entries were recorded on Robert's books or in the check stubs at the time of reconciliation.

To reconcile the bank statement, Robert must do the following.

1.	Write in the ending bank balance:	$5,575.39
2.	Add deposit in transit, March 31:	+ 371.50
	Subtotal:	$5,946.89
3.	Subtract outstanding checks:	

1885	$ 20.00
1888	32.14
1893	150.16
1894	10.00
1896	48.50

	Total:	− 260.80
4.	Determine adjusted bank balance:	$5,686.09
5.	Write in the ending checkbook balance:	$5,957.88
6.	Add the amount of the error on check 1872 ($90 − $60 = $30):	+ 30.00
	Subtotal:	$5,987.88
7.	Subtract the bank statement debits:	

a.	Cash withdrawal, owner	$160.00
b.	Insurance premium	137.79
c.	Bank service charge	4.00

	Total deductions:	− 301.79
8.	Determine adjusted checkbook balance:	$5,686.09

The Bank of the Sierras

Auburn Branch
P.O. Box 319
Auburn, CA 95604

Robert's Pastries
12 Gold Blossom Hill
Newcastle, CA 95658

CHECKING	10753-05366 Custom Checking Plan—Flat Fee	Tax ID 123–45–6789

SUMMARY		
Previous Statement Balance on 02–28		2,651.80
Total of 22 Deposits for		8,140.20
Total of 49 Checks for		4,914.82
Total of 3 Other Debits for		301.79
Statement Balance on 03–31		5,575.39
Instant Cash Available—City Bank Card # –4019–132–190–428		100.00

CHECKS/ OTHER DEBITS

Checks

Check Number	Date Posted	Amount	Check Number	Date Posted	Amount
1842	03–01	321.00	1871	03–19	124.82
1843	03–02	547.00	1872	03–19	60.00
1847*	03–04	35.68	1873	03–20	20.00
1848	03–05	56.49	1874	03–20	68.94
1849	03–05	50.00	1875	03–21	18.02
1850	03–06	65.29	1876	03–21	30.16
1851	03–07	47.77	1877	03–22	120.00
1852	03–09	40.00	1878	03–22	17.53
1853	03–09	36.95	1879	03–24	37.31
1854	03–10	20.01	1880	03–24	30.63
1855	03–10	34.39	1881	03–24	83.14
1857*	03–11	20.00	1882	03–25	30.00
1858	03–11	150.00	1883	03–25	000.00
1859	03–13	35.00	1884	03–26	19.95
1860	03–13	16.00	1886*	03–26	547.00
1861	03–13	20.11	1887	03–27	466.62
1862	03–15	17.00	1889*	03–27	36.95
1863	03–16	20.15	1890	03–28	271.28
1864	03–17	30.00	1891	03–29	52.87
1865	03–17	11.66	1892	03–29	50.00
1866	03–17	48.02	1895*	03–30	549.00
1867	03–18	100.00	1897*	03–30	84.64
1868	03–19	50.00	1898	03–30	45.85
1869	03–19	32.46	1899	03–30	25.00
1870	03–19	20.13			

CHECKS/ OTHER DEBITS

Other Debits

Date Posted	Transaction Description	Amount
03–10	Bank of the Sierras Automated Teller Trans. 003140 on 03–10 Customer 811887496 at Terminal 107501—Cash Withdrawal	160.00
03–12	Ins. Prem. New York Life March 11 C0092172	137.79
03–31	Service Charge	4.00

DEPOSITS/ OTHER CREDITS

Deposits

Date Posted	Amount	Date Posted	Amount
03–01	475.80	03–16	351.07
03–02	340.18	03–17	348.32
03–03	353.06	03–18	360.24
03–04	321.17	03–19	366.80
03–05	350.60	03–22	490.14
03–08	482.10	03–23	340.06
03–09	330.18	03–24	350.64
03–10	340.79	03–25	353.90
03–11	320.18	03–26	360.08
03–12	365.01	03–29	365.20
03–15	403.50	03–30	370.18

Required Journal Entries

When reconciliation is complete and the correct cash account balance has been determined, certain journal entries have to be made to bring the books up to date. Normally, a journal entry will be required for every correction made on the checkbook portion of the reconciliation. For Robert's Pastries, the general journal entries are as follows:

GENERAL JOURNAL					Page *8*
Date	Description	Post. Ref.	Debit	Credit	
Mar. *31*	*Cash*		30 —		
	Utilities Expense			30 —	
	To Correct Incorrect Amount on Check 1872				
31	*Robert Cummings, Drawing*		160 —		
	Insurance Expense		137 79		
	Miscellaneous Expense		4 —		
	Cash			301 79	
	To Record Amounts Previously Omitted: See Bank				
	Reconciliation, March 31				

The first entry debiting Cash and crediting Utilities Expense for $30 was made because too much was subtracted from the check stubs: a $60 check was recorded as a $90 check. Therefore, $30 has to be added back to the check stubs and the Cash account, and the Utilities Expense account has to be corrected.

The other entry is to record cash expenditures that were listed on the bank statement. When these entries are posted, the books will be up to date. The ledger account for Cash will be equal to the corrected bank statement balance. The corrections must also be recorded in the check stubs so that the checkbook will agree with the ledger account for Cash.

T-Account Bank Statement Reconciliation

A simple T-account form may be used when reconciling the bank statement if a printed form is not available. It simply lists the ending bank balance and any additions to or subtractions from it on the left-hand side of the T and the ending checkbook balance and any additions or subtractions on the right-hand side of the T. For Robert's Pastries, a T-account reconciliation looks like this.

Robert's Pastries
Bank Reconciliation
March 31, 19XX

Bank balance, 3/31	$5,575.39	Checkbook balance, 3/31		$5,957.88
Add: Deposit in transit, 3/31	+ 371.50	Add: Error on check 1872		+ 30.00
	$5,946.89			$5,987.88
Deduct:		Deduct:		
Outstanding checks		Cash withdrawal	$160.00	
1885 $ 20.00		Insurance premium	137.79	
1888 32.14		Service charge	4.00	
1893 150.16				−301.79
1894 10.00				
1896 48.50	− 260.80			
		Adjusted checkbook		
Adjusted bank balance	$5,686.09	balance		$5,686.09

THE PETTY CASH FUND

petty cash
a fund that is kept on hand and out of which small cash payments may be made

Although business owners are advised to pay most bills by check, writing a check would not be the best thing to do for some payments. For example, payments to the mail carrier for postage due, payments for telegrams or newspapers delivered, or payments for small items of supplies would best be made with cash. For such expenditures, a special cash fund is established called **petty cash.**

The amount of money put into the petty cash fund depends on the needs of the business. If there is a danger of theft, the petty cash fund should be kept small and should be reimbursed often. If there is no danger of theft, the owner may choose to establish a fund that will last through the month.

Establishing the Fund

To establish the petty cash fund, a check is written and cashed and the money is put into a strong box or some other safe place. The transaction is recorded in the cash payments journal as a debit to Petty Cash and a credit to Cash. The entry simply takes money from one cash account and puts it into another. The account, Petty Cash, is an asset and will be listed on the balance sheet with the other assets.

Petty Cash will not be debited again, after the original entry to establish the fund, unless it is decided to increase the amount of money kept in the fund. Following is the entry establishing the petty cash fund.

			CASH PAYMENTS JOURNAL								Page 10	
Date	Check No.		Account Titles	Post. Ref.	Sundry Accounts Debit	Accounts Payable Debit	Purchases Debit	Purchases Discount Credit			Cash Credit	
19XX Oct.	1	1075	Petty Cash		75 —						75 —	

Making Petty Cash Payments

Vouchers are kept with the petty cash so that all payments made out of the fund will be recorded. If, for example, $6 is paid out of petty cash for the monthly charge for a local newspaper, a voucher would be filled out as follows.

Petty Cash Voucher

No. _1_   Date _Oct. 3, 19XX_

Paid to _Bay Area Press_

Amount Paid _6.00_

Account Debited _Miscellaneous Expense_

Approved by   Payment Received by
_RC_   _Sandy Odette_

Usually one or two persons will be designated as having access to the petty cash fund and who will make cash payments from it. A designated person should initial each voucher as payment is made, as should the person receiving the cash. Making one or two persons responsible for the fund and having the payee sign each voucher gives some internal control over the cash.

The Petty Cash Disbursements Register

disbursements
payments or expenditures

Although some companies prefer to simply put the vouchers into their various categories and find totals for each category, many firms require that petty cash disbursements be recorded in a register similar to the cash payments journal. Following on page 372 is a petty cash **disbursements** register for the month of March.

The amount of the fund, $75, is entered on the first line of the register. Each expenditure is recorded in the column titled Payments and also under its appropriate column heading. When petty cash is replenished at the end of the month or sooner, each column is totaled. Crossfooting is performed to ensure that no errors have been made before the journal entry is prepared.

Distribution of Payments		Total of Payments Column
Supplies	$ 7.65	
Delivery Expense	15.65	
Miscellaneous Expense	17.00	
Sundry	30.00	
Total	$70.30 =	$70.30

Replenishing the Petty Cash Fund

The petty cash fund may be replenished at any time and should be replenished when the funds are low, which may or may not be at the end of the month. Even if the fund is not particularly low at the end of the month (or at the end of the accounting period), petty cash should be reimbursed so that the proper expense accounts may be debited before the trial balance is prepared.

The entry to replenish the petty cash fund will appear in the cash payments journal. The accountant will debit the accounts for which expenditures from the fund have been made and will credit Cash. The information for the entry is taken from the petty cash disbursements record, where each column total represents cash spent for a particular expense during the period. The expenses

PETTY CASH DISBURSEMENTS REGISTER FOR MONTH OF MARCH

Date	Voucher No.	Explanation	Receipts	Payments	Distribution of Payments — Supplies 140	Delivery Exp. 640	Misc. Exp. 690	Sundry Debits — Acct. No.	Amount
19XX Mar. 1		To Establish Fund	$75 00						
3	1	Bay Area Press		6 00			6 00		
5	2	Sam Strauss—Cleaning		10 00				615	10 00
6	3	E & L Stationery		4 50	4 50				
9	4	United Delivery		8 40		8 40			
12	5	Sam Strauss—Cleaning		10 00				615	10 00
18	6	Burke's Drug Store		3 15	3 15				
20	7	Bay Area Press		6 00			6 00		
20	8	U.S. Postmaster		5 00			5 00		
25	9	Belmont Delivery		7 25		7 25			
30	10	Robert Cummings, Drawing		10 00				360	10 00
		Totals	75 00	70 30	7 65	15 65	17 00		30 00
		Balance, March 31		4 70					
			75 00	75 00					
Mar. 31		Balance	4 70						
		To Replenish, March 31	70 30						
Apr. 1		Balance	75 00						

listed in the sundry column will also be journalized at this time. The petty cash disbursements record is not a formal journal; it is similar to a worksheet, a place where the accountant summarizes the information about petty cash. Until the entry to reimburse petty cash is made in the cash payments journal, no formal record has been made of the petty cash expenditures.

Date	Check No.	Account Titles	Post. Ref.	Sundry Accounts Debit	Accounts Payable Debit	Purchases Debit	Purchases Discount Credit	Cash Credit
		CASH PAYMENTS JOURNAL						Page 10
19XX Mar. 31	1104	*Supplies*		7 65				
		Delivery Expense		1 5 65				
		Miscellaneous Expense		1 7 —				
		Robert Cummings,						
		Drawing		1 0 —				
		Cleaning Expense		2 0 —				7 0 30

When the petty cash fund is replenished, the account Petty Cash is not debited again. The ledger account for Petty Cash will contain the same balance that it had originally (in this case, $75) unless it is decided to make the fund either larger or smaller. The credit to Cash, $70.30, represents a check written and cashed for that amount. The amount of $70.30 will be put back into the petty cash fund for use in the next period.

THE CHANGE FUND

Most businesses have on hand a change fund. It is cash that stays in the cash register and in the safe so that change may be made for customers. The journal entry to establish the change fund is as follows.

CASH PAYMENTS JOURNAL									Page *10*
Date	Check No.	Account Titles	Post. Ref.	Sundry Accounts Debit	Accounts Payable Debit	Purchases Debit	Purchases Discount Credit	Cash Credit
19XX Oct. 1	1076	*Change Fund*		2 0 0 —				2 0 0 —

denominations
units in a system of money (dimes, quarters, nickels, and so on)

The bookkeeper will decide what money **denominations** are necessary and prepare a list before going to the bank. The list will show the quantity of each denomination desired and the total dollar value. It may look like the following.

Quantity	Denominations		Dollar Value
2	$20 bills	=	$ 40.00
4	$10 bills	=	40.00
4	$5 bills	=	20.00
40	$1 bills	=	40.00
3 rolls	quarters ($10 each)	=	30.00
4 rolls	dimes ($5 each)	=	20.00
4 rolls	nickels ($2 each)	=	8.00
4 rolls	pennies ($.50 each)	=	2.00
Total			$200.00

The $200 will be placed in the cash register to be used for making change for customers. Assume that at the end of the day on October 7, the cash register tape shows total sales of $490.13. The amount of money, then, that should be in the cash register is $690.13 (sales plus $200 in the change fund). The actual cash when counted, however, is $685.13; the register is $5 short. The entry to record the day's sales will debit Cash for $485.13, debit Cash Short and Over for $5, and credit Sales for $490.13 and will be recorded in the cash receipts journal.

Date	Account Titles	Post. Ref.	Sales Credit	Sales Tax Payable Credit	Cash Short and Over Dr./(Cr.)	Cash Debit
CASH RECEIPTS JOURNAL						**Page 12**
19XX Oct. 1			3 0 0 —	1 5 —	50	3 1 4 50
2			3 2 0 —	1 6 —	(1 0 —)	3 4 6 —
3			4 8 0 —	2 4 —	4 —	5 0 0 —
4			5 1 8 —	2 5 90	1 —	5 4 2 90
5			5 9 0 —	2 9 50	(5 —)	6 2 4 50
6			5 0 2 —	2 5 10		5 2 7 10
7			4 1 7 20	2 0 86	2 0 —	4 1 8 06

This cash receipts journal has a special column for recording shortages and overages. Remember that the Cash Short and Over account may have either a debit or a credit balance, because it is debited for shortages and credited for overages. The column head is titled Cash Short and Over Dr./(Cr.). Credit entries in the column will be enclosed in parentheses to indicate they are credits. When the column is totaled at the end of the accounting period, the accountant will determine whether the account has a debit or a credit balance. After the day's receipts are added, the $200 change fund is put back into the cash register. The accountant may need to make a trip to the bank to ensure that enough change is on hand for the following day's business.

The T-accounts for the three Cash accounts are as follows.

Cash		101
10/31 Balance 3,462		

Petty Cash		105
10/31 Balance 75		

Change Fund		110
10/31 Balance 200		

Each of these accounts appears on the balance sheet for Super Cookies on July 31, 19XX, as follows.

Super Cookies
Balance Sheet
July 31, 19XX

Assets

Cash	$3,588
Petty Cash	75
Change Fund	200
Notes Receivable	4,300
Accounts Receivable	780

Total Assets $37,641

SUMMARY

Businesses generally pay bills by check. The check stubs and the canceled checks provide valuable information for the accountant. The stubs are used when preparing the journal entries for cash payments, the stubs and canceled checks are used when reconciling the bank statement, and the canceled checks provide proof of payment.

To maintain strong internal control, certain persons should be designated to authorize payment and write checks. Also checks should be serially numbered to make it obvious when any are missing.

Once a business is established, deposits of cash should be made daily. The depositor may wish to use an automated teller machine or a night depository, so that she or he will not be restricted to regular banking hours. Daily deposits of cash help reduce the possibility of theft.

A restrictive endorsement should be stamped on incoming checks as soon as they are received. Again, this helps to safeguard against theft, because the restrictive endorsement prohibits further circulation.

The bank will send the depositor a bank statement once a month. This provides the depositor with the opportunity to reconcile the business records with those of the bank. Once reconciliation is complete, the depositor may be relatively sure that the reconciled cash balance is the correct one.

In addition to a checking account, many businesses establish a petty cash fund out of which small cash payments may be made. Payments from this fund are recorded on a voucher and in a petty cash disbursements register.

If cash sales are made, then a change fund is necessary. This fund provides small cash denominations (nickels, dimes, quarters, one- and five-dollar bills, and so on) so that accurate change may be given to a customer. Cash, petty cash, and the change fund appear on the balance sheet as three separate asset accounts.

Review of Accounting Terminology

Following is a list of the accounting terminology for this chapter.

automated	endorsement
blank endorsement	full endorsement
canceled checks	outstanding checks
denominations	petty cash
deposits in transit	reconciliation
disbursements	restrictive endorsement
drawee	serial
drawer	

Fill in the blank with the correct word or term from the list.

1. An endorsement that names a new payee is a/an _____.

2. A fund that is kept on hand for making small cash payments is called _____.

3. An endorsement that prohibits further circulation of a check by stating "For Deposit Only" is a/an _____.

4. An endorsement that contains only a signature is a/an _____.

5. Checks that have been paid by the bank are called _____.

6. Another word for payments or expenditures is _____.

7. Units in a system of money, such as a dime or a quarter, are referred to as _____ of money.

8. Checks that have not yet been presented to the bank for payment are called _____.

9. The act of bringing into agreement is _____.

10. Numbers arranged in a series are _____ numbers.

11. Deposits that have been made but do not appear on the bank statement are referred to as _____.

12. The person who signs the check is the _____ of the check.

13. The bank in which checking account funds are kept is the _____ of the check.

14. The signature of the payee of a check written on its back is a/an _____.

15. When electronic devices are used to control a machine, the machine is said to be _____.

Match the following words and terms on the left with the definitions on the right.

16. automated
17. blank endorsement
18. canceled checks
19. denominations
20. deposits in transit
21. disbursements
22. drawee
23. drawer
24. endorsement
25. full endorsement
26. outstanding checks
27. petty cash
28. reconciliation
29. restrictive endorsement
30. serial

a. an endorsement that contains only a signature
b. checks that have been paid by the bank
c. checks not yet presented to the bank for payment
d. an endorsement that names a new payee
e. when electronic devices are used to control a machine
f. units in a money system
g. in a series
h. an endorsement that prohibits further circulation
i. deposits that do not appear on the bank statement
j. the act of bringing into agreement
k. cash fund out of which small cash payments may be made
l. expenditures
m. the payee's signature on the back of a check
n. person who signs the check
o. bank in which checking account funds are kept

Exercises

Exercise 10.1

preparing deposit ticket and recording cash register sales

On May 22, at the end of the business day, the cash register for Mom's Auto Parts showed total sales of $472.18. The actual cash on hand was $682.18, which included a $200 change fund that would be placed back into the cash register. The daily deposit included the following: $2.18 in coins; $150.00 in currency; and three checks: ABA 11–35, $96.14; ABA 11–35, $83.04; and ABA 11–16, $150.82. In the cash receipts journal, prepare the entry to record the day's sales and prepare a deposit ticket for the daily deposit of cash. Use journal page 5.

Exercise 10.2

calculating balance of Cash Short and Over account

Following is the cash receipts journal for the first week in October showing the total cash sales and the cash short and over for each day. Assuming that Cash Short and Over had a zero balance on October 1, what is the balance of the account on October 7? Is it a debit or credit balance?

	CASH RECEIPTS JOURNAL						Page 22
Date	Account Titles	Post. Ref.	Sales Credit	Sales Tax Payable Credit	Cash Short and Over Dr./(Cr.)	Cash Debit	
19XX Oct. 1			3 0 0 —	1 5 —		50	3 1 4 50
2			3 2 0 —	1 6 —	(1 0 —)		3 4 6 —
3			4 8 0 —	2 4 —	4 —		5 0 0 —
4			5 1 8 —	2 5 90	1 —		5 4 2 90
5			5 9 0 —	2 9 50	(5 —)		6 2 4 50
6			5 0 2 —	2 5 10			5 2 7 10
7			4 1 7 20	2 0 86	2 0 —		4 1 8 06
			3 1 2 7 20	1 5 6 36	1 0 50		3 2 7 3 6 6
					Debit		

Exercise 10.3

answering questions about the Change Fund account

Marcy Lennon owns a small specialty store called Pets 'n People. She sells accessories for pets. In the past, Marcy has had one cash register in the store with a change fund of $150 in it. On July 1, however, Marcy enlarged her store and bought a second cash register. She wants to put $150 in this register also. Answer the following questions.

a. To establish a change fund for the second cash register, what accounts should be debited and credited, and for how much?

b. What will be the balance in the Change Fund account after the journal entry in Step a has been made?
c. On which financial statement will the Change Fund account appear?

Exercise 10.4
preparing check stubs and checks

The balance in the checkbook for Mario's Cleaners on July 5, 19XX, was $2,782.78. Mario wrote checks and made deposits as follows on July 6, 7, and 8.

Date	Check No.	Amount	Payee	Reason	Amount of Deposit
July 6	5632	$575.00	B & L Enterprises	Rent	
July 6					$322.71
July 7	5633	196.42	Key West Power Co.	Utilities	
July 7					271.06
July 8	5634	100.00	Mario Vesuvio	Drawing	
July 8					529.40

Prepare the check stubs and write the checks for Mario's Cleaners for July 6, 7, and 8. Calculate the new cash balance each day. Sign the checks with your name, assuming that you are Mario's accountant and are authorized to write checks on his account.

Exercise 10.5
determining amounts in bank reconciliation

When the bank statement is received on March 2, it shows a balance of $4,116.80 on February 28 before reconciliation. After reconciliation, the adjusted checkbook balance is $4,120.04. If there was one deposit in transit of $520.50, what was the total amount of the outstanding checks, assuming there were no other adjustments to be made to the bank statement?

Exercise 10.6
determining amounts in bank reconciliation

After the bank statement was reconciled, the adjusted bank balance was $2,792.58. The checkbook balance before reconciliation was $2,286.58. The bank collected a note for $500 plus $10 in interest for the depositor. If there were no other adjustments to be made to the checkbook, what was the amount of the bank service charge?

Exercise 10.7
analyzing bank statement reconciliation

When reconciling the bank statement, tell whether the following would be additions to the bank statement, subtractions from the bank statement, additions to the checkbook, or subtractions from the checkbook.

	Add to Bank Statement	Subtract from Bank Statement	Add to Checkbook	Subtract from Checkbook
a. Outstanding checks	_____	_____	_____	_____
b. Check printing charge	_____	_____	_____	_____
c. A collection made by the bank for the depositor	_____	_____	_____	_____
d. A check written for $72.98 and recorded in the check stubs as $79.28	_____	_____	_____	_____
e. A deposit in transit	_____	_____	_____	_____
f. Bank service charges	_____	_____	_____	_____
g. A check written for $543.56 and recorded in the check stubs as $534.56	_____	_____	_____	_____
h. An automatic check for an insurance premium included with the canceled checks	_____	_____	_____	_____

Exercise 10.8
preparing entry to establish and replenish petty cash fund

Heinrich Zimler owns Heinrich's Foreign Auto Sales. On August 1, he decides to establish a petty cash fund of $150. On August 31, after the petty cash vouchers have been categorized and totaled for the month, the expenditures are found to be $18.00 for postage, $30.75 for owner's drawing, $10.80 for delivery expense, $16.42 for supplies, $12.00 for a magazine subscription for customers' use, and $6.00 for a newspaper subscription for the waiting room. Prepare the entry in the cash payments journal, page 8, to (a) establish the petty cash fund on August 1 (check 1075) and (b) to replenish the fund on August 31 (check 1146). Account titles are Cash, 101; Petty Cash, 105; Supplies, 140; Heinrich Zimler, Drawing, 320; Postage Expense, 640; Miscellaneous Expense, 650; and Delivery Expense, 660.

Exercise 10.9
preparing entry to replenish and enlarge petty cash fund

The petty cash fund for Betty's Barber Shop had a balance of $25.00 on September 1, 19XX. On September 9, Betty noticed that the fund was nearly used up. The totals of the petty cash disbursements register showed the following: Postage Expense, 640, $4.20; Miscellaneous Expense, 650, $5.00; and Entertainment Expense, 690, $15.45. Betty decided to make the fund $50.00 larger so that it would not have to be replenished so often. Prepare an entry in the cash payments journal, page 9, on September 9 that will both replenish the petty cash fund and enlarge the fund by $50.00. Use check 1902.

Exercise 10.10
classifying accounts

Identify each of the following accounts as an asset (A), contra asset (CA), liability (L), owner's equity (OE), revenue (R), contra revenue (CR), cost of goods sold (CGS), contra purchases (CP), or expense (E). Also tell what the normal balance (debit or credit) is for each account and on what financial statement (Balance Sheet or Income Statement) it appears.

Account Titles	Classification	Normal debit or credit balance?	Which financial statement?
1. Petty Cash			
2. Sales			
3. Purchases			
4. Merchandise Inventory			
5. Sales Returns and Allowances			
6. Change Fund			
7. Supplies Used			
8. Owner, Drawing			
9. Payroll Taxes Payable			
10. Purchases Discounts			
11. Credit Card Discount Expense			
12. Freight In			
13. Accumulated Depreciation			
14. Prepaid Insurance			
15. Sales Discounts			
16. Unearned Revenue			
17. Interest Income			
18. Notes Payable			
19. Supplies			
20. Notes Receivable			

Problems

Problem 10.1
preparing bank statement reconciliation and making required journal entries

Zorba's Delicatessen received a bank statement on November 2, 19XX. The bank balance for October 31 was $4,982.02. The checkbook balance at the time of reconciliation was $4,547.14. When reconciling, the following were found: four outstanding checks, 1742—$462.81, 1745—$198.40, 1746—$42.69, and 1747—$51.08; two deposits in transit, October 30, $300.00 and October 31, $119.60; a bank service charge, $4.50; a check printing charge, $6.00; a $90.00 automatic check for an insurance premium; and a $200.00 note receivable left with the bank for collection had been paid in full at the bank.

Instructions

1. *Prepare a bank statement reconciliation in T-account form for Zorba's Delicatessen.*

2. *Prepare the necessary entries in the general journal to bring the books up to date after reconciliation. Use journal page 11. Bank service charges may be debited to Miscellaneous Expense. A partial chart of accounts includes the following: Cash, 101; Notes Receivable, 120; Insurance Expense, 650; and Miscellaneous Expense, 670.*

Problem 10.2
preparing bank statement reconciliation and making required journal entries

Geri Speir owns Fillie's Frocks, a western wear store. On June 2, Geri received the bank statement. It showed a balance on May 31 of $6,420.95. The checkbook balance at the time of reconciliation was $6,434.11. When reconciling, Geri found one deposit in transit of $645.80. There were five outstanding checks: 2016, $29.40; 2020, $150.00; 2025, $490.00; 2026, $10.50; and 2027, $65.04. The bank service charge was $6.50, and there was a check printing charge of $8.50. When comparing the canceled checks with the check stubs, Geri noticed that check 1998, written on May 15 to Western Wear in payment of an account payable, was actually written for $75.87 but was recorded in the check stubs and in the cash payments journal as $78.57. Geri also noticed that she forgot to record a $100.00 cash withdrawal from an automated teller on May 27 (the cash was for personal use).

Instructions

1. *Prepare a bank statement reconciliation in T-account form for Fillie's Frocks.*

2. *Prepare the necessary entries in the general journal to bring the books up to date after reconciliation. Use journal page 27. All bank service charges may be debited to Miscellaneous Expense. A partial chart of accounts includes the following: Cash, 101; Accounts Payable, 210; Geri Speir, Drawing, 310; and Miscellaneous Expense, 640.*

Problem 10.3
preparing bank statement reconciliation and making required journal entries

Adrian Wodetzki, owner of A–Z Novelties, reconciled her bank statement on January 31. The January 31 bank balance was $3,240.60. The checkbook balance at the time of reconciliation was $3,203.59. During reconciliation, Adrian noted that the bank service charge was $5.00. Also, a note receivable left at the bank for collection had been paid in full, $600.00 plus $60.00 interest. There were two deposits in transit: January 30, $649.28 and January 31, $596.81. The bank charge for check printing was $8.00. There were three outstanding checks: 972, $450.00; 973, $95.40; and 974, $150.00. When comparing the canceled checks with the check stubs, Adrian noticed that two errors had been made. Check 952, written on January 10 in payment of the electric bill, was actually written for $98.20 but was recorded in the check stubs and in the cash payments journal as $89.20. Check 965, written on January 19 in payment for a desk for the office, was actually written for $370.32 but was recorded in the checkbook and in the cash payments journal as $390.32. An automatic check for $70.30 in payment of an insurance premium was included with the canceled checks.

Instructions   *1. Prepare a bank statement reconciliation in T-account form for A–Z Novelties.*

   2. Prepare the necessary entries in the general journal to bring the books up to date after reconciliation. Use journal page 33. All bank charges may be debited to Miscellaneous Expense. A partial chart of accounts includes the following: Cash, 101; Notes Receivable, 110; Office Furniture, 170; Interest Income, 420; Utilities Expense, 650; Insurance Expense, 660; Miscellaneous Expense, 670.

Problem 10.4
recording in petty cash disbursements register and replenishing petty cash fund

The following petty cash transactions occurred in October for the Jackson House of Guitars, owned by Herb Jackson.

Oct. 1   established a petty cash fund of $100.00; check 1716
Oct. 3   paid $5.00 for delivery charges; voucher 1
Oct. 4   owner took $20.00 cash for personal use; voucher 2
Oct. 7   paid $7.50 for newspaper subscription for customer's use; voucher 3
Oct. 10   paid $15.00 to have windows washed; voucher 4
Oct. 12   paid $5.00 for postage stamps; voucher 5
Oct. 15   paid $9.50 for express mail charges; voucher 6
Oct. 18   owner took a customer to lunch, $17.80; voucher 7
Oct. 21   paid $3.60 for office supplies; voucher 8
Oct. 25   mailed a package to a customer, $3.70; voucher 9
Oct. 27   paid $8.00 for an ad in a shoppers' newspaper; voucher 10

Instructions   *1. Record the entry in the cash payments journal to establish the petty cash fund on October 1. Use page 18 for the journal.*

   2. Record in a petty cash disbursements register the initial $100.00 deposit into the fund and the disbursements for the month. Use *page 10 for the register. Column headings in the register should include postage expense, delivery expense, and entertainment expense. A partial chart of accounts includes Cash, 101; Petty Cash, 110; Office Supplies, 120; Herb Jackson, Drawing, 310; Advertising Expense, 610; Delivery Expense, 620; Cleaning Expense, 630; Postage Expense, 640; Entertainment Expense, 650; and Subscription Expense, 660.*

3. *Total and rule the petty cash disbursements register.*

4. *Prepare the October 31 entry in the cash payments journal, check 1762, to replenish the petty cash fund.*

5. *Complete the petty cash register by indicating the October 31 balance, the deposit into the fund, and the balance on November 1.*

Problem 10.5

recording in petty cash disbursements register and replenishing and enlarging petty cash fund

The following petty cash transactions occurred in January for Cowhide Products, owned by Marge Wade.

Jan. 1   established a petty cash fund of $50.00; check 2640

Jan. 2   paid $4.00 for office supplies; voucher 100

Jan. 5   paid $12.00 for a magazine subscription for customers' use; voucher 101

Jan. 6   owner took a customer to lunch, $15.20; voucher 102

Jan. 7   paid $3.20 for office supplies; voucher 103

Jan. 9   bought postage stamps, $6.00; voucher 104

Jan. 14   owner withdrew $5.00 for personal use; voucher 105

Jan. 15   replenished the petty cash fund and made it $50.00 larger; check 2682

Jan. 17   owner took a client to lunch, $16.40; voucher 106

Jan. 19   paid $15.00 postage to have parcels sent to a customer; voucher 107

Jan. 20   bought $6.40 in office supplies; voucher 108

Jan. 24   owner withdrew $10.00 for personal use; voucher 109

Jan. 25   took packages to the post office for mailing; cost, $8.70; voucher 110

Jan. 26   bought a fern for the store, $17.50 (debit Miscellaneous Expense); voucher 111

Jan. 27   bought plant food for the fern, $3.90 (debit Miscellaneous Expense); voucher 112

Jan. 31   sent flowers to a customer in the hospital, $19.70 (debit Miscellaneous Expense); voucher 113

Instructions

1. *Record the entry in the cash payments journal to establish the petty cash fund on January 1. Use page 13 for the journal.*

2. *Record in a petty cash disbursements register the initial $50.00 deposit into the fund and the disbursements from January 1 through 14. Use page 12 for the register. Column headings for the register should include office supplies, postage expense, and miscellaneous expense. A partial chart of accounts includes Cash, 101; Petty Cash, 110; Office Supplies, 120; Marge Wade, Drawing, 310; Advertising Expense, 610; Postage Expense, 640; Entertainment Expense, 650; Subscription Expense, 660; and Miscellaneous Expense, 670.*

3. *Total and rule the petty cash register.*

4. *Prepare the January 15 entry in the cash payments journal to replenish the petty cash fund and to make the fund $50.00 larger. Use page 14 for the journal and check 2682.*

5. *Complete the petty cash disbursements register for January 1 through 14 by writing in the amounts required to replenish the fund and to make the fund $50.00 larger. The new balance on January 15 will be $100.00.*

6. *Continuing on with the month's transactions in a new petty cash disbursements register, page 13, record the disbursements from January 15 through 31. Total and rule the register again.*

7. *Prepare the entry in the cash payments journal on January 31, check 2731, to replenish the petty cash fund and restore it to a $100.00 balance.*

8. *Record in the petty cash disbursements register, page 13, the balance on January 31, the deposit into the fund, and the balance on February 1.*

Comprehensive Problem 2

for Review of Chapters 7

through 10

Georgia Hawthorne owns a business called Hobby House, which is a novelty store that sells model kits for cars, planes, and railroad equipment; accessories for model kits; miniature furniture and houses; unusual games and puzzles; and other novelty items. The chart of accounts and account balances for Hobby House on December 1, 19XX, and the schedules of accounts receivable and payable showing the balance owed on December 1 follow. The December transactions follow the schedules of accounts receivable and payable. Read all of the instructions that follow the transactions before you begin work on the problem.

Hobby House
Chart of Accounts and Account Balances
December 1, 19XX

101	Cash	$15,040.21	
105	Petty Cash	0	
110	Change Fund	300.00	
120	Accounts Receivable	924.30	
130	Prepaid Insurance	0	
140	Office Supplies	642.50	
150	Office Equipment	12,400.00	
160	Store Equipment	18,600.00	
170	Office Furniture	2,790.00	
180	Van	21,800.00	
210	Notes Payable		$30,620.00
220	Accounts Payable		1,942.00
230	Sales Tax Payable		605.40
301	Georgia Hawthorne, Capital		39,329.61
310	Georgia Hawthorne, Drawing		
410	Revenue from Sales		
420	Sales Returns and Allowances		
510	Purchases		
520	Freight In		
530	Purchases Returns and Allowances		
540	Purchases Discounts		
610	Rent Expense		
620	Utilities Expense		
630	Interest Expense		
640	Wages Expense		
650	Advertising Expense		
660	Delivery Expense		
670	Subscription Expense		
680	Postage Expense		
690	Entertainment Expense		

Hobby House
Schedule of Accounts Receivable
December 1, 19XX

Jane Claiborne	$275.15
Phillip Dewey	291.05
Patrick O'Toole	143.50
Helen Zermatt	214.60
Total	$924.30

Hobby House
Schedule of Accounts Payable
December 1, 19XX

Adult Toys	$ 842.00
Model Supplies	668.00
The Toy Place	432.00
Total	$1,942.00

Transactions

Dec.	1	issued check 4066 for $280 to Business Insurance Company in payment for a two-year fire insurance policy
Dec.	1	sold merchandise on account to Patrick O'Toole on sales invoice 32046; $52 plus 4 percent sales tax
Dec.	1	received a check from Phillip Dewey for $291.05 in full payment of his account
Dec.	1	issued check 4067 for $100 to establish a petty cash fund (enter receipt of the $100 into the petty cash disbursements register after the check is recorded)
Dec.	2	purchased merchandise for resale from Adult Toys for $1,408 on invoice 29-082 dated December 2; terms 2/10, n/30
Dec.	2	issued check 4068 for $50 to Mercury's Trucking Company for delivering the purchase from Adult Toys
Dec.	3	issued check 4069 for $1,400 for December rent
Dec.	4	issued check 4070 to Model Supplies for $654.64 in full payment of November 29 purchase of $668 less a 2 percent discount
Dec.	5	issued check 4071 to Adult Toys for $825.16 in full payment of November 30 purchase of $842 less a 2 percent discount
Dec.	5	sold merchandise on account to Jane Claiborne on sales invoice 32047; $76.50 plus 4 percent sales tax
Dec.	6	paid $6.50 for monthly subscription for the local newspaper; used petty cash voucher 1
Dec.	7	sold merchandise for the week for $3,642.50 cash plus 4 percent sales tax
Dec.	8	issued check 4072 for $275.60 to City Electric for electricity for the month
Dec.	9	received a check from Helen Zermatt for $100 in partial payment of her account
Dec.	9	issued check 4073 for $30.50 to A & S Suppliers for office supplies

Dec. 9 issued check 4074 to The Toy Place for $432 in full payment of December 1 balance; no discount is granted by The Toy Place

Dec. 10 spent $8.20 for postage; used petty cash voucher 2

Dec. 10 sold merchandise on account to Phillip Dewey on sales invoice 32048; $125 plus 4 percent sales tax

Dec. 11 issued credit memorandum 603-A to Phillip Dewey for $20 plus 4 percent sales tax relating to invoice 32048 dated December 10

Dec. 11 received a check from Jane Claiborne for $150 in partial payment of her account

Dec. 12 issued check 4075 for $1,379.84 to Adult Toys in full payment of invoice 29-082 dated December 2

Dec. 12 purchased merchandise for resale from Model Supplies for $1,540 on invoice 333-AA dated December 12; terms 2/10, n/30

Dec. 13 received a check from Patrick O'Toole for $143.50 in partial payment of his account

Dec. 14 issued debit memorandum 321-13 to Model Supplies for $120 for merchandise returned to them

Dec. 14 took a customer out to lunch; $18.90; used petty cash voucher 3

Dec. 15 sold merchandise for the week for $4,016.50 cash plus 4 percent sales tax

Dec. 15 issued check 4076 for $970 for monthly payment on the outstanding note; $459 is for interest expense and the rest is for reduction of the principal

Dec. 16 issued check 4077 for $500 in payment of semimonthly wages

Dec. 17 issued check 4078 for $605.40 in payment of balance owed for sales tax payable on December 1

Dec. 17 issued check 4079 to Georgia Hawthorne for $1,600 for her personal use

Dec. 18 sold merchandise on account to Helen Zermatt on sales invoice 32049; $70 plus 4 percent sales tax

Dec. 19 purchased merchandise for resale from The Toy Place for $2,622 on invoice 78-32001 dated December 19; terms net 30

Dec. 21 sold merchandise for the week for $4,906.50 cash plus 4 percent sales tax

Dec. 21 owner took another customer out to lunch; $17.50; used petty cash voucher 4

Dec. 22 issued credit memorandum 604-A to Helen Zermatt for $10 plus 4 percent sales tax relating to invoice 32049 dated December 18

Dec. 22   issued check 4080 to Model Supplies for $1,391.60 in full payment of invoice 333-AA dated December 12 less the return on December 14

Dec. 22   owner purchased a word processor and computer from Computer World for use in the office at a total cost of $10,700; paid no cash down, but signed a 3-year, 15 percent note for the purchase

Dec. 23   issued check 4081 to The Daily Journal for $150 for advertising for December

Dec. 23   issued check 4082 to Model Supplies for $785.65 for cash purchase of merchandise for resale; invoice 384-AA

Dec. 24   paid $8.25 for delivery expense; used petty cash voucher 5

Dec. 24   purchased merchandise for resale from Adult Toys for $2,750 on invoice 29-185 dated December 24; terms 2/10, n/30

Dec. 24   issued check 4083 to Mercury's Trucking Company for $50 for delivering the purchase from Adult Toys

Dec. 26   sold merchandise on account to Patrick O'Toole on sales invoice 32050; $190 plus 4 percent sales tax

Dec. 27   received a check from Patrick O'Toole for $54.08 in full payment of invoice 32046 dated December 1

Dec. 28   paid $30 for a magazine subscription; used petty cash voucher 6

Dec. 28   issued check 4084 for $625 in payment of wages

Dec. 28   sold merchandise for the week for $3,760.50 cash plus 4 percent sales tax

Dec. 28   issued check 4085 to The Toy Place for $1,232.16 for cash purchase of merchandise for resale; invoice 78-36040

Dec. 29   received a check from Helen Zermatt for $100 in partial payment of her account

Dec. 30   purchased merchandise for resale from Model Supplies for $3,250 on invoice 412-AA dated December 30; terms 2/10, n/30

Dec. 31   received a check from Jane Claiborne for $50 in partial payment of her account

Dec. 31   issued check 4086 for $89.35 to replenish the petty cash fund (stop now and total and rule the petty cash register; see instruction 9)

Instructions   *1. Copy the account names, numbers, and balances into the general ledger.*

2. Copy the names and balances into the accounts receivable and accounts payable subsidiary ledgers. Post to the subsidiary ledgers immediately after each transaction.

3. *Record sales on account in a sales journal, page 11, with the following column headings: sales credit, sales tax payable credit, and accounts receivable debit. Hobby House is required to collect 4 percent sales tax on all sales. Terms of sale are net 30.*

4. *Record credit purchases of merchandise for resale in a single-column purchases journal, page 10. Georgia always pays within the discount period when terms are offered.*

5. *Record all cash receipts in a cash receipts journal, page 12, with the following column headings: sundry credits, accounts receivable credit, sales credit, sales tax payable credit, and cash debit.*

6. *Record all cash payments in a cash payments journal, page 13, with the following column headings: sundry debits, accounts payable debit, purchases debit, purchases discounts credit, and cash credit.*

7. *Record all transactions that do not belong in a special journal in a general journal, page 24.*

8. *Record all payments out of petty cash in the petty cash disbursements register, page 14. Use the following column heads: receipts, payments, subscription expense, postage expense, entertainment expense, and sundry debits.*

9. *On December 31, total and rule the petty cash disbursements register, and then issue check 4086 for $89.35 to replenish the fund.*

10. *Total, crossfoot (where required), and rule the sales, purchases, cash receipts, and cash payments journals.*

11. *Perform all the required summary and individual posting from the special journals.*

12. *Perform all the required posting from the general journal.*

13. *Prepare a trial balance of the general ledger on December 31.*

14. *Prepare a schedule of accounts receivable on December 31 and compare the total with the balance in the Accounts Receivable control account in the general ledger.*

15. *Prepare a schedule of accounts payable on December 31 and compare the total with the balance in the Accounts Payable control account in the general ledger.*

CHAPTER 11

**W**orksheets, Financial Statements, and Closing Entries for a Merchandising Business

LEARNING OBJECTIVES

When you have completed this chapter, you should

1. have a better understanding of accounting terminology.

2. be able to prepare a ten-column worksheet for a merchandising business.

3. have a basic understanding of cost of goods sold.

4. be able to prepare an income statement for a merchandising business.

5. be able to prepare a classified balance sheet.

6. be able to calculate current ratio and working capital.

7. be able to journalize and post the adjusting and closing entries for a merchandising business.

The material presented in this chapter completes the accounting cycle for a merchandising business. The accounting cycle, remember, refers to the sequence of accounting procedures that are performed during an accounting period. The cycle begins when a transaction occurs and is journalized and ends with the closing of the books. The steps in the accounting cycle, from beginning to end, are as follows.

1. Journalize transactions.
2. Post transactions.
3. Prepare a worksheet that includes
   a. A trial balance.
   b. Adjustments.
   c. An adjusted trial balance.
   d. Income statement calculations.
   e. Balance sheet calculations.
4. Prepare an income statement.
5. Prepare a balance sheet.
6. Prepare schedules of accounts receivable and accounts payable.
7. Journalize and post the adjusting entries.
8. Journalize and post the closing entries.
9. Prepare a post-closing trial balance.

This chapter will concentrate on preparing the worksheet and financial statements and journalizing and posting the closing entries for a merchandising business. The worksheet for Ron's Appliances for the month ended June 30, 19XX, follows. The trial balance is prepared directly from the ledger on June 30. Once it is complete and in balance, it should be double ruled. Look over the worksheet and then read the discussion material about Merchandise Inventory and the adjustments.

RON'S APPLIANCES
WORKSHEET
FOR MONTH ENDED JUNE 30, 19XX

Acct. No.	Account Titles	Trial Balance Debit	Trial Balance Credit	Adjustments Debit	Adjustments Credit
101	Cash	11600 —			
110	Notes Receivable	7200 —			
120	Accounts Receivable	13600 —			
130	Merchandise Inventory	46000 —			
140	Supplies	1960 —			a. 640 —
150	Prepaid Insurance	3100 —			b. 100 —
160	Office Equipment	28000 —			
160A	Accumulated Depreciation: Off. Equip.		5500 —		c. 500 —
170	Delivery Equipment	57000 —			
170A	Accumulated Depreciation: Del. Equip.		11250 —		c. 750 —
180	Building	130000 —			
180A	Accumulated Depreciation: Bldg.		7500 —		c. 500 —
210	Notes Payable		25000 —		
220	Accounts Payable		5150 —		
240	Unearned Revenue		3500 —	d. 900 —	
250	Mortgage Payable		90000 —		
310	Ron Renner, Capital		124390 —		
320	Ron Renner, Drawing	6000 —			
410	Sales		104100 —		d. 900 —
420	Sales Returns and Allowances	2100 —			
430	Sales Discounts	2900 —			
501	Purchases	58000 —			
510	Freight In	2000 —			
520	Purchases Returns and Allowances		620 —		
530	Purchases Discounts		2400 —		
610	Rent Expense	3500 —			
620	Utilities Expense	750 —			
630	Wages Expense	5700 —		e. 200 —	
	Totals	379410 —	379410 —		
650	Supplies Used			a. 640 —	
660	Insurance Expense			b. 100 —	
670	Depreciation Expense			c. 1750 —	
230	Wages Payable				e. 200 —
				3590 —	3590 —
	Net Income				

	Adjusted Trial Balance		Income Statement		Balance Sheet	
	Debit	Credit	Debit	Credit	Debit	Credit
	11600—				11600—	
	7200—				7200—	
	13600—				13600—	
	46000—		46000—	45100—	45100—	
	1320—				1320—	
	3000—				3000—	
	28000—				28000—	
		6000—				6000—
	57000—				57000—	
		12000—				12000—
	130000—				130000—	
		8000—				8000—
		25000—				25000—
		5150—				5150—
		2600—				2600—
		90000—				90000—
		124390—				124390—
	6000—				6000—	
		105000—		105000—		
	2100—		2100—			
	2900—		2900—			
	58000—		58000—			
	2000—		2000—			
		620—		620—		
		2400—		2400—		
	3500—		3500—			
	750—		750—			
	5900—		5900—			
	640—		640—			
	100—		100—			
	1750—		1750—			
		200—				200—
	381360—	381360—	123640—	153120—	302820—	273340—
			29480—			29480—
			153120—	153120—	302820—	302820—

THE MERCHANDISE INVENTORY ACCOUNT ON THE WORKSHEET

The Merchandise Inventory figure that appears on the trial balance represents the balance in the account on June 1 and is referred to as the beginning inventory. The beginning inventory appears on the worksheet as a debit in three places: on the original trial balance, on the adjusted trial balance, and on the income statement, where it will be used in calculating cost of goods sold.

At the end of the period, June 30 in this case, the periodic inventory was taken, and the value of the actual merchandise on hand was $45,100. This is referred to as the ending inventory and is the current value of the asset. It appears on the worksheet in two places: as a credit on the income statement, where it will be used in the cost of goods sold calculation and as a debit on the balance sheet, where it represents the actual value of merchandise on hand.

The merchandise inventory appears five times on the worksheet: four times as a debit and once as a credit.

Beginning Inventory Appears	Ending Inventory Appears
As a **debit** on the trial balance.	As a **debit** on the balance sheet.
As a **debit** on the adjusted trial balance.	As a **credit** on the income statement.
As a **debit** on the income statement.	

ADJUSTMENTS ON THE WORKSHEET

Adjustments are made at the end of the accounting period to bring certain accounts up to date. Each adjustment involves both an income statement account and a balance sheet account. Following is a brief explanation of the adjustments on the worksheet for Ron's Appliances.

a. This adjustment records the amount of supplies used during June by debiting Supplies Used and crediting Supplies for $640. The value of the ending inventory of supplies is the figure that should appear on the adjusted trial balance and on the balance sheet.

b. This adjustment records the insurance expense for June by debiting Insurance Expense and crediting Prepaid Insurance for $100.

c. This adjustment records depreciation expense for June on all the depreciable assets (office equipment, delivery equipment, and the building). The debit in each case is to Depreciation Expense and the credit is to the contra-asset account, Accumulated Depreciation. The three debits to Depreciation Expense may be added together and shown as one figure, ($1,750), on the worksheet, but the credits must be made individually to the Accumulated Depreciation accounts ($500, $750, and $500).

d. At some point in the past, Ron received cash in advance of actually delivering the merchandise. This transaction was recorded at the time as a debit to Cash and as a credit to the liability account, Unearned Revenue. This adjusting entry is to transfer a portion ($900) of the balance in Unearned Revenue to Sales, an earned revenue account.

e. This adjustment records wages expense that have accrued at the end of the accounting period by debiting Wages Expense and crediting Wages Payable for $200.

Once the adjustments are all entered on the worksheet, the adjustments column should be totaled and ruled.

COMPLETING THE WORKSHEET

The next step involves combining the original trial balance with the adjustments for the adjusted trial balance. (If necessary, you may wish to review Chapter 5 for details on preparing the worksheet.) Once the adjusted trial balance is complete and in balance, extensions may be made to the balance sheet and income statement columns of the worksheet. Extensions include entering the beginning merchandise inventory as a debit on the income statement and entering the ending inventory as a credit on the income statement and a debit on the balance sheet.

When extensions are complete, the income statement columns are totaled and the net income (or net loss) is determined. A net income figure is entered as a debit on the income statement and as a credit on the balance sheet. Finally, the remaining parts of the worksheet are totaled and ruled.

COST OF GOODS SOLD

After the worksheet is complete, the accountant may wish to prepare the financial statements. Before discussing the income statement for a merchandising business, however, a discussion about cost of goods sold is in order. When an item is sold by a retail store, several things have to be taken into consideration before a net income or loss figure can be determined. In addition to determining the related expenses, the *cost of the merchandise sold* must be calculated.

For example, assume that you buy a used car from a friend for $1,200. You pay $800 to have it painted, $150 to have it tuned, and $350 for new tires. Then you place a $50 ad in the newspaper offering to sell the car for $3,500. After a week's time, you sell the car for $3,400. To calculate your net income, you would do the following.

Revenue from Sale of Car		$ 3,400
Minus Cost of Car		−1,200
Gross Profit		$ 2,200
Minus Expenses		
Painting	$800	
Tune-up	150	
Tires	350	
Ad in Paper	50	
Total Expenses		−1,350
Net Income from Sale		$ 850

gross profit
net sales minus cost of goods sold

The **gross profit** is profit *before* expenses have been deducted; it is simply the revenue minus the cost of the item sold. When a large item such as an automobile is sold, the direct cost of the merchandise sold is relatively easy to figure. When a store sells smaller items that are difficult to identify individually, a different procedure is used to calculate cost of goods sold.

Calculation for Cost of Goods Sold

Before the cost of goods sold can be calculated, three things must be known: (1) the cost of the beginning inventory, (2) the cost of the net purchases, and (3) the cost of the ending inventory.

Cost of Goods Sold		
Beginning Inventory	$ 21,500	What the merchant had to start with.
Add: Net Purchases	46,200	Add what was purchased during the period.
Total Goods Available for Sale	$ 67,700	Everything that was available for sale during the period.
Minus: Ending Inventory	−19,600	Minus what was left at the end of the period.
Cost of Goods Sold	$ 48,100	Equals the cost of what was sold.

Goods Available for Sale

When the net purchases for the period is added to beginning inventory, the result is the total goods that were available for sale. The total goods available for sale does not equal the cost of goods sold, however, because not every item that was available for sale was sold. Some items remain in the store at the end of the accounting period; these items represent ending inventory, or the remaining goods. When the ending inventory, or remaining goods, is subtracted from all the goods that were available for sale, the result is the goods sold, or the *cost* of goods sold. The goods available for sale represents both the goods sold and the goods not sold, because it represents *everything that was available for sale in the store during the entire accounting period.*

THE INCOME STATEMENT

The income statement for a merchandising business contains three main sections: (1) the revenue section, (2) the cost of goods sold section, and (3) the expense section. The three sections appear in this order.

1.   Sales
2. − Cost of Goods Sold
    Gross Profit
3. − Expenses
    Net Income (or Net Loss)

The gross profit, remember, is profit before related expenses are deducted; it is the net sales minus cost of goods sold. The income

RON'S APPLIANCES
WORKSHEET (PARTIAL)
FOR MONTH ENDED JUNE 30, 19XX

Acct. No.	Account Titles	Adjusted Trial Balance Debit	Credit	Income Statement Debit	Credit
101	Cash	11600 —			
110	Notes Receivable	7200 —			
120	Accounts Receivable	13600 —			
130	Merchandise Inventory	46000 —		46000 —	45100 —
140	Supplies	1320 —			
150	Prepaid Insurance	3000 —			
160	Office Equipment	28000 —			
160A	Accumulated Depr.: Off. Equip.		6000 —		
170	Delivery Equipment	57000 —			
170A	Accumulated Depr.: Del. Equip.		12000 —		
180	Building	130000 —			
180A	Accumulated Depr.: Bldg.		8000 —		
210	Notes Payable		25000 —		
220	Accounts Payable		5150 —		
240	Unearned Revenue		2600 —		
250	Mortgage Payable		90000 —		
310	Ron Renner, Capital		124390 —		
320	Ron Renner, Drawing	6000 —			
410	Sales		105000 —		105000 —
420	Sales Returns and Allowances	2100 —		2100 —	
430	Sales Discounts	2900 —		2900 —	
501	Purchases	58000 —		58000 —	
510	Freight In	2000 —		2000 —	
520	Purchases Returns and Allowances		620 —		620 —
530	Purchases Discounts		2400 —		2400 —
610	Rent Expense	3500 —		3500 —	
620	Utilities Expense	750 —		750 —	
630	Wages Expense	5900 —		5900 —	
	Totals				
650	Supplies Used	640 —		640 —	
660	Insurance Expense	100 —		100 —	
670	Depreciation Expense	1750 —		1750 —	
230	Wages Payable		200 —		
		381360 —	381360 —	123640 —	153120 —
	Net Income			29480	
				153120 —	153120 —

statement is prepared directly from the worksheet, where many of the calculations have already been made. A partial worksheet showing the income statement columns for Ron's Appliances appears on page 404.

The net income has already been calculated. The accountant can now prepare the formal income statement for Ron's Appliances directly from the worksheet.

The following income statement for Ron's Appliances contains the three main elements: (1) revenue, (2) cost of goods sold, and (3) expenses.

Ron's Appliances
Income Statement
For Month Ended June 20, 19XX

Revenue from Sales				
Sales			$105,000	
Less: Sales Returns and Allowances		$ 2,100		
Sales Discounts		2,900	− 5,000	
Net Sales				$100,000
Cost of Goods Sold				
Merchandise Inventory, June 1, 19XX			46,000	
Purchases		58,000		
Freight-In		2,000		
Delivered Cost of Purchases		60,000		
Less: Purchases Returns and Allowances	$ 620			
Purchases Discounts	2,400	− 3,020		
Net Purchases			56,980	
Cost of Merchandise Available for Sale			102,980	
Less: Merchandise Inventory, June 30, 19XX			− 45,100	
Cost of Goods Sold				57,880
Gross Profit				42,120
Expenses				
Rent Expense			3,500	
Utilities Expense			750	
Wages Expense			5,900	
Supplies Used			640	
Insurance Expense			100	
Depreciation Expense			1,750	
Total Expenses				12,640
Net Income				$ 29,480

The cost of goods sold section contains the calculation for net purchases, which makes the income statement appear to be more complicated than it really is. The following shows the three main elements of the cost of goods sold section: (1) beginning inventory, (2) net purchases, and (3) ending inventory.

Cost of Goods Sold

1.	**Merchandise Inventory, June 1, 19XX**			**$46,000**
	Purchases		$58,000	
	Freight In		2,000	
	Delivered Cost of Purchases		60,000	
	Less: Purchases Returns and Allowances	$ 620		
	Purchases Discounts	2,400	− 3,020	
2.	**Net Purchases**			**56,980**
	Total Cost of Merchandise Available for Sale			102,980
3.	**Less: Merchandise Inventory, June 30, 19XX**			**45,100**
	Cost of Goods Sold			$57,880

THE CLASSIFIED BALANCE SHEET

The balance sheet, too, is prepared directly from the worksheet. The accounts have already been adjusted, and the net income (or net loss) has already been calculated. The balance sheet portion of the worksheet for Ron's Appliances follows on page 407.

classified
separated into categories

Assets and liabilities are **classified** on the balance sheet. That is, assets and liabilities are separated into categories: for assets, the categories are (1) current assets and (2) plant and equipment; and for liabilities, the categories are (1) current liabilities and (2) long-term liabilities.

Current Assets

liquid asset
an asset that is cash or easily converted into cash

Current assets are listed on the balance sheet in their order of liquidity. A **liquid asset** is cash or one that can easily be converted into cash. Therefore Cash is always listed first, followed by Notes Receivable, Accounts Receivable, and Merchandise Inventory. The other current assets may be listed in any order.

Plant and Equipment

Items of plant and equipment are assets held for use in producing other assets. Those items of plant and equipment that are depreciable are shown with their Accumulated Depreciation accounts as illustrated on page 408.

RON'S APPLIANCES
WORKSHEET (PARTIAL)
FOR MONTH ENDED JUNE 30, 19XX

Acct. No.	Account Titles	Adjusted Trial Balance Debit	Adjusted Trial Balance Credit	Balance Sheet Debit	Balance Sheet Credit
101	Cash	11600 —		11600 —	
110	Notes Receivable	7200 —		7200 —	
120	Accounts Receivable	13600 —		13600 —	
130	Merchandise Inventory	46000 —		45100 —	
140	Supplies	1320 —		1320 —	
150	Prepaid Insurance	3000 —		3000 —	
160	Office Equipment	28000 —		28000 —	
160A	Accumulated Depr.: Off. Equip.		6000 —		6000 —
170	Delivery Equipment	57000 —		57000 —	
170A	Accumulated Depr.: Del. Equip.		12000 —		12000 —
180	Building	130000 —		130000 —	
180A	Accumulated Depr.: Bldg.		8000 —		8000 —
210	Notes Payable		25000 —		25000 —
220	Accounts Payable		5150 —		5150
240	Unearned Revenue		2600 —		2600 —
250	Mortgage Payable		90000 —		90000 —
310	Ron Renner, Capital		124390 —		124390 —
320	Ron Renner, Drawing	6000 —		6000 —	
410	Sales		105000 —		
420	Sales Returns and Allowances	2100 —			
430	Sales Discounts	2900 —			
501	Purchases	58000 —			
510	Freight In	2000 —			
520	Purchases Returns and Allowances		620 —		
530	Purchases Discounts		2400 —		
610	Rent Expense	3500 —			
620	Utilities Expense	750 —			
630	Wages Expense	5900 —			
	Totals				
650	Supplies Used	640 —			
660	Insurance Expense	100 —			
670	Depreciation Expense	1750 —			
230	Wages Payable		200 —		200 —
		381360 —	381360 —	302820 —	273340 —
	Net Income				29480 —
				302820 —	302820 —

Plant and Equipment

Office Equipment	$ 28,000		
Less: Accumulated Depreciation: Office Equipment	− 6,000	$ 22,000	
Delivery Equipment	57,000		
Less: Accumulated Depreciation: Delivery Equipment	− 12,000	45,000	
Building	130,000		
Less: Accumulated Depreciation: Building	8,000	122,000	
Total Plant and Equipment			$189,000

Plant and equipment items are recorded originally at their historic cost. The balance sheet shows the historic cost, the accumulated depreciation, and the book value. If a firm owns land, it will show on the balance sheet beneath the last depreciable item listed.

Current and Long-Term Liabilities

Current liabilities are those that are due within a relatively short period of time, usually one year. Current liabilities are paid out of current assets. On the balance sheet, Notes Payable (that portion that is due within one year) is listed first, followed by Accounts Payable. The other current liabilities are listed in no particular order. A portion of the Mortgage Payable is usually listed as a current liability, but only the amount that is due and payable within one year.

Long-term liabilities are those that are due after one year's time. Mortgage Payable and Notes Payable (those portions due after one year's time) usually fall into this category.

Owner's Equity

There are no changes in presentation of owner's equity on the balance sheet. However, many business owners prepare a separate statement of owner's equity and show only the ending capital on the balance sheet. The balance sheet for Ron's Appliances follows.

Ron's Appliances
Balance Sheet
June 30, 19XX

Assets

Current Assets

Cash	$ 11,600	
Notes Receivable	7,200	
Accounts Receivable	13,600	
Merchandise Inventory	45,100	
Supplies	1,320	
Prepaid Insurance	3,000	
Total Current Assets		$ 81,820

Plant and Equipment

Office Equipment	$ 28,000		
Less: Accumulated Depreciation: Office Equipment	− 6,000	22,000	
Delivery Equipment	57,000		
Less: Accumulated Depreciation: Delivery Equipment	− 12,000	45,000	
Building	130,000		
Less: Accumulated Depreciation: Building	− 8,000	122,000	
Total Plant and Equipment			189,000
Total Assets			$270,820

Liabilities

Current Liabilities

Notes Payable	$ 25,000	
Accounts Payable	5,150	
Wages Payable	200	
Unearned Revenue	2,600	
Mortgage Payable (current portion)	12,000	
Total Current Liabilities		$ 44,950

Long-Term Liabilities

Mortgage Payable		78,000
Total Liabilities		$122,950

Owner's Equity

Ron Renner, Capital, June 1, 19XX	$124,390	
Add: Net Income	29,480	
Subtotal	153,870	
Less: Ron Renner, Drawing	6,000	
Ron Renner, Capital, June 20, 19XX		147,870
Total Liabilities and Owner's Equity		$270,820

CURRENT RATIO

current ratio
one of the indicators of short-term debt-paying ability; obtained by dividing current assets by current liabilities

The **current ratio** is a good indicator of a firm's ability to pay its debts when they are due; it is determined by dividing total current assets by current liabilities. For Ron's Appliances, the current ratio is:

$$\frac{\text{Current Assets}}{\text{Current Liabilities}} = \frac{\$81,820}{\$44,950} = 1.82{:}1.$$

The 1.82:1 figure (rounded to the nearest hundredth) indicates that current assets are 1.82 times as much as current liabilities. Most lenders and other readers of financial statements are concerned with the current ratio and would like to see it be around 2:1 (twice as many current assets as current liabilities), because the current liabilities must be paid out of the current assets. A current ratio of 3:1 would be a strong current position, while a ratio of 1:1 would be weak. A 1:1 ratio indicates that every dollar of current assets is targeted for payment of short-term debt and nothing would be left over for emergencies or working capital.

WORKING CAPITAL

working capital
one of the indicators of short-term debt-paying ability; obtained by subtracting current liabilities from current assets

The excess of current assets over current liabilities is **working capital.** For Ron's Appliances, it is:

$$\text{Current Assets} - \text{Current Liabilities} = \text{Working Capital.}$$
$$\$81,820 \quad - \quad \$44,950 \quad = \quad \$36,870.$$

The working capital figure is, like the current ratio, an indication of a firm's short-term financial strength. It represents an amount of cash that a firm may put into, for example, volume buying, inventories, advertising, or favorable credit terms to customers.

CLOSING ENTRIES

The previous discussion of closing entries showed that there are four entries to be made for a service business. They are entries to (1) close all revenue accounts, (2) close all expense accounts, (3) transfer profit or loss to the capital account, and (4) transfer the balance of drawing to the capital account.

The first two closing entries are a little different for a merchandising business, because all of the cost of goods sold accounts must be closed in addition to the revenue and expense accounts. However, there are still four general journal entries required to close the books of a merchandising business, and they are made directly from the worksheet as before:

1. Close each account that appears in the credit column of the income statement.
2. Close each account that appears in the debit column of the income statement.
3. Transfer the profit or loss to the capital account.
4. Transfer the balance of the drawing account to the capital account.

Only the first two entries are different from those of a service business; the last two are exactly the same. The following shows the income statement columns of the worksheet for Ron's Appliances.

RON'S APPLIANCES
WORKSHEET (PARTIAL)
FOR MONTH ENDED JUNE 30, 19XX

Acct. No.	Account Titles	Adjusted Trial Balance Debit	Adjusted Trial Balance Credit	Income Statement Debit	Income Statement Credit
101	Cash	11600 —			
110	Notes Receivable	7200 —			
120	Accounts Receivable	13600 —			
130	Merchandise Inventory	46000 —		46000 —	45100 —
140	Supplies	1320 —			
150	Prepaid Insurance	3000 —			
160	Office Equipment	28000 —			
160A	Accumulated Depr.: Off. Equip.		6000 —		
170	Delivery Equipment	57000 —			
170A	Accumulated Depr.: Del. Equip.		12000 —		
180	Building	130000 —			
180A	Accumulated Depr.: Bldg.		8000 —		
210	Notes Payable		25000 —		
220	Accounts Payable		5150 —		
240	Unearned Revenue		2600 —		
250	Mortgage Payable		90000 —		
310	Ron Renner, Capital		124390 —		
320	Ron Renner, Drawing	6000 —			
410	Sales		105000 —		105000 —
420	Sales Returns and Allowances	2100 —		2100 —	
430	Sales Discounts	2900 —		2900 —	
501	Purchases	58000 —		58000 —	
510	Freight In	2000 —		2000 —	
520	Purchases Returns and Allowances		620 —		620 —
530	Purchases Discounts		2400 —		2400 —
610	Rent Expense	3500 —		3500 —	
620	Utilities Expense	750 —		750 —	
630	Wages Expense	5900 —		5900 —	
	Totals				
650	Supplies Used	640 —		640 —	
660	Insurance Expense	100 —		100 —	
670	Depreciation Expense	1750 —		1750 —	
230	Wages Payable		200 —		
		381360 —	381360 —	123640 —	153120 —
	Net Income			29480 —	
				153120 —	153120 —

The First Closing Entry

The first closing entry debits each account that appears in the credit column of the income statement; the total is credited to Income Summary. Check marks are placed on the worksheet next to the amounts as they are journalized.

			GENERAL JOURNAL						Page *6*
Date			Description	Post. Ref.		Debit		Credit	
19XX			***Closing Entries***						
June	*30*		*Merchandise Inventory*	130		4 5 1 0 0 —			
			Sales	410		1 0 5 0 0 0 —			
			Purchases Returns and Allowances	520		6 2 0 —			
			Purchases Discounts	530		2 4 0 0 —			
			Income Summary	360				1 5 3 1 2 0 —	
			To Close Income Statement Accounts with						
			Credit Balances and to Enter the Ending						
			Inventory on the Books						

After this first closing entry has been posted, the Merchandise Inventory account will look like this.

Merchandise Inventory   130

6/1	Balance		46,000
6/30	Closing	GJ6	45,100

The effect of the first closing entry on the Merchandise Inventory account is to transfer the value of the ending inventory to the account. The beginning inventory figure is removed from the account in the second closing entry.

The Second Closing Entry

The second closing entry credits every account that appears on the debit side of the income statement and debits Income Summary. The following shows the income statement columns of the worksheet. Check marks have been placed opposite the accounts in the worksheet debit and credit columns for which closing entries have been made.

RON'S APPLIANCES
WORKSHEET (PARTIAL)
FOR MONTH ENDED JUNE 30, 19XX

Acct. No.	Account Titles	Adjusted Trial Balance Debit	Adjusted Trial Balance Credit	Income Statement Debit	Income Statement Credit
101	Cash	11600 —			
110	Notes Receivable	7200 —			
120	Accounts Receivable	13600 —			
130	Merchandise Inventory	46000 —		46000 ✓	45100 ✓
140	Supplies	1320 —			
150	Prepaid Insurance	3000 —			
160	Office Equipment	28000 —			
160A	Accumulated Depr.: Off. Equip.		6000 —		
170	Delivery Equipment	57000 —			
170A	Accumulated Depr.: Del. Equip.		12000 —		
180	Building	130000 —			
180A	Accumulated Depreciation: Bldg.		8000 —		
210	Notes Payable		25000 —		
220	Accounts Payable		5150 —		
240	Unearned Revenue		2600 —		
250	Mortgage Payable		90000 —		
310	Ron Renner, Capital		124390 —		
320	Ron Renner, Drawing	6000 —			
410	Sales		105000 —		105000 ✓
420	Sales Returns and Allowances	2100 —		2100 ✓	
430	Sales Discounts	2900 —		2900 ✓	
501	Purchases	58000 —		58000 ✓	
510	Freight In	2000 —		2000 ✓	
520	Purchases Returns and Allowances		620 —		620 ✓
530	Purchases Discounts		2400 —		2400 ✓
610	Rent Expense	3500 —		3500 ✓	
620	Utilities Expense	750 —		750 ✓	
630	Wages Expense	5900 —		5900 ✓	
	Totals				
650	Supplies Used	640 —		640 ✓	
660	Insurance Expense	100 —		100 ✓	
670	Depreciation Expense	1750 —		1750 ✓	
230	Wages Payable		200 —		
		381360 —	381360 —	123640 ✓	153120 ✓
				29480 —	
				153120 —	153120 —

GENERAL JOURNAL				Page **6**
Date	Description	Post. Ref.	Debit	Credit
19XX	**Closing Entries**			
30	Income Summary	360	1 2 3 6 4 0 —	
	Merchandise Inventory	130		4 6 0 0 0 —
	Sales Returns and Allowances	420		2 1 0 0 —
	Sales Discounts	430		2 9 0 0 —
	Purchases	501		5 8 0 0 0 —
	Freight In	510		2 0 0 0 —
	Rent Expense	610		3 5 0 0 —
	Utilities Expense	620		7 5 0 —
	Wages Expense	630		5 9 0 0 —
	Supplies Used	650		6 4 0 —
	Insurance Expense	660		1 0 0 —
	Depreciation Expense	670		1 7 5 0 —
	To Close Income Statement Accounts with Debit			
	Balances and to Close out Beginning			
	Merchandise Inventory			

After the second closing entry has been posted, the Merchandise Inventory account appears as follows.

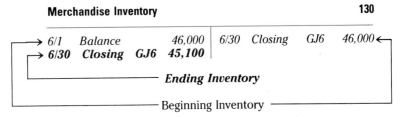

Merchandise Inventory   **130**

| 6/1 | Balance | | 46,000 | 6/30 | Closing | GJ6 | 46,000 |
| 6/30 | Closing | GJ6 | 45,100 | | | | |

Ending Inventory

Beginning Inventory

The account now reflects the value of the ending inventory. The ending inventory for this period becomes the beginning inventory of the next period.

The Third and Fourth Closing Entries

The third closing entry transfers the profit (or loss) to the owner's capital account, and the fourth transfers the balance of the drawing account to the owner's capital account.

GENERAL JOURNAL					Page *6*									
Date	**Description**	Post. Ref.	**Debit**						**Credit**					
19XX	*Closing Entries*													

30	*Income Summary*	*360*		2	9	4	8	0	—						
	Ron Renner, Capital	*310*									2	9	4	8	0	—
	To Transfer Net Income to Capital														
30	*Ron Renner, Capital*	*310*			6	0	0	0	—						
	Ron Renner, Drawing	*320*										6	0	0	0	—
	To Transfer Balance of Drawing to Capital														

After the third closing entry is posted, the Income Summary account is closed as follows.

Income Summary   **360**

| 6/30 | Closing | GJ6 | 123,640 | 6/30 | Closing | GJ6 | 153,120 |
| 6/30 | Closing | GJ6 | 29,480 | | | | |

The General Ledger after the Adjusting and Closing Entries Are Posted

The adjusting and closing entries are shown now, followed by T-accounts representing the general ledger after they have been posted.

GENERAL JOURNAL				Page 5	
Date	Description	Post. Ref.	Debit	Credit	
19XX	**Adjusting Entries**				
June 30	Supplies Used	650	640 —		
	Supplies	140		640 —	
	To Record Supplies Used for June				
30	Insurance Expense	660	100 —		
	Prepaid Insurance	150		100 —	
	To Record Insurance Expense for June				
30	Depreciation Expense	670	1750 —		
	Accumulated Depreciation: Off. Equip.	160A		500 —	
	Accumulated Depreciation: Del. Equip.	170A		750 —	
	Accumulated Depreciation: Bldg.	180A		500 —	
	To Record Depreciation Expense				
30	Unearned Revenue	240	900 —		
	Sales	410		900 —	
	To Transfer a Portion of Unearned				
	Revenue to Sales				
30	Wages Expense	630	200 —		
	Wages Payable	230		200 —	
	To Record Accrued Wages				

GENERAL JOURNAL				Page 6
Date	**Description**	**Post. Ref.**	**Debit**	**Credit**
19XX	**Closing Entries**			
June 30	*Merchandise Inventory*	130	45100 —	
	Sales	410	105000 —	
	Purchases Returns and Allowances	520	620 —	
	Purchases Discounts	530	2400 —	
	Income Summary	360		153120 —
	To Close Income Statement Accounts with			
	Credit Balances and to Enter the Ending			
	Inventory on the Books			
30	*Income Summary*	360	123640 —	
	Merchandise Inventory	130		46000 —
	Sales Returns and Allowances	420		2100 —
	Sales Discounts	430		2900 —
	Purchases	501		58000 —
	Freight In	510		2000 —
	Rent Expense	610		3500 —
	Utilities Expense	620		750 —
	Wages Expense	630		5900 —
	Supplies Used	650		640 —
	Insurance Expense	660		100 —
	Depreciation Expense	670		1750 —
	To Close Income Statement Accounts with			
	Debit Balances and to Close out			
	Beginning Merchandise Inventory			
30	*Income Summary*	360	29480 —	
	Ron Renner, Capital	310		29480 —
	To Transfer Net Income to Capital			
30	*Ron Renner, Capital*	310	6000 —	
	Ron Renner, Drawing	320		6000 —
	To Transfer Balance of Drawing to Capital			

Assets

Cash   101

6/30 Balance	11,600	

Notes Receivable   **110**

| 6/30 | Balance | 7,200 | | | | |

Accounts Receivable   **120**

| 6/30 | Balance | 13,600 | | | | |

Merchandise Inventory   **130**

| 6/1 | Balance | | 46,000 | 6/30 | Closing | GJ6 | 46,000 |
| 6/30 | Closing | GJ6 | 45,100 | | | | |

Supplies   **140**

| 6/1 | Balance | 1,960 | 6/30 | Adjusting | GJ5 | 640 |
| | 1320 | | | | | |

Prepaid Insurance   **150**

| 6/1 | Balance | 3,100 | 6/30 | Adjusting | GJ5 | 100 |
| | 3000 | | | | | |

Office Equipment   **160**

| 6/30 | Balance | 28,000 | | | | |

Accumulated Depreciation: Office Equipment   **160A**

			6/1	Balance		5,500
			6/30	Adjusting	GJ5	500
						6,000

Delivery Equipment   **170**

| 6/30 | Balance | 57,000 | | | | |

Accumulated Depreciation: Delivery Equipment   **170A**

		6/1	Balance		11,250
		6/30	Adjusting	GJ5	750
					12,000

Building   **180**

| 6/30 | Balance | 130,000 | | |
| | | | | |

Accumulated Depreciation: Building   **180A**

		6/1	Balance		7,500
		6/30	Adjusting	GJ5	500
					8,000

Liabilities and Owner's Equity

Notes Payable   **210**

| | | 6/30 | Balance | 25,000 |

Accounts Payable   **220**

| | | 6/30 | Balance | 5,150 |

Wages Payable   **230**

| | | 6/30 | Adjusting | GJ5 | 200 |

Unearned Revenue   **240**

| 6/30 | Adjusting | GJ5 | 900 | 6/1 | Balance | 3,500 |
| | | | | | 2600 | |

Mortgage Payable   **250**

| | | 6/30 | Balance | 90,000 |

Ron Renner, Capital   **310**

6/30	Closing	GJ6	6,000	6/1	Balance		124,390
				6/30	Closing	GJ6	29,480
							153,870
						147,870	

Ron Renner, Drawing   **320**

6/30	Balance		6,000	6/30	Closing	GJ6	6,000

Income Summary   **360**

6/30	Closing	GJ6	123,640	6/30	Closing	GJ6	153,120
6/30	Closing	GJ6	29,480				

Revenue, Cost of Goods Sold, and Expense Accounts
Revenue

Sales   **410**

6/30	Closing	GJ6	105,000	6/30	Balance		104,100
				6/30	Adjusting	GJ5	900

Sales Returns and Allowances   **420**

6/30	Balance		2,100	6/30	Closing	GJ6	2,100

Sales Discounts   **430**

6/30	Balance		2,900	6/30	Closing	GJ6	2,900

Cost of Goods Sold

Purchases   **501**

6/30	Balance		58,000	6/30	Closing	GJ6	58,000

Freight In   **510**

6/30	Balance		2,000	6/30	Closing	GJ6	2,000

Purchases Returns and Allowances   **520**

6/30	Closing	GJ6	620	6/30	Balance		620

Purchases Discounts   **530**

6/30	Closing	GJ6	2,400	6/30	Balance		2,400

Expenses

Rent Expense   **610**

6/30	Balance		3,500	6/30	Closing	GJ6	3,500

Utilities Expense   **620**

6/30	Balance		750	6/30	Closing	GJ6	750

Wages Expense   **630**

6/30	Balance		5,700	6/30	Closing	GJ6	5,900
6/30	Adjusting	GJ5	200				

Supplies Used   **650**

6/30	Adjusting	GJ5	640	6/30	Closing	GJ6	640

Insurance Expense   **660**

6/30	Adjusting	GJ5	100	6/30	Closing	GJ6	100

Depreciation Expense   **670**

6/30	Adjusting	GJ5	1,750	6/30	Closing	GJ6	1,750

THE POST-CLOSING TRIAL BALANCE

All the revenue, cost of goods sold, and expense accounts have zero balances after the closing entries are posted. In addition, the capital account has been brought up to date (by adding the net income and subtracting the drawing), and the drawing account has been closed. The only accounts that remain open are the assets, liabilities, and owner's capital.

The post-closing trial balance is prepared to ensure that debits equal credits in the accounts that remain open—the balance sheet accounts—before work is started for the next accounting period. It should be prepared directly from the ledger after the closing entries are posted. Following is the post-closing trial balance for Ron's Appliances.

Ron's Appliances
Post-Closing Trial Balance
June 30, 19XX

Cash	$ 11,600	
Notes Receivable	7,200	
Accounts Receivable	13,600	
Merchandise Inventory	45,100	
Supplies	1,320	
Prepaid Insurance	3,000	
Office Equipment	28,000	
Accumulated Depreciation: Off. Equip.		$ 6,000
Delivery Equipment	57,000	
Accumulated Depreciation: Del. Equip.		12,000
Building	130,000	
Accumulated Depreciation: Bldg.		8,000
Notes Payable		25,000
Accounts Payable		5,150
Wages Payable		200
Unearned Revenue		2,600
Mortgage Payable		90,000
Ron Renner, Capital		147,870
Totals	$296,820	$296,820

SUMMARY

The complete accounting cycle includes (1) journalizing, (2) posting, (3) preparing a worksheet with adjustments, (4) preparing an income statement, (5) preparing a balance sheet, (6) preparing schedules of accounts receivable and accounts payable, (7) journalizing and posting adjusting entries, (8) journalizing and posting closing entries, and (9) preparing a post-closing trial balance.

The worksheet for a merchandising business contains both the beginning and ending merchandise inventories. The beginning inventory figure is obtained from the general ledger and appears on the worksheet as a debit on the trial balance, the adjusted trial balance, and the income statement. The ending inventory figure, obtained by a physical count or an estimate, appears on the worksheet in two places: as a credit on the income statement and as a debit on the balance sheet. The inventory figures are used when calculating cost of goods sold on the income statement.

The income statement for a merchandising business contains three major sections: (1) revenue, (2) cost of goods sold, and (3) expenses. Revenue minus cost of goods sold produces the gross profit figure, and expenses subtracted from gross profit produces the net profit figure. The cost of goods sold is calculated as follows.

$$
\begin{array}{l}
 \text{Beginning Inventory} \\
\underline{+\ \text{Net Purchases}} \\
 \text{Cost of Merchandise Available for Sale} \\
\underline{-\ \text{Ending Inventory}} \\
 \text{Cost of Goods Sold}
\end{array}
$$

The income statement is prepared directly from the income statement columns of the worksheet, as is the balance sheet. The asset section of the balance sheet is classified into current assets and plant and equipment. Current assets are cash, items that can be converted into cash, or items that will be used up within one year's time. Plant and equipment includes assets that are used in the production of other assets; such items might be furniture, office equipment, delivery vehicles, land, and so on. Items of plant and equipment, when depreciable, are shown on the balance sheet at their historic cost. Accumulated depreciation is subtracted from cost, and the book value is calculated on the balance sheet.

Liabilities are also classified into two categories: current and long term. Current liabilities must be paid within one year's time, and long-term liabilities will be due after one year.

The current ratio is an indicator of a firm's short-term debt-paying ability and is calculated by dividing current assets by current liabilities. A ratio of 2:1 is considered to be adequate; a ratio of 3:1 is considered to be strong. Another indicator of short-term debt-paying ability is the working capital figure, which is obtained by subtracting current liabilities from current assets. Working capital represents the portion of current assets that are not targeted for paying current liabilities.

The closing entries, prepared directly from the income statement columns of the worksheet, accomplish the following.

1. All the revenue and contra-revenue accounts are closed.
2. All the cost of goods sold accounts are closed (these include purchases and contra-purchases accounts).
3. All the expense accounts are closed.
4. The Merchandise Inventory account is brought up to date by closing out the beginning inventory and entering the ending inventory figure on the books.
5. The Drawing account is closed.
6. The Capital account is brought up to date by adding the net income, or deducting the net loss, and by deducting drawing.

Once the closing entries are posted, the only remaining step in the accounting cycle is to prepare a post-closing trial balance. It ensures the equality of debits and credits in the ledger accounts that remain open—all of the balance sheet accounts except drawing.

Review of Accounting Terminology

Following is a list of the accounting terminology for this chapter.

classified   liquid asset
current ratio   working capital
gross profit

Fill in the blank with the correct word or term from the list.

1. The _____ is obtained by dividing current assets by current liabilities and is an indicator of short-term debt-paying ability.
2. Net sales minus cost of goods sold equals _____.
3. Current assets minus current liabilities is called the _____ and is an indicator of a firm's short-term debt-paying ability.

4. When items are separated into categories, they are said to be
   _____.

5. A/an _____ is cash or is easily converted to cash.

Match the following words and terms on the left with the definitions on the right.

6. classified
7. current ratio
8. gross profit
9. liquid asset
10. working capital

a. separated into categories
b. net sales minus cost of goods sold
c. cash or easily converted into cash
d. current assets minus current liabilities
e. current assets divided by current liabilities

Exercises ═══

Exercise 11.1
journalizing adjusting entries

Record the adjusting entries in a general journal (page 6) for the month of September 19XX for Ma and Pa Grocery. Use the following account titles: Supplies, Prepaid Insurance, Prepaid Advertising, Accumulated Depreciation: Computer, Unearned Revenue, Wages Payable, Grocery Revenue, Depreciation Expense, Insurance Expense, Advertising Expense, Supplies Used, and Wages Expense.

a. The computer, purchased on January 2 of this year for $8,000, is expected to be useful for four years and will have a salvage value of $2,000.

b. On September 1 of this year, Ma and Pa Grocery received a check for $2,000 from a local orphanage. The money was for supplies and groceries to be delivered after September 1 and was credited to Unearned Revenue. During September, $800 worth of groceries were delivered to the orphanage.

c. On January 2 of this year, $1,800 was paid for a two-year insurance policy.

d. On September 1 of this year, $900 was paid for three months of advertising.

e. Three days' wages of $210 per day had accrued at the end of September.

f. The balance in the Supplies account on September 1 was $440. Additional supplies were purchased on September 18 for $120 and on September 24 for $70. The value of the supplies on hand on September 30 was $310.

Exercise 11.2
classifying accounts

Tell on which section of the balance sheet each of the following accounts appears. The sections should be identified as current assets (CA), plant and equipment (PE), current liabilities (CL), long-term liabilities (LTL), or owner's equity (OE). Also tell what the normal account balance is for each account listed.

Account Titles	Which section of the balance sheet?	Normal account balance?
1. Prepaid Insurance	_____	_____
2. Owner's Drawing	_____	_____
3. Accounts Payable	_____	_____
4. Building	_____	_____
5. Cash	_____	_____
6. Unearned Revenue	_____	_____
7. Accumulated Depreciation	_____	_____
8. Office Furniture	_____	_____
9. Mortgage Payable (all due in 10 years)	_____	_____
10. Merchandise Inventory	_____	_____

Now tell on which section of the income statement each of the following accounts appears. Sections should be identified as revenue (R), cost of goods sold (CGS), or expense (E). Also tell the normal account balance for each.

Account Titles	Which section of the income statement?	Normal account balance?
11. Sales Discounts	_____	_____
12. Purchases Discounts	_____	_____
13. Wages Expense	_____	_____
14. Sales Returns and Allowances	_____	_____
15. Merchandise Inventory	_____	_____
16. Sales	_____	_____
17. Supplies Used	_____	_____
18. Freight In	_____	_____
19. Purchases	_____	_____
20. Purchases Returns and Allowances	_____	_____

Exercise 11.3
analyzing the Merchandise Inventory account

The Merchandise Inventory account for Sam's Glass Shop shows a debit balance on February 1 of $17,640. Answer the following questions about this account.

a. What is the account classification for merchandise inventory?

b. How is the dollar value of the ending merchandise inventory determined?

c. The beginning merchandise inventory figure appears on the ten-column worksheet in three different places. What are those three places?

d. Assuming that the value of Sam's merchandise inventory on February 28 is $16,500, on which two worksheet columns will this ending inventory figure appear?

e. Where will the merchandise inventory figure appear on the financial statements?

Exercise 11.4
determining order of steps in the accounting cycle

Following are the steps in the accounting cycle. Rearrange them in correct order, numbering each. As an example, the first is (1) journalize period's regular transactions.

Prepare trial balance, calculate adjustments, and complete worksheet.

Prepare a balance sheet.

Prepare a post-closing trial balance.

Journalize period's regular transactions.

Journalize and post closing entries.

Post regular transactions to ledger.

Prepare an income statement.

Journalize and post adjusting entries.

Prepare schedules of accounts receivable and payable.

Exercise 11.5
calculating net sales and net purchases

Given the following account balances, calculate (1) net sales and (2) net purchases.

Cash	$10,550
Sales Discounts	1,470
Purchases Discounts	3,880
Sales	94,000
Freight-In	3,190
Merchandise Inventory	31,000
Purchases	49,600
Sales Returns and Allowances	2,630
Purchases Returns and Allowances	4,020

Exercise 11.6
calculating cost of goods sold

From the following account balances, prepare the cost of goods sold section of an income statement for the month of August 19XX.

Purchases	$29,400
Merchandise Inventory, August 31	12,300
Purchases Returns and Allowances	410
Freight In	1,100
Purchases Discounts	290
Merchandise Inventory, August 1	11,400

Exercise 11.7
analyzing asset accounts

Following are the asset and liability accounts and their balances as of May 31, 19XX, after the adjusting entries have been posted for Carlo's Italian Restaurant. Determine (1) the dollar amount of current assets, (2) the dollar amount of current liabilities, (3) the current ratio, (4) the working capital, and (5) the total dollar value of plant and equipment as it would appear on the balance sheet.

Cash	$ 9,120
Accounts Payable	2,500
Merchandise Inventory	9,235
Equipment	15,000
Accumulated Depreciation: Equipment	2,300
Payroll Taxes Payable	320
Supplies	940
Accounts Receivable	3,630
Wages Payable	550
Prepaid Insurance	500
Furniture	7,500
Accumulated Depreciation: Furniture	1,800
Mortgage Payable ($6,000 due within 12 months)	50,000
Land	75,000

Exercise 11.8
journalizing closing entries

Following are the income statement columns of the May 19XX worksheet for Goodlife Vitamins owned by Nancy Swanson. The balance of the owner's drawing account on May 31, 19XX, was $3,600. Prepare the closing entries to: (1) close all accounts with credit balances and enter the ending merchandise inventory on the books, (2) close all accounts with debit balances and remove the beginning inventory from the books, (3) transfer the net income to the owner's capital account, and (4) transfer the balance of drawing to capital. Use general journal page 31.

	Income Statement	
	Debit	Credit
Merchandise Inventory	13,700	14,100
Sales		47,000
Sales Returns and Allowances	410	
Sales Discounts	520	
Purchases	29,000	
Freight In	1,100	
Purchases Returns and Allowances		330
Purchases Discounts		260
Rent Expense	1,800	
Advertising Expense	2,010	

Continued.

	Income Statement	
	Debit	**Credit**
Salary Expense	2,740	
Supplies Used	390	
Depreciation Expense	1,740	
Utilities Expense	330	
Totals	53,740	61,690
Net Income	7,950	
	61,690	61,690

Exercise 11.9
journalizing closing entries

Following are the income statement columns of the March 19XX worksheet for Puffy Pastries owned by Sam Yee. The balance of the owner's drawing account on March 31 was $1,500. Prepare the closing entries to: (1) close all accounts with credit balances and enter the ending inventory figure on the books, (2) close all accounts with debit balances and remove the beginning inventory figure from the books, (3) transfer the net loss to the owner's capital account, and (4) transfer the balance of drawing to capital. Use general journal page 56.

	Income Statement	
	Debit	**Credit**
Merchandise Inventory	3,000	2,100
Sales		14,300
Sales Returns and Allowances	390	
Purchases	8,000	
Purchases Discounts		740
Rent Expense	1,100	
Utilities Expense	310	
Salary Expense	1,200	
Supplies Used	140	
Depreciation Expense	3,500	
	17,640	17,140
Net Loss		500
	17,640	17,640

Problems

Problem 11.1
posting closing entries

Following are the closing entries and the related T-accounts for Higgins' Grocery on January 31, 19XX.

Date		Description	Post. Ref.	Debit	Credit
		GENERAL JOURNAL			**Page 13**
		Closing Entries			
Jan.	*31*	Merchandise Inventory		12100 —	
		Sales		25000 —	
		Purchases Returns and Allowances		480 —	
		Purchases Discounts		165 —	
		Income Summary			37745 —
		To Close Income Statement Accounts with Credit			
		Balances and to Enter the Ending Inventory on			
		the Books			
	31	Income Summary		34210 —	
		Merchandise Inventory			13400 —
		Sales Returns and Allowances			1400 —
		Sales Discounts			900 —
		Purchases			16500 —
		Rent Expense			900 —
		Utilities Expense			380 —
		Advertising Expense			520 —
		Insurance Expense			210 —
		To Close Income Statement Accounts with Debit			
		Balances and to Close out the Beginning			
		Merchandise Inventory			
	31	Income Summary		3535 —	
		Henry Higgins, Capital			3535 —
		To Transfer Net Income to Capital			
	31	Henry Higgins, Capital		2200 —	
		Henry Higgins, Drawing			2200 —
		To Transfer the Balance of Drawing to Capital			

Merchandise Inventory	130
1/31 Balance 13,400	

Purchases	510
1/31 Balance 16,500	

Higgins, Capital	310
	1/31 Balance 15,200

Purchases Returns and Allowances	520
	1/31 Balance 480

Henry Higgins, Drawing	320
1/31 Balance 2,200	

Purchases Discounts	530
	1/31 Balance 165

Income Summary	330

Rent Expense	610
1/31 Balance 900	

Sales	410
	1/31 Balance 25,000

Utilities Expense	620
1/31 Balance 380	

Sales Returns and Allowances	420
1/31 Balance 1,400	

Advertising Expense	630
1/31 Balance 520	

Sales Discounts	430
1/31 Balance 900	

Insurance Expense	640
1/31 Balance 210	

Instructions

1. *Post the closing entries to the T-accounts provided. As posting is completed, be sure to place account numbers in the journal and the journal page number (GJ13) in the T-accounts.*

2. *After posting has been completed, answer the following questions.*

   a. *What is the balance of the Income Summary account after posting has been completed?*

b.   What is the balance of the Merchandise Inventory account after posting has been completed?

c.   Which income statement accounts remain open after posting has been completed?

d.   What is the balance of the drawing account after posting has been completed?

e.   What is the balance of the capital account on January 31, 19XX?

f.   What is the dollar amount of the net income for January?

Problem 11.2
journalizing closing entries and preparing income statement

Following are the income statement columns of the worksheet for Koffee Kitchen, owned by Raymond White, for the month of February 19XX.

		Income Statement	
		Debit	**Credit**
130	Merchandise Inventory	11,400	10,600
410	Sales		27,400
420	Sales Returns and Allowances	600	
430	Sales Discounts	730	
501	Purchases	14,200	
510	Freight In	540	
520	Purchases Returns and Allowances		190
530	Purchases Discounts		510
610	Rent Expense	850	
620	Utilities Expense	240	
630	Wages Expense	1,500	
640	Advertising Expense	1,000	
650	Supplies Used	190	
660	Insurance Expense	70	
670	Depreciation Expense	850	
		32,170	38,700
	Net Income	6,530	
		38,700	38,700

Instructions

1.   Journalize the four required closing entries. Use general journal page 6. The balance of the owner's drawing account on February 28 is $3,400.

2.   Prepare an income statement for the month.

Problem 11.3

preparing classified balance sheet and calculating current ratio and working capital

Following are the balance sheet columns of the worksheet for Special Effects, a retail store owned by Betsy Rawlings, on September 30, 19XX.

		Balance Sheet	
		Debit	Credit
101	Cash	9,350	
110	Notes Receivable	5,700	
120	Accounts Receivable	5,120	
130	Merchandise Inventory	24,600	
140	Supplies	730	
150	Prepaid Insurance	1,500	
160	Office Equipment	14,000	
160A	Accumulated Depreciation: Office Equipment		5,000
170	Store Equipment	21,000	
170A	Accumulated Depreciation: Store Equipment		6,000
180	Building	55,000	
180A	Accumulated Depreciation: Building		16,400
210	Notes Payable		14,600
220	Accounts Payable		6,200
230	Wages Payable		470
240	Unearned Revenue		1,370
250	Mortgage Payable		42,000
310	Betsy Rawlings, Capital		43,980
320	Betsy Rawlings, Drawing	3,650	
		140,650	136,020
	Net Income		4,630
		140,650	140,650

Instructions

1. *Prepare a classified balance sheet as of September 30, 19XX. The balance in Notes Payable is due in 6 months and $12,000 of the balance in Mortgage Payable is due within the next 12 months. Include a complete statement of owner's equity on the balance sheet.*

2. *Determine the current ratio. (Round to the nearest tenth of a percent.) Does it indicate a strong or a weak current position?*

3. *Detemine the dollar amount of working capital.*

Problem 11.4

completing the accounting cycle from worksheet through post-closing trial balance

Following are the trial balance columns of the worksheet for the month of April 19XX for Gail Greenwood, owner of Woman Source, a bookstore.

		Trial Balance	
		Debit	**Credit**
101	Cash	10,400	
110	Notes Receivable	9,600	
120	Accounts Receivable	3,300	
130	Merchandise Inventory	31,000	
140	Supplies	760	
150	Prepaid Insurance	2,300	
160	Office Equipment	27,000	
160A	Accumulated Depreciation: Office Equipment		6,750
170	Delivery Equipment	40,000	
170A	Accumulated Depreciation: Delivery Equipment		9,375
180	Building	35,000	
180A	Accumulated Depreciation: Building		1,500
210	Notes Payable		40,000
220	Accounts Payable		5,100
240	Unearned Revenue		1,800
250	Mortgage Payable		30,000
310	Gail Greenwood, Capital		67,265
320	Gail Greenwood, Drawing	4,400	
410	Sales		60,000
420	Sales Returns and Allowances	690	
430	Sales Discounts	1,600	
501	Purchases	49,000	
510	Freight In	2,500	
520	Purchases Returns and Allowances		1,110
530	Purchases Discounts		980
610	Rent Expense	1,400	
620	Utilities Expense	370	
630	Wages Expense	3,160	
640	Advertising Expense	1,400	
		223,880	223,880

Instructions

1. Enter the account names, numbers, and balances into T-accounts representing a general ledger and onto the trial balance columns of a worksheet. In addition to the accounts listed on the trial balance, add the following: Supplies Used, 650; Insurance Expense, 660; Depreciation Expense, 670; Wages Payable, 260; and Income Summary, 330.

2. *Calculate the adjustments for April and enter the amounts in the adjustments columns of the worksheet. The necessary information is:*
   a. *The supplies inventory on April 30 is $310.*
   b. *A two-year insurance policy was purchased on March 1 of this year for $2,400.*
   c. *Office equipment was purchased on January 2 of last year; cost, $27,000; life, 5 years; no salvage value.*
   d. *Delivery equipment was purchased on January 4 of last year; cost, $40,000; life, 4 years; salvage value, $10,000.*
   e. *A building was purchased on January 2 of last year; cost, $35,000; life, 20 years; salvage value, $11,000.*
   f. *Wages payable on April 30 are $760.*
   g. *$800 of the unearned revenue has been earned during April.*

3. *The value of the merchandise inventory on April 30 is $34,000. Enter the inventory figures in their appropriate places on the worksheet.*

4. *Complete the worksheet.*

5. *Prepare an income statement for Woman Source for the month of April 19XX.*

6. *Prepare a statement of owner's equity for Woman Source for the month of April 19XX.*

7. *Prepare a classified balance sheet for Woman Source as of April 30, 19XX. Include only the ending capital figure in the owner's equity section. $12,000 of the balance in Notes Payable is due within 12 months, and the mortgage is all due and payable in 10 years.*

8. *Journalize and post the adjusting entries. Use general journal page 48.*

9. *Journalize and post the closing entries. Use general journal page 49.*

10. *Prepare a post-closing trial balance.*

Problem 11.5
preparing financial statements, journalizing closing entries, and calculating current ratio and working capital

Following are the income statement and balance sheet columns of the worksheet for Pete Stavros, owner of Stavros Imports, for the month of August 19XX.

	Income Statement		Balance Sheet	
	Debit	Credit	Debit	Credit
Cash			15,340	
Notes Receivable			14,290	
Accounts Receivable			6,050	
Merchandise Inventory	12,290	15,450	15,450	
Supplies			1,020	
Prepaid Insurance			1,900	
Office Equipment			24,000	
Accumulated Depreciation: Office Equipment				7,400
Store Equipment			34,000	
Accumulated Depreciation: Store Equipment				17,500
Building			42,000	
Accumulated Depreciation: Building				20,600
Notes Payable				36,200
Accounts Payable				3,030
Wages Payable				1,420
Unearned Revenue				1,140
Mortgage Payable				25,700
Pete Stavros, Capital				44,420
Pete Stavros, Drawing			2,490	
Sales		49,740		
Sales Returns and Allowances	600			
Sales Discounts	500			
Purchases	35,000			
Freight In	1,960			
Purchases Returns and Allowances		1,610		
Purchases Discounts		700		
Rent Expense	1,500			
Utilities Expense	590			
Wages Expense	5,640			
Depreciation Expense	4,470			
Advertising Expense	1,940			
Insurance Expense	160			
Repairs Expense	3,120			
Supplies Used	600			
Totals	68,370	67,500	156,540	157,410
Net Loss		870	870	
	68,370	68,370	157,410	157,410

Instructions 1. *Prepare an income statement for Stavros Imports for the month of August 19XX.*

2. *Prepare a classified balance sheet for Stavros Imports on August 31, 19XX, assuming that $12,000 of the balance in Notes Payable is due within a year's time and that $6,000 of the balance in Mortgage Payable is due within a year's time.*

3. *Journalize the closing entries on August 31. Use general journal page 29.*

4. *Determine the current ratio. (Round to the nearest tenth of a percent.)*

5. *Determine the dollar amount of working capital.*

CHAPTER 12

Payroll: Employee Deductions

LEARNING OBJECTIVES

When you have completed this chapter, you should

1. have a better understanding of accounting terminology.

2. have an understanding of the employer-employee relationship.

3. be able to calculate gross earnings.

4. be able to calculate employee deductions for FICA and federal income taxes.

5. be able to calculate net wages.

6. be able to complete a payroll register.

7. be able to prepare the journal entry to record the gross wages, employee deductions, and net wages.

The accounting system chosen for payroll must easily and quickly provide accurate records of the rate of pay, hours worked, and deductions for each employee so that paychecks will be timely and accurate. The system chosen must be able to promptly produce the withholding statements and the necessary government reports. It must also have built-in safeguards against payroll fraud.

Labor costs and the related payroll taxes constitute a large portion of the total operating costs of most businesses. Preparing the payroll and necessary government forms is costly and time consuming. These tasks are made more difficult by the many federal and state laws that relate to filing timely reports and making regular deposits of funds withheld from employees' wages. Employers must keep accurate records of each employee's earnings and deductions, as well as records for the total payroll. Their books must be open to government audit at all times.

For example, the Internal Revenue Service (IRS) requires that employers withhold certain taxes each payroll period, deposit those taxes regularly and before the established deadlines, and file reports relating to the payroll and amounts withheld. If an employer does not meet the deadline for depositing withheld taxes, a 10 percent penalty is assessed. If an employer willfully overstates on an IRS form the amount of money deposited, a 25 percent penalty may be charged the employer, perhaps along with other penalties.

CIRCULAR E: EMPLOYER'S TAX GUIDE

The Internal Revenue Service (Department of the Treasury) provides employers with the necessary information for withholding taxes from employees' wages. It publishes a booklet titled *Circular E: Employer's Tax Guide* that is provided to employers. The *Circular E* is regularly updated as tax laws and withholding rates change. It contains topics such as: Are You an Employer?; Who Are Employees?; Taxable Wages; Taxable Tips; Figuring Withholding; Depositing Taxes; and so on.

The *Circular E* also contains the withholding tables for federal income tax and FICA (social security) tax. A toll-free number is provided in the telephone directory for ordering forms and tax booklets. Proprietors, managers, and those employees involved in preparing the payroll should be familiar with the contents of the *Circular E*.

INTERNAL CONTROL OVER PAYROLL

Owners of small businesses may be able to maintain strong internal control over the payroll by calculating the amounts owed and writing the checks personally. Such owners are usually present at the place of business each day and know which employees are there. In larger companies, maintaining strong internal control is more difficult. The basic principles of internal control may be applied, however. Separation of duties is of primary importance— keeping track of time, preparing the payroll, keeping records, and distributing the payroll checks should be handled by different employees.

For hourly employees, a reliable method of keeping track of hours worked must be devised. Employees may simply sign in under the supervision of the manager, or a time clock may be used. A time clock prints on a time card when the employee arrives at work, when he or she checks out for lunch and returns from lunch, and when he or she leaves for the day. Someone should supervise the time clock to ensure that one employee does not punch in or out for another.

divert
to turn aside from a course or direction

collusion
a secret agreement for a fraudulent purpose

Any time cash is involved, the possibility of fraud exists. For example, the employee who writes the payroll checks may prepare duplicate checks for one or more employees and keep (and cash) the extra checks. The employee may also make out a check to a fictitious person and **divert** the funds to the payroll employee. **Collusion** with other employees may result in the payroll employee writing checks for more than the employees have earned and then taking a kickback from the overpaid employees.

Because of the many possibilities for fraud, employers must exercise great care when devising a payroll system. Separation of duties will help prevent those fraudulent transactions that require collusion of two or more employees.

EMPLOYER IDENTIFICATION NUMBER

Employers who are required to report employment taxes to the Internal Revenue Service and give tax statements to their employees must have an employer identification number, which may be applied for on Form SS-4 available at Social Security or IRS offices.

The identification number should be included on all correspondence and forms submitted to the IRS relating to employment taxes.

THE EMPLOYER-EMPLOYEE RELATIONSHIP

employer
the person who directs the work of others; has the right to hire and fire

employee
the person whose work is directed by the employer

independent contractor
one who is hired but who directs his or her own activities

An **employer** is a person or organization who receives the services of an employee. The employer normally provides the place to work and the required tools. The employer assigns duties and tasks to the employee and sees to it that he/she is held accountable for those duties and tasks. An employer may dismiss an employee and has the right to tell the employee when, where, and how a job is to be done. An **employee** performs services for an employer.

An **independent contractor,** on the other hand, is someone who is hired to do a specific job but may decide how the job is to be completed. Plumbers, doctors, tutors, repair persons, and accountants fall into this category.

The distinction between employees and independent contractors is important, because employers are required by law to withhold certain taxes from wages paid to employees, but they are not required to withhold payroll taxes from fees paid to independent contractors.

SALARIES AND HOURLY WAGES

salary
earnings stated in terms of a month or year

wage
earnings stated in hourly terms

Although the terms *salary* and *wage* are often used interchangeably, **salary** normally refers to earnings that are stated in monthly or yearly terms. Usually management, teachers, engineers, and supervisory personnel are paid a salary. The term **wage** usually refers to earnings that are stated on an hourly basis.

THE FAIR LABOR STANDARDS ACT

The Fair Labor Standards Act (also called the Wage and Hour Law) states that employers who are engaged in interstate commerce must pay their employees at least time and a half for hours worked over 40 each week. Certain categories of workers are not covered by the Fair Labor Standards Act; often management and supervisory personnel are expected to put in as many hours as the job requires without an **overtime** payment. Union contracts may have requirements more strict than the federal or state laws. Such contracts may call for double time for hours worked over 40 each week or for hours worked over eight in any one day.

overtime
earnings for hours worked over 40 in a week

CALCULATING THE GROSS PAYROLL

Gross payroll is the total amount earned by all employees before any deductions are taken. Assume that Wright's Accounting Service has six employees: two are management and are paid a yearly salary; four are accountants who are paid an hourly wage, with time and a half paid for all hours worked over 40 in a week. The gross payroll for the last week in February is calculated as follows.

Management Personnel	
Susan Harris	$31,200 salary per year
	$31,200 ÷ 52 = $600 per week
Anthony LaMarca	$26,000 salary per year
	$26,000 ÷ 52 = $500 per week

Wage Earners	
Richard McIntosh	$6.10 per hour, worked 50 hours
Carolyn Seaver	$8.40 per hour, worked 45 hours
Thomas Wyman	$6.30 per hour, worked 60 hours
Virginia Colter	$6.30 per hour, worked 65 hours

regular earnings
earnings for hours worked up to 40 in a week

Each hourly employee is paid time and a half for hours worked over 40 in a week. To calculate each employee's weekly gross wage, determine: (1) the **regular earnings,** which is the hourly rate times 40 hours (or less, if the employee worked under 40 hours during the week); (2) the overtime premium, which is the hourly overtime rate times the number of hours worked overtime; and (3) the gross wage, the total of the regular and the overtime wage. Following are the calculations for Richard McIntosh's gross wage. Management personnel are salaried and do not receive overtime pay.

McIntosh

1. Determine regular wage:

   $6.10 × 40 hours = $244.00

2. Determine overtime wage:

   $6.10 × 1.5 = $9.15
   $9.15 × 10 hours =   <u>91.50</u>

3. Determine gross wage:

   $244.00 + $91.50 =   <u>$335.50</u>

   The total gross payroll for Wright's Accounting Service for the last week in February is as follows.

Employee	Gross Wages
Susan Harris	$ 600.00
Anthony LaMarca	500.00
Richard McIntosh	335.50
Carolyn Seaver	399.00
Thomas Wyman	441.00
Virginia Colter	488.25
Total	$2,763.75

Calculating the gross payroll is just the first step in the process. Once the gross wages have been calculated, the bookkeeper must calculate each employee's deductions.

EMPLOYEE PAYROLL DEDUCTIONS

Federal Insurance Contributions Act (FICA)

In 1935, the Federal Insurance Contributions Act, commonly called the Social Security Act, was passed by Congress. It was designed primarily to provide a fixed, steady income for persons 65 years of age or older. The law has been altered over the years to include coverage for widowers and widows, disabled persons, and children of disabled or deceased parents.

The social security tax is levied on both employer and employee and is a certain percent of total earnings up to a maximum amount. For example, in 1977, employers withheld 5.85 percent of the first $16,500 earned; in 1980, they withheld 6.65 percent of the first $29,700 earned; in 1983, they withheld 6.7 percent of the first $35,700 earned; in 1987, they withheld 7.15 percent of the first $43,800 earned; and in 1988, they withheld 7.51 percent of the first $45,000 earned. Once an employee has earned the maximum amount that is taxable under FICA, then she or he is not liable for any more FICA taxes that year. In this text, we will assume that the FICA tax rate is 7.5 percent of the first $45,000 earned by each employee.

The amount of the FICA tax may be determined by referring to the tables in the *Circular E: Employer's Tax Guide,* or they may be calculated for each employee by multiplying the current rate times the employee's earnings. Using the latter method, the social security taxes for the employees of Wright's Accounting Service are calculated by multiplying 7.5 percent (.075) times each employee's gross earnings.

Employee	Gross Earnings	FICA Tax		
Harris	$600.00	.075 × $600.00	=	$ 45.00
LaMarca	500.00	.075 × 500.00	=	37.50
McIntosh	335.50	.075 × 335.50	=	25.16
Seaver	399.00	.075 × 399.00	=	29.93
Wyman	441.00	.075 × 441.00	=	33.08
Colter	488.25	.075 × 488.25	=	36.62
Total				$207.29

When multiplying to find the amount of FICA tax, answers should be rounded to the nearest penny. For example, when Virginia Colter's social security tax was determined, the following occurred.

1. .075 × $488.25 = $36.61875

2. $36.61875 rounded to the nearest penny = $36.62

When rounding to the nearest penny, look at the digit immediately to the right of the hundredths position. If that number is 0, 1, 2, 3, or 4, simply drop all the unnecessary digits. If the number is 5, 6, 7, 8, or 9, round up one penny.

Number Is	Digit to the Right of the Hundredths Position Is	Number Rounded to the Nearest Penny Is
$31.3775	$31.3775	$31.38
29.324	29.324	29.32
4.6987	4.6987	4.70
.793	.793	.79

Wages Over the Maximum FICA Taxable Amount

FICA taxes must be paid by an employee only up to the maximum taxable amount, after which time no more FICA tax is required in that year. Assume, for example, that the rate is 7.5 percent and the maximum taxable amount is $45,000. FICA taxes for Nick Pandis, who earns $55,800 per year and is paid monthly, are calculated as follows.

1. Determine monthly salary:

$$\$55,800 \div 12 = \$4,650$$

2. Determine when during the year Nick will have earned the maximum taxable amount by dividing the maximum taxable amount by Nick's monthly salary:

$$\$45,000 \div \$4,650 = 9.6774 \ldots\ldots$$

The answer to the division, 9.67 (rounded), indicates that Nick will pay FICA taxes through September (the ninth month) and into October (9.67 indicates about nine and two-thirds months).

3. Determine how much tax Nick has paid through September by multiplying his monthly salary by 9:

$$\$4,650 \times 9 = \$41,850$$

4. Determine how much tax Nick will have to pay in October, the last month he will have to pay FICA taxes for this year, by sub-

tracting what he has earned through September ($41,850) from the total taxable amount:

$$\$45,000 - \$41,850 = \$3,150$$

The result indicates that Nick will be taxed on $3,150 in October, even though his earnings are still $4,650 for the month. His total FICA tax, then, for October, will be:

$$\$3,150 \times .075 = \$236.25$$

In November and December, Nick will not be required to pay additional FICA tax, because he has already been taxed on the maximum amount, $45,000.

Federal Income Tax Withholding

In 1913, the Sixteenth Amendment to the Constitution was passed, allowing the federal government to tax the incomes of its people. Then, however, payroll taxes were not withheld by employers; instead, employees had to pay the total amount due at the end of the year. It was not until 1943 that employers were required to withhold both income tax and FICA tax from the wages of their employees.

Before the federal income tax withholding for each employee can be determined, the gross wage, the length of the pay period, the marital status, and the number of withholding allowances claimed by the employee must be known. A **withholding allowance** allows an employee to **exempt** a certain amount of her or his wages from income tax. One allowance may be claimed for the employee, one for the employee's spouse (if that person does not claim the exemption), and one for each dependent child. The *Circular E: Employer's Tax Guide* provides additional information.

When an employee begins work, he or she will fill out and sign a Form W-4, Employee's Withholding Allowance Certificate. The W-4 will show the employee's name, address, social security number, and number of withholding allowances claimed by the employee. A Form W-4 for Susan Harris, employed by Wright's Accounting Service, follows.

withholding allowance
an amount deducted from gross earnings for which no federal income tax is withheld

exempt
to free from an obligation

------- Cut here and give the certificate to your employer. Keep the top portion for your records. -------

Form W-4
Department of the Treasury
Internal Revenue Service

Employee's Withholding Allowance Certificate
▶ For Privacy Act and Paperwork Reduction Act Notice, see reverse.

OMB No. 1545-0010

1 Type or print your full name	2 Your social security number
Susan Elaine Harris	*351-30-2177*

Home address (number and street or rural route)
413 East Festival Avenue

City or town, state, and ZIP code
Ashland, OR 97520

3 Marital Status
☐ Single ☑ Married
☐ Married, but withhold at higher Single rate
Note: *If married, but legally separated, or spouse is a nonresident alien, check the Single box.*

4 Total number of allowances you are claiming (from line G above, or from the Worksheets on back if they apply) . . . **4** *4*

5 Additional amount, if any, you want deducted from each pay . . . . **5** $ *-0-*

6 I claim exemption from withholding because (check boxes below that apply):
  a ☐ Last year I did not owe any Federal income tax and had a right to a full refund of **ALL** income tax withheld, **AND**
  b ☐ This year I do not expect to owe any Federal income tax and expect to have a right to a full refund of
     ALL income tax withheld. If both a and b apply, enter the year effective and "EXEMPT" here . . . ▶ Year 19
  c Are you a full-time student? . . . . ☐ Yes ☐ No

Under penalties of perjury, I certify that I am entitled to the number of withholding allowances claimed on this certificate or, if claiming exemption from withholding, that I am entitled to claim the exempt status.

Employee's signature ▶ *Susan Elaine Harris*   Date ▶ *March 1*   , 19 **XX**

7 Employer's name and address (Employer: Complete 7, 8, and 9 only if sending to IRS)
Wrights Accounting Service
182 Bard Avenue
Ashland, OR 97520

8 Office code

9 Employer identification number
78-468157

If an employee does not complete and sign a Form W-4, the employer is required to withhold income tax for that employee using one withholding allowance if the employee is single and two withholding allowances if the employee is married.

The actual amount of the federal income tax to be withheld may be determined in several ways. The most common method is to refer to the wage bracket tables in the *Circular E.* The tables are separated into varying pay periods and as to the marital status of employees. The wage bracket tables from the *Circular E* for married and for single persons for a weekly payroll period are reproduced on pages 452 through 455. Let's now determine the amount of income tax withholding for the employees of Wright's Accounting Service.

SINGLE Persons–WEEKLY Payroll Period

And the wages are–		And the number of withholding allowances claimed is–										
At least	But less than	0	1	2	3	4	5	6	7	8	9	10
		The amount of income tax to be withheld shall be–										
$0	$25	$0	$0	$0	$0	$0	$0	$0	$0	$0	$0	$0
25	30	1	0	0	0	0	0	0	0	0	0	0
30	35	2	0	0	0	0	0	0	0	0	0	0
35	40	3	0	0	0	0	0	0	0	0	0	0
40	45	3	0	0	0	0	0	0	0	0	0	0
45	50	4	0	0	0	0	0	0	0	0	0	0
50	55	5	0	0	0	0	0	0	0	0	0	0
55	60	6	0	0	0	0	0	0	0	0	0	0
60	65	6	1	0	0	0	0	0	0	0	0	0
65	70	7	1	0	0	0	0	0	0	0	0	0
70	75	8	2	0	0	0	0	0	0	0	0	0
75	80	9	3	0	0	0	0	0	0	0	0	0
80	85	9	4	0	0	0	0	0	0	0	0	0
85	90	10	4	0	0	0	0	0	0	0	0	0
90	95	11	5	0	0	0	0	0	0	0	0	0
95	100	12	6	0	0	0	0	0	0	0	0	0
100	105	12	7	1	0	0	0	0	0	0	0	0
105	110	13	7	2	0	0	0	0	0	0	0	0
110	115	14	8	3	0	0	0	0	0	0	0	0
115	120	15	9	3	0	0	0	0	0	0	0	0
120	125	15	10	4	0	0	0	0	0	0	0	0
125	130	16	10	5	0	0	0	0	0	0	0	0
130	135	17	11	6	0	0	0	0	0	0	0	0
135	140	18	12	6	1	0	0	0	0	0	0	0
140	145	18	13	7	1	0	0	0	0	0	0	0
145	150	19	13	8	2	0	0	0	0	0	0	0
150	155	20	14	9	3	0	0	0	0	0	0	0
155	160	21	15	9	4	0	0	0	0	0	0	0
160	165	21	16	10	4	0	0	0	0	0	0	0
165	170	22	16	11	5	0	0	0	0	0	0	0
170	175	23	17	12	6	0	0	0	0	0	0	0
175	180	24	18	12	7	1	0	0	0	0	0	0
180	185	24	19	13	7	2	0	0	0	0	0	0
185	190	25	19	14	8	3	0	0	0	0	0	0
190	195	26	20	15	9	3	0	0	0	0	0	0
195	200	27	21	15	10	4	0	0	0	0	0	0
200	210	28	22	16	11	5	0	0	0	0	0	0
210	220	29	24	18	12	7	1	0	0	0	0	0
220	230	31	25	19	14	8	3	0	0	0	0	0
230	240	32	27	21	15	10	4	0	0	0	0	0
240	250	34	28	22	17	11	6	0	0	0	0	0
250	260	35	30	24	18	13	7	1	0	0	0	0
260	270	37	31	25	20	14	9	3	0	0	0	0
270	280	38	33	27	21	16	10	4	0	0	0	0
280	290	40	34	28	23	17	12	6	0	0	0	0
290	300	41	36	30	24	19	13	7	2	0	0	0
300	310	43	37	31	26	20	15	9	3	0	0	0
310	320	44	39	33	27	22	16	10	5	0	0	0
320	330	46	40	34	29	23	18	12	6	1	0	0
330	340	47	42	36	30	25	19	13	8	2	0	0
340	350	49	43	37	32	26	21	15	9	4	0	0
350	360	50	45	39	33	28	22	16	11	5	0	0
360	370	52	46	40	35	29	24	18	12	7	1	0
370	380	55	48	42	36	31	25	19	14	8	3	0
380	390	58	49	43	38	32	27	21	15	10	4	0
390	400	60	51	45	39	34	28	22	17	11	6	0
400	410	63	53	46	41	35	30	24	18	13	7	1
410	420	66	55	48	42	37	31	25	20	14	9	3
420	430	69	58	49	44	38	33	27	21	16	10	4
430	440	72	61	51	45	40	34	28	23	17	12	6
440	450	74	64	53	47	41	36	30	24	19	13	7
450	460	77	67	56	48	43	37	31	26	20	15	9
460	470	80	69	59	50	44	39	33	27	22	16	10
470	480	83	72	62	51	46	40	34	29	23	18	12
480	490	86	75	65	54	47	42	36	30	25	19	13
490	500	88	78	67	57	49	43	37	32	26	21	15
500	510	91	81	70	60	50	45	39	33	28	22	16
510	520	94	83	73	62	52	46	40	35	29	24	18
520	530	97	86	76	65	55	48	42	36	31	25	19
530	540	100	89	79	68	58	49	43	38	32	27	21

(Continued on next page)

SINGLE Persons–WEEKLY Payroll Period

And the wages are–		And the number of withholding allowances claimed is–										
At least	But less than	0	1	2	3	4	5	6	7	8	9	10
		The amount of income tax to be withheld shall be–										
$540	$550	$102	$92	$81	$71	$60	$51	$45	$39	$34	$28	$22
550	560	105	95	84	74	63	53	46	41	35	30	24
560	570	108	97	87	76	66	55	48	42	37	31	25
570	580	111	100	90	79	69	58	49	44	38	33	27
580	590	114	103	93	82	72	61	51	45	40	34	28
590	600	116	106	95	85	74	64	53	47	41	36	30
600	610	119	109	98	88	77	67	56	48	43	37	31
610	620	122	111	101	90	80	69	59	50	44	39	33
620	630	125	114	104	93	83	72	62	51	46	40	34
630	640	128	117	107	96	86	75	65	54	47	42	36
640	650	130	120	109	99	88	78	67	57	49	43	37
650	660	133	123	112	102	91	81	70	60	50	45	39
660	670	136	125	115	104	94	83	73	62	52	46	40
670	680	139	128	118	107	97	86	76	65	55	48	42
680	690	142	131	121	110	100	89	79	68	58	49	43
690	700	144	134	123	113	102	92	81	71	60	51	45
700	710	147	137	126	116	105	95	84	74	63	53	46
710	720	150	139	129	118	108	97	87	76	66	55	48
720	730	153	142	132	121	111	100	90	79	69	58	49
730	740	156	145	135	124	114	103	93	82	72	61	51
740	750	158	148	137	127	116	106	95	85	74	64	53
750	760	161	151	140	130	119	109	98	88	77	67	56
760	770	164	153	143	132	122	111	101	90	80	69	59
770	780	167	156	146	135	125	114	104	93	83	72	62
780	790	170	159	149	138	128	117	107	96	86	75	65
790	800	172	162	151	141	130	120	109	99	88	78	67
800	810	175	165	154	144	133	123	112	102	91	81	70
810	820	178	167	157	146	136	125	115	104	94	83	73
820	830	181	170	160	149	139	128	118	107	97	86	76
830	840	184	173	163	152	142	131	121	110	100	89	79
840	850	186	176	165	155	144	134	123	113	102	92	81
850	860	189	179	168	158	147	137	126	116	105	95	84
860	870	193	181	171	160	150	139	129	118	108	97	87
870	880	196	184	174	163	153	142	132	121	111	100	90
880	890	199	187	177	166	156	145	135	124	114	103	93
890	900	203	190	179	169	158	148	137	127	116	106	95
900	910	206	193	182	172	161	151	140	130	119	109	98
910	920	209	197	185	174	164	153	143	132	122	111	101
920	930	212	200	188	177	167	156	146	135	125	114	104
930	940	216	203	191	180	170	159	149	138	128	117	107
940	950	219	207	194	183	172	162	151	141	130	120	109
950	960	222	210	198	186	175	165	154	144	133	123	112
960	970	226	213	201	189	178	167	157	146	136	125	115
970	980	229	217	204	192	181	170	160	149	139	128	118
980	990	232	220	208	195	184	173	163	152	142	131	121
990	1,000	236	223	211	198	186	176	165	155	144	134	123
1,000	1,010	239	226	214	202	189	179	168	158	147	137	126
1,010	1,020	242	230	217	205	193	181	171	160	150	139	129
1,020	1,030	245	233	221	208	196	184	174	163	153	142	132
1,030	1,040	249	236	224	212	199	187	177	166	156	145	135
1,040	1,050	252	240	227	215	203	190	179	169	158	148	137
1,050	1,060	255	243	231	218	206	193	182	172	161	151	140
1,060	1,070	259	246	234	222	209	197	185	174	164	153	143
1,070	1,080	262	250	237	225	212	200	188	177	167	156	146
1,080	1,090	265	253	241	228	216	203	191	180	170	159	149
1,090	1,100	269	256	244	231	219	207	194	183	172	162	151
1,100	1,110	272	259	247	235	222	210	198	186	175	165	154
1,110	1,120	275	263	250	238	226	213	201	189	178	167	157
1,120	1,130	278	266	254	241	229	217	204	192	181	170	160
1,130	1,140	282	269	257	245	232	220	208	195	184	173	163
1,140	1,150	285	273	260	248	236	223	211	198	186	176	165
1,150	1,160	288	276	264	251	239	226	214	202	189	179	168
1,160	1,170	292	279	267	255	242	230	217	205	193	181	171
1,170	1,180	295	283	270	258	245	233	221	208	196	184	174
1,180	1,190	298	286	274	261	249	236	224	212	199	187	177
1,190	1,200	302	289	277	264	252	240	227	215	203	190	179

$1,200 and over

MARRIED Persons–WEEKLY Payroll Period

And the wages are–		And the number of withholding allowances claimed is–										
At least	But less than	0	1	2	3	4	5	6	7	8	9	10
		The amount of income tax to be withheld shall be–										
$0	$60	$0	$0	$0	$0	$0	$0	$0	$0	$0	$0	$0
60	65	1	0	0	0	0	0	0	0	0	0	0
65	70	1	0	0	0	0	0	0	0	0	0	0
70	75	2	0	0	0	0	0	0	0	0	0	0
75	80	3	0	0	0	0	0	0	0	0	0	0
80	85	4	0	0	0	0	0	0	0	0	0	0
85	90	4	0	0	0	0	0	0	0	0	0	0
90	95	5	0	0	0	0	0	0	0	0	0	0
95	100	6	0	0	0	0	0	0	0	0	0	0
100	105	7	1	0	0	0	0	0	0	0	0	0
105	110	7	2	0	0	0	0	0	0	0	0	0
110	115	8	2	0	0	0	0	0	0	0	0	0
115	120	9	3	0	0	0	0	0	0	0	0	0
120	125	10	4	0	0	0	0	0	0	0	0	0
125	130	10	5	0	0	0	0	0	0	0	0	0
130	135	11	5	0	0	0	0	0	0	0	0	0
135	140	12	6	1	0	0	0	0	0	0	0	0
140	145	13	7	1	0	0	0	0	0	0	0	0
145	150	13	8	2	0	0	0	0	0	0	0	0
150	155	14	8	3	0	0	0	0	0	0	0	0
155	160	15	9	4	0	0	0	0	0	0	0	0
160	165	16	10	4	0	0	0	0	0	0	0	0
165	170	16	11	5	0	0	0	0	0	0	0	0
170	175	17	11	6	0	0	0	0	0	0	0	0
175	180	18	12	7	1	0	0	0	0	0	0	0
180	185	19	13	7	2	0	0	0	0	0	0	0
185	190	19	14	8	2	0	0	0	0	0	0	0
190	195	20	14	9	3	0	0	0	0	0	0	0
195	200	21	15	10	4	0	0	0	0	0	0	0
200	210	22	16	11	5	0	0	0	0	0	0	0
210	220	23	18	12	7	1	0	0	0	0	0	0
220	230	25	19	14	8	2	0	0	0	0	0	0
230	240	26	21	15	10	4	0	0	0	0	0	0
240	250	28	22	17	11	5	0	0	0	0	0	0
250	260	29	24	18	13	7	1	0	0	0	0	0
260	270	31	25	20	14	8	3	0	0	0	0	0
270	280	32	27	21	16	10	4	0	0	0	0	0
280	290	34	28	23	17	11	6	0	0	0	0	0
290	300	35	30	24	19	13	7	2	0	0	0	0
300	310	37	31	26	20	14	9	3	0	0	0	0
310	320	38	33	27	22	16	10	5	0	0	0	0
320	330	40	34	29	23	17	12	6	1	0	0	0
330	340	41	36	30	25	19	13	8	2	0	0	0
340	350	43	37	32	26	20	15	9	4	0	0	0
350	360	44	39	33	28	22	16	11	5	0	0	0
360	370	46	40	35	29	23	18	12	7	1	0	0
370	380	47	42	36	31	25	19	14	8	2	0	0
380	390	49	43	38	32	26	21	15	10	4	0	0
390	400	50	45	39	34	28	22	17	11	5	0	0
400	410	52	46	41	35	29	24	18	13	7	1	0
410	420	53	48	42	37	31	25	20	14	8	3	0
420	430	55	49	44	38	32	27	21	16	10	4	0
430	440	56	51	45	40	34	28	23	17	11	6	0
440	450	58	52	47	41	35	30	24	19	13	7	2
450	460	59	54	48	43	37	31	26	20	14	9	3
460	470	61	55	50	44	38	33	27	22	16	10	5
470	480	62	57	51	46	40	34	29	23	17	12	6
480	490	64	58	53	47	41	36	30	25	19	13	8
490	500	65	60	54	49	43	37	32	26	20	15	9
500	510	67	61	56	50	44	39	33	28	22	16	11
510	520	68	63	57	52	46	40	35	29	23	18	12
520	530	70	64	59	53	47	42	36	31	25	19	14
530	540	71	66	60	55	49	43	38	32	26	21	15
540	550	73	67	62	56	50	45	39	34	28	22	17
550	560	74	69	63	58	52	46	41	35	29	24	18
560	570	76	70	65	59	53	48	42	37	31	25	20
570	580	77	72	66	61	55	49	44	38	32	27	21
580	590	79	73	68	62	56	51	45	40	34	28	23
590	600	80	75	69	64	58	52	47	41	35	30	24
600	610	82	76	71	65	59	54	48	43	37	31	26

(Continued on next page)

MARRIED Persons–**WEEKLY** Payroll Period

And the wages are–		And the number of withholding allowances claimed is–										
At least	But less than	0	1	2	3	4	5	6	7	8	9	10
		The amount of income tax to be withheld shall be–										
$610	$620	$83	$78	$72	$67	$61	$55	$50	$44	$38	$33	$27
620	630	85	79	74	68	62	57	51	46	40	34	29
630	640	87	81	75	70	64	58	53	47	41	36	30
640	650	90	82	77	71	65	60	54	49	43	37	32
650	660	93	84	78	73	67	61	56	50	44	39	33
660	670	95	85	80	74	68	63	57	52	46	40	35
670	680	98	88	81	76	70	64	59	53	47	42	36
680	690	101	91	83	77	71	66	60	55	49	43	38
690	700	104	93	84	79	73	67	62	56	50	45	39
700	710	107	96	86	80	74	69	63	58	52	46	41
710	720	109	99	88	82	76	70	65	59	53	48	42
720	730	112	102	91	83	77	72	66	61	55	49	44
730	740	115	105	94	85	79	73	68	62	56	51	45
740	750	118	107	97	86	80	75	69	64	58	52	47
750	760	121	110	100	89	82	76	71	65	59	54	48
760	770	123	113	102	92	83	78	72	67	61	55	50
770	780	126	116	105	95	85	79	74	68	62	57	51
780	790	129	119	108	98	87	81	75	70	64	58	53
790	800	132	121	111	100	90	82	77	71	65	60	54
800	810	135	124	114	103	93	84	78	73	67	61	56
810	820	137	127	116	106	95	85	80	74	68	63	57
820	830	140	130	119	109	98	88	81	76	70	64	59
830	840	143	133	122	112	101	91	83	77	71	66	60
840	850	146	135	125	114	104	93	84	79	73	67	62
850	860	149	138	128	117	107	96	86	80	74	69	63
860	870	151	141	130	120	109	99	88	82	76	70	65
870	880	154	144	133	123	112	102	91	83	77	72	66
880	890	157	147	136	126	115	105	94	85	79	73	68
890	900	160	149	139	128	118	107	97	86	80	75	69
900	910	163	152	142	131	121	110	100	89	82	76	71
910	920	165	155	144	134	123	113	102	92	83	78	72
920	930	168	158	147	137	126	116	105	95	85	79	74
930	940	171	161	150	140	129	119	108	98	87	81	75
940	950	174	163	153	142	132	121	111	100	90	82	77
950	960	177	166	156	145	135	124	114	103	93	84	78
960	970	179	169	158	148	137	127	116	106	95	85	80
970	980	182	172	161	151	140	130	119	109	98	88	81
980	990	185	175	164	154	143	133	122	112	101	91	83
990	1,000	188	177	167	156	146	135	125	114	104	93	84
1,000	1,010	191	180	170	159	149	138	128	117	107	96	86
1,010	1,020	193	183	172	162	151	141	130	120	109	99	88
1,020	1,030	196	186	175	165	154	144	133	123	112	102	91
1,030	1,040	199	189	178	168	157	147	136	126	115	105	94
1,040	1,050	202	191	181	170	160	149	139	128	118	107	97
1,050	1,060	205	194	184	173	163	152	142	131	121	110	100
1,060	1,070	207	197	186	176	165	155	144	134	123	113	102
1,070	1,080	210	200	189	179	168	158	147	137	126	116	105
1,080	1,090	213	203	192	182	171	161	150	140	129	119	108
1,090	1,100	216	205	195	184	174	163	153	142	132	121	111
1,100	1,110	219	208	198	187	177	166	156	145	135	124	114
1,110	1,120	221	211	200	190	179	169	158	148	137	127	116
1,120	1,130	224	214	203	193	182	172	161	151	140	130	119
1,130	1,140	227	217	206	196	185	175	164	154	143	133	122
1,140	1,150	230	219	209	198	188	177	167	156	146	135	125
1,150	1,160	233	222	212	201	191	180	170	159	149	138	128
1,160	1,170	235	225	214	204	193	183	172	162	151	141	130
1,170	1,180	238	228	217	207	196	186	175	165	154	144	133
1,180	1,190	241	231	220	210	199	189	178	168	157	147	136
1,190	1,200	244	233	223	212	202	191	181	170	160	149	139
1,200	1,210	247	236	226	215	205	194	184	173	163	152	142
1,210	1,220	249	239	228	218	207	197	186	176	165	155	144
1,220	1,230	252	242	231	221	210	200	189	179	168	158	147
1,230	1,240	255	245	234	224	213	203	192	182	171	161	150
1,240	1,250	258	247	237	226	216	205	195	184	174	163	153
1,250	1,260	261	250	240	229	219	208	198	187	177	166	156
1,260	1,270	263	253	242	232	221	211	200	190	179	169	158

$1,270 and over

Susan Harris is married and claims four withholding allowances. On the wage bracket table for married persons, find the amount of Susan's wage in the left-hand column. The entry reads *at least $600 but less than $610.* With your finger, follow across the column until you reach the amount listed under four withholding allowances. The amount of federal income tax to be withheld for Susan Harris is $59. Continue with this process, making sure you are using the correct wage bracket tables for the employee's marital status, until you have determined the federal income tax to be withheld for each employee. The payroll calculations for Wright's Accounting Service now appear as follows.

| | | | | Deductions | |
Employee	Marital Status	Number of Withholding Allowances	Gross Wages	FICA Tax	Federal Income Tax
Harris	M	4	$ 600.00	$ 45.00	$59.00
LaMarca	S	3	500.00	37.50	60.00
McIntosh	S	6	335.50	25.16	13.00
Seaver	S	1	399.00	29.93	51.00
Wyman	M	0	441.00	33.08	58.00
Colter	S	4	488.25	36.62	47.00
Totals			$2,763.75	$207.29	$288.00

Miscellaneous Payroll Deductions

Many other deductions might be taken in addition to deductions for FICA and federal income taxes. For example, an employee may have money deducted for the following: state income tax, city income tax, savings, union or professional dues, insurance premiums, contributions to a charity, or loan payments.

THE PAYROLL REGISTER

The bookkeeper uses the payroll register much as a worksheet, summarizing on it all the information necessary for calculating the gross and net wages. The payroll register for the last week in February for Wright's Accounting Service follows.

Wright's Accounting Service

Payroll Register

For Week Ended March 31, 19XX

Employee	Hours Worked	Hourly Wage	Regular Earnings	Overtime Earnings	Total Earnings	Marital Status	Number of Allowances	FICA Tax	Federal Income Tax	Medical Insurance	Union Dues	Total Deductions	Net Pay
Harris	Mgmt.		600.00	0	600.00	M	4	45.00	59.00	25.00	0	129.00	471.00
LaMarca	Mgmt.		500.00	0	500.00	S	3	37.50	60.00	25.00	0	122.50	377.50
McIntosh	50	6.10	244.00	91.50	335.50	S	6	25.16	13.00	25.00	6.25	69.41	266.09
Seaver	45	8.40	336.00	63.00	399.00	S	1	29.93	51.00	20.00	6.25	107.18	291.82
Wyman	60	6.30	252.00	189.00	441.00	M	0	33.08	58.00	25.00	6.25	122.33	318.67
Colter	65	6.30	252.00	236.25	488.25	S	4	36.62	47.00	25.00	6.25	114.87	373.38
Totals			2,184.00	579.75	2,763.75			207.29	288.00	145.00	25.00	665.29	2,098.46

Steps in Completing the Payroll Register

The payroll register is completed in this order.

1. Calculate each employee's regular, overtime, and total wages. Total each of these columns before determining payroll deductions.

2. Prove the accuracy of your work at this point by adding the total regular earnings to the total overtime earnings. Your answer must be the total earnings. For Wright's Accounting Service, the calculations are as follows.

Total Regular Earnings. . . .	$2,184.00
Total Overtime Earnings . . .	579.75
Total Earnings	$2,763.75

3. Determine the payroll deductions for each individual employee and total each individual deductions column.

4. Calculate the total deductions for each employee and determine the column total.

5. Before continuing, add the totals of the individual deductions columns. The sum must equal the total of the total deductions column; otherwise, an error has been made and must be found before continuing. For Wright's Accounting Service, this calculation is as follows.

Total FICA Tax	$207.29
Total Federal Income Tax . .	288.00
Total Insurance Deductions .	145.00
Total Union Dues	25.00
Total Deductions	$665.29

6. Calculate the net wages for each employee by subtracting his or her total deductions from total earnings; then find the column total.

7. Prove that the column total is accurate by subtracting the total of the total deductions column from the total of the total earnings column.

Total Earnings	$2,763.75
Total Deductions	665.29
Net Wages	$2,098.46

The accuracy of the work must be checked at each appropriate step in the preparation of the payroll register. If column totals are proved at intervals along the way, mistakes are much easier to find.

THE JOURNAL ENTRY TO RECORD GROSS WAGES AND EMPLOYEES' DEDUCTIONS

Once the payroll register has been completed, the bookkeeper has all the necessary information for the journal entry. The total gross earnings represents the employer's total wages expense for the week. The amounts withheld from employees' salaries represent liabilities, because each amount must be submitted to a government agency, insurance company, employee union, and so on, by the employer. The entry to record the week's payroll for Wright's Accounting Service is as follows.

GENERAL JOURNAL				Page 39	
Date	Description	Post. Ref.	Debit	Credit	
Feb. 28 _19XX_	Wages Expense		2 7 6 3 75		
	FICA Taxes Payable			2 0 7 29*	
	Federal Income Taxes Withheld			2 8 8 —	
	Medical Insurance Premiums Withheld			1 4 5 —	
	Union Dues Withheld			2 5 —	
	Wages Payable			2 0 9 8 46	
	To Record Gross and Net Wages for Week Ended				
	February 28				

*This amount is not exactly 7.5 percent of the gross wages because of rounding in individual employees' deductions.

THE PAYROLL CHECKING ACCOUNT

Many firms have a separate payroll checking account. After the entry to record the gross wages, deductions, and net wages has been recorded, the following entry will be made in the cash payments journal.

					CASH PAYMENTS JOURNAL				Page *14*
Date	Check No.	Account Titles	Post. Ref.	Sundry Accounts Debit	Accounts Payable Debit	Purchases Debit	Purchases Discount Credit	Cash Credit
19XX									
Feb. *28*	*2471*	*Wages Payable*		*2 0 9 8 46*				*2 0 9 8 46*

A check is now written for the net amount of the payroll, $2,098.46, and deposited in a special payroll checking account. Individual checks will then be written for the employees on the payroll checking account. After all payroll checks are cashed, the payroll checking account will have a zero balance. Having a separate payroll checking account makes bank statement reconciliation simpler for both accounts.

SUMMARY

The cost of the payroll and the related payroll taxes constitutes a large portion of the total operating costs of most businesses; thus, the system chosen must provide accurate information both quickly and easily. Strong internal control over payroll is essential to protect the owner against payroll fraud, and the books must be open to government inspection. In short, accounting for payroll is an important function; owners and managers must be familiar with the laws regulating it to avoid costly penalties.

Employers are required to withhold from the wages of most employees both FICA (social security) taxes and federal income taxes. These taxes must be remitted to the proper government agency within certain time limits. For the employer to be able to deduct the correct amount for federal income taxes, each employee must fill out and file with the employer a Form W-4, which shows the employee's marital status and the number of withholding allowances claimed. If the employer does not have a Form W-4 on file for an employee, one exemption is claimed for single employees and two exemptions for married employees.

Much of the information that an employer needs concerning payroll and payroll deductions is found in the Department of the Treasury's booklet *Circular E: Employer's Tax Guide,* which may be obtained free of charge from the Internal Revenue Service. The *Circular E* contains, among other things, tax tables for determining the amount of FICA and federal income taxes.

For certain employees, employers are required by the Fair Labor Standards Act to pay time and a half for hours worked over a weekly total of 40. The entire payroll may be calculated on a payroll register. From the register, the checks are written and the journal entry to record the payroll is made. The entire gross payroll is debited to Wages Expense, and amounts withheld from employee's earnings are credited to liability accounts.

Review of Accounting Terminology

Following is a list of the accounting terminology for this chapter.

collusion	overtime
divert	regular earnings
employee	salary
employer	wage
exempt	withholding allowance
independent contractor	

Fill in the blank with the correct word or term from the list.

1. Earnings for the first 40 hours in a week are called _____.

2. A/an _____ may have his or her work directed by the employer.

3. A word that means to free from an obligation is _____.

4. Earnings for hours worked over a weekly total of 40 hours are referred to as _____.

5. A/an _____ may direct the activities of an employee and may hire and fire the employee.

6. Earnings stated in terms of a month or year are referred to as _____.

7. Earnings stated in terms of an hourly payment are referred to as _____.

8. An employer may hire a/an _____ to perform services for a fee, but the employer will probably not direct the activities of this person, nor will the employer withhold payroll taxes on payment.

9. A/an _____ exempts a certain amount of an employee's paycheck from federal income tax.

10. To turn aside from a course or direction is to _____.

11. A secret agreement for a deceitful or fraudulent purpose is referred to as _____.

Match the following words and terms on the left with the definitions on the right.

12. collusion
13. divert
14. employee
15. employer
16. exempt
17. independent contractor
18. overtime
19. regular earnings
20. salary
21. wage
22. withholding allowance

a. to turn aside from a course
b. the person who hires and fires
c. earnings for the first 40 hours in a week
d. to free from an obligation
e. earnings stated in terms of an hourly payment
f. a secret agreement for a fraudulent purpose
g. an exemption from gross earnings on which no income tax is paid
h. earnings for over 40 hours a week
i. the person whose work is directed by the employer
j. one who is hired but who directs his or her own work activities
k. earnings stated in terms of a month or year

Exercises

Exercise 12.1
determining regular, overtime, and gross earnings

For each employee listed, determine the regular earnings, overtime earnings, and gross earnings. Assume overtime is paid at time and a half for all hours worked over a weekly total of 40.

Employee	Hours Worked	Hourly Wage	Regular Earnings	Overtime Earnings	Gross Earnings
Wickham	48	$6.30	_____	_____	_____
McDonald	50	7.10	_____	_____	_____
Murray	42	9.60	_____	_____	_____
Kauffman	46	6.80	_____	_____	_____

Exercise 12.2
determining FICA and federal income tax withholding

For the first payroll period of the year, determine the FICA tax and income tax withholding for each employee listed. For the FICA tax, assume a rate of 7.5 percent based on the first $45,000 earned in a year. Round to the nearest penny where required. Use the wage bracket tables to determine the amount of federal income tax withholding.

Employee	Marital Status	Number of Withholding Allowances	Gross Earnings	FICA Withholding	Federal Income Tax Withholding
Douglas	M	3	$832	_____	_____
Werner	M	5	500	_____	_____
Olsen	S	3	335	_____	_____
Jenkins	S	6	562	_____	_____
Wade	S	1	925	_____	_____
Bartz	M	0	745	_____	_____

Exercise 12.3
calculating gross and net wages

Margaret Pritchin is single and claims three withholding allowances. She earns $9.40 an hour and is paid time and a half for hours worked over a weekly total of 40. Calculate Margaret's net pay for a week in which she works 47 hours. Figure FICA at 7.5 percent of her gross pay (round to the nearest penny) and figure federal income tax withholding by using the wage bracket tables. Also, Margaret has the following amounts withheld from her paycheck: $7.90 for state income tax, $5.00 for union dues, and $25.85 for medical insurance.

Exercise 12.4
calculating regular, overtime, and gross earnings

The Auburn Company has a four-day workweek. Time and a half is paid for all hours worked over a daily total of 10. Calculate the regular earnings, overtime earnings, and gross earnings for each of the following employees of the Auburn Company. Also calculate the total regular earnings, overtime earnings, and gross earnings.

Employee	Hours Worked M	Tu	W	Th	Hourly Wage	Regular Earnings	Overtime Earnings	Gross Earnings
a. Habib	10	10	12	12	$ 5.20	_____	_____	_____
b. Wiggins	10	10	14	10	5.76	_____	_____	_____
c. Jackson	12	12	12	12	6.14	_____	_____	_____
d. Drummer	14	12	10	10	10.80	_____	_____	_____
Totals						_____	_____	_____

Exercise 12.5
determining gross and net earnings

Determine the regular earnings, overtime earnings, and gross earnings for the following employees of the Mohave Crafts Company for the week ended March 5. Then determine the FICA and federal income tax withholding, the total deductions, and net wages for each employee. Also determine total gross earnings, total federal income tax and FICA tax withheld, total deductions, and total net earnings. Employees are paid time and a half for hours worked over 40 in a week. Assume a FICA tax rate of 7.5 percent of the first $45,000 earned. Use the tables in the text to determine federal income tax withholding. When necessary, round amounts to the nearest penny.

Employee	Hours Worked	Hourly Rate	Marital Status	Number of Withholding Allowances	Regular Earnings	Overtime Earnings	Gross Earnings
Diaz	45	$ 7.60	S	3	_____	_____	_____
Haig	47	10.80	M	0	_____	_____	_____
Hawes	34	10.50	S	1	_____	_____	_____
Reid	44	14.20	S	4	_____	_____	_____
Totals					_____	_____	_____

Employee	FICA Withholding	Federal Income Tax Withholding	Total Deductions	Net Wages
Diaz	————	————	————	————
Haig	————	————	————	————
Hawes	————	————	————	————
Reid	————	————	————	————
Totals	————	————	————	————

Exercise 12.6
determining gross and net earnings

On a payroll register, determine the regular earnings, overtime earnings, and gross earnings for the employees of the Logan Eatery. Also determine the deductions for federal income tax and FICA tax, and the net earnings for the week ended April 14. Also calculate the total gross earnings, total federal income tax and FICA tax deductions, total deductions, and total net pay. Employees are paid double time for hours worked over 40 in a week. Assume a FICA tax rate of 7.5 percent of the first $45,000 earned. Use the tables in the text to determine the amount of federal income tax withholding. In addition to FICA and federal income taxes, each employee elects to have $23 withheld from his or her paycheck for union dues. Also, single employees with more than one exemption and all married employees have $29 withheld for medical insurance premiums; single employees with zero or one exemption have $19.50 withheld. Employee Munyer has $20 per week withheld for savings and employee Smith has $25 withheld. When necessary, round amounts to the nearest penny.

Employee	Hours Worked	Hourly Rate	Marital Status	Number of Withholding Allowances
Munyer	49	$12.60	M	0
Pounds	44	14.20	S	1
Smith	30	16.00	S	4
Harris	46	18.40	M	6

Exercise 12.7
calculating FICA tax to be withheld

The FICA tax is 7.5 percent based on the first $45,000 earned in a year. Calculate the amount of FICA tax for employees of the Winslow Company for the first week in November, given the following payroll data. Round to the nearest penny where required.

Employee	Gross Earnings through October	Earnings This Pay Period	Total FICA Tax to Be Withheld
a. Brasher	$42,900	$1,020	_____
b. Gerke	28,230	675	_____
c. Robinson	44,950	1,070	_____
d. Gonzales	46,950	1,120	_____
e. Martin	34,600	825	_____

Exercise 12.8
calculating FICA tax

Calculate the amount of FICA tax due for the following employees in November and December. The FICA tax is 7.5 percent of the first $45,000 earned in a year.

Employee	Gross Earnings through October	Monthly Salary	FICA Tax in November	FICA Tax in December
a. Suan	$40,850	$4,085	_____	_____
b. Hess	51,600	5,160	_____	_____
c. Church	38,750	3,875	_____	_____
d. McCool	44,100	4,410	_____	_____

Exercise 12.9
preparing journal entry to record payroll

Prepare the general journal entry to record the wages payable for the week ended March 28 from the following information taken from the payroll register of East Coast Real Estate. Use the following account titles: Wages Expense, FICA Taxes Payable, Federal Income Taxes Withheld, State Income Taxes Withheld, Union Dues Withheld, and Wages Payable. Use journal page 6.

Total Regular Earnings	$2,368.50
Total Overtime Earnings	512.48
FICA Tax Withheld	216.07
Federal Income Tax Withheld . .	562.41
State Income Tax Withheld . . .	105.23
Union Dues Withheld.	350.00

Problems

Problem 12.1
*preparing payroll
register*

Following is the necessary information for the preparation of the payroll register for the Rocklin Gravel Company for the week ended March 4.

Employee	Total Hours	Hourly Rate	Regular Earnings	Overtime Earnings	Total Earnings	Marital Status	Number of Withholding Allowances
Morrow	Mgmt.		————	————	1,000	M	3
Kauffman	Mgmt.		————	————	800	S	4
Murray	50	10.40	————	————	————	M	2
Garton	40	11.60	————	————	————	M	7
Garrett	48	12.50	————	————	————	S	1
Weaks	54	15.30	————	————	————	S	5
Totals			————	————	————		

Employee	FICA Tax	Federal Income Tax	Medical Insurance	Union Dues	Total Deductions	Net Pay
Morrow	————	————	27.50	0	————	————
Kauffman	————	————	27.50	0	————	————
Murray	————	————	27.50	7.50	————	————
Garton	————	————	27.50	7.50	————	————
Garrett	————	————	20.40	7.50	————	————
Weaks	————	————	27.50	7.50	————	————
Totals	————	————			————	————

Instructions

1. *Complete the payroll register. For each employee, calculate the gross and net earnings. Nonmanagement employees receive time and a half for hours worked over 40 in a week. FICA tax is 7.5 percent of the first $45,000 earned. Use the tables in the text to determine federal income tax withholding.*

2. *Prepare the general journal entry (page 106) to record the gross wages, employee deductions, and net pay. Account titles required are FICA Taxes Payable, Wages Payable, Federal Income Taxes Withheld, Medical Insurance Premiums Withheld, Union Dues Withheld, and Wages Expense.*

Problem 12.2

preparing payroll register

The following information is available for ABC Products for the week of October 10–16, 19XX.

Employee	Hours Worked	Hourly Wage	Marital Status	Number of Withholding Allowances
Hagen	36	$19.50	M	0
Jones	44	17.00	S	4
Davis	48	16.30	S	6
Lloyd	31	16.00	M	3
Ray	51	12.50	S	1

Instructions

1. *Complete a payroll register for ABC Products for the week of October 10–16, 19XX. Each employee is paid time and a half for hours worked over a weekly total of 40. Round calculations to the nearest penny where required.*
    a. *Calculate regular earnings, overtime earnings, and gross earnings.*
    b. *Calculate FICA withholding at 7.5 percent of gross earnings. Assume no employee has earned over $45,000.*
    c. *Figure the amount of federal income tax withholding by using the wage bracket tables.*
    d. *Include in the deductions $26.90 for medical insurance premiums for single persons with more than one exemption and for all married persons; deduct $18.15 for medical insurance premiums for single persons with zero or one exemption.*
    e. *Calculate total deductions.*
    f. *Calculate net pay.*
    g. *Calculate totals for the columns that are required for checking the accuracy in the payroll register.*

2. *Prepare the general journal entry to record the wages payable. Use journal page 33. Account titles required are FICA Taxes Payable, Wages Payable, Federal Income Taxes Withheld, Medical Insurance Premiums Withheld, and Wages Expense.*

Problem 12.3
*preparing payroll
register; certain
employees
approaching FICA
maximum*

The following information is available on December 10 for Time-share, a firm employing six people.

Employee	Hours Worked	Hourly Wage	Union Dues	Medical Insurance	Earnings at End of Previous Week	Marital Status	Number of Withholding Allowances
Robinson	45	$20.10	$6.35	$30.50	$44,800	M	6
Parrott	46	14.20	6.35	30.50	36,700	M	3
Stokes	30	27.80	6.35	30.50	49,600	S	4
Samudio	30	14.40	6.35	30.50	16,800	S	5
Baney	40	10.60	6.35	19.70	14,640	S	1
Klein	30	27.70	6.35	30.50	44,450	M	1

Instructions   1. *Complete a payroll register for Timeshare for the week of December 4–10, 19XX. Each employee is paid time and a half for hours worked over a weekly total of 40. Round calculations to the nearest penny where required.*

  a.   Calculate regular earnings, overtime earnings, and gross earnings.

  b.   Calculate FICA withholding at 7.5 percent of gross earnings up to $45,000 a year. Several employees are approaching or have exceeded the maximum taxable amount for FICA.

  c.   Figure the amount of federal income tax withholding by using the wage bracket tables.

  d.   Figure state income tax withholding to be 20 percent (.20) of the amount of federal income tax withholding.

  e.   Include in your calculations for total deductions the amounts withheld for union dues and medical insurance premiums.

  f.   Calculate total deductions.

  g.   Calculate net pay.

  h.   Calculate totals for the columns that are required for checking the accuracy of the payroll register.

 2. *Prepare the general journal entry to record the wages payable. Use journal page 19. Account titles required are FICA Taxes*

Payable, Federal Income Taxes Withheld, Medical Insurance Premiums Withheld, Union Dues Withheld, State Income Taxes Withheld, Wages Payable, and Wages Expense.

Problem 12.4

preparing payroll register; certain employees approaching FICA maximum

The following payroll information is available for the Shirt House on November 30, 19XX.

Employee	Hours Worked	Hourly Wage	Savings	Union Dues	Medical Insurance	Earnings at End of Previous Week	Marital Status	Number of Allowances
Arthur	Mgmt.		$40.00	0	$26.40	$50,700	S	4
Lewis	32	$24.30	20.00	$9.00	19.80	44,640	S	1
Olague	55	11.30	0	9.00	26.40	24,708	M	6
Wong	54	6.00	0	9.00	26.40	12,520	S	2
Medina	40	5.30	5.00	9.00	19.80	10,176	S	1

Instructions

1. Complete a payroll register for the Shirt House on November 30, 19XX. Employees, except management, are paid double time for hours worked over a weekly total of 40. The manager, Arthur, earns $1,078.72 each week. Round calculations to the nearest penny where required.

a. Calculate regular earnings, overtime earnings, and gross earnings.

b. Calculate FICA withholding at 7.5 percent of gross earnings up to $45,000 a year. Several employees are approaching or have exceeded the maximum taxable amount for FICA.

c. Figure the amount of federal income tax withholding by using the wage bracket tables.

d. Figure the state income tax to be 15 percent (.15) of the amount of the federal income tax withholding.

e. Include in your calculations amounts withheld for union dues, savings, and medical insurance premiums.

f. Calculate total deductions.

g. Calculate net pay.

h. Calculate totals for the columns that are required for checking the accuracy of the payroll register.

2. *Prepare the general journal entry to record the wages payable. Use journal page 17. Account titles required are FICA Taxes Payable, Federal Income Taxes Withheld, Employee Savings Withheld, Union Dues Withheld, State Income Taxes Withheld, Medical Insurance Premiums Withheld, Wages Payable, and Wages Expense.*

CHAPTER 13

Payroll: Employer Taxes and Other Obligations

LEARNING OBJECTIVES

When you have completed this chapter, you should

1. have a better understanding of accounting terminology.

2. have a basic understanding of the employer's obligation for payroll taxes.

3. be able to calculate the employer's tax liability for FICA and for federal and state unemployment taxes.

4. be able to prepare the journal entry to record the employer's payroll tax expense.

5. be able to prepare Form 941, which shows the tax liability for FICA taxes and for federal income taxes for timely remittance to the Internal Revenue Service.

6. be able to prepare Form 940, which shows the tax liability for federal unemployment insurance for timely remittance to the Internal Revenue Service.

7. be able to calculate the estimated and actual amounts of the workers' compensation premium and prepare the related journal entries.

Employers, as well as employees, are liable for certain payroll taxes. While amounts withheld from employees' earnings are liabilities, amounts levied on the employer are expenses and will appear on the income statement as reductions to gross income.

The employer is responsible for keeping accurate payroll records and filing the appropriate forms with the Internal Revenue Service at regular intervals. For late payments of payroll taxes, the employer may be charged a fine and may have to pay interest on amounts owed. Information relating to required employment taxes, tax rates and bases, required forms and their due dates, and so on, is contained in the *Circular E: Employer's Tax Guide.*

EMPLOYER'S PAYROLL TAXES

The employer's payroll taxes are based on the earnings of employees. The three main categories of employer taxes are (1) FICA tax, (2) federal unemployment tax, and (3) state unemployment tax. The amount of each is determined by applying a certain rate based on earnings up to a maximum amount for each employee. All payroll taxes are paid on a calendar year (January 1 through December 31) regardless of whether an employer's fiscal year is the same as the calendar year.

FICA (Social Security) Tax

Form 941
form on which employers report to the IRS the FICA and federal income taxes withheld, deposited, and due

The employer pays FICA tax on each employee's earnings at the same rate and on the same maximum amount as does the employee (7.5 percent based on the first $45,000 earned). Amounts withheld from employees for FICA tax and federal income tax, as well as the employer's share for FICA taxes, are reported to the Internal Revenue Service quarterly on **Form 941.** The Internal Revenue Service will mail preaddressed forms to employers; the forms include the employer's identification number.

Federal Unemployment Tax

Taxes levied under the Federal Unemployment Tax Act (FUTA) are designed to aid persons who are temporarily unemployed. In this text, we will assume a FUTA tax rate of 6.0 percent applied to the first $7,000 earned by each employee. However, the rate and base are subject to change. The current amounts can always be found in

Form 940
form on which employers report to the IRS federal unemployment taxes deposited and due

the *Circular E.* The federal unemployment tax *must not be deducted from employees' wages,* as it is a tax on the employer.

Federal unemployment taxes are reported on **Form 940** by February 2 following the close of the calendar year for which the taxes are due. The IRS will mail preaddressed forms to employers who filed returns the year before.

State Unemployment Tax

Taxes are also levied under the State Unemployment Tax Act (SUTA). All the states participate in the unemployment insurance program. While the federal government oversees the program, the state governments are responsible for paying the unemployment benefits. The SUTA rates vary, but in this text, we will assume a rate of 5.4 percent of the first $7,000 earned by each employee. Again, this is a tax on the employer, not the employee.

Amounts paid by employers to a state unemployment insurance fund may be deducted from the amount owed to the federal unemployment insurance fund; however, the amount deducted may not exceed 5.4 percent of the first $7,000 earned by each employee. The actual amount to be paid to the federal fund is calculated as follows.

Federal Unemployment Insurance Rate	6.0%
Minus State Unemployment Insurance Rate	−5.4
Actual Rate Paid to Federal Fund	.6%

Calculation of Employer's Payroll Taxes

After the gross wages have been determined, the amount of the employer's payroll tax expense is calculated by multiplying the gross wages times the rate for FICA tax, federal unemployment tax, and state unemployment tax. The gross wages in the following illustration were taken from the payroll register for Wright's Accounting Service in Chapter 12. No employee has earned over $7,000.

FICA Tax: $2,763.75 × .075	$207.28
Federal Unemployment Tax: $2,763.75 × .006	16.58
State Unemployment Tax: $2,763.75 × .054	149.24
Total Payroll Tax Expense	$373.10

In each case, the amount of the tax has been rounded to the nearest penny.

Journal Entry to Record Employer's Payroll Tax Expense

Once the tax amounts have been determined, a journal entry is prepared to record the amount of the employer's payroll tax expense. The entry to record the payroll tax expense for Wright's Accounting Service follows.

		GENERAL JOURNAL			Page 39
Date	Description	Post. Ref.	Debit	Credit	
Feb. 28	Payroll Tax Expense		373 10		
	FICA Taxes Payable			207 28	
	Federal Unemployment Taxes Payable			16 58	
	State Unemployment Taxes Payable			149 24	
	To Record Employer's Payroll Tax Expense				

The total of the employer's payroll taxes is an *expense,* because it is the employer who must pay these taxes. The amounts withheld from employee's earnings are not recorded as an expense, because the employee pays those amounts. In both cases, though, taxes are recorded as liabilities, because the employer is responsible for actually sending the amounts due to the appropriate federal or state taxing agency. For this particular payroll, the total expense involved for the employer may be calculated as follows.

Gross Wages Expense	$2,763.75
Total Payroll Tax Expense	373.10
Total Payroll Expense	$3,136.85

Calculating Taxable Wages

For each employee, an individual earnings record is kept. It contains gross and net earnings, all deductions for each payroll period, and monthly and quarterly totals for each item. The **cumulative** earnings provides important information for the bookkeeper. Unemployment taxes are based on the first $7,000 earned in a cal-

cumulative
increasing by successive addition; resulting from accumulation

endar year by each employee, and FICA taxes are based on the first $45,000 earned. Once an employee has exceeded the maximum earnings, then the employer is no longer required to pay unemployment or FICA tax on that individual for the remainder of the year. By referring to the individual earnings record, the bookkeeper will know how much of each employee's wage is taxable for each payroll period.

On the following page is the individual earnings record for Herbert Weinstock of Adam 'N' Eve's Natural Foods for October and November.

When the payroll register has been completed and the cumulative earnings for each employee have been determined, the calculations may be made to determine the amount of the employer's payroll taxes. Assume the following information for Adam 'N' Eve's Natural Foods on November 26, 19XX.

Adam 'N' Eve's Natural Foods
Calculation of Employer's Payroll Taxes
Week of November 24–30, 19XX

Employee	Gross Earnings through Last Pay Period	Gross Earnings This Pay Period	Year-to-Date Earnings	Taxable Wages This Pay Period For:	
				FICA	State and Federal Unemployment
Weinstock	$47,000	$1,000	$48,000	$ 0	$ 0
O'Connor	44,600	800	45,400	400	0
Wong	6,850	640	7,490	640	150
Adolfi	27,430	730	28,160	730	0
Merino	4,210	500	4,710	500	500
				$2,270	$650

The amounts in the columns for Taxable Wages This Pay Period were determined separately for each employee. For unemployment taxes, the employer must pay taxes for the first $7,000 earned by each employee; and for FICA, the employer pays taxes for the first $45,000 earned. Once these amounts have been exceeded, no more taxes are required for the remainder of the calendar year. For this pay period, for example, only $400 of O'Connor's earnings of $800 is subject to FICA tax, because taxes have already been paid on the

Employee's Individual Earnings Record

Name __Weinstock, Herbert Thomas__   Employee No. __6432-8__ Date Employed __January 1, 19XX__

Address __17 West Atlantic Street, Jersey City, NJ__   Social Security No. __987-66-4231__

Marital Status __Married__   No. of Exemptions __3__

Phone No. __643-1728__ Date of Birth __8/14/45__   Pay Rate __$1,000 per week__

Date Terminated _____

Period Ending	Hours Worked Reg.	OT	Regular Earnings	Overtime Earnings	Total Earnings	Fed. Inc. Tax	FICA	Union Dues	Hosp.	Savings	Deductions	Net Pay	Check No.	Cumulative Earnings
10/5	40		1,000.00	0	1,000.00	159.00	75.00	26.00	28.00	50.00	338.00	662.00	1234	40,000.00
10/12	40		1,000.00	0	1,000.00	159.00	75.00	26.00	28.00	50.00	338.00	662.00	1378	41,000.00
10/19	40		1,000.00	0	1,000.00	159.00	75.00	26.00	28.00	50.00	338.00	662.00	1429	42,000.00
10/26	40		1,000.00	0	1,000.00	159.00	75.00	26.00	28.00	50.00	338.00	662.00	1522	43,000.00
Oct. Totals			4,000.00		4,000.00	636.00	300.00	104.00	112.00	200.00	1,352.00	2,648.00		
11/2	40		1,000.00	0	1,000.00	159.00	75.00	26.00	28.00	50.00	338.00	662.00	1603	44,000.00
11/9	40		1,000.00	0	1,000.00	159.00	75.00	26.00	28.00	50.00	338.00	662.00	1699	45,000.00
11/16	40		1,000.00	0	1,000.00	159.00	0	26.00	28.00	50.00	263.00	737.00	1809	46,000.00
11/23	40		1,000.00	0	1,000.00	159.00	0	26.00	28.00	50.00	263.00	737.00	1922	47,000.00
11/30	40		1,000.00	0	1,000.00	159.00	0	26.00	28.00	50.00	263.00	737.00	2002	48,000.00
Nov. Totals			5,000.00		5,000.00	795.00	150.00	130.00	140.00	250.00	1,465.00	3,535.00		

$44,600 earned through the last pay period. The $400 *taxable amount* is determined as follows.

Total Taxable Amount	$45,000
Amount on Which Taxes Have Already Been Paid	−44,600
Remaining Amount That Is Taxable for This Year	$ 400

The total *taxable* wages for unemployment taxes are $650, and taxable wages for FICA are $2,270. The payroll tax expense for Adam 'N' Eve's Natural Foods for the week ending November 30, 19XX, is calculated as follows.

Federal Unemployment Tax: .006 × $650	$ 3.90
State Unemployment Tax: .054 × $650	35.10
FICA Tax: .075 × $2,270.	170.25
Total Payroll Tax Expense	$209.25

The employer will record this payroll tax expense at the time the wages are paid. However, the unemployment taxes and the FICA taxes will not be paid at the same time the wages are paid. The payroll taxes will be recorded and carried on the books as liabilities until they are paid at a later time.

The Journal Entries to Record Payroll Tax Expense and Wages Expense

The journal entry to record the employer's payroll tax expense is as follows.

	GENERAL JOURNAL				Page *30*
Date	**Description**	**Post. Ref.**	**Debit**	**Credit**	
19XX *Nov.* 30	**Payroll Tax Expense**		2 0 9 25		
	FICA Taxes Payable			1 7 0 25	
	Federal Unemployment Taxes Payable			3 90	
	State Unemployment Taxes Payable			3 5 10	
	To Record Payroll Tax Expense				

A second journal entry is required to record the wages expense and amounts withheld from employees' wages. The journal entry for Adam 'N' Eve's Natural Foods is as follows.

Date	Description	Post. Ref.	Debit	Credit
GENERAL JOURNAL				**Page 30**
19XX Nov. 30	Wages Expense		3 6 7 0 —	
	FICA Taxes Payable			1 7 0 25
	Federal Income Taxes Withheld			6 3 0 —
	Union Dues Withheld			1 3 0 —
	Hospitalization Premiums Withheld			1 1 6 —
	Employee Savings Withheld			9 0 —
	Wages Payable			2 5 3 3 75
	To Record Gross and Net Wages for Week Ended November 30			

The total amounts debited to Payroll Tax Expense and to Wages Expense will appear on the income statement as a deduction from revenue. The balances in Wages Payable, FICA Taxes Payable, Federal Unemployment Taxes Payable, State Unemployment Taxes Payable, Federal Income Taxes Withheld, Union Dues Withheld, Hospitalization Premiums Withheld, and Employees' Savings Withheld are liabilities and will appear on the balance sheet until they are paid.

THE GENERAL LEDGER ACCOUNTS RELATING TO PAYROLL

After the entries to record the payroll tax expense and wages expense have been journalized and posted, the T-accounts appear as follows.

Expenses Resulting from the Payment of Wages

Wages Expense   680

11/30	*GJ30*	*3,670.00*		*Employer's wages expense for this payroll period.*

Payroll Tax Expense   690

11/30	*GJ30*	*209.25*		*Employer's payroll tax expense for this payroll period.*

Liabilities Resulting from the Payment of Wages

Wages Payable   215

	11/30	*GJ30*	*2,533.75*	*Employees' net wages.*

FICA Taxes Payable   220

	11/30	*GJ30*	*170.25*	*Withheld from employees' wages.*
	11/30	*GJ30*	*170.25*	*Employer's tax.*

Federal Income Taxes Withheld   225

	11/30	*GJ30*	*630.00*	*Withheld from employees' wages.*

Federal Unemployment Taxes Payable   230

	11/30	*GJ30*	*3.90*	*Employer's federal unemployment tax.*

State Unemployment Taxes Payable   235

	11/30	*GJ30*	*35.10*	*Employer's state unemployment tax.*

Union Dues Withheld   **250**

	11/30	GJ30	130.00	*Withheld from employees' wages.*

Hospitalization Premiums Withheld   **255**

	11/30	GJ30	116.00	*Withheld from employees' wages.*

Employees Savings Withheld   **265**

	11/30	GJ30	90.00	*Withheld from employees' wages.*

DEPOSITING PAYROLL TAXES

After an employer applies for his or her employer identification number, the IRS will send a printed coupon book to the employer that shows the business name, address, and employer identification number. These coupons are used when making payment to the government for payroll taxes.

depository
a place where something may be deposited for safekeeping

The IRS designates certain banks or other financial institutions to be **depositories** for the payroll taxes. Employers may make payment at the Federal Reserve bank for the area in which the business is located. In most cases, then, amounts due for payroll taxes will be deposited (or paid) at one of the designated financial institutions rather than submitted directly to the government.

Regular deposits of federal payroll taxes must be made for FICA taxes (both the amounts withheld from employees' wages and the employer's portion), for federal income taxes withheld from employees' wages, and for federal unemployment taxes. Regular deposits must also be made for state taxes; these include state income taxes withheld and state unemployment insurance taxes. In this text, however, we will concentrate only on the federal taxes, as the various states have different rules and regulations.

Form 941

FICA taxes and federal income taxes withheld are reported to the IRS on Form 941; it shows the employer's name, address, and employer identification number. In addition, total wages subject to income tax withholding and taxable FICA wages (up to $45,000 for each employee) are listed. Amounts deposited with a financial institution are shown, as well as the date of deposit.

quarterly
every three months

Form 941 must be sent to the IRS **quarterly.** The due dates for remitting it are as follows.

For Quarter	Ending	Due Date for Filing Form 941
January-February-March	March 31	April 30
April-May-June	June 30	July 31
July-August-September	September 30	October 31
October-November-December	December 31	January 31

Actual payments of FICA taxes and federal income taxes withheld are made at regular intervals, depending on how much money is owed to IRS. If at the end of the quarter, total undeposited taxes for the quarter are less than $500, these taxes do not have to be deposited, but may be paid to the IRS when the Form 941 is remitted. If at the end of any month, total undeposited taxes are between $500 and $3,000, then the amount owed must be deposited within 15 days after the end of the month.

eighth-monthly period
the month divided into eight parts representing due dates for depositing FICA and federal income taxes

The IRS divides the months into eight parts for taxpayers who owe more than $3,000 in FICA and federal income taxes each month. The eight parts are referred to as **eighth-monthly periods** and are as follows.

Eighth-Monthly Period	Dates in the Month
1	1st through 3rd
2	4th through 7th
3	8th through 11th
4	12th through 15th
5	16th through 19th
6	20th through 22nd
7	23rd through 25th
8	26th through the last

If at the end of any eighth-monthly period total undeposited taxes are $3,000 or more, the taxes must be deposited within three banking days after the end of that eighth-monthly period. Weekends and local and legal holidays are not counted as part of the three banking days.

A completed Form 941 follows on page 485 for a warehouse named Beaumont Blackies owned by Jake Black. Amounts withheld for FICA and federal income taxes are between $500 and $3,000 each month, thus the tax owed must be deposited within 15 days after the end of each month.

The top of the Form 941 contains information about the business: name, address, employer's identification number, and so on. The numbered lines (1 through 19) ask for specific information relating to the pay period. The lines filled in by Jake Black are as follows.

Line 1a   Shows total number of employees working during this pay period (January 1 through March 31).

Line 2   Shows total wages, tips, taxable fringe benefits, and other compensation paid to employees.

Line 3   Shows total income tax withheld.

Line 6   Shows total taxable FICA wages paid. That amount is multiplied by 15 percent to obtain the total amount owed; it includes both employee and employer portions.

Line 8   Shows total FICA taxes (including taxes withheld on tips, if any).

Line 10   Shows adjusted total for FICA taxes (plus or minus any previous over- or underpayments, and so on).

Lines 14, 16 Show total taxes owed (income tax withheld, FICA tax withheld from employees, and employer's portion of FICA tax).

Line 17   Shows total deposits made. (These were made by Jake Black within 15 days following the end of each month.)

Line 18   Shows amount due. For Jake Black, nothing is due when the Form 941 is submitted, because all taxes have been deposited as required.

The Record of Federal Tax Liability at the bottom of Form 941 shows the tax liability for each month of the quarter. When total

Form **941**

Department of the Treasury
Internal Revenue Service

4141

Employer's Quarterly Federal Tax Return

▶ For Paperwork Reduction Act Notice, see page 2.

Please type or print

Your name, address, employer identification number, and calendar quarter of return. (If not correct, please change.)

Name (as distinguished from trade name)
Jake Black

Trade name, if any
Beaumont Blackie's

Address and ZIP code
16 River Road
Beaumont, TX 77704

Date quarter ended
March 31, 19XX

Employer identification number
62-544320

OMB No. 1545-0029

T	
FF	
FD	
FP	
I	
T	

If address is different from prior return, check here ▶ ☐

IRS Use

If you are not liable for returns in the future, check here . . . ▶ ☐   Date final wages paid . . . . ▶

Complete for First Quarter Only

1a	Number of employees (except household) employed in the pay period that includes March 12th ▶	1a		7
b	If you are a subsidiary corporation AND your parent corporation files a consolidated Form 1120, enter parent corporation employer identification number (EIN) . . ▶	1b	—	
2	Total wages and tips subject to withholding, plus other compensation . . . . . . ▶	2	23,640	20
3	Total income tax withheld from wages, tips, pensions, annuities, sick pay, gambling, etc. . . ▶	3	4,017	78
4	Adjustment of withheld income tax for preceding quarters of calendar year (see instructions) . . ▶	4	-0-	
5	Adjusted total of income tax withheld	5	4,017	78
6	Taxable social security wages paid . . . $ *23,640.20* × 15%(.15)	6	3,546	03
7a	Taxable tips reported . . . . . . $ _____ × 7.5%(.075)	7a	-0-	
b	Tips deemed to be wages (see instructions) . . $ _____ × 7.5%(.075)	7b	-0-	
c	Taxable hospital insurance wages paid . . . $ _____ × 2.9%(.029)	7c	-0-	
8	Total social security taxes (add lines 6, 7a, 7b, and 7c)	8	3,546	03
9	Adjustment of social security taxes (see instructions for required explanation)	9	-0-	
10	Adjusted total of social security taxes (see instructions)	10	3,546	03
11	Backup withholding (see instructions) . . . . ▶	11	-0-	
12	Adjustment of backup withholding tax for preceding quarters of calendar year	12	-0-	
13	Adjusted total of backup withholding	13	-0-	
14	Total taxes (add lines 5, 10, and 13) . . . . ▶	14	7,563	81
15	Advance earned income credit (EIC) payments, if any	15	-0-	
16	Net taxes (subtract line 15 from line 14). **This must equal line IV below** (plus line IV of Schedule A (Form 941) if you have treated backup withholding as a separate liability).	16	7,563	81
17	Total deposits for quarter, including overpayment applied from a prior quarter, from your records ▶	17	7,563	81
18	Balance due (subtract line 17 from line 16). This should be less than $500. Pay to IRS . . ▶	18	-0-	
19	If line 17 is more than line 16, enter overpayment here ▶ $ _____ and check if to be:			
	☐ Applied to next return or ☐ Refunded.			

Record of Federal Tax Liability (Complete if line 16 is $500 or more.) See the instructions under rule 4 for details before checking these boxes.

Check only if you made eighth-monthly deposits using the 95% rule ▶ ☐   Check only if you are a first time 3-banking-day depositor ▶ ☐

Date wages paid		Tax liability (*Do not show Federal tax deposits here.*)					
		First month of quarter		Second month of quarter		Third month of quarter	
1st through 3rd	A		I		Q		
4th through 7th	B		J		R		
8th through 11th	C		K		S		
12th through 15th	D		L		T		
16th through 19th	E		M		U		
20th through 22nd	F		N		V		
23rd through 25th	G		O		W		
26th through the last	H		P		X		
Total liability for month	I	*2,519.17*	II	*2,496.82*	III	*2,547.82*	
IV Total for quarter (add lines *I*, *II*, and *III*) . . . . ▶						*7,563.81*	

Under penalties of perjury, I declare that I have examined this return, including accompanying schedules and statements, and to the best of my knowledge and belief, it is true, correct, and complete.

Signature ▶ *Jake Black*   Title ▶ *Owner*   Date ▶ *4/14/XX*

taxes due each month are less than $3,000, the amount due may be shown on the total lines I, II, and III at the bottom of the record. The total due for the quarter (IV) is the same for Beaumont Blackie's as the total deposits made (Line 17). Once the form has been completed, Jake must sign it and send it to IRS.

Form 940

The IRS mails preaddressed Forms 940 to employers each year for reporting federal unemployment tax. Form 940 must be filed by February 2 of each year; however, if timely deposits of amounts due have been made, the due date is February 10.

If the total federal unemployment tax liability for any of the first three quarters is more than $100, the amount must be deposited by the last day of the first month following the close of the quarter. If the amount owed is $100 or less at the end of the calendar quarter, it should be held and added to the amount due for the following quarter. When that amount reaches $100, it must be deposited by the end of the month following the last month of that quarter. The completed Form 940 for Beaumont Blackies is on page 487.

The top of the form contains specific information about Beaumont Blackies: name, address, employer identification number, and so on. Lines that require an explanation are as follows.

Part I

Line 1 Includes total payments made to employees during the calendar year, even if the wages were not taxable.

Line 2 Shows those payments that are not subject to FUTA (see the *Circular E* for complete information).

Line 3 Shows all wages paid to individual employees over $7,000; these amounts are not taxable.

Part II

Line 1 Is where the total tax due is calculated.

Line 4 Shows the amount deposited during the year for FUTA.

Line 5 Shows any FUTA tax still due.

Form **940**

Department of the Treasury
Internal Revenue Service

**Employer's Annual Federal
Unemployment (FUTA) Tax Return**

▶ For Paperwork Reduction Act Notice, see page 2.

OMB No. 1545-0028

T	
FF	
FD	
FP	
I	
T	

If incorrect, make any necessary change. ▶

Name (as distinguished from trade name)
Jake Black

Trade name, if any
Beaumont Blackie's

Address and ZIP code
16 River Road
Beaumont, TX 77704

Calendar year
19XX

Employer identification number
62-544320

A Did you pay all required contributions to your state unemployment fund by the due date of Form 940? (See instructions if none required.) . . ☑ Yes ☐ No

If you checked the "Yes" box, enter amount of contributions paid to your state unemployment fund . . . . ▶ $ _____ *2,652* | *34*

B Are you required to pay contributions to only one state? . . . . ☑ Yes ☐ No

If you checked the "Yes" box: (1) Enter the name of the state where you are required to pay contributions . . . . . ▶ _____ *Texas*

(2) Enter your state reporting number(s) as shown on state unemployment tax return. ▶ _____ *94-631096*

C If any part of wages subject to FUTA tax is not subject to state unemployment tax, check the box . . . . ▶ ☐

Part I	**Computation of Taxable Wages and Credit Reduction (To be completed by all taxpayers.)**			
1	Total payments (including exempt payments) during the calendar year for services of employees	1	*94,560*	*80*
2	Exempt payments. (Explain each exemption shown, attaching additional sheets if necessary.) ▶ _____	2	*—0—*	
3	Payments for services of more than $7,000. Enter only the excess over the first $7,000 paid to individual employees not including exempt amounts shown on line 2. Do not use the state wage limitation.	3	*45,560*	*80*
4	Total exempt payments (add lines 2 and 3)	4	*45,560*	*80*
5	**Total taxable wages** (subtract line 4 from line 1). (If any part is exempt from state contributions, see instructions.)▶	5	*49,000*	*00*

6 Additional tax resulting from credit reduction for unpaid advances to the states listed (by two-letter Postal Service abbreviations). Enter the wages included on line 5 above for each state and multiply by the rate shown. (See the instructions.)

(a) IL _____ x .012= _____   (c) OH _____ x .011= _____   (e) WV _____ x .011= _____

(b) LA _____ x .009= _____   (d) PA _____ x .012= _____

| 7 | Total credit reduction (add resulting amounts from lines 6(a) through 6(e) and enter here and in Part II, line 2 or Part III, line 4). ▶ | 7 | *—0—* | |

Part II	**Tax Due or Refund (Complete if you checked the "Yes" boxes in both questions A and B and did not check the box in C, above.)**			
1	FUTA tax. Multiply the wages in Part I, line 5, by .006 and enter here	1	*294*	*—*
2	Enter amount from Part I, line 7	2	*—0—*	
3	**Total FUTA tax** (add lines 1 and 2)	3	*294*	*—*
4	Minus: Total FUTA tax deposited for the year, including any overpayment applied from a prior year (from your records)	4	*279*	*46*
5	**Balance due** (subtract line 4 from line 3). This should be $100 or less. Pay to IRS . . . . . ▶	5	*14*	*54*
6	**Overpayment** (subtract line 3 from line 4). Check if it is to be: ☐ Applied to next return, or ☐ Refunded . . ▶	6	*—0—*	

Part III	**Tax Due or Refund (Complete if you checked the "No" box in either question A or B or you checked the box in C, above. Also complete Part V.)**			
1	Gross FUTA tax. Multiply the wages in Part I, line 5, by .06	1		
2	Maximum credit. Multiply the wages in Part I, line 5, by .054	2		
3	Enter the smaller of the amount in Part V, line 11, or Part III, line 2	3		
4	Enter amount from Part I, line 7	4		
5	**Credit allowable** (subtract line 4 from line 3). (If zero or less, enter 0.)	5		
6	**Total FUTA tax** (subtract line 5 from line 1)	6		
7	Minus: Total FUTA tax deposited for the year, including any overpayment applied from a prior year (from your records)	7		
8	**Balance due** (subtract line 7 from line 6). This should be $100 or less. Pay to IRS . . . . . ▶	8		
9	**Overpayment** (subtract line 6 from line 7). Check if it is to be: ☐ Applied to next return, or ☐ Refunded. . ▶	9		

Part IV	**Record of Quarterly Federal Tax Liability for Unemployment Tax (Do not include state liability.)**				
Quarter	First	Second	Third	Fourth	Total for Year
Liability for quarter	$ *141.84*	$ *137.62*	$ *14.54*	*—0—*	$ *294.00*

If you will not have to file returns in the future, write "Final" here (see general instruction "Who Must File") and sign the return. ▶

Under penalties of perjury, I declare that I have examined this return, including accompanying schedules and statements, and to the best of my knowledge and belief, it is true, correct, and complete, and that no part of any payment made to a state unemployment fund claimed as a credit was or is to be deducted from the payments to employees.

Signature ▶ *Jake Black*   Title (Owner, etc.) ▶ *Owner*   Date ▶ *2/1/XX*

Form **940**

Part IV

This section gives the record of the tax liability for each calendar quarter. The liability decreases as employees earn over $7,000.

The Form 940 is signed by Jake and submitted to the IRS.

Journal Entries to Record Payment of Payroll Taxes

The journal entry to record payment of FICA and federal income taxes for the third month of the first quarter follows.

			CASH PAYMENTS JOURNAL						Page 40
Date	Check No.	Account Titles	Post. Ref.	Sundry Accounts Debit	Accounts Payable Debit	Purchases Debit	Purchases Discount Credit	Cash Credit
19XX *Apr.* 14	3614	FICA Taxes Payable		1 0 9 0 80				2 5 4 7 82
		Federal Income Taxes Withheld		1 4 5 7 02				

The actual check will be written to the bank or other financial institution in which the taxes are to be deposited.

The journal entry on February 2 to record payment of the federal unemployment taxes due when Form 941 is submitted to the IRS requires a debit to Federal Unemployment Taxes Payable and a credit to Cash. Again, the check will be written to the financial institution that serves as a depository for the taxes.

			CASH PAYMENTS JOURNAL						Page 50
Date	Check No.	Account Titles	Post. Ref.	Sundry Accounts Debit	Accounts Payable Debit	Purchases Debit	Purchases Discount Credit	Cash Credit
19XX *Feb.* 2	4912	Federal Unemployment Taxes Payable		1 4 54				1 4 54

FORM W-2, WAGE AND TAX STATEMENT

Form W-2
form given by employer to each employee showing gross wages and FICA and federal income taxes withheld

Employers must give a **Form W-2** to each employee from whom income tax and/or social security tax was withheld. The Form W-2 shows, among other things, total wages paid, any tips reported, income tax withheld, and FICA tax withheld.

The Form W-2 shows wages for the calendar year; a copy must be given to each employee by January 31 of the year following the payment of the wages. If an employer fails to give the Form W-2 to an employee when required, he or she may be fined $50. The maximum penalty is $100,000 per calendar year. Each time the employer fails to put correct informaton on the Form W-2, he or she may be assessed a $5 penalty. The maximum penalty is $20,000 per calendar year. It is unlawful for an employer to willfully fail to supply an employee with a Form W-2 or to willfully supply false information on the form. A completed Form W-2 for an employee of Beaumont Blackies follows.

1 Control number 22222	For Paperwork Reduction Act Notice, see back of Copy D. OMB No. 1545-0008	For Official Use Only ▶	
2 Employer's name, address, and ZIP code Jake Black Beaumont Blackie's 16 River Road Beaumont, TX 77704	3 Employer's identification number 62-5443320	4 Employer's state I.D. number 94-631096	
	5 Statutory employee / Deceased / Pension plan / Legal rep. / 942 emp. / Subtotal / Deferred compensation / Void		
	6 Allocated tips —0—	7 Advance EIC payment —0—	
8 Employee's social security number 351-30-2177	9 Federal income tax withheld $1,683.24	10 Wages, tips, other compensation $12,948.00	11 Social security tax withheld $971.10
12 Employee's name (first, middle, last)	13 Social security wages $12,948.00	14 Social security tips —0—	
	16 (See Instr. for Forms W-2/W-2P)	16a Fringe benefits incl. in Box 10 —0—	
Juan Ortega Sanchez 4729-D Front Street Beaumont, TX 77704	17 State income tax —0—	18 State wages, tips, etc. —0—	19 Name of state
15 Employee's address and ZIP code	20 Local income tax —0—	21 Local wages, tips, etc. —0—	22 Name of locality

Form **W-2 Wage and Tax Statement**

Copy A For Social Security Administration   Dept. of the Treasury—IRS

WORKER'S COMPENSATION INSURANCE

worker's compensation insurance
insurance premium paid by employer for payments to employees for job-related injuries or illnesses

Most employers are required to carry **worker's compensation insurance,** which provides certain payments to employees who are injured on the job or who become sick as a result of something job related. The worker's compensation insurance rates are based on the degree of risk involved in the various job categories. For example, restaurant kitchen workers (because of the possibility of cuts, falling, burns, and so on) have a higher risk of becoming injured on the job than would a movie usher; thus, the restaurant owner would pay a higher worker's compensation insurance rate per kitchen worker than the movie-house owner would pay per usher. The premium is normally paid one year in advance, based on the year's estimated gross payroll.

Assume that the estimated payroll for the year for a business is $185,000 and that the worker's compensation rate is .3 percent (or 30 cents on every $100). The premium for the year would be determined as follows.

$$.003 \times \$185,000 = \$555$$

The journal entry to record the premium would debit Prepaid Insurance for $555 and credit Cash. If at the end of the year the bookkeeper determines that the actual wages for the year were $190,050, an additional premium would be required because the original premium was based on total wages of $185,000. The additional premium payment is calculated as follows.

---

1. Figure the extra amount on which premium is to be calculated:

    $$\$190,050 - \$185,000 = \$5,050$$

2. Multiply rate times additional premium:

    $$.003 \times \$5,050 = \$15.15$$

The journal entry to record the additional premium will debit Insurance Expense for $15.15 and credit Cash. If the actual payroll is less than the amount estimated, the company would be entitled to a refund.

SUMMARY

Many federal and state regulations require certain types of records to be kept and numerous forms to be filled out on a regular basis. Employers are liable for paying certain taxes related to payroll. Taxes that must be paid by the employer are debited to an account called Payroll Tax Expense.

Employers are liable for paying FICA tax on their employees at a rate that is equal to that the employees pay. Employers are also required to pay federal unemployment tax (FUTA) of .6 percent of the first $7,000 earned by each employee and state unemployment tax (SUTA) of 5.4 percent of the first $7,000 earned.

FICA taxes and federal income taxes withheld are paid at regular intervals at banks or other financial institutions selected by the federal government to be depositories of such taxes. The amount of wages paid and taxes withheld and due is reported quarterly to the IRS on Form 941. Federal unemployment taxes are deposited quarterly, and total wages paid and FUTA deposits are reported annually to the IRS on Form 940.

For each employee, an individual earnings record is kept. It shows for each pay period the gross and net wages, all deductions, and accumulated earnings. The accumulated earnings are used to determine when an employee has reached the maximum taxable earnings for unemployment and FICA taxes.

In addition to payroll taxes, employers are required to pay a worker's compensation insurance premium. This insurance provides certain payments to employees who are injured or who become sick while on the job. The premium is based on the gross payroll and the degree of risk involved in the job.

Employers must issue to each employee by January 31 of the year following the payment of the wages a Form W-2, Wage and Tax Statement, which shows total earnings and amounts withheld for FICA and federal and state income tax.

Review of Accounting Terminology

Following is a list of the accounting terminology for this chapter.

cumulative	Form 941
eighth-monthly period	Form W-2
depository	quarterly
Form 940	worker's compensation insurance

Fill in the blank with the correct word or term from the list.

1. The form on which the employer reports FICA and federal income tax withheld, deposited, and due is called _____.

2. A word that means resulting from accumulation is _____.

3. The form on which the employer reports federal unemployment tax deposited and due is called _____.

4. IRS divides the months into eight segments for depositing FICA and federal income taxes; each segment is called a/an _____.

5. Every three months may be termed _____.

6. A form given by the employer to the employee showing total wages paid, FICA tax withheld, and federal, state, and local income taxes withheld is referred to as _____.

7. A designated bank or other financial institution where payroll taxes may be paid is referred to as a/an _____.

8. Insurance provided by the employer to compensate employees who suffer work-related injuries or illnesses is referred to as _____.

Match the following words and terms on the left with the definitions on the right.

9. cumulative
10. eighth-monthly period
11. depository
12. Form 940
13. Form 941
14. Form W-2
15. quarterly
16. worker's compensation insurance

a. form on which employer reports to the IRS the FICA tax and federal income tax withheld, deposited, and due
b. every three months
c. January 1–3; January 4–7; January 8–11; and so on
d. provides compensation to employees for job-related illnesses or injuries
e. resulting from accumulation
f. a financial institution where payroll taxes may be deposited
g. form on which employer reports federal unemployment tax liability
h. a form given to employees showing total wages paid for the calendar year and FICA and income tax withheld

Exercises

Exercise 13.1
calculating payroll tax expense

The gross payroll for the week ended February 6 for the Moorpark Delicatessen was $2,760.42. No employee has earned over $7,000. Calculate the employer's FICA, federal unemployment tax, state unemployment tax, and total payroll tax expense for the week. FICA taxes are 7.5 percent of the first $45,000 earned by each employee; federal unemployment tax is .6 percent of the first $7,000 earned; and state unemployment tax is 5.4 percent of the first $7,000 earned. Round all calculations to the nearest penny.

Exercise 13.2
preparing journal entries for wages expense and payroll tax expense

Gross wages for the Reedley Insurance Company for the week ended May 10 were $5,760.48. FICA taxes for the employer and employee are 7.5 percent of the first $45,000 earned; federal unemployment tax is .6 percent of the first $7,000 earned; and state unemployment tax is 5.4 percent of the first $7,000 earned. $1,460 was withheld from employees' wages for federal income tax.

a. Prepare the general journal entry (page 48) to record the gross wages, employee deductions, and net wages.

b. Prepare the general journal entry to record the employer's payroll tax expense. Round tax amounts to the nearest penny when necessary. Assume no employee has earned over $7,000.

Exercise 13.3
calculating taxable earnings for FICA, FUTA, and SUTA

Following are the total earnings for the employees of the Boston Software Company for the year ended December 31, 19XX.

Employee	Year's Earnings
Powell.	$ 52,740
Schaw	21,980
Medeiros.	47,250
Peugh	19,600
Total	$141,570

The FICA tax rate is 7.5 percent of the first $45,000 earned and is imposed on both employee and employer. The FUTA tax is .6 percent of the first $7,000 earned by each employee, and the SUTA rate is 5.4 percent of the first $7,000 earned by each employee. Federal income taxes withheld were $24,396, and state income taxes withheld were $3,842.

a.   Calculate the taxable earnings for FICA, FUTA, and SUTA.

b.   Calculate the total taxes paid by the employees.

c.   Calculate the total amount of payroll taxes paid by the employer. Round to the nearest penny where necessary.

Exercise 13.4
preparing journal entries to record wages expense and payroll tax expense

Following is payroll information for the week ending February 21 for the New Jersey Bakery.

Gross Wages	$6,491.50
Medical Insurance Premiums Withheld	240.00
Employee Savings Withheld	300.00
Federal Income Taxes Withheld	973.50
State Income Taxes Withheld	129.80

FICA taxes are 7.5 percent of the first $45,000 earned by each employee; FUTA taxes are .6 percent of the first $7,000 earned; and SUTA taxes are 5.4 percent of the first $7,000 earned.

a.   Prepare the general journal entry (page 33) to record the wages expense and employee deductions.

b.   Prepare the general journal entry to record the employer's payroll tax expense. No employee has earned over $7,000. Round to the nearest penny where necessary.

Exercise 13.5
calculating taxable earnings and payroll tax expense

Following is the payroll information for the Rosebud Tailors for the week ended November 19. Employer's FICA taxes are 7.5 percent of the first $45,000 earned by each employee; federal unemployment tax is .6 percent of the first $7,000 earned; and state unemployment tax is 5.4 percent of the first $7,000 earned.

a.   Determine the total taxable earnings for the Rosebud Tailors for this payroll period.

b.   Calculate the amount of the employer's FICA tax, federal unemployment tax, state unemployment tax, and total payroll tax expense for this payroll period.

Employee	Cumulative Earnings for Year up to Current Payroll Period	Total Earnings This Pay Period	Taxable Earnings	
			FICA	Unemployment
Blackmun	$49,400	$1,030	_____	_____
O'Day	44,200	960	_____	_____
Reilley	6,740	820	_____	_____
Serrano	25,600	560	_____	_____
Al-Hoty	6,420	920	_____	_____

Exercise 13.6
calculating payroll tax expense

Gross wages for the Commerce Ceramic Works for the week ended December 6 are $40,642.40. Of this amount, $7,400.50 is not subject to FICA taxes and $29,622.45 is not subject to federal or state unemployment tax. Calculate the amount of the employer's total payroll tax expense if the rate for FICA is 7.5 percent of the first $45,000 earned, the rate for federal unemployment is .6 percent of the first $7,000 earned, and the rate for state unemployment is 5.4 percent of the first $7,000 earned. Round amounts to the nearest penny when necessary.

Exercise 13.7
preparing journal entry to record worker's compensation premium

The Tucson Cleaners pays a worker's compensation premium of .4 percent (.004) of its annual payroll, which was estimated to be $75,500 for the current year. At the end of the year, the actual payroll for the year was $82,690.75.

a. Prepare the entry in the cash payments journal (page 36) on January 6, Year 1, to record issuance of check 3161 for the cash purchase of the insurance policy.

b. Record the entry in the cash payments journal (page 48) on January 7 of Year 2 issuing check 5614 for the cash payment for the additional premium.

Problems

Problem 13.1
preparing individual earnings record

Roberta Sanderson is single, claims three withholding allowances, and earns $760 a week. Her address is 3091 Orange Grove Avenue, Sacramento, CA 95841. Her social security number is 496-03-7110. FICA taxes are 7.5 percent of the first $45,000 earned in a year. In addition, Roberta has $24.40 per week withheld for hospitalization insurance and $50.00 per week for savings.

Instructions   1. Calculate Roberta's deductions and net pay for the week ended January 7. For federal income tax withholding, use the tables provided in Chapter 12.

2. Assuming Roberta's gross and net pay are the same each week, complete the individual earnings record for January, assuming pay periods are January 7, 14, 21, and 28. Calculate totals for the month.

3. Enter the weekly figures on the individual earnings record for February, assuming the pay periods fall on February 4, 11, 18, and 25. Calculate totals for the month.

4. Enter the weekly and monthly figures on the individual earnings record for March, assuming the pay periods fall on March 4, 11, 18, and 25.

5. Calculate the gross wages, deductions, and net pay for the first quarter.

Problem 13.2
journalizing to record wages expense and payroll tax expense; posting

The Corsicana Sporting Equipment Store had the following payroll data for the week ended January 14. No employee has earned over $7,000.

Gross Wages	$6,429.80
Employee Deductions	
FICA	482.24
Federal Income Taxes Withheld	964.47
Insurance Premiums Withheld.	400.00
Savings Withheld	375.00

The T-accounts relating to payroll for the Corsicana Sporting Equipment Store for the first week of business (ending January 7) are as follows.

Wages Payable		250	**Federal Income Tax Withheld**		260
1/7	*4,120.92*	*1/7* *4,120.92*		*1/7*	*940.00*

FICA Taxes Payable		255	**Employees' Insurance Premiums Withheld**		265
		1/7 *473.18*		*1/7*	*400.00*
		1/7 *473.18*			

Employees' Savings Withheld   270

1/7	375.00

Federal Unemployment Taxes Payable   275

1/7	37.85

State Unemployment Taxes Payable   280

1/7	340.69

Wages Expense   670

1/7 6,309.10	

Payroll Taxes Expense   680

1/7 851.72	

Instructions

1. *Prepare the general journal entry (page 196) to record the gross wages expense, the employees' deductions, and the net wages for the week. Credit the net wages to Wages Payable.*

2. *Prepare the general journal entry to record the employer's payroll tax expense. FICA taxes are 7.5 percent of the first $45,000 earned; federal unemployment insurance taxes are .6 percent of the first $7,000 earned; and state unemployment taxes are 5.4 percent of the first $7,000 earned. Round amounts to the nearest penny if necessary.*

3. *Post the general journal entries to the T-accounts provided.*

Problem 13.3
determining taxable wages and journalizing payroll tax expense

Following is the payroll data for the week ending March 29 for the Pecos Trading Company.

	Earnings up to Present	Gross Earnings This Pay Period	Taxable Earnings	
Employee			FICA	Unemployment
Medina	$6,720	$520	_____	_____
Dillon	8,975	690	_____	_____
Olague	9,420	724	_____	_____
Wong	6,815	524	_____	_____

Instructions 1. *Determine the taxable wages for FUTA (.6 percent of the first $7,000 earned by each employee) and for SUTA (5.4 percent of the first $7,000 earned by each employee).*

2. *Determine the taxable wages for FICA (7.5 percent of the first $45,000 earned by each employee).*

3. *Prepare a general journal entry to record the wages expense and employee deductions, assuming $416 was withheld for federal income taxes and $76 for state income taxes.*

4. *Prepare a general journal entry to record the employer's payroll tax expense.*

Problem 13.4

calculating employees' deductions and net pay and journalizing wages expense and payroll tax expense

Following is the payroll data for the Manassas Uniform Company for the week ended October 30.

Employee	Marital Status	Number of Withholding Allowances	Earnings up to Present	Gross Earnings This Pay Period
Carlos	M	2	$44,250	$1,005
Wing	S	0	44,770	1,065
Storey	M	3	6,720	531
Grubbs	S	4	4,209	473

FICA	Fed. Inc. Tax	Hosp. Premiums	Total Ded.	Net Pay	Taxable Earnings FICA	Unemployment
____	____	24.40	____	____	____	____
____	____	19.60	____	____	____	____
____	____	24.40	____	____	____	____
____	____	24.40	____	____	____	____

Instructions 1. *Calculate each employee's payroll deductions and net pay. For FICA taxes, use 7.5 percent of the first $45,000 earned for each employee. Figure federal income tax withholding by using the tables in Chapter 12.*

2. *For the employer, determine the amount of taxable wages for each employee for FICA and for federal and state unemploy-*

ment. FICA taxable wages are 7.5 percent of the first $45,000 earned by each employee; federal unemployment taxes are .6 percent of the first $7,000 earned; and state unemployment taxes are 5.4 percent of the first $7,000 earned.

3. Prepare the journal entry (page 64) to record the gross wages, employee deductions, and net pay.

4. Prepare the journal entry to record the employer's payroll tax expense.

Problem 13.5
recording transactions relating to payment of wages and depositing of payroll taxes

Cowboy Buck's employs eight people. FICA taxes are based on 7.5 percent of the first $45,000 earned by each employee in a year; state unemployment taxes are 5.4 percent of the first $7,000 earned; and federal unemployment taxes are .6 percent of the first $7,000 earned. Assume that no employee has earned over $7,000 by the end of March. The T-accounts that relate to payroll and their March 1 balances are as follows.

Cash   110

3/1 Balance 10,600	

Payroll Cash   120

FICA Taxes Payable   205

	3/1 Balance 795.00

Employees' Income Taxes Withheld   210

	3/1 Balance 620.00

Federal Unemployment Taxes Payable   215

	3/1 Balance 63.60

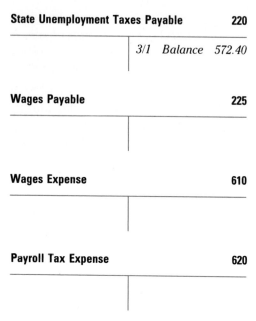

State Unemployment Taxes Payable   220

	3/1 Balance 572.40

Wages Payable   225

Wages Expense   610

Payroll Tax Expense   620

The following transactions relating to payroll occurred in March and April.

Mar. 15 issued a check for monthly deposit for amounts owed for FICA tax and employees' income tax withheld

Mar. 15 recorded semimonthly wages expense, amounts withheld for employees' deductions, and net wages; gross wages, $3,050.00; employees' federal income tax withheld, $420.00; FICA tax withheld, $228.75 (credit wages payable for the net wages)

Mar. 15 recorded the employer's payroll tax expense; no employee earned over $7,000

Mar. 15 recorded the issuance of a check for $2,401.25 payable to the payroll checking account (debit Payroll Cash, credit Cash)

Mar. 15 issued individual checks to pay employees (For this entry, debit Wages Payable and credit Payroll Cash for $2,401.25. In actual practice, a separate check would have to be written for each employee.)

Mar. 31 recorded semimonthly wages expense, amounts withheld from employees' wages, and net wages; gross wages, $3,120.00; employees' federal income tax withheld, $422.00; FICA tax withheld, $234.00

Mar. 31 recorded the employer's payroll tax expense; no employee earned over $7,000

Mar. 31 recorded the issuance of a check for $2,464.00 payable to the payroll checking account

Mar. 31 issued individual checks to pay employees (See similar entry on March 15.)

Apr. 15 issued a check for monthly deposit for amounts owed for FICA tax and employees' income taxes withheld

Apr. 30 issued a check for deposit of federal unemployment taxes for the period January through March

Apr. 30 issued a check for amount owed for the quarter for state unemployment taxes

Instructions

1. *Enter the account names and March 1 balances in the T-accounts.*

2. *Journalize each transaction in a general journal (page 86). Post to the T-accounts immediately after each transaction, so that you will know how much is owed for various taxes.*

3. *Answer the following questions after all the entries have been journalized and posted to the T-accounts.*

   a. *What was the total wages expense for March?*

   b. *What was the total payroll tax expense for March?*

   c. *What amount was remitted to the IRS for FICA taxes for March? What portion of that was expense?*

Problem 13.6

preparing Forms 941 and 940

Sylvia Bucknell owns a business called the Plant Doctors, which is located at 6432 Madison Road, Augusta, Maine 04330. Sylvia employs eight people. Her federal employer's identification number is 98-346210, and her state identification number is 10-431692. Payroll data for the Plant Doctors includes the following information for the last quarter of the year. For FICA and employees' income tax withheld:

Pay Date	Tax Liability	Amount Deposited	Date of Deposit
October 5	$1,445.03		
October 31	1,445.03	$2,890.06	November 11
November 15	1,486.02		
November 30	1,486.02	2,972.04	December 12
December 15	1,442.47		
December 31	1,442.47	2,884.94	January 10

Total wages paid during the quarter were $30,500.10. No employee has earned over $45,000.00. Total income tax withheld was $4,172.02.

For federal unemployment tax, total wages paid during the calendar year were $120,490.06; payments for wages in excess of $7,000 were $64,490.06. Amount paid to state unemployment fund was $3,024.00 (payments required only to Maine). Record of deposits for federal unemployment tax:

Quarter	Tax Liability	Amount Deposited	Date of Deposit
First	$180.73	$180.73	April 30
Second	129.14	129.14	July 31
Third	26.13		Amount remitted with Form
Fourth	0		940 on February 10

Instructions

1. Prepare a Form 941, Employer's Quarterly Federal Tax Return, for the Plant Doctors to be submitted to the Internal Revenue Service on January 31 for the last quarter of the year. Assume that no tips were reported and that there were no adjustments or advanced earned income credits (Line 15).

2. Prepare a Form 940, the Employer's Annual Federal Unemployment (FUTA) Tax Return, for the Plant Doctors to be submitted to the Internal Revenue Service on February 10 for the calendar year. Assume that no refunds are due.

3. Sign both forms with your name and the title Accountant.

Comprehensive Problem 3

for Review of Chapters 11

through 13

Deer Creek Girls' Wear has been in business since January 1, Year 1, and is owned by Helen Bonner. It is located at 4319 Aspen Highway in Bishop, California 93544. Accounts are adjusted and closed monthly. Following are the accounts and their balances as of March 31, Year 1, before adjusting and closing entries have been journalized and posted. All transactions have been recorded for March except the payroll for the week ended March 31.

Deer Creek Girls' Wear
Trial Balance
March 31, 19XX

Acct. No.	Account Title	Debit	Credit
101	Cash	$ 23,950.00	
105	Payroll Cash	0	
110	Notes Receivable	10,800.00	
120	Accounts Receivable	19,400.00	
125	Merchandise Inventory	49,600.00	
130	Supplies	980.00	
135	Prepaid Insurance	2,000.00	
140	Building	90,000.00	
140A	Accumulated Depreciation: Building		$ 625.00
150	Store Equipment	80,000.00	
150A	Accumulated Depreciation: Store Equipment		1,000.00
160	Delivery Equipment	75,000.00	
160A	Accumulated Depreciation: Delivery Equipment		2,500.00
170	Office Equipment	30,000.00	
170A	Accumulated Depreciation: Office Equipment		1,000.00
180	Land	50,000.00	
201	Notes Payable		38,000.00
210	Accounts Payable		11,700.00
215	Unearned Revenue		1,500.00
220	Wages Payable		0
230	FICA Taxes Payable		1,455.60
240	Employees Income Taxes Withheld		1,332.00
250	Medical Insurance Premiums Withheld		578.00
260	Union Dues Withheld		475.00
270	FUTA Taxes Payable		174.72
280	SUTA Taxes Payable		524.00
290	Mortgage Payable		155,000.00
310	Helen Bonner, Capital		179,268.72
320	Helen Bonner, Drawing	4,620.00	
330	Income Summary		0
401	Sales		135,000.00
410	Sales Returns and Allowances	5,750.00	
420	Sales Discounts	2,290.00	
501	Purchases	69,700.00	
520	Freight In	2,420.00	
530	Purchases Returns and Allowances		4,910.00
540	Purchases Discounts		1,280.00
610	Rent Expense	3,000.00	
615	Utilities Expense	940.00	
620	Payroll Tax Expense	1,310.04	
630	Wages Expense	9,704.00	
640	Advertising Expense	2,750.00	
650	Insurance Expense	609.00	
660	Repairs Expense	1,500.00	
670	Depreciation Expense	0	
680	Supplies Used	0	
	Totals	$536,323.04	$536,323.04

Deer Creek's employees are salaried and are paid on Friday of each week. There are five pay periods in March. No employee has earned over $7,000. Following is the payroll information for the week ended March 31.

Employee Name	Gross Wages	Marital Status	Number of Exemptions
Duvall	$510.00	M	2
McInroe	490.00	S	3
Schwartz	400.00	M	0
Suzuki	500.00	S	0
Yee	526.00	S	2

Union dues of $23.75 are withheld each week for each employee. Medical insurance premiums are $24.60 for all married persons and for single employees with more than one exemption; premiums are $17.20 for single employees with one or zero exemptions.

Instructions

1. *Enter the account titles and balances into a general ledger.*

2. *Calculate the payroll for the week ended March 31 on a payroll register. Assume an FICA rate of 7.5 percent of the first $45,000 earned. No employee has earned over $45,000. Use the federal income tax withholding tables in Chapter 12.*

3. *Prepare the general journal entry (page 19) on March 31 to record the gross wages and employee deductions. Credit Wages Payable for the net wages.*

4. *Prepare the general journal entry on March 31 to record the employer's payroll tax expense. The FICA rate is 7.5 percent of the first $45,000 earned by each employee; the federal unemployment tax (FUTA) rate is .6 percent of the first $7,000 earned; and the state unemployment tax (SUTA) rate is 5.4 percent of the first $7,000 earned. No employee has earned over $7,000. Round the tax amounts to the nearest penny where required.*

5. *Prepare the entry in the general journal on March 31 to deposit the net wages into the payroll checking account (debit Payroll Cash and credit Cash).*

6. *Prepare the entry that records checks issued to individual employees (debit Wages Payable and credit Payroll Cash).*

7. Post to the general ledger the journal entries made in instructions 3, 4, 5, and 6.

8. Prepare a trial balance of the ledger on the first two columns of a worksheet. Do not list accounts with zero balances.

9. When the trial balance is complete and in balance, calculate the monthly adjusting entries from the following information; enter the correct debit and credit amounts on the adjustments columns of the worksheet.

   a. The ending inventory of supplies is $625.

   b. An insurance policy costing $2,400 was purchased on January 2 for a 12-month period.

   c. All depreciable assets were purchased the first week in January and are depreciated by the straight-line method. Their useful lives and salvage values are as follows.

Asset	Useful Life	Salvage Value
Building	20 years	$15,000
Store Equipment	10 years	20,000
Delivery Equipment	4 years	15,000
Office Equipment	4 years	6,000

   d. On February 10, a customer paid $1,500 in advance for merchandise that was to be delivered in March and April. $1,000 of the merchandise was delivered on March 29 (credit Sales).

10. The value of the ending merchandise inventory is $45,200. Enter the inventory figures in their correct places in the income statement and balance sheet columns of the worksheet and complete the worksheet.

11. Prepare an income statement for the month ended March 31, 19XX.

12. Prepare a classified balance sheet as of March 31, 19XX. Include a complete statement of owner's equity. The monthly payment on the mortgage is $1,750 and on the note, $1,000 a month.

13. Calculate the current ratio (round to the nearest 10th of a percent). Indicate whether the ratio reveals a strong or a weak current position.

14. *Calculate the working capital.*

15. *Journalize and post the adjusting entries on general journal page 20.*

16. *Journalize and post the closing entries. Continue on page 20.*

17. *Prepare a post-closing trial balance.*

18. *Prepare the entry on April 15 in the general journal (page 25) to record the deposit (payment) of the FICA taxes and employees' income taxes due for the month of March.*

19. *Prepare the entry on April 15 in the general journal to record the deposit (payment) of the state unemployment taxes due for the month of March. Continue on page 25.*

20. *Prepare the entry on April 30 in the general journal (page 25) to record the deposit (payment) of the federal unemployment taxes due for the first quarter.*

21. *Prepare Form 941 on April 30 giving the quarterly information about gross wages, FICA taxes withheld and due, and employees' income taxes withheld and due. Following is the information required for Form 941.*

	January	February	March
FICA Taxes, Employee	$ 727.80	$ 727.80	$ 909.75
FICA Taxes, Employer	727.80	727.80	909.75
Employees Income Tax Withheld	1,332.00	1,332.00	1,665.00
Total.	$2,787.60	$2,787.60	$3,484.50
Date Deposited	February 14	March 14	April 15

Total wages subject to withholding were $31,538. Employer's identification number is 98-792039.

CHAPTER 14

Internal Control and the Voucher System of Accounting

Each year billions of dollars are lost by American businesses through employee carelessness, mistakes, and dishonesty. A strong system of internal control is essential to minimize such losses, and once the system is in place both employees and employer benefit from it. The employees have less temptation to steal assets in a well-organized business, and honest employees will not be suspect when theft or fraud occurs because a good system of internal control pinpoints responsibility and has daily checks and balances.

An internal control system establishes procedures to protect a company's resources from theft, waste, and inefficiency; ensures that accounting data is accurate; and evaluates employees and departments to determine their level of performance and whether they are complying with company policy. The system should be set up so that one employee's work is checked by another with as little duplication of effort as possible.

PRINCIPLES OF INTERNAL CONTROL

An accurate system of accounting for cash is an essential ingredient of internal control. Proper cash management helps to ensure solvency, maintains enough cash on hand to operate efficiently, and puts excess cash to work through various investments. Cash, because it is especially susceptible to theft, requires special procedures. Some of the basic principles of internal control for cash are as follows.

1. No employee should handle all phases of a transaction from beginning to end.
2. Cash should be deposited daily.
3. Cash payments should be made by check.
4. The functions of receiving and paying should be kept separate.
5. One employee should be designated to verify the amount of a cash payment, and another employee should be designated to write the check.
6. The function of accounting should be kept separate from the handling of cash or other assets.
7. Specific routines should be established for handling cash, and a designated employee should check regularly to make sure they are being followed as set up.

In addition, a training program should be in effect for every employee so that each person knows exactly what is expected and why certain procedures are necessary. Only experienced, capable employees should be trusted with important internal control positions. All such employees should be required to take a vacation each year, and during their absence, some other trusted employee should perform the duties of the person on vacation as an important check.

Prenumbered sales tickets, checks, invoices, purchase orders, and so on, should be used so that it is immediately evident when one is missing. Posting reference notations should be used for all transactions so that they may be easily traced from beginning to end.

The person who is in charge of ordering merchandise should not be the one who receives the merchandise when it is delivered. Ideally more than one employee will be involved in receiving deliveries. The merchandise delivered should be checked against that ordered, and the invoice should be checked for mathematical errors.

The system of internal control involves all aspects of the business. Once established, it should be reviewed by management on a regular basis to ensure that it is working as planned.

THE VOUCHER SYSTEM

voucher
a document that shows significant facts about a transaction and that has spaces for signatures verifying the accuracy of the invoice and approving it for payment

A system of establishing control over liabilities and cash payments is the **voucher** system. A voucher is issued for every transaction that requires a payment of cash. Before payment can be made, the voucher must be checked for accuracy, approved for payment, and recorded. If a purchase invoice is involved, the voucher has spaces for initials that verify that the invoice has been checked for mathematical accuracy, that the goods received are the goods ordered, that credit terms are as agreed on, and so forth. A check cannot be issued unless the voucher has been approved according to the procedures established.

The voucher system would not be appropriate for small businesses because of the large amount of paperwork and subdivision of duties required. The small business owner is normally present on a daily basis and is the person responsible for supervising and maintaining a system of internal control. The voucher system is most suitable for medium-sized and large businesses.

The voucher system has its own built-in controls. For example, all payments are made by check and only after a step-by-step process that involves several people. Approved purchase orders are required before merchandise can be ordered. All bills and invoices must be accompanied by a voucher that has been verified and approved for payment. Accounting is done by someone other than the persons involved in verifying vouchers, approving them for payment, and writing the checks. Only certain experienced employees are involved in verifying payment of a voucher.

The Vouchers Payable Account

In the voucher system, the Accounts Payable account is replaced with Vouchers Payable. Every cash payment requires a voucher and is credited to Vouchers Payable. For example, when the rent is to be paid, a voucher is prepared showing the reason for payment, the account(s) to be debited, and the amount of the payment. Vouchers Payable is always credited when a voucher is prepared. The voucher must be initialed by the person responsible for authorizing payment. The voucher will indicate that Rent Expense should be debited and Vouchers Payable should be credited. When the check is issued for payment of the rent, Vouchers Payable will be debited and Cash credited. If office equipment is purchased, the voucher will indicate that Office Equipment is to be debited and Vouchers Payable is to be credited. For merchandise purchased for resale, Purchases is debited and Vouchers Payable is credited. When the balance sheet is prepared, the title Accounts Payable is normally used instead of Vouchers Payable because it is more widely understood by persons using the balance sheet.

Preparing and Approving the Voucher

One of the significant features of the voucher system is that it provides strong control over cash payments. Before a check is written in payment of an invoice, for example, a voucher must be prepared and attached to the invoice. The voucher shows the invoice number, date, amount, and the name and address of the firm to whom payment will be made. In addition, one or more individuals initial the voucher when the goods are delivered to indicate that the goods have arrived as indicated on the invoice. The voucher is then forwarded to the person responsible for checking the invoice

extensions
result obtained when
quantity ordered is
multiplied by unit
price on an invoice

extensions, totals, and discount amount. After this has been completed, the voucher and the invoice are sent to the accounting department, which will indicate which account(s) is to be debited to record the voucher (Vouchers Payable will be credited). Still another individual may be designated to check the whole process up to this point. When the invoice is ready for payment, the voucher as approved will be entered on a special form called the voucher register.

Assume that Bloomington Clothes Mart uses the voucher system and receives a shipment of sweaters from the Peoria Woolen Supply House. When the shipment arrives on November 18, the person responsible for verifying that the merchandise received is the same as the merchandise indicated on the invoice attaches voucher number 598 to the invoice and carefully checks the incoming goods. The invoice date, number, terms, and amount are indicated on the voucher along with the creditor's name and address. In addition, the voucher is initialed to indicate that the goods have been checked on arrival. The initials indicate that nothing is damaged and that all merchandise listed on the invoice is accounted for. Following is the invoice from Peoria Woolen Supply House.

PEORIA WOOLEN SUPPLY HOUSE
13475 East River Road
Peoria, Illinois 61601

Sold to: *Bloomington Clothes Mart*
3990 West Commerce Street
Bloomington, IL 61701

Invoice No. W-75632

Date: *Nov. 17*

Customer Order No. *P-42790*

Terms: *2/10, n/30*

Quantity	Description	Cost per Unit	Total Amount
30	Red Cardigans - Size L - 7963-R	14.95	448.50
10	Navy Cardigans - Size L - 7963-N	14.95	149.50
25	Black Slacks, Ladies, Size 10, 2873-13	29.50	737.50
15	Black Slacks, Ladies, Size 12, 2876-13	29.50	442.50
15	Black Slacks, Ladies, Size 14, 2879-13	29.50	442.50
			2,220.50

After it has been verified that the merchandise listed on the invoice has arrived safely, the invoice extensions are checked by another individual who will initial the voucher after the checking is complete. The voucher for the Bloomington Clothes Mart appears as follows after the extensions have been verified as correct.

BLOOMINGTON CLOTHES MART
3990 West Commerce Street
Bloomington, IL 61701

Payment
Voucher
No. 598

Pay to: _Peoria Woolen Supply House_
13475 East River Road
Peoria, IL 61601

Date: _Nov. 18_

Due Date: _Nov. 27_

Invoice Date: _Nov. 17_

Invoice No.: _W-75632_

Terms: _2/10, n/30_

Gross Amount: _$2,220.50_

Less: Discount _44.41_

Net Amount: _$2,176.09_

Approval

	Approved by	Date
Invoice extensions verified	_JB_	_11/18_
Invoice footings verified	_JB_	_11/18_
Checked against purchase order	_w_	_11/18_
Quantities ordered verified	_w_	_11/18_
Terms as agreed upon	_w_	_11/18_

Accounting

Record as debit to: _Purchases_

Credit: Vouchers Payable

Approved for payment by: _Sdl_

Paid by Check No.:
Date of Check:
Amount of Check:
Entered in Voucher Register by:

Recording, Filing, and Paying the Voucher

tickler file
a file arranged by invoice or voucher due dates

After the voucher has been approved for payment, it is recorded on a form called the voucher register. If the voucher does not have to be paid immediately, it is placed in a **tickler file** where all vouchers are arranged by their due date. This tickler file represents all the accounts payable of the business, and no separate accounts payable subsidiary ledger is kept.

A daily check of the tickler file indicates which vouchers should be paid on any particular day. After the check is written, the check number, amount, and date are entered on the voucher, and the check is recorded in the check register, a form similar to the cash payments journal. The voucher is marked *paid* and is filed in a paid vouchers file either by number or by the name of the payee.

The Voucher Register

Every voucher is recorded in the voucher register after it has been approved. The first column of the voucher register is a vouchers payable credit column, since all vouchers are credited to Vouchers Payable when prepared. The other columns in the voucher register are determined by the needs of the particular company using it. For the following voucher register for the Bloomington Clothes Mart, special columns are provided for recording FICA Taxes Payable, Employee Income Taxes Withheld, Purchases, Freight In, and Wages Expense. There are also miscellaneous debit and credit columns.

When the voucher is paid, Vouchers Payable is debited and Cash is credited and a notation is made in the voucher register alongside the voucher indicating the date and the number of the check issued in payment. Following is the voucher register for the Bloomington Clothes Mart showing the transactions recorded from November 1 through 18. The totals for the month are also included so that posting procedures can be explained.

VOUCHER REGISTER FOR MONTH OF NOVEMBER							
Voucher No.	Date	Payee	Date	Check No.	Vouchers Pay. Cr.	FICA Tax Pay. Cr.	Emp. Inc. Tax Withheld Cr.
586	Nov. 1	Illinois Properties	11/2	1410	1500 —		
587	2	Great Lakes Clothing	11/11	1415	2940 —		
588	2	Stationery House	11/2	1411	300 —		
589	4	Sam McNeal	11/4	1412	500 —		
590	6	Burk's Boots	11/15	1416	760 —		
591	8	Illinois Power Co.	11/8	1413	310 —		
592	10	WGL Radio	11/10	1414	450 —		
593	12	Rantoul Men's Wear	11/22	1422	3620 —		
594	14	Great Lakes Clothing	11/23	1424	1870 —		
595	15	Plains Freight	11/15	1417	500 —		
596	15	Dorothy Swan	11/15	1418	1026 50	94 50	139 —
597	15	Phillip Andrews	11/15	1419	846 25	78 75	125 —
598	18	Peoria Woolen Supply	11/28	1432	2220 50		
		Totals			29416 20	346 50	528 —
					(220)	(225)	(240)

The two columns to the left of the vouchers payable credit column titled Date and Check No. are used to indicate that a check has been written in payment of the voucher. The date the check was written and its number are recorded after the check is recorded in the check register. At a glance, then, one can tell which vouchers have not been paid. Those vouchers are filed in the unpaid vouchers file.

The voucher register for the Bloomington Clothes Mart shows all vouchers through November 18 (the last voucher shown in the illustration) have been paid. A quick check will show that all invoices have been paid within the discount period. The purchase invoices dated November 21 through November 30 with terms of 2/10, n/30 are very likely to be paid in December. When the check is written in payment of those vouchers, the check number and date of the check will be entered in the November voucher register.

Page 33

| Purchases Dr. | Freight In Dr. | Wages Exp. Dr. | Other Accounts | | | |
			Account Titles	PR	Dr.	Cr.
			Rent Expense	610	1 5 0 0 —	
2 9 4 0 —						
			Supplies	140	3 0 0 —	
			Sam McNeal, Drawing	320	5 0 0 —	
7 6 0 —						
			Utilities Expense	620	3 1 0 —	
			Advertising Expense	630	4 5 0 —	
3 3 7 0 —	2 5 0 —					
1 8 7 0 —						
	5 0 0 —					
		1 2 6 0 —				
		1 0 5 0 —				
2 2 2 0 50						
18 8 7 7 70	1 6 1 1 —	4 6 2 0 —			5 1 8 2 —	—
(5 0 1)	(5 2 0)	(6 6 0)			(X)	

Totaling, Crossfooting, Ruling, and Posting the Voucher Register

When the vouchers for the period have all been recorded, the columns of the voucher register are totaled. Crossfooting is required just as with the special journals to prove that the total of the debit columns is equal to the total of the credit columns. For the Bloomington Clothes Mart voucher register, crossfooting is as follows.

Debit Column Totals	Credit Column Totals
$18,877.70	$29,416.20
1,611.00	346.50
4,620.00	528.00
5,182.00	
$30,290.70	$30,290.70

Once crossfooting is complete, the voucher register is double ruled across all columns except the ones titled payee and account titles. Summary posting is performed for all column totals except the miscellaneous debit and credit columns. As posting is completed, the account number in parentheses is placed under the column total. The amounts in the miscellaneous debit and credit columns must be posted individually. An X is placed beneath these columns. The posting reference for the voucher register is VR. No posting is required to a subsidiary ledger because one does not exist with the voucher system. The file of unpaid vouchers replaces the accounts payable subsidiary ledger.

The Check Register

The check register is similar to the cash payments journal, except that checks are only written in payment of bills that are accompanied by approved vouchers. Every entry in the check register is a debit to Vouchers Payable and a credit to Cash. As the entry is recorded, the number of the voucher being paid is entered in the column titled Voucher No. Because the voucher register has special columns that categorize the expenditures as expenses, purchases of merchandise or assets, and so on, this process does not need to be repeated in the check register. If the business always takes advantage of credit terms, however, another column is required in the check register for purchases discounts. Following is a portion of the check register for November for the Bloomington Clothes Mart.

					Vouchers Payable	Purchases Discount	Cash
					CHECK REGISTER		Page 58
Date	Check No.	Payee	Voucher No.		Debit	Credit	Credit
19XX Nov. 1	1408	Urbana Men's Store	572		2470 —	49 40	2420 60
1	1409	University Village	574		1800 —	36 —	1764 —
2	1410	Illinois Properties	586		1500 —		1500 —
2	1411	Stationery House	588		300 —		300 —
4	1412	Sam McNeal	589		500 —		500 —
8	1413	Illinois Power Co.	591		310 —		310 —
10	1414	WGL Radio	592		450 —		450 —
11	1415	Great Lakes Clothing	587		2940 —	58 80	2881 20
15	1416	Burk's Boots	590		760 —	15 20	744 80
15	1417	Plains Freight	595		500 —		500 —
15	1418	Dorothy Swan	596		1026 50		1026 50
15	1419	Phillip Andrews	597		846 25		846 25
		Totals			26420 90	377 54	26043 36
					(220)	(510)	(110)

canceled
a check or voucher that is perforated or stamped *paid*

perforated
pierced or punched with holes

After a voucher has been paid, it should be **canceled.** This requires that the voucher be stamped *paid,* **perforated,** or otherwise obviously marked to indicate that it has been paid. Canceling a voucher in this fashion prevents it from being recirculated for payment a second (or third) time.

Totaling, Crossfooting, Ruling, and Posting the Check Register

The check register is totaled, crossfooted, and ruled at the end of the period. The totals of the columns are then posted to the appropriate accounts in the general ledger. The posting reference for the check register is CkR.

The Schedule of Vouchers Payable

As indicated earlier, no accounts payable subsidiary ledger is used with the voucher system; the tickler file of unpaid vouchers is used in its place. At the end of the accounting period, a schedule of vouchers payable is prepared, however, which lists the vouchers by number, creditor's name, and amount. This information is taken directly from the unpaid vouchers in the tickler file. The total of the schedule of vouchers payable must agree with the balance in the Accounts Payable account in the general ledger. (Remember, Vouchers Payable is shown on the balance sheet as Accounts Payable.) As a final check, the schedule of vouchers payable should be compared with the voucher register. All the vouchers not marked as paid in the voucher register should be listed on the schedule of vouchers payable.

SPECIAL HANDLING PROBLEMS WITH THE VOUCHER SYSTEM

In the voucher system, handling routine transactions presents no problem. A voucher is attached to incoming invoices, the process of checking and verification takes place, and the voucher is approved for payment and entered in the voucher register; finally it is paid, entered in the check register, and filed. The routine is rigid, but its strong point is that it helps maintain strong internal control over cash. One drawback is that certain kinds of transactions are awkward to handle.

Purchases Returns and Allowances

Assume that the Bloomington Clothes Mart purchases $1,300 in merchandise from the Great Lakes Clothing Warehouse with credit terms of 2/10, n/30. The merchandise is delivered on December 4, but a portion of it must be returned because the goods were not as ordered. A debit memorandum for $300 is prepared immediately, before the voucher is prepared and recorded, and attached to the invoice. Then $300 is deducted from the face amount of the invoice. When the voucher is prepared, it will indicate that Purchases is to be debited for $1,000 and Vouchers Payable credited for $1,000. The debit memorandum and the invoice will be attached to the voucher. Returns are easy to handle if they occur before the voucher is prepared, approved, and recorded.

If the decision to return merchandise purchased is made after the voucher has been recorded, a different procedure is required. Assume that on December 6, Bloomington Clothes Mart purchased merchandise costing $2,500 from the Lincoln Bootery with credit terms of 2/10, n/30. Voucher number 642 is prepared and approved, and the purchase is entered in the voucher register as shown.

									VOUCHER REGISTER FOR MONTH OF DECEMBER				Page *34*	
Voucher No.	Date	Payee	Date	Check No.	Vouchers Pay. Cr.	FICA Tax Pay. Cr.	Emp. Inc. Tax Withheld Cr.	Purchases Dr.
	19XX		19XX					
642	Dec. 6	Lincoln Bootery			2500 —			2500 —

Assume further that on December 8, Bloomington Clothes Mart decided to return $500 of the December 6 shipment of goods from the Lincoln Bootery. The entry requires a credit to Purchases Returns and Allowances for $500 and a debit to Vouchers Payable. Because the voucher system is in use, however, it is not that simple. Vouchers are approved before they are entered in the voucher register; thus the old voucher has to be canceled and a new one prepared and approved, as checks can only be issued for the amount shown on the approved voucher. The transaction, then, requires that a new voucher be prepared and approved (number 651) indicating that Vouchers Payable is to be debited for $2,500 to cancel the old voucher; Vouchers Payable is to be credited for $2,000 to record the new voucher; and Purchases Returns and Allowances is to be credited for $500 to record the return. A notation is made in the date and check number columns opposite the original voucher number 642 to indicate that it has been canceled by a new voucher. The original entry and the entry recording the issuing of a new voucher follows.

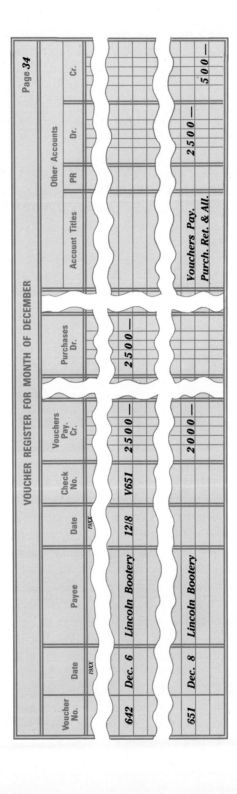

VOUCHER REGISTER FOR MONTH OF DECEMBER

Voucher No.	Date 19XX	Payee	Date 19XX	Check No.	Vouchers Pay. Cr.	Purchases Dr.	Account Titles	Other Accounts		
								PR	Dr.	Cr.
642	Dec. 6	Lincoln Bootery	12/8	V651	2 5 0 0 —	2 5 0 0 —				
651	Dec. 8	Lincoln Bootery			2 0 0 0 —		Vouchers Pay. Purch. Ret. & All.		2 5 0 0 —	5 0 0 —

Notes Payable

Assume that on December 1, voucher number 635 is recorded in the voucher register of the Bloomington Clothes Mart debiting Purchases and crediting Vouchers Payable for $5,000 for a purchase of merchandise from the Springfield Clothes Horse. Terms are 2/10, n/30. On the due date of the invoice, December 31, the manager of the Bloomington Clothes Mart decides to put off payment of the invoice and gives a 12 percent, 60-day note in payment. The entries on December 1 and December 31 in the voucher register are as follows.

VOUCHER REGISTER FOR MONTH OF DECEMBER

Voucher No.	Date	Payee	Check No.	Date	Vouchers Pay. Cr.	Purchases Dr.	Account Titles	PR	Other Accounts Dr.	Other Accounts Cr.
	19XX			19XX						
635	Dec. 1	Springfield Clothes Horse	12/31 by note		5000—	5000—				
	31						Vouchers Pay. Notes Payable		5000—	5000—

A notation must be made in the voucher register on December 31 when the note is issued. The notation is made opposite voucher number 635 indicating that it has been canceled by the issuance of a note payable. The date of the note is entered in the date column and *by note* is written in the check number column as indicated.

When the note becomes due on March 1, a new voucher must be prepared and approved before a check can be written in payment. When the voucher is prepared and approved, it will be recorded in the voucher register as follows.

Voucher No.	Date	Payee	Date	Check No.	Vouchers Pay. Cr.		Other Accounts		
							Account Titles	PR	Dr.
1041	*19XX* Mar. 1	Springfield Clothes Horse	*19XX*		5100 —		Notes Payable Interest Expense		5000 — 100 —

When the check is written in payment of the note, it will be recorded in the check register.

Partial Payments

Often, a voucher is issued in payment of a purchase only to be canceled because the full amount cannot be paid when due. Assume, for example, that on January 5 the Bloomington Clothes Mart bought office equipment on account costing $7,500 from Business Furniture Company with terms of n/30. Voucher number 710 was prepared, and an entry was made in the voucher register debiting Office Equipment for $7,500 and crediting Vouchers Payable. The voucher was placed in the tickler file under its February 4 due date. On February 4, the manager wanted more time for payment, because she felt there was not enough cash on hand to pay the full amount, and she arranged for payment to be made in three installments. One-third would be paid on February 4, one-third on March 4, and the last third on April 4. Three new vouchers were issued (numbers 796, 797, and 798). The original voucher was canceled by recording a debit to Vouchers Payable of $7,500 and indicating in the date column that voucher number 710 had been replaced with vouchers 796, 797, and 798 for $2,500 each. The first $2,500 voucher (number 796) was approved and paid immediately (February 4) and filed in the paid vouchers file. Vouchers 797 and 798 are placed in the tickler file under their due dates. Following are the entries in the voucher register and the check register for the Bloomington Clothes Mart on January 5 and February 4.

Voucher No.	Date	Payee	Date	Check No.	Vouchers Pay. Cr.	Account Titles	PR	Dr.	Cr.
	19XX		19XX			Other Accounts			
710	Jan. 5	Business Furniture Co.	2/4	V796 –798	7500 —	Office Equipment		7500 —	
796	Feb. 4	Business Furniture Co.	2/4	1618	2500 —	Vouchers Payable		7500 —	
797		Business Furniture Co.			2500 —				
798		Business Furniture Co.			2500 —				

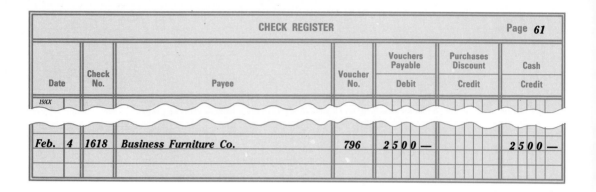

				CHECK REGISTER				Page *61*

Date	Check No.	Payee	Voucher No.	Vouchers Payable Debit	Purchases Discount Credit	Cash Credit
19XX						
Feb. 4	*1618*	*Business Furniture Co.*	*796*	*2500 —*		*2500 —*

RECORDING PURCHASES AT THE NET AMOUNT

gross method
recording purchases at their gross amount and recording the discount if the invoice is paid within the due date

net method
recording purchases at their gross amount less the purchases discount; if the invoice due date is missed, the discount lost is recorded

When purchasing merchandise for resale, the Purchases account may be debited for the gross amount and the discount, if any, is credited to Purchases Discounts at the time of payment of the invoice. This method of recording purchases, called the **gross method,** makes no mention when a due date is missed and the discount is lost. Many accountants consider this a shortcoming of the gross method of recording purchases and prefer to use the **net method.** The net method assumes that the best management of cash requires that all discounts offered be taken, thereby eliminating the need to record a purchases discount. Purchases are simply recorded at their net amount (the gross amount of the invoice less the discount). If for some reason the due date is missed, however, a purchases discount lost will be recorded, calling the lost discount to the attention of management.

Assume that the Bloomington Clothes Mart uses the net method of recording purchases. On March 2, merchandise totaling $840 is purchased from the Mississippi Retail Suppliers with terms of 2/10, n/30. At the time of the purchase, voucher number 1075 is prepared indicating a debit to Purchases and a credit to Vouchers Payable for $823.20. The discount is subtracted before the voucher is prepared and approved. The entry is as follows.

VOUCHER REGISTER FOR MONTH OF MARCH									Page *37*
Voucher No.	Date	Payee	Date	Check No.	Vouchers Pay. Cr.	FICA Tax Pay. Cr.	Emp. Inc. Tax Withheld Cr.	Purchases Dr.	
	19XX		*19XX*						
1075	*Mar. 2*	*Miss. Retail Suppliers*			*8 2 3 20*			*8 2 3 20*	

When the invoice falls due on March 12, a check is written and entered in the check register debiting Vouchers Payable and crediting Cash for $823.20.

This method works very well when the invoices are paid within the due date. A problem occurs, however, when they are not. Assume that the Bloomington Clothes Mart did not pay the invoice of the Mississippi Retail Suppliers within the discount date. The total amount owed, then, is $840, the amount of the original invoice. Because the invoice was recorded at its net amount of $823.20, the amount to be paid does not agree with the amount originally recorded. A special account called Purchases Discounts Lost is used to record the difference between the gross and net amounts of the invoice. The entry in the check register on March 31 to record payment of the Mississippi Retail Suppliers invoice is as follows.

					CHECK REGISTER					Page *62*
Date	Check No.	Payee			Voucher No.	Vouchers Payable Debit		Purchases Discount Lost Debit		Cash Credit
19XX										
Mar. *31*	*1798*	*Mississippi Retail Suppliers*				*8 2 3 20*		*1 6 80*		*8 4 0* —

The account Purchases Discounts Lost is classified as an expense and appears along with the other expenses on the income statement. The net method of recording purchases has the advantage of pointing out to management the cost of not paying invoices within the discount period.

A Comparison of the Gross and Net Methods of Recording Purchases

The following summary is provided as a review of the gross and net methods of recording purchases. Assume that the Bloomington Clothes Mart purchased $3,750 of merchandise for resale on March

2 with terms of 2/10, n/30. In general journal form, the gross and net methods of recording purchases are illustrated.

Gross Method		
Original Purchase		
Mar. 2 Purchases	3,750	
Accounts Payable		3,750
2/10, n/30		
Payment within Discount Period		
Mar. 10 Accounts Payable	3,750	
Purchases Discounts		75
Cash		3,675
Payment within Discount Period		
Payment after Discount Period		
Mar. 30 Accounts Payable	3,750	
Cash		3,750
Payment after Discount Period		
Net Method		
Original Purchase		
Mar. 2 Purchases	3,675	
Accounts Payable		3,675
2/10, n/30		
Payment within Discount Period		
Mar. 12 Accounts Payable	3,675	
Cash		3,675
Payment within Discount Period		
Payment after Discount Period		
Mar. 30 Accounts Payable	3,675	
Purchases Discounts Lost	75	
Cash		3,750
Payment after Discount Period		

SUMMARY

Employee carelessness, dishonesty, and mistakes cost American businesses billions of dollars each year. To minimize the losses, management must take steps to ensure a strong system of internal control. Such a system will establish procedures to protect the company's assets from theft, waste, and inefficiency. Proper cash management is one of the most important features of a good internal control system, because cash is especially susceptible to theft.

The use of the voucher system is one way for medium- and large-sized businesses to help maintain control over cash expenditures. Before any payment can be made, a voucher must be prepared and approved for payment. If a purchase invoice is involved, it is checked to make sure that the goods have arrived safely, that everything on the invoice is accounted for, that the extensions are accurate and the discount is as agreed on, and so on.

Once the voucher is prepared and approved, it is entered in the voucher register. The voucher register has special columns to record the appropriate debit and credit amounts. It is treated like a special journal, and at the end of the accounting period, summary posting is performed. When a voucher is paid, the check is recorded in the check register and an indication is made in the voucher register opposite the voucher that is being paid. The check register, too, is summary posted at the end of the accounting period.

All vouchers are credited to Vouchers Payable when recorded in the voucher register. As they are paid, they are placed in a paid vouchers file. Vouchers that are waiting for payment are placed in a tickler file in which they are filed according to their due date. Each day, the tickler file is checked to see if any voucher requires payment. The tickler file of unpaid vouchers replaces the accounts payable subsidiary ledger. At the end of the accounting period, a schedule of accounts payable may be prepared by listing the vouchers that are in the tickler file. After a voucher has been paid, it should be canceled and filed, so that it may not be recirculated for payment again.

When merchandise is returned after the purchase has been recorded in the voucher register, the original voucher must be canceled by a debit to Vouchers Payable and a new voucher must be issued for the original amount minus the return.

Review of Accounting Terminology

Following is a list of the accounting terminology for this chapter.

canceled	perforated
extensions	tickler file
gross method	voucher
net method	

Fill in the blank with the correct word or term from the list.

1. The results obtained when the quantity is multiplied by the unit price on an invoice are _____.

2. A file of unpaid vouchers arranged by their due dates is a/an _____.

3. A check or voucher marked or perforated to prevent further use is said to be _____.

4. A voucher that has been pierced or punched with holes is _____.

5. Recording purchases at their full invoice amount and recording the discount if paid within the due date is called the _____.

6. A document that shows significant facts about a transaction and has spaces for signatures verifying the invoice's accuracy is a/an _____.

7. A method of recording purchases at their gross amount less the discount is called the _____.

Match the following words and terms on the left with the definitions on the right (lists continue on following page).

8. canceled	a. a file arranged by due dates
9. extensions	b. items multiplied by their unit price
10. gross method	
11. net method	c. a method of recording purchases that does not reveal discounts lost
12. perforated	
13. tickler file	

14. voucher

    d. punched with holes

    e. perforated or stamped paid

    f. a document accompanying invoices that has spaces for signatures that verify invoice terms, extensions, and so on

    g. a method of recording purchases that does not show purchases discounts

Exercises

Exercise 14.1
recording transactions in voucher register (gross method for recording purchases)

Following are a partial list of accounts in the ledger of Independence Foreign Auto Parts and a partial list of transactions for January. Record the transactions in a voucher register, page 13. Use the gross method for recording purchases.

101	Cash	510	Freight In
120	Office Supplies	520	Purchases Discounts
170	Office Equipment	610	Utilities Expense
180	Van	620	Rent Expense
210	Vouchers Payable	630	Repairs Expense
220	Employee Income Taxes Withheld	640	Wages Expense
230	FICA Taxes Withheld		
501	Purchases		

Transactions

Jan. 1 prepared voucher 2017 for $1,200 to Missouri Realty for January rent

Jan. 1 prepared voucher 2018 for $126 to Light and Power Company for electricity bill

Jan. 1 prepared voucher 2019 for $750 to German Auto for parts purchased for resale; terms 2/10, n/30

Jan. 2 prepared voucher 2020 for $120 to Truman Company for office supplies

Jan. 3 prepared voucher 2021 for $2,460 to Sports Cars, Inc., for merchandise for resale; terms 1/10, n/30

Jan. 3 prepared voucher 2022 for $145 to Missouri Hauling for delivering merchandise from Sports Cars, Inc.

Jan. 4 prepared voucher 2023 for $470 to Kansas City Transmissions for repairs to the van

Jan. 5 prepared voucher 2024 for $1,850 to Capital Computers for a new printer

Jan. 6 prepared voucher 2025 for $377.50 to Kevin Hahn for the week's wages; $37.50 was withheld for FICA tax and $85 for federal income tax

Exercise 14.2
recording transactions in check register

Record the following January payments in the check register, page 15, for Independence Foreign Auto Parts. Refer to the partial chart of accounts and the transactions presented in Exercise 14.1. Purchases are recorded by the gross method.

Jan. 1 wrote check 2491 in payment of voucher 2017
Jan. 1 wrote check 2492 in payment of voucher 2018
Jan. 2 wrote check 2493 in payment of voucher 2020
Jan. 3 wrote check 2494 in payment of voucher 2022
Jan. 4 wrote check 2495 in payment of voucher 2023
Jan. 5 wrote check 2496 in payment of voucher 2024
Jan. 6 wrote check 2497 in payment of voucher 2025
Jan. 10 wrote check 2498 in payment of voucher 2019
Jan. 11 wrote check 2499 in payment of voucher 2021

Exercise 14.3
recording purchases (gross method) and returns in voucher register

a. Record the purchases and subsequent returns in the voucher register (page 3) of the Royal Sports Company. Use the gross method for recording purchases.

Mar. 3 issued voucher A-759 for purchase of merchandise from Sports Shoes Company; total cost, $1,750; terms 2/10, n/30

Mar. 4 returned $750 of the merchandise purchased from Sports Shoes Company on voucher A-759; issued voucher A-771 to Sports Shoes Company for $1,000; voucher A-759 is to be canceled and the return recorded

Mar. 6 issued voucher A-802 to Court Clothes for purchase of merchandise; total cost, $2,680; terms 1/10, n/30

Mar. 7 returned $500 of the merchandise purchased from Court Clothes on voucher A-802; issued voucher A-813 for $2,180; voucher A-802 is to be canceled and the return recorded

b. Record payments in the check register (page 6) of Royal Sports Company for the following transactions. Refer to the transactions in part a.

Check No.	Date of Check	In Payment of Voucher No.
920	March 12	A-771
921	March 15	A-813

Exercise 14.4

recording transaction to exchange note for voucher

On May 1, Hudson Bay Electrical issued voucher 4209 to Erie Electric for the purchase of merchandise for resale costing $7,400. Terms were 2/10, n/30. On May 31, the manager decided that more time was needed in which to pay the invoice and signed a 90-day, 12 percent note to obtain the extra time. On August 29, voucher 4601 was issued in payment of the note. Interest expense of $222 was recorded at this time. Record in the voucher register for Hudson Bay Electrical the following: voucher 4209 issued on May 1, the issuance of the note on May 31, and voucher 4601 issued on August 29.

Exercise 14.5

recording purchases (gross method) and subsequent payment in general journal form

Record the following transactions in general journal form for the Mountain Cider Company. Purchases are recorded by the gross method.

July 4   purchased merchandise from Apple House costing $2,950 on invoice 79-864; terms 2/10, n/30

July 8   purchased merchandise from Apple House costing $1,610 on invoice 79-999; terms 2/10, n/30

July 14   wrote check 3221 in full payment of invoice 79-864

July 31   wrote check 3516 in full payment of invoice 79-999

Exercise 14.6

recording purchases (net method) and subsequent payment in general journal form

Record the transactions listed in Exercise 14.5 in general journal form for the Mountain Cider Company assuming that purchases are recorded by the net method.

Exercise 14.7

recording purchases (net method) and subsequent payment in voucher register and check register

Record the following transactions for Girl's Wear in a voucher register (page 9) and in a check register (page 11). Purchases are recorded by the net method.

Sept. 1   issued voucher 1642 payable to Coastal Gifts for a $2,740 purchase of merchandise; terms 1/15, n/30

Sept. 9 issued voucher 1689 payable to Pacific Products for a $1,560 purchase of merchandise; terms 2/10, n/30

Sept. 15 issued check 929 in full payment for voucher 1642

Sept. 30 issued check 987 in full payment for voucher 1689

Exercise 14.8

recording issuance of four vouchers to cancel a previous voucher and pay in installments

On April 16, Paxton Barstools bought merchandise for resale costing $6,000 from Loda Furniture with terms of n/30. On May 16, the manager of Paxton Barstools arranged for payment of the invoice to be spread out in four installments of $1,500 each. The first installment would be paid on May 16, the second on May 31, the third on June 15, and the fourth on June 30.

a. In the voucher register of Paxton Barstools, prepare the April 16 entry recording the issuance of voucher 3561 for the purchase of merchandise by the gross method.

b. Prepare the May 16 entry recording the issuance of vouchers 4045, 4046, 4047, and 4048 for the four installments. Note in the voucher register that voucher 3561 has been canceled.

c. Prepare the May 16 entry in the check register to record check 6493 written in payment of voucher 4045. Make a notation in the voucher register that voucher 4045 has been paid.

Problems

Problem 14.1

recording transactions in voucher register and check register (gross method)

Central Supply has the following unpaid vouchers as of August 1, 19XX; they were issued for the purchase of merchandise.

Voucher No.	Voucher Date	Payee	Terms	Amount
2116	July 28	Andrews Electrics	2/15, n/30	$1,520
2128	July 30	Wards Lighting	1/10, n/30	1,849

Following is a partial chart of accounts for Central Supply.

101	Cash	520	Freight In
220	Vouchers Payable	530	Purchases Returns and Allowances
230	FICA Taxes Payable	540	Purchases Discounts
240	Employees Income Taxes Withheld	610	Rent Expense
350	Dale Sanders, Drawing	620	Utilities Expense
510	Purchases	630	Wages Expense

Following are the transactions for August. Purchases are recorded by the gross method.

Aug. 1   issued voucher 2135 for $1,200 to Royal Realtors for the August rent

Aug. 1   issued voucher 2136 for $575 to Andrews Electrics for purchase of merchandise; terms 2/15, n/30

Aug. 2   issued check 4145 in payment of voucher 2135

Aug. 3   issued voucher 2137 for $320 to City Utilities for electricity bill

Aug. 5   issued voucher 2138 for $1,000 to Dale Sanders, owner of Central Supply, for his personal use

Aug. 6   issued check 4146 in payment of voucher 2137

Aug. 7   issued check 4147 in payment of voucher 2138

Aug. 8   issued check 4148 in payment of voucher 2128

Aug. 10 issued voucher 2139 for $950 to Wards Lighting for merchandise purchased; terms 1/10, n/30

Aug. 11 issued check 4149 in payment of voucher 2116

Aug. 12 issued voucher 2140 to record return of $150 of the merchandise purchased on voucher 2139, Wards Lighting; voucher 2139 must be canceled and a new one for $800 must be issued

Aug. 15 issued voucher 2141 to Ellen Bates for semimonthly net wages of $736.25; FICA tax of $71.25 and federal income tax of $142.50 were withheld (debit Wages Expense $950)

Aug. 15 issued check 4150 in payment of voucher 2141

Aug. 18 issued voucher 2142 for $2,640 to Main Appliances for merchandise purchased; terms 2/10, n/30

Aug. 20 issued check 4151 in payment of voucher 2140

Aug. 23 issued voucher 2143 for $225 to Edison Telephone company for the phone bill

Aug. 25 issued check 4152 in payment of voucher 2136

Aug. 27 issued check 4153 in payment of voucher 2142

Aug. 30 issued voucher 2144 for $1,740 to Wards Lighting for merchandise purchased; terms 1/10, n/30

Aug. 31 issued voucher 2145 for semimonthly net wages to Ellen Bates for $736.25; FICA tax of $71.25 and federal income tax of $142.50 were withheld

Aug. 31 issued check 4154 in payment of voucher 2145

Instructions   *1. Enter the August transactions in a voucher register (page 71) and in a check register (page 110). (Do not enter July vouchers in the voucher register.) Except for July vouchers 2116 and*

2128, make notations in the voucher register when vouchers are paid. Purchases are recorded by the gross method.

2. *Total, crossfoot, and rule the voucher register and the check register.*

Problem 14.2
recording transactions in voucher register and check register (net method)

Wing Produce has the following unpaid vouchers as of February 28, 19XX. The vouchers were issued for purchases of merchandise.

Voucher No.	Voucher Date	Payee	Terms	Gross Amount
649	February 22	Arnie's Grocery	2/10, n/30	$1,000
670	February 27	B & B Market	1/10, n/30	1,500
676	February 28	Sil's Fast Foods	1/15, n/30	1,800

Purchases are recorded by the net method. The schedule of vouchers payable on February 28 is as follows.

Wing Produce
Schedule of Vouchers Payable
February 28, 19XX

649	Arnie's Grocery	$ 980
670	B & B Market	1,485
676	Sil's Fast Foods	1,782
	Total	$4,247

Following is a partial chart of accounts for Wing Produce.

101	Cash	501	Purchases
140	Prepaid Insurance	510	Freight In
205	Notes Payable	520	Purchases Discounts Lost
210	Vouchers Payable	610	Wages Expense
220	FICA Taxes Payable	620	Rent Expense
230	Employees Income Taxes Withheld	630	Utilities Expense
320	Barbara Wing, Drawing	640	Advertising Expense

Following are the transactions for March.

Mar. 1 issued voucher 681 for $1,000 to Barbara Wing, owner, for her personal use

Mar. 1   issued voucher 682 for $2,500 to Coastal Real Estate for August rent

Mar. 2   issued check 2101 in payment of voucher 681

Mar. 2   issued check 2102 in payment of voucher 682

Mar. 4   issued check 2103 in payment of voucher 649

Mar. 6   issued voucher 683 to Arnie's Grocery for purchase of merchandise costing $1,400; terms 2/10, n/30 (record purchases by the net method)

Mar. 7   issued voucher 684 for $425 to Ray's Trucking for delivering merchandise from Arnie's Grocery

Mar. 7   issued check 2104 in payment of voucher 684

Mar. 9   issued check 2105 in payment of voucher 670

Mar. 11 issued voucher 685 to Atlantic Market for purchase of merchandise costing $2,300; terms 2/10, n/30

Mar. 12 issued voucher 686 for $800 to National Insurance Company for fire insurance for the next 12 months.

Mar. 15 issued voucher 687 for $350 to People's Electric for payment of electricity bill

Mar. 15 issued check 2106 in payment of voucher 686

Mar. 15 issued check 2107 in payment of voucher 687

Mar. 16 issued check 2108 in payment of voucher 683

Mar. 19 issued voucher 688 for $500 to the Daily Tribune for advertising

Mar. 20 issued voucher 689 to Sil's Fast Foods for purchase of merchandise costing $2,200; terms 1/15, n/30

Mar. 21 issued check 2109 for payment of voucher 688

Mar. 21 issued 60-day, 14 percent note payable for $2,300 to Atlantic Market in settlement of voucher 685 (record the purchases discount lost in the Other Accounts debit column)

Mar. 23 issued check 2110 in payment of voucher 676

Mar. 25 issued voucher 690 to Atlantic Market for purchase of merchandise costing $800; terms 2/10, n/30

Mar. 27 issued voucher 691 for $210 to Bell Phone Company for phone bill

Mar. 28 issued check 2111 in payment of voucher 691

Mar. 29 issued voucher 692 to Arnie's Grocery for purchase of merchandise costing $420; terms 2/10, n/30

Mar. 30 issued voucher 693 to B & B Market for purchase of merchandise costing $1,740; terms 1/10, n/30

Mar. 31   issued voucher 694 to Robert Christofer for $1,572.50 for his monthly wage; FICA tax of $157.50 and federal income tax of $370 were withheld (debit Wages Expense for $2,100)

Mar. 31   issued check 2112 in payment of voucher 694

Instructions   1.   *Enter the March transactions in a voucher register (page 13) and in a check register (page 17). Do not enter February vouchers in the voucher register. Except for vouchers 649, 670, and 676, make notations in the voucher register when vouchers are paid. Purchases are recorded by the net method.*

2.   *Total, crossfoot, and rule the voucher register and the check register.*

3.   *Prepare a schedule of vouchers payable in alphabetical order as of March 31. Refer to the voucher register to obtain the numbers and the amounts of the vouchers that remain unpaid at the end of the month. The balance in the Vouchers Payable account on March 31 is $5,096.20.*

Problem 14.3
recording transactions in voucher register (gross method) and check register; posting; preparing schedule of vouchers payable

Everglades Industries has the following unpaid vouchers as of April 30, 19XX.

Voucher No.	Voucher Date	Payee	Terms	Gross Amount
1651	April 23	Florida Office Supply	2/15, n/30	$2,760
1665	April 26	Gulf Products	1/15, n/30	1,950
1680	April 28	Petersburg Products	2/10, n/30	1,730
1694	April 30	Panhandle Paper	2/10, n/30	3,400

A partial ledger and account balances are as follows.

Acct. No.	Account Titles	Balance
101	Cash	$22,490
130	Supplies	875
180	Office Equipment	12,640
201	Notes Payable	4,600
210	Vouchers Payable	9,840
220	FICA Taxes Payable	420
230	Employees Income Taxes Withheld	448
320	Warren Sandusky, Drawing	
501	Purchases	
505	Freight In	
510	Purchases Discounts	
520	Purchases Returns and Allowances	
610	Rent Expense	
615	Utilities Expense	
620	Wages Expense	

Transactions for May are as follows. Purchases are recorded by the gross method.

May 1   issued voucher 1703 to North State Properties for $2,000 for rent

May 1   issued voucher 1704 for $1,500 to Warren Sandusky, owner, for his personal use

May 2   issued check 4690 in payment of voucher 1703

May 3   issued check 4691 in payment of voucher 1651

May 4   issued check 4692 in payment of voucher 1704

May 6   issued vouchers 1705, 1706, 1707 for $1,300 each to Hardware, Inc., for purchase of computer; voucher 1705 is due in 10 days; 1706 is due in 30 days; and 1707 is due in 60 days; no discount is allowed

May 8   issued voucher 1708 for $3,750 to Florida Office Supply for purchase of merchandise; terms 2/15, n/30

May 9   issued voucher 1709 for $390 to Florida Power Company for payment of electricity bill

May 11 issued voucher 1710 to Gulf Products for $4,500 for merchandise purchased; terms 2/15, n/30

May 11 issued check 4693 in payment of voucher 1665

May 13 issued check 4694 in payment of voucher 1709

May 14 issued voucher 1711 to Eileen Goodman for $1,071 for semimonthly wages; $105 was withheld for FICA taxes and $224 for

	federal income taxes (debit Wages Expense for $1,400)
May 15	issued check 4695 in payment of voucher 1711
May 15	issued voucher 1712 for $868 payable to Jacksonville First Bank for deposit of FICA and federal income taxes (debit FICA Taxes Payable for $420 and debit Employees Income Taxes Withheld for $448)
May 15	issued check 4696 in payment of voucher 1705
May 15	issued check 4697 in payment of voucher 1712
May 19	issued voucher 1713 for $420 to Petersburg Products for purchase of merchandise; terms 2/10, n/30
May 20	issued voucher 1714 for $320 to Petersburg Products to record the return of $100 of merchandise purchased on voucher 1713; voucher 1713 must be canceled
May 22	issued voucher 1715 for $170 to Best Office Wares for purchase of supplies for the office; terms 2/15, n/30
May 23	issued 90-day, 12 percent note payable to Florida Office Supply in payment of voucher 1708
May 24	issued voucher 1716 for $176 to Florida Phone Company in payment of phone bill
May 25	issued vouchers 1717, 1718, and 1719 for $1,500 each to Gulf Products to obtain a time extension in payment of voucher 1710; voucher 1717 is due in 30 days; 1718 is due in 45 days; and 1719 is due in 60 days; no discount is allowed
May 26	issued check 4698 in payment of voucher 1716
May 26	issued voucher 1720 for $2,700 to Southern Supply for merchandise purchased; terms 2/10, n/30
May 27	issued voucher 1721 for $2,200 to record return of $500 of merchandise purchased from Southern Supply on voucher 1720; voucher 1720 must be canceled
May 27	issued voucher 1722 for $875 to Gulf Products for merchandise purchased; terms 1/15, n/30
May 28	issued check 4699 in payment of voucher 1714
May 30	issued voucher 1723 to Eileen Goodman for $1,071 for semimonthly wages; $105 was withheld for FICA taxes and $224 for federal income taxes
May 30	issued voucher 1724 for $99 to Overnite Trucking for delivering merchandise from Gulf Products
May 30	issued check 4700 in payment of voucher 1680
May 31	issued check 4701 in payment of voucher 1723
May 31	issued check 4702 in payment of voucher 1724

Instructions

1. *Record transactions in a voucher register (page 39) and in a check register (page 62). Do not enter April vouchers in the voucher register. Except for vouchers 1651, 1665, 1680, and 1694, make notations in the voucher register when vouchers are paid.*

2. *Total, crossfoot, and rule the voucher register and the check register.*

3. *Post the voucher register in this fashion.*
   a. *Post the totals to the appropriate general ledger accounts and place the ledger account numbers beneath the column totals. Enter VR39 in the PR column of the ledger accounts.*
   b. *Post the amounts in the other debit and credit columns individually. Place the ledger account numbers in the PR column of the voucher register opposite the account titles. Place an X beneath the other column totals.*

4. *Post the totals of the check register and place the ledger account number in parentheses beneath the column total. Enter CkR62 in the PR column of the ledger accounts.*

5. *Prepare a schedule of vouchers payable by listing in alphabetical order the unpaid vouchers in the voucher register. Compare the total with the balance in the Vouchers Payable account in the general ledger.*

Problem 14.4

recording transactions in voucher register (net method) and check register; posting; preparing schedule of vouchers payable

Barstow Children's Outlet has the following unpaid vouchers as of July 31, 19XX. Purchases are recorded by the net method.

Voucher No.	Voucher Date	Payee	Terms	Gross Amount	Net Amount
321	July 11	Ely Kids' Klothes	2/10, n/30	$5,000	$4,900.00
327	July 29	Reno Boys' Wares	1/15, n/30	2,120	2,098.80

Following are a partial chart of accounts and account balances.

105	Cash	$34,640.19
110	Prepaid Insurance	0
120	Supplies	920.00
130	Office Equipment	12,760.00
201	Notes Payable	0
210	Vouchers Payable	6,998.80
220	FICA Taxes Payable	402.00
230	Employees Income Taxes Withheld	428.80
501	Purchases	
510	Freight In	
600	Purchases Discounts Lost	
610	Wages Expense	
620	Rent Expense	
630	Utilities Expense	
640	Advertising Expense	
650	Interest Expense	

Transactions for August are as follows. Purchases are recorded by the net method.

Aug. 1 issued $5,000, 30-day, 12 percent note payable to Ely Kids' Klothes in payment of voucher 321 (debit Purchases Discounts Lost for $100 because the invoice was not paid within the discount period)

Aug. 1 issued voucher 374 to Nevada Limited for $2,700 for rent

Aug. 1 issued check 617 in payment of voucher 374

Aug. 2 issued voucher 375 to Desert Products for purchase of merchandise costing $2,310; terms 2/10, n/30 (record by the net method)

Aug. 3 issued voucher 376 to Western States Freight for $360 for delivering purchase made on August 2

Aug. 4 issued check 618 in payment of voucher 376

Aug. 7 issued voucher 377 to Nevada Power for $295 for payment of electric bill

Aug. 8 issued voucher 378 for $500 to Reno Union for advertising

Aug. 9 issued check 619 in payment of voucher 377

Aug. 9 issued check 620 in payment of voucher 378

Aug. 9 issued voucher 379 for $1,800 to Nevada Insurance Company for payment of two-year fire insurance policy

Aug. 11 issued check 621 in payment of voucher 375

Aug. 13 issued check 622 in payment of voucher 379

Aug. 15 issued voucher 380 for $830.80 payable to Nevada National Bank for payment of FICA and employees income tax due

(debit FICA Taxes Payable for $402 and debit Employees Income Taxes Withheld for $428.80)

Aug. 15   issued voucher 381 to Ely Kids' Klothes for purchase of merchandise costing $4,970; terms 2/10, n/30

Aug. 15   issued voucher 382 to Betty Beverage for $1,025.10 for semimonthly wages; FICA tax of $100.50 and federal income tax of $214.40 were withheld (debit Wages Expense for $1,340)

Aug. 15   issued check 623 in payment of voucher 382

Aug. 15   issued check 624 in payment of voucher 380

Aug. 17   issued voucher 383 for $8,100 to Sands Computers for purchase of a computer and printer; terms n/30

Aug. 18   issued voucher 384 for $145 to Office Warehouse for purchase of supplies; terms n/30

Aug. 20   issued check 625 in payment of voucher 384

Aug. 23   issued voucher 385 to Desert Products for purchase of merchandise costing $2,240; terms 2/10, n/30

Aug. 24   issued voucher 386 for $150 to Nevada Telephone for phone bill

Aug. 24   issued check 626 in payment of voucher 386

Aug. 25   issued voucher 387 to Ely Kids' Klothes for purchase of merchandise costing $980; terms 2/10, n/30

Aug. 26   issued vouchers 388, 389, and 390 for $2,700 each to obtain an extension of time in which to pay voucher 383, Sands Computers; voucher 388 is due immediately; 389 is due on September 30; and 390 is due on October 31; no discount is allowed

Aug. 26   issued check 627 in payment of voucher 388

Aug. 30   issued voucher 391 to Betty Beverage for $1,025.10 for semimonthly wages; FICA tax of $100.50 and federal income tax of $214.40 were withheld

Aug. 31   issued check 628 in payment of voucher 327

Aug. 31   issued check 629 in payment of voucher 391

Aug. 31   issued check 630 in payment of voucher 381

Aug. 31   issued voucher 392 in payment of August 1 note to Ely Kids' Klothes (first calculate the interest due!)

Aug. 31   issued check 631 in payment of voucher 392

Instructions   1.   *Record transactions in a voucher register (page 27) and in a check register (page 35). Do not enter July vouchers in the voucher register. Except for vouchers 321 and 327, make notations in the voucher register when vouchers are paid. Record purchases by the net method.*

2. *Total, crossfoot, and rule the voucher register and the check register.*

3. *Post the voucher register in this fashion.*
    a. *Post the totals to the appropriate general ledger accounts and place the ledger account numbers beneath the column totals. Enter VR27 in the PR column of the ledger accounts.*
    b. *Post the amounts in the other debit and credit columns individually. Place the ledger account numbers in the PR column of the voucher register opposite the account titles. Place an X beneath the other column totals.*

4. *Post the totals of the check register and place the ledger account number in parentheses beneath the column total. Enter CkR35 in the PR column of the ledger accounts.*

5. *Prepare a schedule of vouchers payable by listing in alphabetical order the unpaid vouchers in the voucher register. Compare the total with the balance in the Vouchers Payable account in the general ledger.*

CHAPTER 15

Inventory Valuation

When you have completed this chapter, you should

1. have a better understanding of accounting terminology.

2. be able to tell what effects an error in inventory valuation will have on net income.

3. be able to determine the cost of the ending inventory by the specific identification method, the average cost method, the first-in, first-out (FIFO) method, and the last-in, first-out (LIFO) method.

4. be able to determine the cost of the ending inventory by the lower-of-cost-or-market rule.

5. be able to estimate the value of the ending inventory by the retail method and by the gross profit method.

6. be able to keep records for a perpetual inventory system.

The Merchandise Inventory account is the only account that appears on both the income statement and the balance sheet. On the balance sheet, the ending inventory is listed as a current asset; on the income statement, both the beginning and ending inventories are used to calculate cost of goods sold.

In most businesses, the value of the ending inventory is determined at regular intervals by a physical count; this is called a periodic inventory. The number of items in each category is determined, and that number is multiplied by the cost of each item to arrive at the total cost of the inventory. These processes, you may recall, are called *taking the inventory* and *pricing the inventory*. When the periodic inventory system is being used, debits are made to the Purchases account when merchandise is acquired. The cost of the goods sold is not calculated until the value of the ending inventory is determined and the income statement is prepared. The periodic inventory system is normally used by businesses that sell numerous items of relatively low unit value, such as a hardware or grocery store.

Businesses with relatively few items of high unit value for sale (such as automobiles or diamonds), normally maintain a perpetual inventory system that keeps track at all times of the number of units on hand and their cost. Under this system, when merchandise is bought, its cost is debited to the Merchandise Inventory account; when goods are sold, their cost is debited to a Cost of Goods Sold account and the Merchandise Inventory account is credited. In this chapter, the emphasis will be on periodic inventory systems.

THE EFFECTS OF INVENTORY VALUATION ON NET INCOME

On the income statement, ending inventory is subtracted from cost of goods available for sale to arrive at the cost of goods sold figure.

Beginning Inventory	$ 39,000
+ Net Purchases	+ 86,000
Cost of Goods Available for Sale	$125,000
− Ending Inventory	− 54,000
Cost of Goods Sold	**$ 71,000**

The cost of goods available for sale figure represents both goods sold and goods not sold. The cost of the goods *not* sold, the ending inventory, is subtracted from the cost of the goods *available* for sale to determine the cost of the goods that were sold.

If the ending inventory is incorrectly valued, it will have a direct effect on the net income for the period. Assume, for example, that the ending inventory of the Vintage Auto Racers' Supply House is actually $54,000, but in taking and pricing the inventory, it was erroneously determined to be $64,000. In other words, the ending inventory is overstated by $10,000. The following income statements reveal the effects of an overstatement of the ending inventory.

Vintage Auto Racers' Supply House
Income Statement
For Year Ended December 31, Year 1

	With Ending Inventory Stated Correctly		With Ending Inventory Overstated	
Sales		$100,000		$100,000
Cost of Goods Sold				
Beginning Inventory	$ 39,000		$ 39,000	
Purchases	+ 86,000		+ 86,000	
Cost of Goods Available for Sale	$ 125,000		$125,000	
Less:				
Ending Inventory	**−54,000**		**−64,000**	
Cost of Goods Sold		− 71,000		− 61,000
Gross Profit on Sales		**$ 29,000**		**$39,000**
Operating Expenses		13,000		13,000
Net Income		**$ 16,000**		**$26,000**

A careful study of the income statement for Vintage Auto Racers' Supply House shows that when the ending inventory is overstated, the cost of goods sold will be understated and that the gross and net income will be overstated. If the reverse were true, if the ending inventory were *under*stated, the net income would also be understated by the same amount.

The ending inventory for the current accounting period becomes the beginning inventory for the next accounting period. When the ending inventory is incorrect, then the beginning inventory for the next period is incorrect. For the Vintage Auto Racers' Supply House, the $10,000 overstated ending inventory will become a $10,000 overstated beginning inventory in Year 2. The effects of a $10,000 overstatement of beginning inventory are shown as follows:

Vintage Auto Racers' Supply House
Income Statement
For Year Ended December 31, Year 2

	With Beginning Inventory Stated Correctly		With Beginning Inventory Overstated	
Sales		$ 120,000		$120,000
Cost of Goods Sold				
Beginning Inventory	**$54,000**		**$64,000**	
Net Purchases	+ 91,000		+ 91,000	
Cost of Goods Available for Sale	$145,000		$155,000	
Less: Ending Inventory	− 59,000		− 59,000	
Cost of Goods Sold		− 86,000		− 96,000
Gross Profit on Sales		**$34,000**		**$24,000**
Operating Expenses		− 17,000		− 17,000
Net Income		**$17,000**		**$ 7,000**

When the beginning inventory is *over*stated, the net income is *under*stated by the same amount. By the same token, when beginning inventory is *under*stated, the net income will be *over*stated. When beginning inventory is misstated, then the figures for cost of goods available for sale and gross profit will also be wrong.

When the ending inventory of Year 1 is incorrect, that error is carried forward to Year 2. Although the total net income for the two years will be the same as if no error had been made, the picture presented by the income statements will be highly inaccurate. The net income figure appears to be fluctuating greatly, when in fact, it is an accounting error that makes it appear so. For the Vintage Auto Racers' Supply House, the two-year income statement data is as follows.

	With Inventory Correctly Stated, Net Income Will Be . . .	With Inventory Incorrectly Stated, Net Income Will Be . . .
Year 1	$16,000	$26,000
Year 2	17,000	7,000
Total for 2 Years	$33,000	$33,000

When the inventories are correctly stated, the net income for each of the two years is stable. When they are incorrectly stated, however, the net income picture is distorted considerably. The Vintage Auto Racers' Supply House appears to be operating far less profitably the second year when, in fact, it has maintained and even improved on its net income position the second year.

For management and owners, the financial statements must reflect an accurate picture of what is occurring each accounting period. Correct inventory valuation methods will help ensure accuracy in reporting. The following summarizes the effects of misstatements in inventory valuation.

	When Ending Inventory Is Understated	When Ending Inventory Is Overstated	When Beginning Inventory Is Understated	When Beginning Inventory Is Overstated
Net Income Is	Understated	Overstated	Overstated	Understated

METHODS OF VALUING THE INVENTORY

There are many different methods for determining the cost of the inventory. If the number of items for sale is small, then the specific identification method may be used. This method is not practical, however, for a clothing store, a variety store, a hardware store, and so on. Pricing the inventory is complicated by the fact that items for sale were purchased at different times and at different prices, and there is no way to determine exactly which items are left and at what price they were purchased. Thus, several methods have been devised to calculate the cost value of the ending inventory. Each method produces a different ending inventory figure, and thus a different net income. Merchants may choose which method best suits their purposes. The following inventory data will be used to illustrate the various methods of pricing the inventory.

	Number of Units	Cost per Unit	Total Cost
Beginning Inventory	100	$50	$ 5,000
Purchases			
Purchase, February 2	20	55	1,100
Purchase, April 9	105	60	6,300
Purchase, July 18	80	65	5,200
Purchase, October 26	40	70	2,800
Total Goods Available for Sale	345		$20,400
Number of Units Sold	215		
Units in Ending Inventory	130		

Specific Identification Method

When the units in the ending inventory can be pinpointed to a particular purchase date, they may be valued at the prices shown on the purchase invoices. This may or may not be the method chosen by the accountant, however. Assume that 500 wool sweaters of a certain type are on hand at the end of the accounting period. These were purchased at various times by the merchant in prices ranging from $40 to $60. If the sweaters are sold for $95 each, is the gross profit $55 or $35? The specific identification method is best used with items that are of high unit value, such as automobiles.

   Assume the following data in calculating the cost of the ending inventory by the specific identification method.

Inventory Items on Hand	Calculation of Cost	Total Cost
25 Units from Beginning Inventory	25 × $50	$1,250
16 Units from February 2 Purchase	16 × 55	880
20 Units from April 9 Purchase	20 × 60	1,200
40 Units from July 18 Purchase	40 × 65	2,600
29 Units from October 26 Purchase	29 × 70	2,030
Ending Inventory (Specific Identification)	130	$7,960

The preceding inventory data can be used to determine that the goods available for sale (beginning inventory plus purchases) are $20,400; thus the cost of goods sold by the specific identification method is as follows.

Goods Available for Sale	$20,400
Minus Ending Inventory	− 7,960
Cost of Goods Sold	$12,440

Average Cost Method

This method of inventory valuation averages the cost of all items available for sale during the period. The total goods available for sale figure is divided by the total number of units available for sale to determine the weighted-average cost per unit. The cost per unit is then multiplied by the number of units in the ending inventory.

Total Goods Available for Sale	$20,400.00
Total Units Available for Sale	345
Average Unit Price: $20,400 ÷ 345 =	$59.13
Average Unit Price × Number of Units in Ending Inventory: $59.13 × 130 =	$7,686.90

The value of the ending inventory, using the average cost method, is $7,686.90. This figure is not the same as the one obtained by using the specific identification method. Each one produces a different cost of goods sold, and thus a different net profit.

Goods Available for Sale	$20,400.00
Minus Ending Inventory	− 7,686.90
Cost of Goods Sold	$12,713.10

A common criticism of the average cost method is that it gives no more weight to prices at the end of the accounting period (current prices) than it does to prices at the beginning of the period.

First-in, First-out Method

The first-in, first-out (FIFO) method assumes that the first merchandise purchased is the first merchandise sold. Thus, the merchandise on hand, the ending inventory, is made up of the most recently purchased items. This method assumes that merchants will try to get rid of their oldest merchandise first to make room for the new. The calculation for the FIFO method is as follows.

Inventory Items on Hand	Calculation of Cost	Total Cost
40 Units from October 26 Purchase	40 × $70	$2,800
80 Units from July 18 Purchase	80 × 65	5,200
10 Units from April 9 Purchase	10 × 60	600
Ending Inventory (FIFO)	130	$8,600

inflation
a period of rising prices

This method of inventory valuation may be used by any merchant, even if the flow of goods sold is not first-in, first-out. During a period of **inflation,** the FIFO method presents a higher ending inventory figure than other methods. When a relatively *large* amount is assigned to the ending inventory, a relatively *small* amount is assigned to cost of goods sold (Goods Available for Sale − Ending Inventory = Cost of Goods Sold). This results in a higher net income, and many accountants argue that the method should not be chosen for that reason. A lower net income figure results in lower taxes and thus in more cash being available to replace the merchandise that has been sold. In an inflationary period, the cost of replacing merchandise sold is constantly rising.

In support of the FIFO method, it may be said that the ending inventory is valued at a cost that more accurately reflects the current prices. The calculation for cost of goods sold using the FIFO method of inventory valuation is as follows.

Goods Available for Sale	$20,400
Minus Ending Inventory	− 8,600
Cost of Goods Sold	$11,800

Last-in, First-out Method

The last-in, first-out (LIFO) method assumes that the last merchandise purchased is the first merchandise sold—an unlikely assumption. During a period of inflation, the cost of the ending inventory by this method will be low because the first merchandise purchased was bought at lower prices. Following is the calculation for the LIFO method of inventory valuation.

Inventory Items on Hand	Calculation of Cost	Total Cost
100 Units from Beginning Inventory	100 × $50	$5,000
20 Units from February 2 Purchase	20 × 55	1,100
10 Units from April 9 Purchase	10 × 60	600
Ending Inventory (LIFO)	130	$6,700

Although the flow of goods sold does not match the last-in, first-out assumption, a great deal of support exists for the use of the LIFO method because it produces a lower ending inventory figure and a cost of goods sold that reflects current market prices. The *lower* the ending inventory, the *higher* the cost of goods sold and the *lower* the net income. During a period of inflation, accountants argue, the cost of goods sold should reflect current high (and rising) prices. The calculation for cost of goods sold using the LIFO method follows.

Goods Available for Sale	$20,400
Minus Ending Inventory	− 6,700
Cost of Goods Sold	$13,700

Comparing the Methods of Inventory Valuation

Four common methods of determining the value of the ending inventory have been discussed. Each produces a different ending inventory value, a different cost of goods sold, and a different gross and net profit. The following income statement data compares the results of the four methods. Assume that sales for the accounting period are $25,000.

	Specific Identification Method	Average Cost Method	First-in, First-out Method	Last-in, First-out Method
Sales	$ 25,000	$ 25,000.00	$ 25,000	$ 25,000
Cost of Goods Sold				
Beginning Inventory	$ 5,000	$ 5,000.00	$ 5,000	$ 5,000
Net Purchases	15,400	15,400.00	15,400	15,400
Cost of Goods Available for Sale	$ 20,400	$ 20,400.00	$ 20,400	$ 20,400
Less: Ending Inventory	**− 7,960**	**− 7,686.90**	**− 8,600**	**− 6,700**
Cost of Goods Sold	$ 12,440	$ 12,713.10	$ 11,800	$ 13,700
Gross Profit	**$12,560**	**$12,286.90**	**$13,200**	**$11,300**
Expenses	− 7,000	− 7,000.00	− 7,000	− 7,000
Net Income	**$ 5,560**	**$ 5,286.90**	**$ 6,200**	**$ 4,300**

This comparison of different methods of inventory valuation, based on a period of rising prices, shows clearly that using the LIFO method will produce the greatest cost of goods sold and the least amount of gross profit and net income. Under the same economic conditions, using the FIFO method will assign the *least* amount to cost of goods sold and the *greatest* amount to gross profit and net income. If prices are falling, the results will be the opposite.

Which Inventory Valuation Method Is Best?

It is not possible to say which method of valuation is best. Accountants will select a method considering the effect each will have on the balance sheet and the income statement. On the income statement, the inventory figures are used in calculating cost of goods sold—or in matching costs against revenue. The inventory method chosen may have a significant effect on net income. On the balance sheet, the inventory is listed as one of the current assets.

The current ratio, a comparison of the current assets to the current liabilities, is used to determine the short-term debt-paying ability of a business.

Consistency in Valuing Inventories

consistency principle
using the same accounting method consistently

Although merchants and accountants have a wide range of choices when determining which inventory valuation method to use, they may not arbitrarily change methods once one has been adopted. The **consistency principle** requires that once an accounting method is chosen, it will be used consistently when reporting to management, investors, lenders, and so on. If this were not the case, accounting methods could be changed regularly to present more favorable pictures of the company's operating results or net worth; also, comparisons of financial statements from one year to the next would be impossible.

disclosure principle
accounting principle which states that all relevant information not obvious in the financial statements be included as footnotes in them

If a company does choose to change its method of inventory valuation, the change should be disclosed in footnotes to the financial statements and the effect on net income should be shown. The **disclosure principle** requires that all information that is necessary for the reader of the financial statements to correctly interpret them be included in the footnotes.

LOWER-OF-COST-OR-MARKET RULE

So far, the discussion of inventory valuation has centered on cost as the basis for pricing the inventory. Sometimes, however, another basis may be used. Assume, for example, that the replacement cost of inventory items, referred to as the current market value, has fallen. If such is the case, the merchant may have to lower selling prices, too, and may even have to sell the items at a loss. In this case, accountants may prefer to value the inventory at the actual cost price or the current market price, whichever is lower.

conservatism
selecting the accounting option which presents the less favorable financial position

This method of inventory valuation illustrates **conservatism** in asset valuation. Ideally accountants base their figures on objective evidence, but when their individual judgments are required, they will tend toward the option which produces the lower figure for asset valuation or income determination, or the less favorable financial position.

There are many considerations when using the lower-of-cost-or-market rule, which will be covered in a later accounting course. It is possible, for example, that the current replacement cost (market price) may decline while actual selling prices do not.

Application of Lower-of-Cost-or-Market to the Total Inventory

When the total inventory is the basis for the valuation, the number of individual items in each category is listed and multiplied by (1) the actual cost per item and (2) the actual current market price. The total cost and the total market price are then determined, and the inventory is valued at the lower of the two figures.

		Unit Cost		Total Cost	
Item	**Quantity**	**Cost Price**	**Market Price**	**Cost Price**	**Market Price**
W	25	$250	$210	$ 6,250	$ 5,250
X	20	500	565	10,000	11,300
Y	125	125	150	15,625	18,750
Z	200	225	175	45,000	35,000
Totals				$76,875	$70,300

If the lower-of-cost-or-market rule is applied to the inventory as a whole, then the valuation will be $70,300; the current replacement cost of the inventory is lower than the actual cost.

Application of the Lower-of-Cost-or-Market Rule on an Item-by-Item Basis

The lower-of-cost-or-market rule may be applied to the inventory on an item-by-item basis, rather than to the inventory as a whole. This method is illustrated as follows.

Item	Quantity	Unit Cost		Total Cost		Lower of Cost or Market
		Cost Price	Market Price	Cost Price	Market Price	
W	25	$250	$210	$ 6,250	$ 5,250	$ 5,250
X	20	500	565	10,000	11,300	10,000
Y	125	125	150	15,625	18,750	15,625
Z	200	225	175	45,000	35,000	35,000
Total						$65,875

The inventory valuation is different when the lower-of-cost-or-market rule is applied on an item-by-item basis ($65,875 as opposed to $70,300 when the rule is applied to the inventory as a whole). Either method is acceptable; individual preference will determine which is used.

ESTIMATING THE VALUE OF THE ENDING INVENTORY

Many times management wants to know the value of the ending inventory without having to undergo the expensive and time-consuming act of physically counting the merchandise. For example, if financial statements are prepared monthly, physically counting the merchandise once or twice a year and estimating it at the other times may be sufficient.

There are other instances when an estimation of the ending inventory is necessary or desirable. If, for example, the merchandise in a store is destroyed by fire, the value of the inventory must be estimated. Frequently an estimation is used after an actual physical count as a double check on the taking and pricing of the inventory.

The Gross Profit Method of Estimating the Ending Inventory

When using the gross profit method, accountants assume that the *rate* of gross profit is about the same from period to period. The rate of gross profit is determined by dividing the dollar amount of the gross profit by the dollar amount of net sales. (Net sales on the income statement is always considered to be 100 percent.)

Net Sales	$200,000	100%	
Minus Cost of Goods Sold	−120,000	− 60%	(120,000 ÷ 200,000 = .60)
Gross Profit	$ 80,000	40%	(80,000 ÷ 200,000 = .40)

The gross profit rate (40 percent) plus the cost of goods sold rate (60 percent) equals 100 percent; this is because cost of goods sold is subtracted from net sales (100 percent) to arrive at the gross profit figure.

$$\text{Sales} - \text{Cost of Goods Sold} = \text{Gross Profit}$$

Thus, when the rate of gross profit is known, the rate for cost of goods sold must also be known because one is subtracted from 100 percent (net sales) to get the other.

The normal procedure for determining Cost of Goods Sold is to subtract the ending inventory from the Cost of Goods Available for Sale as follows.

Cost of Goods Sold	
Beginning Inventory	$ 75,000
Plus Net Purchases	+ 40,000
Cost of Goods Available for Sale	$115,000
Minus Ending Inventory	**−74,000**
Cost of Goods Sold	**$41,000**

When using the gross profit method for estimating the ending inventory, the cost of goods sold will be subtracted from the cost of goods available for sale to determine the value of the ending inventory. The preceding cost of goods sold calculation shows that this is the opposite of what is done on the income statement where ending inventory is subtracted from goods available for sale to determine the amount of the cost of goods sold.

The steps in estimating the value of the ending inventory by the gross profit method are as follows.

1. Using the general ledger records, determine the cost of goods available for sale by adding the beginning inventory to the net purchases.

2. Using the gross profit percentage from previous periods, determine the cost of goods sold percentage by subtracting the gross profit percentage from 100 percent.

3. Multiply the cost of goods sold percentage by the net sales to determine the dollar value of cost of goods sold.

4. Subtract the cost of goods sold from the cost of goods available for sale to arrive at the estimated ending inventory figure.

Assume that Shirts Unlimited had a beginning inventory of $100,000 on April 1. Net purchases in April are $40,000 and net sales are $65,000. Assume further that Shirts Unlimited has a normal gross profit rate of 45 percent of net sales. With this information, the value of the inventory on April 30 may be determined by the gross profit method as follows.

1. Calculate the cost of goods available for sale.

Beginning Inventory	$100,000
Plus Net Purchases	+ 40,000
Cost of Goods Available for Sale	$140,000

2. Calculate the cost of goods sold percentage.

$$\text{Net Sales} - \text{Gross Profit} = \text{Cost of Goods Sold}$$
$$100\% \quad - \quad 45\% \quad = \quad 55\%$$

3. Calculate the cost of goods sold.

$$\text{Net Sales} \times \text{Cost of Goods Sold Percentage}$$
$$\$65,000 \times \quad 55\% \, (.55) = \$35,750$$

4. Deduct cost of goods sold from the cost of goods available for sale to arrive at the estimated ending inventory.

$140,000
− 35,750
$104,250

The Retail Method of Estimating the Ending Inventory

Many retail stores, such as department stores, use this method for estimating the value of the ending inventory. Store owners must keep records showing the value of the beginning inventory and purchases at both cost and retail (selling price). By adding beginning inventory to net purchases, the cost of goods available for sale may be determined; in this case, cost of goods available for sale will reflect both cost and retail price. If actual sales are subtracted from total goods available for sale at retail, then the result will be the ending inventory. The ending inventory obtained in this manner will be valued at the *retail* price; thus, it must be converted to cost before it will be useful for presentation on the financial statements. Following are the steps for estimating the value of the ending inventory by the retail method. Assume that net sales for the period are $48,000.

1. **Determine the cost of goods available for sale for the period at both cost price and retail (selling price).**

	Cost Price	Retail Price
Goods Available for Sale		
Beginning Inventory	$ 30,000	$ 44,000
Net Purchases	+ 21,000	+ 31,000
Cost of Goods Available for Sale	**$51,000**	**$75,000**

2. **Deduct net sales ($48,000) from the cost of goods available for sale at retail to determine the ending inventory at retail.**

		− 48,000
Ending Inventory at Retail		**$ 27,000**

3. **Determine cost percentage. It is the ratio of cost to selling price and is obtained by dividing cost by selling price.**

$$\$51,000 \div \$75,000 = .68 = 68\%$$

4. **Convert ending inventory at retail to ending inventory at cost by using the cost percentage.**

$$.68 \times \$27,000 = \$18,360$$

Ending Inventory at Cost	**$18,360**

When merchants place price tags on their merchandise, they normally indicate only the selling price on the tag. When this is the case, the actual physical inventory will be taken at retail rather than at cost prices, and the retail method for estimating the value of the ending inventory may be used to convert the retail price of the inventory to the cost price. This method is much simpler than locating invoices and looking up the cost price of each item in the ending inventory. The procedure for converting the value of the ending inventory from retail to cost is the same as shown in steps 3 and 4 of the previous illustration. The retail method always assumes that the goods available for sale figure has been used to determine the cost percentage (the ratio of cost to selling price).

THE PERPETUAL INVENTORY SYSTEM

The perpetual inventory system is used by firms that sell items of high unit cost. Each time merchandise for resale is bought, its cost is debited to the account Merchandise Inventory. When merchandise is sold, two entries are required: one debits Cost of Goods Sold and credits Merchandise Inventory, thereby updating the inventory account; and the other debits Accounts Receivable (or Cash) and credits Sales. Assume that ten television sets are purchased at a cost of $300 each. The entry to record the purchase under the perpetual inventory system would be as follows.

	GENERAL JOURNAL			Page 49	
Date	Description	Post. Ref.	Debit	Credit	
19XX *Mar.* 4	*Merchandise Inventory*		3000 —		
	Accounts Payable			3000 —	
	To Record Purchase of Ten Television Sets;				
	Item C-521				

Assume further that two days after the purchase, one of the television sets is sold on account for $420. The following two entries are required at the time of sale.

GENERAL JOURNAL					Page 50	
Date	Description	Post. Ref.	Debit		Credit	
19XX Mar. 6	Accounts Receivable		4 2 0 —			
	Sales				4 2 0 —	
	To Record Sale of Item C-521					
6	Cost of Goods Sold		3 0 0 —			
	Merchandise Inventory				3 0 0 —	
	To Record Cost of Item C-521; Television Set					

With the perpetual inventory system, the cost of goods sold is available for every item at the time of sale. A subsidiary ledger is maintained in which a record is kept of all items purchased and sold—the purchase date, the unit cost, the sale date, the cost of the item sold, the number of units remaining, and the cost of units remaining in stock. The Merchandise Inventory account is a control account; every time merchandise is purchased, the account is debited; and when merchandise is sold, it is credited (for the cost). The balance in the Merchandise Inventory account should equal the total of the balances in the subsidiary ledger for merchandise.

If the number of items sold on account is large enough to warrant it, a special cost of goods sold column may be added to the sales journal. At the time of recording the sale, the bookkeeper will refer to the subsidiary ledger to determine the cost of the item sold. At the end of the accounting period, the cost of goods sold will not have to be calculated as with the periodic inventory system; the dollar amount will be available by simply referring to the ledger account for Cost of Goods Sold. The ending inventory figure is available, too, simply by referring to the Merchandise Inventory account. Strong internal control, however, demands that perpetual inventory records be verified by a physical inventory at regular intervals.

Following is a subsidiary ledger card for Item B-489, a product in an appliance store. Records are maintained on the first-in, first-out basis. Every time Item B-489 is purchased, the number of units and their cost is recorded and a balance is calculated. When Item B-489 is sold, the number of units sold and their cost are recorded; also, the number of items *remaining* in stock and their cost are calculated, using the FIFO method. The number of items on hand and their total cost are always available when using the perpetual inventory system.

| Item | B-489 | | | | | | Maximum No. | 35 | |
| | | | | | | | Minimum No. | 7 | |

| | ITEMS PURCHASED | | | ITEMS SOLD | | | BALANCE | | |
Date	Units	Unit Cost	Total	Units	Unit Cost	Total	Units	Unit Cost	Balance
2/1							20	$100	$2,000
2/6				4	$100	$400	16	$100	$1,600
2/10	12	$105	$1,250				16 / 12	{$100 / $105	$2,860
2/15				13	$100	$1,300	3 / 12	{$100 / $105	$1,560
2/22				3 / 5	$100 / $105	$300 / $525	7	$105	$735
2/28	18	$110	$1,980				7 / 18	{$105 / $110	$2,715

A careful study of the subsidiary ledger card for Item B-489 shows that the beginning inventory consisted of 20 units costing $100 each. On February 6, four units were sold, leaving 16 units. On February 10, 12 items were purchased; the inventory then consisted of 16 units costing $100 each and 12 units costing $105 each. On February 15, when 13 items were sold, those items were taken from the $100 inventory because we are using the FIFO method. This left three items costing $100 each and 12 costing $105 each. When the next sale of eight items was made, this depleted the three items remaining in the $100 category, plus five taken from the $105 group. Only seven items remain after this sale, and because seven is the minimum "safe level," more merchandise is ordered, this time at a cost of $110. The ending inventory, then, contains seven items costing $105 each and 18 items costing $110 each.

The Merchandise Inventory account will contain the total figures for all the subsidiary ledger cards and will provide a check on the accuracy of the subsidiary ledger, just as the Accounts Receivable and Accounts Payable control accounts do. Again, a periodic inventory must be taken at regular intervals to help ensure against theft or employee fraud.

The inventory records of many companies are kept on computer. At the time of sale, the item number is entered on the cash register and the number of those items in inventory is instantly calculated, along with the total cost. When this system is used, however, a periodic physical inventory is still required to maintain strong internal control.

SUMMARY

The Merchandise Inventory account appears on the income statement as part of the calculation for cost of goods sold and on the balance sheet as a current asset. It is the only account that appears on both financial statements, and a misstatement of its cost directly affects the dollar amount of the gross and net income. Because the ending inventory figure is subtracted from the cost of goods available for sale on the income statement to determine the cost of goods sold, a misstatement of the ending inventory will cause a misstatement of cost of goods sold and gross and net income. If the ending inventory is erroneously *overstated* by $5,000, then gross and net income will also be *overstated* by $5,000. If ending inventory is *understated* by $5,000, then gross and net income will be *understated* by $5,000. Conversely, if the beginning inventory is *overstated* by $5,000, then the gross and net income figures will be *understated* by $5,000; and if beginning inventory is *understated* by $5,000, then gross and net income will be *overstated* by $5,000. Thus, the importance of accurately taking and pricing the inventory (or estimating it) cannot be overstressed.

The value of the ending inventory may be determined by many different methods. The specific identification method is used by stores that sell relatively few different items that have a high unit value. This method assumes that each item sold can be identified as coming from a particular purchase. This method calculates a very accurate cost of goods sold figure, but is not practical for most stores.

The average cost method determines a weighted-average cost for each item in the inventory by dividing the total cost of the goods available for sale by the total number of items for sale. The average cost per unit is then multiplied by the total number of units in the ending inventory to determine the value of the ending inventory.

The first-in, first-out (FIFO) method of inventory valuation assumes that the first merchandise purchased will be the first sold. Thus, the ending inventory consists of the most recently purchased items. This method, during a period of inflation, produces a higher ending inventory figure than the other methods, and thus a higher net income. A criticism of this method states that a high net income is not realistic in a period of rising prices, because larger and larger amounts of cash must be spent to replace items sold and the cost of goods sold should realistically reflect that.

The last-in, first-out method assumes that the last merchandise purchased is the first merchandise sold. Although this is not realistic in terms of the physical movement of merchandise, the method does produce a lower ending inventory figure and thus a lower net income. Thus, the LIFO method is commonly used by merchants. Their justification is that a higher cost of goods sold figure and thus a lower gross and net income is realistic because during a period of inflation the cost of replacing merchandise is constantly rising.

The consistency principle of accounting maintains that whichever method is chosen should be used consistently so that financial statements may be intelligently compared. If a change in inventory methods is made, then the disclosure principle requires that the information be presented in a footnote to the financial statements, because such a change may have dramatic effects on the net income.

Conservatism usually prevails when assets are valued; thus the lower-of-cost-or-market rule was devised. This method of inventory valuation allows the lowest of the cost or the market price to be used when valuing the ending inventory.

Because periodic inventories are costly and time consuming, merchants will choose to estimate the value of the ending inventory most of the time. The periodic inventory is then used to verify that the estimates are accurate. One method of estimating the ending inventory is the gross profit method, which assumes a relatively stable gross profit percentage. The gross profit percentage is subtracted from 100 percent (net sales) to determine the percentage for cost of goods sold. The cost of goods sold percentage is multiplied by the net sales to determine the dollar amount of cost of goods sold; that amount is then subtracted from the goods available for sale to determine the value of the ending inventory.

Another method for estimating the value of the ending inventory is the retail method. This method determines the cost of goods available for sale at both cost and retail from the information in the general ledger accounts. The sales are then subtracted from the goods available for sale at retail to determine the value of the ending inventory at retail prices. By using the ratio of cost price to sales, the ending inventory at retail is converted to cost.

Many stores choose to use the perpetual inventory system. Electronic cash registers help by updating inventory records as each sale is made. When using this method, the Merchandise Inventory account is debited each time merchandise for resale is purchased. When merchandise is sold, two entries are required—one to record the sale price and one to update the inventory account and to record the cost of goods sold.

Review of Accounting Terminology

Following is a list of the accounting terminology for this chapter.

conservatism   disclosure principle
consistency principle   inflation

Fill in the blank with the correct word or term from the list.

1. The accounting principle which states that once an accounting method has been chosen that it be used regularly is the _____.

2. The tendency of an accountant to select the accounting option which produces the least favorable financial position is referred to as _____.

3. A period of rising prices is referred to as a period of _____.

4. The principle which states that all information be disclosed in footnotes if that information is necessary for correct interpretation of the financial statements is referred to as the _____.

Match the following words and terms on the left with the definitions on the right.

5. conservatism

6. consistency principle

7. disclosure principle

8. inflation

a. the tendency of accountants to select the accounting option which presents the least favorable financial position

b. the principle which states that once an accounting method is chosen, it will be used consistently

c. a period of rising prices

d. the principle which states that all relevant accounting information not evident in the financial statements themselves will be disclosed in footnotes

Exercises

Exercise 15.1
calculating income statement amounts

From the following account titles and balances, calculate (a) net sales, (b) net purchases, (c) cost of goods available for sale, (d) cost of goods sold, and (e) gross profit for the month of June 19XX.

Sales	$104,000
Sales Returns and Allowances	1,800
Sales Discounts	2,200
Purchases	55,000
Freight In	3,000
Purchases Returns and Allowances	750
Purchases Discounts	1,700
Merchandise Inventory, June 1	42,000
Merchandise Inventory, June 30	40,500

Exercise 15.2
calculating gross profit and cost of goods sold percentages

Net sales are $50,000, net purchases are $35,000, beginning inventory is $40,000, and ending inventory is $39,000. Calculate (a) the gross profit percentage and (b) the cost of goods sold percentage.

Exercise 15.3
determining cost percentage

Beginning inventory is $25,000 at cost price and $42,000 at retail price. Net purchases are $20,000 at cost and $30,000 at retail.

a. Calculate goods available for sale at cost and at retail.
b. Using the goods available for sale figures, determine the cost percentage (ratio of cost to retail prices).

Exercise 15.4
calculating ending inventory using specific identification and average cost methods

Following are the data relating to the inventory of Power Products for the year.

	Number of Units	Cost per Unit	Total Cost
Beginning Inventory,			
January 1	9,000	$5.00	$ 45,000
Purchase, February 14	18,000	5.20	93,600
Purchase, April 9	37,000	5.35	197,950
Purchase, July 20	26,000	5.70	148,200
Purchase, November 2	9,500	6.00	57,000
Total Goods Available for			
Sale	99,500		$541,750
Number of Units Sold	58,000		
Ending Inventory,			
December 31	41,500		

a. Figure the cost of the ending inventory using the specific identification method assuming that 4,000 units on hand are from the February 14 purchase; 17,000 are from the April 9 purchase; 15,500 are from the July 20 purchase; and 5,000 are from the November 2 purchase.
b. Calculate the cost of the ending inventory using the average cost method of inventory valuation. Round the cost per unit to the nearest penny.

Exercise 15.5
calculating ending inventory using the FIFO and LIFO methods

Using the inventory data in Exercise 15.4, compute the value of the ending inventory using (a) the FIFO method of inventory valuation and (b) the LIFO method.

Exercise 15.6
calculating ending inventory using the average cost, FIFO, and LIFO methods

Beginning inventory and purchases for the year for Big Jack Tools are as follows.

	Number of Units	Cost per Unit	Total Cost
Beginning Inventory, January 1	520	$10.00	$ 5,200
Purchase, February 28	1,040	10.90	11,336
Purchase, May 20	1,510	11.40	17,214
Purchase, August 31	900	11.70	10,530
Purchase, November 19	460	12.20	5,612
Goods Available for Sale	4,430		$49,892
Number of Units Sold	2,700		
Ending Inventory, December 31	1,730		

Calculate the value of the ending inventory by (a) the average cost method (round to the nearest cent); (b) the FIFO method; and (c) the LIFO method.

Exercise 15.7
calculating ending inventory using the lower-of-cost-or-market rule

The following information is available about items in the ending inventory of Court Clothes on December 31.

		Cost per Unit	
Item	Number of Units	Cost	Market
L	130	$ 92	$ 98
M	75	310	290
N	70	220	245
O	84	450	495

a. Calculate the value of the ending inventory using the lower-of-cost-or-market rule applying the rule to the inventory as a whole.

b. Calculate the value of the ending inventory using the lower-of-cost-or-market rule applying the rule on an item-by-item basis.

Exercise 15.8
estimating ending inventory using the retail method

Harold's Plumbing Supplies wishes to estimate the value of the ending inventory on October 31. Following are the data compiled by Harold's bookkeeper. Calculate the value of the ending inventory by the retail method.

	Cost Price	Retail Price
Merchandise Inventory, September 30	$450,000	$750,000
Net Purchases, October	307,200	512,000
Net Sales, October		690,000

Exercise 15.9
estimating ending inventory using the gross profit method

After a major fire on March 30, Wilson's Pet Supplies wishes to estimate the value of its ending inventory. The accounting records show the cost of the inventory on March 1 was $60,000, net purchases during March were $130,000, and net sales were $178,000. During the past several years, the gross profit rate was, on the average, 35 percent of net sales. Calculate the cost of the ending inventory using the gross profit method.

Exercise 15.10
journalizing for a perpetual inventory system

Wizard Electronics uses the perpetual inventory system. When goods for resale are purchased, Merchandise Inventory is debited and Cash or Accounts Payable is credited. When goods are sold, two entries are made: (1) the first debits Accounts Receivable (or Cash) and credits Sales for the sale price; and (2) the second debits Cost of Goods Sold and credits Merchandise Inventory for the *cost* of the merchandise that was sold. Record in a general journal (page 28) the following transactions for Wizard Electronics.

July 1 Purchased eight video recorders on account, item VR-42435, at $290 each

July 4 Purchased ten compact disc players on account, item CD-60421, at $210 each

July 6 Sold one video recorder for $400 cash, item VR-42435

July 9 Sold one compact disc player on account for $340; item CD-60421

Exercise 15.11
determining effect of errors in ending inventory valuation

Sales are $120,000, beginning inventory is $49,000, net purchases are $92,000, and ending inventory is $53,000.

a. Calculate the cost of goods available for sale and the gross profit.

b. If the ending inventory is erroneously overstated by $5,000, what will the gross profit figure be?

c. If the ending inventory is erroneously understated by $5,000, what will the gross profit be?

Exercise 15.12
determining effect of errors in beginning inventory valuation

Sales are $69,000, beginning inventory is $26,000, net purchases are $45,000, and ending inventory is $24,000.

a. Calculate the cost of goods available for sale and the gross profit.

b. If the beginning inventory is erroneously overstated by $5,000, what will the gross profit be?

c. If the beginning inventory is erroneously understated by $5,000, what will the gross profit be?

Problems

Problem 15.1
calculating the value of ending inventory using the average cost, FIFO, and LIFO methods

Inventory data for Sports Car Accessories are as follows.

	Number of Units	Cost Per Unit	Total Cost
Inventory, January 1	1,100	$ 9.00	$ 9,900
Purchase, March 4	640	9.60	6,144
Purchase, May 17	1,560	10.20	15,912
Purchase, September 30	730	10.80	7,884
Purchase, December 1	920	11.10	10,212
Goods Available for Sale	4,950		$50,052
Units Sold	3,110		
Inventory, December 31	1,840		

Instructions

1. *Compute the cost of the ending inventory by the average cost method of inventory valuation. (Round cost per unit to the nearest cent.)*

2. *Compute the cost of the ending inventory by the FIFO method.*

3. *Compute the cost of the ending inventory by the LIFO method.*

4. *Answer the following questions about the methods of inventory valuation.*

   a. *Which method of inventory valuation produces the most realistic cost of goods sold in the light of rising prices?*

   b. *Which method of inventory valuation produces the least amount of gross profit in the light of rising prices?*

Problem 15.2
comparing gross profit, net income, and percentages using the LIFO and FIFO methods of inventory valuation

Following are the data for goods available for sale for the Shenandoah Feed Store for the month of August 19XX.

Beginning Inventory	$27,000
Net Purchases	+59,000
Cost of Goods Available for Sale	$86,000

Ending inventory calculated by the LIFO method of inventory valuation is $23,100; by the FIFO method, it is $31,600. Net sales for the period are $85,000 and expenses are $12,750.

Instructions

1. Assuming the LIFO method of inventory valuation, calculate (a) cost of goods sold, (b) gross profit, (c) net income, (d) gross profit percentage, and (e) net income percentage.

2. Assuming the FIFO method of inventory valuation, calculate (a) cost of goods sold, (b) gross profit, (c) net income, (d) gross profit percentage, and (e) net income percentage.

Problem 15.3
determining effects of errors in beginning and ending inventory valuations

The income statement data for La Plata Beauty Supplies for Years 1 and 2 follow.

	Year 1		Year 2	
Sales		$200,000		$220,000
Cost of Goods Sold				
Beginning Inventory	$ 80,000		$115,000	
Net Purchases	+165,000		+155,000	
Cost of Goods Available				
for Sale	$245,000		$270,000	
Ending Inventory	−115,000		−95,000	
Cost of Goods Sold		$130,000		175,000
Gross Profit		$ 70,000		$ 45,000
Expenses		−30,000		−32,000
Net Income		$ 40,000		$ 13,000

Instructions

1. Assume that at the end of Year 1, the ending inventory of $115,000 is overstated by $10,000. Considering the effect that

such an error would have, calculate the correct (a) cost of goods sold, (b) gross profit, and (c) net income for Year 1.

2. After determining the corrected gross and net income for Year 1, calculate the correct (a) gross profit percentage and (b) net income percentage.

3. Assume further that the beginning inventory for Year 2 is overstated by $10,000. Considering the effect that such an error would have, calculate the correct (a) cost of goods sold, (b) gross profit, and (c) net income for Year 2.

4. After determining the corrected gross and net income for Year 2, calculate the correct (a) gross profit percentage and (b) net income percentage. Round to the nearest tenth of a percent when necessary.

5. Assuming that the owner's capital account at the beginning of Year 1 was $72,400 and that drawing was $12,650 during Year 1 and $17,870 during Year 2, calculate the correct ending capital figures for Year 1 and Year 2.

Problem 15.4
estimating the value of ending inventory using the gross profit method

The warehouse of the Ft. Lauderdale Company was destroyed by fire on August 31 of Year 3. The management offices, filing cabinets, computers, and accounting records were not damaged. Ft. Lauderdale Company's last periodic inventory was taken on December 31 of Year 2. The accountants gathered the following information from the company records so that the value of the ending inventory could be estimated before preparing financial statements after the fire.

Inventory, January 1, Year 3	$200,000
Net Purchases	+ 80,000
Goods Available for Sale	$280,000

The gross profit rate for the past three years has been consistently 40 percent. Sales from January 1 to August 31 are $162,000; Sales Returns and Allowances are $7,400; and Sales Discounts are $4,600.

Instructions *Determine the value of the ending inventory by the gross profit method.*

Problem 15.5
estimating the value of ending inventory using the retail method

Following are some of the income statement data at cost and at retail for the month of March for Bridgeton Sweaters, a retail store.

	Cost	Retail
Beginning Inventory	$25,350	$40,025
Net Purchases	+24,650	+39,975
Goods Available for Sale	$50,000	$80,000

Sales for the month were $37,920.

Instructions　*Estimate the cost of the ending inventory by the retail method of inventory valuation. Round to the nearest tenth of a percent where required.*

Problem 15.6
preparing an inventory card and journal entries for the perpetual inventory system

Inver Hills Cycle Shop uses a perpetual inventory system. Purchases and sales of each type of product are kept on an inventory card. Following is the record of the beginning inventory, purchases, and sales for the month of September.

Item CY 40-176

Sept.　1　inventory, 12 units costing $90 each
Sept.　5　sold nine units at $120 each
Sept.　9　purchased ten units on account at $100 each
Sept. 17　sold eight units at $130
Sept. 20　purchased 13 units on account at $105
Sept. 28　sold seven units at $140
Sept. 30　purchased five units on account at $110

Instructions　*1.　On an inventory card, record the beginning inventory, purchases, and sales of Item CY 40-176 for the month of September. Assume the FIFO system.*

2.　Record the transactions for purchases and sales in a general journal, page 71. Assume that purchases were all on account and that sales were for cash. Remember, when recording sales, two entries are required: one to record the actual sale and one to record the cost of goods sold.

ccounts Receivable Valuation

LEARNING OBJECTIVES

When you have completed this chapter, you should

1 have a basic understanding of the functions of a credit department.

2. be able to write off an uncollectible amount using the direct charge-off method.

3. have a basic understanding of the valuation account Allowance for Doubtful Accounts.

4. be able to estimate uncollectible accounts expense using the percentage of net sales method and the aging of accounts receivable method.

5. be able to write off an uncollectible account using the allowance method.

6. be able to determine the net realizable value of Accounts Receivable and present Accounts Receivable and Allowance for Doubtful Accounts on the balance sheet.

7. be able to prepare the journal entry to exhange an account receivable for a note receivable.

8. be able to record the default of a note receivable.

Most Americans make purchases on credit. In fact, many people would not be able to buy a new car or a home without it. The extension of credit for all types of items has been partly responsible for the rapidly expanding business economy over the years. Retail stores have found that they can greatly increase their profits by extending credit; in most cases they make money on the items sold and on the interest charged the customer.

One of the costs of the businesses extending credit, unfortunately, is the cost of bad debts. A business cannot know for sure when granting credit to a customer whether he or she will pay. This chapter examines the various accounting methods of dealing with accounts receivable and uncollectible accounts.

THE CREDIT DEPARTMENT

Obviously, stores do not want to grant credit to persons who are not likely to pay their debts, thus credit departments are established to determine which customers are worthy of receiving credit privileges and how much credit should be granted to each. To make a decision as to whom credit should be granted, credit departments call on the services of a national credit-rating institution such as Dun and Bradstreet, Inc., or local credit bureaus or credit-rating agencies. Such agencies keep current files on credit customers and establish credit ratings. They will also conduct special investigations if asked.

If a business customer asks for credit, the credit department will analyze the financial statements, looking carefully at the trend of operating results. Those audited by certified public accountants are preferable to those that have not been audited.

UNCOLLECTIBLE ACCOUNTS

No matter how thorough the credit department is, inevitably some customers will not pay— they are referred to as *uncollectible accounts* or *bad debts*. A certain amount of uncollectible accounts expense is expected and is in no way alarming. If a company had

no bad debts at all, it could be suspected that the credit department was being too conservative in granting credit and costing the
company money in lost sales.

THE DIRECT CHARGE-OFF METHOD OF RECORDING
UNCOLLECTIBLE ACCOUNTS

Under this method, when a customer's account is determined to be
uncollectible, it is simply written off at that time by a debit to
Uncollectible Accounts Expense and a credit to Accounts Receivable. This method is satisfactory for a company that sells all or
most of its products or services for cash, or for a company that has
very little uncollectible accounts expense. The Tax Reform Act of
1986 stipulates that the direct charge-off method is the only acceptable method for determining taxable income.

Assume, for example, that B. J. Swensen declared bankruptcy
and his past-due account of $550 was determined on April 1 to be
uncollectible. The general journal entry to record the bad debt is
as follows.

GENERAL JOURNAL					Page 47
Date	Description	Post. Ref.	Debit	Credit	
19XX *Apr.* 1	*Uncollectible Accounts Expense*		550 —		
	Accounts Receivable/B. J. Swensen			550 —	
	To Write Off Past-Due Account				

Failure to record the entry would result in expenses being understated and net income and assets being overstated. If, at some
later date, B. J. Swensen finds himself in a position to pay the debt,
the accounts receivable will be reentered on the books by reversing the original April 1 entry writing off his account. Also at that
time, the receipt of the cash will be recorded. The entries are as
follows on November 15.

GENERAL JOURNAL					Page 75	
Date	Description	Post. Ref.	Debit		Credit	
19XX *Nov.* 15	*Accounts Receivable/B. J. Swensen*		5 5 0 —			
	Uncollectible Accounts Expense				5 5 0 —	
	To Reinstate Account					
15	*Cash*		5 5 0 —			
	Accounts Receivable/B. J. Swensen				5 5 0 —	
	To Record Payment in Full					

MATCHING BAD DEBT LOSSES WITH REVENUE

The direct charge-off method is not an acceptable method for most companies because its use violates the matching principle, which requires that the expenses for a particular accounting period be deducted from the revenue generated during that same time period. A bad debt that arises from a sale in Year 1 should be treated as an expense in Year 1. Because when granting credit a business cannot know which accounts will become uncollectible, an estimate should be made of the *amount* of the bad debts expected. The amount of estimated uncollectible accounts expense is recorded as an adjusting entry.

ALLOWANCE FOR DOUBTFUL ACCOUNTS

valuation
assessing the value of something

net realizable value
accounts receivable minus allowance for doubtful accounts

The adjusting entry to record the estimated bad debts requires a debit to Uncollectible Accounts Expense and a credit to an account called Allowance for Doubtful Accounts. Allowance for Doubtful Accounts is a contra-asset account; it is also referred to as a **valuation** account because it subtracts from Accounts Receivable on the balance sheet to determine the **net realizable value** of that account. While the Uncollectible Accounts Expense account will be closed into the Income Summary account each period, the balance of Allowance for Doubtful Accounts will appear on the balance sheet in the following manner.

Hobbs Clothing for Children
Partial Balance Sheet
December 31, Year 4

Current Assets		
Cash		$ 80,000
Notes Receivable		64,000
Accounts Receivable	$125,000	
Less: Allowance for Doubtful Accounts	6,250	118,750
Merchandise Inventory		349,000
Total Current Assets		$712,390

The Allowance for Doubtful Accounts, which has a credit balance, subtracts from Accounts Receivable to produce the net realizable value, $118,750.

THE CONSERVATIVE APPROACH TO ESTIMATING UNCOLLECTIBLE ACCOUNTS

When preparing a balance sheet, conservatism refers to the fact that bankers or other creditors would prefer to see assets valued at the lower end of a reasonable range of values. If, for example, a loan is granted to a customer based on high asset values and the customer is later unable to pay, the lender will look on the balance sheet as being at fault for helping to justify the loan. The larger the balance in Allowance for Doubtful Accounts, the lower the balance will be in Accounts Receivable. When conservatism is applied to the balance sheet, it is also applied to the income statement. A larger Uncollectible Accounts Expense account will result in a lower net income.

THE ALLOWANCE METHOD OF ESTIMATING UNCOLLECTIBLE ACCOUNTS EXPENSE

There are several acceptable methods for estimating the amount of uncollectible accounts expense. One method assumes that a certain percentage of net sales will be uncollectible; another classifies the accounts receivable into age groups, determining how far past due each account is and what percentage of each age group will be uncollectible; and still another assumes a percentage of total accounts receivable will be uncollectible.

Percentage of Net Sales Method

The percentage of net sales method is referred to as the income statement approach to estimating uncollectible accounts expense and is a relatively easy method to use. Assume, for example, that for the past several years 1.5 percent of net sales of the Oxnard Shoe Company has been uncollectible. Following are the December 31 account balances for the related accounts before adjusting entries are made on Year 4.

	Debit	Credit
Sales		$542,000
Sales Returns and Allowances	$4,500	
Sales Discounts	3,700	
Allowance for Doubtful Accounts		915

Net sales for Year 4 amount to $533,800 ($542,000 − $4,500 − $3,700). One and one-half percent of net sales is $8,007 ($533,800 × .015). The following adjusting entry for the Oxnard Shoe Company will be made to record the bad debts for the year.

GENERAL JOURNAL					Page *129*
Date	Description	Post. Ref.	Debit	Credit	
Dec. *31*	*Uncollectible Accounts Expense*		8 0 0 7 —		
	Allowance for Doubtful Accounts			8 0 0 7 —	
	To Record Uncollectible Accounts Expense for the				
	Year— $542,000— ($4,500 + $3,700) × .015				

The percentage of net sales method for valuing accounts receivable stresses the relationship between net sales and uncollectible accounts expense. The percentage used (1.5 percent in this case) will be reviewed each year to determine if it remains valid. If there is a period of high inflation, for example, the percentage may have to be increased because customers will have decreasing ability to pay their debts. When estimating the amount of uncollectible accounts expense by the percentage of net sales method, ignore any balance that appears in Allowance for Doubtful Accounts.

Writing Off an Uncollectible Account

When the credit department decides that a customer's account is uncollectible, it should be written off, which means that the account will be brought to a zero balance. This is accomplished by a debit to Allowance for Doubtful Accounts and a credit to Accounts Receivable (which will be posted to both the general ledger and the accounts receivable subsidiary ledger). Uncollectible Accounts Expense is not debited when the account is written off, because the entire year's expense has been estimated already and debited to Uncollectible Accounts Expense as an adjusting entry. For the Oxnard Shoe Company, $8,007 would have been included among the deductions from revenue on the income statement prepared after the adjusting and closing of the books. The Uncollectible Accounts Expense account would have been closed along with the other expenses at the end of Year 4, but the Allowance for Doubtful Accounts, a contra-asset account, will show a balance of $8,922 ($8,007 plus the December 31 balance of $915) at the beginning of the next accounting period, Year 5.

Assume that on January 14, Year 5, the $500 account of Peter Hawes is determined to be uncollectible by the Oxnard Shoe Company accountants. The journal entry to write off the account is as follows.

GENERAL JOURNAL					Page 142
Date	Description	Post. Ref.	Debit	Credit	
19XX **Jan. 14**	*Allowance for Doubtful Accounts*		500 —		
	Accounts Receivable/Peter Hawes			500 —	
	To Write Off Past-Due Account				

The Allowance for Doubtful Accounts looks like this after the entry is posted.

Allowance for Doubtful Accounts

1/14/Yr. 5	*500*	*12/31/Yr. 4 Bal.*	*915*
		12/31/Yr. 4 Adj.	*8,007*

Each time an account is written off, Allowance for Doubtful Accounts is debited. If the uncollectible accounts estimate is exact, the account will have a zero balance at the end of the accounting period. It would be extremely unusual, however, for any estimate to be exact, so the account usually has a balance at the end of the period. Assume the following write-offs for the Oxnard Shoe Company for Year 5.

Allowance for Doubtful Accounts

1/14/Yr. 5	500	12/31/Yr. 4	Bal.	915
2/24/Yr. 5	1,400	12/31/Yr. 4	Adj.	8,007
4/8/Yr. 5	2,000			8,922
6/20/Yr. 5	650		972	
8/1/Yr. 5	2,500			
11/11/Yr. 5	900			
	7,950			

The credit balance of the account after the last write-off is $972. This was, then, a very close estimate of bad debts; a credit balance in the account at the end of the accounting period indicates that bad debts were overestimated. A debit balance indicates that uncollectible accounts were underestimated. Again, the balance in Allowance for Doubtful Accounts at the time of the adjusting entry should be ignored when estimating the amount of uncollectible accounts expense by the percentage of net sales method.

Aging Accounts Receivable

Another method used to estimate uncollectible accounts expense is referred to as the balance sheet approach and involves determining the age of all of the customers' accounts. Aging the accounts receivable is a process whereby an accountant determines how many accounts are not yet due, how many are 30, 60, or 90 days past due, and how many are over 90 days past due. Following is the accounts receivable aging schedule for the Tucson Saddlery Company.

Tucson Saddlery Company
Accounts Receivable Aging Schedule
December 31, Year 6

Customer Name	Total	Not Yet Due	1–30 Days Past Due	31–60 Days Past Due	61–90 Days Past Due	Over 90 Days Past Due
Abbott	$ 400	$ 400				
Costa	1,000	950	$ 50			
Davidson	1,980	1,000	980			
Gregory	5,700		1,200	$1,800	$1,700	$1,000
Nguyen	850	850				
St. James	1,425	825	600			
Sanchez	3,275	2,000	1,000	275		
All Others	9,880	4,940	2,865	1,185	500	390
Totals	$24,510	$10,965	$6,695	$3,260	$2,200	$1,390
Percentage	100%	45%	27%	13%	9%	6%

From past experience, an accountant may determine what percentage of each age category will be uncollectible. Logically, the further past due an account is, the less likely it is to be collected. Assume, for example, that for accounts not yet due, 2 percent are estimated to be uncollectible; for accounts 1–30 days past due, 4 percent are estimated to be uncollectible; for accounts 31–60 days past due, 9 percent are estimated to be uncollectible; for accounts 61–90 days past due, 20 percent are estimated to be uncollectible; and for accounts over 90 days past due, 50 percent are estimated to be uncollectible. From this information, the total estimated amount of uncollectible accounts expense may be determined as follows.

Tucson Saddlery Company
Age Groups of Accounts Receivable
December 31, Year 6

	Amount	Percentage Estimated To Be Uncollectible	Dollar Value of Estimated Uncollectible Accounts
Net yet due	$10,965	2	$ 219.30
1–30 days past due	6,695	4	267.80
31–60 days past due	3,260	9	293.40
61–90 days past due	2,200	20	440.00
Over 90 days past due	1,390	50	695.00
Totals	$24,510		$1,915.50

Once the estimated amount of uncollectible accounts has been determined, then the adjusting entry may be prepared. Unlike the income statement approach, which uses a percentage of net sales, when using the balance sheet approach, the accountant must first refer to the ledger account Allowance for Doubtful Accounts. If that account has a balance in it (which for all practical purposes, it will have), it must be taken into consideration.

Assume, for example, that Allowance for Doubtful Accounts appears as follows before the Year 6 adjusting entries have been posted for the Tucson Saddlery Company.

Allowance for Doubtful Accounts

	12/31 Bal. 450

From the aging of the accounts receivable, accountants for the Tucson Saddlery Company determined that uncollectible accounts would be $1,915.50 for the year. The $450 credit balance in Allowance for Doubtful Accounts indicates that for the previous year, their estimate was too large. Therefore, for this year, the $450 is subtracted from the new estimate, $1,915.50, to arrive at the amount of uncollectible accounts expense ($1,915.50 − $450.00 = $1,465.50). The adjusting entry is as follows.

GENERAL JOURNAL				Page 63
Date	Description	Post. Ref.	Debit	Credit
19XX Dec. 31	Uncollectible Accounts Expense		1 4 6 5 50	
	Allowance for Doubtful Accounts			1 4 6 5 50
	To Record Uncollectible Accounts Expense for			
	the Year— ($1,915.50 − $450.00 = $1,465.50)			

If the Allowance for Doubtful Accounts had a debit balance when the new estimate was determined, indicating that for the previous year the estimate was too small, then the balance would be added to the new estimate. Assume that the Allowance for Doubtful Accounts appears as follows.

Allowance for Doubtful Accounts

12/31 Bal. *450*	

The adjusting entry under these circumstances is as follows.

GENERAL JOURNAL						Page *63*
Date	Description	Post. Ref.	Debit		Credit	
19XX *Dec.* *31*	*Uncollectible Accounts Expense*		*2 3 6 5 50*			
	Allowance for Doubtful Accounts				*2 3 6 5 50*	
	To Record Uncollectible Accounts Expense for the					
	Year— ($1,915.50 + $450.00 = $2,365.50)					

Aging the accounts receivable emphasizes the relationship between bad debts and accounts receivable and thus is referred to as the balance sheet approach to valuing accounts receivable. This method is more accurate than the income statement approach, which takes a percentage of net sales each period. Aging the accounts receivable may alert management to problems related to uncollectible accounts. If, for example, the percentage of accounts over 90 days past due rose from 5 percent to 10 percent, it may be a signal to review credit policies.

NET REALIZABLE VALUE OF ACCOUNTS RECEIVABLE

Assume that the balance of accounts receivable for the Costa Mesa Clothiers is $7,500, and that the balance of Allowance for Doubtful Accounts is $800 on May 1, Year 8. The net realizable value of accounts receivable, then, is $6,700 ($7,500 − $800). Assume further that on May 11, the $400 account of Sara Poindexter is deemed to be worthless and is written off with the following entry.

GENERAL JOURNAL					Page *74*
Date	Description	Post. Ref.	Debit	Credit	
19XX *May* *11*	*Allowance for Doubtful Accounts*		*4 0 0 —*		
	Accounts Receivable/Sara Poindexter			*4 0 0 —*	
	To Write Off Past-Due Account				

The net realizable value of accounts receivable *does not change* after the write-off, as can be seen from the following.

	Before Write-Off	After Write-Off
Accounts Receivable	$7,500	$7,100
Less: Allowance for Doubtful Accounts	800	400
Net Realizable Value	$6,700	$6,700

The net realizable value does not change when an account is written off because Accounts Receivable and Allowance for Doubtful Accounts are reduced by the same amount. The write-off merely confirms the earlier estimate of bad debt losses, but does not record the expense again. The net realizable value is determined when the adjusting entry is made debiting Uncollectible Accounts Expense and crediting Allowance for Doubtful Accounts.

EXCHANGING AN ACCOUNT RECEIVABLE FOR A NOTE RECEIVABLE

A customer may ask for an extension of time for paying her or his account. In many cases, the merchant will grant the time extension but will ask the customer to sign a note and agree to pay interest on the money owed for the duration of the note.

Assume, for example, that Jake Hatfield owes the Austin Feed Store $3,500 and Jake's account is 120 days past due. On May 1, Jake asks for a 90-day time extension in which to pay his account.

The Austin Feed Store management agrees to the extension if Jake will sign a promissory note and pay 10 percent interest. The transaction to record the issuance of the note is as follows.

GENERAL JOURNAL							Page *41*
Date		Description	Post. Ref.	Debit		Credit	
19XX *May*	*1*	*Notes Receivable*		3 5 0 0 —			
		Accounts Receivable/Jake Hatfield				3 5 0 0 —	
		To Record Exchange of Account Receivable for a					
		90-Day, 10% Note					

Receiving Payment for the Note and Interest

When the note falls due on July 30, Jake must pay the principal (amount borrowed) plus the accrued interest. The interest is calculated as follows.

$$\text{Principal} \times \text{Rate} \times \text{Time} = \text{Interest}$$
$$\$3{,}500 \times .10 \times 90/360 = \$87.50$$

The amount to be paid to the Austin Feed Store is calculated as follows.

$$\text{Principal} + \text{Interest} = \text{Amount Due}$$
$$\$3{,}500.00 + \$87.50 = \$3{,}587.50$$

The journal entry on the books of the Austin Feed Store to record the receipt of money for the note and interest follows.

GENERAL JOURNAL							Page *53*
Date		Description	Post. Ref.	Debit		Credit	
19XX *July*	*30*	*Cash*		3 5 8 7 50			
		Notes Receivable				3 5 0 0 —	
		Interest Income				8 7 50	
		To Record Payment in Full of Note Plus Interest					

Defaulting on a Note Receivable

default
when the maker of a
note does not pay at
note's maturity

If a person does not pay a note on its maturity, he or she is said to **default.** If Jake Hatfield defaults on the note upon its maturity (July 30), the accountant will remove the note from the file and record it once more as an account receivable in the following manner.

GENERAL JOURNAL			Page *53*	
Date	Description	Post. Ref.	Debit	Credit
19XX *July 30*	*Accounts Receivable/Jake Hatfield*		*3 5 8 7 50*	
	Notes Receivable			*3 5 0 0 —*
	Interest Income			*8 7 50*
	To Record Default of 90-Day, 10% Note			

liquid
cash or easily con-
vertible to cash

This entry ensures that the notes receivable are all current and highly **liquid,** as they should be. The accounts receivable ledger will show the default, as a record is kept in it of all accounts receivable transactions with a particular customer.

Interest income is recorded because the Austin Feed Store still expects to collect both the principal and interest from Jake. If the account is finally declared to be a bad debt, then Allowance for Doubtful Accounts will be debited and Accounts Receivable credited for $3,587.50.

SUMMARY

Most Americans use credit on a regular basis, buying at least their major purchases (a home or car) with it. Businesses generally prefer to grant credit because it increases sales revenue and generates income from interest. On the other hand, the business has an added expense of uncollectible accounts. When extending credit, business management does not know which customers will not pay. Larger firms establish a credit department to determine which customers should receive credit privileges. The credit department maintains files on customers, establishes credit ratings, and uses the services of local and national credit-rating institutions.

Despite careful screening of customers, however, businesses expect that some will not pay. If it were otherwise, it could be suspected that the credit department was too conservative in granting credit and that many sales were lost because of this.

Accounting methods for uncollectible accounts have been developed over the years. The direct charge-off method may be used by small businesses and those who have very few bad debts. When an accountant decides that a customer's account is not collectible, an entry is made debiting Uncollectible Accounts Expense and crediting Accounts Receivable. This method is not acceptable for companies with large uncollectible accounts because it violates the matching principle which requires that the expenses for a particular accounting period be matched against the revenue for that same period. Thus, a bad debt that arises in Year 1 should be offset against the revenue from Year 1.

To accomplish this, an estimate is made of the amount of uncollectible accounts expense expected. The estimates are based on company history and may be a percentage of net sales, or may be determined by aging the accounts receivable. Once the estimate is determined, an adjusting entry is made debiting Uncollectible Accounts Expense and crediting Allowance for Doubtful Accounts. Allowance for Doubtful Accounts is a valuation account. It subtracts from accounts receivable on the balance sheet to produce the net realizable value of accounts receivable; it is classified as a contra-asset.

When estimating the amount of uncollectible accounts, accountants use the conservative approach which tends to value assets at the lower end of a reasonable range of values.

Under the allowance method, when a customer's account is determined to be uncollectible, Allowance for Doubtful Accounts is debited and Accounts Receivable is credited. The Allowance for Doubtful Accounts account begins the period with a credit balance, and if estimates of bad debts were exact, it would have a zero balance at the end of the year. This is seldom, if ever, the case, however, and Allowance for Doubtful Accounts finishes the accounting period with a balance. A credit balance indicates that bad debts were overestimated, and a debit balance indicates that they were underestimated. The balance in the account is ignored when estimating by using the income statement method (percentage of net sales or net credit sales); it must be taken into consideration, however, when using the balance sheet method (aging of accounts receivable).

If a customer decides to pay a debt after it has been written off, his or her account must first be reinstated by debiting Accounts Receivable and crediting Allowance for Doubtful Accounts before recording the receipt of the cash on account. The net realizable value of accounts receivable (Accounts Receivable minus Allowance for Doubtful Accounts) does not change when a customer's account is written off. It changes only when the adjusting entry debiting Uncollectible Accounts Expense and crediting Allowance for Doubtful Accounts is made.

Often when a customer needs more time to pay an account than originally agreed upon, a note receivable will be issued in exchange for the account receivable. The note will be for a specific time period and will usually stipulate a certain rate of interest. The accounting entry will debit Notes Receivable and credit Accounts Receivable; at the time of payment of the note, a credit to Interest Income will be recorded. If the maker of the note defaults, then the account receivable will be reinstated by a debit to Accounts Receivable and credits to Notes Receivable and Interest Income. This ensures that the notes receivable file is current and highly liquid, and that the accounts receivable file contains a complete record of transactions with each customer.

Review of Accounting Terminology

Following is a list of the accounting terminology for this chapter.

default	net realizable value
liquid	valuation

Fill in the blank with the correct word or term from the list.

1. An estimate of the value of an account is a/an _____.

2. An asset which is either cash or easily convertible into cash is referred to as a/an _____ asset.

3. The actual amount expected to be collected is the _____ of accounts receivable.

4. When the maker of a note does not pay at the note's maturity, he or she is said to _____.

Match the following words and terms on the left with the definitions on the right.

5. valuation	a. cash or easily convertible into cash
6. net realizable value	b. estimation of the worth of an account
7. default	c. when the maker of a note does not pay at the note's maturity
8. liquid	d. Accounts Receivable minus Allowance for Doubtful Accounts

Exercises

Exercise 16.1
journalizing uncollectible account by direct charge-off method

The San Antonio Bakery decided to write off the $750 account of the Breakfast House. San Antonio Bakery uses the direct charge-off method.

a. Prepare the general journal entry on April 18 to record the write-off.

b. If the accountant fails to write off this account, will net income be overstated or understated as a result? Will assets be overstated or understated as a result?

Exercise 16.2
journalizing uncollectible account by allowance method

Assume that the San Antonio Bakery uses the allowance method for writing off bad debts. If the $750 account of the Breakfast House is determined to be worthless, what general journal entry will be made on April 18 to write off the account?

Exercise 16.3
calculating net realizable value of accounts receivable

On January 1, the San Diego Bagel Works had accounts receivable totaling $24,300 and a balance in Allowance for Doubtful Accounts of $1,700. On January 19, the account of the California Eatery in the amount of $375 is written off.

a. Make the general journal entry to record the write-off of the account.

b. Calculate the net realizable value of accounts receivable before and after the write-off.

Exercise 16.4
writing off uncollectible account and subsequently reinstating it

The Moorpark Cycle Shop uses the allowance method for valuing accounts receivable. On July 14, the $420 account of Tanya Shreves was determined to be worthless and written off.

a. Prepare the general journal entry to write off the account.

b. On October 31, Tanya pays the $420 previously owed to the Moorpark Cycle Shop. Prepare the general journal entries to reinstate Tanya's account receivable on the books and record the cash received.

Exercise 16.5
journalizing adjusting entry to record uncollectible accounts expense by income statement method

At the end of Year 6, before adjusting entries are made, Reedley Auto Accessories Shop had recorded sales of $450,000; sales returns and allowances of $2,750; and sales discounts of $5,050. Reedley uses the income statement approach to estimating bad debts, and experience shows that approximately 1 percent of net sales will be uncollectible.

a. Prepare the adjusting entry to record Uncollectible Accounts Expense if the Allowance for Doubtful Accounts has a credit balance at year end of $650.

b. Prepare the adjusting entry to record Uncollectible Accounts Expense if the Allowance for Doubtful Accounts has a debit balance at year end of $510.

Exercise 16.6
calculating uncollectible accounts expense using income statement and balance sheet approaches

The trial balance of the Costa Mesa Gift Shop shows the following at the end of Year 9 before adjusting entries are prepared.

Account Titles	Debit	Credit
Sales		$575,000
Sales Returns and Allowances	$ 4,960	
Sales Discounts	5,050	
Accounts Receivable	143,750	
Allowance for Doubtful Accounts		1,590

Calculate the uncollectible accounts expense for the year assuming the following:

1. The income statement approach: 1.5 percent of net sales is estimated to be uncollectible.

2. The income statement approach: 1 percent of total credit sales is estimated to be uncollectible (65 percent of total sales are on account). Do not subtract Sales Returns and Allowances or Sales Discounts for the calculation.

3. The balance sheet approach: aging of the accounts receivable indicates an estimate of uncollectible accounts of $5,750.

Exercise 16.7
journalizing uncollectible accounts expense and write-off of account

The unadjusted trial balance of the Pima Novelty Shop showed the following at the end of Year 4.

Account Titles	Debit	Credit
Sales		$1,420,000
Sales Returns and Allowances	$ 21,600	
Sales Discounts	24,830	
Allowance for Doubtful Accounts	1,980	
Accounts Receivable	150,760	

An aging of the accounts receivable estimates that $14,600 will be uncollectible for the year.

a. Prepare the general journal entry on December 31 to record the uncollectible accounts expense using the balance sheet approach.

b. Prepare the general journal entry on February 3, Year 5, to write off the $740 account of Tom Gentry.

c. Calculate the net realizable value of accounts receivable both before and after the write-off of Tom Gentry's account.

Exercise 16.8
journalizing default on note and subsequent write-off

On September 1, the Hillsboro Book Warehouse agreed to give a 12 percent, 60-day note to the Book Worm in exchange for its past-due account receivable of $1,500. On October 31, the Book Worm defaulted on the note. The accountant for the Hillsboro Book Warehouse prepared the general journal entry to reinstate the account receivable of the Book Worm. On December 4, the Hillsboro Book Warehouse decided that the account was uncollectible and wrote it off. Prepare the general journal entries for the Hillsboro Book Warehouse on September 1, October 31, and December 4.

Problems

Problem 16.1
journalizing for uncollectible accounts expense by income statement method and subsequent write-offs

The Provo Electrical Supply makes all sales on credit and has in the past estimated uncollectible accounts expense to be 1 percent of net sales. This year (Year 5), however, there is a large debit balance in Allowance for Doubtful Accounts indicating that the previous year's estimates have been understated. The accountants, therefore, decided to raise the percentage to 1.5 percent of net sales for this year's estimate of uncollectible accounts. Related accounts and balances for the Provo Electrical Supply are as follows.

Account Titles	Debit	Credit
Accounts Receivable	$110,000	
Allowance for Doubtful Accounts	2,400	
Sales		$775,000
Sales Returns and Allowances	7,840	
Sales Discounts	8,690	

Instructions

1. *Prepare the year end adjusting entry to record uncollectible accounts expense.*

2. *Prepare the general journal entry on March 4, Year 6, to write off the balance of the account of the Utah Light House, which has recently declared bankruptcy. Its account balance is $895, of which $120 cash is received via the bankruptcy court.*

3. *Prepare the general journal entry on May 9, Year 6, to write off the $640 account of the Salt Lake Contractor's Supply.*

4. *Prepare the general journal entries on September 1, Year 6, to reinstate the account of the Salt Lake Contractor's Supply and to record the receipt of a check for $640.*

Problem 16.2
journalizing for uncollectible accounts expense by balance sheet method

The Chicago Printing Factory uses the balance sheet approach to estimate bad debts. An aging of the accounts receivable reveals the following for Year 9.

Accounts not yet due	$ 84,900
Accounts 1–30 days past due	44,600
Accounts 31–60 days past due	18,700
Accounts 61–90 days past due	4,230
Accounts over 90 days past due	8,640
Total Accounts Receivable	$161,070

Past experience shows that the following percentages will be uncollectible.

Account Status	Percentage Uncollectible
Accounts not yet due	2.0%
Accounts 1–30 days past due	5.0
Accounts 31–60 days past due	9.5
Accounts 61–90 days past due	30.0
Accounts over 90 days past due	50.0

Instructions

1. *Calculate the estimated amount of uncollectible accounts expense on December 31, Year 9.*

2. *Prepare the adjusting entry on December 31, Year 9, assuming the Allowance for Doubtful Accounts has a credit balance of $1,350.*

3. *Prepare the adjusting entry on December 31, Year 9, assuming the Allowance for Doubtful Accounts has a debit balance of $1,642.*

4. *Prepare the general journal entry on March 29, Year 10, to write off the account of Hillsdale Paper Company in the amount of $542.75.*

Problem 16.3
aging accounts receivable and calculating uncollectible accounts expense; journalizing subsequent write-off of account

Following is the necessary information on December 31 for aging the accounts receivable of the Peoria Sporting Goods store for Year 7.

Account Name	Total Owed	Not Yet Due	1–30 Days Past Due	31–60 Days Past Due	61–90 Days Past Due	Over 90 Days Past Due
Diaz	$4,600	$ 600	$2,500	$1,500		
Estevez	2,960	850	1,000	600	$ 510	
Falwell	920					$920
Haig	1,460	650	394	416		
Lucas	1,970	1,970				
Miller	2,860	125	940	430	1,065	300
Petrovich	1,680	1,200	480			
Santos	740	740				
Zion	3,420	2,350	800	270		
Totals						
Percentage of Total						

From past experience, the accountants for Peoria Sporting Goods know that the following percentages will be uncollectible: approximately 1 percent (.01) of accounts not yet due will be uncollectible; 4 percent (.04) of accounts 1–30 days past due; 9 percent (.09) of accounts 31–60 days past due; 20 percent (.20) of accounts 61–90 days past due; and 45 percent (.45) of accounts over 90 days past due.

Instructions

1. Calculate the totals for each of the columns on the aging schedule.

2. Determine what percentage each column total is of the total accounts receivable by dividing the column total by the total accounts receivable. Round percentages to the nearest tenth of a percent.

3. Calculate the amount of uncollectible accounts expense. Round amounts to the nearest cent if necessary.

4. Prepare the adjusting entry on December 31, Year 7, to record the uncollectible accounts expense. Assume the Allowance for Doubtful Accounts has a debit balance of $575 before the adjusting entry.

5. Word is received that Falwell has declared bankruptcy. A check for $150 is received from the court in partial settlement of her account. Prepare the general journal entries on April 1, Year 8, to record the receipt of the $150 and to write off the balance of Falwell's account.

Problem 16.4
calculating net realizable value of accounts receivable after write-offs

The account balance in Accounts Receivable on January 1, Year 5, for the East Peoria Flower and Gift Shop was $29,650; the credit balance in Allowance for Doubtful Accounts was $889.50. On January 2, the $75 account of Eliza Higgins was written off; on March 31, the $196.50 account of Tom Shephard was written off; on June 14, the $230 account of Pat Shroeder was written off; on October 10, the $90 account of Susan Yee was written off; and on November 11, the $85 account of Sam Chan was written off.

Instructions

1. *Calculate the net realizable value of accounts receivable on January 1 and on November 11 after the account of Sam Chan is written off. Assume there were no transactions other than those listed above.*

2. *On December 31, an aging of the accounts receivable showed that $950 was estimated to be uncollectible. Using the balance sheet approach, prepare the adjusting entry to record the uncollectible accounts expense after calculating the balance in Allowance for Doubtful Accounts.*

3. *Assume that the East Peoria Flower and Gift Shop used the income statement approach to estimating bad debts. Sales are $125,600, Sales Returns and Allowances are $1,800; and Sales Discounts are $1,250. The Allowance for Doubtful Accounts has a debit balance of $142 on December 31. Uncollectible accounts are estimated to be 1 percent of net sales. Prepare the adjusting entry to record the uncollectible accounts expense under these circumstances.*

Problem 16.5
journalizing transactions for sales, default on note, and subsequent collection

The Pueblo Shop makes sales for cash and on account. It uses the income statement approach for estimating bad debts. The Allowance for Doubtful Accounts shows a credit balance on January 1, Year 10, of $2,750. The following transactions relate to Andrew Guthrie's account in Year 10.

Mar. 1   sold merchandise to Andrew Guthrie on account; $700
Apr. 10   sold merchandise to Andrew Guthrie on account; $1,950
Aug. 1   accepted a 60-day, 12 percent note from Andrew for the amount owed on account
Sept. 30 declared the August 1 note in default; reinstated Andrew's account receivable

Oct. 30   received payment in full from Andrew for the full value of the September 30 account receivable plus an additional 12 percent interest for the time period from September 30 through October 30

Instructions   *Record in general journal form each of the transactions relating to Andrew Guthrie.*

CHAPTER 17

Notes Receivable and Notes Payable

LEARNING OBJECTIVES

When you have completed this chapter, you should

1. have a better understanding of accounting terminology.

2. have an increased understanding of promissory notes and their use.

3. be able to account for notes receivable and the subsequent interest income.

4. be able to account for notes payable and the subsequent interest expense.

5. be able to calculate due dates and the number of days in discount periods and adjustment periods.

6. be able to account for bank discounting of a note and net proceeds.

7. be able to calculate the interest and prepare the adjusting entries to record interest receivable and interest payable.

The extensive use of credit is typical of modern businesses. Certain types of merchandise are bought and sold on open account, while other types are bought and sold on the installment plan or by the issuance of a note. Large retailers, such as Wards or Sears, sell millions of dollars worth of merchandise on the installment plan, with customers taking 12, 24, or 36 months (or longer) to pay. Firms that sell high-priced goods, such as automobiles, furniture, boats, or farm equipment, frequently accept notes (with interest) as payment for their product. The use of credit stimulates the economy as individuals and businesses may buy now and pay later.

THE PROMISSORY NOTE

A promissory note is a negotiable instrument. For it to be negotiable, it must have the following characteristics: (1) it must be in writing and must be signed by the maker (the borrower); (2) it must contain an unconditional promise to pay a certain amount of money; (3) it must be payable at a definite time in the future or on demand; and (4) it must be payable to the bearer or to some specific person or firm. A sample promissory note appears in Chapter 9 on page 328.

Notes may be interest-bearing or non-interest-bearing. The formula for finding interest, you will remember from Chapter 9, is:

$$\text{Interest} = \text{Principal} \times \text{Rate} \times \text{Time}.$$

The principal is the amount borrowed, the rate is the annual rate of interest to be paid, and the time refers to the number of days, months, or years that the maker has in which to pay back the principal along with any interest due. The interest rate and the time period will be stated on the face of the note.

When a note is issued, the maker will refer to it as a note payable and payments of interest will be debited to Interest Expense. The payee (the lender) will refer to it as a note receivable and interest received will be credited to Interest Income.

NOTES RECEIVABLE

Businesses may issue notes receivable for a variety of reasons. Although a note is not as good as cash, it is highly liquid and may generate interest income. Loans may be granted to a business on the basis of the value of their notes receivable, or the notes may be discounted (sold) to obtain the cash.

Notes receivable may be given for the following reasons: (1) a customer may wish an extension of time during which to pay his or her account receivable; (2) a loan may be given to a customer or to an employee; or (3) merchandise may be sold by accepting a note receivable. Notes receivable is a current asset and appears on the balance sheet.

Interest Rates

Interest rates vary widely, sometimes as much as one or two points over night. The Federal Reserve Board exercises some control over the economy by adjusting interest rates. To combat inflation, it raises the interest rate; and to stimulate the economy, it lowers the rate. When interest rates are low, individuals are more likely to purchase a home or an automobile, and businesses are more inclined to purchase equipment, buildings, or machinery.

prime rate
the interest rate
charged to the largest
and most financially
sound customers

The interest rate charged by banks to their largest and most financially sound customers is referred to as the **prime rate.** Smaller or less financially secure companies will pay an interest rate that is several points higher than the prime rate.

Exchange of an Account Receivable for a Note Receivable

Assume that the Kitchen Supply House sells to retailers both for cash and on account. Assume further that El Paso Cutlery has a past-due account receivable amounting to $12,500. On May 1, the account receivable is exchanged for a 120-day, 12 percent, note receivable. The transaction on the books of the Kitchen Supply House is as follows.

		GENERAL JOURNAL			Page
Date		**Description**	**Post. Ref.**	**Debit**	**Credit**
19XX May	*1*	*Notes Receivable*		*1 2 5 0 0 —*	
		Accounts Receivable/El Paso Cutlery			*1 2 5 0 0 —*
		Exchanged 120-Day, 12% Note For Past-Due			
		Account			

Calculating the Due Date of a Note

The due date of the El Paso Cutlery note is August 29 and is figured as follows.

Number of days in May	31
Date of note, May 1	− 1
Number of days left in May	30
Number of days in June	30
Number of days in July	+31
Subtotal	91
Number of days needed to equal 120	+29 days into August
Total required number of days	120

Recording Receipt of Cash for Principal and Interest

Assume that on August 29, the maturity date, El Paso Cutlery sends a check to Kitchen Supply House for the principal and interest owed. The entry on the books of Kitchen Supply House follows.

		GENERAL JOURNAL				Page	
Date		**Description**	**Post. Ref.**	**Debit**		**Credit**	
19XX *Aug.*	*29*	*Cash*		1 3 0 0 0 —			
		Notes Receivable				1 2 5 0 0 —	
		Interest Income				5 0 0 —	
		Received Payment in Full for El Paso Cutlery					
		Note and Interest					
		(12,500 × .12 × 120/360 = $500)					

Calculating Interest

The interest on the El Paso Cutlery note was calculated as follows.

$$I = \quad P \quad \times R \times \quad T$$
$$I = 12{,}500 \times .12 \times 120/360$$
$$I = 12{,}500 \times .12 \times 120 \div 360$$
$$I = \$500$$

Renewing a Note at Maturity

If El Paso Cutlery had been unable to pay the note and interest at its maturity, a new note could have been issued by Kitchen Supply House, which would collect on August 29 only the interest owed. Assuming that an extra 60 days was granted to El Paso Cutlery for payment, the following entry would be made on the books of Kitchen Supply House.

GENERAL JOURNAL				Page	
Date	Description	Post. Ref.	Debit	Credit	
19XX Aug. 29	*Cash*		*500 —*		
	Notes Receivable		*12500 —*		
	Notes Receivable			*12500 —*	
	Interest Income			*500 —*	
	Issued New 60 Day, 12% Note to El Paso Cutlery;				
	Collected Interest Due				
	(12,500 × .12 × 120/360 = $500)				

When a new note is issued, the old one is canceled and the maker signs a new note. Although the entry does not change the balance in notes receivable, it nevertheless must be made, as it alerts management that a new note has been issued and it ensures that all notes receivable are current.

Adjusting Entries for Interest Receivable

Assume that Kitchen Supply House has an accounting period of one month. Adjusting entries must take into consideration any interest that is receivable. For example, for the 120-day note receivable of El Paso Cutlery issued on May 1, adjusting entries would have to be made on May 31, June 30, and July 31, or, at the end of each accounting period. The adjusting entries will record a debit to Interest Receivable and a credit to Interest Income, and each will be calculated for the exact number of days in the adjustment period. Interest amounts are always rounded to the nearest penny. Calculations are as follows.

May 31 Adjustment   Number of days in adjustment period—30 days (May 1–31)

$$\begin{aligned} \text{Interest} &= \quad P \quad \times R \times \quad T \\ &= 12{,}500 \times .12 \times 30/360 \\ &= \$125 \end{aligned}$$

June 30 Adjustment   Number of days in adjustment period—30 days in June

$$\begin{aligned} \text{Interest} &= \quad P \quad \times R \times \quad T \\ &= 12{,}500 \times .12 \times 30/360 \\ &= \$125 \end{aligned}$$

July 31 Adjustment   Number of days in adjustment period—31 days in July

$$\begin{aligned} \text{Interest} &= \quad P \quad \times R \times \quad T \\ &= 12{,}500 \times .12 \times 31/360 \\ &= \$129.17 \text{ (rounded to nearest penny)} \end{aligned}$$

The general journal entries to record the adjusting entries at the end of May, June, and July are as follows.

	GENERAL JOURNAL						Page	
Date	Description	Post. Ref.	Debit		Credit			
	Adjusting Entries							
19XX May 31	_Interest Receivable_		1 2 5 —					
	Interest Income				1 2 5 —			
	El Paso Cutlery Note							
	(12,500 × .12 × 30/360 = $125.00)							
June 30	_Interest Receivable_		1 2 5 —					
	Interest Income				1 2 5 —			
	El Paso Cutlery Note							
	(12,500 × .12 × 30/360 = $125.00)							
July 31	_Interest Receivable_		1 2 9 17					
	Interest Income				1 2 9 17			
	El Paso Cutlery Note							
	(12,500 × .12 × 31/360 = $129.17)							

The Interest Income account will be closed at the end of each accounting period, but the Interest Receivable account will remain open until cash is received for the note and interest. Interest receivable is a current asset and appears on the balance sheet. The Interest Receivable account of Kitchen Supply House appears as follows on August 1.

Interest Receivable   135

5/31 125.00	
6/30 125.00	
7/31 129.17	
(379.17)	

When El Paso Cutlery makes payment for the note and interest on August 29, Kitchen Supply House will have to take into consideration when recording the receipt of the cash that interest income and interest receivable have been recorded at the end of each accounting period. The debit balance of the Interest Receivable account is $379.17. That account must be closed on August 29 because when the interest is paid, it is no longer receivable. Also at this time, interest income must be recorded for the 29 days in August ($12{,}500 \times .12 \times 29/360 = \$120.83$). The Kitchen Supply House entry to record receipt of payment for the note and interest is as follows.

GENERAL JOURNAL				Page	
Date	Description	Post. Ref.	Debit	Credit	
Aug. 29	*Cash*		1 3 0 0 —		
	Interest Receivable			3 7 9 17	
	Interest Income			1 2 0 83	
	Notes Receivable			12 5 0 0 —	
	Received Payment in Full for El Paso Cutlery				
	Note and Interest: To Record August Interest				
	(12,500 × .12 × 29/360 = \$120.83)				

After the entry is posted, the Interest Receivable account will be closed.

Interest Receivable   135

5/31	125.00	8/29	379.17
6/30	125.00		
7/31	129.17		

The total interest income recorded since the note was issued on May 1 is \$500. For May, June, and July, the interest income was recorded as an adjusting entry, and in August, the last 29 days of interest income was recorded when payment for the note and interest was received from El Paso Cutlery. The interest income as recorded in May, June, July, and August is as follows.

On May 31	\$125.00	Adjusting Entry
On June 30	125.00	Adjusting Entry
On July 31	129.17	Adjusting Entry
On August 29	120.83	Entry recording receipt of cash for note and interest
Total	\$500.00	

Interest income appears on the income statement in the "other income" category, which follows the net income from operations.

Dishonored Note

dishonored
a dishonored note is one on which the maker defaults when the note is due

If the maker of the note is unable to pay at the note's maturity, the note is said to be **dishonored** and the principal and interest are debited to Accounts Receivable. Assume, for example, that Kitchen Supply House issued a $6,000, 10 percent, 60-day note receivable to Restaurant Pottery Company on August 16. At the note's maturity, Restaurant Pottery Company was in bankruptcy and could not pay. At that time, Kitchen Supply House made the following entry.

GENERAL JOURNAL					Page	
Date	Description	Post. Ref.	Debit		Credit	
19XX *Oct.* *15*	*Accounts Receivable/Restaurant Pottery Co.*		*6 1 0 0 —*			
	Notes Receivable				*6 0 0 0 —*	
	Interest Income				*1 0 0 —*	
	To Record Dishonored 60-Day, 10% Note					
	(6,000 × .10 × 60/360 = $100.00)					

If the account receivable is later determined to be uncollectible, it will be written off by a debit to Uncollectible Accounts Expense (or Allowance for Doubtful Accounts) and a credit to Accounts Receivable.

Discounting Notes Receivable

Once a note receivable is issued, the payee may not demand payment until the due date of the note. However, because notes receivable are negotiable instruments, they may be discounted (sold) to a bank or other financial institution. The bank will charge a fee for discounting the note and will collect the principal and interest at its maturity from the maker of the note.

Assume that on Feburary 14, Kitchen Supply House issued a $7,500, 13 percent, 90-day note receivable to Texas Barstools. On April 5, Kitchen Supply House management decided that it needed cash and so decided to discount the Texas Barstools note. The Rio Grande Bank agreed to discount the note at 15 percent. The five steps necessary to calculate the **net proceeds,** the amount of cash Kitchen Supply House will receive from the sale of the note, are as follows.

net proceeds
the amount of cash received when a note is discounted

1. Find the due date of the note.

Number of days in February	28
Date of note	-14 (February 14)
Number of days left in February	14
Number of days in March	31
Number of days in April	30
Subtotal	75
Number of days needed in May	15 (May 15)
Total days in time of note	90

maturity value
the principal and interest due at a note's due date

2. Find the **maturity value** of the note.

$$I = \quad P \quad \times \ R \ \times \quad T$$
$$I = 7{,}500 \times .13 \times 90/360$$
$$I = \$243.75$$

$$\text{Maturity Value} = \text{Principal} + \text{Interest}$$
$$MV = \$7{,}500.00 + \$243.75$$
$$MV = \$7{,}743.75$$

3. Determine the discount period, the number of days from the day of discount to the due date of the note.

February 14   Discount Date—April 5   Due Date—May 15

Discount Period
April 5–May 15
40 Days

Number of days in April	30
Discount date, April 5	− 5
Days remaining in April	25
Days in May until due date	15
Days in discount period	40

discount
the amount charged by a financial institution when a note is sold (or discounted)

4. Determine dollar amount of **discount.**

Discount = Maturity Value × Discount Rate × Days in Discount Period
Discount =   7,743.75   ×   .15   ×   40/360
Discount = $129.06 (rounded to nearest penny)

5. Determine dollar amount of net proceeds.

Net Proceeds = Maturity Value − Discount
Net Proceeds = $7,743.75   − $129.06
Net Proceeds = $7,614.69

Journalizing Discounted Note Receivable

Once the net proceeds has been determined, the bank will issue a check for $7,614.69 to Kitchen Supply House. The entry on the books of Kitchen Supply House is as follows.

GENERAL JOURNAL				Page	
Date	Description	Post. Ref.	Debit	Credit	
19XX Apr. 5	*Cash*		7614 69		
	Notes Receivable			7500 —	
	Interest Income			114 69	
	To Record Discounting of Texas Barstools				
	90-Day, 13% Note at Discount Rate of 15% by				
	Rio Grande Bank: Contingent Liability Created:				
	Note Due on May 15.				
	(7,743.75 × .15 × 40/360 = $129.06)				
	(7,743.75 − $129.06 = $7,614.69)				

If the net proceeds are less than the face value of the note, a debit to Interest Expense (rather than a credit to Interest Income) may be required. Assume in the previous example of the $7,500, 13 percent, 90-day note dated February 14 that the note was discounted on March 16 at 20 percent. The net proceeds are calculated as follows.

1. Find the due date of the note.
   It is May 15 (see previous example).

2. Find the maturity value of the note.
   It is $7,743.75 (see previous example).

3. Determine the number of days in the discount period.

Number of days in March	31
Discount date, March 16	−16
Days remaining in March	15
Days in April	30
Days in May until due date	+15
Days in discount period	60

4. Determine dollar amount of discount.

Discount = Maturity Value × Discount Rate × Days in Discount Perio

$258.13   =   7,743.75   ×   .20   ×   60/360

5. Determine dollar amount of net proceeds.

Net Proceeds = Maturity Value − Discount

$7,485.62   = $7,743.75   − $258.13

The general journal entry to record the receipt of cash as a result of discounting the note under these circumstances is as follows.

GENERAL JOURNAL				Page			
Date	Description	Post. Ref.	Debit		Credit		
19XX **Mar.** 16	**Cash**		7 4 8 5 62				
	Interest Expense		1 4 38				
	Notes Receivable				7 5 0 0 —		
	To Record Discounting of Texas Barstools						
	90-Day, 13% Note at Discount Rate of 20% by						
	Rio Grande Bank; Contingent Liability Created;						
	Note Due on May 15.						
	(7,743.75 × .20 × 60/360 = $258.13)						
	(7,743.75 − $258.13 = $7,485.62)						

contingent liability
a liability that may develop, contingent on the actions of another person or firm

When Kitchen Supply House discounted the note receivable on April 5 at the Rio Grande Bank, it became contingently liable for payment of the note at its maturity. A **contingent liability** is one that may develop into a real liability if the maker of the discounted note does not pay the bank at the note's maturity. If, for example, the note is dishonored by Texas Barstools, Kitchen Supply House will have to pay the Rio Grande Bank and then try to collect from Texas Barstools. But if Texas Barstools pays the Rio Grande Bank the $7,743.75 maturity value of the note on the due date (May 15), then the contingent liability of Kitchen Supply House will disappear.

The existence of a contingent liability must be disclosed to readers of the financial statements; if the contingent liability turns into an actual one, it could have a major impact on the business. Contingent liabilities are included as footnotes in the financial statements. The contingent liability of Kitchen Supply House might be shown as the following footnote.

Footnote 1: On April 30, 19XX, Kitchen Supply House was contingently liable for a Texas Barstools note receivable discounted on April 5 with a maturity value of $7,743.75.

If Texas Barstools should default on the note's due date, May 15, Kitchen Supply House will make the following entry after paying the Rio Grande Bank.

GENERAL JOURNAL					Page	
Date	Description	Post. Ref.	Debit		Credit	
19XX May 15	Accounts Receivable/Texas Barstools		7743 75			
	Cash				7743 75	
	To Record Dishonored Note at Rio Grande Bank					

If it later becomes evident that the money cannot be collected from Texas Barstools, the account will be written off as a bad debt.

NOTES PAYABLE

Notes payable may be issued to a supplier to gain an extension of time for payment of an open account, may be given for merchandise or property purchased, or may be given when a loan is obtained. Notes payable due within a year's time are listed as current liabilities on the balance sheet, and notes due after a year's time are listed as long-term liabilities.

Recording a Note Payable Given as Evidence of a Loan

Assume that on December 2, Year 9, Kitchen Supply House borrowed $5,000 at 12.5 percent for 60 days from the First Texas Bank. The entry on Kitchen Supply House's books is as follows.

GENERAL JOURNAL					Page	
Date	Description	Post. Ref.	Debit		Credit	
19XX Dec. 2	Cash		5000 —			
	Notes Payable				5000 —	
	Borrowed $5,000 at 12.5% for 60 Days from					
	First Texas Bank					

At the time of borrowing, no interest expense is recorded. However, the interest expense accrues daily, and at the end of the accounting period (December 31), an adjusting entry will be made to record the interst expense, even though it does not have to be paid until January 31, Year 10. The entry on the books of Kitchen Supply House follows.

GENERAL JOURNAL					Page
Date	Description	Post. Ref.	Debit		Credit
	Adjusting Entries				
19XX Dec. 31	_Interest Expense_		50 35		
	Interest Payable				50 35
	First Texas Bank Note				
	_(5,000 × .125 × 29/360 = $50.35)_				

The Interest Expense account will be closed out at the end of December with all the other expenses. Interest payable will show on the balance sheet as a current liability until the note is paid at its due date (January 31). The Interest Payable account appears as follows on January 31.

Interest Payable   245

_____|_____

                        | 12/31   Adjusting   50.35

The entry on the books of Kitchen Supply House to record payment of the note and interest on January 31 must both remove the $50.35 balance in the Interest Payable account and record the interest expense for the 31 days in January. The entry is as follows.

GENERAL JOURNAL				Page	
Date	Description	Post. Ref.	Debit	Credit	
19XX Jan. 31	Interest Payable		50 35		
	Interest Expense		53 82		
	Notes Payable		5000 —		
	Cash			5104 17	
	Paid in Full First Texas Bank Note and Interest:				
	Recorded January Interest				
	(5,000 × .125 × 31/360 = $53.82)				

Renewing a Note at Maturity

Assume that Kitchen Supply House purchased $2,500 worth of merchandise for resale from the Cookware Wholesaler on December 11, Year 9. The manager made a $500 cash down payment and signed a 30-day, 11 percent note for the balance. The entry to record this transaction is as follows.

GENERAL JOURNAL				Page	
Date	Description	Post. Ref.	Debit	Credit	
19XX Dec. 11	Purchases		2500 —		
	Cash			500 —	
	Notes Payable			2000 —	
	Signed $2,000, 30-Day, 11% Note at Cookware				
	Wholesaler				

The following is the adjusting entry to record interest expense on December 31, Year 9.

GENERAL JOURNAL					Page	
Date	Description	Post. Ref.	Debit		Credit	
	Adjusting Entries					
19XX *Dec.* *31*	*Interest Expense*		1 2 22			
	Interest Payable				1 2 22	
	Cookware Wholesaler Note					
	(2,000 × .11 × 20/360 = $12.22)					

When the note falls due on January 10, Year 10, Kitchen Supply House asks for an extension of time in which to pay and the Cookware Wholesaler agrees if partial payment of the note is made along with the interest due. Kitchen Supply House agrees to pay $500 cash toward the principal and the interest due and agrees to sign a new 60-day note with a higher 15 percent interest rate. The entry on the books of Kitchen Supply House is as follows.

GENERAL JOURNAL					Page	
Date	Description	Post. Ref.	Debit		Credit	
19XX *Jan.* *10*	*Notes Payable*		2 0 0 0 —			
	Interest Expense		6 11			
	Interest Payable		1 2 22			
	Cash				5 1 8 33	
	Notes Payable				1 5 0 0 —	
	To Record Partial Payment of Cookware					
	Wholesaler's December 11 Note and Interest					
	and Signing of a New 60-Day, 15% Note:					
	To Record January Interest					
	(2,000 × .11 × 10/360 = $6.11)					

On the books of the Kitchen Supply House, the Interest Payable account is closed, and the January 10 entry records ten days' interest expense for Year 10. The old Notes Payable account (balance $2,000) is closed and the Notes Payable account on January 10 has a balance of $1,500.

Notes Receivable and Notes Payable Registers

If a business holds several notes, then separate notes receivable and notes payable registers are maintained to keep track of the notes. The notes receivable register will show the date of the note, the maker, the time of the note, the amount of the note, the interest rate, the due date, and the date of discount or the day payment is received for the note. Following are the notes receivable and notes payable registers for the St. Paul Stationery and Office Supply Company.

Notes Receivable Register

Date of Note	No.	Maker	Time	Amount	Rate	Due Date	Discounted	Date Paid
Yr. 1								
2/19	1	Cards, Etc.	3 mos.	$3,000	13.0%	5/19	____	5/19
4/16	2	Paper Products	90 days	4,700	10.5	7/15	____	7/15
9/15	3	Letters, Inc.	6 mos.	7,200	10.0	3/15, Yr. 2	____	____
11/3	4	Cards, Etc.	1 year	5,000	10.5	11/3, Yr. 2	____	____
12/1	5	Paper Greetings	60 days	3,750	12.0	1/30, Yr. 2	____	____

Notes Payable Register

Date of Note	No.	Payee	Time	Amount	Rate	Due Date	Date Paid
Yr. 1							
3/30	50	Minnesota Savings	6 mos.	$ 4,500	10%	9/30	9/30
10/1	51	1st National Bank	5 yrs.	12,000	9	10/1, Yr. 6	____
11/14	52	Minnesota Savings	60 days	3,250	12	1/13, Yr. 2	____

Adjusting Entries for Interest Receivable and Interest Payable

St. Paul Stationery and Office Supply Company adjusts and closes its books at the end of the year; following are the calculations for the adjustments for interest receivable and interest payable.

Notes Receivable   Note 3, Calculations for Adjustment Period

Total days in September	30
Date of note	−15
Days left in September	15
Days in October	31
Days in November	30
Days in December	31
Total days until Year End	107

Calculation for Interest Receivable

$$I = 7,200 \times .10 \times 107/360$$
$$I = \$214.00$$

Note 4, Calculation for Adjustment Period

Total days in November	30
Date of note	− 3
Days left in November	27
Days in December	+31
Total days until Year End	58

Calculation for Interest Receivable

$$I = 5,000 \times .105 \times 58/360$$
$$I = \$84.58$$

Note 5, Calculations for Adjustment Period

Total days in December	31
Date of note	− 1
Total days until Year End	30

Calculation for Interest Receivable

$$I = 3,750 \times .12 \times 30/360$$
$$I = \$37.50$$

Notes Payable   Note 51, Calculations for Adjustment Period

Days in October	31
Date of note	− 1
Days left in October	30
Days in November	30
Days in December	+31
Total days until Year End	91

Calculation for Interest Payable

$$I = 21{,}000 \times .09 \times 91/360$$
$$I = \$273.00$$

Note 52, Calculations for Adjustment Period

Days in November	30
Date of note	−14
Days left in November	16
Days in December	+31
Days until Year End	47

Calculation for Interest Payable

$$I = 3{,}250 \times .12 \times 47/360$$
$$I = \$50.92$$

The December 31 year-end adjusting entries relating to interest for the St. Paul Stationery and Office Supply Company are as follows.

		GENERAL JOURNAL				Page	
Date		Description	Post. Ref.	Debit		Credit	
19XX		*Adjusting Entries*					
Dec.	31	*Interest Receivable*			3 3 6 08		
		Interest Income					3 3 6 08
		Note 3: 7,200 × .10 × 107/360 = $214.00					
		Note 4: 5,000 × .105 × 58/360 = 84.58					
		Note 5: 3,750 × .12 × 30/360 = 37.50					
	31	*Interest Expense*			3 2 3 92		
		Interest Payable					3 2 3 92
		Note 51: 12,000 × .09 × 91/360 = $273.00					
		Note 52: 3,250 × .12 × 47/360 = 50.92					

SUMMARY

Modern businesses rely heavily on the use of credit. Goods and services are bought and sold on open account, on the installment plan, and by issuing notes. The use of credit stimulates the economy and generates interest income for the seller or lender.

A promissory note may be issued when selling or purchasing. It is a negotiable instrument and must be in writing and signed by the maker; it must contain an unconditional promise to pay a specific amount of money; it must be payable at a certain future date or on demand; and it must be payable to the bearer or to a specific person or firm. Notes are usually interest-bearing; interest rates are stated in annual terms.

Notes receivable are liquid assets and may be issued to customers who need an extension of time during which to pay their accounts; they may be issued as loans to a customer or to an employee; or they may be issued when merchandise is sold.

The Federal Reserve Board exercises control over the economy by raising or lowering interest rates. The prime rate is that charged to the largest and most financially sound customers; smaller companies usually pay an interest rate several points higher than the prime rate.

The formula for calculating interest is: Interest = Principal $\times$ Rate $\times$ Time (I = P $\times$ R $\times$ T). The principal is the amount borrowed, the rate is the interest rate charged, and the time is the length of time the payee holds the note before payment in full is required.

When a firm holds interest-bearing notes receivable, interest income is generated on a daily basis. As a result, adjusting entries must be made at the end of each accounting period debiting Interest Receivable and crediting Interest Income. Interest receivable is a current asset, and interest income is a revenue account that appears in the other income section of the income statement.

If a note is dishonored at its maturity, the payee will transfer the principal and interest owed to accounts receivable. If it becomes evident at a later date that the money will not be collectible, the account is written off as a bad debt.

Notes receivable, because they are highly liquid, may be discounted (sold) at a bank or other financial institution. The bank will charge a specific discount rate for the number of days it is required to hold the note; the amount of the discount is subtracted from the maturity value of the note to determine the net proceeds payable to the original payee of the note.

When a note receivable is discounted, a contingent liability is created. The contingent liability will become an actual one in the event that the maker of the note fails to pay the bank at the note's maturity. Contingent liabilities should be shown as footnotes to the financial statements.

Interest-bearing notes payable accrue interest expense on a daily basis, and as a result, an adjusting entry must be prepared at the end of the accounting period debiting Interest Expense and crediting Interest Payable for each outstanding note payable. To make adjusting entries easier for interest expense and interest income, separate registers are kept for notes receivable and notes payable. These registers list each note, its date, its number, the maker or payee, the time of the note, the amount, the rate, and the due date.

Review of Accounting Terminology

Following is a list of the accounting terminology for this chapter.

contingent liability   maturity value
discount   net proceeds
dishonored   prime rate

Fill in the blank with the correct word or term from the list.

1. When the maker of a note defaults at the note's maturity, the note is said to be _____.

2. The principal plus the interest at a note's due date is referred to as the note's _____.

3. A note receivable that is discounted creates a/an _____.

4. The maturity value minus the bank discount equals the _____ of the note.

5. The amount the bank charges when it buys a note receivable is referred to as the _____.

6. The interest rate charged to the largest and most financially sound institutions is referred to as the _____.

Match the following words and terms on the left with the definitions on the right.

7. contingent liability

8. discount

9. dishonored

10. maturity value

11. net proceeds

12. prime rate

a. maturity value × discount rate × discount period

b. a defaulted note

c. maturity value minus bank discount

d. a liability that *may* arise as a result of the action of another person or firm

e. the interest rate charged the largest and most financially sound firms

f. principal plus interest at note's due date

Exercises

Exercise 17.1
calculating interest

Calculate the ordinary simple interest for the following notes. (Assume a 360-day year and 30-day months.)

Note	Amount	Interest Rate	Time	Interest
A	$ 7,650	10.0%	60 days	_____
B	10,740	12.0	4 months	_____
C	15,140	11.5	6 months	_____
D	3,720	10.5	90 days	_____

Exercise 17.2
calculating due dates and maturity values

Determine the due date and maturity value for each of the following notes. Round to the nearest penny where required.

Note	Date	Amount	Interest Rate	Time	Due Date	Maturity Value
E	January 27	$2,500	9.0%	60 days	_____	_____
F	March 18	6,420	8.5	90 days	_____	_____
G	July 20	7,600	7.5	90 days	_____	_____
H	September 14	1,760	10.0	120 days	_____	_____

Exercise 17.3
exchanging accounts receivable for notes receivable

On June 30, the Hyannisport Marine accepted a $6,400, 10.5 percent, 60-day note from the Port Suppliers in settlement of its open account.

a. Prepare the general journal entry for Hyannisport Marine to record the issuing of the note.

b. Determine the note's due date.

c. Prepare the general journal entry for Hyannisport Marine on the due date to record the receipt of cash for the principal and interest owed.

Exercise 17.4
renewing note receivable at maturity

On August 14, the Long Island Donut Dunker issued a $2,500, 12 percent, 30-day note receivable to New York Bob's Sweete Shoppe in settlement of its open account.

a. Prepare the general journal entry for Long Island Donut Dunker to record issuing the note.

b. Calculate the due date of the note.

c. Calculate the maturity value of the note.

d. On the due date of the note, New York Bob's Sweete Shoppe asks for a 60-day extension of time in which to pay the amount owed. It agreed to pay the interest due at this time, and a new 60-day, 15 percent note receivable is issued. Prepare the general journal entry for the Long Island Donut Dunker to record the transaction.

Exercise 17.5
preparing adjusting entry for interest receivable

On December 31, the Princeton Fashion House holds two notes receivable.

Note	Date	Amount	Interest Rate	Time
P. Dubois	November 21	$4,650	12%	90 days
K. Turner	December 16	6,420	10	90 days

Princeton Fashion House adjusts and closes its books once a year on December 31. Prepare the adjusting entry to record interest receivable on December 31.

Exercise 17.6
journalizing note receivable, interest receivable, and receipt of principal and interest

On July 2, the Rock Hill Leather Shop sold $5,450 in merchandise to the South Carolina Sheepskin Products Company, which made a $500 cash down payment and signed a 60-day, 12 percent note for the balance.

a. Prepare the general journal entry for the Rock Hill Leather Shop to record the sale of the merchandise.

b. Prepare the adjusting entry on July 31 to record the interest receivable.

c. Prepare the general journal entry on August 31 to record the receipt of cash for the note and interest.

Exercise 17.7
journalizing a dishonored note

On March 18, the Trinidad Shoe Company sold $7,000 in merchandise to the Cal Bootery. The Cal Bootery paid $1,000 cash down and signed a 6-month, 11 percent note for the balance. On the note's due date, the Cal Bootery was in bankruptcy and could not pay.

a. Prepare the general journal entry on March 18 for the Trinidad Shoe Company to record the sale of the merchandise.

b. Prepare the general journal entry to record the dishonoring of the note at its due date.

Exercise 17.8
calculating net proceeds

The Corning Company sold merchandise to the Hawthorne Company amounting to $8,100 on April 9 and accepted a 90-day, 9 percent note as payment. On May 9, the Corning Company discounted the note at the City National Bank at 12 percent. Calculate (a) the due date of the Hawthorne note; (b) the maturity value; (c) the number of days in the discount period; (d) the amount of the bank discount (round to the nearest penny); and (e) the net proceeds of the note.

Exercise 17.9
journalizing sale of merchandise by note and subsequent discounting of the note

The Norfolk Haberdashery sold merchandise totaling $4,630 to the Grand Island Hat House on September 4. Grand Island Hat House paid $630 cash down and signed a 60-day, 10.5 percent note for the balance. On September 20, Norfolk Haberdashery discounted the note at the Nebraska National Bank at 15 percent.

a. Record in general journal form for Norfolk Haberdashery the sale of merchandise on September 4.

b. Calculate the note's due date.

c. Calculate the maturity value.

d. Calculate the number of days in the discount period.

e. Calculate the amount of the discount (round to the nearest penny).

f. Calculate the net proceeds.

g. On September 20, record in general journal form the discounting of the note by Norfolk Haberdashery.

Exercise 17.10
journalizing borrowing cash, adjusting for interest payable, and subsequent payment of note and interest

On December 1, the Hesston Apparel Company borrowed $2,000 at 9 percent for 60 days from the First Kansas Bank. Hesston Apparel Company adjusts and closes its books annually on December 31.

a. Prepare the general journal entry for Hesston Apparel on December 1 to record the receipt of the cash.

b. Prepare the adjusting entry on December 31 to record the interest payable.

c. Prepare the general journal entry on January 30 to record payment to the First Kansas Bank of the note and interest.

Exercise 17.11
journalizing purchase of merchandise with note, adjusting entry for note payable, and renewal of note at maturity

On December 10, the Chocolate Factory purchased $4,420 in merchandise from the East Coast Sweet Supplies Company by paying $1,000 cash down and signing a 30-day, 11 percent note payable for the balance.

a. Prepare the general journal entry to record the purchase of merchandise on December 10.

b. Prepare the adjusting entry for the Chocolate Factory on December 31 to record the interest payable. Round the interest amount to the nearest penny if necessary.

c. On January 9, the Chocolate Factory asked for a time extension in which to pay its note. East Coast Sweet Supplies Company agreed to issue a new 60-day, 14 percent note if Chocolate Factory would pay the interest due on the old note on January 9. Chocolate Factory agreed to this. Prepare the general journal entry for Chocolate Factory to record the paying of the interest and the signing of the new note.

Problems

Problem 17.1
journalizing various notes receivable and interest

The Texas City Produce Company had the following transactions relating to notes receivable for Year 5.

Jan. 13 sold $5,000 in merchandise to San Antonio Supermarkets; received $2,000 cash and accepted a 30-day, 10 percent note receivable for the balance

Feb. 12 received interest only from San Antonio Supermarkets and issued it a new 60-day, 15 percent note receivable

Mar. 10 issued a 60-day, 10 percent note receivable to Texas Discount Groceries in exchange for its past-due account receivable of $4,610

Apr. 13 recorded the dishonoring of the February 12 note from San Antonio Supermarkets

May 9 received payment in full for the March 10 note and interest from Texas Discount Groceries

June 2 received payment from San Antonio Supermarkets for its dishonored note due on April 13; additional interest at 15 percent is received on the balance in accounts receivable from April 13 to June 2

Sept. 29   sold $8,200 in merchandise to Texas Discount Groceries, which paid $2,000 cash down and signed a 60-day, 9 percent note for the balance

Nov. 28   received payment in full from Texas Discount Groceries for its September 29 note and interest

Instructions   *Record the transactions in general journal form for the Texas City Produce Company. No adjusting entries are required in this problem. Round interest amounts to the nearest penny if necessary.*

Problem 17.2
journalizing various notes receivable and adjustments for interest receivable

The Chicago Exotic Gift Shop had the following transactions relating to notes receivable during Year 9. Its books are adjusted and closed at the end of each month.

May 19   sold $3,150 in merchandise to the Hinsdale Candle Company; received $500 cash and accepted a 30-day, 10 percent note for the balance

May 31   prepared the adjusting entry to record interest receivable on the Hinsdale Candle Company note

June 18   received payment in full for the note and interest of the Hinsdale Candle Company

July 11   granted a time extension to Chicago Flowers 'n Things for its account receivable of $4,270; issued a 60-day, 10 percent note

July 31   prepared the adjusting entry to record interest receivable on the Chicago Flowers 'n Things note

Aug. 21   sold $7,500 in merchandise to the Lake Michigan Wickery; received $2,500 cash and issued a 60-day, 9 percent note

Aug. 31   prepared the adjusting entry to record interest receivable on the Chicago Flowers 'n Things and the Lake Michigan Wickery notes

Sept. 9   received payment in full for the July 11 note and interest from Chicago Flowers 'n Things

Sept. 30   prepared the adjusting entry to record interest receivable on the August 21 note from Lake Michigan Wickery

Oct. 20   received cash from Lake Michigan Wickery for the August 21 note and interest

Instructions   *Prepare the Year 9 general journal entries relating to notes receivable for the Chicago Exotic Gift Shop. Round interest amounts to the nearest penny if necessary.*

Problem 17.3
calculating net proceeds and journalizing the discounting of three notes

The Parkersburg Kiddie Klothes Store had the following notes receivable during Year 6.

Note	Date	Amount	Interest Rate	Time
B. Graham	June 10	$7,000	10%	90 days
S. Ying	June 20	5,000	12	90 days
P. Polanski	June 28	8,350	11	60 days

On July 20, Parkersburg Kiddie Klothes Store discounted all three notes at 14 percent at the West Virginia National Bank.

Instructions
1. Calculate the (a) due date, (b) maturity value, (c) discount period, (d) discount amount, and (e) net proceeds for each note. Round interest amounts to the nearest penny if necessary.
2. Prepare the general journal entry to record the receipt of cash for the notes from the West Virginia National Bank.
3. Indicate how the financial statements would be affected by this transaction.

Problem 17.4
journalizing various notes payable

The Bismarck Hardware had the following transactions relating to notes payable in November of Year 4.

Nov. 9 borrowed $15,000 at 12 percent for 60 days from the North Dakota Central Bank

Nov. 15 purchased merchandise totaling $7,500 from Dakota Hand Tools; paid $2,000 cash down and signed a 60-day, 10 percent note for the remainder owed

Nov. 20 purchased merchandise totaling $5,600 from the Plains Mower Shop; paid $1,000 cash down and signed a 60-day, 10.5 percent note for the balance owed

Instructions
1. Record the November entries relating to notes payable for Bismarck Hardware in a general journal.
2. Assuming that Bismarck Hardware adjusts and closes its books monthly, prepare the adjusting entries on November 30 and December 31 to record interest payable on the notes. Round interest amounts to the nearest penny if necessary.
3. Prepare the general journal entries on January 8, January 14,

and January 19, Year 5, to record the payment of the notes and interest. Remember to take into consideration the adjusting entries for interest payable.

Problem 17.5
journalizing various notes receivable and payable and adjusting for interest receivable and payable

Following are the notes receivable and notes payable registers of the Pittsburgh Apparel Company for Year 7.

Notes Receivable Register

Date of Note	No.	Maker	Time	Amount	Rate	Due Date	Discounted	Date Paid
Yr. 7								
3/16	14	Pant Company	6 mos.	$7,200	10%	9/16, Yr. 7	_____	9/16, Yr. 7
6/14	15	Fashion Plate	90 days	5,000	9	9/12, Yr. 7	_____	9/12, Yr. 7
11/16	16	Blouse House	90 days	6,500	11	2/14, Yr. 8	12/16, Yr. 7	_____
12/1	17	Pant Company	60 days	8,000	12	1/30, Yr. 8	_____	_____

Notes Payable Register

Date of Note	No.	Payee	Time	Amount	Rate	Due Date	Date Paid
Yr. 7							
11/1	109	Pennsylvania National Bank	90 days	$10,000	10%	1/30, Yr. 8	____
12/15	110	Pittsburgh Savings and Loan	120 days	5,000	12	4/14, Yr. 8	____

Instructions

1. *Prepare the general journal entry on December 16, Year 7, to record the receipt of cash for the discounting of the Blouse House note (#16) at 13 percent at the Pittsburgh City Bank. Round interest amounts to the nearest penny if necessary.*

2. *Pittsburgh Apparel Company adjusts and closes its books annually on December 31. Prepare the general journal entry on December 31 to record the interest receivable on the December 1 note of Pant Company (#17).*

3. *Prepare the adjusting entry on December 31 to record interest payable on the Pennsylvania National Bank note (#109) and the Pittsburgh Savings and Loan note (#110).*

4. *Record the receipt of cash on January 30, Year 8, for the Pant*

Company note and interest (#17). Round interest amounts to the nearest penny if necessary.

5. *Record the payment of cash on January 30 and April 14, Year 8, for notes payable #109 and #110 to the Pennsylvania National Bank and the Pittsburgh Savings and Loan. Round interest amounts to the nearest penny if necessary.*

Problem 17.6
journalizing various notes receivable and payable and adjusting for interest receivable and payable

The Mt. Hood Sporting Goods Store had the following transactions relating to notes during Year 6. Its practice is to adjust and close its books annually on December 31.

Jan. 19 purchased $9,000 in merchandise from the Mountain Sports Company; paid $3,000 cash down and signed a 90-day, 10 percent note for the balance owed

Feb. 27 sold $7,450 in merchandise to the Oregon Ski Shop; received $2,000 cash and issued a 60-day, 12 percent note for the balance

Mar. 1 purchased $6,500 in merchandise from Snow Sports, Inc.; paid no cash down and signed a 90-day, 10 percent note in payment

Mar. 16 borrowed $10,000 from the Oregon National Bank for 6 months at 12 percent

Apr. 19 paid the interest due on the January 19 note of Mountain Sports Company and paid in addition $2,000 cash toward the principal; a new, 60-day, 14 percent note was signed for the remaining amount owed on the principal

Apr. 28 received word that the Oregon Ski Shop was in bankruptcy; its February 27 note and interest due today is transferred to accounts receivable in the hope that the money will eventually be collected

May 30 wrote a check for the full amount due to Snow Sports, Inc., for the principal and interest on the March 1 note

June 18 wrote a check for the principal and interest due on the April 19 note of Mountain Sports Company

Aug. 26 received a check from Oregon Ski Shop for the full amount due (principal and interest) on its dishonored note, which was transferred to accounts receivable on April 28; in addition, 15 percent interest was received on the balance in accounts receivable from April 28 through August 26.

Sept. 16 wrote a check for the principal and interest due on the March 16 note to Oregon National Bank

Nov. 1   purchased $12,000 in merchandise from the Mountain Sports Company; paid $5,000 cash down and signed a 90-day, 10 percent note for the balance owed

Dec. 1   sold $6,000 in merchandise to the Oregon Ski Shop; received $1,500 cash down and issued a 60-day, 12 percent note for the balance

Instructions   1.   *Prepare the general journal entries to record the transactions for the Mt. Hood Sporting Goods Store for Year 6. Round all interest amounts to the nearest penny if necessary.*

2.   *Prepare the adjusting entry on December 31 to record interest payable on the November 1 note from Mountain Sports Company.*

3.   *Prepare the adjusting entry on December 31 to record interest receivable on the December 1 note to the Oregon Ski Shop.*

CHAPTER 18

aluation of Plant
and Equipment

When you have completed this chapter, you should

1. have a better understanding of accounting terminology.

2. be able to apportion the cost to land and buildings when they are purchased together.

3. be able to calculate depreciation by the straight-line and accelerated methods.

4. be able to calculate depreciation for midyear purchases of assets.

5. be able to calculate depreciation expense after revision of depreciation rates.

6. be able to differentiate between revenue and capital expenditures.

7. be able to calculate depreciation rates after extraordinary repairs.

Assets acquired to be used in the operation of a business and that are not for sale are referred to as *plant and equipment,* or as *property, plant, and equipment.* Examples include buildings, land, equipment, trucks and autos, and furniture and fixtures. Plant and equipment may also be called **fixed assets.**

fixed assets
plant and equipment
assets

Most items of plant and equipment are depreciable assets and may be thought of as providing services to the company over a number of years. Purchasing a building, for example, gives the company office and storage space, and as a result of ownership of the building, no rent has to be paid. Owning the building may be viewed as a prepayment of rent over a period of years, and the cost of the building will gradually be converted to expense through the regular recording of depreciation. In this way, depreciable assets are much like prepaid expenses.

The same item may be a depreciable asset for one company, but not for another. For example, a tractor in the showroom of an implement dealer is an item of inventory, but that same tractor purchased by a paving company for use in road work is an item of plant and equipment whose cost will eventually be transferred to depreciation expense. Most items of plant and equipment are depreciable assets; the notable exception with which you are familiar is land. There are also intangible assets in the plant and equipment category—items such as patents, copyrights, trademarks, franchises, goodwill, and so on—whose cost will normally be spread over the life of the asset. Intangibles will be covered in Chapter 19.

INVESTMENTS

Often, businesses invest in other businesses. Such investments might be in the form of stocks, bonds, or notes. If the investments are temporary ones, they will be listed in the current assets section of the balance sheet as **marketable securities** (or marketable equity securities). If the investments are expected to be held for a long time, they will be included under a special balance sheet heading entitled Investments.

marketable securities
temporary investments
in another company

CATEGORIZING PLANT AND EQUIPMENT

real property
real estate; land and buildings

personal property
autos, furniture, fixtures, and so on; non-real estate assets

tangible asset
assets with a physical substance

intangible asset
assets that are non-physical and noncur-rent

Plant and equipment may be categorized into real property and personal property. **Real property** is real estate—land and anything that is attached to it. **Personal property** includes everything else—autos, equipment, furniture, and so on.

Plant and equipment may be further categorized as tangible or intangible. A **tangible asset** is one with a physical substance; tangible items of plant and equipment include land, which is not depreciable, and machinery, trucks, furniture, buildings, and so on, which are depreciable.

An **intangible asset** has two characteristics—it is nonphysical and noncurrent, and it includes such things as patents, copyrights, franchises, and goodwill. Accounts receivable, prepaid advertising, and other prepaid expenses are *not* intangible assets because they do not have both characteristics of intangible assets; they are non-physical, but they do not qualify as intangible assets because they are current.

THE COST OF PLANT AND EQUIPMENT

The cost of plant and equipment includes the amount paid for the asset (less any discount received) and any other normal expenditures necessary to get the asset into condition for use in the business. Such other expenditures may include sales tax, insurance costs while the asset is being transported, installation charges, the costs of assembling, and the costs of trial runs. When such expenses are debited to an asset account, they are said to be capitalized and will be recovered over several accounting periods as they will be transferred to depreciation expense over the useful life of the asset. If a related expenditure is *not* a normal and reasonable one, then it should not be included in the cost of the asset. For example, if an employee drops an item of equipment while it is being placed into service, that is not a normal and reasonable expenditure and would not be included in the asset's cost, but would be written off as an expense of the period.

Assume that a car dealership in Anaheim ordered several microcomputers from a firm in Long Beach. The list price of the computers was $29,500, and credit terms were 2/10, n/60. Sales tax was 6 percent, freight charges were $375, and installation charges were

$1,200. During the installation process, one of the car dealership's employees dropped a computer and caused $500 damage. Calculation of the cost of the computers is as follows.

List price of the computers	$29,500.00
Less 2 percent discount (.02 × $29,500)	− 590.00
Net price of computers	$28,910.00
Plus:	
Sales Tax (.06 × $28,910)	1,734.60
Freight Charges	375.00
Installation Charges	1,200.00
Total cost of computers	$32,219.60

The asset account Computer will be debited for $32,219.60 and Cash will be credited to record the acquisition. If the computers had been a charge purchase rather than a cash one, the interest expense would not be considered to be a part of the cost of the asset.

The costs required to get an asset ready for use are considered to be part of the depreciable cost of the asset. These costs are capitalized, along with the purchase price of the asset, and will be allocated to depreciation expense over the useful life of the asset. The matching principle requires that the expenses of a particular accounting period be matched against the revenue earned during that same time period. All regular maintenance charges after the asset has been placed in service are debited to expense.

LAND

When land is purchased with no building on it, the cost of the land includes the charges that are connected with the purchase. Such charges might include the commissions of real estate persons, escrow fees, any delinquent taxes paid by the purchaser, legal fees, and any fees spent for clearing, grading, draining, or surveying the property. Assessments for permanent improvements to the land such as sewers, sidewalks, paved streets, and curbs are also debited to the Land account.

Improvements that are not permanent in nature, or that are not directly associated with a building, however, are debited to an account called Land Improvements and are subject to depreciation. Such improvements include fences, outdoor lighting systems, parking lot surfaces, and trees and shrubs. If a building is to be constructed on the land, a separate Building account must be established to record the cost of construction.

PURCHASING LAND WITH A BUILDING ON IT

apportion

to divide into portions according to a formula

appraise

to place a value on

Land is assumed to have an unlimited life and thus is not depreciable. When land is purchased with a building on it, part of the total purchase price must be allocated to the land and the rest to the building. Usually, however, the purchase price does not stipulate separate prices for land and building. The buyer must **apportion** a part of the total cost price to the land and a part to the building.

Therefore, the buyer must **appraise** the asset. An appraisal will help establish how much of the purchase price should be allocated to the land and to the building. For example, assume that an acre of real estate with buildings on it is purchased for $2,500,000. The purchase was a good one, as an independent appraiser placed a value on the land at $1,885,000 and on the buildings at $1,015,000. To determine how much to apportion to the land and the buildings on the books, a percentage is used based on the total appraised value, $2,900,000 ($1,885,000 + $1,015,000). Percentages for cost allocation are calculated as follows.

1. Divide the appraised value of the land by the total appraised value.

$$1,885,000 \div 2,900,000 = .65$$

2. Divide the appraised value of the buildings by the total appraised value.

$$1,015,000 \div 2,900,000 = .35$$

The land represents 65 percent of the total appraised value and the buildings, 35 percent. Once the percents have been determined, the cost allocation may be made simply by multiplying the appropriate percentage by the actual cost of the property.

	Percentage of Total Value	Calculation for Cost Apportionment	Cost on the Books
Land	65%	.65 × $2,500,000	$1,625,000
Buildings	35	.35 × 2,500,000	875,000

The journal entry to record the purchase will debit Land for $1,625,000 and will debit Buildings for $875,000. The credit entry will be to Cash, Notes Payable, or a combination of the two, depending on how the property was paid for.

If the land being purchased has on it old buildings that are not useful to the buyer, the cost of those buildings plus the cost of removing them from the property will be debited to the Land account.

BUYING BUILDINGS WITH THE INTENT OF REPAIRING THEM

If buildings are purchased with the idea of repairing them to make them suitable for use, then the repairs will be debited to the Building account and the cost of the building and the repairs will be charged to depreciation expense over the life of the building. If, however, repairs are made after the buildings have been placed in use, they will be recorded as maintenance expense.

DEPRECIATION

When items of plant and equipment (with the exception of land) are purchased, it is assumed that they will be useful for a certain number of years. Their original cost is debited to an asset account, but that cost will be transferred to depreciation expense over the period of years in which services are received from the asset. The matching principle requires that costs be allocated to the period in which services are rendered.

internal transaction
a transaction for which nothing occurs externally

Journalizing depreciation expense is an **internal transaction,** because nothing occurs externally to cause the accountant to record it. There is no sale, no purchase, no borrowing—in other words, no outside person or business is involved. The rest of the adjusting entries and the closing entries are other examples of internal transactions.

Causes of Depreciation

The major causes of depreciation are physical deterioration, obsolescense, or inadequacy. Physical deterioration refers to the fact that as an asset is used it will wear out, no matter how well it is maintained. Exposure to sun, wind, rain, snow, and other climatic conditions causes further deterioration.

obsolescence
out of date; no longer useful because of technological improvements

Obsolescence refers to the fact that certain products are no longer useful because they have become out of date or they have been replaced by something new that is far more efficient. Computers are good examples of items of equipment that may become obsolete and have to be replaced before they actually wear out. Computer **technology** has grown rapidly during the past few years, and equipment that is state of the art one year may be out of date the next.

technology
the application of science in industry or commerce

If a company experiences rapid growth, some of its assets may become inadequate even though they have not worn out physically. An obsolete or inadequate asset will have to be replaced just as one which has physically deteriorated.

Depreciation as an Allocation of Costs

Regardless of whether an asset deteriorates or becomes obsolete, depreciation will be recorded. The recording of depreciation is not meant to place a value on an asset, but it is meant to allocate the cost of the asset to the periods in which services will be received from it.

When depreciation is recorded, Depreciation Expense is debited and the contra-asset account Accumulated Depreciation is credited. Failure to record this adjusting entry causes an overstatement of net income and assets. While the entry itself does not affect current assets or current liabilities, when the asset is fully depreciated or must be replaced, current assets must be expended to replace it.

Book Value

The cost of an asset minus its accumulated depreciation equals its book value. The total of plant and equipment on the balance sheet is the total of the book values of the depreciable assets. This amount, minus the salvage values of the plant and equipment assets, represents the amount that will be written off as depreciation expense in future periods.

The book value is not meant to approximate market value, which in fact may be much higher than the book value. Often, especially during periods of inflation, buildings become more valuable over the years rather than less valuable. If this is the case, depreciation will nevertheless continue to be recorded until the entire depreciable amount has been allocated to expense.

Methods of Calculating Depreciation

There are several ways in which to compute the amount of depreciation expense. The straight-line method spreads the cost of the asset evenly over its useful life; the units-of-output method allocates cost according to how much the asset is used; and the double-declining balance and the sum-of-the-years' digits methods accelerate the amount of depreciation expense written off during the early years of the asset's life. Different groups of assets may be depreciated by different methods, and it is common practice for accountants to use the straight-line or units-of-output method for their financial statements, but an accelerated method for calculation of income taxes. Logically, the more depreciation expense that is written off in any particular accounting period, the less the net income and the resulting income taxes will be.

Before computing depreciation expense, the cost, the useful life, and the salvage value of the asset must be known. The useful life and the salvage value are estimated and may be decided by past experience or by referring to trade publications or IRS guidelines. If the estimates for useful life or salvage value appear to be grossly in error after a while, they may be changed.

Straight-Line Method   The straight-line method of depreciation writes off the same amount of depreciation expense each accounting period over the life of the asset. The calculation for straight-line depreciation is as follows:

$$\frac{\text{Cost} - \text{Salvage Value}}{\text{Useful Life}} = \text{Depreciation Amount for the Period}$$

residual value
salvage value

The salvage or **residual value** is subtracted from the cost of the asset and the result is divided by the number of years (or months) in the useful life of the asset.

A depreciation schedule is prepared by the accountant when the asset is acquired. It shows the cost of the asset, the depreciation expense for each year, the accumulated depreciation, and the book value for each year of the asset's life. Following is a depreciation schedule for an automobile that was purchased on January 8 at a cost of $29,500. It was estimated to have a useful life of five years and a residual value of $2,500.

Depreciation Schedule
Automobile, Serial No. 7834604002
Straight-Line Method

Year	Depreciation Expense	Calculation	Accumulated Depreciation	Book Value
				Cost: $29,500
1	$5,400	1/5 × $27,000[a]	$ 5,400	$24,100
2	5,400	1/5 × 27,000	10,800	18,700
3	5,400	1/5 × 27,000	16,200	13,300
4	5,400	1/5 × 27,000	21,600	7,900
5	5,400	1/5 × 27,000	27,000	2,500

[a] $29,500 − $2,500 = $27,000 (the depreciable amount).

The total of the accumulated depreciation column at the end of the useful life of the asset must equal the total depreciable amount. Likewise, the balance in the book value column at that time must be equal to the residual value of the asset.

At the end of each accounting period, an adjusting entry is recorded that debits Depreciation Expense and credits Accumulated Depreciation. For the automobile, the entry on December 31 of each of the five years of the asset's life looks as follows.

GENERAL JOURNAL				Page 30
Date	Description	Post. Ref.	Debit	Credit
19XX	*Adjusting Entries*			
Dec. 31	Depreciation Expense		5400 —	
	Accumulated Depreciation: Automobile			5400 —
	To Record Depreciation for the Year			

Depreciation expense is closed along with the other expense accounts, while the balance of Accumulated Depreciation is subtracted from its related asset account on the balance sheet to produce the book value. Accumulated Depreciation is a contra-asset account.

Midyear Purchase Using the Straight-Line Method If the automobile in the preceding example was purchased on October 1 instead of on January 8 and the fiscal year ran from January 1 to December 31, then only three months' depreciation would be recorded the year of purchase. Following is the depreciation schedule assuming the auto was purchased October 1.

Depreciation Schedule
Automobile, Serial No. 7834604002
Midyear Purchase, Straight-Line Method

Year	Depreciation Expense	Calculation	Accumulated Depreciation	Book Value
				Cost: $29,500
1	$1,350	1/5 × $27,000 × 3/12 = $1,350	$ 1,350	$28,150
2	5,400	1/5 × 27,000 = 5,400	6,750	22,750
3	5,400	1/5 × 27,000 = 5,400	12,150	17,350
4	5,400	1/5 × 27,000 = 5,400	17,550	11,950
5	5,400	1/5 × 27,000 = 5,400	22,950	6,550
6	4,050	1/5 × 27,000 × 9/12 = 4,050	27,000	2,500

As a result of the midyear purchase, the depreciation schedule covers six different years, but only 60 months in all. The first and sixth years together record twelve months' depreciation expense, and the entire depreciation schedule records the full five years', or 60 months, depreciation.

The Straight-Line Rate of Depreciation   The calculation for the depreciation for the automobile shows the fraction "1/5" multiplied by the depreciable amount. Often, however, percentages are used rather than fractions. Assume, for example, that in the preceding example a percentage were to be used. It may be calculated in any of several different ways. The easiest way is to divide the life of the asset into 100 percent, and then multiply the rate by the depreciable amount to find the depreciation. For example, in the preceding example of the automobile with a five-year life, the calculation would be as follows:

$$100\% \div 5 \text{ (years)} = 20\% \text{ (rate of depreciation)}$$
$$.20 \times \$27,000 = \$5,400$$

The Units-of-Output Method of Depreciation   This method allows the depreciation amounts to relate directly to how much the asset is used. Assume, for example, a truck is bought by a construction company to haul materials. The truck cost $95,000 and was expected to have a residual value of $5,000 after being driven (used) for 75,000 miles. As with straight-line depreciation, the residual value is subtracted from the cost to determine the depreciable amount and that figure is divided by the number of miles (units) the truck can be used.

$$\frac{\text{Cost} - \text{Residual Value}}{\text{Number of Miles in Useful Life}} = \text{Depreciation per Mile}$$

$$\frac{\$95,000 - \$5,000}{75,000 \text{ miles}} = \$1.20 \text{ depreciation per mile}$$

Assume further that the truck is driven 17,000 miles the first year, 23,000 the second year, 22,500 the third year, and 18,900 the fourth year. The depreciation schedule for the truck is as follows.

Depreciation Schedule
Truck, Serial Number 23P-789235599
Units-of-Output Method of Depreciation

Year	Depreciation	Calculation	Accumulated Depreciation	Book Value
				Cost: $95,000
1	$20,400	17,000 × $1.20 = $20,400	$20,400	$74,600
2	27,600	23,000 × 1.20 = 27,600	48,000	47,000
3	27,000	22,500 × 1.20 = 27,000	75,000	20,000
4	15,000	18,900 × 1.20 = 22,680[a]	90,000	5,000

[a]Even though the fourth year's depreciation calculation is $22,680, only $15,000 may be recorded as depreciation expense for that year ($20,000 − $5,000). When the depreciable amount has been completely transferred to expense, no more depreciation may be recorded for the asset.

Once an asset has been fully depreciated, no more depreciation may be taken on the asset even if it remains in use. This explains the $15,000 depreciation expense for the fourth year of the truck's life. An asset may not be depreciated below its salvage value.

accelerate
to cause to move faster

Accelerated Depreciation To speed something up is to **accelerate** it. Accelerated depreciation refers to the methods that write off large amounts of depreciation expense during the first years of an asset's life and relatively small amounts after that. Accelerating depreciation may be justified because major cash outlays to pay for it may occur during the first years of its life. Also, some accountants feel that the benefits to be derived from an asset are greatest when it is newest and repairs are infrequent, and therefore the greatest amount of depreciation expense should be taken during this time.

The Double-Declining Balance Method of Depreciation This method writes off large amounts of depreciation during the early years of an asset's life. By the same token, it writes off relatively small amounts during the last years of the asset's life.

Assume that the automobile that was depreciated earlier by the straight-line method is depreciated instead by the double-declining balance method. This method is referred to as *double-declining* because twice the straight-line rate is used to calculate depreciation and the rate is multiplied by a declining figure, the book value. *Salvage value is ignored when calculating for double-declining balance; even so, the asset may not be depreciated below residual value.* The automobile cost $29,500, had an estimated life of five years and an estimated residual value of $2,500. The first step when calculating for double-declining balance is to compute the rate of depreciation. This is accomplished by figuring the straight-line rate and then doubling it, as follows.

1. 100% ÷ 5 (years) = 20%, the straight line rate
2. 20% × 2 = 40%, the double-declining balance rate

Depreciation amounts are then calculated by multiplying the double-declining rate the first year by the cost and in succeeding years by the book value, which is always declining. The salvage value is ignored when calculating by the double-declining balance method, but because the asset may not be depreciated below its book value, an adjustment must be made toward the end of the asset's useful life.

Depreciation Schedule
Automobile, Serial No. 7834604002
Double-Declining Balance Method

Year	Depreciation	Calculation	Accumulated Depreciation	Book Value
				Cost: $29,500
1	$11,800	.40 × $29,500 = $11,800	$11,800	$17,700
2	7,080	.40 × 17,700 = 7,080	18,880	10,620
3	4,248	.40 × 10,620 = 4,248	23,128	6,372
4	2,549	.40 × 6,372 = 2,549[a]	25,677	3,823
5	1,323[b]	.40 × 3,823 = 1,529	27,000	2,500

[a]Depreciation amounts are rounded to the nearest dollar.
[b]$3,823 − $2,500 (residual value) = $1,323. The asset should not be depreciated below the residual value.

In the last year of the automobile's life, the depreciation amount had to be adjusted so that the final book value is the same as the residual value of the asset. Depreciating by the double-declining balance method will never bring the book value to zero, because each year only a portion of the **undepreciated cost** is written off. Thus, if the residual value is significant in amount, depreciation should stop when accumulated depreciation is equal to the depreciable amount (the cost minus the residual value).

undepreciated cost
cost minus accumulated depreciation

Calculation for Midyear Purchase by Double-Declining Balance
Assume that the automobile in the preceding illustration was purchased on October 1 instead of on January 8. Again, only a fraction of the entire year's depreciation will be written off the first year. The amount of double-declining balance depreciation expense from October 1 to December 31 during the year of purchase is calculated as follows:

$$.40 \times \$29,500 \times 3/12 = \$2,950$$

The second year's depreciation is calculated by determining the new book value, and then multiplying it by the rate.

$$\$29,500 - \$2,950 = \$26,550 \text{ (book value, December 31, End of Year 1)}$$
$$.40 \times \$26,550 = \$10,620 \text{ (second year's depreciation)}$$

There will be no change in method in calculating depreciation amounts for succeeding years; simply multiply the rate by the book value. The double-declining balance depreciation schedule when the asset is purchased midyear is as follows.

Depreciation Schedule
Automobile, Serial No. 7834604002
Midyear Purchase, Double-Declining Balance Method

Year	Depreciation Expense	Calculation			Accumulated Depreciation	Book Value
						Cost: $29,500
1	$ 2,950	.40 × $29,500 × 3/12	=	$ 2,950	$ 2,950	$26,550
2	10,620	.40 × 26,550	=	10,620	13,570	15,930
3	6,372	.40 × 15,930	=	6,372	19,942	9,558
4	3,823	.40 × 9,558	=	3,823[a]	23,765	5,735
5	2,294	.40 × 5,735	=	2,294	26,059	3,441
6	941[b]	.40 × 3,441	=	1,376	27,000	2,500

[a]Depreciation amounts are rounded to the nearest dollar.

[b]$3,441 − $2,500 (residual value) = $941. The asset should not be depreciated below residual value.

As with a midyear purchase using the straight-line method, depreciation by the double-declining balance method carries over into the sixth year, by which time it is nearly fully depreciated. If the rate of depreciation were higher (say, 50 percent), it is possible the asset would be fully depreciated in the fifth year or before, even with the midyear purchase.

The Sum-of-the-Years' Digits Method of Depreciation   Another accelerated method of depreciation is the sum-of-the-years' digits (SYD) method. Under this method, each year a fraction is multiplied by the depreciable amount. The fraction used is smaller for each succeeding year of the asset's life. For example, in the case of the automobile costing $29,500, having a residual value of $2,500 and a useful life of five years, the depreciation fraction is partially obtained by summing (adding) the digits of the asset's useful life. For a five-year life, the digits $1 + 2 + 3 + 4 + 5$ are added to provide the denominator of the depreciation fraction, 15. The first year's depreciation will be calculated using the fraction 5/15: 5 represents the total number of years in the useful life, and 15 is the sum of the years' digits.

The second year, the fraction (and thus the depreciation expense) will be smaller—4/15. The third year, the fraction will be 3/15; the fourth year, 2/15; and the fifth year, 1/15. The fractions added together equal 15/15: $5/15 + 4/15 + 3/15 + 2/15 + 1/15 = 15/15$. The fraction 15/15, of course, represents 100 percent of the depreciable amount.

With sum-of-the-years' digits, the residual value is subtracted to obtain the depreciable amount. Following is the depreciation schedule for the automobile using the sum-of-the-years' digits method.

Depreciation Schedule
Automobile, Serial No. 7834604002
Sum-of-the-Years' Digits Method

Year	Depreciation Expense	Calculation	Accumulated Depreciation	Book Value
				Cost: $29,500
1	$ 9,000	5/15 × $27,000 = $9,000	$ 9,000	$20,500
2	7,200	4/15 × 27,000 = 7,200	16,200	13,300
3	5,400	3/15 × 27,000 = 5,400	21,600	7,900
4	3,600	2/15 × 27,000 = 3,600	25,200	4,300
5	1,800	1/15 × 27,000 = 1,800	27,000	2,500

A shortcut method may be used to determine the sum of the years' digits. Simply multiply the number of years in the asset's life by the next highest number and divide the result by two. For example, if an asset has a useful life of ten years, the sum of the years' digits from 1 through 10 may be calculated as follows:

$$\frac{10 \times 11}{2} = \frac{110}{2} = 55$$

For an asset with a useful life of 20 years, the sum of the years' digits from 1 through 20 may be figured as follows:

$$\frac{20 \times 21}{2} = \frac{420}{2} = 210$$

If an asset has an estimated useful life of 10 years, under SYD, the depreciation fraction the first year is 10/55; the second year, 9/55; the third year, 8/55; and so on. If the useful life is 20 years, the depreciation fraction the first year is 20/210; the second year, 19/210; the third year 18/210; and so on. The last year of the asset's useful life, the numerator of the fraction will always be 1. The least amount of depreciation is taken the last year of the useful life with accelerated methods of depreciation.

Calculation for Midyear Purchase Using SYD Assume that the $29,500 automobile with a five-year life and a $2,500 residual value was purchased on October 1. The first year's depreciation under SYD would be calculated as follows:

$$5/15 \times \$27,000 \times 3/12 = \$2,250$$

After the depreciation for October 1–December 31 has been recorded, the 5/15 fraction has been used for only three months. Therefore, to continue the acceleration as much as possible, it must be used for the calculation of the second year's depreciation for an additional nine months; the 4/15 fraction will be used for the remaining three months of the second year. The calculation for the second year is as follows:

$$\begin{array}{l} 5/15 \times \$27,000 \times 9/12 = \$6,750 \\ 4/15 \times \$27,000 \times 3/12 = \$1,800 \end{array} = \$8,550$$

The complete depreciation schedule for a midyear purchase using SYD follows.

Depreciation Schedule
Automobile, Serial No. 7834604002
Midyear Purchase, Sum-of-the-Years' Digits Method

Year	Depreciation Expense	Calculation	Accumulated Depreciation	Book Value
				Cost: $29,500
1	$2,250	5/15 × $27,000 × 3/12 = $2,250	$ 2,250	$27,250
2	8,550	5/15 × 27,000 × 9/12 = 6,750		
		4/15 × 27,000 × 3/12 = 1,800	10,800	18,700
3	6,750	4/15 × 27,000 × 9/12 = 5,400		
		3/15 × 27,000 × 3/12 = 1,350	17,550	11,950
4	4,950	3/15 × 27,000 × 9/12 = 4,050		
		2/15 × 27,000 × 3/12 = 900	22,500	7,000
5	3,150	2/15 × 27,000 × 9/12 = 2,700		
		1/15 × 27,000 × 3/12 = 450	25,650	3,850
6	1,350	1/15 × 27,000 × 9/12 = 1,350	27,000	2,500

As with the other depreciation schedules, the total accumulated depreciation must be equal to the total depreciable amount (cost minus residual value) and the ending book value must be equal to the residual value.

FRACTIONAL PERIOD DEPRECIATION

Depreciation is not intended to be exact nor is it intended to place a value on the assets. It is designed to spread the cost of the asset over its useful life. Thus, when an asset is purchased on August 13, it is not necessary for depreciation purposes to calculate the exact number of days in August that the asset is held.

A common method for recording depreciation when the asset is purchased other than at the beginning of the accounting period is to record a full month's depreciation if the asset is purchased on or before the 15th of the month, and to ignore the month for depreciation purposes if the asset is purchased on the 16th or later. Unless otherwise stipulated, this is the method used in this book.

half-year convention
six months' depreciation is recorded the year of purchase, regardless of date of purchase

Another widely used approach is referred to as the **half-year convention.** Under this method, six months' depreciation is recorded for all assets purchased during the year. This method allows similar assets to be depreciated as a group, even though they are purchased at different times during the year. For example, a firm may buy several desktop computers throughout the year for its various offices. Using the half-year convention, the computers may be depreciated as a group, rather than individually.

The half-year convention is used for equipment, autos, furniture, and so on, but may not be used for buildings.

COMPARISON OF DEPRECIATION METHODS

The following illustrates how much more depreciation is written off during the early years of an asset's life when accelerated depreciation methods are used. The double-declining balance method produces the greatest write-off the first years of the asset's life, but it (and the sum-of-the-years' digits method) produces less depreciation expense than the straight-line method the last years of the asset's life.

The illustration following compares the straight-line, sum-of-the-years' digits, and double-declining balance methods of depreciation for the automobile costing $29,500, having a residual value of $2,500 and a useful life of five years.

Comparison of Straight-Line and Accelerated Methods of Depreciation

	Amount of Depreciation Expense		
Year	Straight-Line	Sum-of-the-Years' Digits	Double-Declining Balance
1	$5,400	9,000	$11,800
2	5,400	7,200	7,080
3	5,400	5,400	4,248
4	5,400	3,600	2,549
5	5,400	1,800	1,323

REVISION OF DEPRECIATION RATES

It is not uncommon for the original estimate of the useful life of an asset to be in error. If the error is substantial, the depreciation schedule amounts may have to be revised to reflect either the longer or shorter life of the asset. This is accomplished by spreading the undepreciated cost over the remaining years of the asset's life. No attempt is made to correct past years' depreciation amounts.

Assume, for example, that an asset is acquired on January 9, Year 1, at a cost of $28,000. It is expected to have a useful life of ten years and a residual value of $4,000. After straight-line depreciation has been recorded for three years ($2,400 per year), accountants revise the estimate of useful life to be only three years more. In other words, the estimate of the asset's total useful life has been changed from ten years to six years. There is no change in the estimate of the residual value. The revised depreciation for the remaining three years of the asset's life is calculated as follows.

1. Determine the amount of depreciation taken so far:

$$\$2,400 \times 3 \text{ (years)} = \$7,200 \text{ depreciation recorded first three years}$$

2. Determine the revised depreciation amount:

$$\frac{\text{Cost} - \text{Depreciation Taken so Far} - \text{Residual Value}}{\text{Number of Years Remaining in Asset's Life}} = \text{Revised Depreciation Amount}$$

$$\frac{\$28,000 - \$7,200 - \$4,000}{3} = \frac{\$16,800}{3} = \$5,600 \text{ (revised depreciation amount per year)}$$

In step 2, the undepreciated cost, $16,800, was spread over the remaining three years of the asset's life. At the end of six years, the book value will be equal to the residual value of $4,000.

1st three years' depreciation	$2,400 × 3 = $ 7,200
2nd three years' depreciation	$5,600 × 3 = 16,800
Total depreciation for all six years	$24,000

COST RECOVERY FOR FEDERAL INCOME TAXES

In 1981, Congress changed the rules for depreciation for federal income tax purposes. It devised a new depreciation method called Accelerated Cost Recovery System (ACRS), which was required for figuring income taxes. ACRS does not use the concepts of useful life or residual value; it simply applies a certain percentage each year to the asset's cost. The number of years that an asset is to be depreciated over is determined by referring to a chart that lists various categories of assets and the number of years for which they must be depreciated.

In 1986, Congress passed the Tax Reform Act of 1986, which again made changes in depreciation methods for federal tax purposes. It still allows use of ACRS, but the taxpayer may also elect a straight-line or an accelerated method. It also changed the number of years over which certain assets may be depreciated. If an accelerated method is chosen, double-declining balance is prescribed for most assets (except real estate).

Thus, for assets purchased before December 31, 1980, ACRS may not be used. For assets purchased between December 31, 1980, and January 1, 1987, ACRS is used for federal tax purposes; and for property acquired after January 1, 1987, methods prescribed in the Tax Reform Act of 1986 will be used.

ACRS and the Tax Reform Act were designed to stimulate business by encouraging investment in new items of plant and equipment through the allowance of very rapid depreciation methods. The recovery period (useful life) prescribed in ACRS and the 1986 law are generally much shorter than the actual useful life of assets. This, combined with the high rates allowed, produces a rapid write-off of the cost of the asset.

These depreciation methods used for federal income taxes are not acceptable for financial reporting, because they violate one of the generally accepted accounting principles (GAAP)—the matching principle. A write-off of depreciation expense that is not somewhat realistic in terms of useful life produces an exaggerated, overstated depreciation expense for a few years and a resulting understated net income. As a result, ACRS and the Tax Reform Act methods are not used in the financial statements shown to management, investors, lenders, and so forth.

CAPITAL AND REVENUE EXPENDITURES

capital expenditure
an expenditure that is debited to an asset account and will be transferred to depreciation expense over several accounting periods

betterment
a major improvement to an asset from which services will be received for several accounting periods

revenue expenditure
an expenditure whose benefits are immediate; debited to an expense account

An expenditure is the paying of cash or the incurring of an obligation to pay at some future date. A **capital expenditure** is one that is debited to an asset account. The benefits of a capital expenditure, or capitalizing, will be over a period of several accounting periods. Capital expenditures include the acquisition of plant and equipment. They also include enlargements to existing assets, such as adding new rooms or new wings to existing buildings. Installation of an escalator or an air-conditioning system, referred to as betterments, are also capital expenditures. A **betterment** is an improvement from which services will be received for a period of years and will thus be debited to an asset account.

If the expenditure produces benefits primarily to the current accounting period, it is charged to expense and is referred to as a **revenue expenditure.** Examples are payments for maintenance of equipment such as lubrication, cleaning, or ordinary repairs; the benefits of a revenue expenditure are immediate and will be deducted from the revenue of the current period.

If a revenue expenditure is erroneously recorded as a capital expenditure, expenses of the current period will be understated and the resulting net income will be overstated. On the other hand, if a capital expenditure is incorrectly recorded as a revenue expenditure, expenses will be overstated and net income understated.

Accountants often have difficulty deciding whether a particular payment should be categorized as a capital or a revenue expenditure. Thus many companies establish policies and guidelines for the treatment of expenditures. Normally assets of low unit value, though they might last several years, are debited to expense when purchased, since doing so will have no material effect on net income. Low unit value assets might include such things as pencil sharpeners, wastebaskets, and desk trays.

EXTRAORDINARY REPAIRS

Ordinary repairs are the normal repairs required to keep an asset in good working condition. They include lubrication, cleaning, inspections, and regular maintenance. Extraordinary repairs are those that affect the estimated residual value or the useful life of an asset. For example, a major piece of equipment may receive a major overhaul that will extend its life by several years.

Costly repairs are recorded by debiting Accumulated Depreciation; this has the effect of taking away some of the depreciation recorded earlier and of increasing the book value of the asset. The new book value of the asset (minus any estimated salvage value) should be spread over the remaining years of the asset's life

Assume, for example, that a delivery truck was purchased on January 3, Year 1, for $35,000. It had an estimated useful life of five years and an estimated residual value of $5,000. At the beginning of the fifth year, the engine was rebuilt and other major repairs were made at a cost of $7,500. These repairs extended the useful life an extra two years (seven years in all). There is no change in the estimate of residual value.

For the first four years, $24,000 in depreciation expense was written off:

$$\frac{\$35,000 - \$5,000}{5} = \$6,000 \times 4 = \$24,000$$

The entry to record the depreciation each year debited Depreciation Expense for $6,000 and credited Accumulated Depreciation. The book value at the end of the fourth year was $11,000 ($35,000 − $24,000). The balance in the Accumulated Depreciation account was $24,000.

When the extraordinary repairs were made on January 10, Year 5, the $7,500 was debited to Accumulated Depreciation and credited to Cash. The balance in the Accumulated Depreciation account after the repairs was $16,500.

Accumulated Depreciation:
Delivery Truck   **160A**

Cost of repairs	Year 5	7,500	Year 1 6,000
			Year 2 6,000
			Year 3 6,000
			Year 4 6,000
			16,500

Depreciation first 4 years

The calculation for depreciation expense for the remaining three years is as follows:

$$\frac{\text{Cost} - \text{Accumulated Depreciation} - \text{Residual Value}}{\text{Years Remaining in Useful Life}} = \text{Revised Annual Depreciation}$$

$$\frac{\$35,000 - \$16,500 - \$5,000}{3} = \frac{\$13,500}{3} = \$4,500$$

At the end of the asset's useful life, the Accumulated Depreciation account looks as follows.

Accumulated Depreciation:
Delivery Truck   **160A**

Year 5	7,500	Year 1	6,000
		Year 2	6,000
		Year 3	6,000
		Year 4	6,000
		Year 5	4,500
		Year 6	4,500
		Year 7	4,500
		30,000	

The credits to Accumulated Depreciation total $37,500. This is the total amount debited to Depreciation Expense over the seven-year period. The credit balance of Accumulated Depreciation at the end of the seventh year is $30,000, thus producing a book value equal to the salvage value of the delivery truck, $5,000 ($35,000 − $30,000).

SUMMARY

Plant and equipment, also called fixed assets, are those assets that are not for sale and that are used in the operation of the business. Plant and equipment assets include autos, furniture, buildings, equipment, and land; except for land, the cost of plant and equipment assets will be transferred to expense over the useful life of the asset.

When one business makes a temporary investment in another in the form of stocks, bonds, or notes, this investment is listed in the current assets section of the balance sheet under the title marketable securities.

Plant and equipment includes both real property (real estate) and personal property (equipment, autos, trucks, and so on); it is either tangible or intangible. Tangible assets are those with a physical substance; intangible assets are nonphysical and noncurrent and include patents, copyrights, franchises, and goodwill.

The cost of plant and equipment should include any normal and reasonable expenditures necessary to get the asset into condition for use. These costs, along with the purchase price of the asset, will be allocated to depreciation expense over the useful life of the asset.

When land is purchased with no building on it, its cost should include related charges such as real estate commissions, escrow fees, delinquent taxes, and so on. Also, charges for clearing and draining the land or surveying it should be included as part of the cost, as well as permanent improvements such as sewers and sidewalks. If land is purchased with a building(s) on it, a part of the total cost must be apportioned to the land and the building. An appraisal will help determine the percentage of the cost to allocate to each.

If buildings are purchased that have to be repaired to make them ready for use, the cost of the repairs is debited to the building account and the total cost will be written off to depreciation expense over the useful life of the buildings. Repairs made after the buildings have been put into service are debited to Maintenance Expense.

The recording of depreciation expense, as well as the other adjusting entries and the closing entries, are referred to as internal transactions, because nothing occurs externally to cause the journal entry to be made.

The major causes of depreciation are physical deterioration, obsolescence, and inadequacy, but regardless of whether any of these occur, the cost of the asset will be allocated to the periods in which services will be received from the asset. Failure to record depreciation causes an overstatement of net income and assets.

There are several ways to calculate depreciation. The straight-line method evenly spreads the cost of the asset over its useful life. The units-of-output method allocates cost according to usage of the asset. The sum-of-the-years' digits and double-declining balance methods accelerate the write-off of depreciation expense. Accelerated methods write off large amounts of depreciation the first years of an asset's life when benefits are greatest and when major cash outlays are required to pay for it. Relatively small amounts are written off the last years of the asset's life using accelerated methods.

When assets are purchased other than at the beginning of the accounting period, depreciation may be taken to the nearest whole month, or the half-year convention may be used under which six months' depreciation is taken during the year of purchase, no matter when the acquisition is made. Depreciation is not meant to be exact, nor is it meant to place a value on the asset.

Depreciation rates should be revised if the original estimate of useful life was grossly in error. The remaining undepreciated cost should be spread over the remaining years of useful life.

Congress changed the rules for depreciation for federal income taxes in 1981. A new method of depreciation called Accelerated Cost Recovery System was instituted. Salvage value and useful life were discarded and replaced with a percentage applied to the cost for a certain number of years, usually far fewer than the actual number of years in the life of the asset. The Tax Reform Act of 1986 changed ACRS rules somewhat and allowed the taxpayer to use straight-line or double-declining balance methods for federal tax purposes. For financial statements, however, ACRS is not used because the write-off is too rapid and violates the matching principle.

Expenditures are categorized as capital or revenue expenditures. A revenue expenditure is one that will benefit the current accounting period and is debited to an expense account that will in turn be subtracted from the revenue of the period to obtain net income. Examples include payments for repairs, maintenance, fuel, and so on. A capital expenditure is one that will benefit several accounting periods and is debited to an asset account. Examples include payments for acquisition of assets, major enlargements to buildings, or betterments to buildings (such as the installation of an air-conditioning system).

Major repairs, called extraordinary repairs, that lengthen the useful life of an asset are debited to Accumulated Depreciation.

This increases the book value of the asset, which allows the depreciation taken to be increased and spread over a longer period of time. Extraordinary repairs are capital expenditures.

Review of Accounting Terminology

Following is a list of the accounting terminology for this chapter.

accelerate	marketable securities
apportion	obsolescence
appraise	personal property
betterment	real property
capital expenditure	residual value
fixed asset	revenue expenditure
half-year convention	tangible asset
intangible asset	technology
internal transaction	undepreciated cost

Fill in the blank with the correct word or term from the list.

1. A/an _____ is an expenditure that is debited to an asset account.

2. A/an _____ is a transaction for which nothing external occurs.

3. Assets become out of date; this is one of the major causes of depreciation and is referred to as _____.

4. Real estate is referred to as _____.

5. Investments in the stocks or bonds of another company are referred to on the balance sheet as _____.

6. Another term for salvage value is _____.

7. An expenditure that is debited to expense is a/an _____.

8. To place a value on an asset is to _____ it.

9. A/an _____ has physical substance.

10. An item of plant and equipment is sometimes referred to as a/an _____.

11. Cost minus accumulated depreciation is called the book value or the _____.

12. Depreciation taken for six months during the fiscal year, regardless of the month of purchase, is referred to as the _____.

13. The branch of knowledge that deals with the industrial arts and sciences is referred to as _____.

14. Autos, furniture, equipment, and non-real estate assets are referred to as _____.

15. A/an _____ is nonphysical and noncurrent.

16. To divide into just portions according to a definite rule or formula is to _____.

17. To speed up is to _____.

18. A/an _____ is a major improvement to an existing building such as the adding of a central heating system.

Match the following words and terms on the left with the definitions on the right (columns continue on the following page).

19. accelerate
20. apportion
21. appraise
22. betterment
23. capital expenditure
24. fixed asset
25. half-year convention
26. intangible assets
27. internal transaction

a. autos, trucks, furniture, fixtures, and so forth
b. salvage value
c. depreciation taken for six months during the year of purchase regardless of the date of purchase
d. an expenditure that is debited to expense
e. items of plant and equipment
f. an asset that is nonphysical and noncurrent
g. to cause to move faster
h. adjusting and closing entries; an entry for which no external transaction occurs
i. short-term investments in another business

28. marketable securities

29. obsolescence

30. personal property

31. real property

32. residual value

33. revenue expenditure

34. tangible asset

35. technology

36. undepreciated cost

j. to set a price on

k. an expenditure that is debited to an asset account

l. real estate; land, buildings, and so on

m. the application of science in industry or commerce

n. an asset with physical substance

o. a major improvement to an existing building

p. to divide into just portions according to a definite rule

q. out of date

r. cost minus accumulated depreciation

Exercises

Exercise 18.1
determining cost of equipment

Equipment with a list price of $92,000 is purchased by the Rhode Island Construction Company. Credit terms are 2/10, n/60 and sales tax is 5.5 percent. The Rhode Island Construction Company paid for the equipment within the discount period. Transportation charges to have the equipment brought to the factory were $1,525. An employee who was following the delivery vehicle parked illegally during a stop to check the equipment and was fined $50. Labor charges to install the equipment were $2,100, and testing the equipment immediately after installation cost $1,930. Ninety days after the installation of the equipment, it was inspected and regular maintenance was performed at a cost of $500. Prepare a schedule showing the amount that should be debited to the Equipment account to record its initial cost.

Exercise 18.2
determining cost of land

The Lansing Company purchased land costing $175,000. Real estate fees were 6 percent of the cost; escrow and title company fees were $1,500; $2,750 was spent for clearing the land and another $3,500 for grading it. Trees and shrubs were planted costing $2,900. Legal fees connected with the purchase were $4,000. A fence was built at a cost of $975 which separated the land from adjoining property. Prepare a schedule that shows the amount to be debited to the Land account.

Exercise 18.3
apportioning cost to land and building

The North Carolina Development Company purchased land and a building for a total cost of $1,650,000. An independent appraiser placed a value on the land of $663,000 and a value on the building of $1,287,000. Determine according to the appraisal how much of the cost to apportion to the land and to the building on the books.

Exercise 18.4
preparing a straight-line depreciation schedule

The Purdue Road Builders' fiscal year runs from January 1 to December 31. It purchased a backhoe costing $375,000 on January 4. It was expected to be useful for five years and have a residual value of $25,000.

a. Prepare a straight-line depreciation schedule showing the annual depreciation expense, the calculation for it, the accumulated depreciation, and the book value for each year.

b. Calculate to the nearest month the amount of depreciation expense the first year if the backhoe had been purchased on April 4.

c. Again, assuming the backhoe was purchased on April 4, calculate the amount of depreciation expense to be recognized the first year using the half-year convention.

Exercise 18.5
preparing a units-of-output depreciation schedule

Assume that the Purdue Road Builders decided to depreciate the backhoe in Exercise 18.4 by the units-of-output method. The backhoe had an estimated useful life of 8,000 hours of use and an estimated residual value of $25,000. The first year the backhoe was used 2,080 hours; the second year, 1,972 hours; the third year, 2,200 hours; the fourth year, 1,500 hours; and the fifth year, 1,420 hours. Prepare a units-of-output depreciation schedule showing the annual depreciation, the calculation for it, the accumulated depreciation, and the book value for each year. Do not depreciate the asset below residual value.

Exercise 18.6
preparing a double-declining balance depreciation schedule

The Black Hills Mining company has a fiscal year from January 1 to December 31 and purchased equipment costing $950,000 on January 9. It had a useful life of four years and an estimated salvage value of $75,000.

a. Calculate the double-declining balance rate of depreciation using twice the straight-line rate.

b. Prepare a double-declining balance depreciation schedule for the equipment. Show for each year the depreciation expense, the calculation used to obtain it, the accumulated depreciation, and the book value.

c. Calculate the first and second year's double-declining balance depreciation assuming the equipment was purchased on November 1 of Year 1. Round depreciation amounts to the nearest dollar.

Exercise 18.7
preparing a sum-of-the-years' digits depreciation schedule

Assume the Black Hills Mining Company decided to depreciate the equipment purchased in Exercise 18.6 by the sum-of-the-years' digits method.

a. Prepare a SYD depreciation schedule showing for each year the depreciation, the calculation used to arrive at it, the accumulated depreciation, and the book value.

b. Calculate the first and second year's SYD depreciation assuming the equipment was purchased on November 1. Round depreciation amounts to the nearest dollar.

Exercise 18.8
revising straight-line rate of depreciation

The Portland Cement Company purchased equipment costing $350,000. It was expected to be useful for eight years and would be worth $50,000 at that time. After three years of use, however, it decided that the equipment would be useful for only two more years. No change was made in the estimate for residual value.

a. Using straight-line depreciation, calculate the accumulated depreciation for the first three years.

b. Calculate the revised amount of annual depreciation expense for the remaining two years of the asset's useful life.

Exercise 18.9
identifying capital and revenue expenditures

Identify the following as either a capital expenditure or a revenue expenditure.

a. Added a new wing onto an existing office building at a cost of $160,000.

b. Purchased 20 new wastebaskets for various offices at a total cost of $97.50.

c. Replaced an old stairwell in a building that had been in use for four years with an escalator at a cost of $17,950.

d. Purchased three new batteries for salespersons' cars at a total cost of $105.

e. Paid $275 for regular maintenance of a machine that had been in service six months.

f. Painted salesperson's auto after two years of use.

g. Rebuilt the engine in a four-year-old dump truck at a cost of $2,760. The repairs were expected to increase the useful life of the truck by two years.

h. Painted a building at a cost of $3,200 immediately after purchasing it to make it ready for use.

Exercise 18.10
calculating straight-line depreciation before and after extraordinary repairs

On January 3, Year 1, the New Mexico Silver Company purchased equipment costing $164,000. The equipment was expected to be useful for five years and have a residual value of $40,000. On January 11 of the fifth year, extraordinary repairs were made to the equipment totaling $30,000 cash. The repairs were expected to extend the life of the equipment an extra two years (seven years in all). The estimate of salvage value was revised to be $20,000.

a. Calculate annual straight-line depreciation expense for the first four years.

b. Calculate accumulated depreciation for the first four years.

c. Indicate which accounts will be debited and credited to record the repairs.

d. Determine the balance of the Accumulated Depreciation account after the repairs were made on January 11 of Year 5.

e. Calculate the revised annual depreciation expense for the last three years of the asset's useful life. Round depreciation amounts to the nearest dollar.

Problems ═══

Problem 18.1
determining cost of equipment

On March 1, the Chico Bakery purchased new equipment costing $195,000. Credit terms were 2/10, n/30 and sales tax was 6 percent of the net price paid. Freight charges to get the equipment to Chico were $2,425, and installation labor was $3,960. While installing the equipment, one of the bakery employees hooked it up wrong and when the equipment was turned on, it caused electrical damage amounting to $3,640. Trial runs after the damage was repaired cost $4,600. After the equipment had been operating for 60 days, regular maintenance was performed at a cost of $1,200.

Instructions

1. *Assuming that the Chico Bakery paid within the discount period, prepare a schedule showing the cost of the equipment.*

2. *Prepare the general journal entry to record the acquisition of the equipment if the bakery paid $50,000 cash down and signed a three-year, 10 percent note for the balance.*

3. *Prepare the general journal entry on December 31 to record straight-line depreciation on the equipment assuming the fiscal year is January 1 to December 31. The equipment is estimated to have a useful life of ten years and a residual value of $20,000. Round depreciation amounts to the nearest dollar.*

Problem 18.2
apportioning cost to land and building

On April 13, the Dade County Nursery purchased land with buildings on it for expansion of the nursery. The total purchase price was $825,000. An appraisal placed a value of $592,475 on the land and $319,025 on the buildings.

Instructions

1. *As per the appraisal, determine how much should be apportioned to the land and to the buildings on the books.*

2. *Prepare the general journal entry to record the purchase of the land and buildings if $150,000 cash was paid down and a 20-year, 9.5 percent note was signed for the balance owed.*

3. *Assume that the appraisal showed the buildings to be worth only $75,000 because of disrepair. The Dade County Nursery decided to purchase the land and have the buildings torn down and hauled away to make room for new buildings. The cost of tearing down and removing the buildings was $23,850. In addition, the land had to be cleared and graded at a cost of $5,250. Prepare the general journal entry to record the acquisition of the land if $100,000 cash was paid down and a ten-year, 10 percent note was signed for the balance.*

Problem 18.3
calculating straight-line and units-of-output depreciation

On August 10, Year 6, the Kansas City Pipe Works purchased a truck costing $75,000. Its estimated useful life was four years or 100,000 miles, and its estimated salvage value was $10,000. The truck was driven 8,220 miles between August 10 and December 31 of Year 6; it was driven 26,300 miles in Year 7; 20,429 miles in Year 8; and 18,650 miles in Year 9. The Kansas City Pipe Works has a fiscal year from January 1 to December 31.

Instructions

1. *Prepare the general journal entry to record straight-line depreciation on December 31 for Year 6 (nearest month) and Year 7. Round depreciation amounts to the nearest dollar.*

2. *Prepare the general journal entry to record units-of-output depreciation for Year 6 and Year 7.*

3. *Calculate the maximum amount of units-of-output depreciation that can be taken in Year 10.*

Problem 18.4
calculating double-declining balance and sum-of-the-years' digits depreciation

On January 8, Year 1, the Helena Furniture Warehouse purchased a delivery truck costing $60,000. It was expected to have a useful life of five years, after which time it would be worth $9,000. The Helena Furniture Warehouse has a fiscal year of January 1 to December 31.

Instructions

1. *Prepare a double-declining balance depreciation schedule for the delivery truck for Years 1 through 5. Show for each year the depreciation, the calculation for it, the accumulated depreciation, and the book value.*

2. *Prepare a sum-of-the-years' digits depreciation schedule showing for each year the depreciation, the calculation for it, the accumulated depreciation, and the book value.*

3. *Prepare the general journal entry to record double-declining balance depreciation on December 31 of Year 1 if the truck was purchased on May 8 instead of on January 8.*

4. *Prepare the general journal entry to record sum-of-the-years' digits depreciation for Year 1 if the truck was purchased on May 8 instead of on January 8. Round the depreciation amount to the nearest dollar.*

Problem 18.5
calculating sum-of-the-years' digits and double-declining balance depreciation for midyear purchases

The New Orleans Packing Company has a fiscal year of January 1 to December 31 and purchased manufacturing equipment on September 3 of Year 1 costing $115,000. It was expected to have a useful life of four years and a residual value of $25,000. On October 8, it purchased a refrigerated truck for $125,000. It was expected to have a useful life of five years, after which time it would be worth $20,000.

Instructions

1. *Prepare a sum-of-the-years' digits depreciation schedule for the manufacturing equipment showing the depreciation expense, the calculation for it, accumulated depreciation, and book value for each year of the asset's life. Take into consideration the midyear purchase (nearest month).*

2. *Prepare a double-declining balance depreciation schedule for the refrigerated truck showing the depreciation expense, the calculation for it, accumulated depreciation, and book value for each year of the asset's life. Again, take into consideration the midyear purchase (nearest month).*

3. *Calculate the total amount of depreciation to be taken for the first year on both the equipment and the truck if straight-line depreciation (half-year convention) is used.*

Problem 18.6
revising straight-line depreciation because of change in estimates of useful life and residual value

The Shenandoah Ranch purchased equipment costing $265,000 on January 10 of Year 1. It had an estimated useful life of eight years and an estimated residual value of $50,000. On January 14 of Year 4, accountants decided that the original estimate of useful life was in error. They agreed that because of obsolescence the equipment would be useful for only two more years (five years in all) and revised the estimate of residual value to $15,000.

Instructions

1. *If the fiscal year is January 1 to December 31, prepare the general journal entries on December 31 of Years 1, 2, and 3 to record straight-line depreciation for the equipment. Include your calculations in the explanation for the journal entry.*

2. *Determine the balance of the Accumulated Depreciation account after depreciation has been recorded on December 31, Year 3.*

3. *Prepare the general journal entries on December 31 of Years 4 and 5 to show the revised depreciation amount. Do not round depreciation amounts for this problem. Include your calculations as part of the general journal entry explanation.*

4. *Determine the balance of the Accumulated Depreciation account after depreciation has been taken on December 31, Year 5.*

5. *Determine the amount of the book value of the equipment on the balance sheet prepared on December 31, Year 5.*

Problem 18.7
revising straight-line depreciation because of extraordinary repairs

The Atlanta Publishing House purchased printing equipment costing $86,000 on January 9, Year 1. The equipment was expected to be useful for four years and would have a residual value of $20,000. On January 8 of Year 4, the Atlanta Publishing House paid $28,000 cash for extraordinary repairs to the equipment. The repairs were expected to extend the life of the printing equipment an additional two years (six years in all). The revised estimate of residual value was $12,000.

Instructions

1. Prepare the general journal entries on December 31 of Years 1, 2, and 3 to record the straight-line depreciation. Assume a fiscal year of January 1 to December 31. Include your calculations in the journal entry explanation.

2. Determine the book value of the equipment after depreciation has been recorded for Year 3.

3. Prepare the general journal entry on January 8 of Year 4 to record the extraordinary repairs to the equipment.

4. Determine the book value of the equipment after the extraordinary repairs have been recorded on January 8, Year 4.

5. Prepare the general journal entries on December 31 of Years 4, 5, and 6 to record the depreciation expense. Include your calculations with the journal entry explanation.

6. Determine the book value of the equipment after depreciation has been recorded on December 31 of Year 6.

CHAPTER 19

Disposition of Plant and Equipment, Natural Resources, and Intangible Assets

LEARNING OBJECTIVES

When you have completed this chapter, you should

1. have a better understanding of accounting terminology.

2. be able to prepare entries to record the disposition of assets.

3. be able to calculate and record depletion expense.

4. be able to calculate and record depreciation expense for assets closely related to a wasting asset.

5. have an increased understanding of intangible assets and amortization.

6. be able to prepare the journal entries required as a result of signing an operating lease.

7. be able to prepare the journal entries associated with leasehold improvements and calculate amortization.

8. be able to calculate the amount to be paid for goodwill.

Long-term assets include plant and equipment, natural resources, and intangible assets. Natural resources include timber stands, mines, and oil reserves; intangible assets include patents, copyrights, franchises, and goodwill. In the previous chapter, discussion related to determining the cost of plant and equipment and to spreading that cost over the useful life of the assets. There are many other accounting problems to be considered; this chapter will focus on the disposing of plant assets (plant and equipment) and on natural resources and intangible assets.

PLANT ASSETS

When plant assets become useless because of physical deterioration or obsolescence, they may be discarded, sold, or traded in toward the purchase of a new asset. Each method of disposition requires a slightly different accounting procedure.

Retiring a Fully Depreciated Plant Asset

When a fully depreciated plant asset is retired from service, both its cost and accumulated depreciation must be removed from the books. For example, assume that on January 2, an item of equipment purchased eight years ago at a cost of $12,500 is fully depreciated and is removed from service. The entry to record the retirement from service of the asset is as follows.

GENERAL JOURNAL					Page
Date	Description	Post. Ref.	Debit	Credit	
19XX Jan. 2	Accumulated Depreciation: Equipment		12500 —		
	Equipment			12500 —	
	To Record Retirement from Service				

If an asset is continued in service after it has been fully depreciated, both the asset account and its related accumulated depreciation account are left on the books, but no more depreciation may be taken. The purpose of depreciation, remember, is to spread the cost of the asset over its useful life thereby increasing expenses and lowering net income over those years. The cost of the asset is thus "recovered" through lower income taxes.

Retiring a Plant Asset Not Fully Depreciated

If an asset is removed from service before it is fully depreciated, then its cost and accumulated depreciation should immediately be removed from the books. Also, if it has a scrap or salvage value, that amount should be debited to an account called Salvaged Materials. The remaining undepreciated cost will be debited to an account called Loss on Disposal of Plant Assets.

Assume that equipment purchased five years ago at a cost of $15,000 has an accumulated depreciation account balance of $12,000. The equipment is no longer useful and is to be removed from service immediately. The equipment can be sold for scrap for $2,000. The entry to record the removal of the equipment from service on July 1 is as follows.

		GENERAL JOURNAL			Page
Date		**Description**	**Post. Ref.**	**Debit**	**Credit**
19XX *July*	*1*	*Salvaged Materials*		*2000 —*	
		Accumulated Depreciation: Equipment		*12000 —*	
		Loss on Disposal of Plant Assets		*1000 —*	
		Equipment			*15000 —*
		To Record Retirement from Service			

The Salvaged Materials account is a current asset, and when the equipment is sold for scrap, an entry will be made debiting Cash and crediting Salvaged Materials.

Retiring Plant Assets That Have Been Destroyed

When an asset is destroyed through an accident or by fire or flood, a loss is normally incurred. If there is insurance coverage, the loss is reduced. Assume that an automobile was purchased for $18,000 eighteen months ago and that accumulated depreciation on the auto is $8,800. The automobile caught on fire on July 1 and was destroyed. The insurance company paid $8,500 cash for the automobile after the accident. The entry to remove the auto from the books follows.

GENERAL JOURNAL				Page		
Date	Description	Post. Ref.	Debit		Credit	
July 1	Cash		8500 —			
	Accumulated Depreciation: Auto		8800 —			
	Fire Loss		700 —			
	Automobile				18000 —	
	To Record Loss by Fire and Partial Recovery					
	from Insurance Company					

The loss is calculated by comparing the book value of the auto ($9,200) with the amount received from the insurance company ($8,500). If the payment is less than the book value, then a loss has occurred. If the auto was not insured, the fire loss would be equal to the book value of the auto, $9,200.

Selling a Plant Asset

Companies often sell plant assets. When this occurs, a gain or loss is recognized on the disposition. The gain or loss is calculated by comparing the book value of the asset with the actual sales price. For example, assume that equipment cost $21,500 and had accumulated depreciation of $15,000. At the time of sale on January 3, $5,000 cash is received for the equipment. The calculation for the loss on the disposal is as follows.

Cost of Equipment	$21,500
Less: Accumulated Depreciation	15,000
Book Value of Equipment	$ 6,500
Less: Cash Received	5,000
Loss on Disposal	$ 1,500

The journal entry to record the sale of the asset is as follows.

		GENERAL JOURNAL			Page
Date		**Description**	Post. Ref.	**Debit**	**Credit**
19XX *Jan.*	*3*	*Cash*		5000 —	
		Accumulated Depreciation: Equipment		15000 —	
		Loss on Disposal of Plant Assets		1500 —	
		Equipment			21500 —
		To Record Sale of Equipment			

If the equipment had been sold for $8,500, a gain of $2,000 would be recorded because the cash received would be $2,000 more than the book value.

		GENERAL JOURNAL			Page
Date		**Description**	Post. Ref.	**Debit**	**Credit**
19XX *Jan.*	*3*	*Cash*		8500 —	
		Accumulated Depreciation: Equipment		15000 —	
		Gain on Disposal of Plant Assets			2000 —
		Equipment			21500 —
		To Record Sale of Equipment			

Recording Depreciation to Date of Disposition

When an asset is disposed of, its depreciation must be brought up to date before a gain or loss on the disposition is recognized. Assume that a truck was purchased on January 2, Year 1, at a cost of $29,000. Its useful life was four years and estimated residual value was $5,000. It was sold for $5,500 on March 31, Year 4, and has been depreciated by the straight-line method. Depreciation recorded for Years 1, 2, and 3 was $6,000 per year, or a total of

$18,000. On March 31, Year 4, the date of disposal, an additional three months' depreciation is recorded before recording the disposition.

GENERAL JOURNAL				Page	
Date	Description	Post. Ref.	Debit	Credit	
19XX *Mar.* 31	*Depreciation Expense*		1500 —		
	Accumulated Depreciation: Truck			1500 —	
	To Record 3 Months' Depreciation				

Total accumulated depreciation on March 31, Year 4, is $19,500.

Accumulated Depreciation:	Truck	170A
	Year 1	6,000
	Year 2	6,000
	Year 3	6,000
	Year 4	1,500
	19,500	

The book value of the truck was $9,500 ($29,000 − $19,500) at the time of sale and the sales price was $5,500, a loss of $4,000. Following is the entry to record the disposition.

GENERAL JOURNAL				Page	
Date	Description	Post. Ref.	Debit	Credit	
19XX *Mar.* 31	*Cash*		5500 —		
	Accumulated Depreciation: Truck		19500 —		
	Loss on Disposal of Plant Assets		4000 —		
	Truck			29000 —	
	To Record Sale of Truck				

Trading In Used Assets for Similar New Assets

Autos, trucks, and office equipment are examples of plant assets that are traded in on new assets that are similar in nature. When this occurs, the seller usually gives a trade-in allowance to the buyer for the old asset. The trade-in allowance may or may not be realistic in terms of the value of the asset being traded in. Frequently, the trade-in allowance is artificially high, thus making it appear that a gain is being realized. It is usually assumed, however, that in reality no gain occurs because when a trade-in allowance is high, so is the list price of the new asset being purchased.

For determining taxable income, neither a gain nor a loss is recognized when one asset is exchanged for another similar one. The cost of the new asset on the books is the cash paid for it plus the book value of the old asset.

Assume that a tractor was purchased for $90,000 on January 10 of Year 1. It had a useful life of five years and an estimated salvage value of $15,000. It was depreciated by the straight-line method. On January 4 of Year 5, the tractor was traded in on a new one with a list price of $120,000. A trade-in allowance of $40,000 was given for the old tractor. The cost of the new tractor is determined as follows.

Book Value of Old Tractor

Cost of Old Tractor	$ 90,000
Less: Accumulated Depreciation	
($90,000 − $15,000) ÷ 5 = $15,000 × 4 =	60,000
Book Value of Old Tractor	$ 30,000

Cost of New Tractor

Book Value of Old Tractor	$ 30,000
Plus: Cash Paid for New Tractor	
List Price minus Trade-in Allowance	
$120,000 − $40,000 =	80,000
Cost of New Tractor	$110,000

The journal entry to record the acquisition of the new tractor is as follows.

GENERAL JOURNAL						Page	
Date	Description	Post. Ref.	Debit			Credit	
19XX Jan. 4	Tractor (New)		1 1 0 0 0 0 —				
	Accumulated Depreciation: Tractor (Old)		6 0 0 0 0 —				
	Cash					8 0 0 0 0 —	
	Tractor (Old)					9 0 0 0 0 —	
	To Record Trade-In of Old Tractor for New One						

By comparing the book value of the old tractor ($30,000) with the trade-in allowance ($40,000), it appears that there is a gain of $10,000. When assets are traded in on similar new assets, however, a gain is not recognized. Revenue, remember, is recognized when services or products are sold, and exchanging one asset of production for another does not fit that definition.

Recording a Loss on a Trade-In

For income tax purposes, neither a gain nor a loss is recognized when one asset is traded in on a similar new one. For financial accounting (financial statements), however, a material loss (a relatively large one) *is* recognized.

Assume that equipment costing $100,000 has accumulated depreciation of $65,000 as of August 30, Year 9. On that date, this equipment is traded in on new equipment with a list price of $135,000. A $5,000 trade-in allowance is granted. In this case, the trade-in allowance is $30,000 *less* than the book value. This is considered to be a material loss and should be recorded in the financial statements. The general journal entry to record the transaction is as follows.

GENERAL JOURNAL				Page	
Date	Description	Post. Ref.	Debit	Credit	
19XX Aug. 30	Equipment (New)		135000 —		
	Accumulated Depreciation: Equipment (Old)		65000 —		
	Loss on Disposal of Plant Assets		30000 —		
	Equipment (Old)			100000 —	
	Cash			130000 —	
	To Record Loss on Trade-in of Old Tractor				
	for a New One				

An amount that is material to one company may not be material to another. Materiality depends on company size, gross sales, net income, and other related factors.

NATURAL RESOURCES

natural resources resources provided by nature, such as coal mines, timber stands, oil reserves, or mineral deposits

Natural resources are those provided by nature and include timberlands, coal mines, oil reserves, mineral deposits, and so on. Natural resources are converted into inventory by extracting, cutting, and pumping and are called **wasting assets.** Wasting assets must be physically consumed to turn them into inventory—a tree must be cut down, oil must be pumped from the ground, and coal must be extracted from the earth.

wasting assets assets that must be physically consumed in order to convert them into inventory (timber stands, mines, and so on)

Natural resources appear on the balance sheet under the heading Property, Plant and Equipment under such titles as Coal Deposits or Timber Stands. Their cost includes both the acquisition cost and the cost of exploration and development.

Depletion

depletion the exhaustion of a natural resource

Natural resources do not depreciate as such, but they are depleted as the timber is cut, the oil is pumped, or the coal extracted. **Depletion** refers to the exhaustion of a natural resource and also to the proportional allocation of the cost to the units (barrels, tons, and so forth) removed. When all the oil is pumped from oil reserves, the well is said to be fully depleted. Depletion is recorded by debiting Depletion Expense and crediting Accumulated Depletion.

Calculating Depletion Expense   Depletion Expense is calculated by subtracting the residual value of the natural resource from its cost and dividing the result by the total number of units contained in the natural resource. For example, assume that the Elko mine contains ore deposits and is purchased for $1,300,000. It is estimated that 800,000 tons of ore can be removed from the mine after which time the land will be worth $100,000. If 120,000 tons of ore are mined the first year, the depletion expense is calculated as follows:

$$\frac{\text{Cost of Natural Resource} - \text{Residual Value}}{\text{Total Tons of Ore in Mine}} = \frac{\$1,300,000 - \$100,000}{800,000} = \$1.50$$

$$120,000 \text{ Tons Mined} \times \$1.50 = \$180,000 \text{ Depletion Expense}$$

At the Elko mine, the depletion expense is $1.50 per ton of ore mined. The journal entry to record the depletion expense is as follows.

GENERAL JOURNAL				Page
Date	**Description**	**Post. Ref.**	**Debit**	**Credit**
19XX Dec. 31	Depletion of Ore Deposits		180000 —	
	Accumulated Depletion: Ore Deposits			180000 —
	To Record Depletion Expense for the Elko Mine			
	($1,300,000 − $100,000) ÷ 800,000 = $1.50			
	120,000 tons × $1.50 per ton = $180,000			

The Accumulated Depletion account is a contra asset and subtracts from the cost of the mine on the balance sheet.

The depletion expense of $180,000 will be added to the other costs incurred in removing the ore from the Elko mine to arrive at the cost of goods (ore) available for sale. Other costs might include mining labor, supplies, property taxes, and power costs. The portion of the mined ore that is not sold is reflected on the books as inventory. For example, if 25,000 tons of ore (out of a total of 120,000 extracted at the Elko mine) remain at year end, then the value of the ending inventory of ore (a current asset) will be $37,500 (25,000 × $1.50).

Depreciation of Closely Related Assets   Equipment and buildings erected on a mine or other natural resource site may be useful only at that particular location or while the natural resource is being exhausted. The assets in question should be depreciated over their natural life or the life of the natural resource, whichever is shorter. If depreciation is tied to the natural resources, then the units-of-output method may be used which ties depreciation of closely related assets to the output of the natural resource.

Assume, for example, that a mine is purchased along with the buildings on it. The buildings are estimated to be worth $350,000; their estimated useful life is 20 years; and their residual value is estimated to be only $50,000 because when the mine is exhausted, they will be useful only for salvage materials. The expected life of the mine is 10 years, or 750,000 tons of ore. Since there is no way of telling for sure how many years it will take to exhaust the mine, the building is depreciated according to the output of the mine. Assuming that 85,000 tons of ore are mined the first year, depreciation on the buildings is calculated as follows.

Calculation for Depreciation of Buildings

Relevant Facts

Cost of Buildings	$350,000
Residual Value of Buildings	50,000
Estimated Useful Life of Buildings	20 years
Estimated Life of Mine	10 years
Estimated Capacity of Mine	750,000 tons of ore

$$\frac{\text{Cost of Buildings} - \text{Residual Value}}{\text{Total Tons of Ore in Mine}} = \frac{\$350,000 - \$50,000}{750,000} = \$.40 \text{ per ton}$$

The rate per ton of ore mined is multiplied by the actual tons extracted to arrive at the depreciation expense for the period. Depreciation of the buildings on the mine site will be at $.40 per ton of ore mined. The journal entry to record the depreciation the first year is as follows.

GENERAL JOURNAL					Page	
Date	Description	Post. Ref.	Debit		Credit	
19XX Dec. 31	Depreciation Expense		3 4 0 0 0 —			
	Accumulated Depreciation: Mine Buildings.				3 4 0 0 0 —	
	To Record Depreciation Expense for					
	Mine Buildings					
	($350,000 − $50,000) ÷ 750,000 = $.40					
	$.40 × 85,000 tons = $34,000					

INTANGIBLE ASSETS

Intangible assets, as the phrase suggests, have no physical substance. As discussed earlier, they are both nonphysical and noncurrent. Some assets lack physical substance, but are not classified as intangible assets. Accounts receivable, for example, is nonphysical but it does not qualify as an intangible asset because it is current. Intangible assets include patents, copyrights, franchises, trademarks, leaseholds, and goodwill. Intangibles show on the balance sheet as a subgroup of plant and equipment.

Acquisition of Intangible Assets

Like other assets, intangible assets are recorded on the books at their cost. Any internal costs associated with developing an intangible asset are considered to be revenue expenditures and are written off as expense when incurred.

research and development (R & D)
costs incurred in a planned search for new product knowledge

Research and development (R & D) costs are those costs that are incurred as a result of a planned search for new knowledge and the costs incurred in translating that knowledge into a new product. It is characteristic of American industries to spend billions of dollars a year on research and development. Prior to 1974, R & D costs were capitalized by many companies and listed on the balance sheet as an intangible asset, while other companies wrote them off directly to expense. To solve this problem of inconsistency among companies, the Financial Accounting Standards Board in 1974 ruled that all nonreimbursed research and development costs must be written off as expense when incurred. This ruling allows for easier comparison of the financial statements from different companies.

Amortization of Intangible Assets

amortization
the periodic transferring of the cost of an intangible to expense

The periodic transferring of the cost of an intangible asset to expense is referred to as **amortization.** Amortization is similar to depreciation, and all intangibles must be amortized. The entry to record amortization is a debit to Amortization Expense and a credit to the related asset. Normally an Accumulated Amortization account is not used; the intangible assets are shown on the balance sheet at their book value.

Intangible assets should be amortized over the period of time during which they will be useful or over their legal life, but the period may not exceed 40 years. Straight-line amortization is normally used and is calculated the same way as straight-line depreciation.

Copyrights

copyright
exclusive rights to written work; good for life of creator plus 50 years

A **copyright** is an exclusive right granted by the federal government that gives the owner of the copyright protection from illegal reproductions of written work, design, or literary productions; it is good for the life of the creator plus 50 years. In many cases, the cost of a copyright is minimal and charged to expense. If the copyright is purchased, however, the cost may be material enough to capitalize and spread over the years from which benefits are received.

Patents

patent
exclusive rights to an invention

An exclusive right granted by the federal government to manufacture, sell, lease, or otherwise benefit from an invention is a **patent.** The granting of patents encourages invention; they are good for 17 years and are valuable if they aid in producing revenue.

The purchase of a patent is recorded by debiting the account Patents. Amortization may be spread over the remaining useful life of the patent, but if the benefits to be derived from the patent will be over fewer years, then the shorter time period should be used. If a patent should become worthless before it is fully amortized, its remaining unamortized cost should be written off immediately. In no case will the amortization period exceed 17 years.

Franchises

franchise
a contract giving franchisee the right to conduct a certain type of business in a certain geographical area

A **franchise** is a contract between two parties giving the franchisee the right to conduct a certain type of business in a specific geographical area. The rights may include the use of a name (such as Burger King restaurants), trademark, building design, management instruction, advertising, and so on. The franchise contract may be between an individual and a company, or a franchise may be granted by a governmental agency to a private company to deliver services to a particular area.

The franchisor usually places restrictions on the franchisee that may relate to prices charged, product quality, service area, uniforms, and so on. If the cost of a franchise is relatively small, it may be written off immediately to expense. Frequently, though, franchise costs are substantial. If a lump-sum payment is made for a franchise, it should be amortized over the life of the franchise, but the period may not exceed 40 years. If regular payments are required to the franchisor, they should be debited to a Franchise Expense account.

Trademarks and Trade Names

trademark
a distinctive symbol, logo, or design used to promote a product or company

trade name
a brand name

A **trademark** is a distinctive symbol, design, or logo that is used in the promotion of a particular product or company. A **trade name** is a brand name attached to a product or company. Familiar trademarks include the Ferrari stallion, McDonald's golden arches, and the shell evident at Shell service stations. Trade names that have become common household words include Kleenex, Xerox, and Coca Cola.

To have the permanent, exclusive use of trademarks or trade names, a company must register them with the federal government. If they are developed internally, the actual cost may be small and should be written off to expense. If a trademark or trade name is purchased, however, and the cost is substantial, it should be capitalized and amortized over its useful life or 40 years, whichever is shorter.

Operating Leases

operating lease
a contract giving lessee rights to property or equipment for a specified period of time

An **operating lease** is a contract between the property owner **(lessor)** and the person or company wishing to obtain rights to use the property **(lessee).** An operating lease makes no attempt to transfer ownership at the end of the lease.

lessor
the property owner or the individual or business giving another rights to use property or equipment

lessee
the person or business obtaining property or equipment rights under a lease

A company leasing a building for ten years or an automobile for two years will sign an operating lease. A building lease may require first and last months' rent, or first and last years' rent. Assume, for example, that on January 2, a company signed a ten-year lease for use of a building. Annual rent was $24,000; the lease agreement required first and last years' payments be made in advance, and monthly payments be made thereafter. The entry required at the time of the signing of the lease is as follows.

	GENERAL JOURNAL				Page
Date	Description	Post. Ref.	Debit	Credit	
19XX Jan. 2	Prepaid Rent		24000 —		
	Leasehold		24000 —		
	Cash			48000 —	
	To Record Prepayment of First and Last Year's Rent as per Conditions of Lease				

Each month during the first year of the lease, rent expense is recorded by crediting Prepaid Rent as follows.

	GENERAL JOURNAL				Page
Date	Description	Post. Ref.	Debit	Credit	
19XX Jan. 31	Rent Expense		2000 —		
	Prepaid Rent			2000 —	
	To Transfer $2,000 to Rent Expense				

The Leasehold account is classified as an intangible asset on the balance sheet and represents prepaid rent for the tenth year of the lease. At the beginning of the tenth year, the Leasehold account will be transferred to the current asset section of the balance sheet and rent expense for each month of the tenth year will be recorded as follows.

GENERAL JOURNAL					Page	
Date	Description	Post. Ref.	Debit		Credit	
19XX Jan. 31	Rent Expense		2 0 0 0 —			
	Leasehold				2 0 0 0 —	
	To Transfer $2,000 to Rent Expense					

Often, when a lease is obtained, an additional lump-sum charge is made to the lessee that does not include a specific payment for rent. Such a charge is debited to the Leasehold account and is amortized over the life of the lease. Assume that in the previous example the ten-year lease was granted at an annual charge of $24,000. The first year's rent was required in advance, and an additional $36,000 was required as a lump-sum payment in advance for the right to use the building. The first year's rent is debited to Prepaid Rent, and the lump-sum payment is debited to Leasehold as shown.

GENERAL JOURNAL					Page	
Date	Description	Post. Ref.	Debit		Credit	
19XX Jan. 2	Prepaid Rent		2 4 0 0 0 —			
	Leasehold		3 6 0 0 0 —			
	Cash				6 0 0 0 0 —	
	To Record First Year's Prepaid Rent and $36,000					
	Premium Required to Obtain Lease					

The lump-sum payment is amortized monthly over the life of the lease. At the end of January, rent expense is recorded as follows.

GENERAL JOURNAL				Page	
Date	Description	Post. Ref.	Debit	Credit	
19XX Jan. 31	Rent Expense		2300 —		
	Prepaid Rent			2000 —	
	Leasehold			300 —	
	To Transfer $2,000 to Rent Expense				
	and to Amortize 1/120 of Leasehold Charge				
	to Rent Expense				
	($36,000 ÷ 120 = $300)				

After the first year, Rent Expense will be debited each month for $2,300, Cash will be credited for $2,000, and Leasehold will be credited for $300. The Leasehold account will be fully amortized at the end of the lease.

Leasehold Improvements

leasehold improvement
a physical alteration to leased property by the lessee

A **leasehold improvement** is a physical alteration to leased property that enhances its value but whose ownership will revert to the owner of the property at the end of the lease period. Such improvements may include remodeling a building or the addition of elevators, air conditioning, or carpeting. Such leasehold improvements should be debited to a Leasehold Improvements account. The balance of the account will then be amortized by the straight-line method over the useful life of the leasehold improvements or over the life of the lease, whichever is shorter. Some leases are renewable, and this should be taken into consideration when considering the period of amortization.

Assume that an individual planned to open a restaurant and on January 11 signed a nonrenewable building lease for that purpose for a period of ten years. The lease agreement called for the first and last years' rent of $18,000 a year in advance. After signing the lease agreement, the lessee remodeled the building at a cost of $60,000. The improvements have a useful life of 20 years. The initial prepayment of the first and last years' rent and the cost of the improvements are recorded as follows.

GENERAL JOURNAL						Page	
Date	**Description**	**Post. Ref.**		**Debit**		**Credit**	
9XX *Jan.* *11*	*Prepaid Rent*			1 8 0 0 0 —			
	Leasehold			1 8 0 0 0 —			
	Leasehold Improvements			6 0 0 0 0 —			
	Cash					9 6 0 0 0 —	
	To Record First and Last Years' Rent Expense						
	and the Cost of Leasehold Inprovements						

The leasehold improvements are amortized over the life of the lease and are considered to be an additional charge for rent.

The journal entry showing the rent expense for the first month of operation is as follows.

GENERAL JOURNAL						Page	
Date	**Description**	**Post. Ref.**		**Debit**		**Credit**	
9XX *Jan.* *31*	*Rent Expense*			2 0 0 0 —			
	Prepaid Rent					1 5 0 0 —	
	Leasehold Improvements					5 0 0 —	
	To Transfer $1,500 from Prepaid Rent to Rent						
	Expense and to Amortize 1/120 of Cost of						
	Leasehold Improvements						
	($60,000 ÷ 120 = $500)						

The last year the monthly charge for rent will include a debit to Rent Expense and credits to Leasehold Improvements and Leasehold as follows.

GENERAL JOURNAL				Page	
Date	Description	Post. Ref.	Debit	Credit	
19XX Jan. 31	Rent Expense		2000 —		
	Leasehold			1500 —	
	Leasehold Improvements			500 —	
	To Transfer $1,500 from Leasehold to Rent				
	Expense and to Amortize 1/120 of Leasehold				
	Improvements				

Goodwill

net assets
assets minus liabilities

net identifiable assets
assets minus goodwill minus liabilities

goodwill
an amount paid for a business that is in excess of the value of the net identifiable assets

Goodwill generally refers to the good reputation a company has because of its superior management or outstanding location, product, or service. According to this definition, many businesses possess goodwill, but it will not reflect on their books as an intangible asset unless it has been purchased. When buying an existing company, the purchase price is normally equal to the value of the net identifiable assets. **Net Assets** is total assets minus total liabilities. Because goodwill is not an identifiable asset, **net identifiable assets** is equal to total assets minus goodwill minus liabilities. If more is paid for the business than the fair market value of the net identifiable assets, then the additional payment must be regarded as **goodwill.**

To estimate how much a business is worth, an appraisal of the assets is required by various experts to determine their fair market value. The purchase price is then decided on by subtracting the liabilities from the fair market value of the assets. Sometimes a buyer may be willing to pay more for an existing business than the fair market value of its net assets. If more than the fair market value is paid, it must be assumed that the difference is payment for goodwill.

A buyer may be willing to pay an amount for goodwill if the company being purchased has a rate of return that is higher than similar companies. The rate of return is the rate that a company is expected to earn on its net identifiable assets. For example, assume that the Bull Run Company has assets of $1,750,000 (no goodwill is included) and liabilities of $900,000. The normal rate of return for similar businesses is 15 percent of net identifiable assets. The amount that Bull Run Company should be expected to earn each year, then, is calculated as follows.

Total Assets (excluding goodwill)	$1,750,000
Less: Total Liabilities	− 900,000
Net Identifiable Assets	$ 850,000
Normal Rate of Return, 15%	× .15
Expected Annual Earnings	$ 127,500

If Bull Run Company earns considerably more than $127,500 each year, a prospective buyer may be willing to pay more for the business than the value of the net identifiable assets, $850,000. The additional amount paid will be debited to Goodwill.

Calculating the Amount to Be Paid for Goodwill   Assume that a buyer is interested in the Rocky Mountain Water Company which has net identifiable assets of $2,000,000. The normal rate of return for similar businesses is 12 percent. The Rocky Mountain Water Company has earned an average net income of $290,000 for the past five years. The buyer may calculate goodwill as follows.

Earnings for Similar Companies

Fair Market Value of Net Identifiable Assets	$2,000,000
Normal Expected Rate of Return	× .12
Normal Net Income	$ 240,000

Rocky Mountain Company Earnings in Excess of Normal

Average Annual Earnings for Rocky Mountain Company	$290,000
Average Annual Earnings for Similar Businesses	240,000
Earnings in Excess of Normal	$ 50,000

The Rocky Mountain Company has a rate of return of 14.5 percent. This figure is obtained by dividing the annual earnings by the net identifable assets:

$$\frac{290{,}000}{2{,}000{,}000} = .145 = 14.5\%$$

This information shows that the Rocky Mountain Water Company has had superior earning power for the past five years. The buyer assumes that this will continue for some time into the future and is willing to pay for it. The total purchase price will be a total of the fair market value of the net identifiable assets and the amount to be paid for goodwill. The buyer must determine how long benefits from the goodwill are expected to last, or how long excess earnings are expected to continue. If the buyer assumes that the goodwill will be of benefit for four years after purchase, then the amount to be paid for goodwill is determined by multiplying the earnings in excess of average by the number 4 ($50,000 × 4) to determine the amount to be paid for goodwill. The total purchase price is calculated as follows.

Fair Market Value of Net Identifiable Assets	$2,000,000
Goodwill ($50,000 × 4)	+ 200,000
Total Purchase Price	$2,200,000

The $200,000 is debited to Goodwill and is amortized by the straight-line method over its expected benefit period, four years. The amortization period may not exceed 40 years. If it appears that the benefits from goodwill no longer exist, then the entire amount should be written off to goodwill amortization expense immediately.

SUMMARY

Natural resources and intangible assets are examples of long-term assets and appear on the balance sheet in the plant and equipment category. Timber stands, mines, and oil reserves are examples of natural resources; and patents, franchises, and goodwill are examples of intangible assets.

If an item of plant and equipment is discarded when fully depreciated, the asset account and its related accumulated depreciation account are removed from the books. If the asset is to be sold for scrap, the amount received from the sale is debited to an account called Salvaged Materials; if the asset is not fully depreciated, there may be a loss or a gain on the disposal. Assets that are destroyed by accident must be removed from the books and any cash received from insurance offsets the loss on the disposal.

Assets are often sold. Again, the cost of the asset and its accumulated depreciation account must be removed from the books. The gain or loss on the disposition is determined by comparing the cash received for the asset with its book value. Before calculating the gain or loss, the depreciation must be brought current.

When assets are traded in on similar new assets, neither a gain nor a loss is recorded for income tax purposes, though a material loss will be recorded for financial statement purposes. To calculate the cost to be recorded on the books for the new asset, the book value of the old asset is added to the amount paid for the new asset. The amount paid is determined by subtracting the trade-in allowance from the list price of the new asset.

Natural resources are referred to as wasting assets and are converted into inventory by cutting, extracting, pumping, and so on. Depletion refers to the exhaustion of a natural resource and is recorded periodically based on a units-of-production method which takes into consideration the amount cut, extracted, pumped, and so forth.

Assets closely related to a natural resource, such as buildings on a mine site, are depreciated over their economic life or the life of the natural resource, whichever is shorter. Often, closely related assets will be depreciated by the units-of-production method which ties their depreciation expense to the production of the natural resource.

Intangible assets are long-term assets that are nonphysical and noncurrent. Copyrights, franchises, patents, trademarks, and trade names are all examples of intangible assets. If they are purchased, their cost is capitalized (if it is material in amount) and amortized over their useful life. Amortization is not to exceed 17 years for a patent or 40 years for other intangible assets.

Research and development costs (R & D) are costs incurred in a planned search for knowledge that leads to the development of new products. R & D costs are revenue expenditures and are written off to expense as incurred.

An operating lease gives the right to the lessee to use a piece of property or equipment for a specified number of years and is an intangible asset. Prepayments under the lease agreement are amortized over their useful period. Improvements made to leased property will revert to the owner of the property when the lease has expired. For this reason, they are debited to a Leasehold Improvements account and amortized over the life of the lease.

Goodwill refers to the earnings of a particular company in excess of normal for the industry. Goodwill will be recorded on the books as an intangible asset when it is purchased. It should be amortized over the time period when benefits are derived from it, but the period may not exceed 40 years.

Review of Accounting Terminology

Following is a list of the accounting terminology for this chapter.

amortization	net assets
copyright	net identifiable assets
depletion	operating lease
franchise	patent
goodwill	research and development
leasehold improvement	trademark
lessee	trade name
lessor	wasting assets
natural resources	

Fill in the blanks with the correct word or term from the list.

1. A contract between parties giving one the right to conduct a certain type of business in a particular geographical area is a/an _____.

2. Assets that must be physically consumed in order to convert them to inventory are known as _____.

3. The exhaustion of a natural resource is known as _____.

4. The periodic transferring of the cost of an intangible asset to expense is _____.

5. An exclusive right granted by the federal government to manufacture or sell an invention is a/an _____.

6. Timberlands, coal mines, and oil reserves are examples of _____.

7. A distinctive symbol or logo used in the promotion of a particular company is a/an _____.

8. When an operating lease is negotiated, the property owner is referred to as the _____.

9. When an operating lease is negotiated, the person or business gaining rights to the property is the _____.

10. A planned search by a business for new knowledge and converting that knowledge into a new product is _____.

11. Assets minus goodwill minus liabilities is referred to as _____.

12. A/an _____ protects a writer from illegal reproductions of her or his work.

13. Earnings in excess of normal for the industry are referred to as _____.

14. A brand name attached to a company or product is sometimes referred to as a/an _____.

15. A/an _____ is a contract between a property owner and an individual or business giving the latter rights to the property for a specified period of time.

16. Assets minus liabilities is referred to as _____.

17. An improvement made to leased property is referred to as a/an _____.

Match the following words and terms on the left with the definitions on the right (columns continue on the following page).

18. amortization
19. copyright
20. depletion
21. franchise
22. goodwill
23. leasehold improvement
24. lessee
25. lessor

a. assets minus liabilities
b. resources provided by nature
c. a distinctive symbol or logo
d. the periodic transferring of the cost of an intangible asset to expense
e. the exhaustion of a natural resource
f. assets minus goodwill minus liabilities
g. earnings in excess of normal for the industry
h. a brand name attached to a product

26. natural resources
27. net assets
28. net identifiable assets
29. operating lease
30. patent
31. research and development
32. trade name
33. trademark
34. wasting assets

i. assets that must be physically consumed in order to convert them to inventory

j. a planned search for new knowledge and products

k. a contract allowing the lessee use of property for a specific period of time

l. an improvement to leased property by the lessee

m. a contract giving an individual the right to conduct a certain business in a specific geographical area

n. an exclusive right to manufacture, sell, or otherwise profit from an invention

o. the property owner who grants another use of the property

p. the person who signs a lease and obtains rights to property

q. protects an author or songwriter from illegal reproductions of the work

Exercises

Exercise 19.1
preparing journal entries to dispose of equipment by scrapping

The Mobile Company is retiring from service equipment that cost $15,750. Prepare the general journal entries on January 2 to record the disposition under each of the following assumptions.

a. The balance in Accumulated Depreciation is $15,750 and the equipment is worthless.

b. The balance in Accumulated Depreciation is $13,750 and the equipment is worthless.

c. The balance in Accumulated Depreciation is $12,750 and the equipment is sold for scrap for $1,200 cash.

Exercise 19.2
preparing journal entries to dispose of truck destroyed by fire

A dump truck purchased by the Paducah Hauling Company cost $28,400 two years ago. It is destroyed in an accident on February 9. Prepare the general journal entries to record the disposition of the truck under the following assumptions. (Use the account title Accident Gain or Accident Loss to record the gain or loss upon disposition.)

a. The accumulated depreciation on the dump truck was $9,360 at the time of the accident. The insurance company paid $15,000 cash to Paducah Hauling Company as a result of the accident.

b. The accumulated depreciation on the dump truck was $14,040. The insurance company paid $16,000 cash as a result of the accident.

c. The accumulated depreciation on the dump truck was $17,040. The truck was not insured.

Exercise 19.3
preparing journal entries to dispose of machinery by selling it

A piece of machinery was purchased by the Champaign Auto Wreckers on January 9, Year 1, for $37,600. It was expected to have a useful life of five years and a salvage value of $7,600. Depreciation is recorded annually on December 31. Prepare the general journal entries to record its disposition under the following assumptions.

a. On January 4, Year 4, the machine was sold for $15,000 cash.
b. On January 10, Year 5, the machine was sold for $15,000 cash.
c. On June 30, Year 5, the machine was sold for $4,100.

Exercise 19.4
preparing journal entries to dispose of equipment by trade-in using the income tax method

On April 9, Year 5, the Little Rock Clothing Company traded in equipment that had originally cost $75,000 on similar new equipment. At the time of trade-in, the old equipment had accumulated depreciation of $62,500. Prepare the general journal entries acceptable for federal income taxes to record the acquisition of the new equipment under each of the following assumptions.

a. The new equipment had a list price of $97,600. A trade-in allowance of $17,000 was granted for the old equipment, and cash was paid for the balance.

b. The new equipment had a list price of $97,600, and a trade-in allowance of $7,000 was granted for the old equipment. A two-year, 10 percent note was signed for the balance owed.

Exercise 19.5
preparing journal entry to dispose of auto by trade-in recognizing material loss

An auto originally cost $35,000 and accumulated depreciation on it was $16,500. It was traded in on April 29 on a new auto with a list price of $42,700. The trade-in allowance granted for the old auto was $5,000, and cash was paid for the balance owed. Prepare the general journal entries for financial statement purposes to record the acquisition of the new auto (recognize the material loss).

Exercise 19.6
calculating depletion expense

The Silver City Mine was purchased on January 7, Year 1. It cost $2,500,000 and contained an estimated 500,000 tons of ore. After the ore is extracted, the land will be worth $500,000.

a. Prepare the general journal entry on December 31, Year 1, to record depletion expense if 75,000 tons of ore are extracted.

b. Show how the mine will appear on the balance sheet after depletion is recorded for Year 1.

Exercise 19.7
calculating units-of-output depreciation for building on mine site

Assume that buildings were erected on the Silver City Mine (Exercise 19.6) at a cost of $250,000 and would have a physical life of 20 years and a residual value of $50,000 after the mine was exhausted. Calculate depreciation expense for the first year for the buildings assuming units-of-output depreciation tied to the production of the mine. Again assume a total capacity of 500,000 tons of ore and 75,000 tons extracted the first year.

Exercise 19.8
preparing journal entries to record amortization of intangibles

The Stanford Development Company purchased a patent on January 12, Year 1, for $25,000. Its remaining legal life was ten years. Record amortization under the following conditions.

a. Record amortization expense on December 31, Year 1, assuming the patent is to be amortized fully over its remaining legal life.

b. Record amortization expense on December 31, Year 1, assuming the patent is expected to be useful for four years.

c. Assume that the patent had been amortized at a straight-line rate of 10 percent for a period of five years after purchase. At the end of Year 6, it was decided that no further benefits were to be derived from ownership of the patent, and the balance of the patent account was written off in full.

Exercise 19.9
preparing journal entries relating to lease and leasehold improvements

The Golden Calf Company signed a nonrenewable, ten-year lease on January 2, Year 1, for a building. The first and last years' rent of $27,000 a year was to be paid in cash in advance. Extensive remodeling of the building cost $75,000 cash.

a. Prepare the general journal entry on January 2, Year 1, to record the cash payment for the first and last years' rent.
b. Prepare the general journal entry on January 2, Year 1, to record the expense for remodeling.
c. Prepare the general journal entry on December 31, Year 1, to record the annual rent expense. Include the amortization of the Leasehold Improvements account.
d. Prepare the general journal entry on December 31, Year 10, to record the tenth year's rent expense.

Exercise 19.10
calculating goodwill

A buyer is interested in purchasing the Pittsburgh Metal Products Company. The fair market value of the net identifiable assets is $3,400,000. Average earnings for Pittsburgh Metal Products Company for the past five years were $476,000 a year. For similar businesses, a rate of return of 12 percent on net identifiable assets is normal. Calculate the total purchase price if the buyer is willing to pay for goodwill and assumes that it will be of benefit to the company for a period of five years.

Problems

Problem 19.1
preparing journal entries relating to the disposition of equipment

On January 14, Year 7, the Tampa Restaurant Equipment Company purchased warehouse equipment costing $39,600. It was expected to have a useful life of five years and an estimated residual value of $3,600. It was to be depreciated by the straight-line method. The fiscal year is January 1 to December 31. Depreciation is recorded annually on December 31.

Instructions   *Prepare general journal entries to record the disposition of the equipment under the following circumstances. Bring depreciation up to date where required. Include calculations in the journal explanation.*

1. *On December 30, Year 11, the equipment was discarded. No cash was received.*

2. On January 2, Year 10, the equipment was sold for $14,500 cash.

3. On August 31, Year 10, the equipment was sold for $15,000 cash.

4. On December 30, Year 11, management decided to sell the equipment for scrap for $2,000 (debit Salvaged Materials).

5. On March 31, Year 11, the equipment was traded in on similar new equipment with a list price of $55,000. The trade-in allowance was $13,500 and the balance was paid with a three-year, 10 percent note. Record in a manner acceptable for federal income taxes.

6. On October 1, Year 10, the equipment was traded in on similar new equipment with a list price of $52,500. The trade-in allowance was $8,000. The balance was paid in cash. Record in a manner acceptable for federal income taxes.

Problem 19.2
preparing journal entries relating to the disposition of equipment

The Redwoods Tour Company purchased a customized minibus on April 1, Year 5, for $175,000. It was expected to be useful for four years after which time it would be worth $55,000. It was to be depreciated by the straight-line method. The fiscal year of the Redwoods Tour Company is January 1 to December 31. Adjusting entries are prepared annually on December 31.

Instructions

Prepare the general journal entries to record disposition of the minibus under the following circumstances. Include calculations in the journal explanations.

1. *The minibus was completely destroyed by fire on October 27, Year 6. The Redwoods Tour Company received $99,500 in cash from the insurance company. Depreciation of $22,500 had been recorded on December 31, Year 5. Prepare the general journal entry to bring the depreciation current for Year 6 before preparing the entry to record disposition of the minibus. Use the account title Fire Gain or Fire Loss to record the gain or loss upon disposition.*

2. *The minibus was traded in on a new similar one with a list price of $210,000 on February 28, Year 8. The trade-in allowance granted for the old minibus was $20,000 and the balance was paid in cash. Accumulated depreciation at the end of Year 7 was $82,500. Prepare the general journal entry to bring the*

depreciation current for Year 8. Next, prepare the entry for financial statement purposes to record the disposition of the minibus, recognizing the material loss.

3. *The minibus was sold for cash to a charitable organization on March 31, Year 9, at a price equal to its book value. Record depreciation expense for January 1 to March 31, Year 9, before recording disposition of the minibus.*

Problem 19.3
preparing journal entries for depletion of timber stands and units-of-output depreciation for closely related asset

On January 10, the West Coast Paper Products Company bought a tract of land containing timber for $3,500,000. When the timber reserves are exhausted, the land can be sold for $500,000. A building was constructed on the property at a total cost of $150,000. It had an estimated physical life of 20 years and could be sold for scrap for $30,000 after the timber was exhausted. The timber stands contained 15,000,000 board feet of timber. The building is to be depreciated by the units-of-output method tied to the exhaustion of the timber reserves. The first year, 2,500,000 board feet of timber are cut.

Instructions

1. *Prepare the general journal entry on December 31 to record depletion expense for the first year.*

2. *Prepare the general journal entry on December 31 to record depreciation of the building for the first year.*

Problem 19.4
preparing journal entries to record amortization of intangibles

On January 7, Year 6, the Houston Research Company purchased a patent for $72,000 cash. Its remaining legal life was eight years. On July 1, Year 6, a copyright was purchased at a cost of $100,000 cash from the author of a scientific manual. It was estimated that benefits from the copyright would accure to the Houston Research Company for a period of ten years. Adjusting entries are recorded annually on December 31, and the fiscal year runs from January 1 to December 31.

Instructions

1. *Prepare the general journal entries on December 31, Year 6, to record amortization of the patent and the copyright.*

2. *Assume that on December 31, Year 10, the Houston Research Company decided that the patent held no future benefits to the company. Write off to expense the balance of the account.*

3. *Assume that on December 30, Year 11, the Houston Research Company decided that the copyright held no future benefits to the company. Prepare the general journal entry to write off to expense the balance of the copyright account. Assume that the adjusting entries have not yet been recorded for year 11.*

Problem 19.5
preparing journal entries to record lease, leasehold improvements, amortization, and depreciation

On January 10, Year 1, the Independence Storage Company leased a building for 15 years to be used as a warehouse. The terms of the lease called for the first and last years' rent of $36,000 a year to be paid in advance. At the same time, $120,000 cash was spent for an addition to the building with an estimated physical life of 20 years. Equipment was purchased on July 1 and permanently installed in the remodeled building at a cost of $90,000. At the end of its useful life of eight years, it would have to be replaced. The fiscal year runs from January 1 to December 31.

Instructions

1. *Prepare the general journal entry on January 10 to record the cash payment of the first and last years' rent.*

2. *Prepare the general journal entry on January 10 to record the payment for the building addition.*

3. *Prepare the general journal entry on July 1 to record the purchase of the equipment.*

4. *Prepare the adjusting entry on December 31 to record the first year's rent expense. Include the straight-line amortization of the building and the equipment.*

Problem 19.6
calculating goodwill

The Reno Manufacturing Company had net identifiable assets of $4,250,000 and had earned an average net income of $573,750 per year over the past five years. Similar manufacturing companies normally earn 12 percent on their net identifiable assets. A buyer is willing to pay for the net identifiable assets of the Reno Manufacturing Company plus an amount for goodwill. The goodwill is expected to be of benefit to the buyer for a period of four years.

Instructions

Compute the total purchase price that the buyer is willing to pay for the Reno Manufacturing Company.

CHAPTER 20

Partnership Accounting

LEARNING OBJECTIVES

When you have completed this chapter, you should

1. have a better understanding of accounting terminology.

2. understand the general characteristics of a partnership and the importance of each one.

3. be able to calculate the division of profits, prepare the proper journal entries, and prepare the financial statements.

4. be able to prepare the journal entries for the sale of a partnership interest, the withdrawal of a partner, and the addition of a new partner.

5. be able to prepare the journal entries for a partnership that is going out of business.

Accounting for a partnership is similar to accounting for a single-proprietorship business. A partnership is a contractual arrangement in which two or more persons decide to combine their assets and time to form a business. Many states have adopted a model called the Uniform Partnership Act. This act defines a partnership as "an association of two or more persons to carry on as co-owners a business for profit." It also explains the necessary parts for a contract. Once a contract is written and signed, all parties are legally bound by it. To better understand a partnership, let's examine the major characteristics.

CHARACTERISTICS OF A PARTNERSHIP

A Contractual Agreement

partnership
an association of two or more competent persons who agree to do business as co-owners for profit

A **partnership** is "an association of two or more competent persons who agree to do business as co-owners for profit." It is a voluntary agreement between legally competent parties, and if there is a written agreement, each partner must sign it. Because a partnership is based on agreement, no person can be a partner against his or her will.

Limited Life

The life of a partnership is limited. Because a partnership business is carried on by individuals, it cannot exist separate and apart from these individuals. Should something happen to take away the ability of a partner to contract, the partnership may be terminated. Examples of such situations are death, bankruptcy, and lack of legal capacity. In addition, the life of a partnership may be limited by terms in the original agreement or by unanimous consent of all parties.

Mutual Agency

mutual agency
the ability of each partner, acting as an agent of the business, to enter into and bind it to contracts within the apparent scope of the partnership

Mutual agency exists in a partnership. **Mutual agency** is the legal ability of each partner, acting as an agent of the business, to enter into and bind it to contracts within the scope of the partnership. For instance, Al, Ben, and Charlie are partners in their certified public accounting firm. Ben, as a partner, may bind the partnership by contracting to buy a computer for the business. Even if the other two partners know nothing of this purchase, they are bound to the contract, because a computer is an expected and necessary piece of equipment for an accounting firm. However, the firm would not be bound if Ben should contract to buy land with the expectation that its value will increase, because this transaction is considered to be outside the purpose of an accounting business. In most cases, buying property on speculation is not expected of an accounting firm. Thus, mutual agency is the ability of each partner to bind the partnership in contracts, but only within the scope of the partnership business.

Unlimited Liability

unlimited liability each partner is personally liable for the debts of the partnership

Much like in a single proprietorship, partners have unlimited liability for their business. **Unlimited liability** means that each partner is personally liable for the debts of the business. When a partnership business is unable to pay its debts, the creditors may satisfy their claims from the personal assets of any of the partners. Thus, one partner with personal assets may be called on to pay all the debts to outside creditors of the business. Partners are both jointly and severally liable for partnership debts. The law uses the term *severally* to indicate that any one of the partners can be liable for all the partnership debts. The term *jointly* means that all of the partners are liable together for the partnership debts.

ADVANTAGES AND DISADVANTAGES OF A PARTNERSHIP

A partnership has advantages over other forms of business. By combining the abilities and capital of two or more persons, business potential may be greatly expanded. Also, a partnership is much easier to form than a corporation, because an agreement between parties is all that is required. However, there are several disadvantages—limited life, unlimited liability, and mutual agency are among these and pose potential legal problems that must be considered when forming any new partnership.

PARTNERSHIP ACCOUNTING

Partnership accounting is similar to accounting for a single propri-etorship except for transactions that affect the partners' capital ac-counts. Assets and liabilities are accounted for in the same manner as previously discussed. The owners' equity will include invest-ments of all of the partners. Because a partnership has more than one owner, however, a capital account is set up for each one. Each partner will have a separate capital account and a separate draw-ing account. The accounting equation, Assets = Liabilities + Own-er's Equity is the same, except that owners' equity is the sum of the balances of the partners' capital accounts. Similar to a single owner, the partners (owners) do not receive salaries but rather withdraw assets from the business for their personal needs. Gener-ally, the rules for withdrawals are decided beforehand by the part-ners. For example, assume that Partner Arnold withdraws $5,000 from a partnership firm of which he is a member. The journal entry to show this withdrawal is shown as follows.

GENERAL JOURNAL					Page	
Date	Description	Post. Ref.	Debit		Credit	
Jan. *15*	*Partner Arnold, Drawing*		5000 —			
	Cash				5000 —	
	To Record the Withdrawal of Cash by Partner					
	Arnold					

At the end of the accounting period, the drawing accounts of each partner are closed to their individual capital accounts. Following is the journal entry to close the drawing account of Partner Arnold to his capital account.

GENERAL JOURNAL				Page	
Date	Description	Post. Ref.	Debit	Credit	
19XX Jan. 31	**Partner Arnold, Capital**		5000 —		
	Partner Arnold, Drawing			5000 —	
	To Record the Closing of Arnold's Drawing				
	Account to Capital				

Accounting for a partnership does require some additional calculations and journal entries. Calculations must be made for the division of profits and losses, and journal entries must be made for an addition or withdrawal of partners. In addition, special problems must be solved when a partnership is going out of business. Each of these will be discussed in the following paragraphs.

DIVIDING THE NET INCOME

profit-loss ratio
the method used by the partners to divide profits or losses

The partnership contract must state how the net income or loss is to be divided. The method chosen by the partners for dividing the profits or losses is called the **profit-loss ratio.** There are a number of methods that may be used. The partners may decide to divide profits equally. They may also use the amounts of money invested, the time invested, or the interest and salary allowance methods as a basis for profit sharing. Their agreement should specify the method to be used, which is generally used for both profits and losses unless otherwise provided in the contract. In the absence of a partnership contract, if the partners fail to agree and a dispute arises, the law states that profits and losses will be divided equally.

Dividing Net Income on a Fractional Basis

The easiest way to divide profits is to divide them equally. For example, M. Buck, J. Bagwell, and S. Rose are partners. Buck invested $50,000, Bagwell invested $30,000, and Rose invested $40,000 in their accounting firm. The following balance sheet was prepared on December 31 before adjusting and closing entries for the year had been prepared.

BUCK, BAGWELL, AND ROSE BALANCE SHEET DECEMBER 31, 19XX		
Assets		
Cash	$80000—	
Other Assets	50000—	
Total Assets		$130000—
Liabilities		
Accounts Payable		$ 10000—
Owners' Equity		
Buck, Capital	50000—	
Bagwell, Capital	30000—	
Rose, Capital	40000—	120000—
Total Liabilities and Owners' Equity		$130000—

During the first year of business, expenses were $60,000 and revenues were $96,000. The following T-account illustrates the Income Summary account after all expenses and revenues are closed.

Income Summary

Debits		*Credits*	
12/31	60,000	12/31	96,000
		36,000	
Total expenses for the year		*Total revenue for the year*	

When deducting expenses from revenues, the partnership has earned a net income of $36,000. Revenues (inflows) were $96,000 and expenses (outflows) were $60,000, leaving $36,000 as profits to be divided among the three partners. A calculation is now made to determine how much of the profits will be allocated to each partner's capital account. Remember, profits increase both the assets and the capital of the partnership business. Thus, the profits increase the capital account of each of the partners because they share the business. Once the amount to be divided is determined, a closing entry crediting the capital accounts is required. When net income is to be divided equally, the allocation is determined by dividing the $36,000 by 3 ($36,000 ÷ 3 = $12,000). The Income Summary account is then closed to the capital accounts as follows.

GENERAL JOURNAL				Page
Date	Description	Post. Ref.	Debit	Credit
19XX Dec. 31	Income Summary		3 6 0 0 0 —	
	Buck, Capital			1 2 0 0 0 —
	Bagwell, Capital			1 2 0 0 0 —
	Rose, Capital			1 2 0 0 0 —
	To Record the Closing of the Income Summary			
	to Capital			

Dividing Net Income Based on Amounts Invested

The partners may agree to divide net income according to the amounts invested rather than equally. Remember, a calculation is made for allocating the profits. Once the calculation is made, it is used when closing the Income Summary into the capital accounts. Using the information from the first example, the following steps show the procedure for this calculation.

1. Determine the amounts invested.

Buck	$ 50,000
Bagwell	30,000
Rose	40,000
Total	$120,000

2. Set up fraction. (The denominator is the total amount invested, $120,000, and each partner's individual investment becomes the numerator.)

	Ratio		Profits to be Divided		Total Allocated
Buck	$\dfrac{50,000}{120,000}$	×	$36,000	=	$15,000
Bagwell	$\dfrac{30,000}{120,000}$	×	36,000	=	9,000
Rose	$\dfrac{40,000}{120,000}$	×	36,000	=	12,000
Total to be allocated					$36,000

The general journal entry to close the Income Summary to the capital accounts is as follows.

	GENERAL JOURNAL			Page
Date	Description	Post. Ref.	Debit	Credit
19XX Dec. 31	*Income Summary*		36000 —	
	Buck, Capital			15000 —
	Bagwell, Capital			9000 —
	Rose, Capital			12000 —
	To Record the Closing of the Income Summary			
	to Capital			

Dividing Net Income Using a Fixed Ratio

In the partnership agreement, the contract may specify a fixed ratio to be used to divide the profits or losses. For example, Buck, Bagwell, and Rose decide to use a ratio of 3:2:1, respectively. To use this ratio, convert the ratio into a fraction and multiply it by the net income or loss of the period. The steps for using the ratio to divide the $36,000 of profit are as follows.

1. Determine the fraction from the ratio. Add: $3 + 2 + 1 = 6$ Thus, 6 becomes the denominator of the fraction. The numerators are the numbers in the ratio.

Buck	3/6 or 1/2
Bagwell	2/6 or 1/3
Rose	1/6

2. Make the calculation to determine distribution.

	Fraction		Profits to be Divided		Total Allocated
Buck	1/2	×	$36,000	=	$18,000
Bagwell	1/3	×	$36,000	=	12,000
Rose	1/6	×	$36,000	=	6,000
Total					$36,000

The general journal entry to close the Income Summary to the capital accounts is as follows.

		GENERAL JOURNAL				Page	
Date		Description	Post. Ref.	Debit		Credit	
19XX Dec.	31	**Income Summary**		36000 —			
		Buck, Capital				18000 —	
		Bagwell, Capital				12000 —	
		Rose, Capital				6000 —	
		To Record the Closing of the Income Summary					
		to Capital					

Dividing Net Income Using Interest on Investment and Salary Allowances

Another common way to divide profits is to use an interest percentage and a salary allowance, and divide any remainder equally or according to a fixed ratio. The following example assumes 5 percent (.05) interest on the original investment, salary allowances of $10,000 to each partner, and any remainder to be divided equally. The following shows the calculations made to determine the distribution.

	Share to Buck	Share to Bagwell	Share to Rose	Total
Total Amount to Be Divided				$36,000
Allocated as Interest:				
Buck				
(5% × $50,000)	$ 2,500			
Bagwell				
(5% × $30,000)		$ 1,500		
Rose				
(5% × $40,000)			$ 2,000	
Total Interest				− 6,000
Balance				$30,000
Salary Allowances	10,000	10,000	10,000	− 30,000
Totals to Each	$12,500	$11,500	$12,000	0

There is no remainder to be divided in this instance. The following is the journal entry to close the Income Summary to the capital accounts.

Date	Description	Post. Ref.	Debit	Credit
	GENERAL JOURNAL			**Page**
19XX *Dec.* 31	*Income Summary*		36000 —	
	Buck, Capital			12500 —
	Bagwell, Capital			11500 —
	Rose, Capital			12000 —
	To Record the Closing of the Income Summary			
	to Capital			

Now assume the same facts except that Buck will receive $10,000 salary allowance, Bagwell will receive $8,000, and Rose will receive $9,000. The remainder, if any, will be divided equally. The calculation to determine the distribution would then be as follows.

	Share to Buck	Share to Bagwell	Share to Rose	Total
Total Amount to Be Divided				$36,000
5% Interest	$ 2,500	$ 1,500	$ 2,000	− 6,000
Balance				$30,000
Salary				
Allowance	10,000	8,000	9,000	− 27,000
Balance				$ 3,000
Remainder				
Divided by 3	1,000	1,000	1,000	− 3,000
Totals	$13,500	$10,500	$12,000	0

The general journal entry to close the Income Summary to the capital accounts is as follows.

GENERAL JOURNAL					Page	
Date	Description	Post. Ref.	Debit		Credit	
19XX *Dec.* *31*	*Income Summary*		3 6 0 0 0 —			
	Buck, Capital				1 3 5 0 0 —	
	Bagwell, Capital				1 0 5 0 0 —	
	Rose, Capital				1 2 0 0 0 —	
	To Record the Closing of the Income Summary					
	to Capital					

The methods illustrated thus far are used for calculating the proper allocation of profits to the partners. The use of the salary allowance method does not mean the partners are to withdraw these amounts of salaries. The salary allowances are used solely for the purpose of the calculation for the distribution of net income. The closing of the Income Summary account to the capital accounts of the partners is the end result of the method used to share profits or losses.

PARTNERSHIP FINANCIAL STATEMENTS

The financial statements of a partnership business are similar to those of a single proprietorship. The income statement, the statement of owner's equity, and the balance sheet are shown below using the last illustration and assuming each partner has withdrawn $8,000 for personal expenses.

BUCK, BAGWELL, AND ROSE
INCOME STATEMENT
FOR YEAR ENDED DECEMBER 31, 19XX

Professional Revenue	$9 6 0 0 0 —	
Operating Expenses	6 0 0 0 0 —	
Net Income		$3 6 0 0 0 —
Allocation of Net Income to the Partners:		
M. Buck		
Interest at 5% (.05 × $50,000)	$ 2 5 0 0 —	
Salary Allowance	1 0 0 0 0 —	
⅓ of Remaining Net Income	1 0 0 0 —	
Total		$1 3 5 0 0 —
J. Bagwell		
Interest at 5% (.05 × $30,000)	$ 1 5 0 0 —	
Salary Allowance	8 0 0 0 —	
⅓ of Remaining Net Income	1 0 0 0 —	
Total		$1 0 5 0 0 —
S. Rose		
Interest at 5% (.05 × $40,000)	$ 2 0 0 0 —	
Salary Allowance	9 0 0 0 —	
⅓ of Remaining Net Income	1 0 0 0 —	
Total		1 2 0 0 0 —
Net Income Allocated		$3 6 0 0 0 —

BUCK, BAGWELL, AND ROSE
STATEMENT OF OWNERS' EQUITY
FOR YEAR ENDED DECEMBER 31, 19XX

	Buck	*Bagwell*	*Rose*	*Total*
Capital, January 1, 19XX	5 0 0 0 0 —	3 0 0 0 0 —	4 0 0 0 0 —	1 2 0 0 0 0 —
Add: Additional Investment	0 —	0 —	0 —	0 —
Add: Net Income	1 3 5 0 0 —	1 0 5 0 0 —	1 2 0 0 0 —	3 6 0 0 0 —
Subtotals	6 3 5 0 0 —	4 0 5 0 0 —	5 2 0 0 0 —	1 5 6 0 0 0 —
Deduct: Withdrawals	8 0 0 0 —	8 0 0 0 —	8 0 0 0 —	2 4 0 0 0 —
Capital, December 31, 19XX	5 5 5 0 0 —	3 2 5 0 0 —	4 4 0 0 0 —	1 3 2 0 0 0 —

BUCK, BAGWELL, AND ROSE BALANCE SHEET DECEMBER 31, 19XX		
Assets		
Cash	$92000 —	
Other Assets	50000 —	
Total Assets		$142000 —
Liabilities		
Accounts Payable		$10000 —
Owners' Equity		
M. Buck, Capital	$55500 —	
J. Bagwell, Capital	32500 —	
S. Rose, Capital	44000 —	132000 —
Total Liabilities and Owners' Equity		$142000 —

ACCOUNTING FOR A DEFICIT WHEN DISTRIBUTING NET INCOME

deficit
an abnormal balance
in a capital account

Each illustration thus far has assumed a relatively large net income. In the event the method used for the calculation (such as the one using interest and salary) results in a remainder after interest and salary allowances that is a **deficit** amount (negative), the deficit must be subtracted in the calculation rather than added. Assume for the partnership of Buck, Bagwell, and Rose that the method for distributing net income or loss is to calculate interest at 5 percent of the original investment, give salary allowances of $10,000, $8,000, and $9,000, respectively, and divide any remainder equally. The following example will show the use of this method when profits are only $24,000. The calculation to determine the distribution is as follows.

	Share to Buck	Share to Bagwell	Share to Rose	Total
Total Amount to Be Divided				$24,000
5% Interest	$ 2,500	$ 1,500	$ 2,000	– 6,000
Balance				$18,000
Salary Allowance	10,000	8,000	9,000	– 27,000
Deficit Balance				$(9,000)
Deficit Distributed	(3,000)	(3,000)	(3,000)	9,000
Totals	$ 9,500	$ 6,500	$ 8,000	0

The general journal entry to close the Income Summary to the capital accounts is as follows.

		GENERAL JOURNAL				Page	
Date		Description	Post. Ref.	Debit		Credit	
19XX Dec. 31		Income Summary		24000 —			
		Buck, Capital				9500 —	
		Bagwell, Capital				6500 —	
		Rose, Capital				8000 —	
		To Record the Closing of the Income Summary					
		to Capital					

DISTRIBUTING A NET LOSS

The above example covers only net income. Should a loss occur, the procedure for distributing the loss to the partners' capital account is the same unless the partners agree otherwise. Losses will reduce both assets and capital. Assuming that the partners share profits and losses equally, and assuming a $36,000 loss, the closing entry is as follows.

GENERAL JOURNAL				Page	
Date	Description	Post. Ref.	Debit	Credit	
19XX Dec 31	Buck, Capital		12000 —		
	Bagwell, Capital		12000 —		
	Rose, Capital		12000 —		
	Income Summary			36000 —	
	To Record the Closing of the Income Summary				
	to Capital				

Should additional investments be made by the partners, these investments will increase both the assets and equities of the business. The investment will also increase the capital account of the partner making the additional investment. In the previous example of the statement of owners' equity on page 720, no additional investments were made by the partners; therefore, a zero appeared in the column for additional investments.

WITHDRAWING OR ADDING A PARTNER

A partnership business is based on a contractual agreement among individuals. The partnership ends when these individuals wish to change the contract either by a partner withdrawing from the firm or by a new partner being added to the firm. A partner may withdraw by selling his or her interest or by taking his or her equity in cash or other assets. In addition, a new partner may join the firm either by buying the interest of a present partner or by contributing additional assets. When a partner withdraws from the business by selling his or her interest to another person, all the parties must agree.

account form balance sheet
the format of a balance sheet that shows the major categories—assets, liabilities, and owner's equity—in a horizontal manner

In the examples to follow, the account form balance sheet is used. An **account form balance sheet** shows the three major categories—assets, liabilities, and owner's equity—in a horizontal manner. This format is often used in conjunction with the accounting equation. The assets are presented on the left-hand side, and the liabilities and owner's equity are presented on the right-hand side. The account form balance sheet receives its name from the T-account format used for illustration. The account form balance sheet will be used in this chapter to demonstrate changes in the balance sheet as they occur from the withdrawal of a partner, the addition of a new partner, or a partnership going out of business. The report form of balance sheet has been used thus far (it is presented in a vertical manner). Either of the two formats may be used for the balance sheet. However, the report form is the method used in this text unless specified otherwise. The following paragraphs illustrate various possibilities for changes in the composition of the partnership.

Sale of Partnership Interest

Assume that M. Buck wishes to sell his interest to B. Knight. The balance sheet before this sale is as follows.

BUCK, BAGWELL, AND ROSE
BALANCE SHEET
AUGUST 31, 19XX

Assets		Liabilities & Owners' Equity		
		Liabilities		
Cash	$50000 —	Accounts Payable		$10000 —
Other Assets	80000 —			
		Owners' Equity		
		Buck, Capital	$50000	
		Bagwell, Capital	30000 —	
		Rose, Capital	40000	120000
		Total Liabilities &		
Total Assets	$130000 —	Owners' Equity		$130000 —

Knight has agreed to pay Buck $60,000 for his equity in the business. Bagwell and Rose agree to accept Knight as a partner. The general journal entry to record the transfer is as follows.

GENERAL JOURNAL				Page	
Date	Description	Post. Ref.	Debit	Credit	
19XX *Aug.* *31*	*Buck, Capital*		5 0 0 0 0 —		
	Knight, Capital			5 0 0 0 0 —	
	To Record the Transfer of Buck's Equity in the				
	Partnership to Knight				

After this entry, the old partnership is ended and a new partnership is formed. The only change in the balance sheet will be the substitution of Knight for Buck. After the new partnership is formed, a new contract is written.

Two points should be noted. First, the $60,000 Knight paid Buck was a personal transaction between the two and does not affect the partnership records. The $50,000 equity of Buck is transferred to Knight with the approval of the other two partners. Remember, the business entity concept requires that personal transactions be kept separate from business transactions. The second point to note is that Bagwell and Rose must agree to have Knight as a partner. A partnership is based on agreement of all parties.

Withdrawal of a Partner

The partnership agreement should outline the procedure governing a partner who wishes to withdraw from the business. This may occur when a partner wants to retire or does not wish to continue under the present business arrangements. For example, assume that Rose, with an equity of $40,000, wishes to retire. The partnership contract provides that an audit be made of the business. An audit includes getting all assets appraised to determine market value. In addition, a determination must be made of all liabilities of the partnership. Should the audit reveal that assets and liabilities are different than reflected on the books of the partnership, adjustments are made to the records to determine the true equities of the partners. Once this is accomplished, the contract may provide that assets be distributed to the retiring partner if it does not jeopardize the future profitability of the remaining partners.

In this example, assume that assets and liabilities are the same as presented on the balance sheet on page 714 and that the withdrawal of cash by Rose will not jeopardize the firm's cash position. The general journal entry to record the withdrawal of Rose is as follows.

		GENERAL JOURNAL			Page
Date		Description	Post. Ref.	Debit	Credit
19XX Aug.	31	Rose, Capital		40000 —	
		Cash			40000 —
		To Record the Withdrawal of Rose who Receives			
		Cash Equal to Her Equity			

Sometimes when a partner retires, the remaining partners may not wish to give an amount equal to the retiring partner's equity. The retiring partner may then agree to take an amount less than the value of his or her capital account. If this is the situation, the profit-loss sharing ratio is used to adjust the capital accounts of the remaining partners. Assume that the profits and losses are to be divided equally, and Rose agrees to take $30,000 in cash. The entry to show the withdrawal of Rose for $30,000 cash is as follows.

		GENERAL JOURNAL			Page
Date		Description	Post. Ref.	Debit	Credit
19XX Aug.	31	Rose, Capital		40000 —	
		Cash			30000 —
		Buck, Capital			5000 —
		Bagwell, Capital			5000 —
		To Record the Withdrawal of Rose who			
		Receives Cash Less Than Her Equity			

In the event the two remaining partners are eager to see Rose retire, they may be willing to give more than Rose's equity. Assume that they agree to give Rose $40,000 in cash and a note payable for $10,000. The entry to record this situation is as follows.

Date		Description	Post. Ref.	Debit	Credit
19XX Aug.	31	Rose, Capital		4 0 0 0 0 —	
		Buck, Capital		5 0 0 0 —	
		Bagwell, Capital		5 0 0 0 —	
		Cash			4 0 0 0 0 —
		Notes Payable			1 0 0 0 0 —
		To Record the Withdrawal of Rose who Receives			
		Cash and a Note Payable for Her Equity			

GENERAL JOURNAL — Page

The remaining partners share the additional equity given to Rose as a loss to themselves. Many other variations similar to these can be used. However, whatever method is chosen, assets must equal liabilities and owners' equity at all times.

Adding a New Partner

As shown, a partnership may change by a new individual buying the interest of one of the partners, thus creating a new partnership. Another change that may occur is the decision by the partners to take in a new partner. When a new partner is admitted, a new partnership results and the old one is dissolved. Two situations may occur. First, the new partner will invest cash or other assets equal to the equity he or she is acquiring. The second method requires an investment by the new partner for either more or less than the equity he or she will receive.

Partner Admitted with Investment Same as Equity

Assume that Knight is to invest $40,000 in cash to receive a one-fourth interest in the partnership. The following shows the equity of the present owners.

Buck	$ 50,000
Bagwell	30,000
Rose	40,000
Total	$120,000

After Knight's investment of $40,000, the total equity is $160,000. One-fourth of $160,000 is $40,000, the equity of the new partner. The journal entry to illustrate the addition of Knight under this assumption is as follows.

GENERAL JOURNAL					Page
Date	**Description**	**Post. Ref.**	**Debit**		**Credit**
19XX *Aug.* 31	*Cash*		4 0 0 0 0 —		
	Knight, Capital				4 0 0 0 0 —
	To Record the Addition of Knight as a Partner				
	with a One-Fourth Interest				

After the entry is posted, the assets and equities of the new partnership will appear as follows.

Assets		Liabilities & Owners' Equity		
		Liabilities		
Cash	$ 9 0 0 0 0 —	*Accounts Payable*		$ 1 0 0 0 0 —
Other Assets	8 0 0 0 0 —			
		Owners' Equity		
		Buck, Capital	$ 5 0 0 0 0 —	
		Bagwell, Capital	3 0 0 0 0 —	
		Rose, Capital	4 0 0 0 0 —	
		Knight, Capital	4 0 0 0 0 —	1 6 0 0 0 0 —
		Total Liabilities &		
Total Assets	$17 0 0 0 0 —	*Owners' Equity*		$17 0 0 0 0 —

Bonus to Old Partners

A new partner may be expected to invest more assets than the equity he or she is to receive. This might occur because the equities of the present partners may not reflect the true worth of an already successful business. If this is the case, the partnership is worth more than the records indicate. For example, assume that the present equities are the same as above and that Knight is to invest cash of $36,000 for a one-fifth interest. Knight's equity is determined as follows.

Equities of the present partners	$120,000
Investment of the new partner	36,000
Total equities of the new partnership	$156,000
Equity of Knight	
(1/5 × $156,000 = $31,200)	$ 31,200

Providing the present partners share equally, the bonus of $4,800 (the difference between the cash given, $36,000, and the equity received, $31,200) will be divided by 3 and each capital account of the present partners will be increased by $1,600. The following is the journal entry to admit Knight as one-fifth partner.

		GENERAL JOURNAL			Page
Date		Description	Post. Ref.	Debit	Credit
19XX Aug. 31		Cash		36000 —	
		Buck, Capital			1600 —
		Bagwell, Capital			1600 —
		Rose, Capital			1600 —
		Knight, Capital			31200 —
		To Record the Addition of Knight as Partner			
		with a One-Fifth Interest			

After the entry is posted, the assets, liabilities, and owners' equity are as follows.

Assets		Liabilities & Owners' Equity		
		Liabilities		
Cash	$86000 —	Accounts Payable		$10000 —
Other Assets	80000 —			
		Owners' Equity		
		Buck, Capital	$51600 —	
		Bagwell, Capital	31600 —	
		Rose, Capital	41600 —	
		Knight, Capital	31200 —	156000 —
		Total Liabilities &		
Total Assets	$166000 —	Owners' Equity		$166000 —

Bonus to New Partner

A bonus may be given to a new partner when the new partner is given more equity than his or her cash investment. Assume that Knight invests $20,000 for a one-fourth interest. The equity given to Knight in this case is greater than his investment. Thus Buck, Bagwell, and Rose, who share net income and losses equally, must give up an equal portion of their equity to Knight as determined below.

Equities of present partners	$120,000
Add investment of new partner	20,000
Total equities of the new partnership	140,000
Equity of Knight	
(1/4 × $140,000 = $35,000)	$ 35,000

There is $15,000 difference between the $20,000 cash investment of Knight and total equity of $35,000 he received. The $15,000 is a bonus to Knight. However, the difference must be shared by the present partners as a reduction in their capital accounts. The reduction in the capital accounts is $5,000 each. The entry to record the addition of Knight under these circumstances is as follows.

GENERAL JOURNAL					Page
Date	Description	Post. Ref.	Debit		Credit
19XX Aug. 31	Cash		2 0 0 0 0 —		
	Buck, Capital		5 0 0 0 —		
	Bagwell, Capital		5 0 0 0 —		
	Rose, Capital		5 0 0 0 —		
	Knight, Capital				3 5 0 0 0 —
	To Record the Addition of Knight as a Partner				
	with a One-Fourth Interest				

After the entry is posted, the assets, liabilities, and owners' equity appear as follows.

Assets		Liabilities & Owners' Equity		
		Liabilities		
Cash	$ 7 0 0 0 0 —	Accounts Payable		$ 1 0 0 0 0 —
Other Assets	8 0 0 0 0 —			
		Owners' Equity		
		Buck, Capital	$4 5 0 0 0 —	
		Bagwell, Capital	2 5 0 0 0 —	
		Rose, Capital	3 5 0 0 0 —	
		Knight, Capital	3 5 0 0 0 —	1 4 0 0 0 0 —
		Total Liabilities &		
Total Assets	$15 0 0 0 0 —	Owners' Equity		$15 0 0 0 0 —

This type of situation might occur when the new partner has a special talent or business skill that will increase the profitability of the firm. There are times when a bonus is not recorded at all. Rather, goodwill is recorded and the old partners' capital accounts are increased. This method is seldom used; the bonus method is the preferred method.

Death of a Partner

The death of a partner will automatically end the partnership. The partnership contract should contain provisions for such a situation. The books are closed immediately, and assets are revalued to reflect their current market values. This is done to determine the equity of the deceased partner. The equity of the deceased partner belongs to his or her estate, and the partnership agreement should cover its disposition. Should partners fail to include this in their agreement, the distribution of the deceased partner's equity could threaten the continued existence of the partnership.

GOING OUT OF BUSINESS—LIQUIDATION

liquidation
the total process of going out of business

Partners may determine that it is no longer possible to continue in business. This may occur if the partners have unsettled disputes or the business is no longer profitable and liquidation becomes necessary. **Liquidation** is the total process of going out of business. Thus, liquidation is the legal process of converting assets to cash, paying all creditors, and making final distribution of cash to the partners. This legal process also means that each partner is liable to pay the creditors whether or not there is sufficient cash remaining. Although many different circumstances occur in liquidation, only two are discussed here. In each case, there are four steps to be followed.

1. Convert all assets to cash.
2. Distribute the gains or losses to the partners' capital accounts according to the profit-loss ratio.
3. Pay the creditors.
4. Distribute the remaining cash according to the equities (capital balances) of the partners.

realization
the conversion of non-cash assets to cash

A new account will be used for steps one and two. This account is called the Loss or Gain on Realization. It is a temporary account that is used to assemble the gains or losses that may occur when selling the assets. It is opened upon sale of these assets. It is closed to the partners' capital accounts. **Realization** is the conversion of noncash assets to cash.

Assets Sold for a Gain

The liquidation of a partnership may be illustrated using the following information. Buck, Bagwell, and Rose, the partners in the accounting firm of previous illustrations, have had a bitter dispute over business policies. They decide to dissolve the partnership. To illustrate a liquidation where assets are sold for a gain, assume the following balance sheet before liquidation.

BUCK, BAGWELL, AND ROSE BALANCE SHEET DECEMBER 31, 19XX				
Assets		**Liabilities & Owners' Equity**		
		Liabilities		
Cash	$3 0 0 0 —	Accounts Payable		$1 0 0 0 0 —
Other Assets	10 0 0 0 —			
		Owners' Equity		
		Buck, Capital	$5 0 0 0 0 —	
		Bagwell, Capital	3 0 0 0 0 —	
		Rose, Capital	4 0 0 0 0 —	120 0 0 0 —
		Total Liabilities &		
Total Assets	$13 0 0 0 0 —	Owners' Equity		$13 0 0 0 0 —

Assume that the other assets are sold for $109,000 and the partners share profits and losses equally. The four steps necessary upon liquidation are shown as journal entries.

1. Convert all assets to cash.

		GENERAL JOURNAL			Page
Date		Description	Post. Ref.	Debit	Credit
19XX Dec. 31		Cash		1 0 9 0 0 0 —	
		Other Assets			1 0 0 0 0 0 —
		Loss or Gain on Realization			9 0 0 0 —
		To Record the Sale of Other Assets			

2. Distribute gains or losses to the partners' capital accounts according to the profit-loss ratio.

GENERAL JOURNAL					Page
Date	**Description**	**Post. Ref.**	**Debit**		**Credit**
19XX Dec. 31	*Loss or Gain on Realization*		9 0 0 0 —		
	Buck, Capital				3 0 0 0 —
	Bagwell, Capital				3 0 0 0 —
	Rose, Capital				3 0 0 0 —
	To Record the Closing of the Loss or Gain on				
	Realization Account to the Partners' Capital				
	Accounts				

After posting these two entries, the balance sheet appears as follows.

Assets		*Liabilities & Owners' Equity*		
		Liabilities		
Cash	$13 9 0 0 0 —	**Accounts Payable**		$ 1 0 0 0 0 —
		Owners' Equity		
		Buck, Capital	$ 5 3 0 0 0 —	
		Bagwell, Capital	3 3 0 0 0 —	
		Rose, Capital	4 3 0 0 0 —	1 2 9 0 0 0 —
		Total Liabilities &		
Total Assets	$13 9 0 0 0 —	*Owners' Equity*		$13 9 0 0 0 —

3. Pay the creditors.

GENERAL JOURNAL					Page
Date	Description	Post. Ref.	Debit		Credit
19XX Dec. 31	Accounts Payable		1 0 0 0 0 —		
	Cash				1 0 0 0 0 —
	To Record the Payment of the Creditors				

4. Distribute the remaining cash according to the equities of the partners.

GENERAL JOURNAL					Page
Date	Description	Post. Ref.	Debit		Credit
19XX Dec. 31	Buck, Capital		5 3 0 0 0 —		
	Bagwell, Capital		3 3 0 0 0 —		
	Rose, Capital		4 3 0 0 0 —		
	Cash				1 2 9 0 0 0 —
	To Record the Closing of the Partnership Books				

Once the above entries are posted, every account in the partnership records will have a zero balance, signifying the termination of this business.

Assets Sold for a Loss

Many times a business cannot sell its other assets at the amount carried in the records. Assets will deteriorate with age and therefore are not as marketable as when they were new. Assume that other assets are listed on the balance sheet at $100,000 and that they are sold for $91,000. This is a $9,000 loss to the partners and will result in reducing both their assets and capital accounts. Each of the four steps are presented as journal entries as follows.

1. Convert all assets to cash.

		GENERAL JOURNAL				Page	
Date		Description	Post. Ref.	Debit		Credit	
19XX *Dec.* **31**		*Cash*		91000 —			
		Loss or Gain on Realization		9000 —			
		Other Assets				100000 —	
		To Record the Sale of Other Assets					

2. Distribute the gains or losses to the partners' capital accounts according to the profit-loss ratio.

		GENERAL JOURNAL				Page	
Date		Description	Post. Ref.	Debit		Credit	
19XX *Dec.* **31**		*Buck, Capital*		3000 —			
		Bagwell, Capital		3000 —			
		Rose, Capital		3000 —			
		Loss or Gain on Realization				9000 —	
		To Record the Closing of the Loss to Partners'					
		Capital Accounts					

3. Pay the creditors.

		GENERAL JOURNAL				Page	
Date		Description	Post. Ref.	Debit		Credit	
19XX *Dec.* **31**		*Accounts Payable*		10000 —			
		Cash				10000 —	
		To Record the Payment of the Creditors					

After the above entries are posted, the T-accounts will appear as follows.

Cash		Other Assets		Accounts Payable	
30,000	10,000	100,000	100,000	10,000	10,000
91,000					
(111,000)					

Buck, Capital		Bagwell, Capital		Rose, Capital	
3,000	50,000	3,000	30,000	3,000	40,000
	(47,000)		(27,000)		(37,000)

Loss or Gain on Realization	
9,000	9,000

There is $111,000 left in the Cash account, and the total remaining capital account balances equal $111,000. In step four, the amount of cash to be distributed to each partner is determined by the balance in each partner's capital account.

4. Distribute the remaining cash according to the equities of the partners.

		GENERAL JOURNAL				Page	
Date		Description	Post. Ref.	Debit		Credit	
19XX Dec. 31		Buck, Capital		4 7 0 0 0 —			
		Bagwell, Capital		2 7 0 0 0 —			
		Rose, Capital		3 7 0 0 0 —			
		Cash				1 1 1 0 0 0 —	
		To Record the Closing of the Partnership Books					

After this entry is posted, all the accounts have a zero balance and the partnership is terminated.

A problem may occur if one partner's share of the loss is greater than the balance of his or her capital account. If this is the case, the partner must cover the deficit by paying cash into the partnership. In this situation, a deficit is a debit balance in a partner's capital account. For example, assume the partners Buck, Bagwell, and Rose share profits and losses in a 2:2:1 ratio. If the other assets are shown at $100,000 on the balance sheet and sold for $20,000, a loss of $80,000 must be distributed. The four steps, presented as journal entries, will illustrate this problem and are as follows.

1. Convert all assets to cash.

GENERAL JOURNAL					Page
Date	Description	Post. Ref.	Debit		Credit
19XX *Dec.* 31	*Cash*		20000 —		
	Loss or Gain on Realization		80000 —		
	Other Assets				100000 —
	To Record the Sale of the Other Assets				

2. Distribute the gains or losses to the partners' capital accounts according to the profit-loss ratio.

GENERAL JOURNAL					Page
Date	Description	Post. Ref.	Debit		Credit
19XX *Dec.* 31	*Buck, Capital*		32000—*		
	Bagwell, Capital		32000 —		
	Rose, Capital		16000 —		
	Loss or Gain on Realization				80000 —
	To Record the Closing of the Loss to the				
	Partners' Capital Accounts on a 2:2:1 Ratio				

*Calculation of division of loss:

Buck	2/5 × $80,000 = $32,000
Bagwell	2/5 × $80,000 = 32,000
Rose	1/5 × $80,000 = 16,000

3. Pay the creditors.

GENERAL JOURNAL				Page
Date	Description	Post. Ref.	Debit	Credit
19XX *Dec.* *31*	*Accounts Payable*		*1 0 0 0 0* —	
	Cash			*1 0 0 0 0* —
	To Record the Payment of the Creditors			

After the above entries are posted the T-accounts will appear as follows.

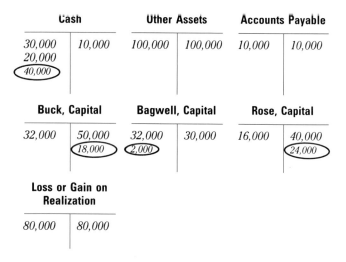

	Cash		Other Assets		Accounts Payable	
	30,000	10,000	100,000	100,000	10,000	10,000
	20,000					
	40,000					

	Buck, Capital		Bagwell, Capital		Rose, Capital	
	32,000	50,000	32,000	30,000	16,000	40,000
		18,000	2,000			24,000

	Loss or Gain on Realization	
	80,000	80,000

Bagwell has a debit balance of $2,000 in his capital account and is liable to the partnership firm for his deficit. If Bagwell has sufficient personal assets and contributes the $2,000 to the firm to cover his debit balance, step four can be completed as follows.

4. Distribute the remaining cash according to the equities of the partners.

a. Payment of cash by Bagwell.

GENERAL JOURNAL					Page	
Date	Description	Post. Ref.	Debit		Credit	
19XX Dec. 31	Cash		2 0 0 0 —			
	Bagwell, Capital				2 0 0 0 —	
	To Record the Cash Contribution of Bagwell					
	to Cover His Liability					

b. Distribute remaining cash.

GENERAL JOURNAL					Page	
Date	Description	Post. Ref.	Debit		Credit	
19XX Dec. 31	Buck, Capital		1 8 0 0 0 —			
	Rose, Capital		2 4 0 0 0 —			
	Cash				4 2 0 0 0 —	
	To Record the Closing of the Partnership					
	Books					

After posting these two entries, all the accounts have a zero balance and the partnership is terminated. However, if Bagwell has no personal assets and cannot pay his liability, Buck and Rose must share this additional loss according to their portion of the profit-loss ratio, which is 2:1. The journal entries for step four under these circumstances are as follows.

4. Distribute the remaining cash according to the equities of the partners.

a.   Distribute the $2,000 loss.

GENERAL JOURNAL					Page
Date	Description	Post. Ref.	Debit		Credit
19XX *Dec.* 31	Buck, Capital		1 3 3 3 —*		
	Rose, Capital		6 6 7 —		
	Bagwell, Capital				2 0 0 0 —
	To Record Bagwell's Liability as a Loss to				
	the Remaining Partners				

*Calculation of division of loss:
  Buck 2/3 × $2,000 = $1,333
  Rose 1/3 × $2,000 =   667

b.   Distribute the remaining cash.

GENERAL JOURNAL					Page
Date	Description	Post. Ref.	Debit		Credit
19XX *Dec.* 31	Buck, Capital		1 6 6 6 7 —		
	Rose, Capital		2 3 3 3 3 —		
	Cash				4 0 0 0 0 —
	To Record the Closing of the Partnership Books				

After the posting of the above entries, all the accounts have a zero balance and the partnership is terminated.

Even though the partner with the deficit cannot pay at the present time, the liability is not eliminated. If the deficit partner becomes able to pay at some time in the future, he or she must do so.

SUMMARY

A partnership is an association of two or more competent persons who agree to do business as co-owners for profit. The partners agree to form a new business and sign a contract stating the terms of their agreement.

The partnership has limited life because it cannot exist separate and apart from the individuals who formed it. Therefore, a partnership ends at the death or bankruptcy of a partner, or when a partner loses his or her capacity to contract.

Accounting for a partnership requires some special considerations. The profits or losses must be divided among the partners. They may decide to divide the profits or losses equally or may use a ratio based on the amounts of their original investments, a fixed ratio, or divide profits and losses using a formula based on interest and salary allowances. If the partners fail to agree on how they are to share profits and losses, the court will require them to be shared equally.

The composition within a partnership business may change. A partner may wish to withdraw or retire. A partner, with the agreement of the remaining partners, may want to sell his or her interest to another party. As the partnership business grows, a new partner may be added. The new partner may invest cash equal to the equity or interest to be received. A new partner may invest cash and receive either a greater equity than the investment or a lower equity than the investment. Any of these events must be reflected on the partnership records.

In addition, a partnership business may not be successful and be forced to terminate. When going out of business, all noncash assets must be sold for cash. A gain or loss may occur by their sale and must be distributed to the capital accounts of the partners according to their profit and loss sharing agreement. All debts must be paid to the creditors before the final distribution of cash to the partners. After the debts are paid, the remaining cash is distributed to the partners according to the balances in their capital accounts.

Review of Accounting Terminology

Following is a list of the accounting terminology for this chapter.

account form balance sheet   partnership
deficit   profit-loss ratio
liquidation   realization
mutual agency   unlimited liability

Fill in the blank with the correct word or term from the list.

1. The total process of going out of business is _____.
2. A/an _____ is an association of two or more competent persons who agree to do business as co-owners for profit.
3. The ability of each partner, acting as an agent of the business, to enter into and bind it to contracts within the apparent scope of the business is _____.
4. _____ is the conversion of noncash assets to cash.
5. The method used by the partners to divide profits or losses is the _____.
6. A/an _____ is an abnormal balance in a capital account.
7. The principle that each partner is personally liable for the debts of the business is called _____.
8. _____ shows the three major categories—assets, liabilities, and owner's equity—in a horizontal manner.

Match the following words and terms on the left with the definitions on the right (columns continue on the following page).

9. account form balance sheet   a. the method used by the partners to divide profits or losses
10. deficit

b. each partner is personally liable for the debts of the business

11. liquidation

12. mutual agency

13. partnership

14. profit-loss ratio

15. realization

16. unlimited liability

c. an association of two or more competent persons who agree to do business as co-owners for profit

d. an abnormal balance in a capital account

e. the conversion of noncash assets to cash

f. the total process of going out of business

g. the ability of each partner, acting as an agent of the business, to enter into and bind it to contracts within the apparent scope of the partnership

h. the format of a balance sheet that shows the assets, liabilities, and owners' equity in a horizontal manner

Exercises

Exercise 20.1
calculating the division of profits

Morton and Long plan to enter into a law partnership, investing $30,000 and $20,000, respectively. They have agreed on everything but how to divide the profits. They are considering the following methods. Calculate the results under each of the following independent assumptions.

a. If the first year's net income is $50,000 and they cannot agree, how should the profits be divided?

b. If the partners agree to share net income according to their investment ratio, how should the $50,000 be divided?

c. If the owners agree to share net income by granting 10 percent interest on their original investments, giving salary allowances of $10,000 each, and dividing the remainder equally, how should the $50,000 be divided?

Exercise 20.2
calculating the division of profits

Assume Morton and Long from Exercise 20.1 use method c to divide profits and net income is $20,000. How should the income be divided?

Exercise 20.3

preparing the general journal entries to record the sale of a partnership

After a number of years, Long, from Exercise 20.1, decides to go with a large law firm and wishes to sell his interest to Brown. Long's equity at this time is $35,000. Morton agrees to take Brown as a partner, and Long sells his interest to Brown for $40,000. Prepare the general journal entry to record the sale of Long's interest to Brown.

Exercise 20.4

preparing the general journal entries to record the withdrawal of a partner

Smith, White, and Saint are partners owning the Book Nook. The equities of the partners are $60,000, $50,000, and $40,000, respectively. They share profits and losses equally. White wishes to retire on May 30, 19XX. Prepare the general journal entries to record White's retirement under each independent assumption.

a. White is paid $50,000 in partnership cash.
b. White is paid $40,000 in partnership cash.
c. White is paid $55,000 in partnership cash.

Exercise 20.5

preparing the general journal entries to record the addition of a new partner

Hall and Mason share profits and losses equally and have capital balances of $60,000 and $40,000, respectively. Taylor is to be admitted and is to receive a one-third interest in the firm. Prepare the general journal entries to record the addition of Taylor as a partner under the following unrelated circumstances.

a. Taylor invests $50,000.
b. Taylor invests $62,000.
c. Taylor invests $47,000.

Exercise 20.6

determining the loss, the distribution of the loss, and the distribution of cash in a partnership going out of business

Martin, Pearson, and Henderson are partners sharing profits and losses in a 2:1:1 ratio. Their capital balances are $30,000, $25,000, and $20,000, respectively. Because of an economic turndown, they have decided to liquidate. After all the assets are sold and the creditors paid, $43,000 cash remains in their business checking account.

a. Determine the amount of their losses by using the accounting equation.
b. Using the profit-loss ratio, determine the amount of loss to be distributed to each partner, and determine their new capital balances.

c.   Determine the amount of cash each partner will receive in the
     final distribution and fill in the blanks below.

Martin will receive cash of   _____
Pearson will receive cash of   _____
Henderson will receive cash of   _____

Exercise 20.7

determining the loss, the distribution of the loss, and the distribution of cash in a partnership going out of business

Baker, Marshall, and Perryman are equal partners beginning their business with investments of $20,000, $15,000, and $8,000, respectively. They have been unprofitable in their business venture and decide they must liquidate. After all the assets are sold and all debts paid, $16,000 cash remains in the business checking account.

a.   Determine the amount of their losses by using the accounting
     equation.

b.   Using the profit-ratio, determine the amount of loss to each
     partner, and determine their new capital balances.

c.   Calculate the amount of cash, if any, each partner will receive
     under the different assumptions below.
     (1) Perryman has personal assets and pays the amount she
          owes to the partnership.

Baker will receive cash of   _____
Marshall will receive cash of   _____
Perryman will receive cash of   _____

(2) Perryman has no personal assets and cannot pay the
     amount she owes to the partnership.

Baker will receive cash of   _____
Marshall will receive cash of   _____
Perryman will receive cash of   _____

Problems

Problem 20.1
determining division of profits, preparing the income statement, and closing the income summary

Jones, Brady, and Bell formed a partnership making investments of $40,000, $60,000, and $80,000, respectively. They believe the net income from their business for the first year will be $81,000. They are considering several alternative plans for sharing this expected profit, which are: (1) divide the profits equally: (2) divide the profits according to their investment ratio; (3) divide the profits by giving an interest allowance of 10 percent on original investments, granting $10,000 salary allowance to each partner, and dividing any remainder equally.

Instructions a. *Prepare a schedule showing distribution of net income under plans 1, 2, and 3. It should have the following headings.*

Plan	Calculations	Jones	Brady	Bell	Total Allocated

b. *Using method 3 above, prepare a partial income statement showing the allocation of net income to the partners (see income statement on page 720 for example).*

c. *Journalize the closing of the Income Summary account using the information from b above.*

Problem 20.2
preparing the general journal entries to record changes in the composition of a partnership

Abner, Black, and Cobb are equal partners with capital balances of $60,000, $50,000, and $50,000, respectively. Cobb wishes to sell his interest and leave the business on July 31 of this year. Cobb is to sell his interest to Williams with the approval of Abner and Black.

Instructions *Prepare the general journal entries, without explanations, to record the following independent assumptions.*

a. *Cobb sells his interest to Williams for $50,000.*

b. *Cobb sells his interest to Williams for $40,000.*

c. *Cobb decides to stay in the partnership but sell one-half of his interest to Williams for $30,000. (Hint: What is the value of half of Cobb's capital account?)*

d. *If Williams is admitted as a new partner, must a new partnership agreement be written? Why?*

Problem 20.3

preparing the general journal entries to close the Income Summary account and preparing an income statement, statement of owners' equity, and a balance sheet

Coleman and Simmons are partners and own the ABC Gift Shop. They formed their partnership on January 2, 19XX, with investments of $50,000 and $25,000, and Simmons investing an additional $5,000 on July 7. They share profits giving 10 percent interest allowance on beginning investments and the remainder on a 2:1 ratio. Following is their trial balance before closing.

ABC GIFT SHOP
TRIAL BALANCE
DECEMBER 31, 19XX

Cash	$19000 —	
Accounts Receivable	5000 —	
Merchandise Inventory		
(Perpetual 12-31-19XX)	60000 —	
Equipment	20000 —	
Accumulated Depreciation: Equipment		$10000 —
Accounts Payable		10000 —
Coleman, Drawing	10000 —	
Simmons, Drawing	10000 —	
Coleman, Capital		50000 —
Simmons, Capital		30000 —
Sales		100000 —
Operating Expenses (control account)	76000 —	
	$200000 —	$200000 —

Instructions

a. Prepare the general journal entries, without explanations, to record the closing of all the nominal accounts (revenue and expense) using the Income Summary account.

b. Prepare a schedule showing the distribution of net income to the partners. It should have the following headings.

Calculations	Coleman	Simmons	Total Allocated

c. Prepare the general journal entries to record the closing of the Income Summary account to the capital accounts, and close the drawing accounts to the capital accounts.

d. *Prepare the partnership income statement showing the alloca-
    tion of net income.*

e. *Prepare the statement of owners' equity.*

f. *Prepare a balance sheet.*

Problem 20.4
*preparing the general
journal entries to
record the withdrawal
of a partner*

Arnold, Cole, and Drake are partners, owning Pizza Plus and sharing profits and losses in a 3:2:1 ratio. The balance sheet, presented
in account form format for this business, is as follows.

	PIZZA PLUS **BALANCE SHEET** **JUNE 30, 19XX**		
Assets		**Liabilities & Owners' Equity**	
		Liabilities	
Cash	$ 0 5 0 0 0 —	*Accounts Payable*	$ 0 0 0 0 —
Delivery Truck #1	$2 5 0 0 0 —		
Accumulated		**Owners' Equity**	
Depreciation:		*Arnold, Capital*	$60 0 0 0 —
Truck #1	1 0 0 0 0 — 1 5 0 0 0 —	*Cole, Capital*	3 0 0 0 0 —
Delivery Truck #2	3 5 0 0 0 —	*Drake, Capital*	1 5 0 0 0 — 10 5 0 0 0 —
Accumulated			
Depreciation:			
Truck #2	7 0 0 0 — 2 8 0 0 0 —		
		Total Liabilities &	
Total Assets	$10 8 0 0 0 —	**Owners' Equity**	$10 8 0 0 0 —

Arnold wishes to withdraw from the firm. Cole and Drake agree.

Instructions *Prepare the general journal entries, without explanations, to record
the June 30 withdrawal of Arnold under the following independent
assumptions.*

a. *Arnold withdraws taking partnership cash of $60,000.*

b. *Arnold withdraws taking cash of $32,000 and truck #2 (debit
    Accumulated Depreciation and credit Truck).*

c. *Arnold withdraws taking cash of $51,000.*

d. *Arnold withdraws taking cash of $25,000 and a $44,000 note given by the partnership.*

e. *Arnold withdraws taking cash of $25,000, a $20,000 note, and truck #1.*

Problem 20.5
preparing the general journal entries to record the addition of a new partner

Green, Keller, and Henley are partners who share profits and losses in a 3:1:2 ratio. Their capital account balances are $60,000, $25,000, and $35,000, respectively. Watts is to be admitted to the firm on March 31, 19XX with a one-fourth interest.

Instructions *Prepare the general journal entries to record the following unrelated assumptions.*

a. *Watts is to be admitted by investing cash of $40,000.*

b. *Watts is to be admitted by investing cash of $30,000.*

c. *Watts is to be admitted by investing cash of $50,000.*

Problem 20.6
preparing the general journal entries to record the sale of assets and final distribution of cash

Bentley, Colby, and Kennedy plan to liquidate their partnership. They share profits and losses on a 3:2:1 ratio. At the time of liquidation, the partnership balance sheet appears as follows.

BENTLEY, COLBY, AND KENNEDY BALANCE SHEET JUNE 30, 19XX				
Assets		**Liabilities & Owners' Equity**		
		Liabilities		
Cash	$23 0 0 0 —	*Accounts Payable*		$30 0 0 0 —
Other Assets	115 0 0 0 —			
		Owners' Equity		
		Bentley, Capital	$48 0 0 0 —	
		Colby, Capital	36 0 0 0 —	
		Kennedy, Capital	24 0 0 0 —	108 0 0 0 —
		Total Liabilities &		
Total Assets	$13 8 0 0 0 —	*Owners' Equity*		$13 8 0 0 0 —

Instructions *Prepare the general journal entries, without explanations, to record (1) the sale of the other assets; (2) the distribution of the loss or gain on realization; (3) the payment to the creditors; and (4) the final distribution of cash. Each of the following are unrelated assumptions. Refer to the text if necessary.*

a. *The other assets are sold for $115,000.*

b. *The other assets are sold for $79,000.*

c. *The other assets are sold for $55,000.*

Problem 20.7
preparing the general journal entries to record the sale of inventory, the distribution of gains or losses, the payment to creditors, and the final distribution of cash

Irby, Jerry, and Kimball are partners in a video rental business, sharing profits and losses in a 2:1:1 ratio. Business has decreased due to the number of other rental stores in their area. They decide it would be best to go out of business. Their December 31, 19XX balance sheet information is as follows.

Balance Sheet Information

Cash	$15,000
Video Inventory	75,000
Accounts Payable	25,000
Irby, Capital	25,000
Jerry, Capital	20,000
Kimball, Capital	20,000

Instructions *Prepare the general journal entries, without explanations, to show: (1) the sale of the noncash assets; (2) the distribution of the losses or gains; (3) the payment to the creditors; and (4) the final distribution of cash under each of the following independent assumptions.*

a. *The video inventory is sold for $63,000.*

b. *The video inventory is sold for $25,000.*

c. *The video inventory is sold for $20,000 and the partner with the deficit can and does pay from personal assets.*

d. *The same assumption as c above, except the partner with the deficit cannot pay.*

CHAPTER 21

Corporations: Characteristics and Formation

LEARNING OBJECTIVES

When you have completed this chapter, you should

1. have a better understanding of accounting terminology.

2. be able to describe the major characteristics of a corporation.

3. be able to list the advantages and disadvantages of the corporate format.

4. understand the differences between common and preferred stock.

5. be able to journalize the issuance of common and preferred stock.

6. be able to journalize stock purchased by subscription.

7. understand the differences among par, book, market, stated, and redemption values.

8. be able to prepare the corporation balance sheet.

At this point in your study of accounting, you have learned about two forms of business organization. In this and the following chapters, you will learn a third type of business formation, the corporation. To review, the three types of business organizations are single proprietorships, partnerships, and corporations. Of the three, corporations have the greatest impact on our economic system because of the volume of dollars they control. Though fewer in number, corporations are the most important form of business organization.

corporation
a separate legal entity
created by law

A **corporation** is a separate legal entity. It is an artificial entity created by law. As such it has the rights, duties, and responsibilities of a person. Because it is a separate legal entity, a corporation, through its agents, may enter into contracts and carry on other business activities. It is also subject to direct federal and state taxation.

ADVANTAGES OF THE CORPORATE FORMAT

Lack of Stockholders' Liability

One of the most important advantages to the corporate format is the limited nature of stockholders' liability. As a separate legal entity, a corporation is responsible for its own acts and its own debts. A shareholder has no personal liability for the corporation's debts. Therefore, a potential investor knows he or she is liable to lose only the amount invested and does not put his or her personal assets in jeopardy when buying stock. This rule does have one exception, which will be discussed later in this chapter.

Ease of Owner Transfers

stock certificate
an intangible representation of the rights
of the owner

A person invests in a corporation by buying stock. This stock is represented by a legal paper called a stock certificate. The **stock certificate** is an intangible representation of the rights of the owner. The certificates can be easily transferred from owner to owner with no effect on the corporation. It is a personal transaction separate and apart from the daily operations of the corporation. Stock exchanges make daily transfers for the owners. An example of a typical stock certificate follows.

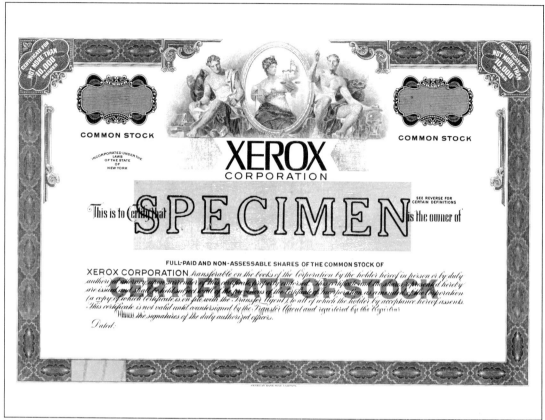

Source: Courtesy of Xerox Corporation.

Length of Corporate Life

A corporation is created by the granting of a charter by a state government. This charter may be for a specific period or any length of time. Because the corporation's life is not dependent on an individual, it may continue as long as the charter permits. A charter may normally be renewed at its expiration, and thus, the corporation can last indefinitely.

No Mutual Agency

Stockholders acting as such may not bind corporations to contracts; only the agents given authority may do so. Stockholders who hold voting stock rights may choose these agents.

Ease of Raising Capital

Limited liability, ease of owner transfers, and length of corporate life are advantages that make it possible for corporations to sell their stock. A corporation may assemble large amounts of capital in this manner. Single owners and partnerships are limited to a relatively small number of individuals, and raising large amounts of capital may be difficult. Normally a corporation's capital accumulation is only limited by its profitability.

DISADVANTAGES OF THE CORPORATE FORMAT

Governmental Control

A corporation is created by the state in which it is incorporated and must abide by that state's regulations. It must also meet federal regulations. The Securities and Exchange Commission of the federal government requires certain standards of conduct by corporations and their agents. This is not true for the single owner or the partnership business.

Taxation

A corporation as a separate entity is taxed by both the state and the federal government. Single proprietors and partners are taxed as individuals for the business profits; the business per se is not taxed. The Internal Revenue Code provides for heavy taxation—up to 50 percent of a corporation's pretax income. In addition, the stockholders of a corporation are taxed again for their individual profits, which are distributed as cash dividends. In other words, the income is taxed twice. First, it is taxed as corporation income and then as personal dividend income to the stockholder. In most cases, double taxation is viewed as a disadvantage of the corporate format.

A set of corporate financial statements is shown in the appendix of this chapter. This appendix illustrates the typical information presented in annual reports of corporations. Stockholders, investors, and analysts review annual reports with great interest.

ORGANIZING A CORPORATION

To organize a corporation, a charter must be secured from a designated official of a particular state. Most states require an application that must meet the legal requirements of the state before a charter can be granted. This application is called the Articles of Incorporation. Among the items required are (1) a unique name, (2) the nature and purpose of the business, (3) the type and classes of stock, and (4) the signatures of at least three subscribers.

subscriber
a potential investor who plans to buy the corporation stock

A **subscriber** is a potential investor who plans to buy the corporation's stock. Sometimes the subscriber is called the promoter or incorporator. If all the legal requirements are met and all the applicable fees are paid, the charter is granted and the corporation comes into legal existence. The subscribers then purchase the corporation's stock and become the stockholders (owners). A meeting is then held to elect a board of directors who become the authorized agents to conduct the affairs of the business. A typical format of the corporate organization is shown on page 758.

The ownership of the corporation rests with its stockholders. The owners manage the business indirectly through their election of the board of directors. A stockholders' meeting is held at least once each year where the stockholders exercise their vote. At this meeting, the board is elected and other business is transacted as provided in the bylaws of the corporation. Some stockholders having voting rights choose not to attend this meeting physically. Instead they delegate an agent to vote in their absence by signing a legal document (such as a power-of-attorney document) called a proxy. A **proxy** is a legal document that gives an agent the right to vote for the stockholder.

proxy
a legal document that gives an agent the right to vote for the stockholder

The board of directors is responsible for the affairs of the corporation. It must act as a collective body and must have a majority present to conduct business. Proxy is not available to a director. The board of directors generally deals only with establishing policy. It delegates the day-to-day activities to the officers and employees. The officers of the corporation carry on the daily activities of the business. The president oversees all the business activities and is directly responsible to the board for the management of the corporation. (See the diagram on the following page.)

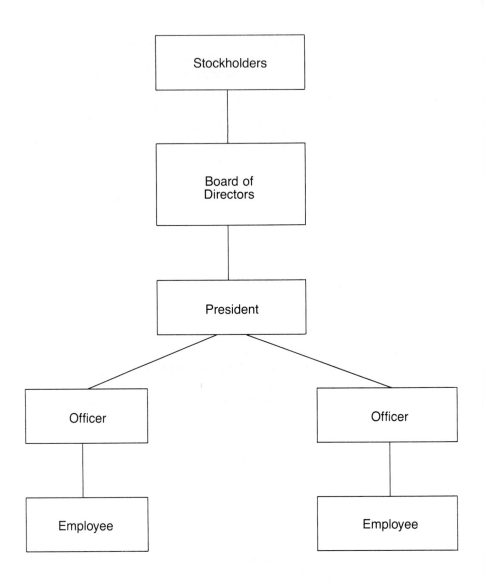

Organization Costs

organization costs
costs incurred to be-
gin a new corporation

A number of costs, such as legal fees, promoter's fees, and amounts paid to the state to secure a charter, must be incurred to organize a corporation. These costs are related and will benefit the business for many years; therefore they are accumulated in one account, **Organization Costs.** Organization Costs is classified as an intangible asset and, like other intangibles, is amortized over a chosen period of time.

Although organization costs are not specifically related to a benefit period, the income tax rules permit corporations to write them off over a period of not less than five and not more than 40 years. Thus many corporations will choose the five-year period over which to write off organization costs, even though the benefit period may in fact be much longer. Since organization costs are not usually large in amount, the principle of materiality allows the shorter write-off period.

To accumulate the costs, each expense is debited to the Organization Costs account. At the end of the accounting period, an adjusting entry is required to amortize this account by the straight-line method. Organization Costs Expense is debited and Organization Costs is credited. No contra account is used for intangible assets. For example, the Organization Costs account has an accumulated balance of $10,000. The calculation to determine the amortization is:

$$\$10,000 \div 5 \text{ yrs.} = \$2,000 \text{ per year.}$$

The general journal entry to record the amortization of the Organization Costs account is as follows.

GENERAL JOURNAL					Page	
Date	Description	Post. Ref.	Debit		Credit	
19XX Dec. 31	Organization Costs Expense		2000 —			
	Organization Costs				2000 —	
	To Record the First Year's Amortization					
	and Adjust Organization Costs					

RECORDS OF STOCK CERTIFICATES

An individual invests in a corporation by buying its stock. The person receives a stock certificate as evidence of the number and class of shares purchased. A corporation may have many stockholders, thus a detailed record must be kept of the name of each owner, the number of shares owned, and the class of stock held.

This information is recorded in a stockholders' ledger or it may be called the stockholders' registrar.

Owners may transfer at will either all or part of the shares they own. To do this, an owner completes and signs a transfer endorsement. When the corporation's transfer agent receives this document, the name of the old stockholder is removed, and the name of the new stockholder is added. A corporation must have a registrar and a transfer agent who keep the stockholders' records up to date. Usually, registrars and transfer agents are large banks or trust companies.

ACCOUNTING FOR A CORPORATION

Accounting for the assets and liabilities of a corporation are basically the same as for that of a single proprietorship or a partnership. The difference is found in the owner's equity section of the balance sheet. Accounting principles require a corporation to distinguish between the stockholders' equity resulting from amounts paid into the corporation through the sale of stock and the amount of stockholders' equity resulting from earnings.

The stockholders' equity section of the balance sheet is divided into two major sections: (1) paid-in or invested capital from the sale of stock and (2) retained earnings (profits retained in the business). Separate accounts are maintained for each of these major sections. To demonstrate corporation accounting as compared with partnership accounting, assume the three partners Buck, Bagwell, and Rose, who share profits and losses equally, decide to incorporate. Buck's capital balance is $50,000, Bagwell's is $30,000, and Rose's is $40,000. There are no liabilities. Assume further that the three purchase 12,000 common shares for $10 each or $120,000 total. The earnings for the first year are $36,000. The T-accounts comparing the capital accounts of a partnership with stockholders' equity accounts of a corporation are as follows.

Partnership Owners' Equity

Buck, Capital	Bagwell, Capital	Rose, Capital
50,000	30,000	40,000
12,000	12,000	12,000

Corporation Stockholders' Equity

Common Stock	**Retained Earnings**
120,000	36,000

A partial balance sheet for each is as follows.

Partnership Owners' Equity		**Corporation Stockholders' Equity**	
Buck, Capital	$ 62,000	Paid-In Capital	
Bagwell, Capital	42,000	Common Stock, $10 par	
Rose, Capital	52,000	value, 12,000 shares	
Total Owners' Equity	$156,000	authorized and issued	$120,000
		Retained Earnings	36,000
		Total Stockholders' Equity	$156,000

The total equity in both cases is the same. Because a corporation is a separate legal entity, the names of its stockholders are of little or no interest to a balance sheet reader and are not shown in the equity section of the corporation balance sheet. Retained Earnings is the capital account used to accumulate profits, and it normally has a credit balance. If it has an abnormal balance, the corporation has experienced losses. If this is the case, the debit balance in the capital account represents a deficit. Profits that are distributed to the owners in the form of dividends are paid from Retained Earnings. The retained earnings and the distribution of dividends are discussed in the following chapter.

ISSUANCE OF CAPITAL STOCK

When a corporation receives its charter, it has the authority to issue a certain amount of stock. This stock is called capital stock. Capital stock is usually issued in two classes: (1) common stock and (2) preferred stock. A corporation will secure authorization to sell more shares than are necessary at the time of organization. This number of shares is called the authorized shares. **Authorized shares** are the maximum number of shares a corporation can issue under its present charter. **Issued stock** is the number of shares that have actually been sold to stockholders. If the issued stock is held by stockholders, it is said to be **outstanding stock.** The number of outstanding shares is used to calculate a dividend. In addition, it is used in a number of other calculations to be discussed later.

authorized shares
the maximum number of shares a corporation can issue under its present charter

issued stock
the number of shares that have actually been sold to stockholders

outstanding stock
the number of issued shares held by stockholders

common stock
the ordinary stock of a corporation

par value
an arbitrary value placed on a share of stock to meet a legal purpose

no par
a class of stock having no par value

stated value
a value placed on a share of no-par stock by the board of directors

Common Stock

When a corporation issues only one class of stock, it is called **common stock.** Common stock is the ordinary stock of a corporation. The charter will specify the authorized number of shares to be issued and whether the stock is par or no-par stock. **Par value** is an arbitrary value placed on a share of stock to meet a legal purpose. **No par** is a class of stock having no par value. However, the board of directors may establish a value for the no-par stock; it is then called **stated value** stock. Thus, the stated value becomes the minimum legal capital for the no-par stock. Each of the above distinctions is important in recording the sale of stock.

Sales of Stock

Journal entries must be prepared when stock is sold for cash or other assets. The general journal entry to record common stock sold for cash is as follows.

GENERAL JOURNAL						Page
Date	Description	Post. Ref.	Debit		Credit	
Jan. **2**	*Cash*		1 2 0 0 0 —			
	Common Stock				1 2 0 0 0 —	
	To Record the Sale of 12,000 Shares of $10					
	Par Value Common Stock at Par					

The general journal entry to record stock sold for other assets is as follows.

	GENERAL JOURNAL												Page				
Date	Description	Post. Ref.	Debit						Credit					
19XX *Jan.* 2	*Equipment*			5 0 0 0	—							
	Building		1 0 0 0 0	—							
	Land		1 5 0 0 0	—							
	Common Stock						1 2 0 0 0 0	—		
	To Record the Issue of 12,000 Shares of $10								
	Par Value Common Stock in Exchange for								
	Miscellaneous Assets								

A corporation may also give shares of its stock to its promoters in exchange for their services in organizing the business. In such a case, the general journal entry is recorded as follows.

	GENERAL JOURNAL												Page				
Date	Description	Post. Ref.	Debit					Credit				
19XX *Jan.* 15	*Organization Costs*		5 0 0 0	—						
	Common Stock						5 0 0 0	—		
	To Record the Issue of 500 Shares of $10								
	Par Value Common Stock to the Promoters in								
	Exchange for Their Services								

minimum legal capital
investment equal to the par value of issued stock

Many stocks have par values. A corporation may choose any amount for its par. It is the arbitrary choice of the corporation, but once the choice is made, it is binding. Par value establishes minimum legal capital. **Minimum legal capital** is equal to the par value of the issued stock. Laws establishing minimum legal capital normally require stockholders to invest assets equal in value to minimum legal capital or be liable to corporation creditors for the difference. Corporation laws governing minimum legal capital were passed to protect creditors who have only the corporation's assets to look to for their claims. Par value establishes this legal capital and is used to record the stock.

Sales of Stock Over Par

Often a corporation will be able to sell a share of stock above par. Selling stock above par is selling stock at a **premium.** Because par does not depict worth or market value, the potential investor may believe the value of the stock is greater than par. Assume 10,000 shares of $10 par value common stock are sold at $15 a share. The general journal entry to record this sale is as follows.

premium
stock sold and issued above its par value

		GENERAL JOURNAL			Page	
Date		Description	Post. Ref.	Debit	Credit	
Jan.	*2*	*Cash*		1 5 0 0 0 0 —		
		Common Stock			1 0 0 0 0 0 —	
		Premium on Common Stock			5 0 0 0 0 —	
		To Record the Sale of 10,000 Shares of $10				
		Par Value Common Stock at $15 per Share				

In this example, minimum legal capital is $100,000 or the amount of 10,000 shares at $10 a share. Because the investor is willing to give more than par, the minimum legal capital has been met, and the excess is recorded in a separate capital account called Premium on Common Stock. In this example, stock is issued for cash. When stock is issued for other assets, the fair market value of the assets is used to record the entry. In the event stock is issued at a price below par, the issue is at a discount. Because the minimum legal capital requirement has not been met, the stockholders may be liable to creditors for the difference. Many states do not legally permit the sale of par value stock below par.

Sales of No-Par Stock

Some states permit corporations to issue no-par stock. This simplifies the accounting, because the purchase price of the stock is used to record the sale and there is no excess to be recorded. If a corporation sells 1,000 shares of no-par common stock for $30 a share, the general journal entry to record this sale is as follows.

		GENERAL JOURNAL				Page	
Date		Description	Post. Ref.	Debit		Credit	
19XX Jan.	20	Cash		3 0 0 0 0 —			
		No-Par Common Stock				3 0 0 0 0 —	
		To Record the Sale of 1,000 Shares of No-Par					
		Common Stock at $30 a Share					

Corporations sometimes choose to set their own minimum legal capital by a resolution in the bylaws. Using the no-par stock example above, assume that the board of directors sets a $15 stated value on its common stock. The general journal entry to record the sale is as follows.

		GENERAL JOURNAL				Page	
Date		Description	Post. Ref.	Debit		Credit	
19XX Jan.	20	Cash		3 0 0 0 0 —			
		No-Par Common Stock				1 5 0 0 0 —	
		Paid-In Capital in Excess of Stated Value				1 5 0 0 0 —	
		To Record the Sale of 1,000 Shares of $15 Stated					
		Value Common Stock at $30 per Share					

Sales of Subscribed Stock

Some potential stockholders may wish to buy stock from the corporation by means of subscription. These investors are asked to sign contracts called subscription contracts. They agree to pay for the stock according to the terms in the contract. The contracts generally call for a down payment and the remainder to be paid later. These transactions are similar to lay-away contracts. In lay-away contracts, periodic payments are made on a purchase and the merchandise is not received until final payment is made. Subscribers pay periodically on the stock, but do not receive their stock until it is paid for in full. Until that time, they are not stockholders and have no stockholders' rights.

To illustrate this type of sale, assume that a corporation accepted subscriptions to 1,000 shares of $10 par value common stock at $12 per share. The contract called for a down payment equal to one-fourth the purchase price and the remainder to be paid in 60 days. The general journal entries to record the down payment and final payment are as follows.

	GENERAL JOURNAL			Page	
Date	Description	Post. Ref.	Debit	Credit	
19XX May 9	Subscriptions Receivable: Common Stock		12000 —		
	Common Stock Subscribed			10000 —	
	Premium on Common Stock			2000 —	
	To Record the Acceptance of Subscriptions to				
	1,000 Shares of $10 Par Value Common Stock				
	at $12 per Share				
May 9	Cash		3000 —		
	Subscriptions Receivable: Common Stock			3000 —	
	To Record the Collection of One-Fourth of Amount				
	Owed as Down Payment on Common Stock				
	Subscribed				
July 8	Cash		9000 —		
	Subscriptions Receivable: Common Stock			9000 —	
	To Record Receipt of Final Payment on				
	Common Stock Subscribed				
July 8	Common Stock Subscribed		10000 —		
	Common Stock (Issued)			10000 —	
	To Record the Issue of 1,000 Shares of $10 Par				
	Value Common Stock Sold Through Subscriptions				

The account Subscriptions Receivable is classified as a current asset, because its collection is anticipated within one year. On the other hand, the Common Stock Subscribed account is a capital account. It is the lay-away account appearing in the stockholders' equity section of the balance sheet until it is removed by the issuance of the stock. A stockholders' equity section of a balance sheet with both issued and unissued stock appears below.

STOCKHOLDERS' EQUITY			
Paid-In Capital			
Common Stock, $10 par value, 20,000 shares			
authorized, 10,000 shares issued and outstanding	$100000 —		
Unissued Common Stock Subscribed	10000 —		
Total Common Stock Issued and Subscribed		$110000 —	
Premium on Common Stock		52000 —	
Total Paid-In and Subscribed Capital		$162000 —	

Common Stockholder Rights

Common stockholders acquire specific rights when they purchase stock. The following is a list of some of these rights.

1. The right to vote.
2. The right to share in residual assets after creditors are paid.
3. The right to receive their pro rata share of dividends declared for common stock.
4. The right to receive the first opportunity to buy any new issue of stock. This right is referred to as the preemptive right.
5. The right to sell or otherwise dispose of their shares.

Preferred Stock

A corporation may issue two classes of stock. If this is the case, one class is called common stock and the other is called preferred stock. The two classes of stock have different rights and are issued to appeal to different types of investors. As the name indicates, preferred stock has a number of preferences over common stock and is almost always sold at its par value. The special characteristics of preferred stock are as follows.

1. Dividends, when declared, are paid first to the preferred stockholders.

2. Preferred stock has first preference on assets after the creditors if the corporation is liquidated.

3. Preferred stock is paid a fixed amount in dividends.

4. Preferred stock may be callable and/or convertible.

5. Preferred stock has no voting rights.

Owners of a single proprietorship or a partnership are taxed according to the net income of their businesses and they receive their profits or returns by withdrawing cash or other assets from the business. The amount withdrawn depends to a large extent on the degree to which the business has been profitable. The board of directors may *choose* to distribute the profits of a corporation to the stockholders in the form of **dividends.** There is no liability for the payment of dividends until the board declares that dividends will be paid. After they are declared, dividends must be paid to the preferred stockholders before they are paid to the common stockholders. If the directors believe, however, that no dividend is warranted, then neither the preferred nor the common stockholders will receive one.

dividends
a return of profits to the stockholders

Because preferred stockholders have first preference on corporate assets during liquidation (after creditors), preferred stock will always be listed first in the stockholders' equity section of the balance sheet as illustrated in Appendix 22A on page 834. This classified balance sheet also contains several new accounts that will be discussed in later chapters.

Cumulative Preferred Stock

cumulative preferred stock
preferred stock on which dividends accumulate annually until paid

Preferred stock may be either cumulative or noncumulative. **Cumulative preferred stock** is stock whose dividends accumulate. The fixed amount per preferred share accumulates from year to year, and the total amount owed to the preferred shareholders must be paid before any amount can be paid to the common shareholders. The corporate charter specifies how dividends are to be paid when declared by the board of directors. Once a dividend is declared, the decision is legally binding on the corporation.

The amount to be paid to preferred stockholders may be stated as a fixed amount per share or as a percentage of the face value of the preferred share. For example, a corporation may agree to pay $8 a share, or it might issue preferred stock with a par value of $100 and pay a yearly dividend of 8 percent. To illustrate the second method, assume that there are 1,000 shares of $100 par value, 9%, cumulative preferred stock. The calculation to determine the dollar amount of the dividend preference per share is:

$$9\% \times \$100 \text{ par} = \$9 \text{ per Share per Year}$$
$$\$9 \times 1{,}000 \text{ Shares Outstanding} = \$9{,}000 \text{ Total Dividend Preference Per Year}$$

An investor in preferred stock could expect to receive $9 per share per year if dividends are declared. In other words, if the investor owns 100 shares, the dividend preference is $900 per year. If the preferred dividend is declared twice each year, the owner would receive $450 two times a year.

Dividends that are not paid when they are declared and due are called *dividends in arrears* and are shown as a footnote on the corporation's balance sheet. For example, assume that a corporation has profits of $0 in its first year, $10,000 in its second year, and $20,000 in its third year. Assume further that the preferred stock is $100 par value, 9%, cumulative, and that 1,000 shares are issued and outstanding. A dividend is declared each year only to cover the preferred stock preference, $9,000. The example below shows the preferred stock dividend distribution and the amount of dividends in arrears each year.

Cumulative Preferred Stock

	Net Income	Declared and Paid to Preferred	Dividends in Arrears
Year 1	0	0	$9,000
Year 2	$10,000	$10,000 (from year 1, $9,000) (from year 2, $1,000)	8,000
Year 3	20,000	17,000 (from year 2, $8,000) (from year 3, $9,000)	0

The unpaid preferred stock dividend will accumulate as a preference on earnings. A corporation is not liable to pay a dividend unless the board of directors makes a formal declaration. Therefore, cumulative dividends do not accrue like interest and are not guaranteed. They are based on profits, and profits are distributed only by the decision of the board of directors. However, once the board declares a cash dividend, it becomes a liability of the corporation.

If cumulative dividends are in arrears, they are a claim against assets by the preferred stockholders. Should the board choose not to pay a cumulative dividend, the dividend in arrears is not a liability and does not appear on the balance sheet. However, the information must appear as a footnote to the balance sheet to meet the full disclosure principle. An example footnote for Year 2 above is as follows.

> *Footnote 10. The cumulative dividend on preferred stock that remains unpaid on this balance sheet date is $8,000. The $8,000 is in arrears and is a claim on assets by preferred stockholders.*

Although the most common type of preferred stock is cumulative, preferred stock may occasionally be noncumulative. When stock is noncumulative, there is no accumulation of cash dividends. If the dividend is not declared and paid, the shareholder loses the dividend and has no further claim on assets for the lost dividend.

Nonparticipating Preferred Stock

Dividends paid to common stockholders are not limited to a certain amount; rather, they are limited only by the earning power of the corporation and the declaration by the board to pay a certain amount in dividends. Preferred stockholders, however, are normally limited to earning their fixed preference (9 percent of par value, for example). When this is the case, the preferred stock is called nonparticipating and may not participate in the earnings of the corporation beyond the amount stated on the stock certificate.

Most preferred stock is nonparticipating, but some corporate charters provide for participating preferred stock, which may be paid additional dividends in excess of the amount stated on the stock certificate. In this instance, participating preferred stockholders share with common stockholders proportionally according to the provisions in the charter. Participating preferred stock is rare.

Redemptive Preferred Stock

redemptive share value
a value specified in the charter for the redemption or retirement of preferred stock

Corporations often issue preferred stock and reserve the right to redeem or retire the stock by paying a specified amount. This specified amount is called the **redemptive share value.** Generally the redemptive value is par plus a premium. For example, a charter might provide for $100 par value preferred stock and establish a redemptive value of $105. If the board of directors chooses to redeem—buy back or call back—the preferred stock from the stockholder, it must pay $105 per share. When the charter gives the board of directors the right to call in or redeem the preferred stock, it is referred to as **callable preferred stock.** The redemption value is a claim on assets by the preferred stockholders and as such will increase their equity in the corporation.

callable preferred stock
a right given to the corporation to buy back preferred stock as provided in the charter

Convertible Preferred Stock

convertible preferred stock
a right given in the charter for the preferred stockholder to convert to a common stockholder

To make the preferred stock attractive to potential investors, it may have **convertible preferred stock** rights. Preferred stockholders may, under provisions provided in the charter, convert (exchange) their preferred shares for common shares. For example, assume 1,000 shares of $50 par value preferred stock have been issued at par. The charter provides that the preferred stockholder may exchange one share of preferred stock for two shares of common stock at par. Assume that a preferred stockholder who owns 200 shares wishes to convert to common stock that is $25 par value. The steps to calculate and the journal entry to record the conversion are as follows.

1. Preferred stock:

$$200 \text{ shares} \times \$50 \text{ par} = \$10,000$$

2. Common stock:

$$2 \times 200 = 400 \text{ shares}$$
$$400 \text{ shares} \times \$25 = \$10,000$$

The journal entry to record the conversion is as follows.

	GENERAL JOURNAL			Page
Date	**Description**	**Post. Ref.**	**Debit**	**Credit**
19XX *Sept.* 11	*Preferred Stock, $50 par*		10000 —	
	Common Stock, $25 par			10000 —
	To Record the Conversion of Preferred Stock to			
	Common Stock on a 2 to 1 Basis as per Charter			

In this situation, the shareholder loses the rights of a preferred stockholder and gains the rights of a common stockholder.

STOCK VALUES

In addition to values previously covered, equity per share values and market values are important to understanding stock values and owners' equities.

Equity per Share

equity per share
a measure of the equity represented by one share of stock in the assets of a corporation

For an individual owner to determine the interest owned in a corporation, the total equity is used to determine the equity on a per-share basis. **Equity per share** is the measure of the equity represented by one share of stock in the assets of the corporation. It is calculated by dividing the total equity by the number of shares outstanding. Assuming one class of stock, the equity per share is calculated as follows.

1. Determine total stockholders' equity = $500,000
2. Determine the total number of common shares outstanding = 100,000 shares
3. Calculate equity per share = $5 per share
   ($500,000 ÷ 100,000 shares = $5)

For example, if John Jones owns 500 shares of common stock, his total interest (equity) in this corporation is $25,000 (500 shares × $5 earnings per share = $25,000). If John paid $20,000 originally, his investment has grown by $5,000. The equity per share is a method owners can use to determine how well their investment is doing. If John wishes to sell all or part of his stock, he will not want to sell for less than $5 per share. Equity per share is often referred to as book value per share.

When more than one class of stock is outstanding, the following steps are used to calculate the equity per share for each type of stock.

1. Determine the total dollar equities of each class.
   a. Determine the total stockholders' equity.
   b. Deduct the dollar preference of the preferred stockholders from the total.
   c. The remainder is the equity of the common stockholders.
2. Determine the total number of outstanding shares.
   a. Determine the total number of preferred shares outstanding.

b. Determine the total number of common shares outstanding.

3. Calculate the equity per share.
   a. Divide 1b by 2a = preferred equity per share.
   b. Divide 1c by 2b = common equity per share.

For example, assume that the corporation's stockholders' equity section appears as follows.

STOCKHOLDERS' EQUITY			
Paid-In Capital			
Preferred Stock, $100 par value, 11% cumulative, nonparticipating, 1,000 shares authorized, issued, and outstanding		$100000 —	
Common Stock, $10 par value, 50,000 shares authorized, 20,000 shares issued and outstanding	$200,000		
Premium on Common Stock	100,000	300000 —	
Total Paid-In Capital			$400000 —
Retained Earnings			40000 —
Total Stockholders' Equity			$440000 —

The following illustrates the calculation for equity per share.

1. Determine the total dollar equities of each class.
   a. Total stockholders' equity $440,000
   b. Deduct the total preference of preferred stock (100,000)
   c. Remainder to common stock $340,000

2. Determine the total number of outstanding shares.
   a. 1,000 preferred shares outstanding
   b. 20,000 common shares outstanding

3. Calculate the equity per share.
   a. Preferred equity per share   = $100
      ($100,000 ÷ 1,000 shares outstanding)
   b. Common equity per share   = $ 17
      ($340,000 ÷ 20,000 shares outstanding)

If cumulative dividends are in arrears or a redemptive value is given, the claims of preferred stockholders will increase. Assume the same example as above except that the preferred dividend is one year in arrears, and the redemptive value is $105. The equity per share for each class of stock is as follows.

1. Determine the total dollar equities of each class.
    a. Total stockholders' equity $440,000
    b. Preferred stock preference
        1. Dividend in arrears:

        $$11\% \times \$100 \text{ par} \times 1,000 \text{ shares} = \$ 11,000$$

        2. Redemption value:

        1,000 shares $\times$ $105 =   105,000 $116,000

    c. Remainder to the common stockholders $324,000
2. Determine the total number of outstanding shares.
    a. 1,000 preferred shares outstanding
    b. 20,000 common shares outstanding
3. Calculate the equity per share.
    a. Preferred equity per share   = $116.00
        ($116,000 ÷ 1,000 shares outstanding)
    b. Common equity per share   = $ 16.20
        ($324,000 ÷ 20,000 shares outstanding)

Market Value

market value
the price for which a share of stock may be bought or sold

The **market value** of a share of stock is the price for which the stock can be purchased or sold. Profits, future prospects of the business, type of industry, and general economic conditions all influence this price.

DONATED CAPITAL

donated capital
a gift of equipment, building, land, or other assets given to the corporation

A corporation may receive additional capital through donations. **Donated capital** is a gift of equipment, building, land, or other assets to the corporation. For example, the Elaineco Corporation is looking for land to build a new plant. The city of Lesleyville agrees to donate land with a market value of $155,000 to the corporation for its plant site. The city is willing to do this because the new plant will employ its citizens. The general journal entry to record this type of gift is as follows.

GENERAL JOURNAL					Page	
Date	Description	Post. Ref.	Debit		Credit	
19XX *Mar.* 11	Land		1 5 5 0 0 0 —			
	Donated Capital				1 5 5 0 0 0 —	
	To Record the Value of Land Donated by the City					
	of Lesleyville					

The corporation will list the land as an asset on its balance sheet and list the donated capital as the last item in the paid-in capital portion of the stockholders' equity section of the balance sheet.

SUMMARY

A corporation is a separate legal entity created by law. As an artificial entity, the business is conducted through the agents of the corporation. This type of business formation has advantages and disadvantages. Lack of stockholders' liability, ease of owner transfers, length of corporate life, and the ease of raising capital are a number of the advantages. A corporation is liable for both state and federal taxes and is regulated closely by the federal government. Taxation and government regulation are both disadvantages of the corporation format.

To form a corporation, a charter must be written and approved by the state in which it is to incorporate. Most states require that the entity have a unique name, be established for a purpose, specify the classes of stock, and provide signatures of three promoters.

Management of the corporation begins by the election of the board of directors by the voting stockholders. The board of directors then chooses the officers, who choose the employees to handle the daily affairs of the business.

Costs are incurred in beginning a new business. Costs such as legal fees, state incorporation fees, and promoter's fees are typical of these costs. Collectively these costs are the organization costs and are amortized over the useful life of the business.

Corporation accounting begins with the sale or the subscribing of the stock. Stock may be subscribed, sold for cash, or sold for other assets. Stock may also be given to the promoters for the benefit of their services. The stock may be common or preferred. Preferred stock has specific preferences over common stock. The rights of each class of stock are detailed in the charter and the stockholders themselves hold stock certificates that also depict these rights.

The balance sheet of a corporation is presented differently from that of a proprietorship or partnership in the capital or the owners' equity section. The equity section of a corporate balance sheet has two major parts: paid-in capital and retained earnings. The paid-in capital portion contains the classes of stock, their preferences, and the number of shares authorized by the charter to be issued. In addition, as shares are sold and issued, the total dollar amount of the invested capital is shown in this section. The retained earnings portion, as the name implies, is the dollar amount of the earnings retained in the business. Stockholders may receive these earnings (or profits) if dividends are declared by the board of directors.

Using the stockholders' equity section of the balance sheet, the equity per share for each class of stock can be determined. By using equity per share, a stockholder can determine how well his or her investment is doing.

Communities often offer a gift of property to corporations as an incentive. These gifts are called donated capital and, when accepted, become a part of the capital of the corporation.

Review of Accounting Terminology

Following is a list of the accounting terminology for this chapter.

authorized shares	minimum legal capital
callable preferred stock	no par stock
common stock	organization costs
convertible preferred stock	outstanding stock
corporation	par value
cumulative preferred stock	premium
dividends	proxy
donated capital	redemptive share value
equity per share	stated value
issued stock	stock certificate
market value	subscriber

Fill in the blank with the correct word or term from the list.

1. The number of issued shares held by the stockholders on which a dividend is to be paid is called _____.

2. A/an _____ is a potential investor who plans to buy the corporation stock.

3. A/an _____ is a separate legal entity created by law.

4. _____ are costs incurred to begin a new corporation.

5. The maximum number of shares a corporation can issue under its present charter is referred to as _____.

6. _____ is a class of stock having no par value.

7. A gift of equipment, building, land, or other assets to the corporation is _____.

8. _____ is a measure of the equity represented by one share of stock in the assets of a corporation.

9. Owners of _____ are given the right in the corporate charter to convert their preferred stock to common.

10. Returns of profits to the stockholders are _____.

11. Stock sold and issued above its par value is sold at a _____.

12. _____ is equal to the par value of issued stock.

13. A value placed on a share of no-par stock by the board of directors is called _____.

14. An intangible representation of the rights of the owner is called a _____.

15. A _____ is a legal document that gives an agent the right to vote for the stockholder.

16. _____ is the number of shares that have actually been sold to stockholders.

17. The ordinary stock of a corporation is called _____.

18. An arbitrary value placed on a share of stock to meet a legal purpose is _____.

19. Preferred stock on which dividends accumulate annually until paid is _____.

20. _____ is a value specified in the charter for the redemption or retirement of preferred stock.

21. A corporation has the right to buy back preferred stock if it is _____.

22. _____ is the price for which a share of stock may be bought or sold.

Match the following words and terms on the left with the definitions on the right (columns continue on the following page).

23. authorized shares
24. callable preferred stock
25. common stock
26. convertible preferred stock
27. corporation
28. cumulative preferred stock
29. dividends
30. donated capital
31. equity per share
32. issued stock
33. market value
34. minimum legal capital
35. no par stock

a. the ordinary stock of a corporation

b. a value placed on a share of no-par stock by the board of directors

c. a legal document that gives an agent the right to vote for the stockholder

d. an investment equal to the par value of issued stock

e. a gift of equipment, building, land, or other assets to the corporation

f. returns of profits to the stockholders

g. a measure of the equity represented by one share of stock in the assets of the corporation

h. stock sold and issued above its par

i. a right given in the charter for the preferred stockholders to convert to common stock

j. a separate legal entity created by law

k. costs incurred to begin a new corporation

l. a class of stock having no par value

m. the number of issued shares held by stockholders

36. organization costs
37. outstanding stock
38. par value
39. premium
40. proxy
41. redemptive share value
42. stated value
43. stock certificate
44. subscriber

n. an intangible representation of the rights of the owner

o. a potential investor who plans to buy the corporation stock

p. the maximum number of shares a corporation can issue under its present charter

q. the number of shares that have actually been sold to stockholders

r. preferred stock on which dividends accumulate until paid

s. a value specified in the charter for the redemption or retirement of preferred stock

t. an arbitrary value placed on a share of stock to meet a legal purpose

u. a right given to the corporation to buy back preferred stock as provided in the charter

v. the price for which a share of stock may be bought or sold

Exercises

Exercise 21.1
preparing the general journal entries to record the sale of stock

Prepare the general journal entries to record the following unrelated assumptions, without explanations.

a. Issued 500 shares of common stock for cash.
1. Common stock, $10 par value issued at par.
2. Common stock, $10 par value issued at $15 per share.
3. Common stock, no par issued at $12 per share.

4. Common stock, $15 stated value issued at $20 per share.

b. Issued 200 shares of $5 par value common stock to the organizers. The board of directors value their services at $1,200.

c. Assume the same facts as b except the common stock is no par.

Exercise 21.2
preparing the general journal entries to record the sale of stock

Prepare the general journal entries to record the following transactions.

a. Exchanged 50,000 shares of $1 par value common stock for the following assets at their fair market values: Equipment, $5,000; Building, $40,000; and Land, $10,000.

b. Assume the same facts as above except the common stock is no par.

Exercise 21.3
preparing the general journal entries to record the subscription sale of stock

On February 25, the Lynn Corporation accepted subscriptions to 100,000 shares of $5 par value common stock for $6.60 a share. In addition, it accepted subscriptions to 1,000 shares of $100 par value, 9% cumulative, nonparticipating preferred stock for par. Each contract provided for one-half of the total price as a down payment and the remainder to be due in 90 days. Prepare the general journal entries to record the following.

a. The subscriptions receivable of both preferred and common stock on February 25.

b. The down payments on February 25.

c. The final payments on May 26.

d. The issuance of the stock on May 26.

Exercise 21.4
determining the cumulative preferred dividends

The Peter Corporation has outstanding 10,000 shares of its $50 par value, 9% cumulative, nonparticipating preferred stock. During the first five years of its operations, the company had net income of: 19X1, none; 19X2, $25,000; 19X3, $50,000; 19X4, $75,000; and 19X5, $75,000.

a. Set up and complete the following table for each of the five years, assuming that Peter Corporation paid all of its net income in dividends.

Year	Net Income	Declared and Paid to Preferred	Dividend in Arrears

b. Set up and complete another table like the table above assuming that the preferred stock is noncumulative.

Exercise 21.5
preparing the stockholders' equity section of the balance sheet

The Tate Corporation's charter authorized it to issue 1,000 shares of $100 par value, 8% preferred stock and 100,000 shares of $5 par value common stock. Selected accounts from the December 31, 19X7 trial balance appear below in alphabetical order.

Accounts Payable	$ 10,000
Accounts Receivable	30,000
Building (Net of Depreciation)	150,000
Cash	70,000
Common Stock	100,000
Unissued Common Stock Subscribed	10,000
Land	50,000
Organization Costs	20,000
Preferred Stock	100,000
Premium on Common Stock	66,000
Retained Earnings	34,000
Subscriptions Receivable: Common Stock	10,000

Select the proper accounts and prepare the stockholders' equity section of the balance sheet.

Exercise 21.6
calculating the equity per share

The stockholders' equity section of the balance sheet of the Sims Corporation is as follows.

STOCKHOLDERS' EQUITY		
Paid-In Capital		
Preferred Stock, $50 par value, 7% cumulative non-participating, 2,000 shares authorized, 1,000 shares issued and outstanding	$ 50000 —	
Common Stock, no par value, 1,000,000 shares authorized, 650,000 issued and outstanding	9750000 —	
Total Paid-In Capital		$9800000 —
Retained Earnings		1200000 —
Total Stockholders' Equity		$11000000 —

a. Calculate the equity per share for the following assuming no dividends are in arrears.
   1. Preferred stock
   2. Common stock

b. Calculate the equity per share for the following assuming that two years of dividends are in arrears.
   1. Preferred stock
   2. Common stock

Exercise 21.7
recording miscellaneous transactions in the general journal

The Dana Corporation received its charter on October 31, 19X8, authorizing the issuance of 500,000 shares of no-par common stock. Record the following miscellaneous transactions in general journal form.

Aug. 31   issued 150,000 shares of common stock at $25 a share for cash

Nov. 11   issued 2,000 shares of common stock to promoters for their services; the board of directors valued their services at $25 a share

Nov. 30   received donated land valued at $350,000 from the city of San Sue

Dec. 1   exchanged 5,000 shares of common stock for a patent valued at $200,000

Exercise 21.8
preparing general journal entry to record exchange of preferred to common stock

A corporation has 5,000 shares of $50 par value, 9% cumulative, nonparticipating, convertible preferred stock. Each preferred share may on December 31, 19X4 exchange one share of preferred stock for two shares of $25 par value common stock. Prepare the general journal entry to record the exchange assuming that all the preferred shareholders convert. Show all calculations.

Problems

Problem 21.1
preparing general journal entries to record various transactions and preparing the stockholders' equity section of the balance sheet

Eric Corporation is authorized to issue 4,000 shares of $100 par value, 9% cumulative, and nonparticipating preferred stock and 50,000 shares of $10 par value common stock. It then completed the following transactions.

June 1   accepted subscriptions to 20,000 shares of common stock at $10 a share; the subscription contracts called for down payments of one-half of the subscription price

June 1   gave the promoters 500 shares of common stock for their services valued at $6,000

June 30   accepted subscriptions to 2,000 shares of the preferred stock at par; the subscription contracts called for 30 percent down payments

Aug. 1   collected the balance due from the common stockholders and issued the stock

Aug. 8   sold 10,000 shares of the common stock for cash at $15 a share

Aug. 15   collected the balance due from the preferred stockholders and issued the stock

Aug. 30   accepted subscriptions to 2,000 shares of the preferred stock at par; the subscription contracts called for 50 percent down payments

Aug. 31   closed the Income Summary account with a credit balance of $20,000 to Retained Earnings

Instructions

1. *Prepare general journal entries to record each transaction without explanations.*

2. *Answer the following questions.*
   a. *How many common shares are outstanding on August 31?*
   b. *How many preferred shares are outstanding on August 31?*

3. *Prepare the stockholders' equity section of the balance sheet as of August 31.*
   (Hint: Set up T-accounts for the capital accounts. Post the general journal entries to the T-accounts, and determine the balance of the accounts.)

Problem 21.2
preparing general journal entries, posting to ledger accounts, and preparing the stockholders' equity section of the balance sheet

Miller Corporation received a charter granting it the right to issue 10,000 shares of $50 par value, 8% cumulative, nonparticipating preferred stock, and 500,000 shares of $1 par value common stock. The following transactions were then completed.

19X1

Mar. 11   issued 55,000 shares of common stock at par for cash

Mar. 15   gave promoters 10,000 shares of common stock for their services; the board of directors valued their services at $12,000

Mar. 18   exchanged 50,000 shares of common stock for assets valued at fair market value; these values are as follows: Equipment, $10,000; Building, $150,000; and Land, $15,000

Dec. 31   closed the Income Summary account with a debit balance of $20,000 to Retained Earnings (Hint: This represents a loss, so Retained Earnings must be debited.)

19X2

Feb. 25   received subscriptions to 1,000 shares of preferred stock at par; a 20 percent down payment is required by the subscription contracts

Mar. 27   sold 1,000 shares of preferred stock at par for cash

Apr. 25   received an additional 20 percent of the amount owed by the preferred stock subscribers of February 25, as required by the subscription contract

Dec. 31   closed the Income Summary account with a credit balance of $80,000 to Retained Earnings (Hint: This represents a net income, so Retained Earnings must be credited.)

Instructions

1. *Prepare the general journal entries to record the above transactions without explanations.*

2. *Post the transactions to the appropriate stockholders' equity ledger accounts.*

3. *Prepare the stockholders' equity section of the balance sheet for the year ended December 31, 19X2.*

Problem 21.3
opening ledger accounts, journalizing and posting journal entries to stockholders' equity accounts, and preparing the stockholders' equity section of the balance sheet

The 19X3 transactions and the stockholders' equity section of the balance sheet for the Morris Corporation as of January 1, 19X3 are as follows.

19X3

Feb. 14   issued 5,000 shares of common stock at $7 a share for cash

Mar. 20   issued 1,000 shares of preferred stock at par for cash

Apr. 15   issued 8,000 shares of common stock at $10 a share for cash

Aug. 31 issued 500 shares of common stock in exchange for a patent valued at $6,000

Sept. 13 received donated land valued at $150,000 from the town of Dalesville

Dec. 31 closed the Income Summary account; the net income for the year is $50,000

STOCKHOLDERS' EQUITY		
Paid-In Capital		
Preferred Stock, $100 par value, 8% cumulative, nonparticipating, 5,000 shares authorized, 1,000 shares issued	$100000—	
Premium on Preferred Stock	5000—	$105000—
Common Stock, $5 stated value, 500,000 shares authorized, 50,000 shares issued	$250000—	
Paid-In Capital in Excess of Stated Value	50000—	300000—
Total Paid-In Capital		$405000—
Deficit in Retained Earnings		(20000—)
Total Stockholders' Equity		$385000—

Instructions

1. *Open T-accounts for the above stockholders' equity section of the balance sheet and enter the balances as given.*

2. *Journalize the transactions without explanations.*

3. *Post the journal entries to the stockholders' equity ledger accounts and balance each account.*

4. *Prepare the stockholders' equity section of the balance sheet as of December 31, 19X3.*

Problem 21.4
preparing the stockholders' equity section of the balance sheet

On December 31, 19X8, the ledger of the Katherine Corporation included the following accounts.

Retained Earnings	$200,000
Notes Receivable	40,000
Common Stock, $10 par value	600,000
Patents	10,000

(Continued)

Organization Costs	20,000
Premium on Common Stock	20,000
Buildings	300,000
Accounts Receivable	8,000
Common Stock Subscribed	40,000
Donated Capital	52,000
Preferred Stock, $100 par value	50,000
Merchandise Inventory	15,000
Subscriptions Receivable: Common Stock	20,000

Instructions *Select the proper items and prepare the stockholders' equity section of the balance sheet as of December 31, 19X8.*

Problem 21.5
calculating the equity per share

Using the stockholders' equity section prepared for Problem 21.4 above, determine the equity per share under the following unrelated assumptions.

1. Determine the equity per share of the preferred and the common stock assuming that the preferred stock is 8% cumulative, nonparticipating, and no dividends are in arrears.

2. Using the same facts as in part 1, determine the equity per share for the preferred and the common stock except that the preferred dividend is one year in arrears.

3. Determine the equity per share of the preferred and the common stock assuming that the preferred stock is 9% noncumulative and nonparticipating and that dividends are two years in arrears.

4. Determine the equity per share of the preferred and the common stock assuming that the preferred stock is 7% cumulative and nonparticipating with a redemptive value of $105 per share and that two years' dividends are in arrears. Assume the charter provides that the redemptive value plus dividends in arrears becomes a claim of the preferred stockholders.

Problem 21.6
answering various review questions

Blake Corporation's common stock is selling on the stock exchange today for $8.50 a share and a newly published stockholders' equity section is as follows.

STOCKHOLDERS' EQUITY		
Paid-In Capital		
Preferred Stock, $10 par value, 8% cumulative,		
nonparticipating, 10,000 shares authorized, issued, and		
outstanding		$1 0 0 0 0 0 —
Common Stock, $5 par value, 50,000 shares		
authorized, issued, and outstanding	$2 5 0 0 0 0 —	
Premium on Common Stock	5 0 0 0 0 —	3 0 0 0 0 0 —
Total Paid-In Capital		$4 0 0 0 0 0 —
Retained Earnings		8 5 0 0 0 —
Total Stockholders' Equity		$4 8 5 0 0 0 —

Instructions   *Answer the following questions.*

1. *What is the market value of the common stock?*

2. *What is the market value of the preferred stock?*

3. *What is the par value of the preferred stock?*

4. *What is the par value of the common stock?*

5. *What was the average price per share paid by the common stockholders?*

6. *If no preferred dividends are in arrears, what is the equity per share of the following: preferred _____ common _____ ?*

7. *If two years were in arrears, what is the equity per share of the following: preferred _____ common _____ ?*

8. *Assume the preferred stock carries the right to the dividend in arrears plus a redemptive value in the amount of $5 per share more than par. Assume further that three years are in arrears. Determine the book value of the following: preferred _____ common _____ .*

9. *What is the minimum legal capital of this corporation?*

10. *Assume the preferred stock is convertible at one share of preferred for two shares of common. How many common shares would the preferred stockholders receive in the conversion?*

Appendix 21A

Corporate Financial

Statements Illustrated

Xerox Corporation
Report of Management

Xerox management is responsible for the integrity and objectivity of the financial data presented in this annual report. The consolidated financial statements were prepared in conformity with generally accepted accounting principles and include amounts based on management's best estimates and judgements.

The Company maintains a system of internal accounting controls designed to provide reasonable assurance that assets are safeguarded against loss or unauthorized use and that financial records are adequate and can be relied upon to produce financial statements in accordance with generally accepted accounting principles. This system includes the hiring and training of qualified people, written accounting and control policies and procedures, clearly drawn lines of accountability and delegations of authority. In a business ethics policy that is communicated annually to all employees, the Company has established its intent to adhere to the highest standards of ethical conduct in all of our business activities.

The Company monitors its system of internal accounting controls with direct management reviews and a comprehensive program of internal audits. In addition, Peat Marwick Main & Co., independent certified public accountants, have examined the financial statements and have reviewed the system of internal accounting controls to the extent they considered necessary to support their report which appears below.

The Audit Committee of the Board of Directors, which is composed solely of outside directors, meets regularly with the independent accountants, representatives of management, and the internal auditors to review audits, financial reporting and internal control matters as well as the nature and extent of the audit effort. The Audit Committee also recommends the engagement of independent accountants, subject to shareholder approval. The independent accountants and internal auditors have free access to the Audit Committee.

David T. Kearns
Chairman and
Chief Executive Officer

Stuart B. Ross
Vice President Finance and
Chief Financial Officer

Report of Independent Certified Public Accountants

To the Board of Directors and Shareholders of Xerox Corporation

We have examined the consolidated balance sheets of Xerox Corporation and consolidated subsidiaries and of Xerox Financial Services, Inc. and subsidiaries as of December 31, 1987 and 1986, and their related consolidated statements of income and cash flows for each of the years in the three-year period ended December 31, 1987. Our examinations were made in accordance with generally accepted auditing standards and, accordingly, included such tests of the accounting records and such other auditing procedures as we considered necessary in the circumstances.

In our opinion, the aforementioned consolidated financial statements appearing on pages 34, 36, 39, 40, 42 and 44-61 present fairly the financial position of Xerox Corporation and consolidated subsidiaries and of Xerox Financial Services, Inc. and subsidiaries at December 31, 1987 and 1986, and the results of their operations and their cash flows for each of the years in the three-year period ended December 31, 1987, in conformity with generally accepted accounting principles consistently applied during the period except for the change in 1986, with which we concur, in the method of accounting for pensions as described in the notes to the financial statements.

Peat Marwick Main & Co.
Stamford, Connecticut
January 25, 1988 except as
to Note 16 on page 52 and
Note 6 on page 58, which
are as of March 3, 1988

KPMG Peat Marwick

Peat Marwick Main & Co.

Xerox Corporation

Xerox Corporation
Consolidated Statements of Income

(In millions, except per share data) Year ended December 31	1987	1986	1985
Income			
Sales	$ 5,702	$4,822	$4,318
Service	2,753	2,292	1,763
Rentals	1,865	2,241	2,595
Equity in income from continuing operations of unconsolidated companies:			
Xerox Financial Services, Inc.	342	278	76
Other	78	48	40
Other Income	126	100	106
Total	10,866	9,781	8,898
Costs and Other Deductions			
Cost of sales	2,940	2,412	2,081
Cost of service	1,274	1,040	871
Cost of rentals	1,168	1,362	1,459
Research and development expenses	722	650	597
Selling, administrative and general expenses	3,571	3,370	3,011
Interest expense	226	212	230
Other, net	44	60	39
Income taxes	262	112	166
Outside shareholders' interests	81	75	63
Total	10,288	9,293	8,517
Income from Continuing Operations	578	488	381
Discontinued Operations	—	(65)	94
Cumulative Effect on Prior Years of Change in Accounting Principles for Pension Costs	—	42	—
Net Income	$ 578	$ 465	$ 475
Income (Loss) per Common Share			
Continuing operations	$ 5.35	$ 4.52	$ 3.47
Discontinued operations	—	(.67)	.97
Cumulative effect on prior years of change in accounting principles for pension costs	—	.43	—
Net Income per Common Share	$ 5.35	$ 4.28	$ 4.44
Average Common Shares Outstanding	99.0	97.3	96.2
Dividends on Preferred Stock	$ 48	$ 48	$ 48

The accompanying notes are an integral part of the consolidated financial statements.

Xerox Corporation

Consolidated Balance Sheets

(In millions) December 31	1987	1986
Assets		
Current Assets		
Cash	$ 309	$ 402
Accounts receivable, net	2,104	1,867
Inventories	1,408	1,389
Other current assets	638	315
Total current assets	4,459	3,973
Finance Receivables Due after One Year, net	300	341
Rental Equipment, net	878	1,070
Land, Buildings and Equipment, net	1,639	1,491
Investment in Xerox Financial Services, Inc., at equity	2,667	2,530
Other Investments, at equity	850	561
Deferred Income Taxes	302	258
Other Assets	503	384
Total Assets	**$11,598**	$10,608

	1987	1986
Liabilities and Common Shareholders' Equity		
Current Liabilities		
Notes payable and current portion of long-term debt	$ 605	$ 306
Accounts payable	470	426
Salaries, profit sharing and other accruals	1,164	1,013
Income taxes	124	89
Unearned income	258	241
Other current liabilities	229	131
Total current liabilities	2,850	2,206
Long-Term Debt	1,539	1,730
Due to Xerox Financial Services, Inc.	418	488
Other Noncurrent Liabilities	592	490
Outside Shareholders' Interests in Equity of Subsidiaries	652	565
$5.45 Cumulative Preferred Stock	442	442
Common Shareholders' Equity	5,105	4,687
Total Liabilities and Common Shareholders' Equity	**$11,598**	$10,608

The accompanying notes are an integral part of the consolidated financial statements.

Xerox Corporation

Consolidated Statements of Cash Flows

(In millions) Year ended December 31	1987	1986	1985
Net Cash Flows From Operating Activities:			
Net income from continuing operations	$ **578**	$ 488	$ 381
Items not requiring (providing) cash included in income:			
Depreciation	**731**	806	849
Outside shareholders' interests in income	**81**	75	63
Net book value of rental equipment sold	**350**	355	355
Equity in income from continuing operations of			
unconsolidated companies, net of dividends	**(286)**	(197)	(15)
Cash provided by operating activities	**1,454**	1,527	1,633
Additions to rental equipment	**(590)**	(704)	(658)
Net (increase) decrease in other working capital	**(212)**	154	(236)
(Increase) decrease in finance receivables due after one year	**41**	(131)	57
Other, net	**(126)**	(137)	(2)
Cash used by operating activities	**(887)**	(818)	(839)
Total	**567**	709	794
Cash Flows from Investing Activities:			
Net income (loss) from discontinued operations	**—**	(65)	94
Items not requiring cash	**—**	63	400
Subtotal	**—**	(2)	494
Additions to land, buildings and equipment	**(347)**	(328)	(293)
Investments in and advances to unconsolidated companies	**(162)**	14	(348)
Other, net	**(24)**	(18)	33
Total	**(533)**	(334)	(114)
Cash Flows from Financing Activities:			
Increase (decrease) in short-term debt, net	**299**	(97)	(252)
Increase in long-term debt	**167**	411	252
Reduction of long-term debt	**(358)**	(264)	(282)
Subtotal	**108**	50	(282)
Dividends on common and preferred stock	**(346)**	(340)	(337)
Net proceeds from sales of Xerox common stock and			
stock of Xerox Canada Inc.	**154**	77	23
Other, net	**(43)**	(27)	(44)
Total	**(127)**	(240)	(640)
Cash Increased (Decreased) During the Year	**(93)**	135	40
Cash at Beginning of Year	**402**	267	227
Cash at End of Year	$ **309**	$ 402	$ 267

The accompanying notes are an integral part of the consolidated financial statements.

Xerox Corporation

Notes to Consolidated Financial Statements

1. Summary of Significant Accounting Policies

Basis of Consolidation. The accounts of all subsidiaries are consolidated, except for the Company's financial services and real estate subsidiaries which are accounted for by the equity method. Investments in corporate joint ventures, and other companies in which the Company has a 20% to 50% ownership, are accounted for by the equity method. The accounts of Latin American subsidiaries are included for their fiscal years which generally end on November 30.

Rank Xerox Limited, Rank Xerox Holding B.V. and their respective subsidiaries and the other subsidiaries jointly-owned by the Company and The Rank Organisation Plc are referred to as Rank Xerox Companies. The accounts of the Rank Xerox Companies are included for their fiscal years ended October 31.

Consolidated financial statements of Xerox Financial Services, Inc. (XFSI), the Company's domestic financial services subsidiary, are presented, beginning on page 53, in support of the carrying value of the Company's investment in, and equity in the earnings of, XFSI.

Income Recognition. Revenues from the sale of equipment under installment contracts and from sales-type leases are recognized at the time of sale or at the inception of the lease, respectively. Revenues from equipment under other leases are accounted for by the operating lease method and are recognized over the lease term. Operating lease plans include maintenance and parts, but generally do not include supplies such as toner and paper which are sold separately. Service revenues are derived primarily from maintenance contracts on the Company's equipment sold to customers. Rental and service revenues from reprographic products vary each month based on the number of copies produced. Sales to third-party lease finance companies of equipment subject to the Company's operating leases are recorded as sales at the time the equipment is accepted by the third party. The Company has agreed to service these units, to perform non-preferential remarketing services and to administer the leases on a compensatory basis.

Inventories. Inventories are carried at the lower of average cost or market.

Rental Equipment, Buildings and Equipment. Rental equipment, buildings and equipment are depreciated over their estimated useful lives. Assets recorded under capital leases are amortized over their lease terms or, if title to the property will ultimately pass to the Company, over their estimated useful lives. Depreciation is computed using principally the straight-line method. Significant improvements are capitalized; maintenance and repairs are expensed. The cost and accumulated depreciation of assets retired or otherwise disposed of are eliminated from the accounts and any resulting gain or loss is credited or charged to income, as appropriate.

Foreign Currency Translation. The Company's subsidiaries in Latin America operate primarily in hyper-inflationary economies and transact a significant amount of business in

U.S. dollars. Accordingly, the U.S. dollar is deemed to be the functional currency of these subsidiaries and all translation gains and losses are taken into income. The financial position and results of operations of the Company's other foreign subsidiaries are measured using local currency as the functional currency. Revenues and expenses of such subsidiaries have been translated at average exchange rates. Assets and liabilities have been translated at current exchange rates, and the related translation adjustments, together with net gains and losses from hedging exposed net asset positions less related tax effects, are being deferred as a separate component of Shareholders' Equity, until there is a sale or liquidation of the underlying foreign investments. The Company has no present plans for the sale or liquidation of significant investments to which these deferrals relate. Aggregate foreign currency exchange gains and losses are included in determining net income. Net aggregate foreign currency exchange gains (losses) were $52 million, $(5) million and $(35) million in 1987, 1986 and 1985, respectively, and are included in Other, net in the consolidated statements of income.

New Accounting Pronouncements. There are several recently issued Statements of the Financial Accounting Standards Board which have not yet been adopted by the Company and its subsidiaries as of December 31, 1987. Of these new Statements the following have particular relevance to the Company:

Statement No. 94 – This Statement will require the Company to consolidate, beginning in 1988, all majority-owned subsidiaries. At the present time the Company does not consolidate XFSI or its real estate and international finance subsidiaries. Statement No. 94 will not affect the Company's net income or shareholders' equity, although the presentation and display of substantially all other financial data will materially change. The industry segment data on page 36 summarize the Company's total revenues, total assets and certain other data on a fully consolidated basis. Short and long-term debt will significantly increase under Statement No. 94 primarily as a result of consolidating Xerox Credit Corporation and the international finance subsidiaries. These subsidiaries are, by nature, highly leveraged relative to the Company and their borrowing capabilities are essentially determined on an independent basis. The Company does not anticipate any changes in its, or its subsidiaries', borrowing capabilities or practices as a result of applying Statement No. 94. Statement No. 94 is required to be retroactively applied.

Statement No. 96 – This Statement – "Accounting for Income Taxes" – will affect the recognition and measurement of income tax expense and deferred tax assets and liabilities and is more fully discussed in the Company's income tax footnote appearing on page 48 and in the accompanying financial statements of XFSI.

Statement No. 97 – This Statement is applicable to the insurance subsidiaries of XFSI and affects the presentation of realized capital gains and losses and the recognition of earned premiums and related expenses of XFSI's life insurance operations. Statement No. 97, which will have no affect on net income, is more fully discussed in the accompanying financial statements of XFSI.

Xerox Corporation

2. Accounts Receivable

Current and long-term receivables consist of the following:

(In millions)	1987	1986
Accounts receivable	$1,475	$1,346
Accrued revenues	542	499
Investment in sales-type leases	653	614
Total	2,670	2,459
Less: Allowance for doubtful accounts	(84)	(75)
Unearned income and other	(182)	(176)
Total receivables, net	2,404	2,208
Less: Net finance receivables due after		
one year	(300)	(341)
Total current accounts receivable, net	$2,104	$1,867

The components of the Company's net investment in sales-type leases included in the consolidated balance sheets at December 31, 1987 and 1986 were as follows:

(In millions)	1987	1986
Total minimum lease payments receivable	$ 653	$ 614
Less: Unearned income and other	(182)	(176)
Allowance for doubtful receivables	(18)	(15)
Net investment in sales-type leases	$ 453	$ 423

Total minimum lease payments receivable are collectible as follows (in millions): 1988-$253; 1989-$193; 1990-$106; 1991-$58; and 1992-$43.

3. Rental Equipment, net

Rental equipment is depreciated over estimated useful lives, generally two to seven years. Changes in rental equipment for the three years ended December 31, 1987 are as follows:

(In millions)	1987	1986	1985
Cost			
Balance at January 1	$2,951	$3,401	$3,799
Additions	590	704	658
Dispositions	(1,077)	(1,291)	(1,138)
Translation and other changes	133	137	82
Balance at December 31	2,597	2,951	3,401
Accumulated Depreciation			
Balance at January 1	1,881	2,164	2,279
Depreciation	411	523	577
Dispositions	(727)	(936)	(783)
Translation and other changes	154	130	91
Balance at December 31	1,719	1,881	2,164
Rental equipment, net	$ 878	$1,070	$1,237

The Company's equipment operating lease terms vary, generally from one to thirty-six months. Minimum future rental revenues on the remaining noncancelable operating leases with original terms of one year or longer are (in millions): 1988-$516; 1989-$205; 1990-$76 and in the aggregate-$797. Total contingent rentals, principally usage charges in excess of minimum rentals for operating leases, amounted to (in millions): 1987-$534; 1986-$582; 1985-$627.

4. Land, Buildings and Equipment, net

The components of land, buildings and equipment follow:

(In millions)	Estimated Useful Lives (years)	1987	1986	1985
Land		$ 89	$ 62	$ 66
Buildings and building equipment	20 to 40	692	621	593
Leasehold improvements	Lease Term	271	249	221
Plant machinery	4 to 12	1,155	1,021	948
Office furniture and equipment	3 to 10	1,122	971	868
Other	3 to 20	133	113	129
Construction in progress		89	122	105
Total		$3,551	$3,159	$2,930

Changes in land, buildings and equipment for the three years ending December 31, 1987 are as follows:

(In millions)	1987	1986	1985
Cost			
Balance at January 1	$3,159	$2,930	$2,779
Additions	347	328	293
Dispositions	(147)	(183)	(241)
Translation and other changes	192	84	99
Balance at December 31	3,551	3,159	2,930
Accumulated Depreciation			
Balance at January 1	1,668	1,507	1,387
Depreciation	320	283	272
Dispositions	(112)	(128)	(159)
Translation and other changes	36	6	7
Balance at December 31	1,912	1,668	1,507
Land, buildings and equipment, net	$1,639	$1,491	$1,423

The Company leases certain land, buildings and equipment under capital leases and operating leases which expire through 2018. Total rent expense under operating leases amounted to (in millions): 1987-$372; 1986-$348; 1985-$309. Future minimum lease payments required under capital leases and operating leases that have initial or remaining noncancelable lease terms in excess of one year at December 31, 1987 are summarized below:

(In millions)	Capital Leases	Operating Leases
1988	$ 33	$ 247
1989	31	202
1990	21	155
1991	15	127
1992	11	107
Later years	67	436
Total minimum lease payments	178	$1,274
Less amount representing interest and executory costs	65	
Present value of net minimum lease payments	$113	

Xerox Corporation

Future minimum sublease income under operating leases with noncancelable lease terms in excess of one year amounted to $41 million at December 31, 1987.

5. Investment in Xerox Financial Services, Inc., at equity

Xerox Financial Services, Inc. (XFSI), is the holding company for the Company's wholly owned domestic financial services subsidiaries, primarily Crum and Forster, Inc., Xerox Credit Corporation, Van Kampen Merritt Inc. and Furman Selz Holding Corporation which was acquired during the third quarter of 1987.

The income (loss) of the XFSI companies included in equity in income from continuing operations of unconsolidated companies in the Company's consolidated statements of income for the years ended December 31, 1987, 1986 and 1985 follows:

(In millions)	1987	1986	1985
Crum and Forster, Inc.	$269	$189	$(16)
Xerox Credit Corporation	83	84	68
Van Kampen Merritt Inc.	14	25	26
Furman Selz Holding Corporation	1	—	—
Xerox Financial Services, Inc.	(25)	(20)	(2)
Total	$342	$278	$ 76

The consolidated financial statements of XFSI are included herein on pages 53 to 61.

6. Other Investments, at equity

Other investments, at equity consist of the following at December 31, 1987 and 1986.

(In millions)	1987	1986
Fuji Xerox Co., Ltd.	$473	$397
Xerox Canada Finance, Inc.	146	60
Rank Xerox Leasing International Companies	138	46
Xerox Real Estate Companies	43	35
Other	50	23
Total	$850	$561

Rank Xerox Limited (RXL) owns 50% of the outstanding stock of Fuji Xerox Co., Ltd. (Fuji Xerox), a corporate joint venture. Fuji Xerox is located in the Far East and operates principally in the Business Equipment business. Condensed financial data for Fuji Xerox for its last three fiscal years are as follows:

(In millions)	1987	1986	1985
Summary of Operations			
Total operating revenues	$2,866	$2,060	$1,419
Costs and expenses	2,627	1,890	1,285
Income before income taxes	239	170	134
Income taxes	139	101	77
Net income	$ 100	$ 69	$ 57
Xerox' equity in net income	$ 50	$ 34	$ 28

Balance Sheets	1987	1986	1985
Assets			
Current assets	$1,504	$1,126	$ 747
Noncurrent assets	964	921	669
Total assets	$2,468	$2,047	$1,416
Liabilities and Shareholders' Equity			
Current liabilities	$1,195	$ 973	$ 704
Long-term debt	63	65	29
Other noncurrent liabilities	257	213	142
Shareholders' equity	953	796	541
Total liabilities and shareholders' equity	$2,468	$2,047	$1,416

Xerox Canada Finance Inc. (XCFI) is wholly owned by Xerox Canada Inc. (XCI), a consolidated subsidiary of the Company. XCFI is engaged in financing accounts receivable arising out of equipment sales by XCI and is in the business of financing leases for third parties. Trade receivables and sales-type leases amounting to $341 million and $300 million were sold or transferred to XCFI from XCI during 1987 and 1986, respectively. During 1987 the Company's equity in XCFI increased primarily due to XCI's investment of $67 million in a new series of XCFI's preferred stock.

As of December 31, 1987 the Company, through RXL, organized fourteen international finance companies which are referred to as the Rank Xerox Leasing International Companies (RXLI) whose purpose is to finance the Rank Xerox Companies' sales of Xerox equipment in a manner similar to the financing activities of XCFI. During 1987 the Company's equity in RXLI increased primarily due to RXL's aggregate investment of $59 million in the various RXLI companies.

Condensed financial data for the Company's unconsolidated real estate and international finance companies included in Other Investments, at equity are set forth below and have been combined based on each entity's respective fiscal year:

(In millions)	1987	1986	1985
Summary of Operations			
Total income	$ 189	$ 81	$ 52
Costs and expenses	130	57	17
Income before income taxes	59	24	35
Income taxes	27	11	17
Net income	$ 32	$ 13	$ 18

Balance Sheets	1987	1986	1985
Assets			
Current assets	$ 451	$205	$223
Noncurrent assets	1,194	625	521
Total assets	$1,645	$830	$744
Liabilities and Shareholders' Equity			
Current liabilities	$ 358	$290	$163
Advances from Xerox	—	2	190
Long-term debt	760	306	105
Other noncurrent liabilities	200	97	82
Shareholders' equity	327	135	204
Total liabilities and shareholders' equity	$1,645	$830	$744

Xerox Corporation

7. Retirement Plans

In 1986 the Company adopted, for its U.S. retirement plans, Statements of Financial Accounting Standards (SFAS) No's. 87 and 88 which respectively establish standards for the determination of pension cost and for the settlement of pension plan obligations. During 1987 these Standards were adopted for the Company's major foreign plans. The Company's policy is to immediately recognize gains and losses resulting from the settlement of pension obligations. The accompanying financial statements of XFSI describe the effect of the new pension standards on the Company's unconsolidated subsidiaries.

U.S. Plans. The Company's major plans are noncontributory, trusteed profit sharing retirement plans to which a defined minimum annual contribution is made; any contributions in excess of such minimum contribution are made based upon a formula related to return on assets. These plans are supplemented by trusteed retirement income guarantee plans which assure a defined monthly income to substantially all U.S. employees at retirement to the extent that such defined benefits are not funded under the related profit sharing plans.

Foreign Plans. Pension coverage for employees of the Company's non-U.S. subsidiaries is provided, to the extent deemed appropriate or as legally required, through separate plans. Obligations under such plans are systematically provided for by depositing funds with trustees, under insurance policies or through the Company's established accrued liabilities. Foreign plans for which SFAS 87 was not adopted in 1987 were, in the aggregate, not material. The market value of foreign pension plans' assets generally exceeds the accumulated benefits of such plans.

The funded status of the Company's retirement plans at December 31, 1987 and 1986 is as follows:

(In millions)	1987	1986*
Actuarial present value of:		
Accumulated benefit obligations		
(substantially all of which are vested)	$2,395	$2,339
Projected benefit obligation	$2,535	$2,498
Plan assets at fair market value	2,860	2,503
Excess of plan assets over projected benefit obligations	325	5
Items not yet reflected in the financial statements:		
Remaining unrecognized net transition asset at date of initial application of SFAS 87	(313)	(318)
Unrecognized prior service cost	89	95
Unrecognized net (gain) loss	(300)	3
Accrued pension costs at December 31	$ (199)	$ (215)

*Restated to include data for non-U.S. Plans.

Included in the funded status are two unfunded plans which have projected benefit obligations of $140 million and $118 million at December 31, 1987 and 1986, respectively.

For its U.S. plans, the Company's policy is to fund the annual profit sharing contribution, which amounted to $93

million and $91 million for 1987 and 1986, respectively, early in the succeeding year. The 1987 contribution, which increases plan assets, will be made on or about March 31, 1988.

The components of pension cost for the Company's retirement plans for the years ended December 31, 1987 and 1986 are as follows:

	1987		
(In millions)	Foreign Plans	U.S. Plans	1986
Defined benefit plans subject to SFAS 87:			
Service cost – benefits earned during the period	$ 25	$105	$ 103
Interest on projected benefit obligation	42	84	275
Actual return on plan assets	(282)	(77)	(297)
Net amortization and deferrals	214	(8)	6
Settlement gains	—	(21)	—
Subtotal	(1)	83	87
Pension cost for defined contribution and foreign plans not subject to SFAS 87	30	2	43
Total	$ 29	$ 85	$ 130

Pension cost for 1985, as determined under the previous accounting methods, was $136 million.

SFAS 87 specifies the use of the projected unit credit actuarial method and requires an annual determination of plan assumptions. Plan benefits for the major U.S. plans are principally determined based upon total years of service and the highest five years of compensation. The projected benefit obligation was determined using assumed discount rates of 9.25% and 8.5% at December 31, 1987 and 1986, respectively. Assumed long-term rates of compensation increases vary from 5.5% to 8.25% and the assumed long-term rates of return on plan assets is 9.5%. Unrecognized net transition assets and prior service costs are being amortized over the average remaining working lives of the plans' participants which is approximately 15 years. Plan assets are primarily invested in marketable equity securities. For the company's major foreign plans the assumed discount rate and long-term rate of return on plan assets was 9.75% at both December 31, 1987 and 1986. Assumed long-term rate of compensation increases vary from 7.0% to 9.0%.

During 1986 the Company announced several amendments to the retirement income guarantee plan for salaried U.S. employees. The principal amendment enhanced the early retirement benefits available to eligible members of the plan by providing five additional years of age and service credits to eligible employees' age and years of service as of December 31, 1986 for purposes of calculating each eligible employee's retirement benefit. For the eligible group the amendment has had the effect of reducing the plan's early retirement age by five years to age 50. The actuarial present value of the cost of this amendment is approximately $75 million. Through December 31, 1987 approximately 1,300 individuals have elected to retire under this amendment.

Xerox Corporation

Postretirement Benefit Plans. The Company provides certain health care and life insurance benefits for retired employees. Substantially all of the Company's U.S. employees and employees in certain foreign countries may become eligible for these benefits if they reach retirement age, with defined minimum periods of service, while still working for the Company. The cost of such benefits is recorded as claims or premiums are paid and amounted to $10 million in 1987, $8 million in 1986 and $7 million in 1985.

8. Income Taxes

The parent Company and its domestic subsidiaries including the unconsolidated financial services and real estate subsidiaries file consolidated U.S. income tax returns. Pursuant to tax allocation agreements, each financial services' subsidiary records its tax provision and makes payments to the Company for taxes due or receives payments from the Company for tax benefits utilized. The following data include income from continuing operations of the Company and its consolidated subsidiaries.

Income from continuing operations before income taxes and outside shareholders' interests consists of the following:

(In millions)	1987	1986	1985
Domestic income	$383	$254	$241
Foreign income	538	421	369
Total	$921	$675	$610

Income tax expense of continuing operations consists of the following:

(In millions)	1987	1986	1985
Federal income taxes			
Current	$ —	$ 63	$ 227
Deferred	(6)	(85)	(204)
Investment tax credits			
Received and deferred, net of recapture and amortization	—	(38)	(18)
Foreign income taxes			
Current	121	122	161
Deferred	141	52	(9)
State income taxes			
Current	7	7	38
Deferred	(1)	(9)	(29)
Total income taxes	$262	$112	$ 166

The Company will have a tax liability of approximately $33 million on its consolidated U.S. income tax return. This liability arises from the income of XFSI.

Deferred income tax expense on income from continuing operations arises from the following items:

(In millions)	1987	1986	1985
Installment sales	$201	$ 51	(174)
Intercompany profits	19	11	34
Depreciation	(36)	(112)	(104)
Other	(50)	8	2
Total	$134	$ (42)	$(242)

A reconciliation of the effective tax rate of continuing operations from the U.S. Federal statutory rate follows:

	1987	1986	1985
U.S. Federal statutory rate	40.0%	46.0%	46.0%
Foreign tax rate differential	8.7	0.7	0.5
Investment tax credits	—	(3.6)	(5.3)
Research and development credits	(1.5)	(1.9)	(2.5)
Equity in income of unconsolidated companies on an after-tax basis	(18.2)	(22.2)	(8.8)
Other	(0.6)	(2.4)	(2.7)
Effective tax rate	28.4%	16.6%	27.2%

On a combined basis, the parent Company and its domestic subsidiaries, including the unconsolidated financial services and real estate subsidiaries, provide U.S. income taxes under the Alternative Minimum Tax. As a result of the allocation agreements, the parent Company and its domestic consolidated subsidiaries, as indicated above, provide taxes using the regular tax system.

Investment tax credits are deferred and amortized as a reduction of the provision for income taxes over the periods during which they are earned. Deferred investment tax credits were fully utilized at the end of 1986 through amortization and recapture. For book purposes, the Company and its unconsolidated financial services subsidiaries have tax credit carryforwards of $30 million, $14 million of which expire in 2002, the remainder have an unlimited carryforward period. These carryforwards are not available for alternative minimum tax purposes. For tax return purposes, the Company has tax credits approximating $102 million which expire in varying amounts from 1998 through 2002. The Tax Reform Act of 1986 may reduce the benefit derived from utilizing these credits.

Total current deferred tax charges included in other current assets at December 31, 1987 and 1986 were $146 million and $99 million, respectively. Deferred income taxes have not been provided on the undistributed earnings of foreign subsidiaries and other foreign investments carried at equity. The amount of such earnings included in consolidated retained earnings at December 31, 1987 was approximately $2.0 billion. These earnings have been substantially reinvested and the Company does not plan to initiate any action which would precipitate the payment of income taxes thereon.

In December of 1987, the Financial Accounting Standards Board issued an accounting pronouncement that significantly changes the accounting rules relating to income taxes. Under the new accounting standard, deferred taxes will be adjusted for the cumulative effect of enacted changes in tax laws or rates. Additionally, net deferred tax assets will only be recognized to the extent that they could be realized by carryback to recover taxes already paid. The Company will be required to adopt the new accounting standard in 1989. When the Company adopts this accounting standard there will be charges to prior years' earnings as a result of the accounting change to value deferred taxes in accordance with the new rules. Restatement of prior years' results is permitted under the new rules, and the Company expects to elect this option.

Xerox Corporation

9. Long-Term Debt

A summary of long-term debt follows:

(In millions)	1987	1986
Consolidated U.S. Operations		
8⅝% sinking fund debentures due 1999(a)	$ 108	$ 108
6% subordinated debentures due 1995 – convertible to common at $92 per share(b)	99	108
5% subordinated debentures due 1988 – convertible to common at $148 per share	74	74
13¼% sinking fund debentures due 2014	100	100
10½% notes due 1988	100	100
10⅝% notes due 1993	100	100
8⅛% notes due 1996	100	100
8⅜% notes due 1996	100	100
Extendible notes due 1998(c)	62	62
Notes payable in Swiss francs due 1989-1991 (6.1% average interest rate at December 31, 1987)	241	187
Capital lease obligations	42	44
Other debt, due 1988-2014 (7.2% average interest rate at December 31, 1987)	144	134
Subtotal	1,270	1,217
Consolidated International Operations		
Various obligations, payable in:		
(Average interest rate at December 31, 1987 in parentheses)		
Canadian dollars, due 1988 (12%)	31	29
Dutch guilders, due 1988-1990 (8.4%)	106	93
European Currency Units, due 1988 (11⅜%)	59	51
German marks, due 1988-1993 (7.5%)	46	38
Pounds sterling, due 1989-1996 (11.0%)	79	75
Swiss francs, due 1993 (5.5%)	79	62
U.S. dollars, due 1988-1995 (7.3%)	125	241
Capital lease obligations	71	64
Other currencies, due 1988-2011 (12.7%)	35	37
Subtotal	631	690
Total	1,901	1,907
Less current portion	362	177
Total long-term debt	$1,539	$1,730

Payments due on long-term debt for the next five years are (in millions): 1988-$362; 1989-$241; 1990-$201; 1991-$265 and 1992-$114. Substantially all long-term debt of the Company is fixed rate debt.

(a) The 8⅝% sinking fund debentures are redeemable by the Company through October 31, 1988 at 102.9% and at reducing percentages thereafter. The Company must redeem a minimum of $12 million annually. At December 31, 1987 a total of $44 million of repurchased debentures was available for sinking fund requirements.

(b) The 6% convertible subordinated debentures are redeemable by the Company, through October 31, 1988, at 100.9% and at reducing percentages thereafter. The Company must redeem a minimum of $8 million annually.

(c) The extendible notes will mature on September 1, 1998 unless the holder elects repayment on September 1, 1989 or on any September 1 thereafter immediately following the end

of a specified interest period. The notes are redeemable, at the election of the Company, at not less than 100% during specified redemption periods. The interest rate through August 31, 1989 is 7.45% and thereafter is adjustable for each specified interest period to a rate not less than 102% of the effective rate on comparable maturity U.S. Treasury obligations.

Certain of the Company's other long-term debt agreements contain various sinking fund requirements, premium payments for early redemption, conversion options, etc. None of these are material to an understanding of the consolidated financial statements of the Company.

10. Notes Payable and Lines of Credit

Short-term borrowings of the Company are as follows:

(In millions)	Balance at End of Year	Weighted Average Interest Rates	
		End of Year	Monthly Average During Year
1987			
Bank notes payable	$128	11.8%	11.2%
Commercial paper	115	7.7%	7.1%
Total	$243	9.8%	9.1%
1986			
Bank notes payable	$ 79	10.4%	11.6%
Commercial paper	50	5.9%	7.2%
Total	$129	8.7%	8.7%
1985			
Bank notes payable	$115	12.9%	12.7%
Commercial paper	219	8.2%	8.9%
Total	$334	9.8%	10.3%

Bank notes payable generally represent foreign currency denominated borrowings of non-U.S. subsidiaries.

The maximum aggregate short-term debt outstanding at any month end was (in millions) $468, $544 and $652 during 1987, 1986 and 1985, respectively. Average short-term borrowings during these years were (in millions) $305, $416 and $504, respectively.

At December 31, 1987, the Company and XCC had unused short-term lines of credit aggregating $150 million with U.S. banks at prime interest rates. The Company maintains compensating balances of not more than 5% of these lines of credit. The Company and XCC also have three revolving credit agreements totaling $1 billion with various banks, generally at prime interest rates, which expire in 1990. Commitment fees vary from ¹⁄₁₆ to ⅛ of 1% per annum on the unused average daily balance. No amounts were outstanding at December 31, 1987 under these agreements. Foreign subsidiaries had unused lines of credit aggregating $523 million in various currencies at prevailing interest rates. Information about the Company's new revolving credit agreement, which was entered into in February of 1988, is included in Note 16 on page 52.

Xerox Corporation

11. Selected Financial Statement Information

(In millions)	1987	1986	1985
Marketable securities included in cash	$ 9	$ 33	$ 45
Inventories			
Finished products	$1,112	$1,086	$1,093
Work in process	127	130	146
Raw materials and supplies	169	173	231
Total inventories	$1,408	$1,389	$1,470
Supplementary expense data			
Advertising	$ 184	$ 194	$ 176
Maintenance and repairs	137	121	105
Taxes, other than payroll and income			
Personal property	19	26	22
Other	58	58	52

(In millions)	1987	1986	1985
Net (increase) decrease in other working capital			
Accounts receivable, net	$(237)	$ (4)	$ 10
Inventories	(19)	62	(203)
Other current assets	(321)	24	(119)
Accounts payable	44	37	94
Salaries, profit sharing and other accruals	171	104	26
Income taxes	35	(40)	(5)
Unearned income	17	35	(6)
Other current liabilities	98	(64)	(33)
Net (increase) decrease in other working capital	$(212)	$154	$(236)
Investment income included in other income	$ 54	$ 54	$ 65

12. Common Shareholders' Equity

The components of common shareholders' equity and the changes therein for the three years ended December 31, 1987 follow:

(Dollars in millions, except per share amounts. Shares in thousands.)	Common Stock Shares	Common Stock Amount	Additional Paid-In Capital	Retained Earnings	Net Unrealized Appreciation of Equity Investments	Translation Adjustments	Total
Balance at December 31, 1984	95,884	$96	$765	$3,760	$17	$(537)	$4,101
Stock option and incentive plans	572		25				25
Net income ($4.44 per share)				475			475
Cash dividends declared —							
Common Stock ($3.00 per share)				(289)			(289)
Preferred stock ($5.45 per share)				(48)			(48)
Net unrealized appreciation of equity investments					61		61
Translation adjustments — net of outside shareholders' interests of $48						61	61
Balance at December 31, 1985	96,456	96	790	3,898	78	(476)	4,386
Stock option and incentive plans	955	2	36				38
Stock purchase and dividend reinvestment plan	240		14				14
Sale of stock by Canadian subsidiary			17				17
Net income ($4.28 per share)				465			465
Cash dividends declared —							
Common Stock ($3.00 per share)				(292)			(292)
Preferred Stock ($5.45 per share)				(48)			(48)
Net unrealized appreciation of equity investments					12		12
Translation adjustments — net of outside shareholders' interests of $67						95	95
Balance at December 31, 1986	97,651	98	857	4,023	90	(381)	4,687
Stock option and incentive plans	510		24				24
Stock purchase and dividend reinvestment plan	1,935	2	131				133
Net income ($5.35 per share)				578			578
Cash dividends declared —							
Common stock ($3.00 per share)				(298)			(298)
Preferred stock ($5.45 per share)				(48)			(48)
Net unrealized depreciation of equity investments					(84)		(84)
Translation adjustments — net of outside shareholders' interests of $97						113	113
Balance at December 31, 1987	100,096	$100	$1,012	$4,255	$ 6	$(268)	$5,105

Common Stock. During 1987 the Company's shareholders approved an increase in the number of authorized shares of $1 par value common stock to 350,000,000 shares from 150,000,000 shares which had been the authorized number since 1982. At December 31, 1987 and 1986, 4.7 million shares and 5.3 million shares, respectively, of an original authorization of 7.9 million shares were reserved for issuance of common stock under the Company's incentive compensation plan and 2.5 million shares were reserved for the conversion of convertible debt. In addition, at December 31, 1987 there were 2.8 million common shares reserved for issuance under the Company's Automatic Dividend Reinvestment and Stock Purchase Plan.

Stock Option and Long-Term Incentive Plans. The Company has a long-term incentive plan (1976 plan) under which eligible employees may be granted incentive stock options, nonqualified stock options, stock appreciation rights (SAR's), performance unit rights and incentive stock rights. These compensation plans are described in the Company's 1988 Proxy Statement. At December 31, 1987 and 1986 1.5 million and 2.2 million shares, respectively, were available for grant of options or rights. Additional data for the stock options and stock rights plans are summarized below:

(In thousands)	Incentive Stock Rights	Stock Options	Average Option Price
Outstanding at January 1, 1987	616	2,434	$48
Granted	21	1,052	68
Cancelled	(38)	(110)	57
Exercised	(55)	(484)	43
Options surrendered for SAR's	—	(238)	40
Outstanding at December 31, 1987	544	2,654	57
Exercisable at December 31, 1987		1,104	
Becoming exercisable in 1988		1,040	

The average unit value when granted of outstanding incentive stock rights was $44. On January 1, 1988 substantially all of these rights became vested.

During 1987, the Company received $21 million from the exercise of stock options.

Net Income Per Common Share. Net income per common share is computed by dividing consolidated net income less dividends on preferred stock by the average number of shares of common stock outstanding during each year. The effect of common stock equivalents (stock options, incentive stock rights and certain convertible debt) and other convertible debt securities are excluded as the potential dilution upon assumed exercise, vesting or conversion thereof is less than 3%.

Retained Earnings. Among the provisions of the several loan agreements are restrictions related to the payment of cash dividends by the Company on common stock. At December 31, 1987 approximately $3.8 billion of consolidated retained earnings was unrestricted.

Preferred Stock Purchase Rights. In April 1987 the Company adopted a shareholder rights plan designed to deter coercive or unfair takeover tactics and to prevent a person or group of persons from gaining control of the Company without offering a fair price to all shareholders.

Under the terms of the plan each common shareholder received a dividend of one preferred stock purchase Right for each outstanding share of the Company's common stock. Each Right entitles the registered holder, under certain circumstances, to purchase from the Company one one-hundredth of a new series of preferred stock at an exercise price of $225.

The Rights may not be exercised until ten days following the earliest of an announcement that a person or affiliated persons has acquired, has commenced or has announced the intention to commence a tender offer to acquire 20% or more of the Company's common shares. If, after the Rights become exercisable, the Company is acquired in a business combination, or alternatively if, in certain circumstances, the Company acquires such person or affiliated persons the Rights entitle the holder to purchase the common stock of the surviving company having a market value two times the exercise price. The Company is entitled to redeem the Rights at $.05 per Right prior to the earlier of the expiration of the Rights in April 1997 or the close of business ten days after the announcement that a 20% position has been acquired. The right to redeem the Rights is reinstated in certain circumstances.

The Rights are non-voting and until they become exercisable, they have no dilutive effect on the earnings per share or book value per share of the Company's common stock.

13. Cumulative Preferred Stock

The Company has 25,000,000 authorized shares of cumulative preferred stock, $1 par value. At December 31, 1987 and 1986, 8,840,205 shares of $5.45 Cumulative Preferred stock were issued and outstanding. These shares have a stated value of $50 per share, are non-voting, have liquidation preference over common stock and are subject to redemption at the stated value through a sinking fund in which the Company must retire 8.18% of the issue cumulatively each year from 1993 through 2002 and the remaining portion in 2003. As discussed in Note 16 on page 52, in early 1988 the Company called for redemption all outstanding shares of the $5.45 Cumulative Preferred stock at a price of $52.725 per share which is equal to the stated value plus a premium of 50% of the annual dividend.

Xerox Corporation
Financial Review

The following discussion summarizes the results as reported in the Company's consolidated financial statements.

Income Improved

A combination of good revenue growth and close attention to basic business factors such as cost control programs produced income gains for both of the Company's principal businesses in 1987. Total income from continuing operations increased 19 percent over the prior year to $578 million. This growth corresponds with $5.35 income per common share from continuing operations in 1987, up from $4.52 in 1986 and $3.47 in 1985.

On a total Company basis, net income in 1986 and 1985 was impacted by operations which were discontinued (see Xerox Corporation Note 15 on page 52), and by the effect of a pension accounting change in 1986 (see Xerox Financial Services, Inc. Note 12 on page 61).

Results of Operations

The financial summary on this page presents the overall organizational contribution to the Company's operating results from the continuing Business Products and Systems (BP&S) business and Xerox Financial Services, Inc. (XFSI). In 1987, BP&S achieved profitability improvement and XFSI continued the profitable expansion of its business. A detailed definition and discussion of industry segments are found below and on pages 37 and 38.

New Accounting Pronouncements

There are several recently issued Statements of the Financial Accounting Standards Board (FASB) which have not yet been adopted by the Company or its subsidiaries. The Standards and their effects on the business are discussed further in Xerox Corporation Notes 1 and 8 and XFSI Note 1, which are found on pages 44, 48 and 56.

Financial Summary

(In millions)	1987	1986	1985
Revenues			
Business Products and Systems			
Business Equipment	$10,320	$ 9,355	$ 8,676
Financing	230	127	81
Total Business Products and Systems	10,550	9,482	8,757
Xerox Financial Services, Inc.			
Insurance	4,072	3,163	2,591
Financing	384	297	313
Investment Banking	119	104	100
Total Xerox Financial Services, Inc.	4,575	3,564	3,004
Total Revenues	$15,125	$13,046	$11,761
Income from Continuing Operations			
Business Products and Systems			
Business Equipment	$ 270	$ 240	$ 335
Financing	28	20	16
Total Business Products and Systems	298	260	351
Xerox Financial Services, Inc.			
Insurance	269	189	(16)
Financing	83	84	67
Investment Banking	15	25	26
Other	(87)	(70)	(47)
Total Xerox Financial Services, Inc.	280	228	30
Total Income from Continuing Operations	$ 578	$ 488	$ 381

This Financial Summary describes the revenue and income contributions from each of the industry segments within BP&S and XFSI. The BP&S revenue and income from Financing includes the results of its financing activities. Most of the financing for domestic sales of Xerox equipment is carried out by Xerox Credit Corporation, whose financing revenue and income are reported within XFSI. Included in the XFSI Income from Continuing Operations as Other, are XFSI holding company interest and other expenses, and allocated interest expense related to the acquisitions of financial services subsidiaries and capital contributions.

Definition of Industry Segments

In 1987 the Company expanded its reporting of industry segments, as defined below.

The Business Equipment segment consists of the development, manufacture, marketing and maintenance of the Company's equipment and related supplies. The Company's products include xerographic copiers and duplicators, electronic and electrostatic printers, workstations, information processing products and systems, electronic typewriters, plotters, facsimile transceivers, networks, computer related services and software.

The Xerox Equipment Financing segment includes the Company's financing activities, either directly or through unconsolidated financing subsidiaries, associated with the sale of Xerox products worldwide.

The Third Party Financing segment consists of the non-Xerox financing activities conducted through unconsolidated financing subsidiaries.

The Insurance segment consists of the Company's unconsolidated insurance subsidiary, Crum and Forster, Inc. (C&F), which is primarily a property and casualty insurer. C&F also provides life insurance products through a wholly-owned subsidiary.

The Investment Banking segment consists of the activities of the Company's unconsolidated subsidiaries, Van Kampen Merritt Inc. and Furman Selz Holding Corporation.

Due to allocation methodologies and other operating conditions, the following information may not be representative of operating profits or assets if the segments were independent companies.

Xerox Financial Services, Inc.

Consolidated Statements of Income

(In millions) Year ended December 31	1987	1986	1985
Income			
Insurance premiums earned	$3,543	$2,685	$2,169
Investment income	505	440	373
Finance and investment banking income	419	355	379
Other income	108	84	83
Total income	4,575	3,564	3,004
Losses and Expenses			
Insurance losses and loss expenses	2,942	2,315	2,160
Insurance acquisition costs and other			
insurance operating expenses	965	818	690
Interest expense	211	188	171
Administrative and general expenses	239	195	180
Total losses and expenses	4,357	3,516	3,201
Operating Income (Loss) from			
Continuing Operations Before Income Taxes	218	48	(197)
Income (Taxes) Benefits	(8)	107	177
Operating Income (Loss) from Continuing Operations	210	155	(20)
Realized Capital Gains of C&F, Net of Income Taxes	132	123	96
Income from Continuing Operations	342	278	76
Discontinued Operations	—	(51)	(111)
Cumulative Effect on Prior Years of Change			
in Accounting Principles for Pension Costs	—	42	—
Net Income (Loss)	$ 342	$ 269	$ (35)

The accompanying notes are an integral part of the consolidated financial statements.

Xerox Financial Services, Inc.
Consolidated Balance Sheets

(In millions) December 31	1987	1986
Assets		
Investments	$ 6,497	$ 5,489
Cash	57	47
Finance receivables, net	2,941	2,181
Premiums receivable, net	750	751
Other receivables, net	775	510
Due from Xerox Corporation, net	241	528
Other assets	926	707
Excess of cost over fair value of net assets acquired	1,069	1,008
Total Assets	**$13,256**	$11,221
Liabilities and Shareholder's Equity		
Liabilities		
Unearned premiums	$ 1,304	$ 1,130
Unpaid losses and loss expenses	3,398	4,268
Notes payable	2,561	1,781
Accounts payable and accrued liabilities	987	1,170
Deferred income taxes	339	342
Total Liabilities	10,589	8,691
Shareholder's Equity	2,667	2,530
Total Liabilities and Shareholder's Equity	**$13,256**	$11,221

The accompanying notes are an integral part of the consolidated financial statements.

Consolidated Statements of Cash Flows

(In millions) Year ended December 31	1987	1986	1985
Net Cash Flows From Operating Activities:			
Net income from continuing operations	$ 342	$ 278	$ 76
Non cash items included in income:			
Increase in unpaid losses and loss expenses	1,151	682	645
Increase in unearned premiums	174	310	120
Depreciation and amortization	75	67	61
Increase (decrease) in deferred income taxes	(3)	(18)	58
Proceeds from pension plan termination	—	97	—
Cash provided by operating activities	1,739	1,416	960
Increase in premiums and other receivables	(264)	(53)	(291)
Increase (decrease) in accounts payable and			
accrued liabilities	(174)	—	357
Due from Xerox Corporation	287	19	(175)
Other, net	(283)	(264)	(216)
Cash used by operating activities	(434)	(298)	(325)
Total	1,305	1,118	635
Cash Flows from Investing Activities:			
Cash used by discontinued operations	(21)	(124)	(46)
Increase in finance receivables	(760)	(195)	(233)
Purchase of investments	(3,598)	(3,680)	(2,283)
Cost of investments sold	2,593	2,675	1,826
Other investments, net	101	(5)	(9)
Investments/advances to unconsolidated affiliates	(200)	—	—
Net equity of businesses acquired	122	35	—
Excess of cost over fair value of net assets			
acquired	(79)	(31)	—
Total	(1,842)	(1,325)	(745)
Cash Flows from Financing Activities:			
Increase in long-term debt	901	600	295
Reduction of long-term debt	(318)	(189)	(91)
Increase (decrease) in short-term debt, net	197	(13)	(53)
Subtotal	780	398	151
Dividends paid to Xerox Corporation	(121)	(108)	(80)
Increase (decrease) in note payable to Xerox			
Corporation	—	(200)	200
Capital contributed by Xerox Corporation	—	200	—
Total	659	290	271
Cash and Short-Term Investments Increased	122	83	161
Cash and Short-Term Investments at Beginning of Year	800	717	556
Cash and Short-Term Investments at End of Year	$ 922	$ 800	$ 717

The accompanying notes are an integral part of the consolidated financial statements.

CHAPTER 22

Corporations: Earnings and Dividends

LEARNING OBJECTIVES

When you have completed this chapter, you should

1. have a better understanding of accounting terminology.

2. understand the nature of retained earnings.

3. be able to make journal entries to appropriate retained earnings.

4. be able to record transactions involving cash and stock dividends.

5. understand stock splits.

6. be able to account for treasury stock.

7. be able to prepare a corporation income statement.

8. be able to calculate earnings per share.

As discussed in Chapter 21, the stockholders' equity section of the balance sheet is made up of two major parts: (1) paid-in or invested capital and (2) retained earnings. Earnings of the corporation occur when more revenues flow into the business than are paid out in expenses. The net difference will increase both the assets of the corporation and the stockholders' equity. A corporation's income statement will list all of the revenue and expense items. In addition, it will show the net income from operations, the federal income tax liability, and the net income after taxes. This is illustrated in Appendix 22B, a corporation income statement, on page 835. The federal income tax owed is shown on a separate line, after the net income from operations. Therefore, the final net income is the remainder after all costs and expenses and federal income taxes have been deducted from revenue. Often net income is referred to as the "bottom line."

retained earnings
the undistributed earnings or losses of a corporation

At the end of an accounting period, the Income Summary account is closed to the capital account, Retained Earnings. **Retained earnings** represents the undistributed earnings or losses of the corporation. To analyze the major transactions that affect retained earnings, a T-account is presented below.

Retained Earnings

Debit	*Credit*
Net Loss	*Net Income*
Cash Dividend	
Stock Dividend	

The major items affecting this account are net income or net loss and both cash and stock dividends. To return a profit to the owners, this account must have a credit balance showing earnings (profits) that are undistributed. The stockholders look to this account to help determine whether they will receive a dividend payment.

APPROPRIATION OF RETAINED EARNINGS

In order for a corporation to pay a dividend, it must have both a credit balance in its Retained Earnings account and sufficient cash on hand or unissued stock. If the cash balance is too low, the board of directors may not declare a dividend even though there

**appropriated
retained earnings**
earnings retained in
the business desig-
nated for a special
purpose

are sufficient retained earnings. The board of directors may decide, too, that a part of the retained earnings should be kept in the corporation for emergencies or for some other specific reason, such as plant expansion. When this is the case, the board of directors will appropriate (or restrict) all or a portion of the retained earnings. **Appropriated retained earnings** are earnings retained in the business for a specific purpose. The purpose is made clear to the stockholders by listing the amount of appropriated retained earnings and the purpose for the appropriation on the balance sheet.

There are many reasons why the board of directors may decide to appropriate retained earnings. For example, the corporation may need to purchase land for a future building site; state law may restrict payment of dividends if the capital of the company would be impaired; or the corporation may have other legal obligations besides the payment of cash dividends to stockholders (such as a bond indenture, which will be discussed in a later chapter).

Assume, for example, that the Sterling Corporation's management wishes to expand its plant facilities. To do this, it plans to designate some of the profits for this purpose. Assume further that Sterling Corporation has a $50,000 credit balance in the Income Summary account and wishes to designate $20,000 of this income for a plant expansion project. The journal entries and the T-accounts involved are as follows.

GENERAL JOURNAL				Page
Date	Description	Post. Ref.	Debit	Credit
19XX *Dec.* 31	*Income Summary*		50 0 0 0 —	
	Retained Earnings			50 0 0 0 —
	To Record the Closing of the Income			
	Summary Account to Retained Earnings			

GENERAL JOURNAL				Page
Date	Description	Post. Ref.	Debit	Credit
Dec. *31* 19XX	*Retained Earnings*		2 0 0 0 0 —	
	Appropriated Retained Earnings:			
	Plant Expansion			2 0 0 0 0 —
	To Record the Designation of $20,000 of			
	Retained Earnings for Plant Expansion			

	Income Summary	Retained Earnings	Appropriated Retained Earnings: Plant Expansion
	50,000 | *100,000*	*20,000* | *50,000*	*20,000*
	50,000	(*30,000*)	

When added together, the two capital accounts, Retained Earnings and Appropriated Retained Earnings, have the same total before and after the entry that records the appropriation. Before the appropriations entry, the total of all earnings retained in the business is $50,000. After the entry, the Retained Earnings account has a balance of $30,000 and the Appropriated Retained Earnings account has a balance of $20,000, which together equal $50,000. The appropriation will leave only $30,000 of the total retained earnings available for dividends. By separating the retained earnings into two accounts, managers are able to convey their intent to the stockholders. Owners will realize that dividends can only be paid from the Unappropriated Retained Earnings account, and they will also understand the purpose for the appropriation by simply looking at the account title, Appropriated Retained Earnings: Plant Expansion.

Corporation laws often require other appropriations of retained earnings. For example, when bonds are issued, the bond contract may call for an appropriation of retained earnings equal to that of the stockholders for bond indebtedness. In addition, a restriction on retained earnings is required by most states when corporations buy back their own stock.

DIVIDEND DISTRIBUTIONS

Cash Dividends

Dividends are a distribution of profits. A cash dividend involves both the cash account and the capital account, Retained Earnings. To pay a cash dividend, two requirements are necessary.

1. Retained Earnings must have a credit balance.
2. Adequate cash must be available to pay the dividend.

The first requirement is a legal one, as most states require a credit balance in the Retained Earnings account. The second requirement is practical. Excess cash must be available to give to the stockholders to pay the cash dividend. As managers of the corporation, the board of directors must determine when enough cash is available to both meet the daily requirements and pay a dividend. If there is adequate cash to pay expenses and pay the dividend, the board of directors may declare the cash dividend. There are three important dates to be considered when declaring a dividend. They are as follows.

1. The date of declaration of the dividend
2. The date of record
3. The date of payment

The board of directors will decide what these three dates will be. On the date of declaration, the board of directors of the corporation makes a formal declaration to pay the dividend. Thereafter, the corporation is liable to pay the dividend. A journal entry is made on this day to show the declaration. The second date is the one used to determine who are the owners of the stock. The names of the owners appearing in the stockholders' registrar on this day will be the ones to receive the dividends. No journal entry is required on this day. The third date is the day the checks will be mailed to the owners, and the journal entry is made to remove the liability. For example, assume the board of directors of the Jonesboro Corporation declares a $.10 per share dividend on December 13 to the stockholders of record of December 18 to be paid on December 31, 19X3. Assume that 100,000 common shares are outstanding. The journal entries to record these transactions are as follows.

1. Date of declaration

GENERAL JOURNAL					Page
Date	Description	Post. Ref.	Debit	Credit	
19XX *Dec.* *13*	*Retained Earnings*		*1 0 0 0 0* —		
	Cash Dividends Payable			*1 0 0 0 0* —	
	To Record the Declaration of a $.10 per Share				
	Dividend on 100,000 Common Shares Outstanding				

2. Date of record—no entry

3. Date of payment

GENERAL JOURNAL					Page
Date	Description	Post. Ref.	Debit	Credit	
19XX *Dec.* *31*	*Cash Dividends Payable*		*1 0 0 0 0* —		
	Cash			*1 0 0 0 0* —	
	To Record Payment of the Dividend Declared				
	on December 13, 19X3				

On the date of declaration, the Retained Earnings account is reduced by the debit showing the expected distribution of profits. Cash Dividends Payable is credited, and this account is classified as a current liability and will remain so until paid. Upon payment of the dividend, the liability is removed by a debit to Cash Dividends Payable and a credit to Cash. If Joyce York owns 1,000 shares, she will receive a check for $100.

Stock Dividends

stock dividend
a distribution by a corporation of its own unissued stock to the stockholders who give nothing in exchange

A **stock dividend** is a distribution by a corporation of its own unissued stock to the stockholders who are required to give nothing in exchange for these shares. When this occurs, it may be because the corporation does not have excess cash to give the owners, but does have authorized and unissued shares of stock. A clear distinction exists between a cash and a stock dividend. A cash dividend reduces both assets and stockholders' equity; a stock dividend has no effect on assets. A stock dividend involves nothing more than a transfer of an amount from retained earnings to paid-in capital. In effect, the shareholders use their profits (retained earnings) to buy the stock. The amount transferred from retained earnings to paid-in capital is determined by the number of shares to be given to the owners and the market price of the stock. To illustrate, assume that the Roberts Corporation has the following stockholders' equity.

STOCKHOLDERS' EQUITY	
Paid-In Capital	
Common Stock, $20 par value, 50,000 shares authorized, 10,000 shares issued and outstanding	$200000 —
Premium on Common Stock	100000 —
Total Paid-In Capital	300000 —
Retained Earnings	78000 —
Total Stockholders' Equity	$378000 —

Assume that on October 31, when the market price is $40 a share, the board of directors declares a 5 percent stock dividend to the November 15 stockholders of record, to be distributed on December 23, 19X8. The calculation of the stock dividend is as follows.

1. 5% × 10,000 shares outstanding = 500 shares to be distributed
2. 500 shares × $40 market price = $20,000
   ($20,000 is the debit to Retained Earnings)
3. 500 shares × $20 par value = $10,000
   ($10,000 is the credit to Common Stock Dividend to Be Distributed at par)
4. $20,000 (from step 2) − $10,000 (from step 3) = $10,000
   ($10,000 is a credit to Premium on Common Stock)

The journal entries to record the declaration and distribution of the stock dividend are as follows.

GENERAL JOURNAL				Page	
Date	Description	Post. Ref.	Debit	Credit	
19XX Oct. 31	Retained Earnings		2 0 0 0 0 —		
	Common Stock Dividend to				
	Be Distributed			1 0 0 0 0 —	
	Premium on Common Stock			1 0 0 0 0 —	
	To Record the Declaration of a 500 Share				
	Stock Dividend at the Market Price of				
	$40 per Share				

Nov. 15   No entry

GENERAL JOURNAL				Page	
Date	Description	Post. Ref.	Debit	Credit	
19XX Dec. 23	Common Stock Dividend to Be Distributed		1 0 0 0 0 —		
	Common Stock			1 0 0 0 0 —	
	To Record the Distribution of the Common Stock				
	Dividend Declared on October 31				

The entries decrease the Retained Earnings account, but increase the Common Stock or Paid-In Capital account, keeping the total stockholders' equity the same. Because there are more common shares outstanding after the stock dividend, the equity per share decreases, but the total stockholders' equity stays the same. The stockholders' equity section of the balance sheet after the stock dividend is as follows.

STOCKHOLDERS' EQUITY		
Paid-In Capital		
Common Stock, $20 par value, 50,000 shares authorized, 10,500 shares issued		
and outstanding		$210000 —
Premium on Common Stock		110000 —
Total Paid-In Capital		320000 —
Retained Earnings		58000 —
Total Stockholders' Equity		$378000 —

The equity per share before the stock dividend is $37.80 per share. The equity per share after the stock dividend is $36.00 per share. For example, assume that John Brown owned 100 shares before the stock dividend. The total number of shares he received is five, and his total equity both before and after the stock dividend is $3,780. Before the stock dividend, he owned 100 shares at $37.80 equity per share for a total equity of $3,780. After the stock dividend, he owned 105 shares at $36 equity per share for a total equity of $3,780.

The account Common Stock Dividend to Be Distributed is classified as a Paid-In Capital Account. It is not to be confused with the Cash Dividends Payable account, which is a liability (see Appendix 22A on page 834). Stock dividends are declared when there are unissued shares and retained earnings, but no excess cash.

Stock Splits

stock split
the calling in of the old stock and issuing additional new stock to take the place of the old stock

A successful corporation may wish to reduce the market price of its stock to make it more attractive to potential investors. This is accomplished by a stock split. A **stock split** is the calling in of the old stock and issuing additional new shares to take the place of the old stock. For example, a corporation having outstanding $20 par value stock selling for $50 a share may call in the old shares and issue two new shares having $10 par value each. The stock split has no effect on paid-in capital, retained earnings, or total stockholders' equity. It will double the number of shares outstanding and should decrease the market price to $25 per share. Only a memorandum entry is necessary to record a stock split. This entry may read as follows:

> *Called in the outstanding $20 par value common stock and issued
> two new shares of $10 par value common stock for each old share.*

In the event there are treasury shares, which are explained in the
following paragraphs, the treasury shares will also split. The cost
per share will then be recalculated to reflect this split. If the treasury shares are reissued, the new cost-per-share basis will then be
used.

TREASURY STOCK

treasury stock
previously issued
stock that is repur-
chased by the corpo-
ration from the
owners

A corporation may decide to buy back some of the stock that it has
previously sold. Such stock is called Treasury Stock. **Treasury
Stock** is previously issued stock that is repurchased by the corporation from the owners; it may be either common or preferred.
Treasury stock may be given to employees as a bonus or to increase the company's earnings per share. Treasury stock is classified as a contra-equity account and will subtract from stockholders' equity on the balance sheet. It reduces both assets and
stockholders' equity. Most states require an appropriation of retained earnings when treasury stock is purchased. The shares repurchased are no longer outstanding and thus are excluded in any
type of dividend declaration, as well as other calculations, such as
equity per share and earnings per share, to be discussed later.
Treasury stock may be held indefinitely, or it may be reissued or
retired.

Purchase of Treasury Stock

When a corporation purchases its own stock, it reduces cash as
well as stockholders' equity. To illustrate, assume that on November 15 Donelly Corporation purchased 500 shares of its own common stock paying $15 per share. The entry to record this purchase
is as follows.

GENERAL JOURNAL					Page	
Date	Description	Post. Ref.	Debit		Credit	
19XX *Nov.* 15	*Treasury Stock*		7 5 0 0 —			
	Cash				7 5 0 0 —	
	To Record the Purchase of 500 Shares of					
	Treasury Stock at $15 per Share					

The cost of the treasury stock is $7,500, which reduces the cash. Because the stock had been previously sold, the paid-in capital account Common Stock includes this stock. After the stock is repurchased, the balance of the contra-equity account Treasury Stock ($7,500) is deducted from total stockholders' equity. The separate account Treasury Stock is used to show the deduction rather than deducting this sum directly from the Common Stock account. Treasury stock will be shown in the stockholders' equity section of the balance sheet as a deduction from stockholders' equity as shown in Appendix 22A on page 834.

Sale of Treasury Stock

A corporation may not wish to hold its own treasury stock but may decide to sell it again. Assume that on December 12 Donelly Corporation sells 250 shares of the treasury stock, which it purchased at $15 per share, for $18 per share. The entry to record this sale is as follows.

GENERAL JOURNAL					Page	
Date	Description	Post. Ref.	Debit		Credit	
19XX *Dec.* 12	*Cash*		4 5 0 0 —			
	Treasury Stock				3 7 5 0 —	
	Paid-In Capital from Sale of Treasury Stock				7 5 0 —	
	To Record the Sale of 250 Shares of Treasury					
	Stock at $18 per Share					

When treasury stock is reissued above cost, the difference is credited to a special account called Paid-In Capital from Sale of Treasury Stock, which is classified as a capital account in the paid-in capital portion of the stockholders' equity section of the balance sheet. The 250 shares reissued will again be outstanding for dividend purposes and for equity per share and earnings per share calculations.

Appropriation of Retained Earnings: Treasury Stock

The purchase of treasury stock will require an equal appropriation of retained earnings. Assume the same facts as before when Donelly Corporation purchased the 500 shares of treasury stock at $15 per share. The entry to show the appropriation is as follows.

	GENERAL JOURNAL			Page	
Date	**Description**	**Post. Ref.**	**Debit**	**Credit**	
19XX *Nov.* *15*	*Retained Earnings*		7 5 0 0 —		
	Appropriation of Retained Earnings for				
	Treasury Stock			7 5 0 0 —	
	To Record the Necessary Appropriation of				
	Retained Earnings for Treasury Stock				

When the treasury stock is reissued, a reversing entry is then made removing the restriction on retained earnings. The reversing entry after the December 12 transaction, which records the reissuing of 250 shares of treasury stock at $18 per share, is as follows.

GENERAL JOURNAL						Page	
Date	Description	Post. Ref.	Debit			Credit	
19XX Dec. 12	Appropriation of Retained Earnings for Treasury Stock		3750	—			
	Retained Earnings					3750	—
	To Record the Removal of the Appropriation						
	of 250 Shares of Treasury Stock Reissued to						
	Stockholders						

FEDERAL INCOME TAXES ON EARNINGS

Corporations are subject to federal income taxes. In addition, some states and municipalities also levy an income tax on the corporation's earnings. A corporation must determine the amount of federal income tax it owes by examining the current Internal Revenue Code. The Internal Revenue Code contains the tax rules and applications to determine the proper tax to be paid. The amount of the tax, when determined, is recorded as an expense and will reduce the earnings of the corporation. At the time the income tax liability is recorded, Federal Income Tax Expense is debited and Federal Income Taxes Payable is credited.

Assume that Donelly Corporation has earnings before taxes of $50,000 and the tax liability is 50 percent of these earnings. The entry to record the payment of this liability to the government is as follows.

GENERAL JOURNAL						Page	
Date	Description	Post. Ref.	Debit			Credit	
19XX Dec. 31	Federal Income Taxes Payable		25000	—			
	Cash					25000	—
	To Record Payment of the 19X7 Federal Income						
	Tax						

The federal income tax is shown separately from the operating expenses and is the last expense to be deducted on the income statement. The reader of the income statement can see the effect of the income tax on earnings, the income from operations, and the net income or bottom line. An illustrative income statement for Sims Computers, Incorporated, appears as Appendix 22B, page 835.

EARNINGS PER SHARE

earnings per share
net income of a corporation stated on a per-share basis for common stock

Earnings per share is the net income of a corporation stated on a per-share basis for common stock. It is calculated only for the common stock of a corporation. Many financial analysts consider earnings per share an important determination of the success of a corporation. It is listed daily in *The Wall Street Journal* for corporations listed by the New York Stock Exchange.

If a corporation has one class of stock, the calculation for earnings per share divides net income by the number of common shares outstanding. Earnings per share is the measure of net income as it relates to each common share outstanding. Assume that net income is $50,000 and there are 10,000 common shares outstanding. The earnings per share calculation is as follows:

$$\$50,000 \div 10,000 = \$5 \text{ Earnings per Share (EPS)}$$

If a corporation has more than one class of stock, preferred cumulative shareholders have a claim on net income for any unpaid dividends. This claim reduces the amount of earnings to the common shareholders. For example, assume that preferred cumulative stockholders have a $2,000 per year dividend preference on earnings that are unpaid, and net income is $50,000. Assume also that there are 10,000 common shares outstanding. The calculation for earnings per share for common stock is as follows:

$$(\$50,000 - \$2,000) \div 10,000 = \$4.80 \text{ EPS}$$

If there are no preferred dividends unpaid, the earnings per share is calculated by dividing the number of common shares outstanding into the net income.

The American Institute of Certified Public Accountants (AICPA), the rule-making body for accountants, requires that every income statement prepared by a corporation contain the earnings per share (EPS) calculation. Accounting Principles Board Opinion 15[1] details the procedure for calculating the EPS under a variety of conditions and mandates its inclusion on every published corporate income statement.

SUMMARY

Earnings of a corporation occur when revenues are greater than expenses and are recorded in a special account titled Retained Earnings. When reading a balance sheet, a stockholder can distinguish between the capital invested in the business and the earnings (profits) retained. A number of things besides profits affect the balance in the Retained Earnings account. A net loss, a cash dividend, and a stock dividend all decrease this account. As earnings accumulate, the board of directors may wish to designate these earnings for special purposes by appropriating retained earnings. A general journal entry is made to appropriate retained earnings and a special appropriation account is used. Once the appropriation is made, the unappropriated earnings are the only earnings available for dividend payments to the stockholders. Legal requirements, such as bond indebtedness and the purchase of treasury stock, also require that appropriations be made by the board of directors.

Cash dividends may be paid from the unappropriated retained earnings. Most states require a credit balance in Retained Earnings before a dividend may be declared. The board of directors must also determine if there is excess cash before declaring a cash dividend. Once a dividend is declared, it becomes a liability of the corporation until paid.

If no excess cash is available, the board of directors may declare a stock dividend. To do this, the corporation must have unissued stock and a credit balance in the Retained Earnings account. The board of directors determines the number of shares to be given to the stockholders. The current market price of a share of stock is used to determine the value of the stock dividend declaration. A stock dividend is a distribution of earnings retained in the business and does not require any cash.

The three dates that must be determined by the board of directors before a dividend can be formally declared are the (1) date of

---

[1]APB Opinion No. 15, "Earnings per Share" (New York: AICPA, 1969).

declaration, (2) date of record, and (3) date of payment. The first date is the day the board of directors formally declares the dividend. On the second date, the stockholders' registrar is used to determine who the owners are on this day. The third date is the day the dividend is to be paid.

A corporation may buy back stock that has been previously sold. These previously issued shares are repurchased from the present owners. These repurchased shares are called treasury stock. Treasury stock is classified as a contra-equity account. On the stockholders' equity section of the balance sheet, it is a reduction of capital.

Total stockholders' equity may be expressed on a per-share basis called equity per share. A corporation having one class of stock divides the total common stockholders' equity by the number of shares outstanding. Equity per share is used by common stockholders to determine their equity or interest in the corporation. If more than one class of stock exists, the preferred stockholders also have a claim on earnings. The claims of the preferred stockholders must be considered in determining the equity per share for the common stockholders.

Review of Accounting Terminology

Following is a list of the accounting terminology for this chapter.

appropriated retained earnings	stock dividend
earnings per share	stock split
retained earnings	treasury stock

Fill in the blank with the correct word or term from the list.

1. Calling in the old stock and issuing additional new stock to take the place of the old stock is called a _____.

2. Net income of a corporation stated on a per-share basis for common stock is called _____.

3. _____ are earnings retained in the business designated for a special purpose.

4. _____ is previously issued stock that is repurchased by the corporation from the owners.

5. Undistributed earnings or losses of a corporation is called _____.

6. A distribution by a corporation of its own unissued stock to the stockholders who give nothing in exchange for these shares is called a _____.

Match the following words and terms on the left with the definitions on the right.

7. appropriated retained earnings
8. earnings per share
9. retained earnings
10. stock dividend
11. stock split
12. treasury stock

a. the calling in of the old stock and issuing additional new stock to take the place of the old stock
b. the undistributed earnings or losses of a corporation
c. previously issued stock that is repurchased by the corporation from the stockholders
d. a distribution by a corporation of its own unissued stock to the stockholders who give nothing in exchange for these shares
e. earnings retained in the business designated for a special purpose
f. net income of a corporation stated on a per-share basis for common stock

Exercises

Exercise 22.1
preparing the general journal entries for appropriations of retained earnings

On September 30, the board of directors of Lewis Corporation decided to designate part of the $586,000 credit balance in the Retained Earnings account for a future plant expansion program.

a. Prepare the journal entry on September 30 to record an appropriation of $65,000 for this purpose.
b. What dollar amount of the retained earnings is available for dividends after the appropriation?

Exercise 22.2
recording in T-accounts selected transactions affecting retained earnings

Set up T-accounts for the following: Cash, Accounts Receivable, Truck, Notes Payable, Common Stock, Retained Earnings, Revenue, Expenses, and Income Summary.

a. Record the following transactions into the T-accounts.
 1. Sold common stock for $25,000 cash.
 2. Sold services for $12,000 on account.
 3. Bought a $30,000 truck, paying $15,000 in cash and giving a note for the remainder.
 4. Paid $10,000 expenses in cash.
 5. Closed the Revenue and Expense accounts.
 6. Closed the Income Summary account.

b. Answer the following questions using the above information.
 1. What is the balance in the Common Stock account?
 2. What is the balance in the Truck account?
 3. What is the balance in the Accounts Receivable account?
 4. What is the balance in the Retained Earnings account?
 5. What is the balance in the Cash account?
 6. Can the corporation declare a legal cash dividend?
 7. Can it pay the dividend?

Exercise 22.3
preparing general journal entries for a cash dividend

The Encop Corporation has 55,000 common shares of stock outstanding. The board of directors declared a $.25 per share cash dividend on March 7 to the stockholders of record on March 11 to be paid on March 27. Prepare the journal entries on March 7 and March 27 to record the declaration and payment of this dividend.

Exercise 22.4
preparing general journal entries for a stock dividend

The Ellen Corporation has $5 par value common stock, 1,000,000 shares authorized, 525,000 issued and outstanding. The board of directors declared a 5 percent stock dividend on June 2 to the stockholders of record on June 19 to be issued on July 3, when the market price of the stock is $7 per share. Prepare the required journal entries on June 2 and July 3 to record these transactions.

Exercise 22.5
preparing various general journal entries and preparing the stockholders' equity section of the balance sheet

On January 31, the stockholders' equity section of the balance sheet of the Holiday Corporation appeared as follows.

STOCKHOLDERS' EQUITY		
Paid-In Capital		
Common Stock, $25 par value, 500,000 shares authorized, 20,000 shares issued		
and outstanding		$5 0 0 0 0 0 —
Premium on Common Stock		1 0 0 0 0 0 —
Total Paid-In Capital		$6 0 0 0 0 0 —
Retained Earnings		1 5 0 0 0 0 —
Total Stockholders' Equity		$7 5 0 0 0 0 —

a. Prepare the necessary journal entries to record the following transactions.

Jan. 31 the board of directors declared a $.05 per share cash dividend to the stockholders of record on February 14 to be paid on February 25

Feb. 4 appropriated $50,000 of retained earnings for plant expansion

Feb. 14 declared a 1 percent stock dividend to the shareholders of record on February 28 to be issued on March 15; the market price is $30 per share

Feb. 25 paid the cash dividend previously declared

Feb. 28 closed the net income of $30,000 from Income Summary to Retained Earnings

Feb. 28 declared a $.05 per share cash dividend to the stockholders of record on March 15 to be paid on March 31 (Hint: Use a T-account for Retained Earnings to help determine the ending balance.)

b. Prepare the stockholders' equity section of the balance sheet as of February 28.

Exercise 22.6
preparing the general journal entries for transactions involving treasury stock and preparing the stockholders' equity section of the balance sheet showing treasury stock

On April 15, the stockholders' equity section of the balance sheet for the Benito Corporation was as follows.

STOCKHOLDERS' EQUITY		
Paid in Capital		
Common Stock, $10 par value, 100,000 shares authorized, 60,000 shares issued and outstanding		$600000 —
Premium on Common Stock		48000 —
Total Paid-In Capital		$648000 —
Retained Earnings		90000 —
Total Stockholders' Equity		$738000 —

On April 15, the corporation purchased 1,000 shares of treasury stock at $17 per share.

a. Prepare the journal entries to record this purchase and the appropriation of retained earnings.

b. Prepare the stockholders' equity section of the balance sheet after the purchase.

c. How many common shares are outstanding after the transactions of April 15?

Exercise 22.7
preparing the general journal entries for the sale of treasury stock

On May 13, the Benito Corporation of Exercise 22.6 sold 500 shares of the treasury stock at $18 per share; and on August 25, it sold the remaining shares at $20 a share. Prepare the journal entries on May 13 and August 25 to record these transactions.

Exercise 22.8
preparing an income statement

The Justin Corporation has the following account balances. Prepare an income statement for the year ended December 31, assuming that the federal income tax rate for this corporation is 50 percent and that 10,000 common shares are outstanding. Include the earnings per share on the Income Statement.

Cost of Goods Sold	$135,000
General Expenses	8,000
Revenue	180,000
Selling Expenses	5,000

Problems

Problem 22.1
preparing the general journal entries for the declaration and payment of a cash dividend

On January 31, 19X8, the stockholders' equity section of the balance sheet for the Linder Corporation was as follows.

STOCKHOLDERS' EQUITY	
Paid-In Capital	
Common Stock, $20 par value, 30,000 shares authorized, 25,000 shares issued	
and outstanding	$500000 —
Premium on Common Stock	90000 —
Total Paid-In Capital	$590000 —
Retained Earnings	230000 —
Total Stockholders' Equity	$820000 —

Instructions

1. *Prepare the general journal entries to record the following transactions*

   Feb. 2 the board of directors declared a $.50 per share cash dividend to the stockholders of record on February 14 to be paid on February 25

   Feb. 2 appropriated $50,000 of retained earnings for a plant expansion program

   Feb. 25 paid the cash dividend declared on February 2

   Feb. 28 closed the Income Summary account, which has a credit balance of $125,000 to Retained Earnings

2. *Answer the following questions.*

   a. *What is the amount of earnings retained in the business on February 28?*

   b. *What is the amount of retained earnings available for dividends? Show all calculations.*

   c. *What is the average price per share of the common stock? Show all calculations.*

Problem 22.2

preparing the general journal entries for various transactions including sale of stock, purchase of treasury stock, declaration and payment of both a cash and stock dividend, and posting to the accounts

The Kelsey Corporation was organized on January 2, 19X8, with 10,000 shares of $50 par value, 12 % cumulative, nonparticipating preferred stock and 50,000 shares of no-par common stock.

Instructions

1. *Prepare the general journal entries to record the following selected transactions without explanations. (Place the letter of each transaction in the date column of the journal.)*

   a. *Issued 10,000 shares of common stock at $12 per share for cash; the board of directors set a $10 stated value for the common stock.*

   b. *Issued 1,000 shares of preferred stock at $50 per share for cash.*

   c. *Repurchased 500 shares of common stock from the estate of a deceased stockholder for $7,500 cash.*

   d. *Closed the Income Summary account, which had a credit balance of $96,000.*

   e. *Declared the yearly cash dividend to the preferred stockholders and declared a $.10 per share cash dividend to the common stockholders.*

   f. *Reissued the treasury stock at $16 per share for cash.*

   g. *Declared a 5 percent stock dividend when the market price was $16 per share.*

2. *Post the transactions into T-accounts with the following account titles: Cash, Cash Dividends Payable, Treasury Stock, Preferred Stock, Common Stock, Common Stock Dividends to Be Distributed, Paid-In Capital in Excess of Stated Value, Paid-In Capital from Sale of Treasury Stock, Retained Earnings, and Income Summary.*

3. *Determine the balance of the Retained Earnings account after the above transactions are posted.*

4. *Prepare the stockholders' equity section of the balance sheet as of December 31, 19X8.*

Problem 22.3

preparing the general journal entries for various transactions and preparing the stockholders' equity section of the balance sheet

The Bender Corporation has a credit balance of $250,000 in retained earnings as of October 1, 19X7. On that date, the corporation had 100,000 authorized shares of $10 par value common stock of which 50,000 shares were issued at $15 per share.

Instructions

1. Prepare the general journal entries to record the following transactions without explanations.

19X7

Oct. 31 the board of directors declared a $.20 per share cash dividend to the stockholders of record on November 15 to be paid on November 30

Nov. 30 paid the cash dividend declared on October 31

Dec. 3 the board of directors declared a 5 percent stock dividend to the stockholders of record on December 15 to be paid on December 23; the market price of the stock on December 3 is $18 per share

Dec. 23 distributed the stock dividend declared on December 3

Dec. 28 the board of directors voted to split the common shares issuing two $5 par value common shares for each $10 par value common share held; the shares are to be mailed to stockholders on December 30

Dec. 30 mailed the new shares to the stockholders

Dec. 31 closed Income Summary account with a credit balance of $86,500 to Retained Earnings (Hint: Using T-accounts simplifies this problem.)

2. Prepare the stockholders' equity section of the balance sheet as of December 31, 19X7.

Problem 22.4

opening the capital accounts, journalizing various transactions, preparing the stockholders' equity section for two years, and calculating earnings per share

The stockholders' equity section of the balance sheet for the Sherry Corporation as of December 31, 19X6 is as follows.

STOCKHOLDERS' EQUITY		
Paid-In Capital		
Preferred Stock, 15%, $50 par value, cumulative		
nonparticipating, 6,000 shares authorized,		
issued, and outstanding	$300000 —	
Common Stock, $5 par value, 300,000 shares authorized,		
150,000 shares issued of which 10,000 are in the treasury	750000 —	
Premium on Common Stock	75000 —	
Total Paid-In Capital		$1125000 —
Retained Earnings		
Appropriated Retained Earnings for Treasury Stock	60000 —	
Unappropriated Retained Earnings	465000 —	
Total Retained Earnings		525000 —
Total Paid-In Capital and Retained Earnings		$1650000 —
Less: Treasury Stock at Cost		60000 —
Total Stockholders' Equity		$1590000 —

Instructions 1. *Enter the following account titles and balances into T-accounts:*

Cash	$490,000
Cash Dividends Payable	0
Treasury Stock	60,000
Preferred Stock	300,000
Common Stock	750,000
Common Stock Dividend to Be Distributed	0
Premium on Common Stock	75,000
Paid-In Capital from Sale of Treasury Stock	0
Appropriated Retained Earnings for Treasury Stock	60,000
Unappropriated Retained Earnings	465,000
Income Summary	0

2. *Prepare the general journal entries to record the following transactions without explanations.*

19X7

Nov. 15   reissued one-half the treasury shares at $7 per share for cash

Dec. 31   Sherry Corporation declared and paid the preferred stock cash dividend and also declared and paid a $.50 cash dividend to the common stockholders

Dec. 31   closed Income Summary with a credit balance of $297,500 into Retained Earnings

19X8

Jan. 8 split the common shares two for one, giving two $2.50 par value shares for each $5 par value share

Dec. 31 declared a 5 percent stock dividend to the stockholders of record on January 15, 19X9, to be distributed on January 31, 19X9; the market price of the stock is $3.50 per share

Dec. 31 Sherry Corporation declared and paid the preferred cash dividend

Dec. 31 paid the annual preferred stock cash dividend

Dec. 31 closed Income Summary with a credit balance of $308,000 to Retained Earnings

3. *Post the transactions into the T-accounts.*

4. *Prepare the stockholders' equity section of the balance sheet as of December 31, 19X7.*

5. *Prepare the stockholders' equity section of the balance sheet as of December 31, 19X8.*

6. *Calculate the earnings per share for 19X7.*

7. *Calculate the earnings per share for 19X8.*

Problem 22.5
completing a worksheet and preparing the income statement and the balance sheet from the worksheet

As of December 31, 19X9, Pill Incorporated has 8 %, $100 par value, cumulative preferred stock. There are 1,000 shares authorized and issued. It also has no par common stock, 500,000 shares are authorized, and 28,275 shares have been issued and are outstanding. The adjusted trial balance for Pill Incorporated is as follows.

	PILL INCORPORATED PARTIAL WORKSHEET FOR YEAR ENDED DECEMBER 31, 19X9	Adjusted Trial Balance	
		Debit	Credit
Cash		$2 25 5 75 —	
Accounts Receivable (Net)		8 5 0 0 0 —	
Equipment		3 9 0 0 0 —	
Accumulated Depreciation: Equipment			$ 1 1 0 0 0 —
Building		4 4 0 0 0 —	
Accumulated Depreciation: Building			4 0 0 0 —
Patent		1 8 5 0 0 0 —	
Accounts Payable			6 4 2 5 —
Income Taxes Payable			2 0 8 8 0 —
Mortgage Payable			5 8 9 5 0 —
Preferred Stock			1 0 0 0 0 0 —
Common Stock			2 5 0 0 0 0 —
Paid-In Capital from Sale of Treasury Stock			3 5 0 0 —
Donated Capital			1 5 0 0 0 —
Retained Earnings			8 6 2 0 0 —
Sales (Net)			2 8 0 0 0 0 —
Cost of Goods Sold		2 1 0 0 0 0 —	
Total Operating Expenses		2 6 5 0 0 —	
Income Tax Expense		2 0 8 8 0 —	
Totals		$8 3 5 9 5 5 —	$8 3 5 9 5 5 —

Instructions

1. Complete the worksheet for Pill, Incorporated, on December 31.

2. Prepare the December 31 income statement, including the earnings per share, assuming there are no preferred dividends in arrears.

3. Prepare the December 31 income statement, including the earnings per share, assuming the preferred dividend is unpaid for 19X9.

4. Prepare a balance sheet assuming the preferred dividend is unpaid for 19X9.

Appendix 22A

SIMS COMPUTERS, INCORPORATED BALANCE SHEET DECEMBER 31, 19XX			
Assets			
Current Assets			
Cash	$ 71620 —		
Marketable Securities (at LCM)	14500 —		
Notes Receivable	6280 —		
Accounts Receivable (Net)	10200 —		
Subscriptions Receivable: Common Stock	3500 —		
Supply Inventory	12500 —		
Prepaid Expenses	2500 —		
Total Current Assets		$121100 —	
Investments and Funds			
Bond Sinking Fund	20000 —		
Filet Corporation: Common Stock	223600 —		
Total Investments and Funds		243600 —	
Plant and Equipment			
Equipment (Net)	206000 —		
Building (Net)	300000 —		
Land	100000 —		
Total Plant and Equipment		606000 —	
Intangible Assets			
Organization Costs	30000 —		
Patent	125000 —		
Total Intangible Assets		155000 —	
Total Assets			$1125700 —

Liabilities

Current Liabilities		
Notes Payable	$ 2 0 0 0 —	
Accounts Payable	5 0 0 0 —	
Dividends Payable	1 8 0 0 —	
Interest Payable	1 5 0 0 —	
Total Current Liabilities		$ 1 0 3 0 0 —
Long-Term Liabilities		
Mortgage Payable, 10%, due 19XX	5 0 0 0 0 —	
Bonds Payable, 8%, due 19XX 80,000		
Less: Unamortized Discount 5,600	7 4 4 0 0 —	
Total Long-Term Liabilities		1 2 4 4 0 0 —
Total Liabilities		$1 3 4 7 0 0 —

Stockholders' Equity

Paid-In Capital			
Preferred Stock, $10 par value, 9%,			
cumulative, nonparticipating, 10,000 shares			
authorized and 2,000 shares issued	$ 2 0 0 0 0 —		
Common Stock, $5 par value, 100,000 shares			
authorized, 75,000 shares issued of which			
1,000 are in the treasury	3 7 5 0 0 0 —		
Premium on Common Stock	1 6 4 1 0 0 —		
Common Stock Dividend to Be Distributed	1 8 9 0 0 —		
Common Stock Subscribed	5 0 0 0 —		
Paid-In Capital from Sale of Treasury Stock	2 0 0 0 —		
Donated Capital	5 4 0 0 0 —		
Total Paid-In and Donated Capital		6 3 9 0 0 0 —	
Retained Earnings			
Unappropriated Retained Earnings	2 4 2 0 0 0 —		
Appropriated for Bonded Indebtedness	8 0 0 0 0 —		
Appropriated for Plant Expansion	3 0 0 0 0 —		
Appropriated for Treasury Stock	8 0 0 0 —		
Total Retained Earnings		3 6 0 0 0 0 —	
Total Paid-In Capital and Retained Earnings		9 9 9 0 0 0 —	
Less: Treasury Stock at Cost		8 0 0 0 —	
Total Stockholders' Equity			9 9 1 0 0 0 —
Total Liabilities and Stockholders' Equity			$1 1 2 5 7 0 0 —

Footnote 10. The cumulative dividend on preferred stock that remains unpaid on this balance sheet date is $1,800. The $1,800 is in arrears and is a claim on assets by preferred stockholders.

Appendix 22B

SIMS COMPUTERS, INCORPORATED INCOME STATEMENT FOR YEAR ENDED DECEMBER 31, 19XX		
Revenues		
Professional Fees	$1 3 3 4 6 0 0 —	
Other Income	2 5 0 0 0 —	
Total Revenue		$1 3 5 9 6 0 0 —
Operating Expenses		
Cost of Goods Sold	1 9 8 4 0 0 —	
Salaries Expense	3 5 8 0 0 0 —	
Travel Expense	1 5 9 4 0 0 —	
Advertising Expense	1 2 5 0 0 0 —	
Supplies Used	7 5 2 5 0 —	
Insurance Expense	1 3 6 2 3 0 —	
Depreciation Expense	2 3 2 0 0 —	
Bond Interest Expense	7 2 0 0 —	
Interest Expense	5 0 0 0 —	
Total Operating Expenses		1 0 8 7 6 8 0 —
Income from Operations		2 7 1 9 2 0 —
Federal Income Taxes		1 3 5 9 6 0 —
Net Income		$1 3 5 9 6 0 —
Earnings Per Share		
Operating Income $3.65[a]		
Net Income 1.81		

[a]Preferred dividend preference:

2,000 Shares × .90 = $1,800

Common Shares Outstanding

75,000 Issued − 1,000 Shares in the Treasury = 74,000

EPS—Calculation for Common Stock

Operating Income: ($271,920 − $1,800) ÷ 74,000 = $3.65

Net Income: ($135,960 − $1,800) ÷ 74,000 = $1.81

CHAPTER 23

Corporations: Issuing Bonds

LEARNING OBJECTIVES

When you have completed this chapter, you should

1. have a better understanding of accounting terminology.

2. understand the difference between stocks and bonds.

3. be able to explain the advantages and disadvantages of issuing bonds.

4. be able to explain why bonds are sold at a discount or at a premium.

5. be able to use present-value tables to calculate the discount or the premium.

6. be able to calculate and journalize the amortization of either the discount or the premium.

7. be able to prepare entries to account for the issuance, the interest payments, the year-end accounting, and the retiring of bonds.

8. be able to define a bond sinking fund and tell how it is used.

The terms *stocks* and *bonds* are commonly referred to in the news media and by those who invest and analyze corporate finance. There are important differences between these two terms. Stocks represent the equity or ownership of a corporation, and stockholders manage the corporation through the board of directors. On the other hand, **bonds** are long-term notes payable that bear interest. The bondholders are creditors of the corporation and as such have no say in management.

bonds
long-term notes payable that bear interest

In the marketplace, stocks are sold by quotations based on dollars and cents. For instance, a share of stock may be quoted and sold at 25-½. This means that one share of stock will sell for $25.50 plus transfer fees. **Transfer fees** are generally handled by a stockbroker and are the costs involved in buying and selling stocks and bonds (transacting an ownership exchange). Stockbrokers act as agents for both buyers and sellers.

transfer fees
the costs involved in transacting an ownership exchange of buying and selling stocks and bonds

Bonds are quoted and sold as a percentage of the **face value.** The face value is the dollar amount appearing on the face of the bond, such as $1,000. The face amount is also referred to as the principal. Assume that a bond has a $1,000 face value and is quoted at 100 percent. The bond will sell for 100 percent times the face value of $1,000, or $1,000. If the bond is quoted at 97 percent, it will sell for $970, below face value at a discount. If the bond is quoted at 107 percent, it will sell for $1,070, selling at a premium.

face value
the dollar amount appearing on the face of the bond; also referred to as principal

METHODS OF LONG-TERM FINANCING

A corporation may need long-term financing for a number of reasons. It may wish to open branches in new areas, buy new capital equipment, or expand its present facility. Whatever the reason, a decision must be made by the board of directors as to the best method to achieve the long-term goals. The board of directors may decide to use one of the following three methods for its long-term financing needs:

1. issue additional common stock
2. issue preferred stock
3. issue bonds

Each of these alternatives has advantages and disadvantages.

Issuing Additional Common Stock

Issuing additional common stock is an easy way to finance a particular project. It has the advantage of the company incurring no debt obligation. However, unissued stock must be available for this purpose. If no additional unissued shares of stock are available, this method may be ruled out at the outset. If they are available, the issuance of additional common shares will spread the ownership and earnings per share over a larger group of stockholders. The present owners may not want to have their interests diluted, which could prove to be a disadvantage. The board of directors must carefully consider the wishes of the present owners.

Issuing Preferred Stock

The board of directors may choose to issue preferred stock, because doing so will not dilute the present common stock ownership and could prove to be an advantage to the present common stockholders. The charter must provide for this method, and unissued preferred shares must be available. This method could prove to be a disadvantage to the common stockholders, however, because preferred stockholders have first claim on declared dividends and first claim on assets after creditors.

Issuing Bonds

The board may consider issuing bonds because bondholders are creditors and do not share in either management or earnings, as do stockholders. In addition, issuing bonds may increase the earnings per share accruing to the common stockholders. Because the interest on bonded indebtedness is deducted before calculating the federal income tax, the amount of income on which the income tax is calculated is reduced. This, of course, reduces the tax liability. A major disadvantage of issuing bonds is incurring additional debt. In addition, bond interest must be paid in a timely manner whether or not there are any earnings. If interest is not paid when due, the bondholders may take legal action to collect.

For example, assume that Beste Corporation will need to secure $1,000,000 to expand its manufacturing facility. Assume further that there are 300,000 shares of authorized common stock with a par value of $10 and 200,000 common shares issued and outstanding. Also, 10,000 shares of 8 percent, $100 par value preferred stock are authorized, but none has been issued. The controller estimates that the corporation can increase its present earnings to $600,000 annually after the expansion is complete. The following three plans are to be considered.

1. Issue 100,000 additional common shares at $10 each.
2. Issue 10,000 shares of 8%, $100 par value preferred stock.
3. Issue $1,000,000 of 8% bonds.

The results of each plan follow.

	Plan 1 (Common Stock)	Plan 2 (Preferred Stock)	Plan 3 (Bonds)
Expected Earnings Before Bond Interest and Income Tax	$600,000	$600,000	$600,000
Deduct Bond Interest Expense	0	0	(80,000)
Income Before Income Tax	600,000	600,000	520,000
Deduct Income Tax (assume 50%)	300,000	300,000	260,000
Net Income	300,000	300,000	260,000
Preferred Stock Dividend Preference	0	(80,000)	0
Earnings Accruing to the Common Stockholders	$300,000	$220,000	$260,000
Earnings per share			
Plan 1 $300,000 ÷ 300,000	$1.00		
Plan 2 $220,000 ÷ 200,000		$1.10	
Plan 3 $260,000 ÷ 200,000			$1.30

The best alternative from the vantage point of the owners (common stockholders) is Plan 3, because earnings per share is greater in Plan 3 than in the other two plans. Because interest is a deductible expense before calculating income tax, the tax saving of $40,000 in effect pays one-half of the $80,000 yearly interest expense of the bonds.

CLASSIFICATION OF BONDS

A corporation may issue several kinds of bonds and will choose the type of bond suited to its own special needs. A contract must be developed that will bind both parties—the bondholder and the

bond indenture
a contract between the corporation and the bondholder that contains the terms of the issue

corporation. This contract is called a **bond indenture** or deed of trust. It contains all the provisions for the type of bond to be issued, including the **contract interest rate** and the interest payment dates. Generally, a bank trust officer will oversee the contract for both parties.

contract interest rate
the rate of interest specified on the bond that applies to the face value

Registered and Coupon Bonds

registered bonds
bonds that are issued in the name of the owner

Bonds may be either registered or coupon. **Registered bonds** are those that are issued in the name of the owner (bondholder) and are recorded with the issuing corporation or the trustee. The list of names will be used when paying the interest when due. If the registered bond is sold, it must be properly endorsed and the trustee must be notified; this allows the trustee to change the records to reflect the name and address of the new owner. **Coupon bonds** obtain their name from the interest coupons attached to the bond. The bondholder detaches the coupon and presents it for the interest payment. In some instances, coupon bonds are called **bearer bonds.** The owner is the person bearing or possessing the bond. Registered bonds are much safer to hold than the coupon bonds because of the possible theft or loss of the interest coupons.

coupon bonds
bonds that pay interest on receipt of the coupons attached to the bond

bearer bonds
bonds where the owner is considered to be the one in possession of the bonds

Secured and Unsecured Bonds

secured bonds
bonds that pledge assets of the corporation as security for the debt

Secured bonds are those that pledge an asset of the corporation, such as land or buildings, as security for the debt. Should the corporation default on the bond, the trustee will take legal action to claim the pledged assets for the bondholders. Secured bondholders have first claim on the pledged assets of the corporation. **Debenture bonds,** also called unsecured bonds, are issued solely on the credit rating of the corporation. Independent credit rating agencies will rate corporations according to their credit worthiness. A debenture bondholder creditor has only the corporation's assets to look to for the debt repayment.

debenture bonds
bonds that are issued solely on the credit worthiness of the corporation

Term and Serial Bonds

term bonds
bonds where the entire issue matures at one time

Term bonds are those where the entire issue matures at one time. For example, assume that a corporation issues $100,000, 8%, ten-year term bonds. These bonds will all mature at the same time. In other words, the bondholders lend $100,000 to the corporation, and the corporation must repay the $100,000 to the bondholders at

serial bonds
bonds where the maturity dates range over a number of years

the end of ten years. **Serial bonds,** the most common type, have maturity dates that range over a number of years. Serial bonds may, for example, mature in 5 years, 10 years, or as long as 20 years. Thus, repayment of the debt may be spread over a number of years. Because of the varied maturity dates, serial bonds appeal to a wide range of investors and generally sell quickly. They also appeal to the corporation because it can spread out the repayment of its debt.

Convertible and Callable Bonds

Bonds must appeal to potential investors if they are to be sold; thus certain provisions may be offered in the bond indenture. For example, bonds may be convertible or callable. **Convertible bonds** are those that can be converted to the stock of the issuing corporation. The details of the conversion, found in the bond indenture, may provide that after the bond has been held for five years, the bondholder can exchange the bond for stock. The conversion rules may further state that for each $1,000 bond exchanged, 90 shares of $10 par value common stock will be issued. If the bondholder converts, he or she is no longer a creditor but instead becomes an owner.

convertible bonds
bonds that can be converted to the stock of the issuing corporation according to the terms of the bond indenture

The bond indenture may give the corporation the option of buying the bonds back from the bondholder before the maturity date; these are referred to as **callable bonds.** In most cases where a bond is callable, the contract will provide a redemption rate in excess of 100 percent. For instance, assume that the contract provides for 105 percent callable bonds that may be repurchased by the corporation after five years. If the corporation chooses to exercise this option, it will have to pay $1,050 for each bond with a face value of $1,000.

callable bonds
bonds that may be redeemed or called in at the option of the corporation

SELLING BONDS

A corporation issuing bonds specifies the contract rate of interest to be paid in the bond indenture. Once this contract interest rate is determined, it is a fixed amount that is paid each interest period.

The corporation will never pay more or less interest, regardless of what the bond may sell for or what the market rate of interest is. In choosing a rate initially, the corporation will check the market rate of interest for this type of obligation. The **market rate of interest** is the current rate of interest a borrower is willing to pay and an investor is willing to receive. Once the contract rate of interest is established, a number of weeks, or even months, may still be needed to get all the details of the bond issue in place. During this time, the market rate of interest may increase or decrease. If the market rate of interest at the time the bonds are to be issued is lower than the contract rate, the bonds will sell for a premium because investors will want the higher (the contract) rate of interest. Thus, the demand for the bonds will be great and investors will be willing to pay more than face value in order to get the higher interest rate. If, on the other hand, the market rate of interest is higher than the contract rate of interest, the bonds will be sold at a discount. Investors will demand the market rate of interest on their investment and in order to get it will not be willing to pay the face amount for the bonds. The present-value method is used to determine the price for which the bonds will actually sell. To fully understand the selling price of the bonds, carefully study Appendix 23A: Present Value Concepts.

market rate of interest
the rate of interest a borrower is willing to pay and an investor is willing to receive

ISSUING BONDS

On the day the bonds are issued, the corporation records the details of the issue. The corporation may sell the bonds at face value, at a discount, or at a premium.

Bonds Sold at Face Value

When bonds are sold at 100 percent of their face value, there is no discount or premium. Assume that on January 2, 19XX, a corporation sells its $100,000, 10%, ten-year bonds at 100 percent. In addition, the bond indenture provides for semiannual interest payments on June 30 and December 31. The general journal entries to record this sale and the first interest payment are as follows.

		GENERAL JOURNAL			Page
Date		**Description**	**Post. Ref.**	**Debit**	**Credit**
19XX *Jan.*	2	Cash		1 0 0 0 0 0 —	
		Bonds Payable			1 0 0 0 0 0 —
		To Record the Sale of 10%, 10-Year Bonds Sold			
		at Face Value			
Jun.	30	*Bond Interest Expense*		5 0 0 0 —	
		Cash			5 0 0 0 —
		To Record the Payment of the Semiannual			
		Interest on Bonds			

The yearly bond interest expense is shown on the income statement. Bonds Payable is shown as a long-term liability on the balance sheet. When the bonds mature at the end of ten years, the general journal entry to record payment of cash to the bondholders is as follows.

		GENERAL JOURNAL			Page
Date		**Description**	**Post. Ref.**	**Debit**	**Credit**
19XX *Jan.*	2	*Bonds Payable*		1 0 0 0 0 0 —	
		Cash			1 0 0 0 0 0 —
		To Record the Payment to Bondholders			
		at Maturity			

Bonds Sold at a Discount

A corporation selling bonds when the prevailing market rate of interest is higher than the contract rate of interest can only sell them at a discount, or at a price less than the face value. Assume that a corporation issues $100,000, 10%, ten-year bonds at $88,530, a discount of $11,470. The general journal entry to record this issue is as follows.

GENERAL JOURNAL					Page	
Date	Description	Post. Ref.	Debit		Credit	
19XX *Jan.* 2	*Cash*		8 8 5 3 0 —			
	Discount on Bonds Payable		1 1 4 7 0 —			
	Bonds Payable				1 0 0 0 0 0 —	
	To Record Sale of 10%, 10-Year Bonds					
	at a Discount					

If the corporation prepares a balance sheet at the time of the sale, the long-term liability section of the balance sheet will appear as follows.

Long-Term Liabilities
    Bonds Payable, 10%, 10-year, due January 2, 19XX $100,000
    Less: Discount on Bonds Payable   11,470 $88,530

Discount on Bonds Payable is classified as a contra-liability account and has a normal debit balance. (Appendix 22A illustrates the long-term liability section of the balance sheet.) Because the corporation does not have the benefit of the full $100,000 for ten years, it will, in reality, cost the corporation more than $10,000 in interest each year. To show this additional cost, the $11,470 discount must be amortized to the Bond Interest Expense account over the life of the issue.

Amortizing the Discount

The corporation in the previous example received cash of $88,530 for its ten-year bonds. However, it must pay back $100,000 to the bondholders at maturity. The difference of $11,470 is an additional cost of issuing the bonds and must be allocated to Bond Interest Expense over the ten years. To amortize the discount, the straight-line method is used; thus $11,470 is divided by ten years. The yearly amortization is divided by two, because interest is paid semiannually. The following is an illustration of how this calculation is made.

$$\$11{,}470 \div 10 \text{ years} = \$1{,}147 \text{ per year}$$
$$\$1{,}147 \div 2 = \$573.50 \text{ on June 30}$$
$$= \$573.50 \text{ on December 31}$$

or

$$\$11{,}470 \div 20 \text{ semiannual periods} = \$537.50$$

The journal entries to record the payment of interest and the amortization of the discount are as follows.

		GENERAL JOURNAL				Page	
Date		Description	Post. Ref.	Debit		Credit	
*Jun.*⁹ˣˣ	30	Bond Interest Expense		5000 —			
		Cash				5000 —	
		To Record the Payment of Semiannual Interest on Bonds					
	30	Bond Interest Expense		573 50			
		Discount on Bonds Payable				573 50	
		To Record the Amortization of the Semiannual Discount on Bonds					
Dec.	31	Bond Interest Expense		5000 —			
		Cash				5000 —	
		To Record the Payment of Semiannual Interest on Bonds					
	31	Bond Interest Expense		573 50			
		Discount on Bonds Payable				573 50	
		To Record the Amortization of the Semiannual Discount on Bonds					

At the end of December, the T-accounts look as follows.

Cash				Bond Interest Expense			Discount on Bonds Payable			
1/1 Balance 88,530	6/30	5,000	6/30	5,000.00		1/2	11,470	6/30	573.50
	12/31	5,000	6/30	573.50				12/31	573.50
			12/31	5,000.00					
			12/31	573.50					
78,530			11,147			10,323			

The total cash paid is $10,000 per year, which is the result of multiplying the contract rate of interest by $100,000. However, because the bonds sold at less than face value, the true cost to the corporation of the borrowing each year was $11,147, which is the balance in the Bond Interest Expense account after the payment of the interest and the amortization of the discount. This is often referred to as the effective interest, or when expressed as a percentile, the effective interest rate. The effective interest rate is the same as the market rate of interest at the time the bonds are sold. The contra-liability account, Discount on Bonds Payable, is amortized over the 10-year period by regular credits to it that reflect the additional (interest) expense. The long-term liability section of the balance sheet at the end of the first year appears as follows.

Long-Term Liabilities		
Bonds Payable, 10%, 10-year, due January 2, 19XX	$100,000	
Less: Unamortized Discount on Bonds Payable	10,323	$89,677

The discount will be amortized twice a year for ten years along with the semiannual payment of interest to the bondholders. The last entry, after ten years, will bring the Discount on Bonds Payable account to a zero balance. The corporation will then pay the bondholders the face amount of $100,000. Remember, when the prevailing market rate of interest is greater than the contract rate of interest, the bonds will sell at a discount. When the bonds sell at a discount, the true cost of the borrowing (the effective interest expense) is greater than the contract rate of interest. The true cost of the debt equals the contract rate of interest paid and the amount of the discount.

Bonds Sold at a Premium

Whenever the market rate of interest is lower than the contract rate of interest, the bonds are sold at a premium. The demand by bondholders for the higher market rate of interest pushes the price at which the bonds will sell above face value. Assume that a corporation issues $100,000, 10%, ten-year bonds at $106,500. The journal entries, the partial balance sheet, and the T-accounts for this issue are as follows.

General Journal Entry at Sale

\multicolumn{7}{c}{GENERAL JOURNAL}						Page
\multicolumn{2}{c}{Date}	Description	Post. Ref.	Debit		Credit
Jan.¹⁹ˣˣ	2	Cash		106500 —		
		Bonds Payable				100000 —
		Premium on Bonds Payable				6500 —
		To Record the Sale of 10%, 10-Year Bonds Sold				
		at a Premium				

Partial Balance Sheet at Sale

Long-Term Liabilities
    Bonds Payable, 10%, 10-year, due January 2, 19XX $100,000
        Add: Premium on Bonds Payable   6,500 $106,500

Journal Entries for Interest and Straight-Line Amortization

\multicolumn{7}{c}{GENERAL JOURNAL}						Page
\multicolumn{2}{c}{Date}	Description	Post. Ref.	Debit		Credit
June¹⁹ˣˣ	30	Bond Interest Expense		4675 —		
		Premium on Bonds Payable		325 —		
		Cash				5000 —
		To Record the Semiannual Interest to				
		Bondholders and the Amortization				
		of the Premium				
		($6,500 ÷ 20 periods)				

GENERAL JOURNAL				Page
Date	**Description**	**Post. Ref.**	**Debit**	**Credit**
_19XX_ _Dec._ 31	Bond Interest Expense		4675 —	
	Premium on Bonds Payable		325 —	
	Cash			5000 —
	To Record the Semiannual Interest to			
	Bondholders and the Amortization			
	of the Premium			

T- Accounts

Cash				Bond Interest Expense			Premium on Bonds Payable			
1/2	106,500	6/30	5,000	6/30	4,675		6/30	325	1/2	6,500
		12/31	5,000	12/31	4,675		12/31	325		
	96,500				9,350				5,850	

As shown in the above T-accounts, the true cost of the borrowing is less than the cash paid to the bondholders. The corporation has $106,500 cash to use for ten years, yet only pays the bondholders the face amount of the bonds, $100,000, at the end of the term. When the $6,500 premium is allocated to expense over the term of the issue, it reduces the bond interest expense by $650 a year, the amount of the amortization. The long-term liability section of the balance sheet after the first year appears as follows.

Long-Term Liabilities		
Bonds Payable, 10%, 10-year, due January 2, 19XX	$100,000	
Add: Unamortized Premium on Bonds Payable	5,850	$105,850

The premium on bonds payable will be amortized twice a year for ten years and after the last period will have a zero balance. The corporation at that time will repay the bondholders the face value of $100,000.

The straight-line method for amortization has been used exclusively in the examples thus far in this chapter. Another method used is the interest method. The Accounting Principles Board of the AICPA ruled in its Opinion 21, Interest on Receivables and Payables, that the interest method be used in all situations, unless the results from using the straight-line method are not materially different than from the interest method. If a substantial difference exists, the interest method must be used.

When the interest method is used to determine bond interest expense, a constant rate is applied each amortization period to the carrying value of the bonds. The constant rate used is the market rate at the time of the sale of the bonded indebtedness. The carrying value of the bonds is multiplied by the market rate of interest for each period. The carrying value of the bonds at any point in time is the face amount of the bonds minus the unamortized discount or plus the unamortized premium. Using the information from the previous two examples, where a $100,000 bond issue was sold first at a discount of $11,470 and then at a premium of $6,500, the interest method calculations for both a discount and a premium appear on pages 851 and 852.

Observe that the market rate of interest on a semiannual basis is used to determine the interest expense each semiannual period. Using the information from the example of the bond sold at a discount on page 844, the discount amortization for the first period is calculated by multiplying the carrying value of $88,530 by the market rate of 12 percent stated on a semiannual basis of 6 percent. The result of this multiplication is the amount of bond interest expense to be recorded in the accounts. Because the contract rate is used to calculate the actual cash payment to the bondholders, this amount is subtracted from the bond interest expense to determine the amount of the amortization of the discount as follows.

First Semiannual Period

Bond Interest Expense (6% of $88,530)	$5,312
Cash Paid to Bondholders	
(5% of $100,000)	(5,000)
Discount Amortization	$ 312

In comparing this first semiannual amortization using the interest method with that of using the straight-line method, it can be seen that the discount amortization by the straight-line method is $573.50 for the first semiannual period, whereas it is $312 by the interest method. With the interest method, as the discount is amortized each interest payment period, the carrying value of the bonds gets larger. As the carrying value increases, so does the

Interest Amortization Table for a Bond Sold at a Discount

Period	(A) Interest Expense to be Recorded	(B) Interest to be Paid to Bondholders	(C) Discount to be Amortized (A − B)	(D) Unamortized Discount (D − C)	(E) End of the Period Carrying Value (E + C)
				$11,470	$88,530
1	$5,312 (6% of $88,530)	$5,000	$312	11,158	88,842
2	5,331 (6% of $88,842)	5,000	331	10,827	89,173
3	5,350 (6% of $89,173)	5,000	350	10,477	89,523
4	5,371 (6% of $89,523)	5,000	371	10,106	89,894
5	5,394 (6% of $89,894)	5,000	394	9,712	90,288
6	5,417 (6% of $90,288)	5,000	417	9,295	90,705
7	5,442 (6% of $90,705)	5,000	442	8,853	91,147
8	5,469 (6% of $91,147)	5,000	469	8,384	91,616
9	5,497 (6% of $91,616)	5,000	497	7,887	92,113
10	5,527 (6% of $92,113)	5,000	527	7,360	92,640
11	5,558 (6% of $92,640)	5,000	558	6,802	93,198
12	5,592 (6% of $93,198)	5,000	592	6,210	93,790
13	5,627 (6% of $93,790)	5,000	627	5,583	94,417
14	5,665 (6% of $94,417)	5,000	665	4,918	95,082
15	5,705 (6% of $95,082)	5,000	705	4,213	95,787
16	5,747 (6% of $95,787)	5,000	747	3,466	96,534
17	5,792 (6% of $96,534)	5,000	792	2,674	97,326
18	5,840 (6% of $97,326)	5,000	840	1,834	98,166
19	5,890 (6% of $98,166)	5,000	890	944	99,056
20	5,944[a]	5,000	944	0	100,000

[a]Remaining unamortized discount.

Interest Amortization Table for a Bond Sold at a Premium

Period	(A) Interest Expense to be Recorded	(B) Interest to be Paid to Bondholders	(C) Premium to be Amortized (B − A)	(D) Unamortized Premium (D − C)	(E) End of the Period Carrying Value (E − C)
				$6,500	$106,500
1	$4,793	$5,000	$207	6,293	106,293
	(4-½% of $106,500)				
2	4,783	5,000	217	6,076	106,076
	(4-½% of $106,293)				
3	4,773	5,000	227	5,849	105,849
	(4-½% of $106,076)				
4	4,763	5,000	237	5,612	105,612
	(4-½% of $105,849)				
5	4,753	5,000	247	5,365	105,365
	(4-½% of $105,612)				
6	4,741	5,000	259	5,106	105,106
	(4-½% of $105,365)				
7	4,730	5,000	270	4,836	104,836
	(4-½% of $105,106)				
8	4,718	5,000	282	4,554	104,554
	(4-½% of $104,836)				
9	4,705	5,000	295	4,259	104,259
	(4-½% of $104,554)				
10	4,692	5,000	308	3,951	103,951
	(4-½% of $104,259)				
11	4,678	5,000	322	3,629	103,629
	(4-½% of $103,951)				
12	4,663	5,000	337	3,292	103,292
	(4-½% of $103,629)				
13	4,648	5,000	352	2,940	102,940
	(4-½% of $103,292)				
14	4,632	5,000	368	2,572	102,572
	(4-½% of $102,940)				
15	4,616	5,000	384	2,188	102,188
	(4-½% of $102,572)				
16	4,598	5,000	402	1,786	101,786
	(4-½% of $102,188)				
17	4,580	5,000	420	1,366	101,366
	(4-½% of $101,786)				
18	4,561	5,000	439	927	100,927
	(4-½% of $101,366)				
19	4,542	5,000	458	469	100,469
	(4-½% of $100,927)				
20	4,531[a]	5,000	469	0	100,000

[a]Remaining unamortized premium.

amount of the bond discount amortization. While it is $312 the first amortization period, it is $944 the last period, and the final carrying value of the bonds is the same as the face value, $100,000.

The interest amortization table on page 852 for a bond sold at a premium illustrates the use of the interest method for amortization of the premium. The semiannual market rate of interest when the bonds sold was 4-½ percent (9 percent annually). This rate was multiplied by the carrying value of $106,500 at the beginning of the bond issue. Because the bonds were sold at a premium, the bond interest expense was less than the amount of cash interest paid to the bondholders.

First Semiannual Period

Cash Paid to Bondholders (5% times $100,000)	$5,000
Bond Interest Expense (Rounded)	
(4-½% times $106,500)	(4,793)
Premium Amortization	$ 207

Again compare the interest method with the straight-line method. Using the information from the example of the bond sold at a premium on page 847, the straight-line amortization is $325, while the interest amortization is $207. For bonds sold at a premium, the interest amortization amount gets larger each year, while the straight-line amount remains the same throughout the life of the bond.

Whenever the interest method is used, a table is developed for use in preparing the semiannual amortization entries. Tables may also be developed for the straight-line method, but are not as essential as are the tables developed for the interest method. Each corporation must decide which method is to be used and then use that method consistently.

The method used for amortization is very important when a corporation is dealing in million-dollar issues. The increase (discount amortization) or the decrease (premium amortization) in the bond interest expense could substantially affect the amount of income a corporation reports.

Accrued Bond Interest Expense

Often bonds are sold where the interest payments do not coincide with the fiscal year (the accounting year end). If such is the case, interest is owed but not yet due to be paid by the end of the year.

Accrued interest must be recognized in the adjusting entries to accurately reflect the total liabilities of the corporation. In addition, an adjusting entry must be prepared to amortize any discount or premium. For example, assume that a corporation issued $500,000 of 9%, ten-year bonds on May 1, 19X7, with interest to be paid semiannually on November 1 and May 1. Assume further that the bonds were sold at face value and that the corporation's fiscal year is January 1 to December 31. The journal entries to record the semiannual interest payment on November 1 and the adjusting entry for the accrued interest on December 31, 19X7, are as follows.

GENERAL JOURNAL					Page
Date	Description	Post. Ref.	Debit	Credit	
19X7 Nov. 1	Bond Interest Expense		22500 —		
	Cash			22500 —	
	To Record the Semiannual Interest Payment				
	on Bonds ($500,000 × .09) ÷ 2				

GENERAL JOURNAL					Page
Date	Description	Post. Ref.	Debit	Credit	
19X7 Dec. 31	Bond Interest Expense		7500 —		
	Bond Interest Payable			7500 —	
	To Record Two Months' Accrued Interest on				
	Bonds ($500,000 × .09) ÷ 12 = $3,750				
	$3,750 × 2 = $7,500				

The bond interest is calculated by multiplying 9 percent by $500,000, which equals $45,000 a year, or $3,750 per month. Two months' interest has accrued since the payment on November 1.

The example included no discount or premium, but if it did, the discount or premium would also be amortized for the two-month period.

REVERSING ENTRIES

After the year-end adjusting and closing procedures, the accountant may decide to prepare reversing entries. Reversing entries are the exact reverse of adjusting entries and are carried out after the books are closed for the current period. They are dated at the beginning of the next accounting period. Reversing entries are optional and are prepared to make the recording of certain routine cash receipts and payments in the following accounting period an easier task.

Assume that the accountant for the corporation in the previous example routinely uses reversing entries and thus reverses the December 31, 19X7, adjusting entry which recorded bond interest expense and bond interest payable. The reversing entry will be dated January 2, 19X8, and will use the same account titles and amounts as the adjusting entry, only they will be reversed. The adjusting entry and its related reversing entry are as follows.

GENERAL JOURNAL				Page	
Date	Description	Post. Ref.	Debit	Credit	
19X7	*Adjusting Entry*				
Dec. 31	**Bond Interest Expense**		7500 —		
	Bond Interest Payable			7500 —	
	To Record Two Months' Accrued Interest				
	on Bonds				
19X8	*Reversing Entry*				
Jan. 2	**Bond Interest Payable**		7500 —		
	Bond Interest Expense			7500 —	
	To Record the Reversal of the Interest Accrued				
	at Year End				

The T-accounts after the adjusting and closing entries have been posted appear as follows. Note that the reversing entries have not yet been posted to the T-accounts.

Bond Interest Expense				Bond Interest Payable	
11/1 Payment 22,500	12/31 Closing 30,000				12/31 Adjusting 7,500
12/31 Adjusting 7,500					

The income statement prepared for the year ended December 31 will reflect the correct amount of interest expense for the year and the balance sheet will show bond interest payable as a current liability. When the new accounting period starts, the reversing entry will remove the current liability and reduce the amount of bond interest expense for the new year.

After the closing entries have been posted, Bond Interest Expense has a zero balance. The Bond Interest Payable account has a balance of $7,500. The reversing entry places an abnormal credit balance in the Bond Interest Expense account and closes the Bond Interest Payable account as follows.

Bond Interest Expense		Bond Interest Payable	
	1/2 Reversing 7,500	1/2 Reversing 7,500	12/31 Adjusting 7,500

When the interest is paid again on May 1, 19X8, the accountant does not have to remember to close the Bond Interest Payable account, because that has already been done with the reversing entry. The entry to record the payment of the May 1 interest will debit Bond Interest Expense and credit Cash for $22,500. After the entry is posted, the account for Bond Interest Expense reflects the correct amount of bond interest for the first five months of 19X8, $15,000.

Bond Interest Expense

If the bonds are sold at a discount or a premium, an adjusting entry must be prepared at year end to record the amortization of the discount or the premium. Assume that the $500,000, 9%, ten-year bond issue is sold at a discount of $12,000 and that interest is paid on May 1 and November 1. Using straight-line, the amortization is $1,200 a year ($600 semiannually or $100 a month). Using this information, the adjusting entry at the end of the year and the reversing entry at the beginning of the next year are as follows.

GENERAL JOURNAL				Page
Date	Description	Post. Ref.	Debit	Credit
19XX	**Adjusting Entries**			
Dec. 31	Bond Interest Expense		7 5 0 0 —	
	Bond Interest Payable			7 5 0 0 —
	To Record Two Months' Accrued Interest on			
	Bonds ($500,000 × .09) ÷ 12 = $3,750			
	$3,750 × 2 = $7,500			
31	Bond Interest Expense		2 0 0 —	
	Discount on Bonds Payable			2 0 0 —
	To Record Two Months' Amortization of Discount			

GENERAL JOURNAL				Page
Date	Description	Post. Ref.	Debit	Credit
19XX	**Reversing Entry**			
Jan. 2	Bond Interest Payable		7 5 0 0 —	
	Bond Interest Expense			7 5 0 0 —
	To Record the Reversal of the Interest Accrued			
	at Year End			

A compound entry could be made on December 31, but only the amount of the accrued interest payable is reversed, not the discount amortization.

Assume the $500,000 issue is sold at a premium of $12,000. The compound adjusting entry for accrued interest and the premium amortization is as follows.

GENERAL JOURNAL				Page	
Date	Description	Post. Ref.	Debit	Credit	
19XX	**Adjusting Entry**				
Dec. 31	Bond Interest Expense		7 3 0 0 —		
	Premium on Bonds Payable		2 0 0 —		
	Bond Interest Payable			7 5 0 0 —	
	To Record Accrued Interest and Amortization				
	of Premium				
	Reversing Entry				
Jan. 2	Bond Interest Payable		7 5 0 0 —		
	Bond Interest Expense			7 5 0 0 —	
	To Record the Reversal of the Interest Accrued				
	at Year End				

Note that the reversing entry credits Bond Interest Expense for $7,500, the amount that will actually be paid on May 1. *The amortization of the premium is not reversed.* Preparing separate entries for the accrued interest and the amortization of the premium or discount usually makes it easier to understand.

REDEMPTION OF BONDS

Bond indentures often provide for the redemption of bonds. They may provide for either the callable option or the convertible option. The bond indenture will provide the detail necessary to account for either of these situations.

Callable Bonds

If bonds are issued with the provision that the corporation may redeem them before maturity, the provision will state either a percentage of face value or specify the prevailing market rate. For example, assume that a corporation buys back a $100,000, 8 percent bond, with an unamortized premium of $2,600 at 102 percent of face value as provided in the contract. The calculation and the general journal entry to record this redemption are as follows.

Calculation

1. Cash required to redeem bonds

Face value of bonds	$100,000
Redemption rate, 102%	× 1.02
Cash required to redeem bonds	$102,000

2. Carrying value of bonds

Face value	$100,000
Plus unamortized premium	2,600
Carrying value	$102,600

3. Gain or loss on redemption

Carrying value	$102,600
Minus cash required to redeem	−102,000
Gain on bond redemption	$ 600

	GENERAL JOURNAL			Page
Date	Description	Post. Ref.	Debit	Credit
19XX Jul. 1	Bonds Payable		100000 —	
	Premium on Bonds Payable		2600 —	
	Cash			102000 —
	Gain on Bond Redemption			600 —
	To Record the Redemption of Bonds Payable			
	at 102% of Face Value			

Now assume that the above corporation has unamortized discount of $2,600 and can buy the bonds at 99-½ percent. The calculation and the general journal entry to record this redemption are as follows.

Calculation

1. Cash required to redeem bonds

Face value of bonds	$100,000
Redemption rate, 99-½%	× .995
Cash required to redeem bonds	$ 99,500

2. Carrying value of bonds

Face value	$100,000
Minus unamortized discount	− 2,600
Carrying value	$ 97,400

3. Gain or loss on redemption

Carrying value	$ 97,400
Minus cash required to redeem	(99,500)
Loss on bond redemption	$ (2,100)

GENERAL JOURNAL				Page
Date	Description	Post. Ref.	Debit	Credit
19XX *Jul.* 1	*Bonds Payable*		100000 —	
	Loss on Retirement of Bonds		2100 —	
	Discount on Bonds Payable			2600 —
	Cash			99500 —
	To Record the Redemption of Bonds Payable			
	at 99-½% of Face Value			

Convertible Bonds

Because bonds must be sold to potential investors, corporations sometimes make them more attractive by giving the owners a right to convert their bonds to stock. Assume that a bond indenture provides that each $1,000 bond may be exchanged for 90 shares of $10 par value common stock. Assume further that bonds of $100,000, with unamortized discount of $5,000, are to be exchanged for stock. The following calculations are made to determine the number of $1,000 bonds to be converted, the number of common shares to be issued, and the dollar amounts to be used for the conversion.

1. Number of bonds converted:

   $100,000 \div \$1,000 = 100$ bonds with a face value of $1,000

2. Number of common shares to be issued:

   100 bonds $\times$ 90 shares $= 9,000$ common shares to be issued

3. Dollar amounts to be used for the general journal entry:
   a. Face value of bonds to be converted $= \$100,000$
   b. Common stock to be issued at par (9,000 shares $\times$ $10 par) $= \$90,000$
   c. Discount on bonds payable to be written off $= \$5,000$
   d. Premium on common stock (excess remaining) $= \$5,000$

The premium on the common stock is determined as follows.

Face value of bonds		$100,000
Less: Par value of common stock	$90,000	
Unamortized discount on bonds	5,000	95,000
Premium on common stock		$ 5,000

The premium is the amount remaining after the par value of the common stock and the discount on bonds payable are subtracted from the face value of the bonds. The general journal entry to record the conversion is as follows.

GENERAL JOURNAL				Page	
Date	Description	Post. Ref.	Debit	Credit	
19XX Aug. 31	**Bonds Payable**		100000 —		
	Common Stock			90000 —	
	Discount on Bonds Payable			5000 —	
	Premium on Common Stock			5000 —	
	To Record the Conversion of Bonds Payable to				
	Common Stock, 90 Shares of $10 Par for Each				
	$1,000 Bond				

The bondholder gives up the rights of a creditor when he or she exercises the convertible option. The corporation no longer has a debt of $100,000 or interest payments to make. In both callable and convertible bond situations, the unamortized discount or premium must be removed from the books. The general procedure is to make the redemption or conversion on the date of the payment of the semiannual interest, so as not to have additional mid-period interest transactions.

APPROPRIATION OF RETAINED EARNINGS FOR BONDS

A number of states require corporations to appropriate an amount equal to the interest payment and accumulation of principal to repay the bondholders. The creditors have only the assets of the corporation to look to for their claims, so the appropriation provides additional protection to the bondholders, because earnings will be retained in the business to repay their debt. The appropriation will help prevent a corporation from paying out all of its earnings as dividends to stockholders. The appropriation can take one of two forms. It may be presented as a footnote to the financial statement, or a general journal entry may be made debiting retained earnings. An example of such a footnote is as follows.

Notes to the financial statements:
Note C: Under the terms of the bond indenture, a part of the retained earnings is appropriated from dividend availability. The amount of $28,500 is therefore appropriated this year for that purpose. This amount will be increased each year as provided by the bond indenture. When the bonds are retired, the appropriation will be removed.

The second method is to actually prepare a general journal entry and record the appropriation into the accounts. The general journal entry and the proper presentation on the balance sheet are as follows.

GENERAL JOURNAL				Page	
Date	Description	Post. Ref.	Debit	Credit	
19XX *Dec.* *31*	*Retained Earnings*		2 8 5 0 0 —		
	Retained Earnings, Appropriated for Bonded	·			
	Indebtedness			2 8 5 0 0 —	
	To Record the Appropriation of Retained				
	Earnings for Bonded Indebtedness According				
	to the Bond Indenture				

Retained Earnings		
Retained Earnings, Appropriated for Bonded Indebtedness	$ 28,500	
Unappropriated Retained Earnings	438,500	
Total Retained Earnings		$467,000

BOND SINKING FUND

bond sinking fund
a special fund set up
by the corporation
and used to repay the
bondholders at the
maturity date

Most bond indentures provide that a special fund be set up to repay the bondholders at the maturity date. This fund is called the **bond sinking fund** and is classified as a long-term investment. The corporation sets aside a certain amount of earnings each year to be deposited in this fund, which is generally managed by a trustee. The trustee invests the funds prudently so as to earn interest income for the corporation. This interest income increases the amount of the fund and helps accumulate the amount necessary to repay the bondholders at maturity. Assume that a corporation issues $100,000, 9%, ten-year bonds. In addition, it sets aside a bond sinking fund from the corporate earnings. If the yearly amount set aside earned no interest, the corporation would need to set aside $10,000 each year to accumulate $100,000 in ten years. However, the trustee invests each year's deposit so that it earns interest. Because each year's deposit earns interest, less than $10,000 must be deposited by the corporation. The present-value tables in Appendix 23A are used by the accountant to determine the amount to be deposited. The amount of the deposit depends on the rate of interest the trustee receives on the investment. Assume that the corporation determines it must set aside a minimum of $7,500 each year. The general journal entry to record this deposit is as follows.

GENERAL JOURNAL					Page	
Date	Description	Post. Ref.	Debit		Credit	
19XX *Dec.* 31	*Bond Sinking Fund*		7 5 0 0 —			
	Cash				7 5 0 0 —	
	To Record the Annual Deposit Necessary					
	to Repay Bondholders at Maturity					

Each year, the trustee will report the earnings status of the fund to the corporation. The interest income earned on the deposit is recorded as other income, and the balance of the fund at year end is reported on the corporation balance sheet.

SUMMARY

A corporation may want additional financing to expand its facility, open new branches, or purchase new equipment and may obtain financing by selling stocks and bonds. Whatever the reason, a decision must be made by management about the best method to use to obtain the needed funds. The board of directors, along with the top management, may decide to issue additional common stock, issue preferred stock, or issue bonds payable. Each alternative has its advantages and disadvantages. Issuing additional common stock spreads the present ownership over more stockholders. Issuing preferred stock creates a claim on corporate assets and a claim on retained earnings. Issuing bonds creates no additional stockholders and thus no sharing in management or retained earnings. However, the bondholders are creditors of the corporation and will have first claim on assets upon liquidation.

When a corporation decides to sell bonds, a contract is written called the bond indenture. This contract covers all the terms of the bond issue. Bonds are long-term liability contracts that require regular interest payments to the bondholders. The amount of interest is stated on the bond and is called the contract rate of interest. Bonds may be classified as registered bonds, coupon bonds, bearer bonds, secured bonds, and debenture bonds. Bonds may be either term or serial. Term bonds all mature at the same time, while serial bonds have maturity dates that range over a number of years. Other bonds that give specific rights are callable bonds and convertible bonds.

The corporation will determine the amount of interest to be paid to the bondholders. However, the market rate of interest at the time the bonds are sold will determine the selling price. When the market rate of interest is higher than the contract rate, the bonds will sell at a discount. When the market rate of interest is lower than the contract rate of interest, the bonds will sell at a premium.

To properly record the bond interest expense, the discount or the premium on bonds payable must be amortized. Two methods are used: the straight-line method and the interest method. The straight-line method may be used if it is not materially different from the interest method. Whichever method is chosen must be used consistently. Accrued interest must be recorded at the end of the accounting period, along with any amortization of discount or premium on the bonds.

A number of states require that an appropriation of retained earnings be made for the bonded indebtedness. Either a footnote to the financial statements is used, or a general journal entry is made for this appropriation. The appropriation is used to set aside earnings that, after the appropriation, cannot be used for any other purpose.

To accumulate the necessary funds to repay the bondholders, a sinking fund account is established. A bond sinking fund is a long-term investment used to accumulate the amount needed to repay the debt at the end of the bond issue. The corporation sets aside a certain amount from its earnings to repay the debt. Generally, a trustee manages the funds for the corporation. The earnings and the fund balance are reported on the financial statements of the corporation.

Bonds are chosen by corporations to obtain needed funds for special purposes. When bonds are sold, they are reported on the financial statements along with the applicable bond interest expense and the amortized discount or premium.

Review of Accounting Terminology

Following is a list of the accounting terminology for this chapter.

bearer bonds	debenture bonds
bond indenture	face value
bond sinking fund	market rate of interest
bonds	registered bonds
callable bonds	secured bonds
contract interest rate	serial bonds
convertible bonds	term bonds
coupon bonds	transfer fees

Fill in the blank with the correct word or term from the list.

1. The dollar amount appearing on the face of the bond is called the _____.

2. _____ are the costs involved in transacting an ownership exchange of buying and selling stocks and bonds.

3. _____ are bonds that are issued in the name of the owner.

4. Long-term notes payable that bear interest are _____.

5. A _____ is the contract between the corporation and the bondholder that contains the terms of the issue.

6. _____ is the rate of interest specified on the bond that applies to the face value.

7. _____ are bonds that pledge an asset of the corporation as security for the debt.

8. Bonds that pay interest on receipt of the coupons attached to the bonds are _____.

9. _____ are bonds where the entire issue matures at one time.

10. Bonds issued solely on the credit worthiness of the corporation are called _____

11. _____ are bonds where the owner is considered to be the one in possession of the bond.

12. _____ are bonds that can be converted to the stock of the issuing corporation according to the terms in the bond indenture.

13. A special fund set up by the corporation and used to repay the bondholders at the maturity date is a/an _____.

14. The rate of interest a borrower is willing to pay and an investor is willing to receive is called _____.

15. _____ may be redeemed or called in at the option of the corporation.

16. Bonds where the maturity dates range over a number of years are _____.

Match the following words and terms on the left with the definitions on the right (columns continue on the following page).

17. bearer bonds
18. bonds
19. bond indenture
20. bond sinking fund
21. callable bonds
22. contract interest rate
23. convertible bonds
24. coupon bonds
25. debenture bonds

a. the contract between the corporation and the bondholder that contains the terms of the issue

b. the costs involved in transacting an ownership exchange of buying and selling stocks and bonds

c. the dollar amount appearing on the face of the bond

d. bonds that pay interest on receipt of the coupons attached to the bond

e. bonds where the owner is considered to be the one in possession of the bonds

f. a special fund set up by the corporation and used to repay the bondholders at the maturity date

g. bonds that may be redeemed or called in at the option of the corporation

h. bonds where the entire issue matures at one time

26. face value
27. market rate of interest
28. registered bonds
29. secured bonds
30. serial bonds
31. term bonds
32. transfer fees

i. bonds that can be converted to the stock of the issuing corporation according to the terms of the bond indenture

j. bonds issued solely on the credit worthiness of the corporation

k. bonds that pledge an asset of the corporation as security for the debt

l. bonds where the maturity dates range over a number of years

m. long-term notes payable that bear interest

n. bonds that are issued in the name of the owner

o. the rate of interest specified on the bond that applies to the face value

p. the rate of interest a borrower is willing to pay and an investor is willing to receive

Exercises

Exercise 23.1
determining the sales price of a bond payable and calculating the annual, semiannual, and monthly interest

On May 1, 19X9, a corporation sold $100,000 of its 7-½%, ten-year bonds payable at 100 percent. Interest is to be paid on November 1 and May 1. Fill in the blanks.

a. The bonds sold for $ _____ cash.

b. The annual interest is $ _____.

c. The semiannual interest is $ _____.

d. The monthly interest is $ _____.

e. The interest accrued by December 31 is $ _____.

Exercise 23.2

preparing the general journal entries necessary in Exercise 23.1

Using the information from Exercise 23.1, prepare the general journal entries required on May 1, November 1, and December 31, 19X9. No explanations are necessary.

Exercise 23.3

preparing the general journal entries for bond discount and premium and straight-line and interest amortization

Assume the same facts as in Exercise 23.1, except that the bonds sold for 96-½ percent.

a. Prepare all the necessary entries on November 1 and December 31, 19X9, assuming straight-line amortization of the bond discount. Round to the nearest dollar where necessary.

b. Prepare all the necessary entries on November 1 and December 31, 19X9, assuming the interest method for amortization of the bond discount is to be used, and the market rate of interest is 8 percent. Round to the nearest dollar where necessary.

c. Assuming the bonds sold for 101 percent of the face value, prepare all the necessary entries on November 1 and December 31, 19X9, assuming straight-line amortization of the bond premium. Round to the nearest dollar where necessary.

d. Assuming the bonds sold for 101 percent of the face value, prepare all the necessary entries for the first year, using the interest method for amortization. The market rate of interest is 7 percent. Round to the nearest dollar where necessary.

Exercise 23.4

calculating the selling price of bonds, straight-line amortization, and bond interest

On January 2 of the current year, a corporation sold $500,000 of its 9-½%, ten-year bonds at a price to reflect a discount of $24,000 and with interest to be paid semiannually.

a. Calculate the selling price of the bonds.

b. Calculate the straight-line amortization of the discount (1) annually and (2) semiannually.

c. Calculate the interest (1) annually and (2) semiannually.

Exercise 23.5

preparing the general journal entries for the interest payment and straight-line amortization using the information from Exercise 23.4

Using the information calculated in Exercise 23.4, prepare the necessary general journal entries for the first year, assuming the interest is paid on June 30 and December 31. (December 31 is also the year end for this corporation.)

Exercise 23.6

preparing the general journal entries for calling in bonds payable

On March 1, 19X4, the Norris Corporation issued $500,000 of its 12%, ten-year callable bonds payable for $476,000. Interest is payable semiannually on March 1 and September 1, and straight-line amortization is used. On March 1, 19X9, after the interest is paid, the bonds are called in at 102 percent of face value. Prepare the general journal entry on March 1, 19X9, to record calling in the bonds. Round amounts to the nearest dollar. (Hint: Use a T-account for Discount on Bonds Payable and post all transactions to it until the bonds are called.)

Exercise 23.7

preparing the general journal entries for the conversion of bonds to stock

On August 31, after the interest payment is made, several of the bondholders of the Elton Corporation decide to exercise their option to exchange their bonds for common stock. The bond indenture calls for 90 shares of $10 par value stock to be exchanged for each $1,000 bond. The bondholders of $500,000 bonds are to convert to stock. These bondholders purchased their bonds at 100 percent of face value. Prepare the general journal entry to record the conversion of these bonds to common stock. Make all the calculations as shown on page 861.

Problems

Problem 23.1

preparing the general journal entries for the issue of bonds at a discount, payment of interest, and year-end closing, and preparing the liability section of the balance sheet

Sunglow Corporation issued $700,000 of 14%, ten-year bonds payable on April 1, 19X8. Interest is paid semiannually on April 1 and October 1. The corporation uses straight-line amortization.

Instructions

1. *Prepare all the necessary general journal entries for each of the following transactions. (Hint: Post entries to T-accounts for Discount on Bonds Payable and Bond Interest Expense.)*

19X8
Apr. 1   sold the bonds for cash at a $24,000 discount
Oct. 1   paid the semiannual interest and amortized the discount
Dec. 31   recorded the adjusting entry for accrued interest and amortization of the discount

Dec. 31   closed the Bond Interest Expense account to Income Sum-
           mary

19X9

Jan. 2   recorded the reversing entry
Apr. 1   paid the semiannual interest and amortized the discount
Oct. 1   paid the semiannual interest and amortized the discount
Dec. 31   recorded the adjusting entry for accrued interest and amorti-
           zation of the discount
Dec. 31   closed the Bond Interest Expense account to Income Sum-
           mary

2. *Prepare the long-term liability section of the balance sheet as
    of December 31, 19X9.*

3. *What amount of bond interest expense is reported on the 19X9
    income statement?*

Problem 23.2

*preparing general
journal entries for
bonds sold at a
premium, the payment
of interest, and the
year-end closing, and
preparing the liability
section of the balance
sheet*

Chucks Corporation issued $950,000 of 16%, ten-year bonds pay-
able on April 1, 19X6. Interest is payable semiannually on April 1
and October 1. The corporation uses straight-line amortization.
Round amounts to the nearest dollar if necessary.

Instructions

1. *Prepare all the necessary entries without explanations for each
    of the following transactions.*

Apr. 1   sold the bonds for cash at a premium of $54,000
Oct. 1   paid the semiannual interest and amortized the premium
Dec. 31   recorded the adjusting entry for the accrued interest and the
           amortization of the premium
Dec. 31   closed the Bond Interest Expense account to Income Sum-
           mary

2. *Prepare the long-term liability section of the balance sheet as
    of December 31, 19X6.*

3. *Prepare the reversing entry necessary on January 2, 19X7.*

Problem 23.3

calculating the amount of discount, the interest method of amortization, and the bond interest, and preparing general journal entries to record sale of bonds and interest payment

In 19X9, a corporation sold $600,000 of its own 8-½%, ten-year bonds on their date of issue, January 2, for $580,462. Interest on these bonds is payable on June 30 and December 31. The bonds were sold when the market rate of interest was 9 percent. The corporation uses the interest method for amortization.

Instructions

1. Calculate the following:
   a. the amount of the discount and the amortization amount for the first two periods
   b. the total amount of the bond interest for the first semiannual period and the second semiannual period

2. Prepare the general journal entries to record the sale of the bonds on January 2 and the first two interest payments (including the amortization) on June 30 and December 31.

3. Prepare the long-term liability section of the balance sheet as of December 31, 19X9.

Problem 23.4

calculating the premium, straight-line amortization, the interest, and preparing the general journal entries and the liability section of the balance sheet.

On March 31, 19X8, a corporation sold $1,000,000 of its 10%, ten-year Bonds Payable for $1,065,000 when the market rate of interest was 9 percent. The interest is to be paid semiannually on March 31 and September 30. The corporation uses straight-line amortization.

Instructions

1. Calculate the following:
   a. the amount of the premium and the amount of the amortization for the first and second periods
   b. the amount of the bond interest to be paid in cash on September 30, 19X8, and on March 31, 19X9
   c. the accrued interest for the three-month period from October 1 to December 31, 19X8

2. Prepare the general journal entries without explanations to
   a. record the sale of the bonds on March 31, 19X8
   b. record the first interest payment on September 30, 19X8
   c. record the December 31, 19X8, adjusting entry for the accrued interest and amortization of the premium
   d. record the reversing entry
   e. record the second interest payment on March 31, 19X9

3. *Prepare the long-term liabilities section of the balance sheet as of December 31, 19X8.*

Problem 23.5

preparing a calculation for amortizing the premium using the interest method, preparing general journal entries and the long-term liability section of the balance sheet

Assume the same facts as in Problem 23.4, except that the corporation uses the interest method for calculating the amortization of the premium.

Instructions

1. *Calculate the following:*
   a. *the amount of the premium and the amount of the amortization of the premium for the first and second periods*
   b. *the amount of the bond interest on September 30, 19X8, and on March 31, 19X9*
   c. *the accrued interest for the three-month period from October 1 to December 31, 19X8*

2. *Prepare the general journal entries without explanations to:*
   a. *record the sale of the bonds on March 31, 19X8*
   b. *record the first interest payment on September 30, 19X8*
   c. *record the December 31, 19X8, adjusting entry for the accrued interest and amortization of the premium*
   d. *record the reversing entry*
   e. *record the second interest payment on March 31, 19X9*

3. *Prepare the long-term liabilities section of the balance sheet as of December 31, 19X8.*

Problem 23.6

preparing the general journal entries for a bond issue sold at a discount, posting to the applicable accounts for three years, and preparing the liability section of the balance sheet

The Lyndee Corporation sold a bond issue on October 1, 19X1. The corporation uses the straight-line method for amortization. Following are the transactions relating to bonds for 19X1, 19X2, 19X3, and 19X4.

19X1

Oct. 1 sold $3,000,000 of its 9-½%, ten-year bonds payable at 97 percent; interest is payable on October 1 and April 1 (Hint: Make all calculations before preparing the entry.)

Dec. 31 recorded the adjusting entry for interest and amortization of the discount

Dec. 31 closed Bond Interest Expense to Income Summary

19X2

Jan. 2   recorded the reversing entry
Apr. 1   paid the semiannual interest and amortized the discount
Oct. 1   paid the semiannual interest and amortized the discount
Dec. 31   recorded the necessary adjusting entry
Dec. 31   closed Bond Interest Expense to Income Summary

19X3

Jan. 2   recorded the reversing entry
Apr. 1   paid the semiannual interest and amortized the discount
Oct. 1   paid the semiannual interest and amortized the discount
Oct. 1   called in one-tenth of the bonds at 98 percent for cash
Dec. 31   recorded the necessary adjusting entry (Remember to recal-
           culate the interest.)
Dec. 31   closed Bond Interest Expense to Income Summary

19X4

Jan. 2   recorded the reversing entry
Apr. 1   paid the semiannual interest and amortized the discount
Oct. 1   paid the semiannual interest and amortized the discount
Dec. 31   recorded the necessary adjusting entry
Dec. 31   closed the Bond Interest Expense to Income Summary

Instructions

1. *Open the following T-accounts: Cash, Bond Interest Payable, Bonds Payable, Discount on Bonds Payable, Bond Interest Expense, and Income Summary.*

2. *Prepare the general journal entries without explanations to record the bond transactions of Lyndee Corporation. Post to the T-accounts after each entry.*

3. *Prepare the long-term liability section of the balance sheet as of December 31, 19X4.*

Problem 23.7
preparing the general journal entries for bonds sold at a premium, posting to the accounts, and determining the balance of certain accounts

The Kelley Corporation sold a $4,000,000, 12%, ten-year bond issue on March 1 at 102 percent. The corporation uses the straight-line method of amortization. Kelley completed the following transactions.

19X1

Mar. 1   sold $4,000,000 of its 12%, ten-year bonds payable at 102 percent; interest is payable on March 1 and September 1
Sept. 1   paid the semiannual interest and amortized the premium

Dec. 31   deposited $350,000 with the trustee; this is an appropriation of retained earnings for the bonded indebtedness

Dec. 31   recorded the necessary adjusting entry

Dec. 31   closed the Bond Interest Expense account to Income Summary

19X2

Jan. 2   recorded the necessary reversing entry

Mar. 1   paid the semiannual interest and amortized the premium

Sept. 1   paid the semiannual interest and amortized the premium

Dec. 31   deposited $350,000 with the trustee

Dec. 31   recorded the necessary adjusting entry

Dec. 31   closed the Bond Interest Expense account to Income Summary

19X3

Jan. 2   recorded the necessary reversing entry

Mar. 1   paid the semiannual interest and amortized the premium

Mar. 1   converted one-tenth of the issue to common stock; each $1,000 bond is to receive 200 shares of $5 par value common stock

Sept. 1   paid the semiannual interest and amortized the premium

Dec. 31   deposited $350,000 with the trustee

Dec. 31   recorded the necessary adjusting entry

Dec. 31   closed the Bond Interest Expense account to Income Summary

Instructions

1. *Open the following T-accounts: Cash, Bond Sinking Fund, Bond Interest Payable, Bonds Payable, Premium on Bonds Payable, Common Stock, Premium on Common Stock, Bond Interest Expense, Income Summary, Retained Earnings, and Appropriated Retained Earnings for Bonded Indebtedness.*

2. *Prepare the general journal entries without explanations for the transactions and post to the T-accounts after each entry. Round amounts to the nearest dollar where necessary.*

3. *Determine the balances of each of the following: Bond Sinking Fund, Bonds Payable, and Premium on Bonds Payable.*

4. *What is the amount of the bond interest expense reported on the 19X3 income statement?*

5. *Prepare the long-term liability section of the balance sheet as of December 31, 19X3.*

Problem 23.8

preparing an interest amortization table, preparing general journal entries for one year, and preparing the long-term liability section of the balance sheet

Assume the same facts as for the Kelley Corporation in Problem 23.7, except that Kelley uses the interest method for calculating the amortization of the premium, and the market rate of interest at the time the bonds were sold was 11-½ percent.

Instructions

1. *Prepare a partial interest amortization table through the first four periods, similar to the one shown in the chapter.*

2. *Prepare the general journal entries for the following transactions.*

19X1

Mar. 1   sold $4,000,000 of its 12%, ten-year bonds payable at 102 percent; interest is payable on March 1 and September 1

Sept. 1   paid the semiannual interest and amortized the premium

Dec. 31   deposited $350,000 with the trustee; this is an appropriation of retained earnings for bonded indebtedness

Dec. 31   recorded the necessary adjusting entry

Dec. 31   closed the Bond Interest Expense account to Income Summary

3. *Prepare the long-term liability section of the balance sheet as of December 31, 19X1.*

Appendix 23A

Present-Value Concepts

THE CONCEPT OF PRESENT VALUE

The concept of present value is based on the time value of money. A profit-motive business will not invest $1 today unless it expects to get back somewhat more than $1 at a later time. The difference between the amount invested and the amount returned is referred to as the interest earned on the investment. Likewise, if a business makes an investment today that will return $1 a year from now, the amount invested *today* has a present value of somewhat less than $1. The amount invested today, the present value, depends on the interest rate of the investment. Assume, for example, a company wishes to have $1,000 one year from now and can receive a 10 percent annual return. The company need only invest approximately $909, at a 10 percent return, for one year to receive the $1,000. This calculation can be made using the interest formula or the present-value formula. The calculation using the interest formula is as follows:

$$I = PRT$$

$$\text{where } I = \text{interest}$$
$$P = \text{principal}$$
$$R = \text{the periodic interest rate}$$
$$T = \text{time}$$

$$I = \$909 \times .10 \times 1$$
$$I = \$90.90$$

By adding the principal of $909 to the interest of $90.90, the total is $999.90 or $1,000 rounded to the nearest dollar. This demonstrates that the present value of $1,000, earning 10 percent interest to be received in one year, is $909.

The calculation using the present-value formula is as follows:

$$Pv = \frac{1}{(1 + i)^n}$$

where Pv = present value of $1 at compound interest

i = the periodic interest rate

n = number of periods

The formula may be applied as follows to calculate the present value of $1,000 in one year's time if the money earns 10 percent.

$$Pv = \frac{1}{(1 + .10)^1}$$

$$Pv = \frac{1}{1.10} = 0.909 \times \$1,000$$

$$Pv = \$909$$

The present value for $1,000 is determined by multiplying 0.909 by the desired amount of $1,000. Thus, $909 is the amount that must be invested today at 10 percent in order to receive $1,000 one year in the future. Assume that the same company wants to know how much they have to invest today in order to have $1,000 two years hence if money is earning 10 percent. The formula is as follows.

$$Pv = \frac{\$1,000}{(1 + .10)^2} = \frac{\$1,000}{1.10 \times 1.10} = \frac{\$1,000}{1.21} = \$826 \text{ (rounded)}.$$

The company must invest $826 today at 10 percent interest compounded annually for two years in order to have $1,000 at the end of the two years. The $826 is the present value of $1,000 at 10 percent, compounded annually, two years hence.

Compound interest is different from simple interest. Simple interest is based on a principal that never changes, while compound interest is computed on the principal plus past interest earned. For this reason, compound interest is referred to as "interest on interest." The more interest periods, the quicker interest will earn interest, thereby causing the investment to grow at a faster pace.

The following example shows the difference between simple interest and compound interest. Assume that (1) $10,000 is invested at 8 percent simple interest for three years and (2) $10,000 is invested at 8 percent compounded annually for three years.

Simple Interest

$$PRT = I$$

$$\$10,000 \times .08 \times 3 = \$2,400 \text{ (total interest)}$$

Compound Interest

Year 1	$10,000.00	Principal	$10,000.00
	× .08	Plus Year 1 Interest	+ 800.00
	$ 800.00	New Principal	$10,800.00
Year 2	$10,800.00	Principal	$10,800.00
	× .08	Plus Year 2 Interest	+ 864.00
	$ 864.00	New Principal	$11,664.00
Year 3	$11,664.00	Principal	$11,664.00
	× .08	Plus Year 3 Interest	+ 933.12
	$ 933.12	New Principal	$12,597.12

When interest is compounded (for more than one period), the result produced is higher than that produced by simple interest. In the example, the compound interest over a three-year period was $2,597.12, as compared to only $2,400 simple interest.

Interest may be compounded any number of times in a year (for example, semiannually, quarterly, monthly, or daily). The more frequently it is compounded, the more interest is produced.

If interest is compounded quarterly at 8 percent, it will be calculated four times a year at 2 percent each period. If it is compounded semiannually at 8 percent, it will be calculated twice a year at 4 percent, and so on.

USING THE PRESENT-VALUE TABLE

The present value is the amount a knowledgeable investor will invest today to receive a future benefit that is greater than the original investment. Although the present-value formula can be used, present-value tables are normally used to make the calculation easier. Following is a table developed for the present value of $1 at a compound interest rate. This table is used any time the amount to be received in the future is a lump sum. The left-hand column is the number of periods hence, and the different interest rates are shown across the top.

TABLE 1   Present Value of $1 at Compound Interest

Periods Hence	4½%	5%	6%	7%	8%	9%	10%	12%	14%	16%
1	0.9569	0.9524	0.9434	0.9346	0.9259	0.9174	0.9091	0.8929	0.8772	0.8621
2	0.9157	0.9070	0.8900	0.8734	0.8573	0.8417	0.8265	0.7972	0.7695	0.7432
3	0.8763	0.8638	0.8396	0.8163	0.7938	0.7722	0.7513	0.7118	0.6750	0.6407
4	0.8386	0.8227	0.7921	0.7629	0.7350	0.7084	0.6830	0.6355	0.5921	0.5523
5	0.8025	0.7835	0.7473	0.7130	0.6806	0.6499	0.6209	0.5674	0.5194	0.4761
6	0.7679	0.7462	0.7050	0.6663	0.6302	0.5963	0.5645	0.5066	0.4556	0.4104
7	0.7348	0.7107	0.6651	0.6228	0.5835	0.5470	0.5132	0.4524	0.3996	0.3538
8	0.7032	0.6768	0.6274	0.5820	0.5403	0.5019	0.4665	0.4039	0.3506	0.3050
9	0.6729	0.6446	0.5919	0.5439	0.5003	0.4604	0.4241	0.3606	0.3075	0.2630
10	0.6439	0.6139	0.5584	0.5084	0.4632	0.4224	0.3855	0.3220	0.2697	0.2267
11	0.6162	0.5847	0.5268	0.4751	0.4289	0.3875	0.3505	0.2875	0.2366	0.1954
12	0.5897	0.5568	0.4970	0.4440	0.3971	0.3555	0.3186	0.2567	0.2076	0.1685
13	0.5643	0.5303	0.4688	0.4150	0.3677	0.3262	0.2897	0.2292	0.1821	0.1452
14	0.5400	0.5051	0.4423	0.3878	0.3405	0.2993	0.2633	0.2046	0.1597	0.1252
15	0.5167	0.4810	0.4173	0.3625	0.3152	0.2745	0.2394	0.1827	0.1401	0.1079
16	0.4945	0.4581	0.3937	0.3387	0.2919	0.2519	0.2176	0.1631	0.1229	0.0930
17	0.4732	0.4363	0.3714	0.3166	0.2703	0.2311	0.1978	0.1456	0.1078	0.0802
18	0.4528	0.4155	0.3503	0.2959	0.2503	0.2120	0.1799	0.1300	0.0946	0.0691
19	0.4333	0.3957	0.3305	0.2765	0.2317	0.1945	0.1635	0.1161	0.0830	0.0596
20	0.4146	0.3769	0.3118	0.2584	0.2146	0.1784	0.1486	0.1037	0.0728	0.0514

The present value of an investment is found by selecting the proper interest rate, selecting the number of periods hence, and determining where they come together on the table. For example, select the 10 percent column, one year hence; where the two come together is the number 0.9091. This is the present value of $1 at a 10 percent interest rate compounded for one year. Assume that $1,000 is desired at the end of two years. The 10 percent column is used, and two periods hence. The number 0.8265 appears where the two join, and this amount must be multiplied by $1,000 to determine the present value of $1,000, which is $826.50. Although some differences may occur in the dollar amounts because of the rounding factors, usually these differences are small. The use of the present-value method is referred to as discounting, and the 10 percent rate is called the discount rate.

Table 1 is used any time the amount to be received in the future is a lump sum amount. Often, however, the amount to be received is in yearly or other periodic increments. Table 2, shown below, is a table of the present value of $1 received periodically for a number of periods.

TABLE 2 Present Value of $1 Received Periodically for a Number of Periods

Periods Hence	4½%	5%	6%	7%	8%	9%	10%	12%	14%	16%
1	0.9569	0.9524	0.9434	0.9346	0.9529	0.9174	0.9091	0.8929	0.8772	0.8621
2	1.8727	1.8594	1.8334	1.8080	1.7833	1.7591	1.7355	1.6901	1.6467	1.6052
3	2.7490	2.7232	2.6730	2.6243	2.5771	2.5313	2.4869	2.4018	2.3216	2.2459
4	3.5875	3.5460	3.4651	3.3872	3.3121	3.2397	3.1699	3.0374	2.9137	2.7982
5	4.3900	4.3295	4.2124	4.1002	3.9927	3.8897	3.7908	3.6048	3.4331	3.2743
6	5.1579	5.0757	4.9173	4.7665	4.6229	4.4859	4.3553	4.1114	3.8887	3.6847
7	5.8927	5.7864	5.5824	5.3893	5.2064	5.0330	4.8684	4.5638	4.2883	4.0386
8	6.5959	6.4632	6.2098	5.9713	5.7466	5.5348	5.3349	4.9676	4.6389	4.3436
9	7.2688	7.1078	6.8017	6.5152	6.2469	5.9953	5.7590	5.3283	4.9464	4.6065
10	7.9127	7.7217	7.3601	7.0236	6.7101	6.4177	6.1446	5.6502	5.2161	4.8332
11	8.5289	8.3064	7.8869	7.4987	7.1390	6.8052	6.4951	5.9377	5.4527	5.0286
12	9.1186	8.8633	8.3838	7.9427	7.5361	7.1607	6.8137	6.1944	5.6603	5.1971
13	9.6829	9.3936	8.8527	8.3577	7.9038	7.4869	7.1034	6.4236	5.8424	5.3423
14	10.2228	9.8986	9.2950	8.7455	8.2442	7.7862	7.3667	6.6282	6.0021	5.4675
15	10.7395	10.3797	9.7123	9.1079	8.5595	8.0607	7.6061	6.8109	6.1422	5.5755
16	11.2340	10.8378	10.1059	9.4467	8.8514	8.3126	7.8237	6.9740	6.2651	5.6685
17	11.7072	11.2741	10.4773	9.7632	9.1216	8.5436	8.0216	7.1196	6.3729	5.7487
18	12.1600	11.6896	10.8276	10.0591	9.3719	8.7556	8.2014	7.2497	6.4674	5.8179
19	12.5933	12.0853	11.1581	10.3356	9.6036	8.9501	8.3649	7.3658	6.5504	5.8775
20	13.0079	12.4622	11.4699	10.5940	9.8182	9.1286	8.5136	7.4694	6.6231	5.9288

For example, what is the present value of a series of five $800 amounts, with each $800 amount to be received at the end of each of five successive years, discounted at a rate of 8 percent? Using Table 2, select the 8 percent column and five periods hence to secure the number 3.9927. The number 3.9927 is the present value of $1 to be received annually at the end of each of five years, discounted at 8 percent. To calculate the total present value of $4,000

($800 received at end of each of five years), multiply 3.9927 by $800 to determine the present value of $3,194.16, or $3,194 rounded.

Table 2 is actually an accumulation of the columns in Table 1. Using the 8 percent discount rate and Table 1, the following illustrates this accumulation.

Using Table 1 and 8 Percent

Periods Hence	Table Amount
1	0.9259
2	0.8573
3	0.7938
4	0.7350
5	0.6806
	3.9926[a]

[a]Slight variation from rounding.

Using Table 1, 8 Percent, and $800

Periods Hence	Principal		Table Amount		Discounted Amount
1	$800	×	0.9259	=	740.72
2	$800	×	0.8573	=	685.84
3	$800	×	0.7938	=	635.04
4	$800	×	0.7350	=	588.00
5	$800	×	0.6806	=	544.48
					$3,194.08

Using Table 2, 8 Percent, and $800

Periods Hence	Principal		Table Amount		
5	$800	×	3.9927	=	$3,194.16[a]

[a]Slight variation from first table because of rounding.

Both tables are rounded to four places for simplicity, but rounding problems may occur because of the number of places in the tables. In a true business situation, present-value tables are used with as many as ten or more places.

PRESENT VALUE OF BONDS

Corporations often sell long-term liability contracts such as bonds payable. These bonds are purchased by investors who invest to receive the cash paid from the contract interest rate each interest period. When the market rate of interest fluctuates, potential investors will pay only the present value for the bonds, which may be more or less than face value, depending on the market rate. The present value of the bonds is equal to the accumulation of the two rights they received when they purchased the bonds. The first is the right to receive their principal back at the end of the term of the bond issue in a lump-sum repayment. Therefore, Table 1 is used to calculate the present value of this first right. The second right is the right to receive the contract interest rate at each of the stated periods of the issue. Because the bondholder receives interest each period for a number of periods, Table 2 is used to calculate the present value of this right. In calculating both of these rights, the current market rate of interest is used. By adding the two amounts together, the lump sum payment and the interest, each of which has been discounted at the market rate of interest, the present value of the issue is determined. The present value of the investment is the amount the potential bondholder is willing to pay and the amount the corporation will receive for the issue.

Bonds Sold for a Discount

A corporation selling bonds when the prevailing market rate of interest is higher than the contract rate of interest can only sell them at a discount. To illustrate how the selling price is determined, assume that the market rate of interest is 12 percent. A corporation offers to sell and issue bonds having a $100,000 face value and a ten-year life, on which interest is to be paid twice each year at the contract rate of interest of 10 percent per year. Following are the calculations for the present value of a $100,000 face value, 10%, ten-year bond sold at a discount.

Present Value of a Bond Sold at a Discount

Present Value of Right 1
Present value of $100,000 to be received 20 periods
   hence, discounted at 6% per period ($100,000 ×
   0.3118) $31,180

Present Value of Right 2
Present value of $5,000 to be received for 20 semiannual
   periods, discounted at 6% per period ($5,000 ×
   11.4699, rounded)   57,350

Present Value of the Bonds $88,530

Face value $100,000
Less present value   − 88,530
Discount on bonds $ 11,470

In purchasing these bonds, the investor will gain the following two rights, as shown above.

1. the right to receive back the face value of $100,000 at the end of the 10 years

2. the right to $5,000 in interest, paid twice each year for 10 years

$$\$100{,}000 \times .10 \div 2 = \$5{,}000, \text{ semiannually}$$

Both of these rights are to receive money in the future. To determine today's value—the present value of the money to be received in the future—the present value of the two amounts is determined using the market rate of interest. If the market rate is 12 percent per year, it is 6 percent when paid semiannually, and in 10 years there are 20 semiannual periods. Using Table 1, the present value table for compound interest, choose the 6 percent column, 20 periods hence. The amount of .3118 is multiplied by $100,000 to calculate the present value of the first right as shown above.

To calculate the present value of the second right, use Table 2, amounts received periodically for a number of years. The amount of 11.4699 is multiplied by the semiannual interest of $5,000 to calculate the present value of the second right. Observe that Table 1 is used for the first right, because there is a lump sum payment of $100,000 to the bondholders at the end of the 20 periods. Table 2 is used for the second right, because there are two periodic payments each year for 10 years. Add the two rights to find the present value of the bond. The present value of the investment is the amount the bond will sell for. This example illustrates that the bond will sell for a discount of $11,470.

Bonds Sold for a Premium

When a corporation issues a bond and the prevailing market rate of interest is below the contract rate of interest, it will sell the bonds at a premium. To illustrate bonds selling at a premium, again assume a 10 percent bond issue with a face value of $100,000 and a ten-year life. Also assume that the market rate of interest is 9 percent annually or 4-½ percent semiannually. Following are the calculations for the present value of a $100,000 face value, 10%, ten-year bond sold at a premium of $6,500.

Present Value of a Bond Sold at a Premium

Present Value of Right 1		
Present value of $100,000 to be received 20 periods hence, discounted at 4-1/2% per period ($100,000 × 0.4146)		$ 41,460
Present Value of Right 2		
Present value of $5,000 to be received for 20 semiannual periods, discounted at 4-½% per period ($5,000 × 13.0079)		65,040 (rounded)
Present Value of Bonds		$106,500
Present value of bond	$106,500	
Face value of bond	100,000	
Premium on bond	$ 6,500	

Exercises

Exercise 23A.1

On January 2 of the current year, a corporation sold $500,000 of its 9-½%, ten-year bonds at a price to reflect a market rate of 12 percent, with interest to be paid semiannually. Calculate the selling price using Table 1 and Table 2. Present your calculations as shown in this appendix.

Exercise 23A.2

A corporation sold $600,000 of its own 8-½%, ten-year bonds on their date of issue, January 2. Interest on these bonds is payable June 30 and December 31. The bonds were sold when the market rate was 9 percent. Calculate the selling price using Table 1 and Table 2. Present your calculations as shown in this appendix.

Exercise 23A.3   On March 31 of the current year, a corporation sold $1,000,000 of its 10%, ten-year Bonds Payable that yielded the buyers a market rate of 9 percent. The interest is to be paid semiannually on March 31 and September 30. Calculate the selling price using Table 1 and Table 2. Present your calculations as shown in this appendix.

CHAPTER 24

Corporations: Short-Term and Long-Term Investments

Corporations may choose to buy the stock of other corporations for investment purposes. These investments may take the form of short-term temporary or long-term investments. **Short-term investments** are those where management expects to hold them for less than one year and generally include common and preferred stock. These investments will be classified as current assets and are considered to be available sources of cash when sold. If management intends to hold investments for longer than a year, the investments are classified in their own category on the balance sheet, **long-term investments.** Such investments may include land or other assets not regularly used in the normal operations of business, funds earmarked for a special purpose (such as a bond sinking fund), or the stock of another corporation.

short-term investments
temporary investments that management expects to hold for less than one year

long-term investments
investments that management expects to hold for longer than one year

ACCOUNTING FOR SHORT-TERM TEMPORARY INVESTMENTS IN STOCK

A corporation having idle cash may choose to invest it in a number of ways, such as placing the funds into a savings account or into a certificate of deposit where they will earn interest. Or management may believe it can achieve a higher return on its investment by buying the stock of another corporation that may increase in market value enough to be a good temporary investment or that may pay high dividends.

When purchased, short-term temporary investments in the stock of another company are recorded at cost (including broker's fees). Later on, if the stock declines in value below its cost, the decline will be shown on the income statement as a loss. If the market value later increases, the increase will be reported as a gain, but a gain above original cost is not recorded. The method for recording stock purchases at cost and the procedure for reporting the portfolios at the lower-of-cost-or-market will be discussed in the following paragraphs.

Purchasing Corporation Stock at Cost

When stock is purchased for either a short-term temporary investment or a long-term investment, it is recorded at total cost, which includes the purchase price and the broker's commission (transfer fees). Because the corporation may invest in the stock of several different corporations, it will record the purchase of each issue at cost. An account titled Marketable Equity Securities is debited when stock is purchased. **Marketable equity securities** are securities, such as common stock, held by a corporation that can be readily bought and sold on a stock exchange.

marketable equity securities
securities held by a corporation that can be readily bought and sold on a stock exchange

The account Marketable Equity Securities is a control account and is classified on the balance sheet as a current asset. A separate subsidiary ledger will be kept showing the exact cost of each purchase or sale. The account Marketable Equity Securities is sometimes referred to as a portfolio, designating that more than one corporate issue has been purchased. To properly account for these temporary purchases, the Financial Accounting Standards Board (FASB), the rule-making body of the AICPA, requires that a specific procedure be used. Statement 12 of the FASB, "Accounting for Certain Marketable Equity Securities,"[1] requires that the purchase be recorded initially at cost. For example, assume that 500 shares of Black Corporation's common stock are purchased as a temporary investment at 25-¼ plus a $150 broker's commission. The entry to record this transaction is as follows.

GENERAL JOURNAL				Page
Date	Description	Post. Ref.	Debit	Credit
19XX *Aug.* *1*	*Marketable Equity Securities*		*12 7 7 5 —*	
	Cash			*12 7 7 5 —*
	To Record the Purchase of 500 Shares of Black			
	Corporation Common Stock at 25-¼			

The calculation of the total cost of this purchase is as follows.

500 shares × $25.25	=	$12,625
Plus Broker's Commission	=	150
Total Cost		$12,775

---

[1] FASB Statement No. 12, "Accounting for Certain Marketable Securities" (Stamford, Conn.: Financial Accounting Standards Board, 1975).

Assume further that the Black Corporation paid a $1 per share dividend to its shareholders on September 30. The entry to record the receipt of this dividend is as follows.

GENERAL JOURNAL				Page	
Date	Description	Post. Ref.	Debit	Credit	
Sept. **30**	**Cash**		500 —		
	Dividend Income			500 —	
	To Record the Receipt of $1 per Share Dividend				
	on 500 Shares of Black Corporation Common				
	Stock				

A stock dividend is not income, however, and no entry recording it should be made. The stock dividend will be noted in the investment portfolio and the cost per share recalculated.

Sale of Marketable Equity Securities

When stock purchased for a temporary investment is sold, the selling price of the stock must be compared with the cost and any gain or loss recorded. Assume that 300 shares of the Black Corporation stock is sold at 30-½ less a $100 broker's commission. The calculation for the sale of marketable equity securities is as follows.

300 shares × $30.50	=	$9,150
Less: Broker's Commission	=	100
Total received from sale		$9,050
Less: Cost of 300 Shares		
$\left(\dfrac{300}{500} \times \$12,\!775 = \$7,\!665 \right)^{a}$		7,665
Gain on Sale of Stock	=	$1,385

[a]The total cost of the 500 shares was $12,775. Of the 500 shares, 300 were sold, or 300/500 of the total. This fraction multiplied by the total cost gives the cost of 300 shares.

$$300/500 \times \$12,\!775 = \$7,\!665$$

The same result may be obtained by dividing the total cost by the total number of shares purchased,

$$\$12,\!775 \div 500 = \$25.55 \text{ cost per share,}$$

and by multiplying the cost per share by the number of shares sold.

$$\$25.55 \times 300 = \$7,\!665$$

This second method is not preferred, however, because of the variations that may occur in answers because of rounding.

The general journal entry to record this sale is as follows.

GENERAL JOURNAL					Page	
Date	Description	Post. Ref.	Debit		Credit	
19XX *Dec.* 1	Cash		9 0 5 0 —			
	Marketable Equity Securities				7 6 6 5 —	
	Gain on Sale of Stock				1 3 8 5 —	
	To Record the Sale of 300 Shares of Black					
	Corporation Common Stock at 30-½					

subsidiary stock investment ledger
a ledger showing the detail of purchases and sales of stock of other corporations

When the issue is purchased, it is recorded in the control account in the general ledger, as well as in a **subsidiary stock investment ledger** detailing the Black Corporation issue. If other corporate stock is purchased, each type will be listed separately as shown on page 894.

When the remaining shares are sold, the selling price is again compared with the cost to determine the gain or loss on the sale. The balances of all the investment accounts, including the $5,110 balance in the Black Corporation account, will be added together to verify the balance in the control account, Marketable Equity Securities. The balance in the control account should be the same as the total of all the investments.

Marketable Equity Securities at Lower-of-Cost-or-Market Valuation

lower-of-cost-or-market
a method of valuation used for marketable equity securities at accounting year end where one or the other is chosen for balance sheet purposes

Accounting for marketable equity securities at the end of the accounting period requires special consideration. Statement 12 of the FASB requires the portfolio to be accounted for by the **lower-of-cost-or-market** rule. To illustrate the procedure, assume that Sims Corporation purchased the stock of three different corporations. The balance of the Marketable Equity Securities account is $27,300 on December 31, 19X8. The specific cost detail taken from the subsidiary stock investment ledger is shown on page 895.

STOCK INVESTMENT ACCOUNT, 19X8

NAME: BLACK CORPORATION
DESCRIPTION: COMMON STOCK

Date	Number of Shares	Certificate Numbers	Price per Share	Total Cost	Date Sold	Sale Price	Gain (Loss)	Dividends Received
8/1	500	48249-48749	25¼	$12775 —				—
9/30	300	48249-48548	30½	7665 —	12/1	$9050 —	$1385 —	$500 —
Balance	200			$5110 —				

	Cost
Eddy Corporation	$ 8,000
Frank Corporation	6,525
Black Corporation	12,775
Total Cost	$27,300

A comparison of the total market price of all the stock in the portfolio, called the aggregate by Statement 12, with the total cost (or aggregate cost) in the portfolio is made as follows.

	Cost	Market
Eddy Corporation	$ 8,000	$ 7,000
Frank Corporation	6,525	6,600
Black Corporation	12,775	12,900
Aggregate	$27,300	$26,500

unrealized loss
a loss that occurs from the lower-of-cost-or-market valuation of marketable equity securities

The difference between the aggregate cost and the aggregate market value of the stock on December 31, 19X8, is $800. This results in an unrealized loss of $800. The term **unrealized loss** is used to show the possibility that if the stock were sold immediately, it would sell at a loss. A corporation must show this potential loss on its balance sheet at the end of the year to properly state the assets the corporation holds. Therefore, an adjusting entry must be made to reduce the cost price to the market value for balance sheet purposes. The adjusting entry and balance sheet presentation are as follows.

GENERAL JOURNAL				Page
Date	**Description**	**Post. Ref.**	**Debit**	**Credit**
19XX Dec. 31	*Unrealized Loss on Marketable Equity Securities*		800 —	
	Allowance to Reduce Marketable Equity			
	Securities to Market			800 —
	To Record the Loss in Value of Temporary			
	Investments by Lower-of-Cost-or-Market			
	Procedures			

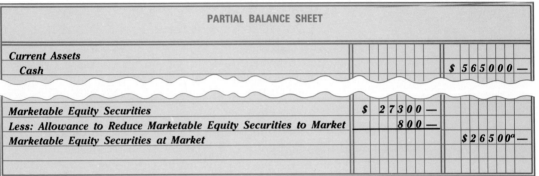

PARTIAL BALANCE SHEET			
Current Assets			
Cash			$ 5 6 5 0 0 0 —
Marketable Equity Securities	$ 2 7 3 0 0 —		
Less: Allowance to Reduce Marketable Equity Securities to Market	8 0 0 —		
Marketable Equity Securities at Market		$ 2 6 5 0 0ª —	

ªMany corporations will show only the net amount, as illustrated in Appendix 22A.

allowance to reduce marketable equity securities to market
an offset account to the Marketable Equity Securities account to show the net value of these securities on the balance sheet

The account Unrealized Loss on Marketable Equity Securities is closed to the Income Summary account in the closing process and will appear on the income statement. The account **Allowance to Reduce Marketable Equity Securities to Market** is classified as a contra-asset account and will appear on the balance sheet as a deduction from the investment account. Where the comparison of aggregate cost and aggregate market is made, the lower-of-cost-or-market value is chosen for valuation. If cost is the lower of the two, no adjusting entry is necessary, and the cost price remains on the balance sheet. If market price is lower, as shown in the previous example, that valuation is used and the unrealized loss is recorded. Assume the following for the Sims Corporation on December 31, 19X9:

	Cost	Market
Gaddy Corporation	$10,000	$11,000
Laurel Corporation	12,000	12,500
Aggregate	$22,000	$23.500

At the end of 19X8, Sims Corporation recorded an unrealized loss on marketable equity securities. At the end of 19X9, there is a gain of $1,500. An unrealized gain is not recorded, except to offset an unrealized loss recorded earlier. The stock that the Sims Corporation held as a temporary investment in 19X8 has been sold, and two different stock purchases have been made in 19X9, as shown. When the cost of the stock is compared with the market value, cost is found to be the lower of the two: thus, the cost of $22,000 must be shown on the balance sheet. Since the account Allowance to Reduce Marketable Equity Securities to Market still has an $800 credit balance from 19X8, it must be removed from the books at the end of 19X9, because at that time the cost is lower than the market, and an allowance account is not necessary. The allowance account is debited to close it, and an unrealized gain account is credited as follows.

GENERAL JOURNAL					Page	
Date	Description	Post. Ref.	Debit		Credit	
19XX Dec. 31	Allowance to Reduce Marketable Equity					
	Securities to Market		8 0 0 —			
	Unrealized Gain on Marketable					
	Equity Securities				8 0 0 —	
	To Record the Recovery of Market to Cost Using					
	the Lower-of-Cost-or-Market Procedures					

unrealized gain
a gain recorded only to the extent that it represents a recovery of an unrealized loss of past years

An **unrealized gain** is recorded only to the extent that it represents a recovery of an unrealized loss of past years. When the total original cost is less than market, an allowance account is not necessary and there will be no unrealized gain or loss.

ACCOUNTING FOR LONG-TERM INVESTMENTS

A corporation may invest in another corporation with the intent of holding the stock for an undetermined length of time. If this is management's intent, the investment will be classified as long term. Assume the Patton Corporation bought 1,000 shares of Byer Corporation's common stock at $25 a share including the broker's commission. The journal entry to record this transaction is as follows.

GENERAL JOURNAL					Page	
Date	Description	Post. Ref.	Debit		Credit	
19XX *Jan.* 2	*Investment in Byer Corporation*		2 5 0 0 0 —			
	Cash				2 5 0 0 0 —	
	To Record the Purchase of 1,000 Shares of Byer					
	Corporation Common Stock at $25					

The account Investment: Byer Corporation is classified as a long-term investment. Because corporations limit their long-term purchases, the account title may include the name of the corporation in which the investment is made.

Long-Term Investments—Consolidations

A corporation may buy enough of the outstanding shares of another corporation to gain control of its operations. For example, if Patton Corporation purchases 51 percent or more of Byer Corporation's outstanding voting common stock, Patton would gain control of Byer. By owning the majority of the voting shares, Patton could elect the board of directors, and thus gain control of all the activities of Byer Corporation. In this situation, Patton Corporation would be known as the **parent corporation** and Byer would be called the **subsidiary corporation.**

parent corporation
a corporation owning enough voting stock of another corporation to control its activities

subsidiary corporation
a corporation where another corporation owns the majority of its voting stock and exercises control over all its activities

There are both legal and tax advantages for a parent corporation controlling a subsidiary corporation. Patton Corporation and Byer Corporation must keep separate accounting records and by law are still two separate legal entities. As legal entities, each has certain rights, duties, and responsibilities as separate corporations. Keeping in mind that the primary advantage of the corporate form of business is limited stockholders' liability, the stockholder in this case (Patton Corporation) is liable to lose only what it invests, and will not be legally liable for the Byer Corporation beyond that amount. In addition to the limited liability advantage, it is also likely that Byer Corporation will have a lower net income upon which the Internal Revenue Service can collect a tax. Because the profits of Byer Corporation will be taxed separately from those of Patton, a lower effective tax may result.

If one corporation has economic control of another, the Securities and Exchange Commission requires publicly held corporate parents to publish their financial statements as if the two corporations were one single economic entity. These statements, the consolidated balance sheet and the consolidated income statement, will be prepared in this text using the equity method of consolidation. A **consolidated balance sheet** is a financial statement showing parent and subsidiary corporations as if they were one economic entity. Appendix 21A illustrates typical financial statements for a corporation.

consolidated balance sheet
a financial statement showing parent and subsidiary corporations as if they were one economic entity

CONSOLIDATED BALANCE SHEET

When a parent corporation controls a subsidiary, they are separate legal and accounting entities, but investors expect the parent company to show the results of all operations under its control. Thus, the parent prepares a consolidated balance sheet combining the assets and liabilities of the parent company and its subsidiaries and prepares a consolidated income statement combining revenue, cost of goods sold, and expenses.

The goal of a consolidated financial statement is to account for two legal entities as if they were one economic unit. When the parent's and the subsidiary corporation's balance sheets are consolidated, duplications are eliminated so the combined figures do not inflate assets or equities. For example, a parent corporation's investment in a subsidiary is evidenced by the common shares recorded on the parent corporation's books as an asset (investment). When preparing a consolidated balance sheet combining the assets, liabilities, and equities of the two entities, it would not be logical to include both the Investment in Common Stock by the parent company and the assets of the subsidiary. To avoid such duplication, one must be eliminated when preparing the consolidated balance sheet.

This elimination is accomplished by using a special worksheet. On this worksheet, the parent's investment is credited, thus eliminating it because the investment in the subsidiary is recorded as an asset, and the subsidiary's common stock and retained earnings are debited, thus eliminating them from the worksheet. The assets and liabilities of the subsidiary remain on the worksheet and will be used for preparing the consolidated balance sheet.

Consolidated Balance Sheet Preparation

To make preparing the consolidated balance sheet easier, a special worksheet is used. Assume that Patton Corporation buys all of the outstanding stock of Byer Corporation—10,000 shares of common stock at $12 a share. Patton records this purchase on its books as follows:

GENERAL JOURNAL					Page
Date	Description	Post. Ref.	Debit	Credit	
19XX *Jan.* 2	*Investment in Byer Corporation*		120000 —		
	Cash			120000 —	
	To Record the Purchase of 10,000 Shares of Byer				
	Corporation Common Stock at $12 per Share				

Byer Corporation records nothing on its books except to change the stockholders' registrar to reflect the new owners of the stock. The worksheet for Patton Corporation follows on page 901.

The only purpose for using this type of worksheet is to consolidate the two legal entities into one economic entity for presentation of the results of operations to stockholders and the Securities and Exchange Commission. The worksheet is not a formal statement, and the entries made on it are not journalized or posted. Observe carefully the two columns used for the elimination process. While several steps may be needed to complete the worksheet, in this first example only one step was demonstrated.

As mentioned previously, the investment of the parent, $120,000, is credited on the worksheet. When extending the figures across to the consolidations amounts column, the original debit of $120,000 (Investment in Byer Corporation) is now offset by a credit of $120,000, thus eliminating the investment. The common stock and the retained earnings of the subsidiary are both debited, which also eliminates them. These two entries on the worksheet are necessary to prevent counting the same resources twice. The com-

PATTON CORPORATION AND SUBSIDIARY COMPANY
Worksheet for a Consolidated Balance Sheet
January 2, 19X8

	Patton	Byer	Eliminations Debit	Eliminations Credit	Consolidations Amounts
Assets					
Cash	150000 —	15000			165000 —
Notes Receivable	10000 —				10000 —
Accounts Receivable	25000 —	10000 —			35000 —
Investment in Byer Corporation	120000 —			@ 120000 —	0
Other Assets	530000 —	105000 —			635000 —
	835000 —	130000 —			845000 —
Liabilities and Equities					
Notes Payable	25000 —				25000 —
Accounts Payable	10000 —	10000 —			20000 —
Common Stock	600000 —	100000 —	@ 100000 —		600000 —
Retained Earnings	200000 —	20000 —	@ 20000 —		200000 —
	835000 —	130000 —	120000 —	120000 —	845000 —

bined amounts on the worksheet are used to prepare a consolidated balance sheet that shows all the assets and equities of both parent and subsidiary.

The following steps may be taken when preparing a consolidated balance sheet.

1. Enter amounts on the worksheet.
    a. Eliminate the investment of the parent against the stockholders' equity of the subsidiary.
    b. Eliminate any other intercompany duplications.
    c. Recognize any excess, called Goodwill.
    d. Recognize any minority interest.

2. Complete the worksheet and prepare the consolidated balance sheet.
    a. Extend totals across to the consolidations amounts column.
    b. Prepare the formal consolidated balance sheet from the last column on the worksheet.
    c. Do not post the eliminating entries. File the worksheet.

These steps can be used in many different situations and are given to aid the student. In step 1, item a, the parent's investment is eliminated and so are the common stock and retained earnings of the subsidiary, as previously discussed. Item b eliminates intercompany transactions between parent and subsidiary. Item c is recorded when the parent has paid more for the stock than the equity per share of the subsidiary. Item d is recorded whenever the corporation buys only a portion of the outstanding stock of the subsidiary and does not own all the outstanding shares.

The worksheet on page 901 illustrates only part of step 1 (item a) and step 2 (item a). Patton Corporation bought all of Byer Corporation's outstanding stock and paid exactly book value for it. (This may not always be the case.) In other words, Patton paid $120,000 for a $120,000 interest in Byer Corporation. To calculate the book value of the subsidiary corporation, the liabilities are subtracted from the assets; the remainder is the book value of Byer Corporation. The book value of Byer Corporation shown on the worksheet is $120,000.

minority interest occurs when the parent corporation does not own all of the subsidiary corporation's outstanding stock

Because Patton Corporation paid exactly book value for Byer's stock, there are no duplications in assets or liabilities to account for, nor is there any minority interest. A **minority interest** occurs when the parent does not own all of the outstanding stock of a subsidiary. Minority stockholders are those who do not own enough stock to exercise any control.

The worksheet is prepared and used as a guide for preparing the consolidated balance sheet. In the worksheet on page 901, when the balances on the worksheet are extended across, combining the debit and credit items, the total assets are $845,000, and the total liabilities and owners' equity are $845,000. This amount is $10,000 greater than the amount for the parent company alone. The $10,000 difference is the claim on Byer's assets by Byer's creditors, represented by Accounts Payable, and must be included when consolidating amounts. The consolidated balance sheet is prepared from the consolidations amounts column on the worksheet as follows.

PATTON CORPORATION AND SUBSIDIARY
Consolidated Balance Sheet
January 2, 19X8

Assets		
Cash	$ 165000 —	
Notes Receivable	10000 —	
Accounts Receivable (Net)	35000 —	
Other Assets	635000 —	
Total Assets		$ 845000 —
Liabilities and Stockholders' Equity		
Liabilities		
Notes Payable	25000 —	
Accounts Payable	20000 —	
Total Liabilities		45000 —
Stockholders' Equity		
Common Stock	600000 —	
Retained Earnings	200000 —	
Total Stockholders' Equity		$ 800000 —
Total Liabilities and Stockholders' Equity		$ 845000 —

In the previous illustration, Patton Corporation purchased 100 percent of Byer Corporation's stock and paid book value for it. This will not always be the case, however. A parent might pay more or less than book value for a subsidiary's stock and may purchase only a portion of it.

To continue to illustrate this concept, assume that Patton Corporation could purchase only 80 percent of the 10,000 outstanding shares of Byer and paid $14 per share, $2 over book value. The following are the calculations (from step 1) that show the dollar amounts to be used on the consolidated worksheet. By making these calculations before preparing the worksheet, all the dollar amounts to be used on the worksheet will be determined beforehand. The worksheet is subsequently used for preparing the consolidated balance sheet.

Calculations

1. Cost to the parent corporation
   to buy the stock:
   (80% × 10,000 shares × $14) = $112,000

2. 80% of book value of shares of
   subsidiary corporation purchased.
   (80% × $120,000) =   96,000

3. Subtract 2 from 1 to get the difference,
   which is debited to Goodwill.
   ($112,000 − $96,000) = $16,000

4. Determine the minority interest:
   20% × book value of subsidiary corporation.
   (20% × $120,000) = $24,000

The worksheet on page 905 shows how the above amounts are used to complete the worksheet.

a. The $112,000 investment in Byer Corporation is credited on the worksheet to remove it from Patton's assets, and common stock and retained earnings are debited to remove them from Byer's equity section.

b, c. Goodwill is debited for $16,000 on the worksheet of Patton Corporation because more was paid for the net assets of Byer than the book value of the stock indicated they were worth. Because the parent owns only 80 percent of the subsidiary's stock, there is a 20 percent minority interest that must be reflected on the consolidated balance sheet. Twenty percent of the book value of Byer Corporation's stock is equal to $24,000 and is recorded on the last line of the worksheet in the stockholders' equity section.

PATTON CORPORATION AND SUBSIDIARY COMPANY
Worksheet for a Consolidated Balance Sheet
January 2, 19X8

	Patton	Byer	Eliminations Debit	Eliminations Credit	Consolidations Amounts
Assets					
Cash	158000 —	15000 —			173000 —
Notes Receivable	10000 —				10000 —
Accounts Receivable	25000 —	10000 —			35000 —
Investment in Byer Corporation	112000 —			(a) 112000 —	0
Other Assets	530000 —	105000 —			635000 —
Goodwill			(b) 16000 —		16000 —
	835000 —	130000 —			869000 —
Liabilities and Equities					
Notes Payable	25000 —				25000 —
Accounts Payable	10000 —	10000 —			20000 —
Common Stock	600000 —	100000 —	(a) 100000 —		600000 —
Retained Earnings	200000 —	20000 —	(a) 20000 —		200000 —
Minority Interest				(c) 24000 —	24000 —
	835000 —	130000 —	136000 —	136000 —	869000 —

After the worksheet is completed, the consolidated balance sheet is prepared from the consolidations amounts columns.

PATTON CORPORATION AND SUBSIDIARY Consolidated Balance Sheet January 2, 19X8		
Assets		
Cash	$ 173000 —	
Notes Receivable	10000 —	
Accounts Receivable (Net)	35000 —	
Other Assets	635000 —	
Goodwill	16000 —	
Total Assets		$ 869000 —
Liabilities and Stockholders' Equity		
Liabilities		
Notes Payable (Current)	$ 25000 —	
Accounts Payable	20000 —	
Total Liabilities		$ 45000 —
Stockholders' Equity		
Minority Interest in Subsidiary	$ 24000 —	
Common Stock	600000 —	
Retained Earnings	200000 —	
Total Stockholders' and Minority Equities		824000 —
Total Liabilities and Stockholders' Equity		$ 869000 —

One other example of like items to be eliminated relates to an intercompany loan.

Assume that on the date of acquisition the parent loans the subsidiary corporation $15,000 in cash. The following journal entries are made on the two separate corporation books.

Parent's Books

GENERAL JOURNAL				Page
Date	Description	Post. Ref.	Debit	Credit
Jan. 2	Notes Receivable: Byer Corporation		15000 —	
	Cash			15000 —
	To Record the Receipt of a 90-Day,			
	Non-interest-bearing Note from Byer Corporation			

Subsidiary's Books

GENERAL JOURNAL				Page
Date	Description	Post. Ref.	Debit	Credit
Jan. 2	Cash		15000 —	
	Notes Payable: Patton Corporation			15000 —
	To Record the Giving of a 90-Day,			
	Non-interest-bearing Note to Patton Corporation			

This loan is an intercompany transfer of $15,000 cash. When consolidating the two balance sheets, it is wrong to include both the $15,000 note receivable of Patton Corporation and the cash of Byer Corporation of $15,000. To do so would overstate the assets on a consolidated basis. It is also wrong to show an additional liability of $15,000 (note payable on the Byer books), because a corporation cannot owe itself on a consolidated balance sheet. The procedure when preparing the worksheet is to eliminate the Note Receivable by a credit and to eliminate the Note Payable by a debit. When the totals are extended, only the $15,000 cash is recorded. This asset is now in the subsidiary's bank account, and no other receivable or payable is shown for purposes of consolidation. The following worksheet on page 908 (item b) illustrates the intercompany elimination.

PATTON CORPORATION AND SUBSIDIARY COMPANY
Worksheet for a Consolidated Balance Sheet
January 2, 19X8

	Patton	Byer	Eliminations Debit	Eliminations Credit	Consolidations Amounts
Assets					
Cash	143000—	30000—			173000—
Notes Receivable	25000—			(b) 15000—	10000—
Accounts Receivable	25000—	10000—			35000—
Investment in Byer Corporation	112000—			(a) 112000—	0
Other Assets	530000—	105000—			635000—
Goodwill			(c) 16000—		16000—
	835000—	145000—			869000—
Liabilities and Equities					
Notes Payable	25000—	15000—	(b) 15000—		25000—
Accounts Payable	10000—	10000—			20000—
Common Stock	600000—	100000—	(a) 100000—		600000—
Retained Earnings	200000—	20000—	(a) 20000—		200000—
Minority Interest				(d) 24000—	24000—
	835000—	145000—	151000—	151000—	869000—

Subsidiary Dividends and Earnings

The previous illustrations are based on the consolidated balance sheet at the time of acquisition. The investment by the parent corporation was initially recorded at cost. Over a period of time, however, the subsidiary may earn a net income and may pay out dividends. This means the equity the parent has in a subsidiary grows accordingly. For consolidated purposes, the cost of the investment account on the parent's books will be adjusted to reflect this increased equity. This process is called the equity method of consolidation. The **equity method of consolidation** is the accounting method used to adjust the cost of the investment of the parent corporation by recording its portion of a subsidiary corporation's net income and the return on the investment by the receipt of cash dividends.

equity method of consolidation
the accounting method used to adjust the cost of the investment of the parent corporation by recording its portion of a subsidiary corporation's net income and the return of investment by the receipt of cash dividends

For example, assume Byer Corporation has net income of $15,000 one year after acquisition by Patton. Assume further that Byer Corporation paid a cash dividend of $5,000 during the year. Because Patton Corporation has an 80 percent interest in the Byer Corporation, its investment in the subsidiary increases by 80 percent of the subsidiary's earnings. In addition, Patton Corporation receives a cash dividend equal to 80 percent of the total Byer Corporation paid ($4,000). This receipt of $4,000 is dividend income to the Patton Corporation and is a return of part of its investment in the subsidiary. Patton Corporation makes the following journal entries on its books to reflect its increased equity in Byer Corporation.

GENERAL JOURNAL					Page	
Date	Description	Post. Ref.	Debit		Credit	
19XX Dec. 31	Investment in Byer Corporation		12000 —			
	Earnings from Investment in Byer Corporation				12000 —	
	To Record 80% of the Net Income Reported					
	by Byer Corporation					
31	Cash		4000 —			
	Investment in Byer Corporation				4000 —	
	To Record the Receipt of 80% of the $5,000					
	Cash Dividend Paid by Byer Corporation					

The following T-accounts used to record the above entries more readily show how the equity method of accounting works.

Parent's Books   Subsidiary's Books

Investment in Byer Corporation   **Common Stock**

| 1/2   112,000 | 12/31   4,000 | | | 1/2   100,000 |

1/2   112,000 | 12/31   4,000
12/31   12,000
⎯⎯⎯⎯⎯
120,000

1/2   100,000

Retained Earnings

12/31   5,000 | 1/2   20,000
              | 12/31   15,000
              ⎯⎯⎯⎯⎯
              30,000

During the year, Byer Corporation had net income of $15,000 and paid out $5,000 in dividends, resulting in a December 31 balance in Retained Earnings of $30,000. The net increase in retained earnings is $10,000 of which 80 percent (or $8,000) is a net increase in equity to Patton as well. The parent's T-account, Investment in Byer Corporation, shows this increased equity by the debit of $12,000 and the credit of $4,000 (a net $8,000 increase). The $12,000 represents Patton Corporation's 80 percent interest in net income, and the $4,000 represents the cash return of that investment. The minority interest shareholders' equity will also increase to $26,000. The consolidated worksheet after one year follows on page 911.

The T-accounts shown above for Patton and Byer Corporations on December 31, 19X8, illustrate that Patton Corporation had no transactions during the year except those recording its increased equity in Byer Corporation and its receipt of $4,000 in dividends. Assume further that Byer Corporation's assets and liabilities did not change during the year and that the note payable to Patton was not paid.

By comparing the two preceding worksheets, we observe the changes in Patton Corporation's and Byer Corporation's balance sheets during the year.

1. Patton Corporation's cash has increased by $4,000, the amount of the cash dividend.

2. Patton Corporation's retained earnings have increased by

PATTON CORPORATION AND SUBSIDIARY COMPANY
Worksheet for a Consolidated Balance Sheet
December 31, 19X8

	Patton	Byer	Eliminations Debit	Eliminations Credit	Consolidations Amounts
Assets					
Cash	147000 —	40000 —			187000 —
Notes Receivable	25000 —			(b) 15000 —	10000 —
Accounts Receivable	25000 —	10000 —			35000 —
Investment in Byer Company	120000 —			(a) 120000 —	0
Other Assets	530000 —	105000 —			635000 —
Goodwill			(c) 16000 —		16000 —
	847000 —	155000 —			883000 —
Liabilities and Equities					
Notes Payable	25000 —	15000 —	(b) 15000 —		25000 —
Accounts Payable	10000 —	10000 —			20000 —
Common Stock	600000 —	100000 —	(a) 100000 —		600000 —
Retained Earnings	212000 —	30000 —	(a) 30000 —		212000 —
Minority Interest				(d) 26000 —	26000 —
	847000 —	155000 —	161000 —	161000 —	883000 —

$12,000, an amount equal to 80 percent of the net income of Byer Corporation (Byer's net income was $15,000).

3. Byer Corporation's cash has increased by $10,000. Byer had cash net income of $15,000 and paid out $5,000 in dividends.

4. Byer Corporation's retained earnings have increased by $10,000, represented by the difference between the net income ($15,000) and the cash paid out in dividends ($5,000).

Consolidating the amounts on the worksheet simplifies the task of preparing the consolidated balance sheet. And referring to the steps presented on page 902 will be helpful when preparing the worksheet to consolidate the parent's and subsidiary's books. Item c of step 2 states: Do not post the eliminating entries (from the worksheet). File the worksheet. This is included to remind you that none of the debit and credit transactions recorded on the worksheet are recorded on the books of the parent or the subsidiary. They remain separate legal and accounting entities. This special worksheet is used solely for the purpose of preparing the consolidated balance sheet. Once the consolidated balance sheet is prepared, the worksheet is filed for future reference.

The discussion has been limited to the equity method of consolidation. Long-term investments may, however, be accounted for in other ways, the discussion of which must be deferred to advanced accounting courses. Today, readers of financial statements must have an understanding of consolidated statements because most major corporations have one or more subsidiaries. Preparation of these statements must conform to the rules of the AICPA and the Securities and Exchange Commission.

SUMMARY

Corporations make short-term and long-term investments in other corporations. Short-term investments are temporary and are expected to be sold in less than one year. If more than one investment is made in short-term securities, a special account is used as a control account. This account is titled Marketable Equity Securities. A subsidiary stock investment ledger is also used and contains the details of each purchase and sale of stock. The cost method is used to record the purchase price of the stock. When the stock is sold, the selling price is compared with the cost price to determine whether a gain or loss has occurred. Details in the subsidiary stock investment ledger are used for this purpose. At the end of the accounting period, the summary totals in the subsidiary ledger are compared with the balance in the control account Marketable Equity Securities to verify the accuracy of the two.

A special valuation procedure must be made of the short-term investments at the end of the accounting year. FASB Statement 12 requires that aggregate cost be compared with aggregate market and that the lower of the two be used for the balance sheet. If cost is the lowest in this comparison, no adjustments are necessary and the investment account will appear at cost on the balance sheet. However, if market is the lowest, an adjusting entry must be made to reduce cost to market. The account Allowance to Reduce Marketable Equity Securities to Market is credited. This account is a contra-asset account and will offset the Marketable Equity Securities account on the balance sheet. When the value on the balance sheet is lower than cost, an unrealized loss occurs and appears on the income statement. If future comparisons result in cost being the lowest, an unrealized gain is recorded and the allowance account is removed. An unrealized gain is recorded only to the extent an unrealized loss has previously occurred.

A long-term investment is one held for longer than one year. A corporation may wish to buy enough stock to be able to control the activities of another corporation. When this occurs, the corporation having control is called the parent corporation, and the corporation being controlled is called the subsidiary corporation. The Securities and Exchange Commission requires a parent corporation to prepare financial statements as if the parent and the subsidiary corporation were one economic entity.

A consolidated worksheet is used to simplify the task of preparing consolidated financial statements. Several steps are used to aid in preparing the worksheet for a consolidated balance sheet. They are: Eliminate the investment of the parent against the stockholders' equity of the subsidiary; eliminate any other intercompany duplication; recognize any excess, called Goodwill; and recognize any minority interest. Then extend all totals across to the consolidations amounts column, and prepare the formal consolidated balance sheet from that column on the worksheet. Do not post the eliminating entries. Finally, file the worksheet.

In addition, a number of calculations are necessary to determine the dollar amounts for cost, book value, goodwill, and minority interest. If the parent corporation does not own all of the outstanding stock of the subsidiary, the remaining stockholders are referred to as the minority interest stockholders. The minority interest of these stockholders must be listed in the equity section of the consolidated balance sheet.

The equity method of consolidation is used to determine the value of the investment after a period of time. When a subsidiary corporation has net income, its equity increases and so will the equity of the parent corporation. The parent corporation will account for its increased equity by increasing its investment account, which appears as an asset on its balance sheet. If the subsidiary corporation pays cash dividends, the parent corporation will decrease its investment account to show a return of part of its investment. The net amount of the investment account will be shown on the consolidated balance sheet. The minority interest will also increase as the subsidiary corporation has net income. Consolidated financial statements are prepared when one corporation owns controlling interest of another corporation. The consolidated financial statements show the two legal entities as if they were one economic entity.

Review of Accounting Terminology

Following is a list of the accounting terminology for this chapter.

allowance to reduce marketable
  equity securities to market
consolidated balance sheet
equity method of consolidation
lower-of-cost-or-market
long-term investments
marketable equity securities
minority interest

parent corporation
short-term investments
subsidiary corporation
subsidiary stock investment
  ledger
unrealized gain
unrealized loss

Fill in the blank with the correct word or term from the list.

1. A/an _____ is a corporation owning enough voting stock of another corporation to control its activities.

2. _____ is a method of valuation used for marketable equity securities at accounting year end, where one or the other is chosen for balance sheet purposes.

3. A financial statement showing parent and subsidiary corporations as if they were one economic entity is called a/an _____.

4. Temporary investments that management expects to hold for less than one year are _____.

5. A/an _____ is a loss that occurs from the lower-of-cost-or-market valuation of marketable equity securities.

6. The offset account to the Marketable Equity Securities account to show the net value of these securities on the balance sheet is called the _____.

7. Investments that management expects to hold for longer than one year are _____.

8. _____ are securities held by a corporation that can be readily bought and sold on a stock exchange.

9. When another corporation owns the majority of its voting stock and exercises control over its activities, this corporation is referred to as a/an _____.

10. A/an _____ occurs when the parent corporation does not own all of the subsidiary corporation's outstanding stock.

11. A/an _____ is a ledger showing the detail of purchases and sales of stock of other corporations.

12. The _____ is the accounting method used to adjust the cost of the investment of the parent corporation by recording its portion of a subsidiary corporation's net income and the return of investment by the receipt of cash dividends.

13. _____ is recorded only to the extent that it represents a recovery of an unrealized loss of past years.

Match the following words and terms on the left with the definitions on the right (columns continue on the following page).

14. allowance to reduce marketable equity securities to market
15. consolidated balance sheet
16. equity method of consolidation
17. lower-of-cost-or-market
18. long-term investments
19. marketable equity securities
20. minority interest
21. parent corporation

a. a loss occurring from the valuation of marketable equity securities using lower-of-cost-or-market valuation

b. a corporation owning enough voting stock of another corporation to control its activities

c. a corporation where another corporation owns the majority of its voting stock and exercises control over its activities

d. an offset account to the Marketable Equity Securities account to show the net value of these securities on the balance sheet

e. temporary investments that management expects to hold for less than one year

f. a method of valuation used for marketable equity securities at accounting year end, where one or the other is chosen for balance sheet purposes

g. investments that management expects to hold for longer than one year

h. a financial statement showing parent and subsidiary corporations as if they were one economic entity

22. short-term investments
23. subsidiary corporation
24. subsidiary stock investment ledger
25. unrealized gain
26. unrealized loss

i. securities held by a corporation that can be readily bought and sold on a stock exchange

j. occurs when the parent corporation does not own all of the subsidiary corporation's outstanding stock

k. a ledger showing the detail of purchases and sales of stock of other corporations

l. an accounting method used to adjust the cost of the investment of the parent corporation by recording its portion of a subsidiary's net income and the return of investment by the receipt of cash dividends

m. recorded only to the extent that it represents a recovery of an unrealized loss of past years

Exercises

Exercise 24.1
recording short-term stock purchases

The Johnson Corporation purchased stocks of other corporations for temporary investment purposes and completed the following transactions. Record each transaction below in general journal form. Account titles required are: Cash, Marketable Equity Securities, and Gain on Sale of Stock.

Jan. 2   purchased for cash 100 shares of Marvin Corporation common stock at $42 plus a $55 broker's commission

Feb. 14   purchased for cash 200 shares of Shelby, Incorporated common stock at $32 plus a $72 broker's commission

Mar. 11   purchased for cash 400 shares of Bay Corporation common stock at $15 plus a $68 broker's commission

Apr. 4   sold Marvin Corporation common stock at $47 less broker's fee of $59.

Exercise 24.2
recording the purchase and sale of short-term securities

The Leonard Corporation purchases common stock of other corporations for temporary investments. Record in general journal form the following transactions. Round amounts to the nearest dollar. Account titles required are: Cash, Marketable Equity Securities, Dividend Income, and Gain on Sale of Stock.

Mar. 27   purchased for cash 600 shares of Elvin Corporation common stock at $12 per share plus broker's fee of $94

Apr. 25   purchased for cash 450 shares of Palmer Corporation common stock at 25-¼ plus broker's fee of $88

Jun. 10   received $1 per share dividend on the Elvin Corporation stock

July 9   sold 250 shares of the Palmer Corporation common stock at 28-¾ less broker's fee of $45

Aug. 18   purchased for cash 100 shares of Berry Corporation common stock at 42-⅛ plus broker's fee of $49.50

Exercise 24.3
recording the purchase of marketable equity securities and preparing a partial balance sheet using the lower-of-cost-or-market method

Joshua Corporation purchases the common stock of other corporations for temporary investments.

a. Record the following 19X7 transactions in general journal form. Round to the nearest dollar where required. Account titles required are: Cash, Marketable Equity Securities, Allowance to Reduce Marketable Equity Securities to Market, Dividend Income, and Unrealized Loss on Marketable Equity Securities.

June 30   purchased for cash 500 common shares of Winter Corporation common stock at 25-½ plus a broker's fee of $75

Sept. 2   purchased for cash 200 shares of Powell Corporation common stock at 12-¼ plus a broker's fee of $40

Oct. 31   received a $.50 per share dividend from the Winter Corporation

b. Prepare the December 31, 19X7, adjusting entry to record the unrealized loss on Marketable Equity Securities using the lower-of-cost-or-market rule. The market values of the stock investments were as follows: Winter Corporation, $24; Powell Corporation, $10.

c. Determine the balance of the Marketable Equity Securities account and prepare the current assets section of the balance sheet for Joshua Corporation on December 31, 19X7, using the following account titles and amounts: Cash, $55,000; Accounts

Receivable (net), $10,000; Prepaid Insurance, $2,500; and Marketable Equity Securities (?).

Exercise 24.4
recording the purchase of marketable equity securities; posting to the control account and the subsidiary accounts; and preparing the adjusting entries using the lower-of-cost-or-market method

The Theo Corporation purchases common stock of other corporations for its investment portfolio.

a. Record the following stock transactions in general journal form. Round to the nearest dollar where required. Open a control account for Marketable Equity Securities and open an account in the subsidiary stock investment ledger as each stock is purchased.

Jan. 15   purchased for cash 1,000 common shares of Elton Corporation at 10-½ plus $325 broker's fee
Feb. 14   purchased for cash 200 common shares of Arnold, Incorporated at 45 plus $275 broker's commission
Mar. 27   received $1 per share dividend from Arnold, Incorporated
Sept. 13 sold 500 shares of Elton Corporation at $15; broker's fee is $175

b. Post to the control account and to the subsidiary stock investment ledger. Other posting to the general ledger is not required.

c. Answer the following questions.
   1. What is the balance in the Elton Corporation subsidiary stock investment ledger account?
   2. What is the balance in the Arnold, Incorporated subsidiary stock investment ledger account?
   3. What is the balance of the control account, Marketable Equity Securities?

d. What is the total revenue received by Theo Corporation from the stock transactions?

e. Assume the market price of Elton is $12 and the market price of Arnold is $52 on December 31. Prepare the required adjusting entry using the lower-of-cost-or-market rule.

Exercise 24.5
determining the eliminating entry for a 100 percent purchase for a consolidated worksheet

Alpha Corporation purchased all of the Beta Corporation's outstanding common stock for $150,000 cash. The stockholders' equity of Beta Corporation contains $100,000 of issued common stock and $50,000 of retained earnings. Describe how the eliminating entry would appear on a consolidated worksheet.

Exercise 24.6

determining the eliminating entry for an 80 percent purchase for a consolidated worksheet

Assume the same facts as Exercise 24.5 except that Alpha Corporation purchased only 80 percent of the outstanding stock of Beta Corporation for $150,000. Describe what the eliminating entries would be on a consolidated worksheet. (Hint: Make the four-step calculation first.)

Exercise 24.7

determining cash dividends, net income, balances, and minority interest

Assume Beta Corporation of Exercise 24.6 has net income of $20,000 during the year after acquisition. Assume it also paid out $10,000 in cash dividends during the year. Answer the following questions.

a.   What is the total dollar amount of cash dividends received by Alpha?

b.   What amount of Beta's net income does Alpha record on its books?

c.   What is the balance of Alpha's ledger account Investment: Beta Corporation?

d.   What is the total equity of the minority interest in Beta after one year?

Problems

Problem 24.1

recording short-term investment purchases and sales, and posting to the general ledger control account and the subsidiary ledger

The Carl Corporation uses its excess cash to invest in temporary securities. Following are the transactions for 19X3.

Jan. 9   purchased for cash 100 common shares of Bagel Corporation at $10 plus a broker's commission of $38 (Open a subsidiary stock investment ledger account and post to the control account and to the subsidiary ledger.)

Feb. 8   purchased for cash 200 common shares of Rolet Corporation at 25-¼ plus a broker's commission of $35

Apr. 21   purchased for cash 650 common shares of Nob, Incorporated, at 24-½ plus a broker's commission of $105

June 10   received a $1 per share dividend from Rolet Corporation

Aug. 1   sold 250 shares of Nob, Incorporated, stock at 30-¼; the broker's commission was $66

Sept. 11   purchased for cash 850 common shares of Clara Corporation at 15-⅛; the broker's commission was $180

Nov. 29   sold all the Bagel Corporation stock at $8; the broker's commission was $35

Instructions
1. *Open a control account for Marketable Equity Securities and open accounts in the subsidiary stock investment ledger as each stock is purchased.*
2. *Record the transactions in general journal form without explanations. Round amounts to the nearest dollar where necessary.*
3. *Post to the control account and to the subsidiary stock investment ledger after each transaction. No other posting to the general ledger is required in this problem.*
4. *Answer the following questions:*
   a. *What is the balance of the control account Marketable Equity Securities?*
   b. *What is the total of all the balances in the subsidiary stock investment ledger?*
   c. *What is the net revenue or net loss to Carl Corporation as a result of the stock transactions in 19X3?*

Problem 24.2
recording short-term investment purchases and sales, preparing the adjusting entry at the end of the accounting period using the lower-of-cost-or-market method, posting to the control and subsidiary accounts, and preparing a partial balance sheet

The Alta Corporation invests in temporary short-term investment securities. The following transactions occurred during the year 19X8.

Jan. 2 purchased for cash 100 shares of Salinas Corporation common stock at 42 plus broker's fee of $45

Feb. 8 purchased for cash 300 shares of Marlen Corporation common stock for $15 per share plus $48 broker's fee

Mar. 7 purchased for cash 1,000 shares of Bud Corporation common stock at 8-¾ plus broker's fee of $225

Jun. 30 received $.75 per share cash dividend on the Salinas stock

July 25 purchased 525 shares of Bear Corporation common stock at 17-½ plus broker's fee of $200

Oct. 31 sold all the Marlen stock at 18-½; broker charges are $110

Dec. 1 sold all the Salinas stock at 50; broker charges are $45

Dec. 31 recorded the adjusting entry necessary using the lower-of-cost-or-market rule; the following quotes are obtained from the stockbroker.

Bud	8-½
Bear	16

Instructions
1. *Open general ledger accounts with the following account titles: Cash, Marketable Equity Securities, Allowance to Reduce Mar-*

ketable Equity Securities to Market, Dividend Income, Gain on Sale of Stock, and Unrealized Loss on Marketable Equity Securities. Open subsidiary ledger accounts as required after each transaction.

2. *Record the transactions in general journal form without explanations. Round to the nearest dollar where required.*

3. *Post all entries to the general ledger and to the subsidiary stock investment ledger.*

4. *Reconcile the Marketable Equity Securities control account to the subsidiary stock investment ledger in the same manner as you would the Accounts Receivable control account and accounts receivable subsidiary ledger.*

5. *Prepare the current asset section of the balance sheet using the following information.*

Cash	$250,000
Marketable Equity Securities	_____
Allowance to Reduce Marketable Equity Securities to Market	_____
Accounts Receivable (Net)	55,000
Merchandise Inventory	129,000
Supplies	45,000
Prepaid Insurance	4,500

Problem 24.3
preparing a consolidated worksheet and a consolidated balance sheet with a 100 percent interest

On January 2, 19X8, the Parent Company purchases 100 percent of the outstanding voting stock of Subsidiary Company. Information from the two companies immediately after acquisition is as follows.

	Parent	Subsidiary
Assets		
Cash	$100,000	$ 20,000
Marketable Equity Securities (LCM)	28,000	0
Accounts Receivable (Net)	32,000	15,000
Merchandise Inventory	200,000	85,000
Plant and Equipment (Net)	300,000	100,000
Investment: Subsidiary Company	200,000	
Total Assets	$860,000	$220,000
Liabilities and Stockholders' Equity		
Accounts Payable	$ 60,000	$ 20,000
Common Stock	600,000	150,000
Retained Earnings	200,000	50,000
Total Liabilities and Stockholders' Equity	$860,000	$220,000

Instructions

1. *Prepare a consolidated worksheet as of January 2, 19X8.*
2. *Prepare a consolidated balance sheet as of January 2, 19X8.*

Problem 24.4
preparing a consolidated worksheet and a consolidated balance sheet with a 90 percent interest

On January 2, 19X7, Perry Company purchased 90 percent of the Sperry Company's outstanding common stock for $286,000. Before the acquisition, each company had the following balance sheets

	Perry	Sperry
Assets		
Cash	$400,000	$ 60,000
Notes Receivable	50,000	0
Accounts Receivable (Net)	20,000	40,000
Inventory	100,000	70,000
Plant and Equipment (Net)	420,000	140,000
Total Assets	$990,000	$310,000
Liabilities and Stockholders' Equity		
Notes Payable	$ 0	$ 0
Accounts Payable	130,000	20,000
Bonds Payable	200,000	0
Common Stock	500,000	200,000
Retained Earnings	160,000	90,000
Total Liabilities and Stockholders' Equity	$990,000	$310,000

Instructions   *1.*   *a.*   *Prepare the general journal entry to record the purchase of the Sperry stock on the Perry books.*

   b.   *Using the above information, prepare the four-step calculation as illustrated in this chapter at date of purchase.*

   c.   *Prepare the consolidated worksheet at date of purchase.*

   d.   *Prepare the consolidated balance sheet at date of purchase using the above worksheet.*

2.   *Assume Perry loans Sperry $10,000 in cash on September 13, 19X7, receiving a note receivable.*

   a.   *Record in general journal form the loan on the Perry books.*

   b.   *Record in general journal form the loan on the Sperry books.*

   c.   *Prepare the consolidated worksheet after the loan, assuming it is now September 30, 19X7.*

   d.   *Prepare the consolidated balance sheet from the above worksheet.*

Problem 24.5
preparing a consolidated worksheet and a consolidated balance sheet with an 80 percent interest

Paddle Sporting Goods Corporation purchased 8,000 of the 10,000 common shares outstanding of Saddle Corporation at 27-½, including broker's commission, on January 2, 19X7. The balance sheets of each company before the purchase by Paddle are presented below.

	Paddle	Saddle
Assets		
Cash	$ 400,000	$ 40,000
Notes Receivable	10,000	0
Accounts Receivable (Net)	160,000	30,000
Merchandise Inventory	190,000	80,000
Plant and Equipment (Net)	380,000	140,000
Total Assets	$1,140,000	$290,000
Liabilities and Stockholders' Equity		
Notes Payable	0	0
Accounts Payable	170,000	30,000
Common Stock	600,000	180,000
Premium on Common Stock	80,000	20,000
Retained Earnings	290,000	60,000
Total Liabilities and Stockholders' Equity	$1,140,000	$290,000

Instructions   *1. a. Record in general journal form the entry to record the purchase of Saddle stock on the Paddle books on January 2, 19X7.*

b. Prepare the four-step calculation as illustrated in the chapter to determine the cost of the stock purchase, the book value of the shares purchased, the goodwill, and the minority interest.

c. Prepare the consolidated worksheet at acquisition.

d. Prepare the consolidated balance sheet at acquisition.

2. Assume it is one year after the purchase of the Saddle stock. The Saddle Corporation has net income of $20,000 and has paid out cash dividends of $10,000 during the year. In addition, on May 31, 19X7, Paddle Corporation loaned Saddle Corporation $10,000 in cash and sold $5,000 of its inventory on account to Saddle at cost.

a. Prepare the general journal entries to record the above transactions on the Paddle Corporation books.

b. What is Paddle's equity in Saddle Corporation on December 31, 19X7?

c. What is the equity of the minority interest in Saddle Corporation on December 31, 19X7?

Problem 24.6
answering review questions

Answer the following questions as a review of this chapter.

1. How does the accountant know whether to classify investments as short term or long term?

2. How are temporary investments reported on the balance sheet?

3. What is the logic of using the lower-of-cost-or-market method for marketable equity securities on the year-end balance sheet?

4. Where does the accountant obtain the market price of stock?

5. When purchasing marketable equity securities, how is the total cost calculated?

6. The total of the account Marketable Equity Securities is $150,000 and the market value of these securities is $148,000. How would this information be reported on the year-end balance sheet?

7. What is the name of the corporation who owns a controlling interest in another corporation?

8. What are two reasons for one corporation owning the controlling interest in another corporation?

9. What is the purpose of the consolidated worksheet?

10. Why aren't the eliminating entries on the consolidated worksheet ever recorded?

11. Why is it necessary to prepare a consolidated balance sheet?

12. What method is used to keep track of the total interest a parent corporation has in a subsidiary corporation?

CHAPTER 25

Corporations:
Statement
of Cash Flows

LEARNING OBJECTIVES

When you have completed this chapter, you should

1. have a better understanding of accounting terminology.

2. be able to state the reasons for preparing a cash-flow statement.

3. be able to describe the direct and the indirect methods for preparing the statement of cash flows, and be able to name the preferred method.

4. be able to name and describe the three major classifications within the cash-flow statement.

5. be able to analyze the necessary accounts to determine the effects of their increases and decreases in the determination of net cash flow from operations using the direct method.

6. be able to analyze net income to determine the inflows and the outflows of cash from operations using the indirect method.

7. be able to explain how noncash items are disclosed in the statement of cash flows for both the direct and the indirect methods.

8. be able to prepare a worksheet using either the direct or the indirect method.

9. be able to prepare the formal statement of cash flows from the worksheet using either the direct or the indirect method.

Cash is one of the most important assets of a business. A company that is able to have excess cash is in an excellent competitive position. To achieve adequate cash flow, a corporation must manage its receipts and payments of cash carefully. Owners, potential investors, and creditors pay close attention to a company's cash position. Owners look for an adequate cash balance for the declaration and payment of dividends. Potential investors will value highly the corporation with a well-managed cash position. Creditors, on the other hand, examine the cash position to determine the ability of a corporation to repay its obligations as they become due. Corporate managers use cash-flow information to evaluate the ability of the corporation to meet unexpected problems and take advantage of new opportunities. A company that brings in more cash than it uses from operations is considered a successful one by decision makers.

Because of the importance of cash, the FASB issued Statement of Financial Accounting Standard No. 95, "Statement of Cash Flows." This standard requires certain businesses to present a statement of cash flows along with its published income statement and balance sheet. The primary objective of the Statement of Cash Flows is to present information based on the cash receipts and cash disbursements during the accounting period and to show the net result as an increase or decrease of cash for each category of the statement. The FASB also stated that financial statements should include the following information:

1. how a business obtains and spends its cash

2. information concerning its borrowing and repayment policies

3. information about the sale and repurchase of ownership securities

4. information about dividend payments and any other distributions to the owners

5. any other information about the liquidity or solvency of the corporation[1]

---

[1]FASB, Statement of Financial Accounting Standards No. 95, "Statement of Cash Flows" (Stamford, Conn., 1987). Copyright by the Financial Accounting Standards Board, High Ridge Park, Stamford, CT 06905, U.S.A.

statement of cash flows
the net cash inflows and the net cash outflows for an accounting period, classified as operating activities, investing activities, and financing activities

The **statement of cash flows** reports the net cash inflows and the net cash outflows for an accounting period. To meet the stated objective of the FASB, the prepared statement of cash flows will include three major categories; the titles are as follows:

1. Cash Flows from Operating Activities
2. Cash Flows from Investing Activities
3. Cash Flows from Financing Activities

All cash inflows and outflows will be shown within the net results in each category, as shown on the illustrative statement on page 933. Because all inflows and outflows of cash are reported, both the beginning balances and the ending balances of an accounting period are reconciled. Using a **comparative balance sheet,** a balance sheet that shows two accounting periods (years) side by side, the reconciliation can begin. Along with the comparative balance sheet, a current income statement is also used. The comparative balance sheet for Flower Corporation showing two years, 19X8 and 19X9, is illustrated on page 932. The current income statement for Flower Corporation is illustrated on page 933. Both the comparative balance sheet and the current income statement are used as examples for this chapter.

comparative balance sheet
a balance sheet that shows two accounting periods side by side

direct method
a calculation of the net cash flows provided or used for operating activities; lists the major classes of cash receipts and subtracts the major classes of disbursements

The FASB also determined that the first part of the statement, Cash Flows from Operating Activities, be prepared using either the direct method or the indirect method. The **direct method** is a calculation of the net cash flows provided or used for operating activities by listing the major classes of cash receipts and subtracting the major classes of disbursements. The **indirect method** begins with net income and then reconciles net income by adding and subtracting certain items to determine the net cash provided or used in the operating activities. However, the FASB recommended that the direct method be used because it is the most informative for the reader of financial statements. Although the FASB recognizes that some corporations use the indirect method, and the FASB will accept its use, it strongly recommends that the direct method be used.

indirect method
begins with net income and then reconciles net income by adding and subtracting certain items to determine the net cash provided or used in the operating activities

cash equivalents
assets readily convertible to a known amount of cash and sufficiently close to maturity to be able to determine market value

The FASB also concluded that cash includes both cash and **cash equivalents.** To qualify as a cash equivalent, the investment must be: (1) readily convertible to a known amount of cash, and (2) sufficiently close to its maturity date so as to be able to determine its market value. Examples are short-term commercial paper, money market funds, and U.S. Treasury bills.

Following are the comparative balance sheet, the income statement, and the statement of cash flows for the Flower Corporation. The balance sheet and income statement are used in the chapter to illustrate the development of the statement of cash flows.

Flower Corporation
Comparative Balance Sheet
December 31, 19X8 and December 31, 19X9

	19X8	19X9
Assets		
Current Assets		
Cash	$ 50,000	$ 65,700
Accounts Receivable (Net)	49,500	57,000
Merchandise Inventory	31,380	32,500
Prepaid Expenses	3,200	3,300
Total Current Assets	$134,080	$158,500
Plant and Equipment		
Equipment	$ 60,000	$ 70,000
Accumulated Depreciation: Equipment	(12,000)	(26,000)
Building	120,000	120,000
Accumulated Depreciation: Building	(3,000)	(6,000)
Land	30,000	30,000
Total Plant and Equipment	$195,000	$188,000
Total Assets	$329,080	$346,500
Liabilities		
Current Liabilities		
Accounts Payable	$ 30,080	$ 31,000
Dividends Payable	8,000	9,000
Total Current Liabilities	$ 38,080	$ 40,000
Long-Term Liabilities		
Mortgage Payable	$ 36,000	$ 35,000
Total Liabilities	$ 74,080	$ 75,000
Stockholders' Equity		
Common Stock, $10 par value	$160,000	$170,000
Premium on Common Stock	40,000	42,000
Retained Earnings	55,000	59,500
Total Stockholders' Equity	$255,000	$271,500
Total Liabilities and Stockholders' Equity	$329,080	$346,500

Flower Corporation
Income Statement
For Year Ended December 31, 19X9

Sales		$560,000
Cost of Goods Sold		310,000
Gross Profit		$250,000
Operating Expenses		
Salaries, Wages, and Other		
Operating Expenses	$195,380	
Depreciation Expense	17,000	
Interest Expense	2,880	
Total Expenses		215,260
Income from Operations before		
Income Taxes		34,740
Income Tax Expense		21,240
Net Income		$ 13,500

Earnings per Share:
From Operations $1.25
Net Income $ .79

Flower Corporation
Statement of Cash Flows—Direct Method
For Year Ended December 31, 19X9

Cash Flows from Operating Activities:		
Cash received from customers	$552,500	
Cash payments for merchandise	(310,200)	
Cash payments for salaries, wages,		
and other operating expenses	(195,480)	
Cash payments for interest expense	(2,880)	
Cash payments for income tax		
expense	(21,240)	
Net cash provided by operating		
activities		$22,700
Cash Flows from Investing Activities:		
Cash purchase of equipment	(10,000)	
Net cash used by investing activities		(10,000)
Cash Flows from Financing Activities:		
Cash received from the sale of		
common stock	12,000	
Cash paid on the mortgage payable	(1,000)	
Cash payment of dividends	(8,000)	
Net cash provided by financing		
activities		3,000
Net increase in cash		$15,700
Cash balance at beginning of 19X9		50,000
Cash balance at end of 19X9		$65,700

THE STATEMENT OF CASH FLOWS

Operating Activities

The first major portion of the statement of cash flows is the operating activities category. **Operating activities** are examined to determine the increases and decreases in cash to achieve the net cash flows from the operating activities for the accounting period. Observe in the first category of the statement of cash flows, Cash Flows from Operating Activities, page 933, that the major classes of inflows of cash are given. For example, the amount of cash received from customers by Flower Corporation is given as $552,500. The major classes of outflows of cash are also given, such as cash payments for merchandise. When the list of receipts of cash and disbursements of cash is complete, the cash disbursements are subtracted from the cash receipts to determine the net cash result— a net increase or a net decrease in cash. On the statement, all the decreases are bracketed to show the amount to be subtracted. As shown in the illustration, the types of cash receipts and cash disbursements are the same as those reported on an income statement. Because the income statement is the financial statement showing the net results of matching the revenues with the expenses, all the cash inflows and outflows from the operating activities are on this statement. The items classified in the first major category of the statement of cash flows are those that involve the production or purchase of goods and the sale of goods and services to customers. In addition, the operating activity category includes those disbursements related to the administration of the business (salaries, interest, etc.). Therefore, all of the accounts that are used in reporting income must be analyzed. Following is a chart of the major cash-flow classifications. It is presented in tne form of a chart to aid in the classification process.

Cash Flow Classification Chart

Operating Activities Classifications

Cash Receipts	Cash Payments
1. Collections of cash sales	1. Payments to suppliers for merchandise inventory
2. Collections from credit customers	2. Payments for services
3. Collections of interest revenue	3. Payments to employees for salaries and wages
4. Collections of cash dividends from stock held as an investment	4. Payments of interest on debt
5. Cash collections from lawsuits	5. Payments of taxes

Investing Activities Classifications

Cash Receipts	Cash Payments
1. Cash from the sale of plant assets	1. Payments to purchase plant assets
2. Cash from the sale of investments	2. Payments to purchase investments
3. Cash from the collection of the principal amount on note receivable	3. Principal amounts loaned to borrowers in the form of notes receivable

Financing Activities Classifications

Cash Receipts	Cash Payments
1. Cash from long-term borrowing	1. Principal amounts paid to long term creditors
2. Cash received from the sale of capital stock	2. Cash paid to stockholders in the form of cash dividends
3. Cash from other short-term borrowing	3. Repayments of cash loans
	4. Cash paid to purchase treasury stock

Investing Activities

investing activities
transactions involving the purchase and sale of plant assets and other productive assets or investments

The second major category on the statement of cash flows is the investing activities. **Investing activities** are transactions involving the purchase and sale of plant assets and other productive assets or investments. Items under this category are those in which cash is received from the sale of plant assets or of marketable securities, and cash collections from principal amounts on loans. In addition, accounts classified as investing are those in which cash is paid out to purchase plant assets and buy marketable securities and other investments. Most of the information needed to analyze these accounts can be found by reconciling the changes in the balances on a comparative balance sheet. By examining the changes in the balances between accounting periods, the cash receipts and the cash payments made during the period can be determined. The second category on the statement of cash flows, Cash Flows from Investing Activities, page 933, shows the major items on this statement, and the cash flow classification chart, page 935, shows all of the major items in this category.

Financing Activities

financing activities
transactions involving borrowing cash on a short- or long-term basis and repaying that loan or the sale of capital stock and the payment of dividends

Financing activities are transactions involving borrowing cash on a short- or long-term basis and repaying that loan, the sale of capital stock, and the payment of dividends. Typical examples of financing activities are transactions with the owners of the corporation and with long-term bondholders. Cash borrowed either on a short-term or long-term basis is also considered a financing activity if it does not involve the payment for merchandise sold in the business. The statement of cash flows on page 933, and the cash flow classification chart, page 935, show the major items in this category.

Noncash Investing and Financing Activities

Important transactions occur that clearly do not involve cash at all. Yet these activities are important in understanding the total financial structure of a business. For example, assume a corporation purchases land, building, and equipment for $250,000. If no cash is given or received, this transaction is not reported on the statement of cash flows. The FASB determined that the noncash portion of investing and financing activities should *not* be reported in the statement of cash flows, but it should be reported on a separate schedule. For example, assume a corporation purchased a new computer for $25,000. It gave $5,000 in cash, a note payable for $8,000, and an old computer with a fair market value and book value of $12,000 for the new computer. On the statement of cash flows only the $5,000 cash expenditure is reported. Because of the importance of these transactions, the FASB concluded that a separate schedule of noncash activities be prepared to show these items. The following schedule of noncash investing and financing activities illustrates how these items may be shown.

ABC Corporation
Schedule of Noncash Investing and Financing Activities

1. The company purchased land, building, and equipment for the fair market value of $250,000 and gave a 9 percent, ten-year note payable in the amount of $250,000.
2. The company exchanged an old computer with a fair market value of $12,000 for a new computer valued at $25,000. An 8 percent, three-year note payable in the amount of $8,000 was given for this computer as well as $5,000 in cash.

When preparing the Schedule of Noncash Investing and Financing Activities, the details of the entire transaction (both the cash and noncash portions) are given. Examples of transactions that must be disclosed as noncash investing and financing activities are as follows.

1. the conversion of preferred stock to common stock
2. the purchase of long-term assets financed by a note payable to the seller
3. the conversion of debt securities to equity securities (e.g., convertible bonds to common stock)
4. the exchange of noncash assets for noncash assets (e.g., a truck for a truck)
5. the purchase of noncash assets in exchange for equity or debt securities (e.g., the purchase of land in exchange for stock or a bond payable)

DEVELOPING THE STATEMENT OF CASH FLOWS BY THE DIRECT METHOD

The Cash account in the general ledger contains all the cash receipts and all the cash disbursements. To begin our analysis, the contents of a typical Cash account is used to show the various types of receipts and payments from this account.

Analyzing the Cash Account

The Cash account for Flower Corporation, with summarized totals for simplicity, is shown below to review its contents.

Cash

Balance Dec. 31, 19X8	50,000	(1) Payments for mer- chandise (summarized)	310,200
(1) Receipts from customers (summa- rized)	552,500	(1) Payments for sala- ries, wages, and other operating expenses (summarized)	195,480
(3) Proceeds from sale of stock	12,000	(1) Payment of interest	2,880
		(1) Payment of income taxes	21,240
		(2) Purchase of equipment	10,000
		(3) Payment on mortgage	1,000
		(3) Payment of dividends	8,000
Balance Dec. 31, 19X9	65,700		

The various receipts of cash are shown by the summarized debit entries. Cash disbursements are also summarized and shown as credits. Each summarized total is categorized according to its position on a statement of cash flows: (1) operating activity, (2) investing activity, and (3) financing activity. From this analysis, one may think a statement of cash flows could be quickly prepared. However, this example is a simple one and could only be used by a very small business. Most corporations have a vast number of individual cash transactions, and reviewing each to determine its proper category would be very time consuming. However, the Cash account, as illustrated, is useful in providing information for the statement of cash flows. To obtain all the information needed, the changes in the noncash accounts must also be analyzed.

Analyzing the Noncash Accounts

Each time a cash transaction is recorded it also affects another account. It may affect a balance sheet account, or it may affect an income statement account. For example, consider the following general journal entries.

GENERAL JOURNAL				Page	
Date	Description	Post. Ref.	Debit	Credit	
(1) Feb. 14	Cash		2000 —		
	Accounts Receivable			2000 —	
	To Record the Collection of Cash from a Credit				
	Customer				
(2) Mar. 3	Cash		12000 —		
	Common Stock			10000 —	
	Premium on Common Stock			2000 —	
	To Record the Sale of 1,000 Shares of Common				
	Stock at $12 per Share				
(3) Apr. 4	Accounts Payable		1200 —		
	Cash			1200 —	
	To Record the Payment of Cash to a Creditor for				
	Merchandise Purchased				
(4) May 10	Equipment		10000 —		
	Cash			10000 —	
	To Record the Cash Purchase of Equipment				

Observe the various noncash accounts involved in each cash transaction. Transaction 1 demonstrates the receipt of cash from a prior sale. Transaction 2 shows the receipt of cash from the sale of common stock. These two transactions are inflows of cash. Transaction 3 is an outflow of cash for a payment on account for a purchase of merchandise. Transaction 4 records the purchase of a truck and is also a cash outflow. By examining transactions 1 and 3, both the cash and noncash portions are determined to be categorized as operating activities. Transaction 2 is classified as an inflow of cash from a financing activity. Transaction 4 affects the noncash plant asset account, Equipment, and is an outflow of cash for an investing activity.

These examples demonstrate the need to analyze the noncash accounts as well as the cash account to determine the necessary information for the statement of cash flows. The revenue and expense items also affect noncash accounts and must therefore be examined; they affect the noncash Retained Earnings account upon closing. Therefore, the income statement accounts will also supply needed information for the statement of cash flows. An examination of the income statement, along with the applicable balance sheet accounts, will give additional information about possible cash flows. For example, the sales amount on the income statement may include cash sales and sales on account, or it may be all credit sales. By determining the change in the Accounts Receivable account balance from one accounting period to another, cash collections from customers can be determined. If the balance of the Accounts Receivable account is unchanged between accounting periods, it may be inferred that the cash collected from customers is the same as the sales revenue reported on the income statement. More detailed information concerning the analysis of non-cash items on the balance sheet and the analysis of the income statement items is given in the following example.

COMPLETE ILLUSTRATION OF THE DIRECT METHOD

Using the information from the comparative balance sheet, page 932, and the income statement, page 933, for Flower Corporation, a complete illustrative example is presented. The objective of this illustration is tc prepare a statement of cash flows that explains the $15,700 increase in cash for 19X9. A list of other related information is given below.

a. The amounts involved in the Accounts Payable account are for merchandise purchases.

b. Equipment was purchased for $10,000 cash.

c. Paid $1,000 on the mortgage payable.

d. Sold 1,000 shares of common stock at $12 per share.

e. Paid $8,000 of cash dividends during the first month of 19X9.

f. Declared $9,000 of dividends payable the last month of 19X9.

g. No assets were sold or discarded.

Operating Activities

The first step in the preparation of the statement of cash flows is to determine the net cash flow from the operating activities. Using the income statement and the related balance sheet items, each item appearing in the statement of cash flows using the direct method, page 933, is discussed below.

Cash Received from Customers   Using the income statement and the changes in the balances of related items on the comparative balance sheet, an analysis is made to determine the cash inflows and outflows. Because sales is the first item on the income statement, both sales and its related balance sheet account, Accounts Receivable, are analyzed first.

On the income statement, the total sales are $560,000. On the comparative balance sheet, the balance of the Accounts Receivable account at the end of 19X8 is $49,500, and the balance at the end of 19X9 is $57,000, which shows an increase of $7,500. Assuming that all sales are on account and using the T-account below for illustration, the cash collections can be determined.

Accounts Receivable (Net)

12/31/19X8 Bal.	*49,500*		
19X9 Sales	*560,000*	*19X9 Collections*	*552,500*
12/31/19X9 Bal.	*57,000*		

This account illustrates that the balance of the Accounts Receivable account increased from $49,500 to $57,000, and that cash receipts from customers are equal to the sales of $560,000, plus the beginning balance of $49,500 and less the ending balance of $57,000. The calculation may be stated as follows.

$$\text{Cash Received from Customers} = \begin{bmatrix} \text{Sales} - \text{Increase in Accounts Receivable Balance} \\ \text{or} \\ \text{Sales} + \text{Decrease in Accounts Receivable Balance} \end{bmatrix}$$

The section on statement of cash flows—direct method, page 933, shows the cash received from customers as $552,500, the first amount on the statement.

Cash Payments for Merchandise   To determine the amount of cash paid for merchandise, we analyze cost of goods sold, merchandise inventory, and accounts payable. If all purchases were made for cash, and there was no change in merchandise inventory from the beginning to the end of the period, then cash payments for merchandise would be the same as the cost of goods sold (Beginning inventory + Net purchases − Ending inventory). This is rare, of course, because merchandise is usually purchased on account and because there is normally a change in the merchandise inventory from the beginning to the end of the period.

To determine the amount of cash paid for merchandise, we must adjust the cost of goods sold for the changes in merchandise inventory and in accounts payable. There are two steps involved in the process. The first step combines the change in merchandise inventory with cost of goods sold to calculate the cost of purchases for the period. The second step combines the change in accounts payable with the cost of purchases calculated in step 1 to calculate the cash paid for merchandise.

The cost of goods sold for Flower Corporation is $310,000. To determine the amount of cash actually paid for merchandise, we must analyze both the merchandise inventory account and the accounts payable account.

Merchandise Inventory

12/31/19X8 Bal.	31,380		
19X9 Purchases	311,120	19X9 Costs of Goods Sold	310,000
12/31/19X9 Bal.	32,500		

The T-account shows that the increase in Merchandise Inventory from 12/31/19X8 to 12/31/19X9 is $1,120 ($32,500 − $31,380), and that this amount must be added to the cost of goods sold to arrive at the total amount of purchases, $311,120. Further, to determine the cash paid for merchandise purchases, the purchases of $311,120 is shown in the Accounts Payable account as follows.

Accounts Payable

		12/31/19X8 Bal.	30,080
19X9 Payments 310,200		19X9 Purchases	311,120
		12/31/19X9 Bal.	31,000

Once the amount of purchases is posted as a credit, the cash payments to creditors for merchandise can be determined. This analysis is stated in two steps as follows:

$$\text{Purchases} = \begin{bmatrix} \text{Cost of Goods Sold} + \text{Increase in Merchandise Inventory} \\ or \\ \text{Cost of Goods Sold} - \text{Decrease in Merchandise Inventory} \end{bmatrix}$$

$$\text{AND}$$

$$\begin{matrix} \text{Cash Payments} \\ \text{for Merchandise} \end{matrix} = \begin{bmatrix} \text{Purchases} + \text{Decrease in Accounts Payable} \\ or \\ \text{Purchases} - \text{Increase in Accounts Payable} \end{bmatrix}$$

After this analysis, the second item in the operating activity category, Cash Payments for Merchandise, is known. Cash Payments for Merchandise appears on the statement of cash flows—direct method, on page 933.

Cash Payments for Salaries, Wages, and Other Operating Expenses

From the Flower Corporation Income Statement, the summarized amount for salaries, wages, and other operating expenses is found to be $195,380. To determine the amount of cash paid out, this total must be combined with changes in the related balance sheet accounts—prepaid expenses and accrued liabilities—that relate to salaries, wages, and other operating expenses. (In this example, there are no accrued liabilities that relate. Therefore, to determine the cash paid, only the change in prepaid expenses is combined with the salaries, wages, and other operating expenses figure from the income statement—$195,380.)

We assume for this analysis that all payments for salaries, wages, and other operating expenses were originally debited to prepaid expenses, though usually that is not the case. To simplify this analysis, the amounts have been summarized. Analyzing the individual accounts would produce the same results as analyzing the summarized totals. The T-account for Prepaid Expenses is shown below.

Prepaid Expenses

12/31/19X8 Bal.	3,200		
19X9 Payments	195,480	19X9 Salaries, Wages, and Other Operating Expenses	195,380
12/31/19X9 Bal.	(3,300)		

The Prepaid Expenses account shows a $100 increase from 19X8 to 19X9, thus the amount paid was $100 more than reported on the income statement. If the amounts paid had been debited directly to the expense accounts rather than to prepaid expense accounts, the total cash spent would still be the same.

In the event that there are accrued liabilities, an additional adjustment is necessary. This adjustment is included in the following calculation.

$$
\text{Cash Paid for Salaries, Wages, and Other Operating Expenses} \begin{cases} \begin{bmatrix} \text{Salaries, Wages, and Other Operating Expenses} \\ + \\ \text{Increase in Prepaid Expenses} \\ \text{or} \\ \text{Salaries, Wages, and Other Operating Expenses} \\ - \\ \text{Decrease in Prepaid Expenses} \end{bmatrix} \\ \text{AND} \\ \begin{bmatrix} \text{Salaries, Wages, and Other Operating Expenses} \\ + \\ \text{Decrease in Accrued Liabilities} \\ \text{or} \\ \text{Salaries, Wages, and Other Operating Expenses} \\ - \\ \text{Increase in Accrued Liabilities} \end{bmatrix} \end{cases}
$$

Cash Payments for Interest and Taxes   The analysis for these two items is similar to the other adjustments, because both require an adjustment should a related liability account appear on the balance sheet. In this example, there is no interest that is payable and there is no income tax payable. Therefore, the amounts on the income statement are the amounts paid out in cash.

Should a related liability appear on the balance sheet, however, such as interest payable or income taxes payable, the following adjustment analysis and calculation must be made.

$$
\text{Cash Paid for Interest and Taxes} \begin{cases} \begin{bmatrix} \text{Expense} + \text{Decrease in a Related Liability} \\ \text{or} \\ \text{Expense} - \text{Increase in a Related Liability} \end{bmatrix} \end{cases}
$$

The amounts paid for interest and income taxes are the last items in the operating activity category. This portion of the statement of cash flows is presented as follows.

Cash Flows from Operating Activities:	
Cash received from customers	$552,500
Cash payments for merchandise	(310,200)
Cash payments for salaries, wages, and other operating expenses	(195,480)
Cash payments for interest expense	(2,880)
Cash payments for income tax expense	(21,240)
Net Cash Provided by Operating Activities	$22,700

The only item remaining on the income statement is depreciation expense. Though rightfully deducted on the income statement, it is not an outflow of cash. It is an offset to the related asset that shows its proper allocation of cost. The following chart contains the various analysis calculations. This chart was developed to show the analysis for each item that is used in the cash flows from the operating activities section of the statement of cash flows.

Direct Method Adjustment Chart

Operating Activity Title	Balance Sheet Account	Income Statement Account	Type of Adjustment to Determine Cash Flow
To Determine Cash Received from Customers	Accounts Receivable	Sales =	$\begin{bmatrix} - \text{ Increase in A/R Balance} \\ \text{or} \\ + \text{ Decrease in A/R Balance} \end{bmatrix}$
To Determine Cash Payments for Merchandise	Merchandise Inventory	Purchases =	$\begin{bmatrix} \text{Cost of Goods Sold + Increase in} \\ \text{Merchandise Inventory} \\ \text{or} \\ \text{Cost of Goods Sold − Decrease in} \\ \text{Merchandise Inventory} \end{bmatrix}$
			AND
	Accounts Payable	Cash Payments for Merchandise =	$\begin{bmatrix} \text{Purchases + Decrease in Accounts Payable} \\ \text{or} \\ \text{Purchases − Increase in Accounts Payable} \end{bmatrix}$
To Determine Cash Payments for Salaries, Wages, and Other Operating Expenses	Prepaid Expenses	Salaries, Wages, and Other Operating Expenses	$\begin{bmatrix} + \text{ Increase in Prepaid Expenses} \\ \text{or} \\ - \text{ Decrease in Prepaid Expenses} \end{bmatrix}$
			AND
	Accrued Liabilities	Salaries, Wages and Other Operating Expenses	$\begin{bmatrix} + \text{ Decrease in Accrued Liabilities} \\ \text{or} \\ - \text{ Increase in Accrued Liabilities} \end{bmatrix}$
To Determine Cash Payments for Interest Expense	Interest Payable	Interest Expense	$\begin{bmatrix} + \text{ Decrease in Interest Payable} \\ \text{or} \\ - \text{ Increase in Interest Payable} \end{bmatrix}$
To Determine Cash Payments for Income Tax Expense	Taxes Payable	Tax Expense	$\begin{bmatrix} + \text{ Decrease in Taxes Payable} \\ \text{or} \\ - \text{ Increase in Taxes Payable} \end{bmatrix}$

Investing Activities

This section of the statement of cash flows requires that an analysis be made of transactions involving the purchase and sale of plant assets and other productive assets or investments. The comparative balance sheet for Flower Corporation on page 932, and the additional information at the beginning of this section will aid in this analysis. Equipment was purchased for $10,000 cash, and no other assets were bought, sold, or discarded. Therefore, in this example, there is only one item—the cash outflow for the purchase of the equipment. Because there is only one item, this portion of the cash flows statement appears as follows.

Cash Flows from Investing Activities:		
Cash purchase of equipment	($10,000)	
Net cash used by investing activities		($10,000)

Should there be other items, as shown on the cash flow classification chart, page 935, only the cash portion, the cash inflow or the cash outflow, will be listed. For example, assume a company purchased a plant asset that cost $80,000 by paying $10,000 in cash and issuing a note payable for the difference as follows.

Purchase of Plant Asset	$80,000
Issued Note Payable to Finance Purchase	(70,000)
Balance Paid in Cash	$10,000

The $10,000 is shown as an outflow of cash under the investing activity category. In addition, assume the same corporation sold marketable equity securities that cost $13,000 for $15,000. The $15,000 is an inflow of cash and is listed as an investing activity. If these were the only items to be listed in this category, the investing activity portion of the statement would be as follows.

Cash Flows from Investing Activities:		
Sale of marketable equity securities	$15,000	
Cash paid for the purchase of plant assets	(10,000)	
Net cash provided by investing activities		$5,000

The noncash portion of these two items is presented on a separate schedule as previously discussed.

Financing Activities

Financing activities are transactions that relate to long-term debt and owners' equity accounts. Items in this category include the $1,000 principal payment on the mortgage, the sale of 1,000 shares of common stock, and the payment of cash dividends.

Payment on the Mortgage   The information already given states that $1,000 was paid on the mortgage, and a review of the comparative balance sheet of the Flower Corporation shows this to be true. Below is the T-account for Mortgage Payable.

Mortgage Payable

	12/31/19X8 *Bal.* *36,000*
19X9 Cash Payment 1,000	
	12/31/19X9 *Bal.* *35,000*

As shown by comparing the two balances, the difference is $1,000. Therefore, a $1,000 cash outflow is shown in this section of the statement of cash flows.

Sale of Common Stock   The comparative balance sheet is used to help analyze this sale. It has been stated previously that this stock was sold for cash. To help analyze the cash inflow, T-accounts are given as follows.

Common Stock

	12/31/19X8 *Bal.* *160,000*
	19X9 Cash Inflow 10,000
	12/31/19X9 *Bal.* *170,000*

Premium on Common Stock

	12/31/19X8 *Bal.* *40,000*
	19X9 Cash Inflow 2,000
	12/31/19X9 *Bal.* *42,000*

The total of $12,000 shown on the statement of cash flows is obtained by adding the increase in the Common Stock account to the increase in the Premium on Common Stock account.

Payment of Cash Dividends   Information provided concerning cash dividends stated that $8,000 was paid in cash during the year and an additional $9,000 was declared. The cash payment of $8,000 is the outflow of cash. To verify that this is correct, T-accounts for both Dividends Payable and Retained Earnings are shown as follows.

Dividends Payable

		12/31/19X8 Bal.	8,000
19X9 Cash Divident Paid	8,000	12/31/19X9 Declared	9,000

Retained Earnings

		12/31/19X8 Bal.	55,000
		19X9 Net Income	13,500
19X9 Cash Dividend Declared	9,000		
		12/31/19X9 Bal.	59,500

The above analysis illustrates the transactions that have occurred. On completion of this analysis, the financing activity portion of the statement of cash flows is as follows.

Cash Flows from Financing Activities:		
Cash received from the sale of common stock	$12,000	
Cash paid on the mortgage payable	(1,000)	
Cash payment of dividends	(8,000)	
Net cash provided by financing activities		$3,000

The complete statement is prepared by combining the three sections and is shown as the statement of cash flows—direct method on page 933.

This type of analysis is possible, but for most corporations, the large number of accounts and the many types of transactions make it difficult to use. To better organize the information, a worksheet is used.

PREPARING A STATEMENT OF CASH FLOWS
WORKSHEET USING THE DIRECT METHOD

The preparation of a worksheet helps to organize the information needed for the formal statement of cash flows. When completed, it also provides proof of the accuracy of the analysis. Although the statement of cash flows can be prepared directly from the ledger accounts, using the worksheet approach helps to eliminate errors that are likely to be made.

The worksheet used to prepare the statement of cash flows is structured differently than the normal worksheet. The completed worksheet for Flower Corporation using the direct method is shown on pages 950–951.

The worksheet is set up in a special way. The balance sheet account balances for 19X8 are listed in the first money column. They are listed with the debit balances first and then the credit balances. The 19X9 balance sheet account balances are listed in the same manner in the fourth column. The middle two columns, analysis of transactions for current year, are used for reconciling the differences in balances between the two years. The 19X9 income statement is recorded below the balance sheets in the analysis of transaction columns, and the statement of cash flows is developed and listed below the income statement.

In the beginning of the worksheet preparation, the middle two columns are blank. Each balance sheet account balance is then reconciled by the amounts shown in the analysis columns. As each noncash item is analyzed, both a debit and a credit entry are made in the analysis columns. In this manner, the worksheet is completed. This worksheet meets several needs. First, it lists every account balance on the worksheet so that all the accounts are analyzed and none are forgotten. Second, it provides the necessary information to prepare the statement of cash flows. Third, it provides the information necessary to report the noncash transactions on a separate schedule as required.

Procedures for Setting Up the Worksheet

The information needed to begin the preparation of the worksheet is found in the Flower Corporation's comparative balance sheet and its income statement, and in the additional information given in the text. The completed worksheet using the direct method, as

FLOWER CORPORATION
WORKSHEET FOR STATEMENT OF CASH FLOWS—DIRECT METHOD
FOR YEAR ENDED DECEMBER 31, 19X9

Account Titles	Dec. 31, 19X8 Account Balances	Analysis of Transactions for Current Year — Debit	Analysis of Transactions for Current Year — Credit	Dec. 31, 19X9 Account Balances
Balance Sheet—Debits:				
Cash	50000 —	(1) 560000 —	(1a) 552500 —	65700 —
Accounts Receivable (Net)	49500 —	(2a) 311120 —	(2) 310000 —	57000 —
Merchandise Inventory	31380 —	(3a) 195480 —	(3) 195380 —	32500 —
Prepaid Expenses	3200 —			3300 —
Equipment	60000 —	(6) 10000 —		70000 —
Building	120000 —			120000 —
Land	30000 —			30000 —
Total Debits	344080 —			378500 —
Balance Sheet—Credits:				
Accumulated Depreciation: Equipment	12000 —		(10) 14000 —	26000 —
Accumulated Depreciation: Building	3000 —		(10) 3000 —	6000 —
Accounts Payable	30080 —	(2b) 310200 —	(2a) 311120 —	31000 —
Dividends Payable	8000 —	(9) 8000 —	(11) 9000 —	9000 —
Mortgage Payable	36000 —	(8) 1000 —		35000 —
Common Stock, $10 par value	160000 —		(7) 10000 —	170000 —
Premium on Common Stock	40000 —		(7) 2000 —	42000 —
Retained Earnings	55000 —	(11) 9000 —	(12) 13500 —	59500 —
Total Credits	344080 —			378500 —
Income Statement:				
Sales			(1) 560000 —	
Cost of Goods Sold		(2) 310000 —		
Salaries, Wages, and Other		(3) 195380 —		
Operating Expenses		(10) 17000 —		
Depreciation Expense		(4) 2880 —		
Interest Expense		(5) 21240 —		
Income Tax Expense		(12) 13500 —		
Net Income				

Statement of Cash Flows:

Operating Activities:		
Cash Received from Customers	(1a) 552500 —	
Cash Payments for Merchandise		(2b) 310200 —
Cash Payments for Salaries, Wages, and Other Operating Expenses		(3b) 195480 —
Cash Payments for Interest Expense		(4) 2880 —
Cash Payments for Income Tax Expense		(5) 21240 —
Investing Activities:		
Cash Purchase of Equipment		(6) 10000 —
Financing Activities:		
Cash Received from Sale of Stock	(7) 12000 —	
Cash Paid On Mortgage Payable		(8) 1000 —
Cash Payment of Dividends		(9) 8000 —
Noncash Investing and Financing Activities:	0 —	0 —
	2529300 —	2529300 —

shown on pages 950–951, should be reviewed along with the following procedures.

1. Begin by writing the words *Balance Sheet Debits* on the first line of the account titles column. All of the debit account names are entered along with the dollar amounts for 19X8 and 19X9. After the debit account names and dollar amounts are entered, add each column to determine the debit totals.

2. Next, write the words *Balance Sheet Credits* on the next line in the account name column. Enter all the credit accounts and the dollar amounts in the appropriate columns for the two years. After all account names and dollar amounts are entered, add each column to determine the credit totals for each year. Compare the debit totals with the credit totals to verify that they are equal and in balance.

3. Below the balance sheet accounts, enter the income statement account titles and the title *Statement of Cash Flows* and the three major categories: Operating Activities, Investing Activities, and Financing Activities. You may wish to leave blank lines for additional items. Below the statement of cash flows, prepare a line for the noncash investing and financing items should there be any. Once this is complete, enter the income statement amounts. Record expenses and costs as debits and revenue as a credit.

   After income statement items are entered, analyze the changes in the related noncash balance sheet accounts. From each analysis, the cash-flow items are recorded on that portion of the worksheet in the correct category. For example, review the sales and accounts receivable entries (1 and 1a) on the completed worksheet for Flower Corporation on pages 950–951.

   If a revenue (or expense) item was received (or paid) in cash, it has no effect on a noncash item so it is immediately entered in the cash-flow section in the correct category. For an example of this, review the interest expense (4) on the worksheet. A debit and a credit must always be entered.

4. A cross-reference of debits and credits is accomplished by assigning a numeral for the original entry and a numeral along with the letter *a* for the analysis portion.

5. After all the amounts are entered, review each balance sheet account to determine whether the beginning and the ending

balances are reconciled. Accounts Receivable, for example, has a December 31, 19X8, balance of $49,500; a debit in the analysis of transactions column of $560,000 (representing credit sales); and a credit in the analysis column of $552,500 (representing collections on account). The balance on December 31, 19X9, is $57,000, thus the account is reconciled ($49,500 + $560,000 − $552,500 = $57,000). If there are balances that do not reconcile, review the additional information given for noncash items. Any adjustment for noncash items can be recorded below the statement of cash flow portion of the worksheet. In this example, there are none.

6. Total the debits and credits in the analysis of transaction columns to prove the equality of debits and credits.

7. From the completed worksheet, prepare the formal statement of cash flows.

Entering the Operating Activities on the Worksheet

To review in detail each entry made in the analysis of transactions columns on the worksheet, the following is presented for study. Each entry appearing in the analysis column is discussed below.

Entering Sales on the Worksheet

1. Sales revenue of $560,000 is entered as a credit across from sales on the income statement part of the worksheet and as a debit of $560,000 across from accounts receivable in the balance sheet section. This is the beginning of the analysis.

1a. By reviewing the Accounts Receivable balance, we see that the only source of a decrease in this account is collections of cash from customers. Therefore, $552,500 is entered in the operating activity portion of the statement of cash flows as a debit, and $552,500 is entered as a credit across from the Accounts Receivable in the balance sheet section. It is assumed that all sales were on account in this example. However, if some sales were for cash, the total cash received would still be sales minus the increase (or plus the decrease) in the Accounts Receivable.

Entering the Cost of Goods Sold   Items 2, 2a, and 2b relate to cash payments for merchandise.

   2.   Cost of goods sold in the amount of $310,000 is entered in the income statement section as a debit. As this results in a sale of merchandise, the Merchandise Inventory account is credited for $310,000.

   2a.   Because all merchandise was purchased on credit, a debit of $311,120 is made to the Merchandise Inventory account and a credit of $311,120 is made to the Accounts Payable account.

   2b.   Because the only decrease in accounts payable is for payments for merchandise, the amount of $310,200 is entered across from accounts payable as a debit and $310,200 is entered as a credit across from cash payments for merchandise in the operating activity portion of the worksheet.

Entering Salaries, Wages, and Other Operating Expenses   Items 3 and 3a relate to cash payments for salaries, wages, and other operating expenses.

   3.   Salaries, wages, and other operating expenses are entered as a debit of $195,380 on the income statement. The Prepaid Expenses account is credited for $195,380.

   3a.   The Prepaid Expenses account is debited for $195,480, and the cash payments for salaries, wages, and other operating expenses is credited for $195,480.

Entering Interest Expense   Item 4 relates to the cash payment for interest.

   4.   The interest expense amount of $2,880 is entered as a debit on the income statement, and the cash payment for interest is credited for $2,880 on the statement of cash flows. Because there is no Interest Payable account, it may be determined that the entire amount was paid in cash.

Entering the Income Tax Expense   Item 5 relates to the cash payment for income taxes.

   5.   The income tax expense is debited for $21,240 on the income statement, and the cash payments for income tax is credited for $21,240 in the operating activity section of the worksheet. Because there is no Income Tax Payable account, all the income tax is assumed to have been paid in cash.

Entering the Investment Activities on the Worksheet   Item 6 relates to the cash purchase of equipment.

6. The Equipment account on the balance sheet section has increased by $10,000 from 19X8 to 19X9. The increase would indicate that equipment has been purchased. From the additional information, it is also found that this equipment was purchased for cash. Across from the Equipment account, a debit of $10,000 is made, and a $10,000 credit is made under the portion for investing activities for cash paid for equipment.

Entering the Financing Activities on the Worksheet   Item 7 relates to the cash received from the sale of common stock. Item 8 relates to the payment on the mortgage and Item 9 to the payment of dividends to the stockholders.

7. Because the stock was sold for cash, the following three entries are made. Across from cash received from sale of common stock, in the financing activity portion of the worksheet, enter a debit of $12,000. Across from the Common Stock account on the balance sheet, enter a credit of $10,000 (1,000 shares of common stock at $10 par), and across from the Premium on Common Stock account, enter a credit of $2,000.

8. Opposite Mortgage Payable on the balance sheet, a debit of $1,000 is entered, and a credit of $1,000 is entered across from the cash paid on mortgage payable on the work sheet.

9. Opposite Dividends Payable on the balance sheet, a debit of $8,000 is entered, and a credit of $8,000 is entered across from the cash payment of dividends on the statement of cash flows.

Entering the Remaining Items for Reconciling   Item 10 relates to depreciation expense and accumulated depreciation, two noncash items. Item 11 relates to dividends payable, and Item 12 relates to the recording of net income.

10. Debit Depreciation Expense for $17,000 ($14,000 for equipment and $3,000 for building). Credit Accumulated Depreciation: Equipment for $14,000, and credit Accumulated Depreciation: Building for $3,000.

11. From the additional information, it is found that $9,000 of cash dividends were declared. Because the Year 9 balance of dividends payable is $9,000, it has not been paid in cash. This account is reconciled by debiting Retained Earnings for $9,000 and crediting Dividends Payable for $9,000.

12. Across from Net Income on the income statement, enter a debit of $13,500, and across from Retained Earnings on the balance sheet, enter a credit of $13,500.

After the last item is entered, each balance sheet item is reconciled. The statement of cash flows may now be prepared from the worksheet. In this example, there are no noncash investing or financing activities.

THE INDIRECT METHOD OF DETERMINING THE NET CASH RESULTS OF OPERATING ACTIVITIES

The FASB recommends the use of the direct method to prepare the statement of cash flows. When this method is used, it also requires that a disclosure be made of net income to net cash provided (used) from operations. The indirect method is precisely determined in that manner. The indirect method begins with net income and then reconciles net income by adding and subtracting certain items to determine the net cash provided (used) in the operating activities. The indirect method applies only to the first category of the statement of cash flows. The other two categories remain the same. Refer to Appendix 21A, page 792, for a specific example.

When using the indirect method, two types of adjustments are necessary: (1) adjustments for changes in noncash operational current assets and noncash operational current liabilities, and (2) adjustments for noncash operating items that neither provide nor use cash. An **operational current asset** is a current asset directly related to an income statement item. For example, accounts receivable is an operational current asset because it is directly related to sales, while marketable equity securities is not. An **operational current liability** is a current liability directly related to an income statement item. For example, accounts payable is an operational current liability because it is directly related to purchases, while dividends payable is not.

Following is the statement of cash flows using the indirect method for Flower Corporation.

operational current asset
a current asset directly related to an income statement item

operational current liability
a current liability directly related to an income statement item

Flower Corporation
Statement of Cash Flows—Indirect Method
For Year Ended December 31, 19X9

Cash Flows from Operating Activities:		
Net Income		$13,500
Adjustments to reconcile net income to net cash		
provided by operating activities:		
Increase in accounts receivable	$(7,500)	
Increase in merchandise inventory	(1,120)	
Increase in prepaid expenses	(100)	
Increase in accounts payable	920	
Depreciation expense	17,000	
Total adjustments		9,200
Net cash provided by operating activities		$22,700
Cash Flows from Investing Activities:		
Cash purchase of equipment	(10,000)	
Net cash used by investing activities		(10,000)
Cash Flows from Financing Activities:		
Cash received from the sale of common stock	12,000	
Cash paid on the mortgage payable	(1,000)	
Cash payment of dividends	(8,000)	
Net cash provided by financing activities		3,000
Net increase in cash		$15,700
Cash balance at beginning of 19X9		50,000
Cash balance at end of 19X9		$65,700

The first item under the operating activity category is net income. Analyzed adjustments are added and subtracted from net income to determine the net cash provided by operating activities.

Operational Current Assets and Current Liabilities Adjustments

Flower Corporation is also used for this example. The comparative balance sheet, page 932, and the income statement, page 933, as well as the additional information provided in the chapter, will be used for the illustration.

Operational Current Assets   The first item on the income statement is sales. As in the previous example, all sales are considered to be on account. Credit sales affect the current asset Accounts Receivable. The comparative balance sheet shows that the accounts receivable increased by $7,500. A T-account is used for illustration.

Accounts Receivable

12/31/19X8 Bal.	49,500		
19X9 Charge Sales	560,000	19X9 Cash Collections 552,500	
12/31/19X9 Bal.	57,000		

Using the information from the T-account and recalling the previous analysis of accounts receivable, the amount of cash collected is $7,500 less than the amount of sales revenue. Thus, net income must be reduced (adjusted) by $7,500 to properly reflect the amount of cash generated from operations. Assume, however, that the reverse of the above situation were true. For example, assume sales were $552,500 and cash collections were $560,000. This would mean that the $7,500 must be added to sales to reflect the proper cash receipts. The following is the adjustment calculation.

All Operational Current Assets

When the balance between balance sheet periods	[increases, deduct difference from Net Income]
	[decreases, add difference to Net Income]

This same procedure is used for all the operational current assets.

Operational Current Liabilities   The only operational current liability on the Flower Corporation's comparative balance sheet is Accounts Payable. The Accounts Payable account increased by $920. Recalling the previous analysis of cost of goods sold, merchandise inventory, and accounts payable, the T-account for Accounts Payable is as follows.

Accounts Payable

		12 31 19X8 Bal.	30,080
19X9 Payments 310,200		19X9 Purchases 311,120	
		12 31 19X9 Bal.	31,000

Purchases of merchandise of $311,120 exceed the cash payments on merchandise by $920. Thus, $920 must be added back to net income to help determine the amount of cash actually generated from operations. The following is the adjustment calculation, as also shown on the Statement of Cash Flows—indirect method, page 957.

All Operational Current Liabilities

When the balance between balance sheet periods	[increases, add difference to Net Income] [decreases, deduct difference from Net Income]

Adjustments for Noncash Operating Items Depreciation expense is deducted from revenue when determining net income, yet depreciation requires no cash payment. Because there is no cash used, this expense is added back to net income as an adjustment when preparing the statement of cash flows.

Other items such as patent expense, organizational expenses, goodwill amortization, bond discount amortization, and losses on long-term assets are items where no cash is used and are thus added back to net income as an adjustment to determine the amount of cash generated from operations. Items such as gains on the sale of long-term assets and bond premium amortization are not cash receipts and must be deducted. After all adjustments are analyzed, the operating activity portion of the statement of cash flows is then prepared along with the investing and financing activities portion, which remains the same using either the direct or the indirect method. The following indirect method adjustment chart is useful when determining what is the proper adjustment.

Indirect Method Adjustment Chart
Additions to or Deductions from Net Income
to Determine Cash Generated

Step 1: Operational Current Assets and Current Liabilities

Account	Net Income Adjustment
Decrease in Accounts Receivable (Net)	Add
Decrease in Merchandise Inventory	Add
Decrease in Prepaid Expenses	Add
Increase in Accounts Payable	Add
Increase in Accrued Liabilities	Add
Increase in Accounts Receivable (Net)	Subtract
Increase in Merchandise Inventory	Subtract
Increase in Prepaid Expenses	Subtract
Decrease in Accounts Payable	Subtract
Decrease in Accrued Liabilities	Subtract

Step 2: Noncash Accounts

Account	Net Income Adjustment
Depreciation Expense	Add
Loss on Sales of Noncurrent Assets	Add
Amortization of Patent	Add
Amortization of Discount on Bonds Payable	Add
Amortization of Goodwill	Add
Amortization of Premium on Bonds Payable	Subtract
Gain on Sale of Noncurrent Assets	Subtract

As with the direct method, using a worksheet to analyze and make the adjustments is helpful. A completed worksheet for the Flower Corporation using the indirect method is shown on pages 962–963.

FLOWER CORPORATION
WORKSHEET FOR STATEMENT OF CASH FLOWS—INDIRECT METHOD
FOR YEAR ENDED DECEMBER 31, 19X9

Account	Dec. 31, 19X8 Account Balances	Analysis of Transactions for Current Year Debit	Analysis of Transactions for Current Year Credit	Dec. 31, 19X9 Account Balances
Balance Sheet—Debits:				
Cash	50000 —			65700 —
Accounts Receivable	49500 —	(2) 7500 —		57000 —
Merchandise Inventory	31380 —	(3) 1120 —		32500 —
Prepaid Expenses	3200 —	(4) 100 —		3300 —
Equipment	60000 —	(7) 10000 —		70000 —
Building	120000 —			120000 —
Land	30000 —			30000 —
Total Debits	344080 —			378500 —
Balance Sheet—Credits:				
Accumulated Depreciation: Equipment	12000 —		(6) 14000 —	26000 —
Accumulated Depreciation: Building	3000 —		(6) 3000 —	6000 —
Accounts Payable	30080 —		(5) 920 —	31000 —
Dividends Payable	8000 —	(10) 8000 —	(11) 9000 —	9000 —
Mortgage Payable	36000 —	(8) 1000 —		35000 —
Common Stock, $10 par value	160000 —		(9) 10000 —	170000 —
Premium on Common Stock	40000 —		(9) 2000 —	42000 —
Retained Earnings	55000 —	(11) 9000 —	(1) 13500 —	59500 —
Total Credits	344080 —			378500 —

Statement of Cash Flows:

		Debit		Credit
Operating Activities:				
Net Income	(1)	135000 —		
Increase in Accounts Receivable			(2)	7500 —
Increase in Merchandise Inventory			(3)	1120 —
Increase in Prepaid Expenses			(4)	100 —
Increase in Accounts Payable	(5)	920 —		
Depreciation Expense	(6)	17000 —		
Investing Activities:				
Cash Purchase of Equipment			(7)	100000 —
Financing Activities:				
Cash Paid on Mortgage Payable			(8)	1000 —
Cash Received from Sale of Stock	(9)	12000 —		
Cash Payment of Dividends			(10)	8000 —
Noncash Investing and Financing Activities:		0 —		0 —
		80140 —		80140 —

PREPARING A STATEMENT OF CASH FLOWS WORKSHEET USING THE INDIRECT METHOD

The worksheet is set up using the comparative balance sheet and the income statement of the Flower Corporation. The reconciliation of the balances between the periods and the income statement analysis will provide the information needed to adjust net income to net cash provided by operating activities.

Enter the balance sheet accounts and amounts for 19X8 and 19X9 in the same manner as for the direct method. Enter the three major categories of the statement of cash flows below the balance sheet accounts, leaving adequate space after each for the different items. The following list identifies each item entered in the "Analysis of Transactions for Current Year" columns of the worksheet. The debits and credits are numbered on the worksheet.

1. Net income was $13,500.
2. Accounts Receivable increased by $7,500.
3. Merchandise Inventory increased by $1,120.
4. Prepaid Expenses increased by $100.
5. Accounts Payable increased by $920.
6. Depreciation Expense was $17,000.
7. Equipment was purchased for $10,000 cash.
8. Payment on mortgage payable was $1,000.
9. Sold 1,000 shares of common stock for $12,000.
10. Paid cash dividends of $8,000.
11. Declared $9,000 of cash dividends.

Entering the Analysis of Changes on the Worksheet

After all balances are entered and the major categories written in, use the following sequence for analysis as shown on the completed worksheet on pages 962–963.

1. Enter net income of $13,500 as a debit in the operating activity category, and enter $13,500 as a credit to Retained Earnings on the balance sheet. This is similar to Item 12 of the direct method.

2. Under net income on the statement of cash flows portion of the worksheet, enter the operational current asset analysis by crediting increases and debiting decreases. This is similar to Items 1, 1a, 2, 2a, and 3a of the direct method.

3. Under net income, enter the operational current liability analysis by debiting increases and crediting decreases. This is similar to Item 2b of the direct method.

4. Enter the income statement items that use cash. This is similar to Items 3, 4, and 5 of the direct method.

5. Under net income, enter the items from net income that neither provide cash nor use cash. Expenses not requiring cash are debits, and revenue items not providing cash are credits. This is similar to Item 10 of the direct method.

6. Review the balance sheet account balances to reconcile all remaining entries to the investing or financing activity categories. This is similar to Items 6, 7, 8, 9, and 11 of the direct method.

7. Total the analysis of transaction columns to determine accuracy and prepare the formal statement of cash flows from the worksheet.

The following illustration is a comparison of the direct method and the indirect method for the operating activity portion of the statement of cash flows.

A Comparison of the Direct and the Indirect Method for Preparing the Operating Activities Portion of the Statement of Cash Flows

Direct Method		Indirect Method		
Cash Flows from Operating Activities:		Cash Flows from Operating Activities:		
Cash Received from Customers	$552,500	Net Income		$13,500
Cash Payments for Merchandise	(310,200)	Adjustments to Reconcile Net Income to Net Cash Provided by Operating Activities:		
Cash Payments for Salaries, Wages, and Other Operating Expenses	(195,480)	Increase in Accounts Receivable	$ (7,500)	
Cash Payments for Interest Expense	(2,880)	Increase in Merchandise Inventory	(1,120)	
Cash Payments for Income Tax Expense	(21,240)	Increase in Prepaid Expenses	(100)	
		Increase in Accounts Payable	920	
		Depreciation Expense	17,000	
		Total Adjustments		9,200
Net Cash Provided by Operating Activities	$22,700	Net Cash Provided by Operating Activities		$22,700

SUMMARY

Cash is one of the most important assets of a business. The reporting of the receipt and use of cash is important. The users of financial statements value highly a corporation that manages its cash well. Because of the importance of cash, the FASB requires that a financial statement called the statement of cash flows be prepared along with the balance sheet and the income statement. The statement of cash flows is prepared using three categories for reporting cash. The titles are as follows.

1. Cash Flows from Operating Activities
2. Cash Flows from Investing Activities
3. Cash Flows from Financing Activities

Using a comparative balance sheet and an income statement, an analysis is made to determine the net cash flows in each of the above categories.

First, an analysis is made to determine the proper category for transactions involving cash. Operating activities involve analysis of the noncash balance sheet items related to the income statement items. Investing activities are those involving the purchase and sale of plant assets and other productive assets or investments. Financing activities are those involving borrowing cash on a short- or long-term basis, repayment of those loans, the sale of capital stock or the sale of bonds payable, and the payment of dividends.

The first major portion of the statement of cash flows is the operating activity category. Two methods may be used for its preparation: the direct method or the indirect method. The FASB strongly recommends that the direct method be used.

The direct method is a calculation of the net cash flow provided or used for operating activities and lists the major classes of cash receipts and subtracts the major classes of cash disbursements. The indirect method begins with net income and then adds or subtracts certain items to determine the net cash provided or used in the operating activity.

The statement of cash flows is developed by first examining the operating activities. The noncash items on a comparative balance sheet are compared to determine the changes between periods. These changes are then used to analyze the effects on the amounts appearing on the income statement. The direct method begins by analyzing sales on the income statement and its related balance sheet account, Accounts Receivable, to determine the cash received as collections from customers. The analysis continues until all the income statement items and the related noncash balance sheet items are reconciled. The remaining noncash accounts are analyzed to determine which transactions involve investing and financing activities.

The indirect method may also be used for the operating activities category. This analysis begins with net income and then reconciles the related operational current assets and operational current liabilities to adjust the income statement to a cash statement. The remaining noncash accounts are analyzed to determine the transactions involving investing and financing activities. These last two categories are the same for both the direct method and the indirect method.

A worksheet is used to aid in developing the statement of cash flows. It helps to organize the information needed for the formal statement. The worksheet contains four money columns. Two of the columns are used for the comparative balance sheet amounts. The other two columns are used for the analysis of transactions for the current year. When completed, the worksheet provides proof of accuracy of the analysis.

Review of Accounting Terminology

Following is a list of the accounting terminology for this chapter.

cash equivalents
comparative balance sheet
direct method
financing activities
indirect method

investing activities
operating activities
operational current asset
operational current liability
statement of cash flows

Fill in the blank with the correct word or term from the list.

1. _____ are examined to determine the increases and decreases in cash to achieve net cash flows from the operating activities for an accounting period.

2. The net cash inflows and outflows for an accounting period, classified as operating activities, investing activities, and financing activities, are reported on the _____.

3. A current asset that is directly related to an income statement item is a/an _____.

4. _____ are transactions involving borrowing cash on a short- or long-term basis and repaying that loan or the sale of capital stock and the payment of dividends.

5. _____ is a calculation of the net cash flows provided or used for operating activities and lists the major classes of cash receipts and subtracts the major classes of disbursements.

6. _____ begins with net income and then reconciles net income by adding and subtracting certain items to determine the net cash provided or used in the operating activities.

7. A balance sheet that shows two accounting periods side by side is a/an _____.

8. Transactions involving the purchase and sale of plant assets and other productive assets or investments are _____.

9. Assets readily convertible to a known amount and sufficiently close to maturity to be able to determine market value are _____.

10. A current liability that is directly related to an income statement item is a/an _____.

Match the following words and terms on the left with the definitions on the right (columns continue on the following page).

11. cash equivalents

12. comparative balance sheet

13. direct method

14. financing activities

15. indirect method

16. investing activities

a. items examined to determine the increases and decreases in cash to achieve net cash flows from the operating activities for an accounting period

b. a current asset directly related to an income statement item

c. transactions involving the purchase and sale of plant assets and other productive assets or investments

d. reports the net cash inflows and outflows for an accounting period, classified as operating activities, investing activities, and financing activities

e. a calculation of the net cash flows provided or used for operating activities and a listing of the major classes of cash receipts and disbursements

f. a current liability related to an income statement item

17. operating activities
18. operational current asset
19. operational current liability
20. statement of cash flows

g. transactions involving borrowing cash on a short- or long-term basis and repaying that loan or the sale of capital stock and the paying of dividends

h. a balance sheet that shows two accounting periods side by side

i. begins with net income and then reconciles net income by adding and subtracting certain items to determine the net cash provided or used in the operating activities

j. assets readily convertible to a known amount and sufficiently close to maturity to be able to determine market value

Exercises

Exercise 25.1
classifying operating, investing, and financing activities

Classify the following items as operating (O), investing (I), or financing (F) activities. Use the letters O, I, or F in the space provided.

_____ 1. Net income is $23,200.

_____ 2. Purchased a truck for cash of $15,800.

_____ 3. Paid cash dividends of $4,000.

_____ 4. Made a $2,000 principal payment on the mortgage payable.

_____ 5. Collected a principal payment from a customer on a note receivable.

_____ 6. Sold $100,000 of bonds payable.

_____ 7. Paid $100 of interest expense.

_____ 8. Paid $2,500 of federal income tax.

_____ 9. Equipment was purchased for $4,000 cash.

_____10. Purchased marketable equity securities for $10,000.

Exercise 25.2
analyzing and
calculating cash flows

Analyze and calculate the cash flows for each of the following. (Hint: Use the T-account method.)

a.	Net Credit Sales	$80,000
	Accounts Receivable, January 1	22,000
	Accounts Receivable, December 31	19,000
	Cash received from customers is $ _____	
b.	Cost of Goods Sold	$48,000
	Merchandise Inventory, January 1	12,500
	Accounts Payable, January 1	10,200
	Merchandise Inventory, December 31	13,000
	Accounts Payable, December 31	11,800
	Cash paid for merchandise is $ _____	
c.	Rent Expense	$12,000
	Prepaid Rent, January 1	3,000
	Prepaid Rent, December 31	3,600
	Cash paid for rent is $ _____	
d.	Salaries Expense	$24,000
	Accrued Salaries Payable, January 1	15,000
	Accrued Salaries Payable, December 31	18,000
	Cash paid for salaries is $ _____	

Exercise 25.3
preparing a statement
of cash flows by the
direct method from
miscellaneous
information

Use the following information to prepare a statement of cash flows for Lee Corporation, Year 19X9, using the direct method.

Cash paid for salaries	$106,000
Cash collected from customers	175,000
Cash received from the sale of equipment	3,000
Cash paid for interest expense	2,000
Cash paid for rent expense	10,000
Cash paid for merchandise	55,000
Cash paid for dividends	15,000
Cash received from the sale of stock	20,000
Cash borrowed on long-term mortgage	15,000
Cash paid to purchase a building	15,000
Cash balance, December 31, 19X8	50,000
Cash balance, December 31, 19X9	60,000

Exercise 25.4
using a comparative
balance sheet and an
income statement to
prepare a statement
of cash flows using
the direct method
without a worksheet

The following is a comparative balance sheet for Sands Company for the years ended December 31, 19X6 and December 31, 19X7.

Sands Company
Comparative Balance Sheet
December 31, 19X6 and December 31, 19X7

	19X6	19X7
Assets		
Cash	$ 25,000	$ 35,000
Accounts Receivable (Net)	40,000	38,000
Merchandise Inventory	75,000	85,000
Plant and Equipment	80,000	90,000
Accumulated Depreciation: Plant and Equipment	(20,000)	(26,000)
Total Assets	$200,000	$222,000
Liabilities		
Accounts Payable	$ 40,000	$ 35,000
Bonds Payable	80,000	90,000
Total Liabilities	$120,000	$125,000
Stockholders' Equity		
Common Stock, no par value	$ 50,000	$ 62,000
Retained Earnings	30,000	35,000
Total Stockholders' Equity	$ 80,000	$ 97,000
Total Liabilities and Stockholders' Equity	$200,000	$222,000

Sands Company
Income Statement
For the Year Ended December 31, 19X7

Sales		$112,000
Cost of Goods Sold		67,200
Gross Profit		44,800
Operating Expenses		
Salaries Expense	$22,800	
Depreciation Expense	6,000	
Other Operating Expenses	11,000	
Total Operating Expenses		39,800
Net Income		$ 5,000

Additional information:

a. Bonds payable were issued for $10,000 cash.

b. Sold no-par common stock for $12,000 cash.

c. Purchased equipment costing $10,000.

Using the above information, prepare the statement of cash flows for 19X7 by using the direct method without a worksheet.

Exercise 25.5

preparing a statement of cash flows using the indirect method

Using the information from Exercise 25.4, prepare the statement of cash flows for 19X7 using the indirect method without a worksheet.

Exercise 25.6

using a partial balance sheet to determine the effect on net income using the indirect method

The following is a partial comparative balance sheet for the Continental Corporation for the years 19X5 and 19X6. Using the indirect method, determine the following. (Hint: Refer to the Indirect Method Adjustment Chart on page 960.)

a. Determine the changes in the account balances (+ or −) between the two years and insert the amount of change in column three.

b. Determine the net income effect (+ or −) of each of these changes as it would appear on a statement of cash flows, Accounts Receivable is given as an example. Insert the remaining amounts in column four.

Continental Corporation
Partial Balance Sheet
December 31, 19X5 and December 31, 19X6

	19X5	19X6	Amount of Change	Effect on Net Income
Current Assets				
Cash	$ 60,000	$ 80,000	_____	_____
Accounts Receivable				
(Net)	85,000	110,000	+$25,000	−$25,000
Merchandise Inventory	76,000	72,000	_____	_____
Prepaid Insurance	2,000	1,500	_____	_____
Current Liabilities				
Accounts Payable	$100,000	$114,000	_____	_____
Wages Payable	2,000	3,000	_____	_____
Accrued Interest Expense	1,000	500	_____	_____
Dividends Payable	2,000	3,000	_____	_____

Problems

Problem 25.1
classifying operating, investing, financing, and noncash transactions from miscellaneous information

Classify the following transactions as an operating activity (O), investing activity (I), financing activity (F), or as a noncash transaction (N). Use a plus (+) or a minus (−) to indicate a cash receipt effect or a cash payment effect.

_____ 1. Sold common stock for cash.

_____ 2. Net income is $25,600.

_____ 3. Bought back ten $1,000 bonds payable from the bondholders.

_____ 4. Received the entire principal amount owed on a customer's note receivable.

_____ 5. Traded a truck for a similar truck; no cash was involved.

_____ 6. Paid the interest owed on a long-term mortgage payable.

_____ 7. Sold the marketable securities for cash.

_____ 8. Earned $300,000 in cash sales.

_____ 9. Bought new equipment for cash.

_____10. Collected cash from accounts receivable customers.

_____11. Bought 1,000 shares of XYZ Corporation common stock as a short-term investment for cash.

_____12. Paid $3,000 in cash dividends.

_____13. Exchanged preferred stock for common stock.

_____14. Equipment and building were depreciated in the total amount of $18,000.

_____15. Received $30,000 cash from the sale of an unused building with a net book value of $32,000.

Problem 25.2
using a comparative balance sheet and an income statement to prepare the operating activities section of the statement of cash flows by the direct method

The following is the Simson Corporation comparative balance sheet for the years 19X6 and 19X7.

Simson Corporation
Comparative Balance Sheet
For Years Ending December 31, 19X6 and 19X7

	19X6	19X7
Assets		
Cash	$ 7,300	$ 10,600
Accounts Receivable (Net)	14,350	12,850
Merchandise Inventory	48,100	47,350
Prepaid Rent	1,900	1,600
Equipment	36,100	45,250
Accumulated Depreciation: Equipment	(7,300)	(9,250)
Total Assets	$100,450	$108,400
Liabilities and Stockholders' Equity		
Accounts Payable	26,950	20,400
Mortgage Payable	18,000	13,250
Common Stock, $7.50 par value	37,500	45,000
Premium on Common Stock	0	3,750
Retained Earnings	18,000	26,000
Total Liabilities and Stockholders' Equity	$100,450	$108,400

Simson Corporation
Income Statement
For Year Ending December 31, 19X7

Sales		$288,600
Cost of Goods Sold		173,160
Gross Profit		115,440
Operating Expenses		
Wage Expense	$72,000	
Rent Expense	12,000	
Depreciation Expense	3,150	
Other Operating Expenses	17,290	
Total Operating Expenses		104,440
Net Income		$ 11,000

Related information from the accounts:

a. Fully depreciated equipment that cost $1,200 was discarded, and its cost and accumulated depreciation is removed from the accounts.

b. Equipment costing $10,350 was purchased with cash.

c. The mortgage was reduced by a $4,750 payment.

d. One thousand shares of common stock were issued at $11.25 per share including broker's commission.

e. Cash dividends totaling $3,000 were paid.

f. All sales are credit sales.

g. Wages and other operating expenses were paid in cash.

Instructions *Prepare the operating activities section of the statement of cash flows for 19X7 using the direct method to determine the net increase or decrease in cash.*

Problem 25.3
preparing a statement of cash flows worksheet by the direct method

Using the information from the Simson Corporation of Problem 25.2, complete the following.

1. Set up a worksheet for the direct method.

2. Enter the changes, using transaction reference numbers similar to those used in the chapter, in the analysis of transaction columns of the worksheet and complete the worksheet.

3. Prepare the formal statement of cash flows from the information on the worksheet.

4. Prepare the schedule for noncash investing and financing activities.

Problem 25.4
using a partial balance sheet to determine the effects on net income using the indirect method

The following is a partial balance sheet for Mickey Corporation for December 31, 19X6 and December 31, 19X7.

	19X6	19X7	Amount of Change	Effect on Net Income
Current Assets				
Cash	$ 50,000	$ 55,000	_____	_____
Marketable Securities	15,000	16,000	_____	_____
Accounts Receivable (Net)	18,000	17,000	_____	_____
Merchandise Inventory	26,000	24,000	_____	_____
Prepaid Insurance	3,000	3,200	_____	_____
Total Current Assets	$112,000	$115,200	_____	_____
Current Liabilities				
Notes Payable	$ 5,500	$ 5,500	_____	_____
Accounts Payable	40,000	42,000	_____	_____
Income Tax Payable	12,500	11,200	_____	_____
Dividends Payable	3,000	2,900	_____	_____
Total Current Liabilities	$ 61,000	$ 61,600	_____	_____

Instructions

1. *Determine the changes in the account balances (+ or −) between the two years and insert the amount of dollar change in column three.*

2. *Determine the net income effect (+ or −) of each of the changes as each would appear on a statement of cash flows, and insert the amount in column four. (Hint: Refer to the Indirect Method Adjustment Chart on page 960.)*

Problem 25.5
using a comparative balance sheet and an income statement to prepare the statement of cash flows by the direct method without a worksheet

Horn Corporation's December 31, 19X8 and 19X9 balance sheets carried the following balances.

	19X8	19X9
Debits		
Cash	$ 20,000	$ 40,000
Marketable Equity Securities	20,000	10,000
Note Receivable	5,000	0
Accounts Receivable (Net)	20,000	30,300
Merchandise Inventory	40,000	55,000
Equipment	135,000	145,000
	$240,000	$280,300
Credits		
Accumulated Depreciation: Equipment	$ 13,500	$ 14,500
Accounts Payable	25,000	24,000
Wages Payable	2,000	1,800
Bonds Payable	0	10,000
Preferred Stock	25,000	0
Common Stock, no par	150,000	200,000
Retained Earnings	24,500	30,000
	$240,000	$280,300

Horn Corporation
Income Statement
For Year Ended December 31, 19X9

Sales		$275,000
Cost of Goods Sold		178,750
Gross Profit		96,250
Operating Expenses		
Wages Expense	$52,500	
Depreciation Expense	1,000	
Other Operating Expenses	36,750	
Total Operating Expenses		90,250
Net Income		$ 6,000

Related information:

a. Purchased equipment for cash of $10,000.

b. Sold no-par stock for $25,000 cash.

c. Paid cash dividends of $500.

d. Sold marketable securities that cost $10,000 for $10,000 cash.

e. Collected the principal amount due on a customer's note receivable.

f. The preferred stockholders converted their shares to common stock for equal equity.

g. Sold a five-year bond payable for $10,000 cash.

Instructions

1. *Prepare a statement of cash flows for 19X9 without the worksheet using the direct method.*

2. *Prepare a schedule for the noncash investing and financing activities.*

Problem 25.6
preparing a statement of cash flows by the indirect method without a worksheet

Using the information from Problem 25.5, prepare a statement of cash flows from operating activities using the indirect method to determine the net increase or net decrease in cash.

Problem 25.7
preparing a statement of cash flows worksheet by the direct method

Rusk Corporation's December 31, 19X2 and December 31, 19X3 balance sheets carried the following items.

	19X2	19X3
Debits		
Cash	$ 5,000	$16,800
Accounts Receivable (Net)	3,000	3,800
Merchandise Inventory	12,000	14,000
Equipment	6,000	8,000
Building	15,000	15,000
Total Debits	$41,000	$57,600
Credits		
Accumulated Depreciation: Equipment	$ 600	$ 1,400
Accumulated Depreciation: Building	1,500	3,000
Accounts Payable	3,000	3,200
Wages Payable	500	600
Dividends Payable	200	200
Common Stock	25,000	35,000
Retained Earnings	10,200	14,200
Total Credits	$41,000	$57,600

Rusk Corporation
Income Statement
For Year Ended December 31, 19X3

Sales		$81,000
Cost of Goods Sold		50,400
Gross Profit		33,600
Operating Expenses		
Wages Expense	$15,100	
Depreciation Expense	2,300	
Other Operating Expenses	12,000	
Total Operating Expenses		29,400
Net Income		$ 4,200

The following information is provided for your analysis.

a. Purchased equipment costing $2,000 cash.

b. Sold common stock for $10,000 cash.

c. Paid cash dividends in the amount of $200.

d. Dividends of $200 were declared at the end of the year.

Instructions   1. *Set up a statement of cash flows worksheet using the direct method.*

2. *Enter all changes, using transaction reference numbers similar*

to those used in the chapter, in the transaction analysis columns of the worksheet and complete the worksheet.

3.   *Prepare the formal statement of cash flows from the worksheet.*

Problem 25.8
*preparing a statement
of cash flows
worksheet by the
indirect method*

Using the information from Problem 25.7, complete the following.

1.   Set up a statement of cash flows worksheet using the indirect method.

2.   Enter all changes, using transaction reference numbers similar to those given in the chapter, in the transaction analysis columns of the worksheet and complete the worksheet.

3.   Prepare the formal statement of cash flows from the worksheet.

CHAPTER 26

Corporations: Financial Statement Analysis and Interpretation

Accounting is the language of business, and the financial statements are the instruments used to analyze the success or failure of businesses and their managers. Each set of managers uses the assets to produce the greatest profit possible. How they perform is reflected in the financial statement instruments.

Many different types of groups are interested in the success of a business. Among these are stockholders, potential investors, creditors, stockbrokers, government, unions, financial analysts, and managers. Each group will have an interest in the financial statements, but for a different purpose. For example, a stockholder will be interested in net income, earnings per share, and whether the equity of the business is increasing. Stockholders are also interested in the amount of cash or stock dividends received during the year and the market price of their stock. Potential investors, stockbrokers, and financial analysts are interested in the profitability of one corporation compared with another when making decisions about potential investments.

A creditor, on the other hand, analyzes the ability of the corporation to meet its current or future debt obligations. The government is always interested in the legality of corporations and their fair payment of federal income taxes. Unions look to profits and future expectations of the corporations for their bargaining position for higher wages and benefits. Managers look at the financial statements for potential problem areas and ways to improve not only efficient use of the assets, but also profitability. As can be seen, many different groups will analyze and interpret corporate financial statements for their own individual purposes.

Most of the information gained by the analysis is obtained by studying relationships and making comparisons. Analytical measures are used and are expressed as ratios or percentages. For example, the relationship of $200,000 to $100,000 may be expressed as $200,000/$100,000, or $200,000:$100,000, 2.0, 2:1, or 200 percent. In this text, ratios and percentages are rounded to no more than one decimal place for convenience. When making comparisons by computing ratios or percentages, the analyst must decide if the resultant calculations are good, average, or bad.

The analyst may make a judgment based on information gained from several different sources. For example, Dun & Bradstreet publishes ratios and percentages that may be used for comparison. Many industries have trade associations that regularly publish standard ratios and percentages for that industry. These are considered excellent sources to use. However, a caution is given: When comparing one company with another company, the analyst must be careful that both companies are in the same industry and are relatively the same size. For example, comparing a multinational merchandising company with a small retail store is meaningless. They may be in the same industry, but they are not comparable because of size.

TYPES OF ANALYSIS

comparative financial statements
financial statements showing two or more years side by side

profitability
the ability of a business to earn a reasonable amount of income

Financial statements are compared from one year to another. The change in financial data for two or more years is placed side by side in adjacent columns. Financial statements presented in this manner are called **comparative financial statements.** Examples are shown in the following discussions. In addition, the two most important factors for analysis are solvency and profitability. Solvency as previously defined is the ability of the company to pay its current debt as it becomes due. **Profitability** is the ability of a business to earn a reasonable amount of income. All groups are extremely interested in these two factors.

COMPARATIVE FINANCIAL STATEMENTS

By comparing the financial statements of two or more successive years, analysts can readily see changes. By observing the changes in various items, analysts can make observations about the growth and profitability of the business. This comparison can be improved on by including two more adjacent columns for dollar increases or decreases. The increases or decreases may then be stated in percentages. By preparing comparative statements in this manner, analysts can immediately identify large dollar or percent changes. The comparative balance sheet for Flower Corporation follows.

Flower Corporation
Comparative Balance Sheet
December 31, 19X8 and December 31, 19X9

	19X8	19X9	Amount of Increase (Decrease) during 19X9	Percent of Increase (Decrease) during 19X9
Assets				
Current Assets				
Cash	$150,000	$165,700	$15,700	10.5
Accounts Receivable (Net)	49,500	57,000	7,500	15.2
Merchandise Inventory	31,380	32,500	1,120	3.6
Prepaid Expenses	3,200	3,300	100	3.1
Total Current Assets	$234,080	$258,500	$24,420	10.4
Plant and Equipment				
Equipment (Net)	$ 48,000	$ 44,000	$(4,000)	(8.3)
Building (Net)	117,000	114,000	(3,000)	(2.6)
Land	30,000	30,000	0	0
Total Plant and Equipment	$195,000	$188,000	(7,000)	(3.6)
Total Assets	$429,080	$446,500	$17,420	4.1
Liabilities				
Current Liabilities				
Accounts Payable	$ 30,080	$ 31,000	$ 920	3.1
Dividends Payable	8,000	9,000	1,000	12.5
Total Current Liabilities	$ 38,080	$ 40,000	$ 1,920	5.0
Long-Term Liabilities				
Mortgage Payable	$ 36,000	$ 35,000	$(1,000)	(2.8)
Total Liabilities	$ 74,080	$ 75,000	$ 920	1.2
Stockholders' Equity				
Common Stock, $10 par value	$160,000	$170,000	$10,000	6.3
Premium on Common Stock	40,000	42,000	2,000	5.0
Retained Earnings	155,000	159,500	4,500	2.9
Total Stockholders' Equity	$355,000	$371,500	$16,500	4.6
Total Liabilities and Stockholders' Equity	$429,080	$446,500	$17,420	4.1

Analyzing the Comparative Statement

In the analysis of the comparative balance sheet, the analyst selects the items on the statement showing the largest increases or decreases. An effort is then made to determine the reasons for the changes. For example, in the comparative balance sheet for Flower Corporation above, accounts receivable shows a 15.2 percent increase. The analyst must determine if this is a favorable increase or an unfavorable increase. Did the accounts receivable increase because customers are not paying their accounts promptly enough? If this is the case, the collection of cash from receivables will be slow, and thus, the increase is unfavorable. Did the accounts receivable increase because sales increased? If this is true, then the analyst may determine that the increase is favorable. Other large increases can be examined in the same way to determine whether they are favorable changes or unfavorable changes. The following comparative income statement for Flower Corporation is examined in the same manner.

Flower Corporation
Comparative Income Statement
For Years Ended December 31, 19X8 and 19X9

	19X8	19X9	Amount of Increase (Decrease) during 19X9	Percent of Increase (Decrease) during 19X9
Gross Sales	$670,500	$771,075	$100,575	15.0
Sales Returns and Allowances	10,200	8,500	(1,700)	(16.7)
Net Sales	$660,300	$762,575	$102,275	15.5
Cost of Goods Sold	$495,225	$579,557	$ 84,332	17.0
Gross Profit	$165,075	$183,018	$ 17,943	10.9
Operating Expenses				
Selling Expenses				
Sales Salaries Expense	$ 88,914	$ 94,538	$ 5,624	6.3
Advertising Expense	10,000	15,000	5,000	50.0
Store Supplies Expense	1,500	1,950	450	30.0
Depreciation: Store Equipment	10,000	11,000	1,000	10.0
Total Selling Expenses	$110,414	$122,488	$ 12,074	10.9
General and Administrative Expenses				
Salaries Expense	$ 27,104	$ 33,430	$ 6,326	23.3
Supplies Expense	2,900	900	(2,000)	(69.0)
Depreciation: Office Equipment	3,000	3,000	0	0
Depreciation: Building	3,000	3,000	0	0
Uncollectible Accounts Expense	800	500	(300)	(37.5)
Total General and Administrative Expenses	$ 36,804	$ 40,830	$ 4,026	10.9
Total Operating Expenses	$147,218	$163,318	$ 16,100	10.9
Income before Federal Income Taxes	$ 17,857	$ 19,700	$ 1,843	10.3
Income Tax Expense	$ 5,357	6,200	843	15.7
Net Income	$ 12,500	$ 13,500	$ 1,000	8.0

19X8 Earnings per Share
$12,500 ÷ 16,000 shares = $.78

19X9 Earnings per Share
$13,500 ÷ 16,000 shares = $.84

Flower Corporation's cost of goods sold has increased by 17 percent, while gross profit has increased by 10.9 percent. Further, the increase in cost of goods sold can be compared with the 15.5 percent increase in net sales. Because the increase in cost of goods sold is greater than both the net sales increase and the gross profit increase, an unfavorable trend is occurring and must be remedied if at all possible. In examining other increases, the analyst observes the advertising expense, the store supplies expense, and the increase in general and administrative salaries. Each of these is examined further to determine their reasonableness. For example, did the 50 percent increase in advertising result in greater sales? If the analyst finds the increased advertising expense is directly related to sales, then this increase may be favorable. Another favorable change may be found in the general and administrative supplies expense, which decreased substantially. Further study should be made of the 23.3 percent increase in general and administrative salaries to determine if this is an unfavorable trend. The analyst uses the comparative balance sheet and the comparative income statement to look for favorable or unfavorable trends. Another way to look at a comparative income statement is to examine it vertically, as follows.

Flower Corporation
Comparative Income Statement
For Years Ended December 31, 19X8 and 19X9

	19X8	19X9	19X8 %	19X9 %
Gross Sales	$670,500	$771,075	101.5	101.1
Sales Returns and Allowances	10,200	8,500	1.5	1.1
Net Sales	$660,300	$762,575	100.0	100.0
Cost of Goods Sold	$495,225	$579,557	75.0	76.0
Gross Profit	$165,075	$183,018	25.0	24.0
Operating Expenses				
Selling Expenses				
Sales Salaries Expense	$ 88,914	$ 94,538	13.5	12.4
Advertising Expense	10,000	15,000	1.5	2.0
Store Supplies Expense	1,500	1,950	.2	.3
Depreciation: Store Equipment	10,000	11,000	1.5	1.4
Total Selling Expenses	$110,414	$122,488	16.7	16.1
General and Administrative Expenses				
Salaries Expense	$ 27,104	$ 33,430	4.1	4.4
Supplies Expense	2,900	900	.4	.1
Depreciation: Office Equipment	3,000	3,000	.5	.4
Depreciation: Building	3,000	3,000	.5	.4
Uncollectible Accounts Expense	800	500	.1	.1
Total General and Administrative Expenses	$ 36,804	$ 40,830	5.6	5.4
Total Operating Expenses	$147,218	$163,318	22.3	21.4
Income Before Federal Income Taxes	$ 17,857	$ 19,700	2.7	2.6
Income Tax Expense	5,357	6,200	.8	.8
Net Income	$ 12,500	$ 13,500	1.9	1.8

19X8 Earnings per Share
$12,500 ÷ 16,000 shares = $.78

19X9 Earnings per Share
$13,500 ÷ 16,000 shares = $.84

The percentages presented are all based on net sales. In each percentage column, the net sales figure is used as the base, which is 100 percent. Every amount is then expressed as a percentage of net sales. For example, to determine the cost of goods sold for 19X9 as a percentage of net sales, divide cost of goods sold ($579,557) by net sales ($762,575) to arrive at 76 percent. It could then be said that $.76 of every $1.00 of net sales is the average cost of an item sold.

The analyst examines the percentages item by item between the two periods. Comparing the cost of goods sold percentage in 19X8 of 75 percent with the percentage in 19X9 of 76 percent may be considered unfavorable. Even though sales and net income increased in 19X9, the analyst may consider both unfavorable in comparison to 19X8. In addition to this type of analysis, the analyst will examine the solvency of the business. An examination is made of the working capital and both the current and long-term items on the balance sheet.

SOLVENCY ANALYSIS

Solvency is the ability of a company to pay its current obligations when due. These current obligations include accounts payable, the current portion of mortgage and notes payable, interest payable, taxes payable, wages payable, and dividends payable. Stockholders, potential investors, and especially creditors analyze financial statements for solvency. The analysis for solvency includes all the current items on the balance sheet. For a merchandising company, the current balances are affected by the buying and selling of inventory. For a service company, these balances are impacted by how much and how well the services are performed. To aid in this analysis, the working capital of the business is considered first, and then its composition.

Working Capital

The working capital of a business is the excess of the current assets over the current liabilities and reflects the ability of a business to meet its current obligations. The more important of the working capital items are cash, accounts receivable, and merchandise inventory. When merchandise is sold and accounts receivable are collected, the cash is used to pay the current liabilities, such as the accounts payable. Adequate working capital enables a business to meet its current obligations, take advantage of cash discounts, carry sufficient inventory, and offer favorable credit terms to its customers. A company with a poor working capital position is in a poor competitive position. In fact, inadequate working capital may threaten its very survival.

Working capital is an important consideration in analysis. A business must have an adequate current debt-paying ability with enough excess to meet other requirements. Although the total working capital is important, the quality of the working capital is more important. A working capital example is as follows.

BING CORPORATION PARTIAL BALANCE SHEET DECEMBER 31, 19X4		
Current Assets		
Cash	$	3 5 0 0 0 —
Marketable Securities (LCM)		1 5 0 0 0 —
Notes Receivable		1 0 0 0 0 —
Accounts Receivable (Net)		4 0 0 0 0 —
Merchandise Inventory		9 8 0 0 0 —
Prepaid Expenses		2 0 0 0 —
Total Current Assets	$	2 0 0 0 0 0 —
Current Liabilities		
Notes Payable (Current Portion)	$	2 0 0 0 0 —
Accounts Payable		7 5 0 0 0 —
Wages Payable		5 0 0 0 —
Total Current Liabilities	$	1 0 0 0 0 0 —
Working Capital	$	1 0 0 0 0 0 —

As shown, the working capital total is determined by subtracting the current liabilities from the current assets. To determine the quality of the working capital, the current assets and current liabilities must be analyzed more closely. Several calculations are made to aid in this procedure. Two of these calculations, the current ratio and the quick ratio, are discussed.

Current Ratio

The current ratio is calculated by dividing the current assets by the current liabilities. Using the information from the partial balance sheet of Bing Corporation, the following is the current ratio calculation.

Current Ratio

Total Current Assets	$200,000
Total Current Liabilities	$100,000

Formula: $\dfrac{\text{Current Assets}}{\text{Current Liabilities}}$

Calculation: $\dfrac{\$200,000}{\$100,000} = 2{:}1$

The current ratio is used to express the relationship between the current assets and the current liabilities. Some industries expect to see at least a 2:1 current ratio, which expresses the fact that there are $2 of current assets to every $1 of current liabilities. Another way to express this ratio is to state that there are twice as many current assets as current liabilities. Comparisons may be made by the managers of Bing Corporation from one year to another. They may use the comparative balance sheets to see where improvements occur or where problems arise that need to be corrected.

Quick Ratio

quick ratio
the quick assets divided by the current liabilities

To determine the ability of the company to pay its immediate debt, an analysis is necessary to determine what current assets can be quickly converted to cash to pay the debt. The company does not necessarily intend to do this, but if necessary it could cover its current obligations with cash. The **quick ratio** is found by dividing the quick assets by the current liabilities. Using the information from the Bing Corporation, an analysis of each current asset is made to determine its potential conversion to cash.

Quick Ratio

Cash	$ 35,000
Marketable Securities	15,000
Notes Receivable	10,000
Accounts Receivable	40,000
Total Quick Assets	$100,000
Total Current Liabilities	$100,000

Formula: $\dfrac{\text{Quick Assets}}{\text{Current Liabilities}}$

Calculation: $\dfrac{\$100,000}{\$100,000} = 1{:}1$

The analysis here is simply to see if the current assets are close enough to cash to be able to use them to pay the current liabilities. Generally, a 1:1 ratio is considered satisfactory in most situations.

After this analysis of the working capital, attention is then given to two specific current assets: the accounts receivable and the merchandise inventory. As you know, cash is needed to purchase sufficient inventory; this is true even if it is a credit purchase, because credit purchases must usually be paid with cash within 30 days. If the inventory is sold for cash, the money may then be used to purchase new inventory. If the sale of inventory creates ac-

Circulating Assets

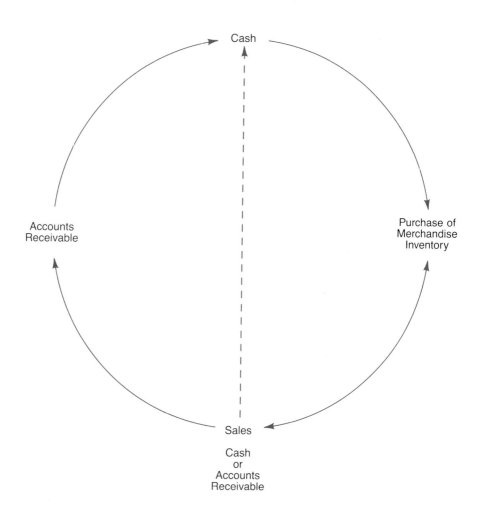

counts receivable, these must be collected in order to have cash again. Because of this constant change of assets from cash to inventory to accounts receivable and back again to cash, these assets are called **circulating assets.** An illustration of this cycle is shown on the previous page.

circulating assets
the cash, inventory, cash sales, credit sales, and accounts receivables as they occur and are converted to cash over time

The analytical procedures developed from the circulating assets are accounts receivable turnover, average days' sales uncollected, inventory turnover, and average number of days to sell inventory.

Accounts Receivable Turnover

accounts receivable turnover
net credit sales divided by average accounts receivable

The **accounts receivable turnover** is calculated by dividing net credit sales by the average accounts receivable. The average balance is determined by averaging the balances at the beginning and ending of the year as follows.

1. Accounts receivable, January 1, 19X2 $44,000

2. Accounts receivable, December 31, 19X2 $40,000

3. Average balance (1 + 2) ÷ 2
    ($44,000 + $40,000) ÷ 2 $42,000

The average balance may also be determined by adding together the balances at the end of each month and dividing the total by twelve. Assume the average accounts receivable for Bing Corporation is $42,000 and the credit sales are $420,000. The calculation for the accounts receivable turnover is as follows.

Accounts Receivable Turnover

Total Net Credit Sales	$420,000
Average Accounts Receivable	$ 42,000

Formula: $\dfrac{\text{Net Credit Sales}}{\text{Average Accounts Receivable}}$

Calculation: $\dfrac{\$420,000}{\$42,000} = 10 \text{ times}$

The accounts receivable turnover is the number of times the accounts receivable has been created and then collected over a year's time. The accounts receivable turnover will be high when accounts receivable are collected rapidly, and low when they are not.

Average Days' Sales Uncollected

average days' sales uncollected
365 days in the year divided by accounts receivable turnover

The accounts receivable turnover shows how quickly a company collects its accounts. Accounts receivable may be further analyzed by calculating the **average days' sales uncollected.** This calculation is made by dividing the accounts receivable turnover into 365 days. Using the accounts receivable turnover for Bing Corporation, the average days' sales uncollected is calculated as follows.

Average Days' Sales Uncollected

Number of Days in Year	365 days
Accounts Receivable Turnover	10 times

Formula: $\dfrac{365\ \text{Days}}{\text{Accounts Receivable Turnover}}$

Calculation: $\dfrac{365\ \text{Days}}{10\ \text{Times}} = 36.5$ days

To determine if 36.5 average days' sales uncollected is favorable or unfavorable, the analyst must know the collection terms of the company. If Bing Corporation has credit terms of 2/10, n30, the 36.5 days' sales uncollected would appear to be unfavorable. Customers are not taking advantage of the 2 percent discount for early payment of their balances, and in addition, the average customer takes 6.5 days longer to pay than the credit terms allow. This results in an unfavorable cash-flow situation because the company must wait longer for its cash than it anticipated when granting the credit terms. The company's manager will look at this calculation to determine how efficient the accounts receivable collections are and to see if every effort is being made to collect the accounts on time. The manager may also check the company's credit granting procedures to see if they are strict enough and check to see if the current procedures are being followed by the employees.

Inventory Turnover

inventory turnover
the cost of goods sold divided by the average inventory

The **inventory turnover** is the number of times the average inventory is sold during an accounting period. It is calculated by dividing average merchandise inventory into the cost of goods sold as follows.

Inventory Turnover

Total Cost of Goods Sold	$315,000
Average Inventory	$ 95,000

Formula: $\dfrac{\text{Cost of Goods Sold}}{\text{Average Inventory}}$

Calculation: $\dfrac{\$315,000}{\$95,000} = 3.3$ times

The cost of goods sold figure is taken from the company's income statement and the average inventory figure is obtained by adding the January 1 and December 31 inventories together and dividing by two.

A high inventory turnover is considered to be desirable because this shows aggressive marketing. However, the analyst must know the type of inventory sold before he or she can make a judgment as to whether the inventory turnover is high, average, or low. If the inventory has a high selling price per item, the inventory will not sell as quickly; thus, the inventory turnover will be low. On the other hand, if the selling price of an item is low, the inventory turnover will be high. If Bing Corporation sells appliances, such as refrigerators, stoves, and microwave ovens, an inventory turnover of 3.3 may be considered favorable or average. Before any judgments are made, industry averages need to be used for comparison to determine if the turnover is high, average, or low.

Average Number of Days to Sell Inventory

average number of days to sell the inventory
the inventory turnover divided into 365 days of the year

A further examination of inventory is desired to calculate the **average number of days to sell the inventory.** This calculation is made by dividing the inventory turnover into 365 days.

Average Number Days to Sell Inventory

Number of Days in Year	365 days
Inventory Turnover	3.3 times

Formula: $\dfrac{365\text{ Days}}{\text{Inventory Turnover}}$

Calculation: $\dfrac{365\text{ Days}}{3.3\text{ Times}} = 110.6$ days

The average number of days to sell the inventory is 110.6 days (rounded) or more than three months. This may be unfavorable, because inventory displayed in the store may become dusty, old, or obsolete very quickly. The person who analyzes the ratios and turnover figures will probably study similar figures from comparable sized companies in the same industry, those figures published by Dun and Bradstreet, and/or those published by trade associations to determine what is average for their particular industry.

By analyzing the working capital, current ratio, quick ratio, and circulating assets, the solvency position of the business is determined. A business must be able to manage in such a way as to be able to pay its current debt as it becomes due. The analyses given have been for one year only, but the analyst may wish to consider the previous years for comparative purposes.

PROFITABILITY ANALYSIS

Owners and others analyzing financial statements are interested in a corporation with growing equity. A corporation grows through the profits it retains in the business. There are several balance sheet and income statement relationships that are analyzed to determine the degree of profitability.

Analysis of Owner and Creditor Equities

An analyst, especially a creditor, is always interested in the share of the company's assets that is contributed by the owners and the share that is contributed by the creditors. Remembering that creditors have first claim on the assets, the dollar contributions of each is of interest. From the balance sheet, the dollar contributions may be clearly seen. Often these dollar amounts become more meaningful when expressed as percentages. These percentages are called equity-debt ratios. The **equity ratio** is calculated by dividing the total assets into the stockholders' equity. The **debt ratio** is calculated by dividing the total assets into the liabilities. An example is presented below for Bing Corporation assuming the following liabilities and owner's equity.

equity ratio
the total assets divided into the stockholders' equity

debt ratio
total assets divided into total liabilities

Equity-Debt Ratio

Total Liabilities	$150,000
Total Stockholders' Equity	325,000
Total Liabilities and Stockholders' Equity	$475,000
Total Assets	$475,000

Equity Formula: $\dfrac{\text{Stockholders' Equity}}{\text{Total Assets}}$ Calculation: $\dfrac{\$325,000}{\$475,000} = 68.4\%$

Debt Formula: $\dfrac{\text{Liabilities}}{\text{Total Assets}}$ Calculation: $\dfrac{\$150,000}{\$475,000} = 31.6\%$

Potential creditors, as well as the present creditors, prefer to see the owners have a higher percentage of equity than the creditors. The greater the equity of the owners, the greater the possibility that the creditors will be able to receive their claims when due. If owners, however, can use borrowed capital to earn a greater return than is required to pay back the debt, then from the owners' viewpoint, a reasonable amount of creditors' equity is desirable.

Rate of Return on Total Assets

rate of return on total assets
net income divided by average total assets

The rate of return on total assets is a measure of the performance of managers in using the assets to produce income. The **rate of return on total assets** is calculated by dividing net income by the average total assets. Assume that the net income of Bing Corporation is $45,600, and that the average total assets are $475,000. The rate of return on total assets is calculated as follows.

Rate of Return on Total Assets

Net Income	$ 45,600
Average Total Assets	$475,000

Formula: $\dfrac{\text{Net Income}}{\text{Average Total Assets}}$

Calculation: $\dfrac{\$45,600}{\$475,000} = 9.6\%$

The average total assets figure is determined by adding the total assets at the beginning of the year to those at the end of the year and dividing the result by two. If the total assets did not fluctuate throughout the year, the year-end total of assets may be used. The rate of return on assets is an important calculation, because using the assets to produce revenue is the primary purpose of management.

Rate of Return on Common Stockholders' Equity

rate of return on common stockholders' equity
net income divided by average common stockholders' equity

The primary purpose for a business is to earn a return for the owners. The **rate of return on common stockholders' equity** is calculated by dividing the net income by average common stockholders' equity. Using the information from Bing Corporation, the rate earned on common stockholders' equity is as follows.

Rate of Return on Common Stockholders' Equity		
Net Income		$ 45,600
Beginning Stockholders' Equity	$279,400	
Ending Stockholders' Equity	$325,000	
Average ($279,400 + $325,000) ÷ 2		$302,200

$$\text{Formula:} \frac{\text{Net Income}}{\text{Average Stockholders' Equity}}$$

$$\text{Calculation:} \frac{\$45,600}{\$302,200} = 15.1\%$$

Compare the 15.1 percent rate of return on the common stockholders' equity with the 9.6 percent on total assets. This greater return to common stockholders resulted from using borrowed money. The use of borrowed capital to increase the earnings applicable to common stockholders is called **leverage.**

leverage
the use of borrowed capital to increase the earnings applicable to the common stockholders

Earnings per Share

Chapter 22 covered the calculation and discussion of earnings per share. To review, the earnings per share is calculated by dividing the number of outstanding common shares into the net income for the year. Assume that the Bing Corporation, having only one class of stock, has 19,000 shares of common stock outstanding; therefore, the earnings per share is $2.40 ($45,600 ÷ 19,000).

Price-Earnings Ratio

price-earnings ratio
the market price per common share divided by earnings per share

The price-earnings ratio is widely used for comparing investment opportunities. The **price-earnings ratio** is calculated by dividing the market price per share of common stock by the earnings per share of that common stock; it is often referred to as the P-E ratio. Assuming that Bing Corporation's common stock is quoted at the market price of $22.00 per share, the calculation for the price-earnings ratio is as follows.

Price-Earnings Ratio

Market Price per Common Share	$22.00
Earnings per Share	$ 2.40

Formula: $\dfrac{\text{Market Price per Common Share}}{\text{Earnings per Share}}$

Calculation: $\dfrac{\$22.00}{\$2.40} = 9.2{:}1$

From this calculation an analyst may say that it takes $9.20 to buy $1 of Bing Corporation earnings. To determine if the P-E ratio of 9.2:1 is good, average, or bad, the analyst may use an industry average. The P-E ratio is quoted on a daily basis because of its importance in the marketplace. Most financial media that quote the daily activity of the stock exchanges will include the P-E ratio as well as the dividend yield.

Dividend Yield

dividend yield
the cash dividend per common share divided by the market price per common share

Another calculation that is quoted in the daily financial press is the dividend yield. To calculate the **dividend yield,** the total cash dividend for the year is divided by the number of outstanding common shares to determine the cash dividend on a per-share basis. The dividend per share is then divided by the market price per common share. For example, assume the cash dividend paid to common stockholders during the year is $1.50 per share. The calculation is as follows.

Dividend Yield

Cash Dividend per Common Share	$ 1.50
Market Price per Common Share	$22.00

Formula: $\dfrac{\text{Cash Dividend per Common Share}}{\text{Market Price per Common Share}}$

Calculation: $\dfrac{\$1.50}{\$22.00} = 6.8\%$

This calculation shows the rate earned from the receipt of cash dividends based on the current market price per share.

SUMMARY

Users of financial information are extremely interested in how well a corporation performs. Its performance is summarized in the published financial statements, where a minimum of two years can be compared. By examining the comparative financial statements, analysts can evaluate and compare one year with the other. This is accomplished by contrasting the dollar changes and the percentage changes between the two accounting periods. In addition, these financial statements can be used to compare one corporation with another. Many different groups are interested in the success of a corporate business. Among these are stockholders, potential investors, creditors, stockbrokers, government agencies, trade unions, financial analysts, and the managers of the corporation. Each group has a different interest and will analyze the financial statements with that interest in mind.

The analysis of the corporation financial statements may take one of two forms. First, the analysis may revolve around the solvency of the corporation (the ability of the corporation to pay its current debt). The circulating assets are analyzed to determine the accounts receivable turnover, the average days' sales uncollected, the inventory turnover, and the average number of days to sell the inventory.

By selling merchandise or rendering a service, a corporation may increase or decrease its assets. Adequate working capital of a corporation is an important aspect to success. Working capital, the excess of current assets over current liabilities, is an important measure of solvency. Other calculations, such as current ratio, quick ratio, inventory turnover, and accounts receivable turnover, are important in understanding the composition of the working capital items. Creditors are among the group of analysts interested in the solvency of a corporation.

The second form of analysis is the profitability analysis. Owners, potential investors, and creditors are among those who are interested in a growing equity of a corporation. A corporation will grow through the net income it retains. Because the assets are used to produce net income, the type of assets and how they are used by management determines its success. The calculation of the rate of return on total assets will aid in the determination of management's success in the use of its assets. In addition, stockholders are interested in the rate of return on their own investments and the equity per share of their stock. The rate of return on common stock will influence the market price of the stock. Often, managers successfully use debt obligations to increase the earnings applicable to the common stockholders. The stockholders can see this reflected in the calculation of earnings per share. By analyzing the financial statements, the reader can determine the current position, as well as the long-term position, of a corporation and compare this position with an industry standard or with the position of a similar corporation.

Summary of Analytical Methods

Title	Method of Calculation	Significance
Working Capital	Current Assets Minus Current Liabilities	Shows the excess of current assets over current liabilities to provide funds for other current needs.
Current Ratio	$\dfrac{\text{Current Assets}}{\text{Current Liabilities}}$	Shows the current debt-paying ability.
Quick Ratio	$\dfrac{\text{Quick Assets}}{\text{Current Liabilities}}$	Shows the current liquid assets available to pay current debt.
Accounts Receivable Turnover	$\dfrac{\text{Net Credit Sales}}{\text{Average Accounts Receivable}}$	Indicates how long it takes a company to collect its accounts.
Average Days' Sales Uncollected	$\dfrac{365\ \text{Days}}{\text{Accounts Receivable Turnover}}$	Shows the average number of days required to collect the accounts receivable.
Inventory Turnover	$\dfrac{\text{Cost of Goods Sold}}{\text{Average Inventory}}$	Indicates the average number of times a company's inventory is sold during an accounting period.
Average Number of Days to Sell the Inventory	$\dfrac{365\ \text{Days}}{\text{Inventory Turnover}}$	Shows the average number of days required to sell the inventory.
Equity Ratio	$\dfrac{\text{Stockholders' Equity}}{\text{Total Assets}}$	Shows the interest the owners have in the corporation expressed as a percent.
Debt Ratio	$\dfrac{\text{Total Liabilities}}{\text{Total Assets}}$	Shows the claims the creditors have on the assets expressed as a percent.
Rate of Return on Total Assets	$\dfrac{\text{Net Income}}{\text{Average Total Assets}}$	Shows the rate of income achieved from the use of the assets to produce revenue.
Rate of Return on Common Stockholders' Equity	$\dfrac{\text{Net Income}}{\text{Average Common Stockholders' Equity}}$	Shows the rate of income achieved from the investment of the common shareholders.
Earnings per Share	$\dfrac{\text{Net Income}}{\text{Number of Common Shares Outstanding}}$	Shows the earnings achieved on each share of common stock presently in the hands of stockholders.
Price-Earnings Ratio	$\dfrac{\text{Market Price per Common Share}}{\text{Earnings per Share}}$	Shows the desirability of owning common stock in the marketplace.
Dividend Yield	$\dfrac{\text{Cash Dividend per Common Share}}{\text{Market Price per Common Share}}$	Shows the rate earned from the receipt of cash dividends based on the current price of the common stock.

Review of Accounting Terminology

Following is a list of the accounting terminology for this chapter.

accounts receivable turnover   equity ratio
average days' sales uncollected   inventory turnover
average number of days to sell   leverage
   the inventory   price-earnings ratio
circulating assets   profitability
comparative financial   rate of return on common
   statements   stockholders' equity
debt ratio   rate of return on total assets
dividend yield   quick ratio

Fill in the blank with the correct word or term from the list.

1. Net income divided by average total assets is the _____ .

2. The _____ is the quick assets divided by the current liabilities.

3. The inventory turnover divided into 365 days of the year is the _____.

4. _____ is 365 days in the year divided by accounts receivable turnover.

5. Net income divided by average common stockholders' equity is the _____.

6. Financial statements showing two or more years side by side are called _____.

7. _____ is the ability of business to earn a reasonable amount of income.

8. Cash, inventory, cash sales, credit sales, and accounts receivables as they occur and are converted to cash over time are called the _____.

9. The use of borrowed capital to increase the earnings applicable to the common stockholders is called _____.

10. The _____ is the total assets divided into the stockholders' equity.

11. The cost of goods sold divided by the average inventory is called the _____.

12. The market price per common share divided by earnings per share is the _____.

13. _____ is the cash dividend per common share divided by the market price per common share.

14. Total assets divided into total liabilities is called the _____ .

15. Net credit sales divided by average accounts receivable is called the _____.

Match the following words and terms on the left with the definitions on the right (columns continue on the following page).

16. accounts receivable turnover

17. average days' sales uncollected

18. average number of days to sell the inventory

19. circulating assets

20. comparative financial statements

21. debt ratio

22. dividend yield

23. equity ratio

24. inventory turnover

25. leverage

a. the quick assets divided by the current liabilities

b. net credit sales divided by average accounts receivable

c. the accounts receivable turnover divided into 365 days in the year

d. the cost of goods sold divided by the average inventory

e. the inventory turnover divided into 365 days of the year

f. total assets divided into the stockholders' equity

g. total assets divided into total liabilities

h. net income divided by average total assets

i. net income divided by average common stockholders' equity

j. the market price per common share divided by earnings per common share

k. the cash dividend per common share divided by the market price per common share

26. price-earnings ratio
27. profitability
28. rate of return on common stockholders' equity
29. rate of return on total assets
30. quick ratio

l. financial statements that show two or more years side by side

m. the ability of business to earn a reasonable amount of income

n. cash, inventory, cash sales, credit sales, and accounts receivable as they occur and are converted to cash over time

o. the use of borrowed capital to increase the earnings applicable to the common stockholder

Exercises

Exercise 26.1
calculating percent increases and decreases of given account balances

Calculate the dollar increase or decrease and the percentage change for the following selected items. Use the following information and round to the nearest whole percent.

	19X6	19X7	Amount of Increase (Decrease) during 19X7	Percent Increase (Decrease) during 19X7
Cash	$56,200	$ 48,900	_____	_____
Notes Receivable	3,000	5,000	_____	_____
Equipment (Net)	74,000	113,500	_____	_____
Mortgage Payable	25,000	22,000	_____	_____

Exercise 26.2
calculating inventory turnover, accounts receivable turnover, average days' sales uncollected, and average number of days to sell the inventory

The following information relates to two years of the Bow Company. The average inventory and the average accounts receivable amounts may be determined using the year-end figures for 19X2 and 19X3.

	19X2	**19X3**
Sales (Credit)	$340,000	$460,000
Cost of Goods Sold	232,000	292,000
Inventory (Year End)	37,000	43,000
Account Receivable (Year End)	38,000	50,000

Calculate the following for 19X3. Round to the nearest tenth of a percent.

a. Inventory turnover

b. Accounts receivable turnover

c. Average days' sales uncollected

d. Average number of days to sell inventory

Exercise 26.3
*calculating working
capital, current ratio,
quick ratio, debt ratio,
and equity ratio*

The following is the comparative balance sheet for the Calco Corporation for the years ending December 31, 19X8 and 19X9.

Calco Corporation
Comparative Balance Sheet
For Years Ended December 31, 19X8 and 19X9

	19X8	**19X9**
Assets		
Cash	$ 40,000	$ 80,000
Accounts Receivable (Net)	160,000	160,000
Inventory	230,000	235,000
Prepaid Insurance	10,000	5,000
Plant and Equipment (Net)	100,000	100,000
Total Assets	$540,000	$580,000
Liabilities and Stockholders' Equity		
Accounts Payable	$200,000	$200,000
Common Stock	320,000	340,000
Retained Earnings	20,000	40,000
Total Liabilities and		
Stockholders' Equity	$540,000	$580,000

a. Calculate (1) the working capital; (2) the current ratio; and (3) the quick ratio for each of the two years.

b. Calculate the debt ratio for year 19X9.

c. Calculate the equity ratio for year 19X9.

Exercise 26.4

calculating rate of return on assets, rate of return on common stockholders' equity, earnings per share, and price-earnings ratio

Assume the following is information from the records of Sims Corporation for the two years ending December 31, 19X4 and 19X5. Round your answers to the nearest tenth of a percent where necessary.

	19X4	19X5
Net Income	$ 43,000	$ 49,500
Average Total Assets	429,500	430,000
Average Stockholders' Equity	350,000	350,000
Common Shares Outstanding	25,000	25,000
Market Price per Share	16	21

a. Determine the rate of return on assets for each of the two years.

b. Determine the rate of return on common stockholders' equity for each of the two years.

c. Calculate earnings per share for each of the two years.

d. Calculate the price-earnings ratio for each of the two years.

Exercise 26.5

calculating dollar changes and percent changes for an income statement

The following is a comparative income statement for Dulux Corporation. Determine the increases and decreases and express them as dollar and percentage changes. Round to the nearest tenth of a percent.

Dulux Corporation
Comparative Income Statement
For Years Ending December 31, 19X8 and 19X9

	19X8	19X9	Amount of Increase (Decrease) during 19X9	Percent Increase (Decrease) during 19X9
Net Sales	$710,000	$830,000	_____	_____
Cost of Goods Sold	422,000	510,200	_____	_____
Gross Profit	288,000	319,800	_____	_____
Selling Expenses	141,200	158,000	_____	_____
General and Administrative				
Expenses	76,400	74,000	_____	_____
Net Income	70,400	87,800	_____	_____

Exercise 26.6
preparing a vertical analysis

Using the comparative income statement from Exercise 26.5, pre-pare a vertical analysis by expressing each item as a percentage of net sales. Use the format shown in the text. Round to the nearest tenth of a percent.

Problems

Problem 26.1
calculating dollar and percent increases or decreases for a comparative balance sheet, working capital, and dividend yield, and analyzing items

The following is a partial comparative balance sheet for Cindy Cor-poration for two years ended December 31, 19X6 and 19X7.

	(1) 19X6	(2) 19X7	(3) Amount of Increase (Decrease) for 19X7	(4) Percent of Increase (Decrease) for 19X7
Current Assets				
Cash	$ 50,000	$ 55,000	_____	_____
Marketable Securities				
(LCM)	15,000	16,000	_____	_____
Accounts Receivable				
(Net)	18,000	17,000	_____	_____
Merchandise				
Inventory	26,000	24,000	_____	_____
Prepaid Insurance	3,000	3,200	_____	_____
Total Current Assets	$112,000	$115,200	_____	_____
Current Liabilities				
Notes Payable	$ 5,500	$ 5,500	_____	_____
Accounts Payable	40,000	42,000	_____	_____
Income Tax Payable	12,500	11,200	_____	_____
Dividends Payable	3,000	2,900	_____	_____
Total Current Liabilities	$ 61,000	$ 61,600	_____	_____

Instructions

1. *Calculate the dollar increase or decrease between the years 19X6 and 19X7 and record in Column 3.*

2. *Calculate the percent increase or decrease between the years 19X6 and 19X7 and record in Column 4. Round to the nearest tenth of a percent.*

3. *Determine the working capital for each of the two years.*

4. *If there are 10,000 common shares outstanding and the market price per share is $5.50, calculate the dividend yield for 19X7*

assuming the dividends have been paid. Round to the nearest tenth of a percent.

5. *In analyzing Cindy Corporation, list the favorable items and the unfavorable items.*

Problem 26.2

calculating dollar and percent increases and decreases for a comparative income statement

The following is a comparative income statement for Santos Corporation for the years ending December 31, 19X8 and 19X9.

Santos Corporation
Comparative Income Statement
For Years Ended December 31, 19X8 and 19X9

	19X8	19X9
Sales	$1,485,165	$1,620,689
Sales Returns and Allowances	10,095	11,148
Net Sales	$1,475,070	$1,609,541
Cost of Goods Sold	901,144	984,163
Gross Profit on Sales	$ 573,926	$ 625,378
Selling Expenses		
Sales Salaries Expense	$ 198,200	$ 205,073
Advertising Expense	27,650	37,100
Depreciation Expense	15,000	25,000
Supplies Expense	8,882	6,400
Total Selling Expenses	$ 249,732	$ 273,573
General and Administrative Expenses		
Administrative Salaries Expense	$ 172,700	$ 192,400
Supplies Expense	6,531	7,976
Depreciation Expense	55,000	55,000
Total General and		
Administrative Expenses	$ 234,231	$ 255,376
Total Operating Expenses	$ 483,963	$ 528,949
Income from Operations		
Before Taxes	$ 89,963	$ 96,429
Federal Income Tax	21,200	23,170
Net Income	$ 68,763	$ 73,259

Instructions

1. *Calculate the dollar amount of increase or decrease between the two years.*

2. *Calculate the percent increase or decrease between the two years. Round to the nearest tenth of a percent.*

Problem 26.3
preparing vertical analysis

Using the comparative income statement from Problem 26.2 for Santos Corporation, complete the following.

1. Prepare a vertical analysis by using net sales as the base year. Express all other items as a percentage of net sales. Round to the nearest hundredth of a percent (two decimal places).
2. List the items that are favorable for 19X9 and those that are unfavorable for 19X9.
3. Explain the choices you made in 2 above.

Problem 26.4
calculating solvency and profitability ratios and analyzing performance

The following is a comparative balance sheet for Market Corporation for the years ending December 31, 19X4 and 19X5. Prepare an analysis and round to two decimal places.

Markus Corporation
Comparative Balance Sheet
For Years Ending December 31, 19X4 and 19X5

	19X4	19X5
Assets		
Cash	$ 35,000	$ 32,000
Accounts Receivable (Net)	15,000	17,000
Merchandise Inventory	57,500	60,000
Plant and Equipment (Net)	135,000	144,000
Total Assets	$242,500	$253,000
Liabilities		
Accounts Payable	$ 10,000	$ 11,000
Wages Payable	2,500	2,000
Total Liabilities	$ 12,500	$ 13,000
Stockholders' Equity		
Common Stock, $10 stated value	$200,000	$200,000
Retained Earnings	30,000	40,000
Total Stockholders' Equity	$230,000	$240,000
Total Liabilities and Stockholders' Equity	$242,500	$253,000

Additional information for the Markus Corporation is as follows.

	19X4	19X5
Net Credit Sales	$150,000	$176,000
Cost of Goods Sold	120,000	140,800
Net Income		25,000
Market Price per Share		13

Instructions

1. *Calculate the current ratio for both years.*
2. *Calculate the quick ratio for both years.*
3. *Calculate the accounts receivable turnover for 19X5.*
4. *Calculate the inventory turnover for 19X5.*
5. *Calculate the rate of return on common stockholders' equity for 19X5.*
6. *Calculate the earnings per share for 19X5.*
7. *Calculate the price-earnings ratio for 19X5.*
8. *Indicate how you would improve the performance of this company.*

Problem 26.5
calculating solvency and profitability ratios and evaluating

The following is a comparative balance sheet for Star Company for the two years ended December 31, 19X6 and 19X7.

Star Company
Comparative Balance Sheet
For Years Ending December 31, 19X6 and 19X7

	19X6	19X7
Assets		
Cash	$ 25,000	$ 35,000
Accounts Receivable (Net)	40,000	38,000
Merchandise Inventory	75,000	85,000
Plant and Equipment (Net)	60,000	64,000
Total Assets	$200,000	$222,000
Liabilities		
Accounts Payable	$ 40,000	$ 35,000
Bonds Payable (Long Term)	80,000	90,000
Total Liabilities	$120,000	$125,000
Stockholders' Equity		
Common Stock, no par	$ 50,000	$ 62,000
Retained Earnings	30,000	35,000
Total Stockholders' Equity	$ 80,000	$ 97,000
Total Liabilities and		
Stockholders' Equity	$200,000	$222,000

Additional information for the Star Company is as follows.

	19X7
Net Income	$ 5,000
Credit Sales	319,200
Cost of Goods Sold	239,400
Market Price per Share	1
Common Stock Shares	
Outstanding	12,400

Instructions   1. *Using the above comparative balance sheet and additional information, calculate the following for 19X7. Round to the nearest tenth of a percent.*
   a.   *Working capital*
   b.   *Current ratio*
   c.   *Quick ratio*
   d.   *Debt ratio*
   e.   *Equity ratio*
   f.   *Accounts receivable turnover and the days' sales uncollected*
   g.   *Inventory turnover and the average number of days to sell the inventory*
   h.   *Book value per share*
   i.   *Earnings per share*
   j.   *Price-earnings ratio*

2.   *What is your evaluation of the year 19X7? Explain.*

Problem 26.6
using solvency and profitability ratios to make comparisons between two corporations

The following are the balance sheets for the Morton Corporation and the Ponder Corporation on December 31, 19X8. These two corporations are in the same industry and are the same size companies. Round all calculations to two decimal places.

	Morton	Ponder
Assets		
Current Assets		
Cash	$150,000	$ 210,000
Accounts Receivable (Net)	193,500	195,700
Merchandise Inventory	410,525	419,250
Prepaid Expenses	4,000	5,500
Total Current Assets	$758,025	$ 830,450
Other Assets		
Building (Net)	$135,000	$ 147,500
Land	17,500	29,500
Patent	20,000	18,000
Total Other Assets	$172,500	$ 195,000
Total Assets	$930,525	$1,025,450
Liabilities		
Current Liabilities		
Notes Payable	$ 30,000	$ 20,000
Accounts Payable	150,000	138,250
Wages Payable	17,500	19,875
Total Current Liabilities	$197,500	$ 178,125
Long-Term Liabilities		
Bonds Payable	$230,000	$ 270,000
Total Liabilities	$427,500	$ 448,125
Stockholders' Equity		
Common Stock, no par	$415,000	$ 465,000
Retained Earnings	88,025	112,325
Total Stockholders' Equity	$503,025	$ 577,325
Total Liabilities and		
Stockholders' Equity	$930,525	$1,025,450

Additional information for these companies is as follows.

	Morton	Ponder
Credit Sales	$ 1,896,300	$ 2,133,130
Cost of Goods Sold	1,257,600	1,257,750
Average Assets	929,422	1,030,200
Average Equity	476,845	551,083
Net Income	74,300	71,084
Market Price per Share	$42.00	$39.75
Common Stock Shares		
Outstanding	16,600 shares	18,600 shares
Total Cash Dividends Paid		
Owners	$ 20,750	$ 18,600

Your rich uncle has just left you $1,000,000. After much thought, you decide to invest a portion of it in corporate stock. You have investigated several companies and have narrowed your search down to Morton and Ponder corporations. In making your final decision, you make the following examination.

Instructions

1. *Examine the current position by calculating the following for each of the two companies.*
   - a. *Current ratio*
   - b. *Quick ratio*
   - c. *Accounts receivable turnover (use the ending balance)*
   - d. *Average days' sales uncollected*
   - e. *Inventory turnover (use the ending balance)*
   - f. *Average number of days to sell the inventory*

2. *Examine the two companies from an owner's viewpoint. Calculate the following for each of the two companies.*
   - a. *Rate of return on total assets*
   - b. *Rate of return on common stockholders' equity*
   - c. *Book value per share*
   - d. *Earnings per share*
   - e. *Price-earnings ratio*
   - f. *Dividend yield*
   - g. *Both the equity ratio and the debt ratio*

3. *Answer the following questions.*
   - a. *Which company has the best current position? Explain.*
   - b. *Which company has the best position from the viewpoint of a potential investor? Explain.*
   - c. *Assuming you can purchase the common stock at the current price, which company is the best investment? Explain.*

4. *Assume you are a loan officer for a bank and that the managers of each of these companies came to you for a $100,000 loan. To which company would you lend the $100,000? Give your reasons.*

Comprehensive Problem 4

for Review of Chapters 21

through 26

The Montgomery Corporation, supplier of pool equipment and pool supplies, has been in operation for five years. The accountant for the company adjusts and closes the books annually on December 31 and uses the periodic inventory system. Following are the balance sheet of the Montgomery Corporation for December 31, 19X5, and the trial balance as of November 30, 19X6.

MONTGOMERY CORPORATION
Balance Sheet
For Year Ended December 31, 19X5

Assets

Current Assets			
Cash			$ 80,506
Marketable Equity Securities			160,000
Accounts Receivable		$342,000	
Less: Allowance for Doubtful Accounts		20,000	322,000
Merchandise Inventory			268,000
Prepaid Insurance			21,000
Total Current Assets			851,506
Investments and Funds			
Bond Sinking Fund		$ 20,000	
Total Investments and Funds			20,000
Plant and Equipment			
Equipment	$200,000		
Less: Accumulated Depr.—Equip.	15,000	$185,000	
Building	400,000		
Less: Accumulated Depr.—Bldg.	20,000	380,000	
Land		100,000	
Total Plant and Equipment			665,000
Intangible Assets			
Patent		$ 24,000	
Total Intangible Assets			24,000
Total Assets			$1,560,506

Liabilities

Current Liabilities			
Accounts Payable		$114,000	
Wages Payable		4,000	
Dividends Payable		8,000	
Bond Interest Payable		12,000	
Total Current Liabilities			$ 138,000
Long-Term Liabilities			
8% Mortgage Payable		$ 62,000	
12%, 10-Year Bonds Payable	$400,000		
Less: Unamortized Discount	12,000	388,000	
Total Long-Term Liabilities			450,000
Total Liabilities			$ 588,000

(Continued)

Stockholders' Equity

Paid-In Capital
  Preferred Stock, 8%, $100 par value—
    1,000 shares authorized and issued $100,000
  Common Stock, $5 par value, 500,000
    shares authorized, 100,000 shares
    issued, of which 2,000 are in the
    treasury   500,000
  Premium on Common Stock   100,000
  Donated Capital   25,000
  Paid-In Capital from Sale of Treasury Stock   5,000
Total Paid-In and Other Contributed Capital $ 730,000

Retained Earnings
  Appropriated for Bonded Indebtedness $ 20,000
  Appropriated for Plant Expansion   20,000
  Appropriated for Treasury Stock   12,000
  Unappropriated Retained Earnings   202,506
      Total Retained Earnings   254,506
Total Paid-In Capital and Retained Earnings   984,506
  Less: Treasury Stock   12,000
  Total Stockholders' Equity   972,506
Total Liabilities and Stockholders' Equity $1,560,506

MONTGOMERY CORPORATION
Trial Balance
November 30, 19X6

Account Titles	Debit	Credit
Cash	137,546	
Marketable Equity Securities	140,000	
Accounts Receivable	350,000	
Allowance for Doubtful Accounts		$20,000
Merchandise Inventory	268,000	
Prepaid Insurance	21,000	
Bond Sinking Fund	20,000	
Equipment	220,000	
Accumulated Depreciation—Equipment		15,000
Building	480,000	
Accumulated Depreciation—Building		20,000
Land	120,000	
Patent	24,000	
Accounts Payable		124,000
Wages Payable		4,000
Dividends Payable		8,000
Bond Interest Payable		0
Income Tax Payable		0
8% Mortgage Payable		0
12% Bonds Payable		400,000
Discount on Bonds Payable	11,100	
Preferred Stock, 8%, $100 Par		100,000
Common Stock, $5 Par		550,000
Premium on Common Stock		110,000
Donated Capital		25,000
Paid-In Capital from Sale of Treasury Stock		5,000
Appropriated Retained Earnings for Bonded Indebtedness		20,000
Appropriated Retained Earnings for Plant Expansion		20,000
Appropriated Retained Earnings for Treasury Stock		12,000
Unappropriated Retained Earnings		202,506
Treasury Stock	12,000	
Sales		820,000
Purchases	482,000	
Wage Expense	114,000	
Uncollectible Accounts Expense	0	
Insurance Expense	0	
Rent Expense	11,000	
Mortgage Interest Expense	4,960	
Bond Interest Expense	36,900	
Depreciation Expense—Equipment	0	
Depreciation Expense—Building	0	
Patent Amortization Expense	0	
Miscellaneous Expense	3,000	
Income Tax Expense	0	
Totals	2,455,506	2,455,506

Only the transactions for the month of December remain to be journalized and posted for 19X6 before the accounting period ends on December 31, 19X6. Following are the December transactions, the information needed for the December adjusting entries, and other related information.

Transactions

Dec. 1   sold $35,000 of merchandise; $25,000 on account and $10,000 for cash

Dec. 12   paid the monthly rent, $1,000

Dec. 13   purchased merchandise in the amount of $15,000 on account

Dec. 15   collected $20,000 from various accounts receivable customers

Dec. 18   sold 1,000 shares of treasury stock at $6 per share

Dec. 18   removed the appropriation for the above treasury stock from retained earnings

Dec. 23   sold merchandise for cash, $20,000

Dec. 26   paid cash for miscellaneous expenses in the amount of $800

Dec. 28   paid the dividends previously declared in the amount of $8,000; declared a $.10 per share cash dividend to the common stockholders of record on January 10 to be paid on January 15, 19X7

Dec. 29   paid the monthly wages expense of $10,000, plus the $4,000 in accrued wages from November

Adjusting Entry Information

1. The allowance for doubtful accounts is to be increased by $2,000.

2. The insurance expense is $1,200.

3. The depreciation expense is calculated to be $15,375 for the equipment and $10,000 for the building.

4. The patent amortization is $2,000.

5. The accrued wages payable for the month of December is $4,200.

6. The accrued bond interest payable is $12,000.

7. The discount amortization is $300.

8. The income tax payable for the year is $23,269.

Related Information
During the year, the following occurred.

1. The December 31, 19X6, inventory is $258,000.

2. The marketable equity securities were sold for cash at their cost of $20,000.

3. Assets were purchased for cash as follows:
   a. Equipment, $20,000
   b. Building expansion, $80,000
   c. Land, $20,000

4. The 8 percent mortgage payable was retired by paying cash of $66,960, which included both the principal and the interest expense.

5. Common stock consisting of 10,000 shares were sold for the cash price of $6 per share.

6. The current market price of the common stock is $10.80.

Instructions

1. *Enter the account names and balances into the general ledger as they are listed on the November 30, 19X6, trial balance.*

2. *Record December transactions in the general journal without explanations and post to the accounts in the general ledger.*

3. *Prepare a trial balance on the first two columns of an eight-column worksheet using the balances in the general ledger at the end of December.*

4. *Record the adjusting entries on the worksheet from the information given above and complete the worksheet.*

5. *Prepare the income statement, including earnings per share, and the balance sheet as of December 31, 19X6.*

6. *Prepare a statement of cash flows worksheet, using the balance sheet for December 31, 19X5, as given above and the balance sheet as of December 31, 19X6. Complete the worksheet using the direct method, and prepare the formal statement of cash flows from the completed worksheet.*

7. *Journalize the adjusting and closing entries, and post to the accounts.*

8. *Prepare a post-closing trial balance.*

9. a. *Make the following calculations for analysis of the financial condition of this corporation. Round the calculation to the nearest hundredth (two decimal places).*
   (1) *Current ratio for the years 19X5 and 19X6*
   (2) *Quick ratio for the years 19X5 and 19X6*
   (3) *Accounts receivable turnover for the year 19X6 (Assume net credit sales were $865,000.)*
   (4) *Merchandise inventory turnover for the year 19X6*
   (5) *Rate earned on total assets, 19X6*

      (6) *Rate earned on common stockholders' equity, 19X6*

      (7) *Equity per share for the years 19X5 and 19X6*

      (8) *Debt ratio for the years 19X5 and 19X6*

      (9) *Equity ratio for the years 19X5 and 19X6*

    (10) *Price-earnings ratio, 19X6*

b.   (1) *What is your assessment of this company's short-term position?*

      (2) *What is your assessment of this company's long-term position?*

      (3) *What recommendations would you suggest? (Hint: Is the balance in the cash account excessive?)*

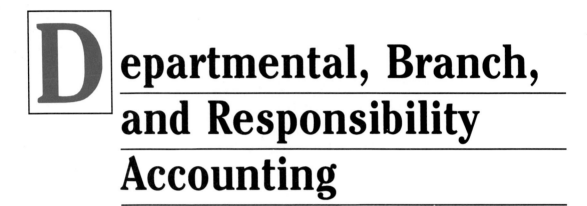

CHAPTER 27

Departmental, Branch, and Responsibility Accounting

In previous chapters our attention was focused on the preparation and analysis of financial statements of corporations. The use of basic financial statements is limited in that they summarize the business activities as a whole. These financial statements tell nothing of the different segments or subunits that comprise a business entity. Information about these segments or subunits is useful to managers in determining profitability, planning, and controlling the operations of the business. This chapter examines the accounting procedures for these subunits. A merchandising firm is an excellent example, because it is generally divided into various departments. Because each department sells a different product or performs a different service, the term *departmental accounting* is used. **Departmental accounting** is the procedure of evaluating the profitability or the cost effectiveness of each department. In the following paragraphs, departmental accounting, branch accounting, and responsibility accounting are discussed.

departmental accounting
the procedure of evaluating the profitability or cost effectiveness of each department of a business

DEPARTMENTAL ACCOUNTING

To determine the profitability of a department, accounting information is recorded in such a way as to identify the revenue, cost of goods sold, and the operating expenses of each department and is accumulated in such a way that an analysis is possible. The information accumulated is used by management to evaluate the profitability or cost effectiveness of the various subunits. In addition, the information is used to hold managers responsible for the results of their departments. Because of this, departmental accounting is also referred to as responsibility accounting. **Responsibility accounting** refers to an accounting process where each manager is held responsible for the costs and expenses under his or her control. Each department is classified as a profit center or a cost center.

responsibility accounting
a system of management where each manager is held responsible for the costs, expenses, and profit of the subunit

profit centers
revenue-producing departments that sell the products or perform the services

Profit centers are revenue-producing departments that sell the products or perform the services. For example, a department store may sell clothes, shoes, furniture, and carpets. All of these departments are profit centers. The sales and the costs of sales are matched to determine the profitability of each department. The profit-centered department is also referred to as the productive de-

cost centers

those departments not directly earning revenue

partment. **Cost centers** are those departments not directly earning revenue. These departments are also known as service departments. Managers spend a great deal of time and effort in reviewing and controlling costs of the service departments, and the service department managers are held responsible for their departmental expenses. For example, the janitorial department does not produce revenue, but it provides an important service to the organization as a whole. The purpose for accumulating the janitorial department expenses is to measure the costs of its operations and provide a basis for controlling these costs.

Departmental Information

A special record-keeping method is used to collect the necessary accounting information for each department. If the business is a merchandising firm, it needs more information than a service firm. Cash registers can be used not only to record the sales of items, but also the cost of those items. A large merchandising business will have its cash register connected directly to the store's central computer system. Thus, the information regarding department sales and cost of goods sold is readily available. These systems also keep perpetual inventory records, because the computer is constantly recording each item that is sold. Keeping the inventory on a perpetual basis provides vital inventory information promptly. This is generally accomplished by a code system of input at the cash register.

For example, the modern grocery store has a product scan system whereby the article being sold contains a code. When the article containing the code is passed over a sensoring device attached to the computerized cash register, it reads the code and instantly records the data. Other department stores use a scanner called a computer wand that resembles a very large pen. The computer wand is also attached to the computerized cash register. The wand is scanned across the code, usually on a price tag attached to the article, and immediately inputs the data. Companies with this capability can obtain the necessary information about revenue, cost of goods sold, and the inventory status immediately. Timely information is important because it gives management the opportunity to move quickly when problems arise.

If a computer is not available, the cash register tapes can be added daily to determine the sales of the various departments, and by using the retail method for inventory valuation, the ending inventory is calculated. The accounting records can provide the information for cost of goods sold and other expenses if the business is not automated. The following is a sales journal with a departmental breakdown of sales. The sales journal is adequate for a fairly small business.

						Sales by Departments		
Date	Sales Ticket Number	Customer	✓	Accounts Receivable Debit	No. 1 Credit	No. 2 Credit	No. 3 Credit
19XX								
Sept. 13	101	*Hawkins*		1 5 0 0 0 —	7 5 0 0 —	7 0 0 0 —	5 0 0 —
Sept. 25	102	*Ferris*		2 5 0 0 —		2 5 0 0 —	
Sept. 30	103	*Harris*		1 0 0 0 —	5 0 0 —		5 0 0 —
Sept. 30		Totals		1 0 0 0 0 0 —	5 0 0 0 0 —	2 0 0 0 0 —	3 0 0 0 0 —

SALES JOURNAL

For a business with a large number of departments, a departmental sales analysis sheet is prepared. The goal of the departmental system is to determine gross profit for each profit-centered department, and then determine the departmental net income. Determination of departmental net income aids management in the evaluation process.

Information Needed for Departmental Income Statements

Special problems arise when preparing departmental income statements. Because each department is treated as if it were a small entity on its own, the departmental income statement must include all revenues and expenses. Revenues of a department and cost of sales is available from the accounting records. The expenses will be one of two kinds, direct or indirect.

direct expenses
those expenses incurred solely for the benefit of a department

Direct expenses are those incurred solely for the benefit of a department. For example, the wage of the salesperson in the shoe department is a direct expense, because it is incurred solely for the benefit of the shoe department. It is considered a direct expense.

indirect expenses
those expenses not directly associated with any particular department

overhead costs
those costs that jointly benefit the entire business

Indirect expenses are those expenses that are not easily identified with a particular department and that benefit all departments. For example, renting the entire building benefits all the departments of the business. The total rent expense must be allocated so that each departmental income statement shows a portion of the rent expense. Indirect expenses are also referred to as the overhead of a business. **Overhead costs** are those costs that jointly benefit the entire business. Examples are rent, heating, lighting, depreciation, utilities, and the total expenses of the service departments.

Allocating Indirect Expenses

Different procedures are used for allocating the indirect expenses or overhead items. The proper basis for allocation must be chosen so that each profit-centered department is allocated its fair share of the expenses. The goal of this allocation is to determine net income for each department. No single method can be chosen; a judgment must be made as to the best procedure in each circumstance. The following are examples of indirect expenses and allocation methods.

Rent Expense   Rent expense is generally allocated on the basis of the floor space occupied by a department and the value of that floor space. A department located by the main entrance of a business has more valuable floor space than a department located in an obscure corner of the building. Because all customers coming in to the store enter through the departments located at or near the entrance, those departments are considered to have more valuable floor space. Some customers may never come into contact with the departments in the back corners of the store or departments that are located on an upper level. Because there is no objective procedure to determine the value of individual departments, a judgment must be made. Often opinions of experts as to the rental values of the space can give a good approximation of the value for purposes of allocating expenses to the departments. For example, assume that the rent expense for the month of September is $4,000 and that there are three departments in this business. Department 1 and Department 2 are located on the first floor, sharing the 3,000 square feet of floor space equally. Department 3 is located entirely on the second floor. For our example, the value of the first-floor space is determined to be 60 percent of the total of $4,000. Using this information, the allocation is as follows.

Value of Floor Space

Department 1	
Department 2	60% of $4,000 = $2,400
Department 3	40% of $4,000 = $1,600

Space and Value Allocation

Department	Square Footage		Cost to Allocate		Total
Department 1	1,500/3,000	×	$2,400	=	$1,200
Department 2	1,500/3,000	×	2,400	=	1,200
Department 3	3,000/3,000	×	1,600	=	1,600
Total of Rent Allocated					$4,000

On a departmental income statement, the rent expense of $4,000 for the month of September is allocated according to the above calculation. Department 1 is allocated $1,200; Department 2, $1,200; and Department 3, $1,600.

Advertising Expense   Advertising is a necessary expense for a merchandising business. Some advertising is of a general nature, and some advertising is more direct. If the shoe department advertises a shoe sale, the advertising may be considered as a direct expense for this department. However, general advertising must be allocated in some fair manner. Allocating general advertising on the basis of total sales per department has proved to be an adequate basis. For example, assume that the general advertising for the month of September is $1,000. The allocation is as follows.

Sales by Departments

Department 1	$ 50,000
Department 2	20,000
Department 3	30,000
Total Sales	$100,000

Advertising Expense Allocation on the Basis of Sales

Department	Fraction of Sales		Amount Allocated		Total
Department 1	50,000/100,000	×	$1,000	=	$ 500
Department 2	20,000/100,000	×	1,000	=	200
Department 3	30,000/100,000	×	1,000	=	300
Total of Advertising Allocated					$1,000

As shown, the total sales is the denominator of the fraction that is multiplied by the total advertising expense, and each individual department's sales is the numerator. On a departmental income statement, Department 1 is allocated $500 as advertising expense, Department 2 is allocated $200, and Department 3 is allocated $300.

Depreciation Expense   A department may use depreciable assets for its sole benefit. In this case, the depreciation expense of that asset is a direct expense of the department. Assume, however, that the company owns its building. Because the building benefits all the departments, the depreciation expense on the building must be allocated to the various departments. A good basis for this allocation is the same basis as used for rent: the amount of space and the value of that space.

Heating, Cooling, and Lighting Expense   Heating, cooling, and lighting expense benefit all the departments and is also an overhead cost that must be allocated to the departments. The floor space occupied is generally a fair basis to use. If some other evidence is present to the contrary, then that evidence is used to determine a fair allocation. For example, a business having a large lamp and lighting department may use a greater amount of electricity than other departments because most lamps will be in operation for marketing purposes. Such a company may wish to install separate meters for this department to determine the number of kilowatt hours accumulated and used for the electricity expense. When this occurs, it is a direct electric expense to the lamp department. However, most companies consider this to be more trouble than it is worth and make a judgment to approximate the electrical expense allocation.

Service Departments   The cost-centered departments provide critical services to the revenue-producing ones, and the cost to perform the services must be allocated to the revenue-producing departments. The following is a list and allocation basis for a number of cost-centered departments.

Department	Allocation Basis
General Office	Sales volume or number of employees in the department
Payroll	Number of employees in the department
Personnel	Number of employees in the department
Purchasing	Dollar amount of purchases or cost of sales for each department
Janitorial	Square footage of floor space occupied by each department

A departmental expense allocation worksheet is used to collect all of this information, make proper allocations, and total the results. The departmental expense allocation worksheet for True Blue Hardware is as follows.

TRUE BLUE HARDWARE DEPARTMENTAL EXPENSE ALLOCATION WORKSHEET FOR YEAR ENDED DECEMBER 31, 19X7			
Undepartmentalized Expense Allocation	Basis for Allocation	Expense Account Balance	General Office
Salaries Expense	Direct	$ 61000 —	$ 15000 —
Supplies Expense	Direct	800 —	100 —
Rent Expense	Floor Space & Value	10000 —	800 —
Utilities Expense	Floor Space	2500 —	167 —
Advertising Expense	Sales	1500 —	0 —
Depreciation: Equipment	Direct	7200 —	2000 —
Insurance Expense	Value of Assets	2000 —	556 —
Total Expenses		$ 85000 —	$ 18623 —
Allocations:			
General Office Expense	Sales		(18623 —)
Janitorial Expense	Floor Space		
Total Expenses to Departments		$ 85000 —	

Preparing the Departmental Expense Allocation Worksheet

To prepare this worksheet, a list of all expenses, both direct and indirect, are entered on the worksheet. In addition, all departments, whether profit- or cost-centered, are listed. Next, the basis for allocation is used to calculate the totals. These totals are then extended across to the various departments. Using the True Blue Hardware worksheet as an example, each item is discussed below in the order in which it is listed. All totals are rounded to the nearest dollar for convenience.

Line 1: Salaries Expense   The first expense on the departmental expense allocation worksheet is salaries expense. Because salaries are direct expenses, these are extended across to the various departments using the payroll records.

Line 2: Supplies Expense   Supplies expense is a direct expense to each department and therefore a calculation is not necessary for allocation. Supplies are issued to each department using a supplies requisition. These requisitions are summarized for each department to determine the total direct expense for that department.

Line 3: Rent Expense   Rent expense is allocated according to floor space and the value of the floor space. It is determined that

Janitorial	Hardware	Housewares	Paint
$ 8000 —	$20000 —	$11000 —	$ 7000 —
400 —	150 —	100 —	50 —
200 —	3825 —	3825 —	1350 —
83 —	833 —	833 —	584 —
0 —	960 —	345 —	195 —
1600 —	1500 —	1500 —	600 —
444 —	417 —	417 —	166 —
$ 10727 —	$27685 —	$18020 —	$ 9945 —
	11919 —	4283 —	2421 —
$ (10727 —)	3973 —	3973 —	2781 —
	$43577 —	$26276 —	$15147 —

10 percent of the total rent expense of $10,000 ($1,000) is to be allocated to the general office and janitorial departments. General office is allocated 80 percent of the total of $1,000, and the remaining 20 percent is allocated to the janitorial department. Thus, general office receives an allocation of $800, and the janitorial department receives an allocation of $200. This allocation is chosen because both service departments are located in space at the rear of the store. The hardware and the housewares departments share the space equally that is located at the front of the store. The paint department is located at the back of the store. Therefore, considering these locations, it is determined that of the $9,000 remaining rent expense, $7,650 is to be divided equally between the hardware and housewares departments, and the remaining $1,350 is to be allocated to the paint department.

Line 4: Utilities Expense   The $2,500 in utilities expense is allocated according to floor space occupied. The total floor space for each department and the utilities expense allocation based on this space is as follows.

Space Occupied

Department	Square Feet
General Office	800
Janitorial	400
Hardware	4,000
Housewares	4,000
Paint	2,800
Total	12,000

Allocation of Utilities Expense

General Office	$800/12,000 \times \$2,500$	=	$ 167[a]
Janitorial	$400/12,000 \times 2,500$	=	83
Hardware	$4,000/12,000 \times 2,500$	=	833
Housewares	$4,000/12,000 \times 2,500$	=	833
Paint	$2,800/12,000 \times 2,500$	=	584
Total			$2,500

[a]Rounded to nearest dollar.

Line 5: Advertising Expense   Advertising expense is allocated on the basis of total sales of the productive departments. Therefore, no allocation is made to the general office or janitorial departments. The following is a list of the sales by departments and the allocation of the advertising expense on this basis.

Sales of Profit-Centered Departments

Department	Sales	% of Sales
Hardware	$170,000	64%
Housewares	60,000	23
Paint	35,000	13
Total sales	$265,000	

Allocation of the Advertising Expense

Hardware	64% ×	$1,500	=	$ 960
Housewares	23 ×	1,500	=	345
Paint	13 ×	1,500	=	195
Total				$1,500

The percent for each department is obtained by dividing the department's sales by the total sales. The percent for the hardware department is calculated as follows:

$$170,000/265,000 = .64 = 64\%$$

The fraction method may also be used in this calculation. For example, the hardware department fraction for this allocation is:

$$170,000/265,000 \times 1,500 = \$960.$$

Line 6: Depreciation Expense Depreciation expense is a direct allocation according to the equipment used in each department as determined by the inventory records. The building is rented in this example. However, should the building be owned, its depreciation expense would be allocated on the basis of the floor space and the value of floor space occupied.

Line 7: Insurance Expense Insurance is allocated according to the value of the assets used in the departments. These values are taken from the inventory records. The assets are listed below, and their values are used to allocate the insurance expense.

Value of Assets

General Office	$20,000
Janitorial	16,000
Hardware	15,000
Housewares	15,000
Paint	6,000
Total	$72,000

Allocation of Insurance Expense

General Office	20,000/72,000 × 2,000	=	$ 556
Janitorial	16,000/72,000 × 2,000	=	444
Hardware	15,000/72,000 × 2,000	=	417
Housewares	15,000/72,000 × 2,000	=	417
Paint	6,000/72,000 × 2,000	=	166
Total			$2,000

After all expenses are allocated to the departments and totaled, the expenses of the two service departments are then allocated to the three revenue-producing departments. For True Blue Hardware, the service departments are General Office with total expenses of $18,623 and Janitorial with total expenses of $10,727. These amounts must be allocated to the revenue-producing departments as follows.

Allocation of General Office Expense on the Basis of Sales

Hardware	64% × $18,623	=	$11,919
Housewares	23 × 18,623	=	4,283
Paint	13 × 18,623	=	2,421
Total			$18,623

Allocation of Janitorial Expense on the Basis of Floor Space

Hardware	4,000 sq.ft.	4,000/10,800 × $10,727	=	$ 3,973
Housewares	4,000 sq.ft.	4,000/10,800 × 10,727	=	3,973
Paint	2,800 sq.ft.	2,800/10,800 × 10,727	=	2,781
Total	10,800 sq.ft.	Total		$10,727

Using the departmental expense allocation worksheet on pages 1032–1033, a departmental income statement can then be prepared as follows.

	Hardware	Housewares	Paint	Combined
TRUE BLUE HARDWARE DEPARTMENTAL INCOME STATEMENT FOR YEAR ENDED DECEMBER 31, 19X7				
Sales	$ 170000 —	$ 60000 —	$ 35000 —	$ 265000 —
Cost of Goods Sold	108750 —	30000 —	26250 —	165000 —
Gross Profit on Sales	$ 61250 —	$ 30000 —	$ 8750 —	$ 100000 —
Gross Profit %	36 %	50 %	25 %	
Operating Expenses				
Salaries Expense	$ 20000 —	$ 11000 —	$ 7000 —	$ 38000 —
Supplies Expense	150 —	100 —	50 —	300 —
Rent Expense	3825 —	3825 —	1350 —	9000 —
Utilities Expense	833 —	833 —	584 —	2250 —
Advertising Expense	960 —	345 —	195 —	1500 —
Depreciation: Equipment	1500 —	1500 —	600 —	3600 —
Insurance Expense	417 —	417 —	166 —	1000 —
General Office Expenses	11919 —	4283 —	2421 —	18623 —
Janitorial Expense	3973 —	3973 —	2781 —	10727 —
Total Operating Expenses	43577 —	26276 —	15147 —	85000 —
Net Income (Loss)	$ 17673 —	$ 3724 —	$ (6397)	$ 15000 —

Departmental Contribution to Overhead

contribution margin
the amount a department's revenue exceeds its direct costs and expenses

The departmental income statement for True Blue Hardware shows that the paint department has a net loss of $6,397. On examination of this loss, it would appear that the paint department should be eliminated because it is not profitable. However, consideration must be given to the contribution this department makes toward the payment of the indirect or overhead expenses. This is called the contribution margin. The **contribution margin** is the amount a department's revenue exceeds its direct costs and expenses. Preparing a departmental income statement by showing departmental contribution to overhead reveals that the paint department made a significant contribution to the overhead expenses. The contribution margin for the paint department is $1,100 and is shown on the following departmental income statement.

TRUE BLUE HARDWARE DEPARTMENTAL INCOME STATEMENT FOR YEAR ENDED DECEMBER 31, 19X7	Hardware	Housewares	Paint	Combined
Sales	$ 170000 —	$ 60000 —	$ 35000 —	$ 265000 —
Cost of Goods Sold	108750 —	30000 —	26250 —	165000 —
Gross Profit on Sales	$ 61250 —	$ 30000 —	$ 8750 —	$ 100000 —
Gross Profit %	36 %	50 %	25 %	
Direct Expenses				
Salaries Expense	$ 20000 —	$ 11000 —	$ 7000 —	$ 38000 —
Supplies Expense	150 —	100 —	50 —	300 —
Depreciation: Equipment	1500 —	1500 —	600 —	3600 —
Total Direct Expenses	$ 21650 —	$ 12600 —	$ 7650 —	$ 41900 —
Departmental Margin	$ 39600 —	$ 17400 —	$ 1100 —	$ 58100 —
Indirect Expenses				
Rent Expense				$ 9000 —
Utilities Expense				2250 —
Advertising Expense				1500 —
Insurance Expense				1000 —
General Office Expenses				18623 —
Janitorial Expense				10727
Total Indirect Expenses				$ 43100 —
Net Income (loss)				$ 15000 —

Because the departmental net income is derived by arbitrarily allocating the overhead items to each department, many managers believe that this way of presenting the income statement is a truer measure of the success of the departments. Although the departmentalized income statement shows a net loss of $6,397, the department actually contributed $1,100 to the payment of the overhead expenses. Because the department has a contribution margin of $1,100, a closer examination must be made before eliminating this department.

Eliminating the Unprofitable Department

Before eliminating a department, managers must review not only the departmental net income and contribution margin, but also the effect on the combined net income. To do this, management must determine what amount of profit and what amount of expenses will really be eliminated if the department is discontinued. Managers realize that allocated indirect expenses cannot be eliminated but must be charged to the remaining departments. Assume for this example that the equipment used by the paint department is transferred to one of the other departments. The result of this analysis is as follows.

Paint Department

Type of Expense	Expense to Be Eliminated	Expense That Must Be Charged to Other Departments
Salaries Expense	$7,000	
Supplies Expense	50	
Rent Expense		$1,350
Utilities Expense		584
Advertising Expense		195
Depreciation Expense		600
Insurance Expense		166
General Office Expense		2,421
Janitorial Expense		2,781
Totals	$7,050	$8,097

If the paint department is eliminated, the $8,097 of allocated expenses must be charged to the remaining departments. In addition, by subtracting the $7,050 in direct expenses from the gross profit of $8,750 of the paint department, the company will lose $1,700 of income by eliminating this department. The following illustrates a pro forma income statement showing the effect on net income if the paint department were to be eliminated.

TRUE BLUE HARDWARE PRO FORMA DEPARTMENTAL INCOME STATEMENT[a] FOR YEAR ENDED DECEMBER 31, 19X7	Hardware	Housewares	Combined
Sales	$ 170 00 —	$ 60 00 —	$ 230 00 —
Cost of Goods Sold	108 75 0 —	30 00 —	138 75 0 —
Gross Profit on Sales	$ 61 25 0 —	$ 30 00 —	$ 91 25 0 —
Direct Expenses			
Salaries Expense	$ 20 00 —	$ 11 00 —	$ 31 00 —
Supplies Expense	15 0 —	10 0 —	25 0 —
Depreciation: Equipment	15 00 —	15 00 —	30 00 —
Total Direct Expenses	$ 21 65 0 —	$ 12 60 0 —	$ 34 25 0 —
Departmental Margin	$ 39 60 0 —	$ 17 40 0 —	$ 57 00 0 —
Indirect Expenses			
Rent Expense			$ 90 00 —
Utilities Expense			22 50 —
Advertising Expense			15 00 —
Depreciation: Equipment[b]			60 0 —
Insurance Expense			10 00 —
General Office Expense			18 62 3 —
Janitorial Expense			10 72 7 —
Total Indirect Expenses			$ 43 70 0 —
Net Income (loss)			$ 13 30 0 —

[a]Without the paint department.

[b]Equipment used in the paint department will now be for general use.

pro forma financial statement
a financial statement prepared to show the effect on net income as if certain assumptions were to occur

A **pro forma financial statement** is one prepared to show the effect on net income "as if" the department were to be immediately eliminated. This pro forma income statement shows the effect on net income if the paint department were eliminated. The net income with the paint department is $15,000, and the net income without the paint department is $13,300. In this situation, management will not eliminate the paint department until (1) a more profitable department can be found to substitute for the paint department or (2) the paint department provides a zero or a negative contribution margin.

BRANCH ACCOUNTING

Many companies expand their present operations by establishing branch offices or stores in different locations. This is quite common, especially for stores in suburban shopping centers.

Accounting Systems for Branch Accounting

Branch accounting is similar to consolidated accounting. Consolidated accounting combines a parent and a subsidiary, whereas branch accounting combines a home office and a branch. In consolidated accounting, the parent has an asset called Investment in Subsidiary. In branch accounting, the home office has an asset called Investment in Branch. Although in practice a company may have many branches, our discussion will entail accounting for one branch.

Two types of systems are used in branch accounting. One is the **centralized** system, where all records are kept by the home office and very few at the branch location. The second system is the **decentralized** system, where each branch maintains its own record-keeping system. This discussion covers only the decentralized system. The following T-accounts show the relationship between the home office investment account and the branch accounts. The asset account Investment in Branch on the home office books is reciprocal to the Home Office Equity account on the branch books.

centralized
a system in branch accounting whereby all the records are kept by the home office

decentralized
a system in branch accounting whereby most of the records are kept by the branch

Branch Records	Home Office Records
Branch Assets	**Investment in Branch**
Assets from Home Office	Assets to Branch / Net Income from Branch
Home Office Equity	
	Investment of Home Office in Branch / Net Income
Income Summary	
Expenses / Net Income—Closing	Revenue

Certain branch transactions require entries on both sets of records, while others require entries on the branch records only.

At the end of the accounting period, financial statements are prepared for the branch office much like those used for departmental accounting. The system is set up so that a combined financial statement is prepared instead of an income statement for each branch. In any case, all the records of the branch are available for the combined financial statements of the home office.

Illustration of Decentralized Branch Accounting

A series of transactions and general journal entries will be used to illustrate branch accounting, assuming a home office and one branch. The illustration will include only the entries in the home office records that affect the branch. An explanation of the transactions is followed by the general journal entries for the branch and the home office and by T-accounts that summarize the results of the transactions.

1. The home office established Branch A by sending $30,000 cash and $50,000 of merchandise inventory (at cost) to the branch. The home office uses a perpetual inventory system. The branch uses a periodic inventory system.

2. The branch purchased $10,000 additional inventory on account; prepaid the rent, $2,000; and prepaid the insurance, $1,200.

3. The branch sold merchandise of $25,000 on account and $25,000 for cash.

4. The branch paid operating expenses of $13,200.

5. The branch collected $12,500 of its accounts receivable.

6. The branch paid $5,000 of its accounts payable.

7. The branch sent $10,000 cash to the home office.

Adjusting Entries

   a. The rent expense is $1,000.
   b. The insurance expense is $600.

Closing Entries

   c. The ending merchandise inventory is $40,000.
   d. The sales account is closed.
   e. Purchases and the rent, insurance, and other operating expenses are closed.
   f. The income summary is closed to the home office account, and the home office records the net income of the branch to its records.

General Journals

	Branch				Home Office		
1.	Cash	30,000		1.	Investment: Branch	80,000	
	Inventory	50,000			Cash		30,000
	Home Office		80,000		Inventory		50,000
2.	Purchases	10,000		2.	no entry		
	Prepaid Rent	2,000					
	Prepaid Insurance	1,200					
	Accounts Payable		10,000				
	Cash		3,200				
3.	Cash	25,000		3.	no entry		
	Accounts Receivable	25,000					
	Sales		50,000				
4.	Operating Expenses	13,200		4.	no entry		
	Cash		13,200				
5.	Cash	12,500		5.	no entry		
	Accounts Receivable		12,500				
6.	Accounts Payable	5,000		6.	no entry		
	Cash		5,000				
7.	Home Office	10,000		7.	Cash	10,000	
	Cash		10,000		Investment: Branch		10,000

Adjusting Entries

	Branch				Home Office		
a.	Rent Expense	1,000		a.	no entry		
	Prepaid Rent		1,000				
b.	Insurance Expense	600		b.	no entry		
	Prepaid Insurance		600				

Closing Entries

	Branch				Home Office		
c.	Inventory (Ending)	40,000		c.	no entry		
	Income Summary		40,000				
	Income Summary	50,000					
	Inventory (Beginning)		50,000				
d.	Sales	50,000		d.	no entry		
	Income Summary		50,000				
e.	Income Summary	24,800		e.	no entry		
	Rent Expense		1,000				
	Insurance Expense		600				
	Purchases		10,000				
	Operating Expenses		13,200				
f.	Income Summary	15,200		f.	Investment: Branch	15,200	
	Home Office		15,200		Revenue from Branch		15,200

Branch T-Accounts

Cash				Accounts Receivable				Inventory				Prepaid Rent			
(1)	30,000	3,200	(2)	(3)	25,000	12,500	(5)	(1)	50,000			(2)	2,000	1,000	(a)
(3)	25,000	13,200	(4)					(c)	40,000	50,000	(c)				
(5)	12,500	5,000	(6)												
		10,000	(7)												

Prepaid Insurance				Accounts Payable				Home Office				Sales			
(2)	1,200	600	(b)	(6)	5,000	10,000	(2)	(7)	10,000	80,000	(1)	(d)	50,000	50,000	(3)
										15,200	(f)				

Purchases				Rent Expense				Insurance Expense				Operating Expenses			
(2)	10,000	10,000	(e)	(a)	1,000	1,000	(e)	(b)	600	600	(e)	(4)	13,200	13,200	(e)

Income Summary			
(c)	50,000	40,000	(c)
(e)	24,800	50,000	(d)
(f)	15,200		

Home Office T-Accounts

Cash				Inventory				Investment: Branch			
(7)	10,000	30,000	(1)			50,000	(1)	(1)	80,000	10,000	(7)
								(f)	15,200		

Revenue from Branch		
	15,200	(f)

After the adjusting entries are posted and the accounts are ruled and balanced, a trial balance is prepared and a worksheet is completed. An income statement and a balance sheet are prepared at this time for the branch, if required. The closing entries are then posted and a new trial balance prepared. The home office will prepare its own combined financial statements that include the branch.

RESPONSIBILITY ACCOUNTING

performance report
a report where the budget expectations are compared with the actual performance of a manager for evaluation purposes

In the beginning of the chapter, responsibility accounting is defined as a system whereby a manager is held accountable for the success of a subunit. This subunit may be a department or a branch. Generally, plans are made that specify the expected revenues and expenses. These plans are in the form of a budget, as shown in Appendix A. The budget is the plan with which actual performance is compared. This comparison shows how well a manager has performed. Reports are developed called performance reports. A **performance report** shows the budget expectations compared with the actual performance. Performance reports are used to evaluate the effectiveness of each manager in the specific area of responsibility.

The XYZ Corporation has ten branch hardware stores. The following diagram illustrates who is responsible for the corporate sales. It also shows the different areas of responsibility. Each manager is only responsible for what that manager can control. Some cost and expense items may be outside the control of a particular manager. When this is the case, the manager is not held responsible for those items.

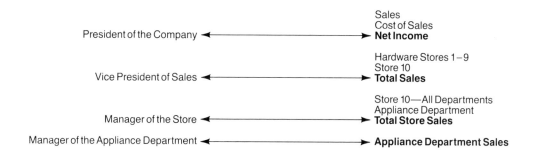

SUMMARY

Departmental accounting is the procedure used for evaluating the profitability or cost effectiveness of each subunit of a business. Accounting information is recorded in such a way as to be able to identify the revenue, expenses, or costs of a department. Profit centers are the revenue-producing departments, and the cost centers are subunits that provide a needed service to the organization as a whole.

Departmental income statements of profit centers are used to aid in the evaluation of these departments. Expenses on the departmentalized income statement are either direct or indirect. Direct expenses are incurred solely for the benefit of a particular department, while indirect expenses are allocated on an established basis. The basis for allocating the indirect expenses is determined by the nature of the item. Often no clear-cut basis is found and a judgment must be made by management. A departmental income statement is used to evaluate the success of the department. Departments that are unprofitable are subject to being eliminated. The department in question is examined carefully by reviewing the department's contribution margin. In addition, a pro forma income statement is prepared to determine the effects on net income if the unprofitable department were to be eliminated. Because the manager is responsible for the success of a subunit, departmental accounting is also referred to as responsibility accounting. Responsibility accounting is a system where each manager is held responsible for the costs and expenses under his or her control.

Companies expand their present operations by establishing subunits such as branch offices. A branch is a self-contained business unit similar to the main business entity. The main business unit is the home office and the subunit is the branch office. To keep track of a branch office, one of two types of accounting systems is used. Whenever the home office maintains the majority of the record keeping, it is a centralized accounting system. The decentralized system of accounting is one where the branch office maintains its own record keeping. In branch accounting, the home office records the investment in the branch office on its records. The branch office records its own transactions, and the title of the equity account on the branch records is Home Office. At the end of an accounting period, the branch office closes the Revenue and Expense accounts to the Income Summary account. The Income Summary is then closed to the Home Office account. The balance of the Home Office account on the branch office records is the same as the balance of the Investment: Branch account on the home office records. Responsibility accounting is also used in branch accounting with each branch manager being held responsible for the performance of the branch.

Review of Accounting Terminology

Following is a list of the accounting terminology for this chapter.

centralized	indirect expenses
contribution margin	overhead costs
cost centers	performance report
decentralized	profit centers
departmental accounting	pro forma financial statement
direct expenses	responsibility accounting

Fill in the blank with the correct word or term from the list.

1. _____ is the procedure of evaluating the profitability or cost effectiveness of each department of a business.

2. Departments not directly earning revenue are called _____.

3. A report where the budget expectations are compared with the actual performance of a manager for evaluation purposes is called a _____.

4. _____ is a system of management where each manager is held responsible for the costs, expenses, and profit of the subunit.

5. A financial statement prepared to show the effect on net income as if certain assumptions occur is called a _____.

6. A system in branch accounting whereby all the records are kept by the home office is called a _____ system.

7. _____ are those expenses incurred solely for the benefit of a department.

8. Costs that jointly benefit the entire business are called _____.

9. Expenses not directly associated with any particular department are _____.

10. _____ is the amount a department's revenue exceeds its direct costs and expenses.

11. A system of branch accounting whereby most of the records are kept by the branch is called a _____ system.

12. Revenue-producing departments that sell the products or perform the services are called _____.

Match the following words and terms on the left with the definitions on the right (columns continue on the following page).

13. centralized
14. contribution margin
15. cost centers
16. decentralized
17. departmental accounting
18. direct expenses
19. indirect expenses
20. overhead costs
21. performance reports
22. profit centers
23. pro forma financial statement

a. the procedure of evaluating the profitability or cost effectiveness of each department of a business

b. a system of management where each manager is held responsible for the costs, expenses, and profit of the subunit

c. revenue-producing departments that sell the products or perform the service

d. those departments not directly earning revenue

e. those expenses incurred solely for the benefit of a department

f. those expenses not directly associated with any particular department

g. the costs that jointly benefit the entire business

h. the amount a department's revenue exceeds its direct costs and expenses

i. a financial statement prepared to show the effects on net income as if certain assumptions occur

j. a system in branch accounting where all the records are kept by the home office

k. a system in branch accounting where most of the records are kept by the branch

24. responsibility accounting

l. reports prepared where the budget expectations are compared with the actual performance of a manager for evaluation purposes

Exercises

Exercise 27.1
calculating the rent expense allocation

A company rents for $50,000 a year a two-story building. The company has four departments located in this building. The rent is allocated on the basis of floor space and value of floor space. It is determined that the first floor be assigned 60 percent of the rent. The floor space is as follows.

Department A	3,000 square feet	located on first floor
Department B	2,000 square feet	located on first floor
Department C	1,000 square feet	located on second floor
Department D	4,000 square feet	located on second floor

Determine the rent allocation for each of the above departments.

Exercise 27.2
calculating the advertising expense allocation

Ratcliff Company advertised a storewide sale at an advertising cost of $9,000. Following are the departmental sales results.

	Sales
Department A	$100,000
Department B	50,000
Department C	20,000
Department D	80,000

If advertising expense is allocated according to each department's percent of total sales, determine the advertising allocation for each department.

Exercise 27.3
calculating the janitorial expense allocation

Using the floor-space information from Exercise 27.1, determine the allocation of $15,000 janitorial expense to Department A, Department B, Department C, and Department D.

Exercise 27.4
allocating two service departments' expense allocations to two revenue departments

Marshall Company has two service departments, Department 1 and Department 2. In addition, it has two revenue-producing departments, Department A and Department B. The total expense of Department 1 is $3,000, and the total expense of Department 2 is $2,000. The expenses of Department 1 are allocated to the productive departments on the basis of twice as much being allocated to Department A as to Department B (a ratio of 2:1). Expenses of Department 2 are evenly distributed between Department A and Department B.

a. Determine the total to be allocated to Department A from Department 1 and Department 2.

b. Determine the total to be allocated to Department B from Department 1 and Department 2.

Exercise 27.5
completing a departmental expense allocation worksheet

General, the service department, is allocated to the two revenue-producing departments on the basis of two-thirds to the Black Department and one-third to the White Department. Complete the expense allocation worksheet showing what portion of General Department's expenses will be allocated to Black Department and what portion to White Department.

Sun Corporation
Departmental Expense Allocation Worksheet
For Year Ended December 31, 19X8

Account Title	Basis for Allocation	Total Expense	General	Black	White
Wage Expense	Direct	$7,000	$1,000	$4,000	$2,000
Rent Expense	Square Footage	2,000	500	1,000	500
Utilities Expense	Square Footage	1,000	250	500	250
Supplies Expense	Direct	200	50	100	50
Total Expenses		——	——	——	——
Allocations:					
General			——	——	——
Total Expenses to Departments		——	——	——	——

Exercise 27.6
preparing a departmental income statement

Sun Corporation's two sales departments, Black Department and White Department, had the following results of operations.

	Black	White
Sales	$50,000	$30,000
Cost of Goods Sold	40,000	24,000
Gross Profit on Sales	$10,000	$ 6,000

a. Using the expense allocation worksheet from Exercise 27.5, prepare a departmental income statement for Sun Corporation, showing the net income or loss for the Black and White departments and the combined net income or loss.

b. Using the expense allocation worksheet from Exercise 27.5, prepare a departmentalized income statement using the departmental margin method.

Exercise 27.7
preparing general journal entries for the branch transactions

Following are the transactions for Branch Number 8 of the Northbay Merchandising Company for the month of February. Prepare the general journal entries without explanations for each transaction for the branch records.

Feb. 1   received from the home office $10,000 cash and merchandise inventory which cost $40,000

Feb. 1   paid the rent for the month of February, $6,000 (debit Rent Expense)

Feb. 9   sold merchandise on account for $12,000 and for cash, $5,000
Feb. 19   collected $6,000 of its accounts receivable
Feb. 20   paid operating expenses of $3,500 cash
Feb. 25   sold merchandise on account for $5,000 and for cash, $2,000
Feb. 26   received from the home office merchandise inventory which cost $25,000
Feb. 28   closed the Revenue, Expense, and Income Summary accounts for the month (no entries are required for merchandise inventory)

Exercise 27.8
preparing general journal entries for the home office transactions

Using the transactions from Exercise 27.7, prepare the general journal entries without explanations for the home office of Northbay Merchandising Company.

Exercise 27.9
defining and giving an example of responsibility accounting

In your own words, define responsibility accounting and give one example of this important concept.

Problems

Problem 27.1
calculating the rent expense allocation

The ABC Company occupies a two-story building with a basement. The departments and the floor space occupied by each department are as follows.

Women's Shoe Department	First floor	1,000 square feet
Cosmetics Department	First floor	2,000 square feet
Dresses Department	First floor	3,000 square feet
Sportswear Department	First floor	4,000 square feet
Men's Shoe Department	Second floor	1,000 square feet
Men's Suits and Sportswear	Second floor	9,000 square feet
General Office	Basement	1,000 square feet
Receiving and Shipping	Basement	2,000 square feet
Linen Department	Basement	3,000 square feet
Housewares Department	Basement	4,000 square feet

The building is leased at an annual rent of $100,000 with 25 percent allocated to the basement, 30 percent to the second floor, and 45 percent to the first floor. Determine the amount to be allocated to each department, based on each department's percent of the total floor space of the first floor, the second floor, or the basement.

Problem 27.2
preparing the departmental expense allocation worksheet

Lee Corporation operates two sales departments, Departments Jay and Kay, and two service departments, S1 and S2. The expenses of the two service departments are allocated evenly to Departments Jay and Kay, and the other indirect expenses are allocated on the basis given below. Following is a list of both direct and indirect expenses for the month of September.

	Basis for Allocation	Expense	S1	S2	Jay	Kay
Salaries	Direct	$ 4,300	$800	$500	$2,000	$1,000
Rent	Square feet	10,000				
Advertising	Sales	4,000				
Insurance	Direct	2,000	300	300	800	600
Supplies	Direct	800	150	150	300	200
Janitorial	Square feet	600				
Other Data:						
Department Space (square feet)			1,000	2,000	4,000	3,000
Department Sales					$150,000	$100,000

Prepare a departmental expense allocation worksheet for the month of September.

Problem 27.3
preparing a departmental expense allocation worksheet, a departmental income statement, and making a recommendation

The Shelby Florist operates three sales departments. The operating expenses and other business data for the year ended December 31, 19X8 are shown below.

	Basis for Allocation	Fresh Flowers	Live Plants	Silk Arrangements	Indirect Expenses
Salaries	Direct	$ 25,000	$ 20,000	$10,000	0
Supplies	Direct	10,000	9,800	6,800	0
Rent	Value of Floor Space				$50,000
Advertising	Direct and Sales	1,000	1,000	1,000	6,000
Insurance	Direct	500	400	300	0
Miscellaneous	Direct and Sales	100	300	200	2,000
Janitorial	Square Feet				12,000

Other data:

	Fresh Flowers	Live Plants	Silk Arrangements
Net Sales	$220,000	$120,000	$60,000
Cost of Goods Sold	110,000	52,500	32,000
Value of Floor Space	50%	30%	20%
Floor Space (square feet)	5,000	3,000	2,000

Instructions

1. *Prepare a departmental expense allocation worksheet.*
2. *Prepare a departmental income statement showing net income or loss for each department.*
3. a. *Prepare a departmental income statement showing the departmental margin for each department.*
   b. *Should the Silk Arrangements Department be discontinued? Explain. (Hint: Prepare a pro forma income statement.)*
4. *Assuming you are the manager responsible for the Silk Arrangements Department, present recommendations for making the department more profitable.*

Problem 27.4
preparing a pro forma income statement for a department and making a recommendation

Jones & Jones Corporation is considering discontinuing Department F. It estimates that the indirect expenses of the company will not change if this department is eliminated. Income information on December 31, 19X9 is as follows.

	Department F		All Other Departments
Sales		$64,000	$977,000
Cost of Goods Sold		42,200	584,000
Gross Profit on Sales		21,800	393,000
Operating Expenses			
Direct Expenses	$16,300		$204,000
Indirect Expenses	9,200	25,500	104,000
			308,000
Income (loss)		($ 3,700)	$ 85,000

Instructions

1. *Prepare a pro forma income statement assuming Department F is eliminated.*

2. *On the basis of your findings, would you as a manager think it advisable to discontinue Department F at this time? Explain.*

Problem 27.5

preparing general journal entries for a branch, posting to the accounts, ruling and balancing, journalizing adjusting and closing entries, preparing a post-closing trial balance, and calculating the balance in the Home Office

The Major Furniture Store is located in the center of Downtown, U.S.A. Because of a population growth in the city suburbs, Major is opening a branch in the northern part of the city. The North Branch is opening on March 1, 19X7. Major uses the periodic inventory method for accounting for merchandise. During the month of March, the following transactions for North Branch were completed.

Mar. 1 received $30,000 in cash and $650,000 of merchandise inventory from the home office at cost

Mar. 2 the branch manager paid the rent of $10,000 for the month of March (debit to Rent Expense)

Mar. 3 the branch manager purchased a one-year insurance policy for $1,200

Mar. 4 sold merchandise for cash, $10,000 and on account, $35,000

Mar. 10 purchased $1,600 of supplies on account

Mar. 15 sold $12,500 of merchandise on account

Mar. 20 received $18,200 cash from collections on accounts receivable

Mar. 25 paid miscellaneous operating expenses of $2,000 and paid salaries of $20,000

Mar. 30 sold $64,000 of merchandise for cash

Mar. 30 paid one-half of the amount owed on supplies bought on March 10

Instructions

1. Open the following accounts in the general ledger of the North Branch: Cash, Accounts Receivable, Merchandise Inventory, Supplies, Prepaid Insurance, Accounts Payable, Home Office, Income Summary, Sales, Rent Expense, Insurance Expense, Supplies Expense, Salaries Expense, and Other Operating Expenses.

2. Record the transactions in the general journal of the North Branch without explanations.

3. Post the journal entries in the general ledger accounts of the North Branch.

4. Journalize the necessary adjusting and closing entries on March 31 without explanations. The supplies inventory on March 31 is $500. The merchandise inventory on March 31 is $596,000.

5. Post the entries of (4) above and determine the balance of each of the ledger accounts.

6. Prepare a post-closing trial balance.

Problem 27.6
preparing general journal entries for the home office transactions using information from Problem 27.5

Using the transaction information from Problem 27.5, complete the following.

Instructions

1. Open the following accounts in the general ledger of the Major Furniture Store (the home office): Cash, Merchandise Inventory, Investment: North Branch, and Revenue from Branch.

2. Record the transactions that relate to the home office in a general journal without explanations.

3. Post the transactions. Verify that the balance in the North Branch Investment account is the same as the balance of the Home Office account on the North Branch records (Problem 27.5).

CHAPTER 28

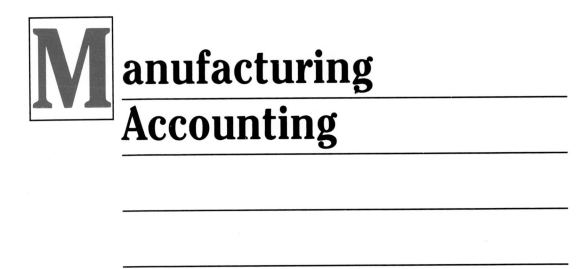

Manufacturing Accounting

LEARNING OBJECTIVES

When you have completed this chapter, you should

1. have a better understanding of accounting terminology.

2. be able to describe what the differences are between the financial statements of a manufacturing business and those of a merchandising business.

3. be able to list and define the three elements of manufacturing costs.

4. be able to list the different manufacturing accounts and tell how each one is used.

5. be able to describe what are the uses of control and subsidiary accounts.

6. be able to prepare a manufacturing statement.

7. be able to complete a worksheet for a manufacturing company.

8. be able to prepare adjusting and closing entries for a manufacturing company.

9. be able to prepare a multiple-step income statement for a manufacturing company.

10. be able to explain the differences between job order cost and process cost accounting systems.

11. be able to describe how costs are allocated to individual jobs and how overhead is distributed.

The service firm or the merchandising firm has been used for illustrative purposes in the chapters studied thus far. In this chapter, attention is given to the manufacturing firm. Manufacturing and merchandising firms are similar because they must sell a product. However, the similarity ends at this point. Major differences occur in the manner in which each type of company acquires the product that is sold. The merchandising company will buy its merchandise inventory in a finished form and sell it in the same condition without any further alteration. The manufacturing company must convert raw material, through some process, into a finished product ready for sale. The costs incurred in the manufacturing process include many different costs other than the cost for raw material.

The main difference between the merchandising and the manufacturing firm is the method of accumulating the cost of the product they sell. Because the merchandise firm buys its goods in a finished condition, costs are easily determined. The cost of the merchandise is determined by the invoice price, where delivery expenses are added and trade discounts deducted. From these items, the cost of the merchandise can be readily determined. The manufacturing concern must combine raw material costs, labor costs, overhead costs, packaging costs, and many other costs to determine the cost of the product until it is finished and ready for sale. The cost of the goods is an important factor for both concerns because the cost of the goods sold is matched with revenue to determine gross profit. The cost of goods sold section of a partial income statement shown below emphasizes the differences in the two types of financial statements.

Merchandising Company		Manufacturing Company	
Cost of Goods Sold		Cost of Goods Sold	
Beginning Inventory	$16,500	Beginning Finished Goods Inventory	$ 28,700
Net Cost of Purchases	36,450 ⟵⟶	Cost of Goods Manufactured (see Manufacturing Statement)	288,512
Goods Available for Sale	52,950	Goods Available for Sale	317,212
Ending Inventory	14,400	Ending Finished Goods Inventory	29,500
Cost of Goods Sold	$38,550	Cost of Goods Sold	$287,712

The major difference, as explained previously, is in the net cost of purchases for the merchandising company and the cost of goods manufactured for the manufacturing company. The arrow in the illustration points this out. The inventories also have different titles. The manufacturing company's inventory account is titled Finished Goods, whereas the merchandising company may use the title Inventory or Merchandise Inventory. Because the manufacturing concern must accumulate many costs in the manufacturing process, parentheses are used to refer the reader to the more detailed manufacturing statement. The **manufacturing statement** shows the detail of all the costs required to manufacture a finished product. A manufacturing statement and a complete income statement, including cost of goods sold, for the Collins Manufacturing Company follow.

manufacturing statement
a statement containing the detail of all the costs incurred in manufacturing a product

COLLINS MANUFACTURING COMPANY INCOME STATEMENT FOR YEAR ENDING DECEMBER 31, 19X9			
Revenue			$ 494139 —
Sales			
Cost of Goods Sold			
Finished Goods Inventory, 12/31/X8	$ 28700 —		
Cost of Goods Manufactured			
(see Manufacturing Statement)	282712 —		
Goods Available for Sale	$ 311412 —		
Finished Goods Inventory, 12/31/X9	29500 —		
Cost of Goods Sold		281912 —	
Gross Profit		212227 —	
Operating Expenses			
Selling Expenses (Control)	$ 88793 —		
General and Administrative Expenses (Control)	72555 —		
Total Operating Expenses		161348 —	
Operating Income		$ 50879 —	
Income Tax		15000 —	
Net Income		$ 35879 —	

COLLINS MANUFACTURING COMPANY MANUFACTURING STATEMENT FOR YEAR ENDING DECEMBER 31, 19X9		
Work-in-Process Inventory, 12/31/X8		$ 10500 —
Raw Materials Used		
Raw Materials Inventory, 1/1/X9	$ 25000 —	
Raw Materials Purchases	140000 —	
Freight In	2200 —	
Raw Material Available for Use	167200 —	
Raw Materials Inventory, 12/31/X9	26000 —	
Raw Materials Used		141200 —
Direct Labor Costs		50215 —
Factory Overhead Costs		
Indirect Labor	$ 17764 —	
Factory Payroll Taxes	6753 —	
Factory Supplies Expense	6808 —	
Factory Insurance Expense	4530 —	
Factory Repairs and Maintenance	10392 —	
Depreciation Expense: Building	13400 —	
Depreciation Expense: Machinery and Equipment	16800 —	
Patent Amortization	5500 —	
Utilities	8850 —	
Total Factory Overhead Costs		90797 —
Total Manufacturing Costs		$ 292712 —
Work-in-Process Inventory, 12/31/X9		(10000) —
Cost of Goods Manufactured		$ 282712 —
Work-in-Process Adjustment Calculation:		
Add Beginning Work-in-Process Inventory		
Deduct Ending Work-in-Process Inventory		

Groups marked: 1, 2, 3, 4

ACCOUNTING FOR MANUFACTURING COSTS

A manufacturing company must have an accounting system for accumulating the costs of manufacturing. Two types of accounting systems may be used: a general accounting system or a cost accounting system. A general accounting system uses a periodic physical inventory to account for raw material, work-in-process, and finished goods at the end of the accounting period. In this system, no effort is made to determine the individual cost per unit. This type of system is discussed at the beginning of this chapter.

Cost accounting systems use perpetual inventory systems and record sufficient detail to determine the cost per individual unit. Two examples of cost accounting systems are job order cost and process cost. Each of the cost accounting systems is discussed in the latter part of this chapter.

ELEMENTS OF MANUFACTURING COSTS

In accumulating the costs of manufacturing, all costs fall into one of three categories. These categories are referred to as the three elements of cost. A manufacturer uses raw materials, direct labor, and factory overhead to produce a finished product.

Three Elements of Cost

1. Direct Raw Material: Direct raw material consists of all raw material used directly in the finished product.
2. Direct Labor: Direct labor refers to the wages of the employees that worked directly on the finished product.
3. Factory Overhead: Factory overhead consists of all other factory costs related to the production of the finished product.

Raw Materials   Raw materials are the commodities used in the manufacture of a product. For our purpose, direct raw material is the raw material that goes directly into the product. To manufacture shoes, for example, the manufacturer will need such raw materials as leather, tacks, glue, synthetic materials, and plastic, to name a few. All of these items must be accumulated as inventory in order to begin the production of manufacturing shoes. All of these commodities are examples of direct raw materials because each can be expected to be used directly in the shoes. Thus, raw materials that go directly into the finished product are called **direct raw materials.** Other types of raw materials that may be used but do not go directly into the finished product are called **indirect raw materials.** Examples of indirect raw materials are oil for the machines, cleaning fluids, and so on. A furniture manufacturer may use indirect raw materials such as sandpaper, solvents, stripper, and other types of chemicals that do not go directly into the finished furniture.

direct raw material
all the raw material used directly in the product being manufactured

indirect raw material
raw material used that does not go directly into the product being manufactured

direct labor
the wages of the employees who work directly on the product being manufactured

Direct Labor   Employees in the factory who produce the finished product are paid by the hour and the accumulation of their wages is called the **direct labor** costs. They use the machinery and the hand tools, and work directly with the product until it is finished. Each of these employees is required to keep an accounting of the units or batches of product he or she has worked with. Thus, units of product can easily be associated with the direct labor costs. Often companies may employ timekeepers to aid the workers in keeping accurate records of the hours they work. Because the timekeepers do not work directly on the product, their wages are overhead costs, and are an example of **indirect labor.**

indirect labor
the wages of the factory employees who do not work directly on the product being manufactured

Factory Overhead   Factory overhead includes all other costs incurred in the factory to manufacture the product. As previously mentioned, raw materials not going directly into the product are indirect expenses and are overhead items. Costs associated with employees who do not work directly on the product are also factory overhead. Listed below are some examples of items considered to be factory overhead.

Indirect labor

Factory supplies

Repairs to factory buildings and equipment

Insurance on factory facilities

Heat, lights, and power

Depreciation of factory equipment

Small tools used in the factory

Taxes on equipment and raw materials of the factory

Amortization of patents

Factory workers' compensation

FICA taxes applicable to factory workers

factory overhead
all the manufacturing costs except direct raw material and direct labor

None of the above costs are costs of selling the product or costs of administration. Selling and general and administrative costs are not considered to be incurred in the manufacturing process. These expenses are classified as operating expenses. Thus, **factory overhead** includes all manufacturing costs except direct material and direct labor costs. Because of the large number of factory overhead accounts, accountants generally use a factory overhead control account in the general ledger and accumulate all the detail in the factory overhead subsidiary ledger. The detail in the subsidiary ledger is then added to obtain a summary total that is recorded in the general ledger account Factory Overhead. An example is presented as follows using T-accounts.

General Ledger	Factory Overhead: Subsidiary Ledger	
Factory Overhead Control	**Indirect Wage Expense**	**Depreciation Expense**
Summary Expense Total	*Total Expense*	*Total Expense*
	Indirect Materials	**Factory Rent Expense**
	Total Expense	*Total Expense*
	Factory Supplies Expense	**Factory Repairs and Maintenance**
	Total Expense	*Total Expense*

Although the summary total is used in the general ledger, the detail from the factory overhead subsidiary ledger is used in the manufacturing statement on page 1060. All overhead costs are accumulated in the same manner that the costs of selling and administrative expenses are accumulated. Special account titles are used to distinguish factory costs from other costs. For example, the inventory account for supplies purchased specifically for factory use may be titled Factory Supplies. Many accounts will be unique to the manufacturing company. All accounts relating directly to the factory and the manufacturing process are gathered together on the manufacturing statement to show the cost of goods manufactured.

MANUFACTURING ACCOUNTS

Some accounts for the manufacturing company will be entirely different from those of the merchandising company. The balance sheet will contain three different types of inventory. These inventory accounts are classified as current assets. The three types of inventories are listed below.

Raw Materials Inventory

Work-in-Process Inventory

Finished Goods Inventory

Raw Materials Inventory

In a general cost accounting system, a periodic inventory system is used. Because of this, a Raw Materials Purchases account will be used. All raw materials purchased during the accounting period will be debited to this account. Freight-In is also debited for freight charges on incoming materials and is considered to be an additional cost of purchasing as discussed in Chapter 8. At the end of the accounting period, the physical inventory is taken and the account Raw Materials Inventory is adjusted through the Income Summary account to reflect the new balance. In addition, the Raw Materials Purchases account and Freight-In are closed along with the other nominal accounts.

Work-in-Process Inventory

work-in-process inventory
goods on hand that remain unfinished

Goods on hand at the end of the accounting period that remain unfinished are referred to as the **work-in-process inventory.** Costs that have already been incurred, such as the raw materials used, some of the direct labor costs, and some of the factory overhead costs, must be accounted for. These costs are similar to prepaid expenses, but are incurred in the process of manufacturing. The costs are accounted for in an inventory account titled Work-in-Process. Work-in-Process is classified as a current asset. When these goods are finished, the costs are transferred to the Finished Goods Inventory account.

Finished Goods Inventory

finished goods inventory
goods that are finished and remain unsold

Goods that are finished products but that remain unsold constitute the **finished goods inventory.** This inventory is the equivalent of a store's merchandise on hand that is still unsold. In a general cost accounting system, a periodic inventory is taken at the end of the accounting period. The Finished Goods Inventory account is then adjusted through the Income Summary account at the time of the closing of the accounts.

In addition to the inventory accounts, there are many expense accounts associated with a manufacturing company. Some of these accounts are Depreciation Expense, Utilities Expense, Supervisor Salaries, Factory Insurance Expense, Repairs and Maintenance Expense, and so on. The manufacturing statement for Collins Manufacturing Company illustrates the types of expenses related to manufacturing companies.

The Manufacturing Statement

An examination of the manufacturing statement on page 1060 reveals that it contains the three elements of cost, plus an adjustment of work-in-process. These elements are shown as (1) raw materials used; (2) direct labor costs; (3) total factory overhead costs; and (4) the work-in-process adjustment. The work-in-process inventory (unfinished product) at the beginning of the accounting period is added to the raw materials used, the direct labor costs, and the total factory overhead costs to calculate the total manufacturing costs of the period. The work-in-process inventory at the end of the accounting period is deducted from the total manufacturing costs of the period to arrive at the cost of goods manufactured.

The cost of goods manufactured is used on the income statement in lieu of purchases, which appears on a merchandising firm's income statement, as illustrated earlier in the chapter. The cost of goods manufactured is used in calculating the cost of goods available for sale. Because the manufacturing statement is an additional financial statement that is used by the manufacturing company, a worksheet is needed more than ever to accumulate all the information from the accounts, including the subsidiary ledger accounts.

Worksheet for a Manufacturing Concern

The income statement and the manufacturing statement must be prepared at the end of the accounting period. By reviewing these two statements for the Collins Manufacturing Company shown earlier, one can see that many accounts are involved in the record keeping for a manufacturing firm. The general ledger and subsidiary ledger accounts are recorded on a worksheet to aid in preparing these financial statements. The worksheet used for a manufacturing company will have one additional set of columns. These columns are the manufacturing statement columns. The worksheet is completed in the same manner as illustrated in Chapter 11, with the exception of the manufacturing statement columns. All the accounts to be shown on the manufacturing statement will be extended to these columns. In turn, the debits and credits of the manufacturing statement columns will be added and extended to the income statement columns. Because the manufacturing statement is a supplemental statement to the income statement, it depicts the total manufacturing costs of the period.

Completing the Worksheet A completed worksheet for the Collins Manufacturing Company is shown on pages 1068–1069. The steps for completing the manufacturing worksheet are outlined below.

1. The general ledger accounts are listed and a trial balance is prepared. The trial balance is recorded on the worksheet in the first two columns.

2. All the information for the adjusting entries is assembled, and the adjusting entries are recorded on the worksheet in the adjustments columns. When all adjustments are recorded, the columns are totaled to determine if debits equal credits.

3. The trial balance and the adjustment amounts are then combined and extended to the financial statement columns on which they will appear. These amounts will be extended to one of three sets of columns as debits or credits. Two decisions must be made for each amount to be extended. The first decision determines whether the account will be extended as a debit or credit, and the second determines on which statement the account will appear. For example, the Factory Supplies Expense amount is a debit and is to be listed on the manufacturing statement. Thus, the debit amount will be extended to the manufacturing statement debit column. All other items appearing on the manufacturing statement will be sorted and extended to their respective debit or credit columns. Raw materials, direct labor, work-in-process, and all factory overhead items are extended to the manufacturing statement columns. Assets, liabilities, and stockholders' equity items are extended

to the balance sheet columns. The finished goods inventory, revenue, and selling and administrative expenses are sorted and extended to the income statement columns.

4. After all the items are sorted, the ending inventory amounts are entered on the worksheet. The raw materials and work-in-process inventories are entered as credits on the manufacturing statement and as debits on the balance sheet. The finished goods inventory is entered as a credit on the income statement and as a debit on the balance sheet. Thus, the new (ending) physical inventory balances appear as current assets on the balance sheet.

5. After all the accounts, including the ending inventory items, are sorted and extended, the manufacturing statement, income statement, and balance sheet debit and credit columns are added. The first columns to be added are the manufacturing statement columns. The debits and credits, when added, should not equal each other. The difference between the balances should be the cost of goods manufactured. The difference should be recorded as a credit beneath the credit total of the manufacturing statement and as a debit on the income statement. The income statement columns are added next. Likewise, they should not be equal because the debits represent costs and expenses and the credits represent revenue and the ending inventory. The difference between the two columns is the net income when the credits are greater than the debits. The term *net income* should be recorded on the far left side beneath the account titles, and the amount should be recorded as a debit beneath the totals on the income statement and as a credit beneath the totals on the balance sheet.

6. After the worksheet is completed, the financial statements are prepared. The adjusting and closing entries are then journalized from the completed worksheet.

COLLINS MANUFACTURING COMPANY
MANUFACTURING WORKSHEET
FOR YEAR ENDED DECEMBER 31, 19X8

	Trial Balance		Adjustments	
	Debit	Credit	Debit	Credit
Cash	20000 —			
Accounts Receivable	58350 —			
Allow. for Uncollect. Accts.		5000 —		
Raw Materials Inventory	25000 —			
Finished Goods Inventory	28700 —			
Work-in-Process Inventory	10500 —			
Prepaid Insurance	10870 —			a 4530 —
Factory Supplies	10200 —			b 6808 —
Machinery and Equipment	84000 —			
Accumulated Depreciation:				
Machinery and Equipment		16800 —		c 16800 —
Building	268000 —			
Accumulated Depreciation: Bldg.		13400 —		d 13400 —
Patents	12500 —			e 5500 —
Accounts Payable		6303 —		
Mortgage Payable		30000 —		
Common Stock		300000 —		
Retained Earnings		60000 —		
Sales		494139 —		
Raw Materials Purchases	140000 —			
Freight-In	2200 —			
Direct Labor	50215 —			
Indirect Labor	17764 —			
Utilities	8850 —			
Factory Payroll Taxes	6753 —			
Factory Supplies Expense			b 6808 —	
Factory Repairs and Maintenance	10392 —			
Patent Amortization			e 5500 —	
Factory Insurance Expense			a 4530 —	
Depreciation Expense:				
Machinery and Equipment			c 16800 —	
Depreciation Expense: Bldg.			d 13400 —	
Selling Expense (Control)	88793 —			
General and Administrative Expense (Control)	72555 —			
Income Tax Expense			f 15000 —	
Income Tax Payable				f 15000 —
	925642 —	925642 —	62038 —	62038 —
Cost of Goods Manufactured				
Net Income				

| Manufacturing Statement | | Income Statement | | Balance Sheet | |
Debit	Credit	Debit	Credit	Debit	Credit
				20000 —	
				58350 —	
25000 —	26000 —				5000 —
				26000 —	
		28700 —	29500 —	29500 —	
10500 —	10000 —			10000 —	
				6340 —	
				3392 —	
				84000 —	
					33600 —
				268000 —	
					26800 —
				7000 —	
					6303 —
					30000 —
					300000 —
					60000 —
			494139 —		
140000 —					
2200 —					
50215 —					
17764 —					
8850 —					
6753 —					
6808 —					
10392 —					
5500 —					
4530 —					
16800 —					
13400 —					
		88793 —			
		72555 —			
		15000 —			
					15000 —
318712 —	36000 —				
	282712 —	282712 —			
318712 —	318712 —	487760 —	523639 —	512582 —	476703 —
		35879 —			35879 —
		523639 —	523639 —	512582 —	512582 —

FINANCIAL STATEMENT PREPARATION

Using the completed worksheet, the manufacturing statement is prepared before the income statement or the balance sheet. Because this is a supplemental statement to the income statement, a proper three-line heading is used. The beginning work-in-process inventory is added to the three elements of cost to arrive at the total manufacturing costs for the period. Work-in-Process Inventory + Raw Materials Used + Direct Labor Costs + Factory Overhead Costs = Total Manufacturing Costs. The ending work-in-process inventory is then deducted to arrive at the cost of goods manufactured. The total cost of goods manufactured is then transferred to the income statement where it is used in the determination of cost of goods sold. Finally, the worksheet is used to prepare the balance sheet.

Adjusting Entries

A general journal entry is made for each adjusting entry. This procedure is the same as for the merchandising company shown in Chapter 11.

Closing Entries

manufacturing summary
a temporary account used for closing all the items appearing on the manufacturing statement

To make the closing process easier and more efficient, a special closing account is used. This temporary account is called the Manufacturing Summary. The **Manufacturing Summary** account is a temporary account used for closing all the items appearing on the manufacturing statement. All amounts in the manufacturing statement columns of the worksheet will be closed to the Manufacturing Summary account first. This will include the adjustments of the raw materials and the work-in-process inventories. The Manufacturing Summary account is then closed to the Income Summary account. All amounts on the income statement columns of the worksheet are also closed to the Income Summary account. The closing process will also adjust the finished goods inventory. The Income Summary account is closed to the Retained Earnings account of the Corporation. Using the worksheet on pages 1068–1069, the following adjusting and closing entries are recorded in the general journal.

		GENERAL JOURNAL			Page
Date		Description	Post. Ref.	Debit	Credit
		Adjusting Entries			
Dec. 31		Factory Insurance Expense		4530 —	
		Prepaid Insurance			4530 —
		To Record the Insurance Expense			
31		Factory Supplies Expense		6808 —	
		Factory Supplies			6808 —
		To Record the Factory Supplies Used			
31		Depreciation Expense: Machinery and Equipment		16800 —	
		Accumulated Depreciation: M & E			16800 —
		To Record the Yearly Depreciation Expense			
31		Depreciation Expense: Building		13400 —	
		Accumulated Depreciation: Building			13400 —
		To Record the Yearly Depreciation Expense			
31		Patent Amortization		5500 —	
		Patents			5500 —
		To Record the Yearly Patent Amortization			
31		Income Tax Expense		15000 —	
		Income Tax Payable			15000 —
		To Record the Income Taxes Payable			

19X9

		GENERAL JOURNAL			Page
Date		Description	Post. Ref.	Debit	Credit
19X9 Dec.	31	**Closing Entries**			
		Manufacturing Summary		3 1 8 7 1 2 —	
		Raw Materials Inventory, 12/31/X8			2 5 0 0 0 —
		Work-in-Process Inventory, 12/31/X8			1 0 5 0 0 —
		Raw Materials Purchases			1 4 0 0 0 0 —
		Freight-In			2 2 0 0 —
		Direct Labor			5 0 2 1 5 —
		Indirect Labor			1 7 7 6 4 —
		Utilities			8 8 5 0 —
		Factory Payroll Taxes			6 7 5 3 —
		Factory Supplies Expense			6 8 0 8 —
		Factory Repairs and Maintenance			1 0 3 9 2 —
		Patent Amortization			5 5 0 0 —
		Factory Insurance Expense			4 5 3 0 —
		Depreciation Expense: Mach. & Equip.			1 6 8 0 0 —
		Depreciation Expense: Building			1 3 4 0 0 —
		To Record Closing Entries			
		Raw Materials Inventory, 12/31/X9		2 6 0 0 0 —	
		Work-in-Process Inventory, 12/31/X9		1 0 0 0 0 —	
		Manufacturing Summary			3 6 0 0 0 —
		To Record Closing Entries			
		Income Summary		4 8 7 7 6 0 —	
		Finished Goods Inventory, 12/31/X8			2 8 7 0 0 —
		Selling Expenses (Control)			8 8 7 9 3 —
		General and Administrative Expense (Control)			7 2 5 5 5 —
		Income Tax Expense			1 5 0 0 0 —
		Manufacturing Summary			2 8 2 7 1 2 —
		To Record Closing Entries			
		Finished Goods Inventory, 12/31/X9		2 9 5 0 0 —	
		Sales		4 9 4 1 3 9 —	
		Income Summary			5 2 3 6 3 9 —
		To Record Closing Entries			
		Income Summary		3 5 8 7 9 —	
		Retained Earnings			3 5 8 7 9 —
		To Close Income Summary to Retained Earnings			

PERIODIC INVENTORY PROBLEMS

Accounting values must be placed on ending inventories at the end of an accounting period. Raw materials inventory is physically counted and priced and the ending inventory is thus determined. Finished goods inventory is also counted. The ending inventory of work-in-process is not as easily determined. These unfinished goods will have some raw materials, some direct labor, and some factory overhead already consumed within the unfinished product. These prepaid costs comprise the inventory asset. Estimating the raw materials that have been used thus far in work-in-process is not too difficult. A responsible manager can estimate an item's percentage of completion in order to estimate the amount of raw materials used. Likewise, a reasonable estimate of the direct labor costs can be made by using the payroll records. Knowledge about how the product is manufactured will help in this estimate.

Estimating overhead, on the other hand, presents a more difficult problem. Because the actual factory overhead total is not known until the end of the accounting year, a fair estimate must be made. This estimate must be made in a timely manner to achieve the third element of cost in the ending work-in-process and finished goods inventories. In making this estimate, many accountants have found that there is a relationship between machine hours used and factory overhead costs or between direct labor costs and factory overhead costs. The theory behind this assumption is that if the employees are present and working, then factory overhead is also occurring. Thus an estimate can be derived from these relationships and can be used until the actual factory overhead is known. Assume that the previous year's total direct labor costs were $100,000 and the total factory overhead costs for the year were $200,000.

$$\text{Formula:} \quad \frac{\text{Total Factory Overhead Costs}}{\text{Total Direct Labor Costs}}$$

$$\text{Solution:} \quad \frac{\$200,000}{\$100,000} = 200\%$$

In comparing these two totals, factory overhead is said to be twice the direct labor cost, or 200 percent of direct labor. If this knowledge about the previous year is used, once the direct labor cost is determined, the factory overhead estimate can be made as well as estimates of the ending inventories of work-in-process and finished goods. Assume that Collins Corporation produces Product A. The supervisor of the plant estimates that 500 of these units in work-in-process have utilized raw materials estimated at $4,000 and direct labor costs estimated at $2,000. The ending work-in-process inventory can be determined by estimating factory overhead. If Collins Corporation uses a 200 percent estimate for factory overhead, the direct labor cost of $2,000 can be multiplied by 200 percent, and the factory overhead estimate of $4,000 can be calculated and used as the third element of cost. The finished goods inventory can also be estimated as follows.

Work-in-Process Estimated Inventory

Product	Estimated Direct Material	Estimated Direct Labor	Estimated Factory Overhead[a]	Quantity	Work-in-Process Inventory 12/31/X9
A	$4,000	$2,000	$4,000	500	$10,000

[a]200% application rate

Finished Goods Estimated Inventory

Product	Estimated Direct Material	Estimated Direct Labor	Estimated Factory Overhead[a]	Quantity	Finished Goods Inventory 12/31/X9
A	$6,000	$4,000	$8,000	750	$18,000

[a]200% application rate

As can be seen from the preceding calculations, the work-in-process and finished goods inventories are made up of three components: (1) estimated direct material, (2) estimated direct labor, and (3) estimated factory overhead.

Predetermined Factory Overhead Rate

As previously discussed, factory overhead must be allocated to the work-in-process and finished goods to determine the cost of the ending inventories. This rate will be applied as an estimate any time factory overhead is required before the end of the year and before the actual factory overhead is known. To wait until the end of the accounting period is not acceptable from the standpoint of presenting timely financial statements. Most corporations prepare interim financial statements monthly. Thus estimates must be made to prepare these statements for analysis and review by management. Because the current manufacturing costs are needed for statement preparation, it is customary to apply the factory overhead estimate by using this predetermined rate. Thus, the **predetermined factory overhead application rate** is the percentage that is used to determine the third element of cost for estimating the ending inventories of work-in-process and finished goods.

predetermined factory overhead application rate
the percentage used to estimate the factory overhead

At the end of the year when the actual amount of factory overhead costs are determined, a comparison must be made with the estimate. If the estimate is inaccurate, a reconciliation must be made adjusting the estimate to the actual costs. If the estimate of factory overhead costs is too high, it is said to be **overapplied factory overhead,** and the estimate must be reduced to actual cost by an adjusting entry. If the estimate is lower than the actual cost, it is said to be **underapplied factory overhead,** and again an adjusting entry must be made to correct the estimate. These adjusting entries are discussed in the following paragraphs about the job order cost system.

overapplied factory overhead
when the overhead estimate exceeds the actual overhead costs

underapplied factory overhead
when the overhead estimate is less than the actual overhead costs

JOB ORDER COST SYSTEM

job order cost
a cost accounting system that accumulates the three elements of cost in such a way as to determine the cost per unit during production

Job order cost is a cost accounting system rather than a general cost system. **Job order cost** is a system of record keeping that accumulates the three elements of cost in such a way as to determine the cost per unit. These manufacturing costs can be identified at the beginning of production, as well as throughout the production of the product. In a general cost system, no effort is made to determine a specific unit cost during the manufacturing process. Only when the units are completed are the costs per unit determined. The job order cost system is used any time the product being manufactured can be identified at the beginning of the process. For example, a job cost system is used for the manufacture of automobiles, computers, television sets, hand-held calculators, refrigerators, and most durable goods.

A job order cost system uses a special and detailed cost record of each individual job to determine its cost. The cost is accumulated on a per-unit basis or is accumulated in batches of like items. For example, a manufacturer may produce 100 copy machines at one time as a specific job for a customer. Costs of producing the 100 copiers, once accumulated, would be divided equally among the 100 machines to determine the cost per machine. The cost per machine is especially important if the batch of 100 copiers is to be sold individually rather than by special order, because cost is needed to help determine the selling price of each unit. Special orders for motors, machinery, and special-order automobiles are types of products where the job order cost system is used and the cost of the specific item is determined.

In a job order cost system, perpetual inventory systems are used for raw materials, work-in-process, and finished goods. Each of these accounts is debited directly for all additions and credited directly for all deductions. Control accounts in the general ledger and subsidiary ledger accounts are important elements in the job order cost accounting system. One of the more important of the control accounts is the Work-in-Process account. The summary totals of the direct materials used, the direct labor used, and the factory overhead used are recorded in this account. These totals comprise the three elements of cost. When the product is finished, its summarized cost is transferred from the Work-in-Process control account to the Finished Goods control account. The expenses related to manufacturing move through work-in-process to finished goods to cost of goods sold. In a job cost accounting system, a special account is used, titled Cost of Goods Sold. A calculation is no longer necessary as in a periodic system. This flow of costs through the perpetual inventory accounts is as follows. A complete review of this illustration is recommended.

General Ledger Control Accounts

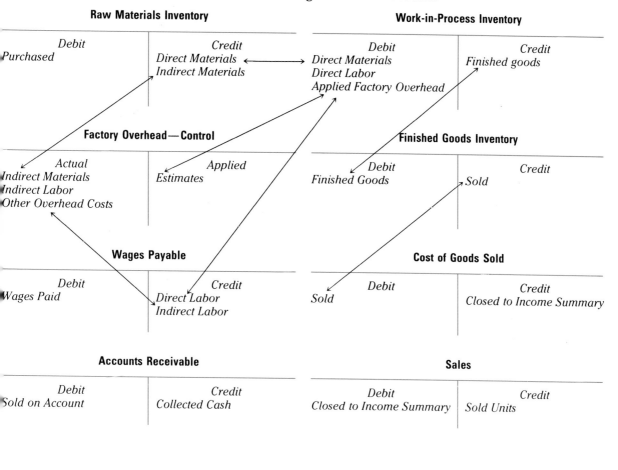

Raw Materials Inventory

Debit	Credit
Purchased	Direct Materials
	Indirect Materials

Work-in-Process Inventory

Debit	Credit
Direct Materials	Finished goods
Direct Labor	
Applied Factory Overhead	

Factory Overhead—Control

Actual	Applied
Indirect Materials	Estimates
Indirect Labor	
Other Overhead Costs	

Finished Goods Inventory

Debit	Credit
Finished Goods	Sold

Wages Payable

Debit	Credit
Wages Paid	Direct Labor
	Indirect Labor

Cost of Goods Sold

Debit	Credit
Sold	Closed to Income Summary

Accounts Receivable

Debit	Credit
Sold on Account	Collected Cash

Sales

Debit	Credit
Closed to Income Summary	Sold Units

Factory Overhead Subsidiary Ledger

Indirect Labor

Debit	Credit
Used	Closed

Indirect Materials

Debit	Credit
Used	Closed

Depreciation Expense: Machinery

Debit	Credit
Used	Closed

Factory Supplies Expense

Debit	Credit
Used	Closed

	Utilities				Factory Repairs and Maintenance	
	Debit	*Credit*			*Debit*	*Credit*
Used		*Closed*		*Used*		*Closed*

	Factory Insurance Expense				Patent Amortization	
	Debit	*Credit*			*Debit*	*Credit*
Used		*Closed*		*Used*		*Closed*

Raw Materials Subsidiary Ledger

	Material A				Material B	
	Debit	*Credit*			*Debit*	*Credit*
Purchased		*Used*		*Purchased*		*Used*
		(Direct or Indirect)				*(Direct or Indirect)*

	Material C				Material D	
	Debit	*Credit*			*Debit*	*Credit*
Purchased		*Used*		*Purchased*		*Used*
		(Direct or Indirect)				*(Direct or Indirect)*

Work-in-Process Subsidiary Ledger

	Job 1			Job 2	
	Debit	*Credit*		*Debit*	*Credit*
	Direct Materials			*Direct Materials*	
	Direct Labor			*Direct Labor*	
	Overhead Applied	*Finished*		*Overhead Applied*	*Finished*

	Job 3	
	Debit	*Credit*
	Direct Materials	
	Direct Labor	
	Overhead Applied	*Finished*

Raw Materials

As shown in the previous materials subsidiary ledger, various types of raw materials are purchased. The control account for raw materials is debited with the summary totals of Material A, Material B, Material C, and Material D. This material is then issued to the individual jobs as direct material by debiting the job and crediting the raw materials account. The summary total of direct material used on the jobs is then debited to the control account Work-in-Process as the first element of cost. Indirect material used is debited to the specific account in the factory overhead subsidiary ledger. The summary of all indirect materials used is then debited to the control account Factory Overhead. An example of a detailed material record is as follows.

Direct Raw Material

			Purchased			Issued			Balance		
								Item:	Material A		
Date 19X9		Ref.	Quantity	Unit Cost	Total Cost	Quantity	Unit Cost	Total Cost	Quantity	Unit Cost	Total Cost
Jan.	2	AA	400	$22.50	$9,000	20	$22.50	$450	380	$22.50	$8,550
Jan.	15	MB				20	$22.50	$450	360	$22.50	$8,100
Jan.	25	AC				4.4	$22.50	$100	356	$22.50	$8,000 (rounded)

Factory Labor

The wages of the factory employees are classified as direct or indirect labor. The account Wages Payable is used to show the earnings of these employees. The total wages of the employees working directly on the product are debited to the jobs on which they worked according to the timekeeper's record. The summary total of the direct labor cost on each job is then debited to the control account Work-in-Process. The indirect labor is recorded in the factory overhead subsidiary ledger as a debit to that account. The summary total of all the indirect labor is then debited to the control account Factory Overhead. An example of a direct labor time sheet follows.

Direct Labor Time Sheet

Employee Name	Mark Brown		SS No.	222-22-2222	

Date	Work Station	Wage per Hour	Time Start	Time Out	Total Cost
1-15	Job 102	$10.00	8:00 a.m.	12 N	$ 40.00
1-15	Job 103	$10.00	1:00 p.m.	2:00 p.m.	$ 10.00
1-15	Job 101	$10.00	2:00 p.m.	4:00 p.m.	$ 20.00
1-15	Job 104	$10.00	4:00 p.m.	5:00 p.m.	$ 10.00

Factory Overhead

A predetermined overhead application rate is used to determine factory overhead. For example, at the end of the month, or whenever a job is completed, the total direct labor for each of the jobs is determined. The overhead rate is then applied to this total to estimate the factory overhead applicable to each job. The overhead rate is multiplied by the direct labor cost to determine the dollar estimate.

At the end of the month, the summary total of factory overhead estimates are debited to the Work-in-Process account and credited to the control account Factory Overhead. As shown on page 1087, instead of the word *debit* on the left side and the word *credit* on the right, the words used are actual (debit) and applied (credit) and are used for illustrative purposes only. In other words, this account is debited for actual factory overhead expenditures and is credited whenever the factory overhead application estimate is recorded.

At the end of the period, the total debits in this account will reflect the total actual expenditures for factory overhead, and the total credits will show the total estimates that have been made. At the end of the year, the debits and the credits must be equal. This concept is discussed along with the job order cost example.

Work-in-Process Subsidiary Ledger

The Work-in-Process control account contains the summary total of the direct material used on each job, the direct labor costs on each job, and the factory overhead applied (estimate). An individual record of each job is needed. This record is called a job cost sheet as shown below. The job cost sheet contains the description of the item, the job number assigned, the date started and completed, and the customer's name or the purpose for manufacturing this job. In addition, it contains the direct materials used, the di-

---

Job Cost Sheet

Quantity and Description: 1 DJK Motor   Job No. 1

Date Started: January 2, 19X8   Date Completed: January 25, 19X8

For: John Jones Corporation—special order to customer specifications

	Direct Materials			Direct Labor		
Date	Requisition Number	Amount	Date	Time Ticket Number	Hours	Amount
1-2	202	$ 500	1-2	402, 403	16	$200
	203	$ 500	1-4	450, 460	16	$200
			1-15	610, 612	16	$200
			1-20	701, 702	16	$200
			1-25	811, 812	16	$200

Summary

Total direct materials used	$	1,000.00
Total direct labor used	$	1,000.00
Factory overhead applied @ 200%	$	2,000.00
Total cost	$	4,000.00

rect labor costs, and the factory overhead estimate. When the job is completed, a summary is prepared of the total costs of the job. The total cost is then transferred from the Work-in-Process account to the Finished Goods account. The job cost sheet record then becomes a part of the finished goods subsidiary ledger.

JOB ORDER COST ACCOUNTING EXAMPLE

The Morton Corporation manufactures small motors as special orders for its customers. Morton uses a job order cost system for cost accumulation purposes. A summary of the transactions and the adjustments for the month of January is given below. The T-accounts following this summary detail the recording in the control accounts and the subsidiary ledgers. In the example, dollar amounts given are small for simplicity. Three special jobs are started on the first work day of January.

a.   Materials Purchase

GENERAL JOURNAL				Page
Date	Description	Post. Ref.	Debit	Credit
Jan. 2	Raw Materials Inventory		18000 —	
	Accounts Payable			18000 —
	To Record the Purchase of Raw Materials			
	on Account			

Summary for the raw materials subsidiary ledger:

Material A	$ 9,000
Material B	3,000
Material C	5,000
Material D	1,000
Total	$18,000

b. Raw Materials Requisitioned for Use

	GENERAL JOURNAL			Page
Date	**Description**	**Post. Ref.**	**Debit**	**Credit**
Jan. 15	*Work-in-Process Inventory*		*3 0 0 0 —*	
	Factory Overhead Control		*1 0 0 0 —*	
	Raw Materials Inventory			*4 0 0 0 —*
	To Record the Use of Materials			

Summary of raw materials requisitioned for use:

By Use:		By Type:	
Job 1	$1,000	Material A	$2,000
Job 2	1,000	Material B	1,500
Job 3	1,000	Material C	250
Total to Jobs	$3,000	Material D	250
Overhead Use	1,000		
Total	$4,000	Total	$4,000

c. Factory Labor

	GENERAL JOURNAL			Page
Date	**Description**	**Post. Ref.**	**Debit**	**Credit**
Jan. 15	*Work-in-Process Inventory*		*2 0 0 0 —*	
	Factory Overhead Control		*2 0 0 0 —*	
	Wages Payable			*4 0 0 0 —*
	To Record the Factory Payroll			

Summary of time tickets:

Job 1	$1,000
Job 2	800
Job 3	200
Total to Jobs	$2,000
Overhead Use	2,000
Total	$4,000

d. Factory Overhead Costs Incurred and Depreciation

GENERAL JOURNAL					Page	
Date	Description	Post. Ref.	Debit		Credit	
Jan. 31	*Factory Overhead Control*		3000 —			
	Accounts Payable				1500 —	
	Accumulated Depreciation: Machinery				1500 —	
	To Record the Actual Expenses and Adjustment					
	for Depreciation					

Summary for factory overhead subsidiary ledger:

Factory Supplies Expense	$ 500
Depreciation Expense: Machinery	1,500
Utilities	1,000
Total Overhead	$3,000

e. Application of Predetermined Overhead Rate (Assume 200%)

GENERAL JOURNAL				Page
Date	Description	Post. Ref.	Debit	Credit
Jan. 31	Work-in-Process Inventory		4000 —	
	Factory Overhead Control			4000 —
	To Record the Application of the Overhead Rate			
	to the Jobs			

Summary of applied overhead to jobs:

Job 1	(200% × $1,000)	=	$2,000
Job 2	(200% × $800)	=	1,600
Job 3	(200% × $200)	=	400
Total Applied			$4,000

f.   Jobs 1 and 2 completed

GENERAL JOURNAL				Page
Date	Description	Post. Ref.	Debit	Credit
Jan. 31	Finished Goods Inventory		7400 —	
	Work-in-Process Inventory			7400 —
	To Record the Transfer of the Completed Jobs			
	to Finished Goods			

Summary of completed jobs:

Job 1		Job 2	
Direct Material	$1,000	Direct Materials	$1,000
Direct Labor	1,000	Direct Labor	800
Factory Overhead	2,000	Factory Overhead	1,600
Total Cost	$4,000	Total Cost	$3,400

Total of Jobs Completed:	Job 1	$4,000	
	Job 2	3,400	
		$7,400	

g.   Sale of Job 1, $5,000 on Account

		GENERAL JOURNAL			Page
Date		**Description**	**Post. Ref.**	**Debit**	**Credit**
Jan.	31	*Cost of Goods Sold*		4000 —	
		Finished Goods Inventory			4000 —
		To Record the Cost of Job 1			
	31	*Accounts Receivable*		5000 —	
		Sales			5000 —
		To Record the Sale of Job 1 on Account			

General Ledger Accounts

Raw Materials Inventory

	Debit			Credit	
(a)	18,000		(b)	4,000	
	(purchases)			(what was used)	

Work-in-Process Inventory

	Debit			Credit	
(b)	3,000		(f)	7,400	
	(direct material)			(jobs completed)	
(c)	2,000				
	(direct labor)				
(e)	4,000				
	(applied factory overhead)				

Factory Overhead Control

Debit (Actual)		Credit (Applied)	
(b)	1,000	(e)	4,000
	(indirect materials)		(applied factory overhead)
(c)	2,000		
	(indirect labor)		
(d)	3,000		
	(other factory overhead)		

Finished Goods Inventory

Debit		Credit	
(f)	7,400	(g)	4,000
	(jobs completed)		(what was sold)

Accumulated Depreciation: Machinery

Debit	Credit	
	(d)	1,500

Accounts Payable

Debit	Credit	
	(a)	18,000
	(d)	1,500

Wages Payable

Debit	Credit	
	(c)	4,000
		(factory labor)

Cost of Goods Sold

Debit		Credit
(g)	4,000	
	(what was sold)	

Accounts Receivable

Debit		Credit
(g)	5,000	
	(sold on account)	

Sales

Debit	Credit	
	(g)	5,000
		(sold)

Factory Overhead Subsidiary Ledger

Indirect Labor			
	Debit	*Credit*	
(c)	2,000		

Indirect Materials			
	Debit	*Credit*	
(b)	1,000		

Factory Supplies Expense			
	Debit	*Credit*	
(d)	500		

Utilities			
	Debit	*Credit*	
(d)	1,000		

Depreciation Expense: Machinery			
	Debit	*Credit*	
(d)	1,500		

Finished Goods Subsidiary Ledger

Job 1			
	Debit	*Credit*	
(f)	4,000	(g)	4,000

Job 2			
	Debit	*Credit*	
(f)	3,400		

Raw Materials Subsidiary Ledger

Material A			
	Debit	*Credit*	
(a)	9,000 *(purchased)*	(b)	2,000 *(used)*

Material B			
	Debit	*Credit*	
(a)	3,000 *(purchased)*	(b)	1,500 *(used)*

Material C			
	Debit	*Credit*	
(a)	5,000 *(purchased)*	(b)	250 *(used)*

Material D			
	Debit	*Credit*	
(a)	1,000 *(purchased)*	(b)	250 *(used)*

Work-in-Process Subsidiary Ledger

Job 1

	Debit			Credit	
(b)	1,000		(f)		4,000
	(direct materials)			(jobs completed)	
(c)	1,000				
	(direct labor)				
(e)	2,000				
	(applied factory overhead)				

Job 2

	Debit			Credit	
(b)	1,000		(f)		3,400
	(direct materials)			(jobs completed)	
(c)	800				
	(direct labor)				
(e)	1,600				
	(applied factory overhead)				

Job 3

	Debit		Credit
(b)	1,000		
	(direct materials)		
(c)	200		
	(direct labor)		
(e)	400		
	(applied factory overhead)		

At the end of the month, the accounts are balanced in preparation for the monthly reporting. The ending inventories of materials, work-in-process, and finished goods have been kept up to date by the perpetual inventory method. The appropriate totals are then used for the monthly financial statements.

Although in the preceding example direct labor costs are used to determine the factory overhead application rate, two other methods may also be used where applicable. The factory overhead application rate may be determined by using machine hours or direct labor hours.

When using the machine hours method, the total number of hours a machine is to be used during the year is calculated. The estimated factory overhead costs for the year are then divided by the total number of machine hours used to calculate a rate per hour. The rate is then multiplied by the number of hours the machine is used during a particular accounting period. Assume, for example, that the total factory overhead for the year is estimated as $200,000, and the total time the machine is expected to be in use is 200,000 hours. The calcuation is as follows:

$$200,000 \text{ hours} \div \$200,000 = \$1 \text{ (rate per machine hour)}.$$

If the machine is used for 2,000 hours during the month of June, the estimate for factory overhead is calculated as follows:

$$2,000 \text{ hours} \times \$1 = \$2,000.$$

The $2,000 is the amount of factory overhead estimated or applied.

The method using direct labor hours is similar. The total expected direct labor hours for the year is divided into the estimated factory overhead for the year to calculate the rate per hour to be applied. The direct labor rate per hour is then multiplied by the number of direct labor hours used during the estimate period.

The accountant will decide the method to be used to estimate factory overhead. In some situations, all three of the previously mentioned methods may be used.

RECONCILING ACTUAL FACTORY OVERHEAD TO ESTIMATE

Throughout the year, an estimate has been used for factory overhead by applying a predetermined rate to the direct labor costs. At the end of the year, the estimate and the actual overhead costs must be examined. Assume the following for the Factory Overhead account at the end of the year.

Factory Overhead Control

	Actual			*Applied*	
12/31	*Balance*	*20,000*	12/31	*Balance*	*12,000*

As shown in this T account, the summary total of the actual factory overhead costs is a $20,000 debit for the year. The $12,000 credit is the summary total of the factory overhead applied during the year. Because the actual costs of $20,000 are $8,000 greater than the estimate of $12,000, the cost of all the jobs manufactured is also $8,000 greater. When this occurs, the cost of the jobs is understated or underapplied. To correct this, an additional cost amount must be added to the cost of goods sold, the finished goods inventory, and the work-in-process inventory. This means that each of these has a greater cost for factory overhead than is presently shown in these accounts. To record the $8,000 additional cost, the factory overhead account must be adjusted and reconciled to a zero balance. This is accomplished by debiting the applicable accounts, as mentioned above, and crediting factory overhead.

Two alternative approaches can be used, both of which are judgments to be made by the accountant. The first approach is to decide that the $8,000 is immaterial. If this is the judgment of the accountant, the following entry is made.

		GENERAL JOURNAL				Page	
Date		Description	Post. Ref.	Debit		Credit	
19XX		*Adjusting Entries*					
Dec.	31	**Cost of Goods Sold**		8 0 0 0 —			
		Factory Overhead—Control				8 0 0 0 —	
		To Record the Reconciliation of Factory Costs					

This entry allocates the entire $8,000 to the cost of goods sold during the year. Because this method allocates all of the underapplied amount to the cost of goods sold, a distortion occurs in the costs of the jobs that are completed during the year.

The second alternative, preferred by most accountants as a fair allocation, is to allocate the $8,000 to cost of goods sold, ending finished goods inventory, and ending work-in-process inventory. Thus each job involved bears a portion of the inaccurate estimate. Using the job cost information from the example on page 1089, the amount of factory overhead applied to each of the three jobs is as follows.

Factory Overhead Applied:

Job 1	$2,000
Job 2	1,600
Job 3	400
Total	$4,000

Allocation of the $8,000 Underapplied Overhead:

Job 1: $\dfrac{\$2,000}{\$4,000}$ $\times$ $\$8,000$ $=$ $\$4,000$

Job 2: $\dfrac{\$1,600}{\$4,000}$ $\times$ $\$8,000$ $=$ $\$3,200$

Job 3: $\dfrac{\$400}{\$4,000}$ $\times$ $\$8,000$ $=$ $\$\ 800$

GENERAL JOURNAL					Page
Date	Account Titles	Post. Ref.	Debit		Credit
19XX	*Adjusting Entry*				
Dec. 31	Cost of Goods Sold (Job 1)		4 0 0 0 —		
	Finished Goods Inventory (Job 2)		3 2 0 0 —		
	Work-in-Process Inventory (Job 3)		8 0 0 —		
	Factory Overhead—Control				8 0 0 0 —
	To Record the Underapplied Overhead to the				
	Various Jobs				

Observe that the costs of each of the three jobs are found in one of the three accounts: cost of goods sold, ending finished goods inventory, or ending work-in-process inventory.

It may also be observed that the second alternative provides a more accurate determination of the costs of each of the jobs. Because the estimate in this example is material, the accountant would adjust the predetermined factory overhead application rate upward for future estimates.

PROCESS COST ACCOUNTING

The second major cost accounting system is the process cost system. As the name indicates, the accumulation of costs of the prod-

process cost
a cost accounting
system in which costs
are assembled ac-
cording to steps in the
manufacturing pro-
cess

uct is based on the step-by-step manner in which the product is manufactured. Thus, **process cost** is a cost accounting system in which costs are assembled according to the steps in the manufacturing process. A process system is used when the product cannot be specifically identified until the final process has occurred. Manufacturing companies that produce flour, cement, paint, refined oil, and sugar are examples where the process cost system is used. Each of these must go through some step-by-step process to become the finished commodity. The following paragraphs give simple illustrations of this system. More detailed information about process cost accounting is covered in advanced accounting courses.

In accumulating the costs, the accountant divides the cost accounting record-keeping system according to the manufacturing steps. These manufacturing steps are often identified as departments. Each department will accumulate its own costs and be responsible for the control of these costs. In the process cost system, the finished product cannot be identified on a per-unit basis until it is finished and packaged.

To illustrate the cost accumulation feature of the process cost system, a simple illustration with T-accounts is used for a paint manufacturing company. Assume that the paint must go through three processes before it is separated into pints, quarts, and gallons. The three-step process is divided into three departments, and the steps are as follows.

Department 1: Mixing			
Debit		Credits	
1 { Direct Material	$3,400	$6,400 Transferred to Department 2	
Direct Labor	1,000		
Factory Overhead[a]	2,000		
2 { Direct Material	$3,500	$6,500 Transferred to Department 2	
Direct Labor	1,000		
Factory Overhead	2,000		
3 { Direct Material	$3,800	$7,400 Transferred to Department 2	
Direct Labor	1,200		
Factory Overhead	2,400		

[a]Factory overhead applied at 200%

Department 2: Heating and Blending

	Debit		Credit
1 ⎰ From Department 1	$6,400	$9,400	Transferred to Department 3
Direct Labor	1,000		
Factory Overhead	2,000		
2 ⎰ From Department 1	$6,500	$9,500	Transferred to Department 3
Direct Labor	1,000		
Factory Overhead	2,000		
3 ⎰ From Department 1	$7,400	$10,400	Transferred to Department 3
Direct Labor	1,000		
Factory Overhead	2,000		

Department 3: Coloration and Packaging

	Debit		Credit
1 ⎰ From Departments 1 and 2	$ 9,400	$14,400	to Finished Goods
Direct Material	500		
Direct Labor	1,500		
Factory Overhead	3,000		
2 ⎰ From Departments 1 and 2	$ 9,500	$14,700	to Finished Goods
Direct Material	700		
Direct Labor	1,500		
Factory Overhead	3,000		
3 ⎰ From Departments 1 and 2	$10,400	$16,800	to Finished Goods
Direct Material	1,000		
Direct Labor	1,800		
Factory Overhead	3,600		

Finished Goods: #303 Red

	Debit		Credit
(1)	15,000 Pints		
	$.96	$14,400	
(2)	15,000 Pints		
	$.98	14,700	
(3)	15,000 Pints		
	$1.12	16,800	

In the above example, three batches of red paint have been produced. The accumulated cost for each batch is debited to finished goods. For example, the first batch begins in the mixing department. The summary of the three elements of cost of the mixing department is $6,400. When Department 1 has completed its process, the total cost is transferred to Department 2. Likewise, the summary costs in Department 2 are added to the total cost from Department 1, and the two totals are transferred to Department 3. In the example, the cost up to this point is $9,400. Department 3 incurs an additional cost of $5,000 to complete the product. When the product is finished, the total cost of $14,400 for the entire first batch is then transferred to finished goods. At this point, the cost per pint of red paint is determined by dividing 15,000 pints into $14,400. It is necessary to know the cost per pint when the paint is sold. The preceding example illustrates the accumulation of the total costs of producing three different batches of red paint.

A review of the example shows that the cost of producing 15,000 pints of red paint steadily increased, with a very large increase occurring in batch three. Because the cost per pint is matched with revenue when the paint is sold, a problem arises as to the proper amount to assign to cost. Assuming that the company sold 18,000 of the 45,000 pints at $1.50 per pint, what is the cost of the 18,000 pints? The cost is determined by whichever valuation method is chosen: FIFO, LIFO, or Weighted Average. Below is an illustration of each, showing the effects on net income.

FIFO		Partial Income Statement	
Cost of Goods Sold:		Sales	$27,000
15,000 @ $.96 =	$14,400	Less: Cost of Goods Sold	17,340
3,000 @ $.98 =	2,940		
Total Cost	$17,340	Gross Profit	$ 9,660

LIFO		Partial Income Statement	
Cost of Goods Sold:		Sales	$27,000
15,000 @ $1.12 =	$16,800	Less: Cost of Goods Sold	19,740
3,000 @ $ .98 =	2,940		
Total Cost	$19,740	Gross Profit	$ 7,260

Weighted Average	Partial Income Statement	
Cost of Goods Sold:	Sales	$27,000
$\dfrac{\$45,900}{45,000 \text{ pints}} = \$1.02$		
	Less: Cost of Goods Sold	18,360
Total Cost (18,000 × $1.02) $18,360	Gross Profit	$ 8,640

This inventory problem does not occur with job order cost because costs can be identified with individual units as they are produced. A judgment must be made in process cost accounting, though, as to the inventory valuation system best suited for a particular product or a particular company.

The records of process cost accounting are kept in such a way that responsibility accounting results. Each of the three departments will have a supervisor who is held responsible for controlling the costs. If the costs of a particular department increase beyond what may be expected, the source of the problem must be found. Once the problem is located, wherever possible, remedial action must be taken. Using our example of the paint manufacturing company on page 1093, assume that Department 1 costs increased more than might be expected. The supervisor must determine why both the direct materials and the direct labor costs increased. Assume the supervisor determines that a new employee spilled some direct material, and because of this accident the direct material cost is greater than usual. In addition, the supervisor authorized the employee to work overtime to clean up the mess. Because new employees must learn the process, the supervisor decides that no remedial action is necessary other than additional training for the new employee.

A look at Department 3 reveals a similar situation. The supervisor of this department, after examining the facts, discovered that a skilled employee acted in a negligent manner by spilling raw materials and by working overtime without authorization to clean up the mess. This employee would probably get a warning notice from the supervisor concerning the conduct and would be more closely supervised thereafter. Because of these two problems, the cost of the paint increased more than was expected. A manager is responsible for controlling costs and must take whatever action is necessary to do so. The accounting records for process cost accounting are set up in such a way as to aid the responsible managers in achieving their cost-control goals.

SUMMARY

Accounting for a manufacturing firm is different from accounting for the merchandising firm. The main difference is the method of accounting for the cost of the products sold. The manufacturing firm combines raw materials costs, direct labor costs, and factory overhead costs to produce the product it sells. All of these costs are accumulated to determine the cost of the goods manufactured. A general accounting system accumulates the total costs and makes no effort to differentiate the cost per unit until the production is complete. The three basic elements of costs are as follows.

1. Direct raw material is the raw material used directly in the finished product.
2. Direct labor is the wages of the employees who worked directly on the finished product.
3. Factory overhead is all other factory costs.

The total cost to manufacture a product is accumulated and appears on the income statement when the product is sold.

Three different inventories appear on the balance sheet: the raw materials inventory, the work-in-process inventory, and the finished goods inventory. The raw materials inventory is an inventory of all unused material. The work-in-process inventory is an inventory of the total costs to date of an unfinished product. The finished goods inventory is an inventory of the finished product that remains unsold. A general accounting system uses a periodic inventory system. Most all manufacturing concerns use control accounts and subsidiary ledger accounts. The main control accounts are the Raw Materials Inventory account, the Work-in-Process Inventory account, the Factory Overhead account, and the Finished Goods Inventory account.

At the end of the accounting period, a manufacturing worksheet is prepared to use in preparing the financial statements. This worksheet contains one extra column for the accumulation of the manufacturing costs. All of the three elements of cost and the adjustment for work-in-process inventory are extended to this column on the worksheet. In addition, a Manufacturing Summary account is used to close all of these items. The Manufacturing Summary is a temporary account used for closing and is itself closed to the Income Summary.

In determining the appropriate amount of factory overhead to be allocated to a job, a predetermined factory overhead application rate is used. This rate is used to estimate the factory overhead when the actual overhead has not as yet been determined. This rate is calculated by dividing the estimated factory overhead costs by the estimated direct labor costs. After the estimate has been applied, a reasonable estimate of factory overhead, as the third element of cost, can be calculated. When the actual overhead cost is known by the end of the accounting period, it must be compared with the estimate and any necessary correction must be made. Whenever the estimate is greater than the actual cost, it is said to be overapplied. Whenever the estimate is less than the actual cost, it is said to be underapplied. Two methods are used to reconcile any difference: (1) a material difference must be allocated to work-in-process inventory, cost of goods sold, and finished goods inventory in some fair manner, or (2) an immaterial difference is closed to the cost of goods sold.

There are two basic cost accounting systems: the job order cost system and the process cost system. Job order cost is a cost accounting system that accumulates the three elements of cost in such a way as to determine the cost per unit during production. Manufacturing an automobile is an example for which job order cost is used. Process cost is a cost accounting system in which costs are assembled according to the steps in the manufacturing process, such as in the manufacture of flour, sugar, or paint. In both of these systems, control and subsidiary ledger accounts are used. The perpetual inventory system is also used, rather than the periodic system.

Review of Accounting Terminology

Following is a list of the accounting terminology for this chapter.

direct labor	manufacturing summary
direct raw materials	overapplied factory overhead
factory overhead	predetermined factory over-
finished goods inventory	head application rate
indirect labor	process cost
indirect raw materials	underapplied factory overhead
job order cost	work-in-process inventory
manufacturing statement	

Fill in the blank with the correct word or term from the list.

1. _____ is a cost accounting system in which costs are assembled according to the steps in the manufacturing process.

2. When the overhead estimate exceeds the actual overhead costs, it is _____.

3. A cost accounting system that accumulates the three elements of cost in such a way as to determine the cost per unit during production is _____.

4. When the overhead estimate is less than actual cost, it is _____.

5. A/an _____ is a statement containing the detail of all the costs to manufacture a product.

6. All manufacturing costs except direct raw materials and direct labor are called the _____.

7. _____ are the raw materials used directly in the finished product.

8. Goods that are finished and remain unsold are _____.

9. _____ are raw materials used that do not go into the finished product.

10. A percentage that is used to estimate factory overhead is the _____.

11. _____ consists of goods on hand that remain unfinished.

12. The wages of the employees working directly on the product being manufactured is referred to as _____.

13. _____ is the wage of factory employees who do not work directly on the product being manufactured.

14. A temporary account used for closing all the items appearing on the manufacturing statement is called the _____.

Match the following words and terms on the left with the definitions on the right (columns continue on the following page).

15. direct labor   a. the factory overhead estimate exceeds the actual costs

16. direct raw materials
17. factory overhead
18. finished goods inventory
19. indirect labor
20. indirect raw materials
21. job order cost
22. manufacturing statement
23. manufacturing summary
24. overapplied factory overhead
25. predetermined factory overhead application rate
26. process cost
27. underapplied factory overhead
28. work-in-process inventory

b. a cost accounting system in which costs are assembled according to the steps in the manufacturing process

c. the wages of the employees who work directly on the product being manufactured

d. goods that are finished and remain unsold

e. a statement containing the detail of all the costs of manufacturing a product

f. goods on hand that remain unfinished

g. raw materials used that do not go directly into the product being manufactured

h. the wages of the factory employees who do not work directly on the product being manufactured

i. all manufacturing costs except direct material and direct labor

j. the overhead estimate is less than the actual overhead cost

k. a cost accounting system that accumulates the three elements of cost per unit during production

l. the percentage used to estimate the factory overhead

m. the raw materials used directly in the product being manufactured

n. a temporary account used for closing all the items appearing on the manufacturing statement

Exercises

Exercise 28.1
preparing a
manufacturing
statement

Gross Manufacturing Company uses a general cost accounting system. Below is a list of selected accounts before closing entries were made on December 31, 19X9.

Administrative Expenses (control)	50,000
Direct Labor	68,000
Raw Materials Inventory, December 31, 19X8	19,000
Raw Materials Inventory, December 31, 19X9	17,000
Raw Materials Purchases	58,000
Factory Supplies Expense	9,000
Federal Income Tax Expense	13,200
Finished Goods Inventory, December 31, 19X8	29,000
Finished Goods Inventory, December 31, 19X9	26,000
Freight-In	2,000
Indirect Labor	25,000
Machinery Repairs	12,000
Rent Expense: Factory Building	14,000
Sales	359,000
Selling Expenses (control)	42,000
Work-in-Process Inventory, December 31, 19X8	23,000
Work-in-Process Inventory, December 31, 19X9	15,000

From the information above, prepare a manufacturing statement.

Exercise 28.2
preparing a
manufacturing
company's income
statement

Using the information from Exercise 28.1, prepare the income statement for December 31, 19X9.

Exercise 28.3
preparing the
manufacturing closing
entries

Using the information from Exercises 28.1 and 28.2, prepare the closing entries without explanations. The Manufacturing Summary and Income Summary accounts are used for this procedure.

Exercise 28.4
preparing a
manufacturing
statement

The following are selected accounts of the Robotworks Manufacturing Company, a manufacturer of toys. From the following information, prepare a manufacturing statement for the month ending July 31, 19X8.

	June 30, 19X8	July 31, 19X8
Direct Labor		$ 63,500
Freight-In		600
Indirect Labor		23,000
Indirect Materials and Supplies		820
Factory Insurance Expense		1,900
Depreciation Expense: Machinery		2,500
Raw Materials Purchases		129,000
Finished Goods Inventory	$15,200	32,600
Raw Materials Inventory	7,000	6,300
Work-in-Process Inventory	5,200	4,100

Exercise 28.5
preparing the manufacturing worksheet, the manufacturing statement, and the income statement

The trial balance for Bayboat Manufacturing Company for December 31, 19X1 is as follows.

	Debits	Credits
Cash	$ 23,000	
Raw Material Inventory	15,000	
Work-in-Process Inventory	11,000	
Finished Goods Inventory	16,000	
Prepaid Insurance: Factory	4,000	
Equipment	185,000	
Accumulated Depreciation: Equipment		$ 30,000
Accounts Payable		5,000
Common Stock, $10 par		100,000
Retained Earnings		20,000
Sales		355,000
Raw Materials Purchases	52,000	
Direct Labor	88,000	
Indirect Labor	10,000	
Factory Supervision	21,000	
Utilities	16,000	
Rent Expense: Factory Building	10,000	
Factory Supplies Expense	0	
Depreciation Expense: Equipment	0	
Income Tax Expense	0	
Selling Expenses (control)	30,000	
Administrative Expenses (control)	29,000	
	$510,000	$510,000

Additional information for the Bayboat Manufacturing Company is as follows.

1. Insurance expense for the period is determined to be $1,500.
2. Depreciation expense on equipment is $2,500.
3. Ending inventories are as follows.

Raw Materials Inventory	$14,000
Work-in-Process Inventory	12,000
Finished Goods Inventory	17,000

4. Income tax expense is $22,000.

   a. Record the trial balance on the worksheet and enter adjusting entries and ending inventories. Extend accounts to the proper statement columns. Total and balance all columns and complete the worksheet.

   b. Prepare the manufacturing statement for December 31, 19X1, from the completed worksheet.

   c. Prepare the income statement for December 31, 19X1, from the completed worksheet.

Exercise 28.6
calculating the factory overhead application rate

Using the following information, compute the factory overhead application rate for Gerry Manufacturing Company.

Previous Year-End Information

Actual Factory Overhead Costs	$402,000
Actual Direct Labor Costs	268,000
Actual Cost of Direct Materials Used	895,000

Exercise 28.7
applying the factory overhead application rate to estimate factory overhead costs

The following jobs were in work-in-process during the month of June. At the end of June, the following amounts of materials and labor were charged against the jobs.

Job 101		**Job 102**		**Job 103**	
Materials	$1,600	Materials	$3,800	Materials	$4,450
Labor	800	Labor	1,200	Labor	2,200

Assume that Jobs 101 and 103 are finished and that Job 101 has been sold for $6,000 on account.

a. Determine the cost of each job assuming the application rate is 150 percent.

b. Determine the following.
   1. Cost of Goods Sold $ _____
   2. Finished Goods Inventory $ _____
   3. Work-in Process Inventory $ _____

Exercise 28.8
determining the cost of goods sold for process costs by FIFO, LIFO, and weighted average

Assume Sweetime Corporation produces refined sugar. It has produced three batches of sugar during the week and has sold 1,550 pounds. The following T-account for finished goods shows the manufacturing results.

Finished Goods Inventory

(1)	1,000 lbs	$3,000
(2)	1,000 lbs	$3,250
(3)	1,000 lbs	$3,900

Calculate the cost of goods sold using the following independent methods.

a. FIFO

b. LIFO

c. Weighted average (round to the nearest penny).

Problems

Problem 28.1
using a partial worksheet to prepare a manufacturing statement and an income statement

The following is a partial worksheet for Lamonz Manufacturing Company for the year ending December 31, 19X5.

	Manufacturing Statement		Income Statement	
LAMONZ MANUFACTURING COMPANY **PARTIAL WORKSHEET** **FOR YEAR ENDED DECEMBER 31, 19X5**	Debit	Credit	Debit	Credit
Raw Materials Inventory	17900 —	17150 —		
Work-in-Process Inventory	23200 —	21350 —		
Finished Goods Inventory			23150 —	27200 —
Sales				552250 —
Raw Materials Purchases	87500 —			
Direct Labor	124000 —			
Indirect Labor	10700 —			
Factory Supervision	28000 —			
Utilities	17600 —			
Machinery Repairs	8750 —			
Rent Expense: Factory	20800 —			
Selling Expenses (Control)			56200 —	
Administration Expenses *(Control)*			33300 —	
Factory Insurance Expense	3500 —			
Factory Supplies Expense	8100 —			
Depreciation Expense: Fact. Mach.	14500 —			
Patent Amortization	5750 —			
Income Tax Expense			18000 —	
	370300 —	38500 —		
Cost of Goods Sold		331800 —	331800 —	
	370300 —	370300 —	462450 —	579450 —
Net Income			117000 —	
			579450 —	579450 —

Instructions   *1. From the information given, prepare a manufacturing statement.*

       2. From the information given, prepare an income statement.

Problem 28.2
preparing the closing entries for Problem 28.1

Using the partial worksheet in Problem 28.1, prepare all the necessary closing entries for Lamonz Manufacturing Company without explanations.

Problem 28.3
preparing a manufacturing worksheet, a manufacturing statement, an income statement, and closing entries

The December 31, 19X8 trial balance for General Manufacturing Company follows.

	Debits	Credits
Cash	$ 28,240	
Accounts Receivable	50,360	
Allowance for Uncollectible Accounts		$ 2,735
Raw Materials Inventory	11,000	
Work-in-Process Inventory	9,000	
Finished Goods Inventory	19,000	
Prepaid Insurance: Factory Equipment	1,285	
Factory Supplies	450	
Plant and Equipment	40,500	
Accumulated Depreciation: Plant and Equipment		8,040
Accounts Payable		16,245
Wages Payable		2,900
Income Tax Payable		0
Bonds Payable		10,000
Common Stock, $10 par		60,000
Retained Earnings		29,865
Sales		266,092
Raw Materials Purchases	71,250	
Direct Labor	40,200	
Indirect Labor	6,980	
Utilities	7,180	
Factory Repairs and Maintenance	3,742	
Indirect Materials	2,795	
Depreciation Expense: Plant and Equipment		
Uncollectible Accounts Expense		
Factory Insurance Expense		
Factory Supplies Expense	0	
Income Tax Expense	0	
Selling Expense (control)	32,965	
Administrative Expense (control)	70,930	
	$395,877	$395,877

Instructions

1. *Enter the trial balance on the worksheet.*

2. *Using the following data, enter the adjusting entries and extend to the proper statement columns. Complete the worksheet.*

   a. *Allowance for uncollectible accounts is increased by $1,000.*

   b. *Factory insurance expense is $485.*

   c. *Factory supplies expense is $250.*

d. *Depreciation expense is $2,060.*

e. *Accrued wages payable: Direct Labor, $205; Indirect Labor, $75.*

f. *Ending Inventories:*

Raw Materials	$ 9,000
Work-in-Process	10,500
Finished Goods	17,000

g. *Federal income tax expense is 15 percent of operating income. Round to the nearest dollar.*

3. *Prepare a manufacturing statement from the completed worksheet.*

4. *Prepare an income statement from the completed worksheet.*

5. *Prepare all the necessary adjusting and closing entries in general journal form. Explanations may be omitted.*

Problem 28.4

calculating the factory overhead application rate for two departments by two different methods and comparing the estimate with the actual overhead

Jergen Company applies factory overhead to jobs on the basis of machine hours in the Cutting Department and on the basis of direct labor costs in the Finishing Department. The following is a list of the estimated factory overhead costs, the direct labor costs, and the total machine hours for the year. In addition, the actual factory overhead costs, the actual direct labor costs, and the actual machine hours used are given for the month of September.

	Cutting	Finishing
Estimated Factory Overhead Costs for the Year	$58,800	$174,636
Estimated Direct Labor Cost for the Year		158,760
Estimated Machine Hours for the Year	12,000	
Actual Factory Overhead Cost for September	7,020	28,250
Actual Direct Labor Cost for September		23,500
Actual Machine Hours for September	1,450	

Instructions

1. a. *Determine the factory overhead application rate for the Cutting Department.*

b. *Determine the factory overhead application rate for the Finishing Department.*

2. *Using the above rates, calculate the total factory overhead applied to the cutting department and to the finishing department.*

3. *Compare the applied (estimated) overhead with the actual overhead for each department and calculate the total dollar differences. State if the difference in each department is over-applied or underapplied.*

Problem 28.5

calculating the factory overhead application rate, applying the estimate to five jobs, calculating the cost of the finished jobs, preparing general journal entries, and determining the finished goods and work-in-process inventories

The Allen Company manufactures kitchen cabinets on a special-order basis. The accountant for the company estimates that factory overhead costs for the year are likely to be $125,000 and the direct labor costs are likely to be $100,000. The company uses a job order system and a perpetual inventory system.

Instructions

1. *Determine the factory overhead applicaton rate to be used for the present year based on direct labor costs.*

2. *The subsidiary job cost ledger is given below.*

Job 10			Job 20		
Direct Materials	1,250		Direct Materials	980	
Direct Labor	2,115		Direct Labor	1,025	
Factory Overhead			Factory Overhead		

Job 30			Job 40		
Direct Materials	1,550		Direct Materials	508	
Direct Labor	2,480		Direct Labor	620	
Factory Overhead			Factory Overhead		

Job 50		
Direct Materials	1,840	
Direct Labor	3,080	
Factory Overhead		

Using the subsidiary job cost ledger, complete the following.

a. *Apply the factory overhead application rate to each job, and post the calculation to the subsidiary ledger. Round to the nearest dollar where necessary.*

b. *Assuming Jobs 10, 30, and 50 are now finished, calculate the total cost for each.*

c. *Prepare the general journal entries without explanations to transfer these jobs to the finished goods inventory.*

3. *Determine the amount of the finished goods inventory.*

4. *Determine the amount of the work-in-process inventory.*

Problem 28.6

recording the general journal entries, posting to both the control accounts and the subsidiary job cost ledger, applying factory overhead, determining the cost of goods sold and ending inventories, and reconciling the Factory Overhead account

The Sims Manufacturing Company uses a perpetual inventory system and completed several transactions relating to the manufacture of Jobs 10, 11, and 12.

Instructions

1. a. *Open the following T-accounts in the general ledger: Cash debit $50,000, Accounts Receivable debit $12,500, Raw Materials Inventory, Work-in-Process Inventory, Finished Goods Inventory, Factory Overhead Control, Accounts Payable credit $5,700, Wages Payable, Sales, and Cost of Goods Sold.*

    b. *Open the following in the work-in-process subsidiary ledger: Jobs 10, 11, and 12.*

2. *Record in general journal form the following transactions and post to the T-accounts and the subsidiary ledger accounts after each entry is made. Explanations may be omitted.*

    a. *Purchased raw materials on account in the amount of $36,000.*

    b. *Materials requisitions were issued as follows.*

Job 10	$2,000
Job 11	2,000
Job 12	2,000
Indirect Materials Used	2,000
Total Materials Used	$8,000

c. *Labor time tickets were used to charge labor to the jobs and indirect labor to factory overhead as follows.*

Job 10	$2,000
Job 11	1,600
Job 12	400
Indirect Labor	2,000
Total Labor	$6,000

d. *Miscellaneous factory overhead expenses paid in cash are $5,000.*

e. *Jobs 10 and 11 were completed. The predetermined factory overhead rate of 200 percent is used and is based on direct labor cost. This rate is applied to all jobs.*

f. *Job 11 was sold and shipped to Arnold Supply on account. The invoice price is $7,500; terms are 2/10, n/30.*

3. *Total and balance all accounts.*

4. *Determine the amount of the following ending inventories: Raw Materials, Work-in-Process, and Finished Goods.*

5. a. *Determine the status of the factory overhead account. Is it overapplied or underapplied? Is the balance material or immaterial?*

   b. *Close the Factory Overhead account using your best judgment. Explain your entry.*

anagement Decisions:
Planning and
Controlling

PLANNING AND CONTROLLING THROUGH BUDGETS

planning
setting goals for the future

controlling
monitoring actual results by comparing them with goals

Planning and controlling a business take a great deal of effort from management. **Planning** is setting goals for the future, and **controlling** is monitoring the actual results by comparing them with the goals. If any unfavorable deviation occurs, managers must take immediate action. Establishing a master budget is one way to plan and control a business.

THE MASTER BUDGET

master budget
the comprehensive overall plan of the business

The **master budget** is the comprehensive overall financial plan of the business. The budget should reflect realistic goals. Each department or subunit of the organization must participate in preparing this budget, and each must realize that it will be held responsible for adhering to the plan. It is useful to have many people participate in preparing the budget so it reflects the ideas, needs, and responsibilities of all the employees. The more employees that participate in the planning, the more likely the business plan will be achieved.

After the budget is prepared, each department must take great care to check its performance throughout the budget period. When problems arise, the manager responsible must be ready to evaluate the problem and take appropriate action. Every well-managed business, whether merchandising or manufacturing, relies heavily on budgets.

The area's budget should be separate so it can be compared with actual performance and evaluated promptly. Different types of businesses and different departments within these companies will have varying budget needs. A typical master budget may include a sales budget, an inventory purchases budget, a capital expenditures budget, and a cash budget.

fixed budget
a budget of future plans used for the entire budget period

rolling budget
a continuous budget adjusted at the end of each accounting period to reflect important changes

When the master budget has been prepared it is a fixed budget. A **fixed budget** is a budget of future plans that is used for the entire budget period. Some companies prepare a type of continuous budget called a rolling budget. A **rolling budget** is a continuous budget adjusted at the end of each accounting period to reflect important changes. We will now discuss each part of a fixed master budget for a merchandising firm, using an illustrative income statement and balance sheet. The statement of budgeted income from operations for Oates Company follows.

OATES COMPANY
Budgeted Income Statement
For the Year Ended December 31, 19X7

Sales (See Sales Budget)		$286,600	
Less: Sales Returns and Allowances	$ 600		
Sales Discounts	1,000	1,600	
Net Sales			$285,000
Cost of Goods Sold:			
Inventory, December 31, 19X6		$ 16,125	
Net Purchases (See Purchases Budget)		217,875	
Cost of Goods Available for Sale		234,000	
Inventory, December 31, 19X7		19,050	
Cost of Goods Sold			214,950
Gross Profit			70,050
Operating Expenses:			
Selling Expenses:			
Sales Salaries Expense	$20,000		
Advertising Expense	5,000		
Store Supplies Expense	540		
Depreciation—Store Equipment	5,000		
Total Selling Expenses		$ 30,540	
General and Administrative Expenses:			
Office Salaries Expense	$ 6,000		
Office Supplies Expense	200		
Rent Expense	4,500		
Insurance Expense	310		
Depreciation—Office Equipment	500		
Total General and Administrative Expenses		11,510	
Total Operating Expenses			42,050
Income from Operations			$ 28,000

The budgeted balance sheet for Oates Company follows.

OATES COMPANY
Budgeted Balance Sheet
December 31, 19X7

Assets		
Cash (See Cash Budget)		$ 31,400
Accounts Receivable (Net)		48,600
Inventory, December 31, 19X7 (See Budgeted Income from Operations)		19,050
Equipment	$181,100	
Less Accumulated Depreciation	10,550	170,550
Total Assets		$269,600

Liabilities and Stockholders' Equity		
Liabilities:		
Accounts Payable	$ 13,600	
Notes Payable	10,000	
Total Liabilities		$ 23,600
Stockholders' Equity:		
Common Stock	$200,000	
Retained Earnings	46,000	
Total Stockholders' Equity		$246,000
Total Liabilities and Stockholders' Equity		$269,600

Preparing the Master Budget

Departmental or subunit budgets must be prepared before preparing the master budget. Some subunits will depend on the information from another subunit to complete their own budgets. For example, the purchasing department must know the sales goals of the sales department before it can order the merchandise to be sold. The following sections discuss the steps required in the budgeting process.

1. Sales budget is prepared

2. a. Inventory purchases budget is prepared
   b. Selling expense budget is prepared
   c. General and administrative expense budget is prepared
   d. Capital expenditure budget is prepared if major expenditures are expected during the coming years

3. Cash budget is prepared, based on the above budgets

4. Budgeted income statement is prepared

5. Budgeted balance sheet is prepared

The Sales Budget

sales budget
an estimate of the merchandise that will be sold and the revenues provided to the company

The **sales budget** is an estimate of the amount of merchandise that will be sold and the revenue that the sales will provide the company. The sales budget details each item to be sold, the number of items to be sold, and the revenue to be received. The following is a sales budget for one product to be sold during the year.

OATES COMPANY
19X7 Yearly Sales Budget for Product XX

Month	Expected Sales (Number of Units)	Price Per Unit	Expected Revenue
January	1,000	$1.00	$ 1,000
February	1,500	1.00	1,500
March	2,000	1.00	2,000
April	2,100	1.00	2,100
May	5,000	1.00	5,000
June	8,000	1.00	8,000
July	10,000	1.00	10,000
August	3,000	1.00	3,000
September	2,000	1.00	2,000
October	1,000	1.00	1,000
November	1,000	1.00	1,000
December	1,000	1.00	1,000
Total	37,600		$37,600

Each product to be sold will be budgeted in this way. The individual budgets will be compiled to create the total sales budget for the year. The completed sales budget for Oates Company is as follows.

OATES COMPANY
Sales Budget, 19X7

Product	Projected Unit Sales	Unit Price	Total Expected Revenue
XX	37,600	$1.00	$ 37,600
YY	42,000	2.00	84,000
ZZ	55,000	3.00	165,000
Total Expected Revenue from Sales			$286,600

After the projected unit sales is determined, the purchasing department can plan its budget for purchasing inventory. The total expected revenue from sales is transferred to the budgeted income statement as the first line item (see page 1114).

The Inventory Purchases Budget

The timing of inventory purchases requires close coordination between the purchasing and sales departments. Purchasing inventory for a full year would be unwise, because the costs involved with the investment in inventory would be very high. Instead, inventories should be maintained within reasonable limits. The timing of the inventory purchases should provide adequate inventory to sell, without overstocking.

For example, consider the yearly budget for Product XX. Product XX's sales are low at the beginning and at the end of the year. Product XX has the largest sales during the summer months. The purchasing department will consider this fluctuation when planning the inventory purchases. Purchases will be made to ensure no more inventory is purchased than is expected to be sold, yet to provide adequate inventory for the high-volume months. An inventory purchases budget for Oates Company follows.

OATES COMPANY
Inventory Purchases Budget, 19X7

	Product XX	**Product YY**	**Product ZZ**	**Combined**
Units Required for Year	37,600	42,000	55,000	134,600
Plus Desired Inventory, 12/31/X7	1,400	6,000	4,000	11,400
	39,000	48,000	59,000	146,000
Less Estimated Inventory, 12/31/X6	1,500	5,500	3,000	10,000
Total Units to Purchase	37,500	42,500	56,000	136,000
Unit Cost	$.75	$1.50	$2.25	
Total Cost of Purchases	$28,125	$63,750	$126,000	$217,875

After the inventory purchases budget has been determined, a more detailed budget is prepared to show when the units should be purchased throughout the year. The total cost of the purchases is then transferred to the budgeted income statement (see page 1114).

Selling and General Administrative Expenses   The budgets for the operating expenses are prepared using the expected employee salaries, supplies, advertising, and depreciation of equipment. After these budgets have been prepared, they are recorded on the budgeted income statement (page 1114).

The Capital Expenditures Budget

A capital expenditures budget is prepared when a company expects to purchase new equipment, produce a new product, or expand its facilities. The analysis of capital budgeting projects is discussed on page 1120. Many companies prepare a capital expenditures budget to project the timing of replacement or additional equipment in future years. Following is a five-year capital expenditures budget for Oates Company.

OATES COMPANY
Projected Capital Expenditures Budget

Type of Purchase	19X2	19X3	19X4	19X5	19X6
Delivery Truck	$20,000				$30,000
Store Fixtures		$15,000		$18,000	
Office Equipment			$10,000		2,000
Total Projections	$20,000	$15,000	$10,000	$18,00ʋ	$32,000

The Cash Budget

The cash budget is vital to a well-managed company, and its importance cannot be overemphasized. Adequate cash must be available to meet current obligations as well as unexpected needs. Poor cash management has resulted in bankruptcy for many businesses, despite their sales or investment in capital assets. Cash managers often allow a balance at the end of each month to provide a safety buffer for mistakes or emergencies. To prepare the cash budget we must first determine the inflows and outflows of cash for a day, a week, a month, or a year. Following is the cash budget for the Oates Company covering only the last three months of the coming year. Assume that the minimum cash balance desired by Oates Company is $30,000. The cash projections for each month help predict when cash may be low.

OATES COMPANY
Cash Budget
For Three-Month Period Ending December 31, 19X7

	October	November	December
Cash Balance (Beginning)	$30,000	$34,050	$37,100
Estimated Cash Receipts:			
Cash Sales	$ 9,500	$10,000	$ 6,000
Collection of Receivables	14,250	17,000	11,500
Other sources	0	0	300
Total Cash Receipts	$23,750	$27,000	$17,800
Total Cash Available	53,750	61,050	54,900
Estimated Cash Expenditures:			
Inventory Costs	$16,200	$20,250	$18,500
Operating Expenses	3,500	3,500	3,500
Other Expenses	0	200	1,500
Total Expenditures	$19,700	$23,950	$23,500
Monthly Cash			
Increase(Decrease)	$ 4,050	$ 3,050	$(5,700)
Cash Balance—End of Month	34,050	37,100	31,400
Excess(Deficiency)[a]	4,050	7,100	1,400

[a]Required ending balance is $30,000.

CAPITAL BUDGETING ANALYSIS

One of the largest costs a business may incur is the cost of buying or replacing capital assets. In making these complicated decisions, the analyst must follow the correct process to make the best possible decision. Many managers use the following procedure.

1. List all the alternatives.
2. Evaluate each alternative objectively.
3. Evaluate each alternative subjectively.
4. Decide.

To make a decision, list all the alternatives and examine each one carefully. Next, consider each alternative objectively, taking into account schedules, costs, and revenues. The next step is the hardest, because likes, preferences, and various subjective situations are difficult to translate into dollars and cents. Evaluating alternatives subjectively is important to the manager and to the expected end results. After all the alternatives have been examined carefully, make a decision. The decision that is made after carefully going through this process will in all likelihood be a good one.

Evaluating and making decisions about the proposals for the purchase of capital assets is called **capital budgeting.** Most capital budget analyses involve the estimated annual net cash flows of the use of the assets. In the following paragraphs we discuss the payback period, the rate of return on average investment, and the discounted cash flow methods to help in this analysis.

capital budgeting
evaluating and making decisions about proposals for the purchase of capital assets

Assume that Chang Corporation is considering the purchase of a piece of equipment for $32,000. The equipment has a useful life of eight years and no residual value; Chang Corporation plans to use straight-line depreciation. The equipment will be purchased in order to produce a new product. Market research shows that the expected sales of the product will produce $3,200 in annual net income, as follows.

CHANG CORPORATION
Estimated Annual Income from Sales of New Product

Estimated Sales		$60,000
Estimated Manufacturing Costs:		
Direct Material	$10,000	
Direct Labor	7,000	
Estimated Depreciation	4,000	
Other Factory Overhead	14,000	
Total Estimated Costs		$35,000
Other Estimated Expenses:		
Selling	$ 8,000	
General and Administrative	11,000	
Total estimated expenses		19,000
Total Cost and Expenses		54,000
Estimated Operating Income		$ 6,000
Estimated Federal Income Tax		2,800
Estimated Net Income		$ 3,200

Using the estimated yearly results Chang Corporation expects operating income to increase by $3,200. However, the analyst also needs to know the annual expected net cash flow from this investment. Net cash flow is calculated by comparing the inflow of cash from revenue and the outflow of cash from costs and expenses.

net cash flow
the net cash generated by cash received as revenues and cash paid out as expenses

In this example, depreciation expense is correctly deducted to calculate operating income, but it has no effect on the outflow of cash. The **net cash flow** is the difference between cash generated by revenues and cash paid out as expenses. Net cash flow for Chang Corporation is calculated by adding depreciation back to net income. The net cash flow in this example is $7,200 (depreciation of $4,000 plus net income of $3,200).

Payback Period

payback period
the length of time to recover the total cost of an investment through yearly cash flow

The **payback period** is the length of time it takes to recover the total cost of the investment (equipment) from the yearly net cash flow. The payback period is computed as follows.

$$\frac{\text{Amount to Be Invested}}{\text{Estimated Net Cash Flow Per Year}} = \text{Payback}$$

$$\frac{\$32,000}{\$7,200} = 4.4 \text{ years}$$

Thus, the payback period is 4.4 years. In other words, under the present situation, the cost of the investment ($32,000) can be recovered in 4.4 years, and management must decide if that is satisfactory. The shorter the payback period, the sooner the cost of the investment can be recovered. If the investment can be recovered quickly, the risk that something may go wrong in selling the new product is reduced. Analyzing the payback period is one way to evaluate the worthiness of an investment.

Rate of Return on Average Investment

As explained in Appendix 23A on page 878, money has a time value. Any investment is expected to earn a satisfactory rate of return over time. Management sets a rate of return goal by determining the minimum return required for any investment. Management calculates the rate of return on an average investment by dividing the net income by the average cost of the investment each year. In the case of an investment in a piece of equipment, depreciation causes a yearly reduction in the carrying value (book value) of the investment.

To calculate the rate of return on average investment, first determine the average investment by adding together the book values of the asset at the beginning of each year of its useful life, and then dividing the sum by the number of years in its useful life. Then divide the average investment into net income to arrive at the rate of return on average investment. The following demonstrates this method and the rate of return on average investment.

Calculation of Average Investment

Year	Beginning Book Value Calculation	Book Value
1		$ 32,000
2	($32,000 − $4,000 Depreciation) =	28,000
3	($28,000 − $4,000 Depreciation) =	24,000
4	($24,000 − $4,000 Depreciation) =	20,000
5	($20,000 − $4,000 Depreciation) =	16,000
6	($16,000 − $4,000 Depreciation) =	12,000
7	($12,000 − $4,000 Depreciation) =	8,000
8	($8,000 − $4,000 Depreciation) =	4,000
Total		$144,000

$$\frac{\$144,000}{\text{8-Year Useful Life}} = \$18,000$$

Calculation of Rate of Return on Average Investment

$$\frac{\text{Estimated Net Income}}{\text{Average Investment}} = \text{Rate of Return on Average Investment}$$

$$\frac{\$3,200}{\$18,000} = 17.8\%$$

A simple average may be used to determine the average investment instead of using the calculation above, which uses the book values at the end of each year of the asset's life. The simple average is determined by dividing the cost of the asset by two; the result is then divided into the estimated net income.

Calculation of Simple Average Investment

$$\frac{\text{Cost of Asset}}{2} = \frac{\$32,000}{2} = \$16,000$$

The average investment is then divided into the estimated net income to determine the rate of return on average investment.

$$\frac{\text{Estimated Net Income}}{\text{Average Investment}} = \frac{\$3,200}{\$16,000} = 20\%$$

Either method may be used. But in either case, management must consider whether the rate of return is adequate in meeting their investment goals.

One problem with this calculation is that it does not take into account the timing of the cash flows. Estimated annual net income or net cash flow does not address the question of when cash receipts are received. Will the revenue be equally distributed throughout the life of the equipment? Will demand for the product occur in the earlier years? A method used to help answer some of these questions is the discounted cash flow method, which uses the present value concept.

Discounted Cash Flow Method

As explained in Appendix 23A on page 878, a corporation would be willing to pay a present amount today for the right to future benefits. The exact amount of the present value can be determined by knowing (1) the length of time of the investment; (2) the amount of the future benefit; and (3) the rate of return desired by management. You may wish to review the present value concept before reading on.

The three requirements for calculating the discounted cash flow for Chang Corporation are (1) a useful life of 8 years; (2) $7,200 net cash flow each year; and (3) a desired rate of return of 16 percent. To buy the equipment, management must invest $32,000. By selling the product the machine produces, it expects to recapture $7,200 net cash flow each year. If management desires a 16 percent rate of return, will the rate of return be met with this investment? Using Table 1 in Appendix 23A on page 881, we calculate the rate of return as follows, assuming net cash flows are received by the end of each year.

Discounted Cash Flow Analysis

Periods Hence	Net Cash Flow	Present Value of $1 at 16%	Present Value of Net Cash Flows
1	$7,200	$0.8621	$ 6,207
2	7,200	0.7432	5,351
3	7,200	0.6407	4,613
4	7,200	0.5523	3,977
5	7,200	0.4761	3,428
6	7,200	0.4104	2,955
7	7,200	0.3538	2,547
8	7,200	0.3050	2,196
Total Present Value			$31,274
Amount to Be Invested			32,000
Negative Net Present Value			$ 726

Using the present value table, we multiply the net cash flow by the present value factor for each period. For example, we calculate the present value of the $7,200 cash flow one year (period) hence: $7,200 × $0.8621 (the present value of $1) – $6,207. The calculation for four years hence is $7,200 × $0.5523 = $3,977. By adding all the present value amounts together, we determine the total present value of $7,200 received annually for 8 years at 16 percent. The total present value is then matched with the cost of the equipment. If the cost of the investment is less than the total present value, the difference is a positive one and meets management's 16 percent goal. In other words, the cost of the investment is recovered and the investment has earned a compounded rate of return of 16 percent. Any time the difference is positive, the investment is considered to be satisfactory. If the difference between the total present value and the equipment cost is negative, however, as in the preceding example, the rate of return chosen has not been met, and the investment is not considered satisfactory.

A shortcut method for calculating the total present value uses Table 2 in Appendix 23A on page 882. Because the net cash flow is the same for each year, the amount for 16 percent 8 periods hence, can be used as follows.

$$\$7,200 \times 4.3436 = \$31,274$$

Alternative investment situations can be compared using cash flow analysis. Management can then choose the best possible alternative. Assume that management can choose among three alternatives with three different cash flow patterns. When the cash flows are not the same for each year, Table 1 must be used for the discounted cash flow analysis. The following example shows uneven discounted cash flows for the three different products under consideration, assuming an investment cost of $18,000 and a discount rate of 12 percent.

	Annual Cash Flows		
Years	Product A	Product B	Product C
1	$ 6,000	$10,000	$ 2,000
2	6,000	8,000	4,000
3	6,000	4,000	8,000
4	6,000	2,000	4,000
Total Cash Flows	$24,000	$24,000	$18,000
	Discounted Cash Flow Analysis at 12 Percent		
1	$ 5,357	$ 8,929	$ 1,786
2	4,783	6,378	3,189
3	4,271	2,847	5,694
4	3,813	1,271	6,355
Total Present Value	$18,224	$19,425	$17,024
Total Investment	18,000	18,000	18,000
Net Present Value	$ 224	$ 1,425	$ (976)

Product A and B each has a positive net present value, meaning that each meets the 12 percent rate of return. Product C, however, has a negative cash flow of $976. From these three alternatives, assuming all other considerations are equal, management is likely to choose Product B.

BREAK-EVEN ANALYSIS

break-even
the sales level at which a company neither earns a profit nor incurs a loss

Another tool managers use to set goals and make decisions is the break-even analysis, also called the cost-volume-profit analysis. **Break-even** analysis is the sales level at which a company neither earns a profit nor incurs a loss. Every company needs to know its break-even and have this information available. Break-even can be stated as the number of units sold at a fixed sales price or as the volume of sales dollars needed to cover all costs and expenses exactly. No company wishes to just break even, but break-even analysis can help answer many questions upper management may ask, such as: What net income will be earned by selling a certain number of units? What sales volume is necessary to achieve a certain level of operating income? What is our margin of safety? What level of sales volume will give the desired net income after tax?

To understand the concept of break-even analysis, assume Bark Company produces a product that incurs $105,000 in fixed costs. Also, assume the following information.

Sales Price per Unit	$350
Less Variable Cost	245
Contribution Margin per Unit	$105

Contribution Rate = 30 percent ($105 ÷ $350)

In the preceding example, the sale of each unit covers the variable cost of $245, and there is $105 left to cover the payment of the fixed overhead. The remainder of $105 is called the contribution margin. The contribution margin per unit is the amount available, after recovery of the variable costs, to recover fixed costs and contribute to profit.

Another way to express contribution margin is as a percentage of sales. In this example, we divide $105 by $350, resulting in a 30 percent **contribution rate.** After the contribution margin and contribution rates have been determined, break-even can be quickly calculated.

contribution rate
the contribution margin expressed as a percentage of sales

To calculate the break-even point stated in units, we use the contribution margin. To calculate break-even stated in sales volume, we use the contribution rate. The calculation of the break-even point in number of units is as follows.

$$\frac{\text{Fixed Overhead}}{\text{Contribution Margin}} = \text{Break-Even in Units}$$

$$\frac{\$105,000}{\$105} = 1,000 \text{ Units}$$

The calculation of the break-even point in volume of sales dollars is as follows.

$$\frac{\text{Fixed Overhead}}{\text{Contribution Rate}} = \text{Sales Dollar Volume}$$

$$\frac{\$105,000}{30\%} = \frac{\$105,000}{.30} = \$350,000$$

To verify this break-even point, we construct a partial income statement as follows.

BARK COMPANY
Partial Income Statement
Break-Even Analysis

Sales (1,000 units × $350)		$350,000
Costs:		
Variable Costs (1,000 × $245)	$245,000	
Fixed Costs	105,000	
Total costs		350,000
Net Income		0

The above formulas can be used to answer many questions. Note, however, that the sales price must remain constant throughout any particular analysis. If the sales price changes, a complete new analysis must be made. If several changes are to be made in sales price, then several analyses must be made, after which the alternatives can be compared.

Using Break-even Analysis

By making a few additions to the previous formulas, a desired amount of operating income may be determined. For example, assume Bark Company wishes to achieve an operating income of $10,500. How many units must be sold to achieve this level of income? What sales volume is required? A demonstration of the use of break-even analysis follows.

Calculation for Number of Units to Be Sold to Achieve a Net Operating Income of $10,500

$$\frac{\text{Fixed Overhead} + \text{Desired Income}}{\text{Contribution Margin}} = \text{Number of Units to Be Sold}$$

$$\frac{\$105,000 + \$10,500}{\$105} = 1,100 \text{ Units}$$

Calculation for Sales Dollar Volume to Achieve a Net Operating Income of $10,500

$$\frac{\text{Fixed Overhead} + \text{Desired Income}}{\text{Contribution Rate}} = \text{Desired Sales Volume}$$

$$\frac{\$105,000 + \$10,500}{.30} = \$385,000$$

BARK COMPANY
Partial Income Statement

Sales (1,100 × $350)		$385,000
Costs:		
Variable Costs (1,100 × $245)	$269,500	
Fixed Costs	105,000	
Total Costs		374,500
Operating Income		$ 10,500

The preceding calculation is used to determine operating income, so management may wish to determine the effects of the federal income tax on the analysis. Assume that Bark Company wishes to have $10,500 net income after taxes and that the taxes are expected to approximate 50 percent of operating income. What sales dollar volume is needed to achieve the desired net income? How many units must be sold? The following example demonstrates this type of analysis.

Calculation for Sales Dollar Volume to Achieve a Net Income of $10,500 after Taxes

$$\frac{\text{Fixed Overhead} + \text{Net Income} + \text{Taxes}}{\text{Contribution Rate}} = \text{Desired Sales Volume}$$

$$\frac{\$105,000 + \$10,500 + \$10,500}{.30} = \$420,000$$

Calculation for Number of Units to Be Sold to Achieve a Net Income of $10,500 after Taxes

$$\frac{\text{Fixed Overhead} + \text{Net Income} + \text{Taxes}}{\text{Contribution Margin}} = \text{Number of Units}$$

$$\frac{\$105,000 + \$10,500 + \$10,500}{\$105} = 1,200 \text{ Units}$$

Management can see from the calculation what sales goal it must achieve to reach the net income desired.

Both of these calculations are not necessary. If one calculation is made, it can be used to determine the other. For example, the sales dollar volume required is $420,000. To determine the number of units that must be sold, simply divide the sales volume by the selling price per unit. Likewise, if the number of units is known, multiply the number of units by the selling price per unit to obtain the desired sales volume.

Margin of Safety

margin of safety
the dollar amount or rate by which sales exceed the break-even point

The **margin of safety** is the amount sales may decrease before the company will incur a loss. Managers can keep abreast of decreasing sales results by knowing the margin of safety. The margin of safety can be stated in dollars or as a rate. For example, assuming the present sales volume is $450,000 and the break-even sales volume is $350,000. The margin of safety in dollars is as follows.

Sales	$450,000
Less Break-Even Sales	350,000
Margin of Safety	$100,000

The margin of safety can also be expressed as a percentage of sales volume as follows.

$$\frac{\text{Sales} - \text{Break-Even Sales}}{\text{Sales}} = \text{Margin of Safety Rate}$$

$$\frac{\$450,000 - \$350,000}{\$450,000} = 22 \text{ Percent (Rounded)}$$

The margin of safety for this example is expressed as 22 percent. If the sales volume decreases by 10 percent, managers will know they are still achieving a profit. However, should the sales volume decrease below the 22 percent margin of safety, a loss is being incurred.

Accounting is the language of business, and a well-designed accounting system can provide the information managers need to make better decisions. Good management decisions are arrived at through planning and control.

Index

Boldface numbers indicate pages on which terms are defined. Italics indicate illustrations.

CHECK FIGURES FOR PROBLEMS

1.1 Total Assets, **$9,550**
1.2 Total Assets, **$16,700**
1.3 Total Assets, **$21,200**
1.4 Total Assets, **$20,575**
1.5 Total Assets, February 1, **$46,605**

2.1 Capital, September 30, **$5,970**
2.2 Capital, June 30, **$8,140**
2.3 Capital, September 30, **$6,494**
2.4 Capital, December 31, **$6,170**
2.5 No check figure.

3.1 Trial Balance Total, **$27,300**
3.2 Trial Balance Total, **$58,577**
3.3 Trial Balance Total, **$67,125**
3.4 Capital, September 30, **$15,704**
3.5 Trial Balance Total, **$39,870**
3.6 No check figure.

4.1 Trial Balance Total, **$304,499**
4.2 Trial Balance Total, **$120,575**
4.3 Trial Balance Total, **$19,475**
4.4 Capital, November 30, **$44,270**
4.5 No check figure.

5.1 Net Income, **$1,049**
5.2 Net Income, **$1,645**
5.3 Net Income, **$2,540**
5.4 Net Income, **$7,710**
5.5 Net Loss, **$85**
5.6 Correct Net Income, **$1,985**

6.1 No check figure.
6.2 Trial Balance Total, **$27,625**
6.3 Capital, December 31, **$16,466**
6.4 Post-Closing Trial Balance Total, **$64,110**
6.5 Net Income **$104**

Comprehensive Problem 1
Trial Balance Worksheet, **$386,782.64**
Net Income, **$2,465.18**
Post-Closing Trial Balance, **$364,060.09**

7.1 Schedule of Accounts Receivable, **$16,175**
7.2 Schedule of Accounts Receivable, **$5,535**
7.3 Schedule of Accounts Receivable, **$1,196.80**
7.4 Schedule of Accounts Receivable, **$12,920**
7.5 Schedule of Accounts Receivable, **$8,975**

8.1 Schedule of Accounts Payable, **$14,775**
8.2 Schedule of Accounts Payable, **$7,430**
8.3 Schedule of Accounts Payable, **$31,075**
8.4 Total Accounts Receivable, Sales Journal, **$2,003.40**
8.5 Schedule of Accounts Receivable, **$3,280**
Schedule of Accounts Payable, **$7,575**

9.1 Cash Receipts Journal, Cash Total, **$17,984.75**
9.2 Cash Payments Journal, Cash Total, **$9,236**
9.3 Balance of Cash Account, December 31, **$5,247.40**
9.4 Cash Payments Journal, Cash Total, **$5,942**
9.5 Cash Account Balance, August 31, **$8,254**

10.1 Adjusted Bank Balance, **$4,646.64**
10.2 Adjusted Bank Balance, **$6,321.81**
10.3 Adjusted Bank Balance, **$3,791.29**
10.4 To Replenish, October 31, **$95.10**
10.5 To Replenish, January 31, **$97.60**

Comprehensive Problem 2
Trial Balance, December 31, **$106,479.25**
Schedule of Accounts Receivable, **$538.51**
Schedule of Accounts Payable, **$8,622**

11.1 No check figure.
11.2 Gross Profit, **$11,230**
11.3 Current Assets, **$47,000**
11.4 Net Income, **$3,285**
11.5 Current Liabilities, **$23,590**

12.1 Net Pay, **$3,237.95**
12.2 Net Pay, **$2,599.06**
12.3 Net Pay, **$3,116.61**
12.4 Net Pay, **$2,322.44**

13.1 Net Pay for Quarter, **$5,959.20**
13.2 Payroll Tax Expense, **$868.03**
13.3 Payroll Tax Expense, **$212.25**
13.4 Net Pay, **$2,302.39**
13.5 Total Payroll Tax Expense, March, **$832.95**
13.6 No check figure.

Comprehensive Problem 3
Net Pay, Week Ended March 31, **$1,676.70**
Total, Adjusted Trial Balance, **$539,962.35**

14.1 Check Register, Cash Credit, **$11,266.81**
14.2 Check Register, Cash Credit, **$12,994.50**
14.3 Check Register, Cash Credit, **$15,153.90**
14.4 Check Register, Cash Credit, **$25,934.80**

15.1 Ending Inventory, FIFO, **$20,034**
15.2 Net Income Percentage, **LIFO, 11%, FIFO, 21%**
15.3 Net Income Percentage, **Year 1, 15%; Year 2, 10.5%**
15.4 Ending Inventory, **$190,000**
15.5 Ending Inventory, **$26,300**
15.6 Balance, Item CY 40-176, September 30, **$1,705**

1143

16.1 December 31, Year 5, Uncollectible Accounts Expense, **$11,377.05**

16.2 December 31, Year 9, Uncollectible Accounts Expense, **$9,943.50**

16.3 December 31, Year 7, Uncollectible Accounts Expense, **$2,057.85**

16.4 December 31, Year 5, Uncollectible Accounts Expense (balance sheet approach), **$737**

16.5 Interest Income, October 30, **$27.03**

17.1 Interest Income, November 28, **$93.00**

17.2 Interest Income, October 20, **$25.00**

17.3 Interest Income, July 20, **$92.74**

17.4 Interest Expense, December 31, **$243.95**

17.5 Interest Income, December 31, **$80.00**

17.6 Interest Expense, December 31, **$116.67**; Interest Income, December 31, **$45**

18.1 Depreciation Expense, December 31, **$16,129**

18.2 No check figure.

18.3 Maximum units-of-output depreciation, Year 10, **$17,160**

18.4 Depreciation Expense, double-declining balance, Year 1, May 8–December 31, **$16,000**

18.5 SYD Depreciation, Year 4, **$15,000**

18.6 Depreciation Expense, December 31, Year 5, **$84,687.50**

18.7 Depreciation Expense, December 31, Year 6, **$17,500**

19.1 (5) Cost of New Equipment, **$50,500**

19.2 (1) Fire Loss, **$28,000**

19.3 Depreciation Expense, December 31, **$20,000**

19.4 Amortization of Patent, December 31, Year 6, **$9,000**

19.5 (4) Rent Expense, **$55,250**

19.6 Goodwill, **$255,000**

20.1 Income Distribution, Jones, Plan 3, **$25,000**

20.2 No check figure.

20.3 Income Distribution, Coleman, **$16,000**

20.4 (e) **Credit Cash for $25,000**

20.5 (b) **Debit Green, Capital for $3,750**

20.6 [b(4)] **Debit Bentley, Capital for $30,000**

20.7 [c(4)] **Debit Jerry, Capital for $6,250**

21.1 Total Stockholders' Equity, **$776,000**

21.2 Total Stockholders' Equity, 19X2, **$402,000**

21.3 Total Stockholders' Equity, 19X3, **$806,000**

21.4 Total Stockholders' Equity, 19X8, **$962,000**

21.5 (4) Equity per Share, Common Stock, **$15.04**

21.6 No check figure.

22.1 [2(a)] Retained Earnings, **$342,500**

22.2 Total Stockholders' Equity, 19X8, **$259,550**

22.3 Total Stockholders' Equity, 19X7, **$1,076,500**

22.4 Earnings per Share, 19X8, **$1.06**

22.5 Net Income, **$22,620**

23.1 Total Long-Term Liabilities, **$680,200**

23.2 Total Long-Term Liabilities, **$999,950**

23.3 Total Long-Term Liabilities, **$581,732**

23.4 Total Long-Term Liabilities, 19X8, **$1,060,175**

23.5 Total Long-Term Liabilities, 19X8, **$1,061,481**

23.6 Total Long-Term Liabilities, 19X4, **$2,645,325**

23.7 No check figure.

23.8 No check figure.

24.1 Marketable Equity Securities Account Balance, **$27,986**

24.2 Total Current Assets, **$500,400**

24.3 Total Assets, **$880,000**

24.4 Total Liabilities and Stockholders' Equity, **$1,039,000**

24.5 Minority Interest, December 31, 19X7, **$54,000**

24.6 No check figure.

25.1 No check figure.

25.2 Net Cash Provided from Operations, **$10,150**

25.3 No check figure.

25.4 No check figure.

25.5 Net Cash Provided from Operations, **($19,500)**

25.6 No check figure.

25.7 No check figure.

25.8 No check figure.

26.1 (4) Dividend Yield per Share, **$.29**

26.2 Net Income, **6.5%**

26.3 Net Income, 19X9, **4.55%**

26.4 (7) Price-Earnings Ratio, **10.4:1**

26.5 [1(i)] Earnings per Share, **$.40**

26.6 No check figure.

Comprehensive Problem 4
Net Income, **$115,996**

27.1 Housewares, **$10,000**

27.2 Total Expenses, Jay Department, **$12,430**

27.3 Silk Department, **$3,900 Loss**

27.4 Net Income, **$75,800**

27.5 Branch Income, **$34,300**

27.6 Investment: North Branch, **$714,300**

28.1 Cost of Goods Sold, **$331,800**

28.2 No check figure.

28.3 Net Income, **$19,954**

28.4 Cutting Department Rate, $4.90; Finishing Department Rate, **110%**

28.5 Finished Goods Inventory, **$21,909**

28.6 Factory Overhead Underapplied, **$1,000**